PRINCIPLES
AND
CASES
OF
THE
LAW
OF
ARREST,
SEARCH,
AND
SEIZURE

The authors have attempted to summarize and present in this text the general principles of the law of arrest, search, and seizure. However, because state law and court decisions vary from state to state, some of the police procedures described may be of questionable legality or not permitted at all under the laws of some states. Therefore, officers are urged to consult with their legal advisers before assuming that procedures acceptable in other jurisdictions may be used in their states.

PRINCIPLES AND CASES OF THE LAW OF ARREST, SEARCH, AND SEIZURE

THOMAS J. GARDNER
Member of the Wisconsin Bar and Practicing Attorney
Police Science Instructor, Milwaukee Area Technical College

VICTOR MANIAN
County Judge, Milwaukee County
Former Assistant and Deputy District Attorney, Milwaukee County
Former Patrolman and Sergeant, Milwaukee Police Department

McGraw-Hill Book Company

New York
St. Louis
San Francisco
Düsseldorf
Johannesburg
Kuala Lumpur
London
Mexico
Montreal
New Delhi
Panama
Rio de Janeiro
Singapore
Sydney
Toronto

Library of Congress Cataloging in Publication Data

Gardner, Thomas J   1921–
   Principles and cases of law of arrest, search, and
seizure.

   1. Searches and seizures—United States. 2. Arrest
—United States. I. Manian, Victor, joint author.
II Title
KF9630.G37   345'.73'052   73-5786
ISBN   0-07-022837-X

PRINCIPLES AND CASES OF THE LAW OF ARREST,
SEARCH, AND SEIZURE

6 7 8 9 0   DODO   8 3 2 1 0

*The editors for this book were Ardelle Clever-
don and Alice V. Manning, the designer was
Marsha Cohen, and its production was super-
vised by James E. Lee. It was set in Cairo by
Monotype Composition Company, Inc.*

This book is dedicated to the many thousands of law enforcement officers who courageously man the outposts of our democracy in a professional and restrained manner during very difficult and trying times

CONTENTS

PREFACE

If one were to describe the qualities of the ideal and perfect law enforcement officer, the description might be as follows. The officer would have the knowledge of a lawyer, doctor, psychiatrist, current affairs specialist, and community relations expert. He would have the skills of a diplomat and conciliator; the judicial temperament of an outstanding judge; the abilities of a weapons expert, a karate master, and a judo teacher. He would have the dedication of a cloistered monk and the compassion of a humanitarian. He would be a patient peacemaker, a skilled adjudicator and, at times, he would have to be a fierce avenger. He would be honest, intelligent, and articulate. In a week's time his duties could include caring for lost children, controlling rioters, giving first aid to the injured, apprehending murderers, arresting narcotics violators, delivering babies, and ticketing speeders.

The public reaction to the law enforcement officer can be admiration, contempt, hatred, respect, open revilement, or gratitude. Yet the average person, regardless of what he thinks of police officers, calls for the assistance of officers in an emergency with the expectation that the officers will know what to do and how to render assistance quickly and effectively.

Dr. Joyce Brothers, a psychologist, points out that some of the common myths concerning law enforcement officers are the "dumb cop" and the "brutal cop." Yet, states Dr. Brothers, the average policeman is, in reality, above average in intelligence and actually less inclined to express feelings through physical violence than other members of his social group are.

The increasing complexities of criminal law and criminal procedural law add to the difficulties of the law enforcement officer's task. He must make quick decisions in complex situations without the benefit of volumes of legal research for guidance. His actions may be reviewed and pondered for days by lawyers, judges, and a jury.

United States Supreme Court Justice Cardozo wrote the following in the 1934 case of *Snyder v. Massachusetts*, 291 U.S. 97, 54 S. Ct. 330, 78 L. Ed. 647:

The law, as we have seen, is sedulous in maintaining for a defendant charged with crime whatever forms of procedure are of the essence of an opportunity to defend. Privileges so fundamental as to be inherent in every concept of a fair trial that could be acceptable to the thought of reasonable men will be kept inviolate and inviolable, however crushing may be the pressure of incriminating proof. But justice, though due to the accused, is due to the accuser also. The concept of fairness must not be strained till it is narrowed to a filament. We are to keep the balance true.

To maintain that proper balance, the law enforcement officer and all other officials in the criminal justice system must be fair, impartial, and just. The United States Supreme Court stated that the police officer:

> ... is the representative not of an ordinary party to a controversy, but of a sovereignty whose obligation to govern impartially is a compelling as its obligation to govern at all; and whose interest, therefore, in a criminal prosecution is not that it shall win a case, but that justice shall be done. As such, he is in a peculiar and very definite sense the servant of the law, the twofold aim of which is that guilt shall not escape or innocence suffer. He may prosecute with earnestness and vigor—indeed, he should do so. But, while he may strike hard blows, he is not at liberty to strike foul ones. It is as much his duty to refrain from improper methods calculated to produce a wrongful conviction as it is to use every legitimate means to bring about a just one. *Berger v. United States.*, 295 U.S. 78, 55 S. Ct. 629, 79 L. Ed. 1314

An effective law enforcement officer must be knowledgeable in his craft. This text is an effort to acquaint the average officer, whose day-to-day activities result in arrest, search, and seizure, with the philosophy and principles of law which determine his authority, provide him with guidelines, and delineate the limits of these activities.

Thomas J. Gardner
Victor Manian

INTRODUCTION

The responsibility of maintaining public order and safety rests primarily on the states, with the federal government having some responsibility and also an obligation under the U.S. Constitution's article IV to protect the states "... on application [from the state] ... against domestic violence."

If all men were angels (to use Madison's metaphor from *The Federalist*) and people were to live in peace and harmony with one another, the task of maintaining public order and safety would be an easy one. But all men are not angels (nor are men governed by angels, as Madison observed), and the problem of maintaining public order has never been an easy one.

In the not too distant past, religious institutions and the family as an institution exerted a very strong influence on American community life. There existed a much stronger ethical commitment to the rule of law (or observing the golden rule, if you will) and also complying with the norms set down by the community. Criminal codes were less than half the size they are today and concerned conduct seriously antisocial in character. Regulation of behavior in other respects was controlled by the family, the church, and even the neighborhood.

With the lessening of the influence of the American religious institutions and the lessening of the influence of the home along with an alarming increase in the number of broken homes, the burden of maintaining public order and safety has shifted to the American criminal justice system. While this shift was taking place, there was an unbelievable array of economic, social, and political changes and phenomena, which also have increased the strain on the overburdened American criminal justice system.

Maintenance of public order and safety is achieved through the use of the police power of the state. The police power is defined as the power and responsibility of the state to promote and provide for public safety, health, and morals. However, the police power is not confined to the suppression of what is offensive, disorderly, or unsanitary but extends also to what is for the greatest welfare of the state. The U.S. Supreme Court stated in the 1949 case of *Kovacs v. Cooper*, 336 U.S.

77, that the "police power of a state extends beyond health, morals and safety, and comprehends the duty, within constitutional limitations, to protect the well-being and tranquillity of a community . . . ."

In order to achieve these goals, the state must vest in the municipal subdivisions the authority and capacity to safeguard public health, safety, and morals by appropriate means. The method and means used by the state and the political subdivisions of the state are valid as long as they do not contravene the U.S. Constitution or infringe upon any of the rights granted or secured by the U.S. Constitution.

Arrest, search, seizure, and detention are methods and means used in the exercise of the police power of the state. The use of these powers by government must be in harmony with the U.S. Constitution; article VI of the Constitution reads as follows:

> This Constitution and the Laws of the United States which shall be made in Pursuance thereof: . . . shall be the supreme law of the land; and the judges in every State shall be bound thereby, any thing in the Constitution or laws of any State to the contrary notwithstanding.

The U.S. Constitution, then, is the supreme law of the land. See Appendix A of this text for the pertinent sections of the U.S. Constitution that secure or grant rights to the individual and, in so doing, define and limit the police power of the states and the federal government.

When the Bill of Rights (the first ten amendments to the U.S. Constitution) was ratified in 1791, it applied only to the federal government and not to the states. Following the Civil War, in 1868, the famous Fourteenth Amendment of the U.S. Constitution was ratified. Sections 1 and 5 of the Fourteenth Amendment read as follows:

> Section 1 All persons born or naturalized in the United States, and subject to the jurisdiction thereof, are citizens of the United States and of the State wherein they reside. No State shall make or enforce any law which shall abridge the privileges or immunities of citizens of the United States; nor shall any State deprive any person of life, liberty or property without due process of law; nor deny to any person within its jurisdiction the equal protection of law.
>
> Section 5 The Congress shall have power to enforce by appropriate legislation, the provisions of this article.

In recent decades, most of the provisions of the Bill of Rights have been made applicable to state actions through the Fourteenth Amendment due process clause. Some of the important U.S. Supreme Court cases interpreting and applying the requirements of the Bill of Rights to the states through the Fourteenth Amendment due process clause are

Gideon v. Wainwright, Mapp v. Ohio, and *Miranda v. Arizona.* The issues involved in these cases concerned interpretation of provisions of the Bill of Rights as made applicable to the states through the Fourteenth Amendment due process clause. The application of the provisions of the Bill of Rights to the states has been referred to as the "nationalization of the Bill of Rights." This process began in the 1920s and probably was completed in the late 1960s or early 1970s.

State constitutions, state laws, and law enforcement procedures within a state must therefore be in harmony with the supreme law of the land, the U.S. Constitution. The final determination as to the interpretation of the U.S. Constitution is made by the Supreme Court of the United States.

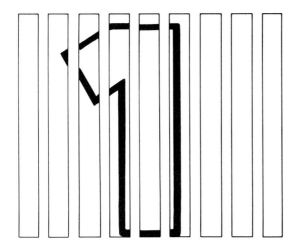

ARREST

1
ARREST AND THE NECESSITY FOR PROBABLE CAUSE

Over 5 million arrests are made every year in the United States by officers of the 40,000 or so law enforcement agencies operating under the laws of the fifty states and the federal government. The President's Commission reported in 1966 in *The Challenge of Crime in a Free Society* (page 18) that the federal government alone has created more than 2,800 crimes and observes that the number of offenses which state and local governments have created are more numerous. Thus, in most jurisdictions in the United States, enforcement of over 6,000 offenses is attempted by various governmental agencies.

WHAT AGENCIES ENFORCE THE LAWS

Many agencies enforce laws having criminal sanctions. Some of the agencies have arrest powers, but most do not. State criminal codes are enforced, primarily, by police and sheriff departments. Local ordinances which create crimes are enforced primarily by police departments. The federal criminal code is enforced by such agencies as the FBI, Secret Service, Bureau of Narcotics, etc., each having statutory jurisdiction and responsibilities in given areas.

State statutes have to be consulted to determine the state agencies charged with enforcement responsibilities of state criminal codes and violations created by the state.

Health, sanitation, fire, and pollution codes which have criminal sanctions are enforced by local, state, and federal agencies given statutory responsibility for their enforcement.

The "policemen" in the business and commercial world include for the most part state and federal agencies. In addition to bank examiners and insurance commissions, such agencies as the Securities and Exchange Commission, the Federal Trade Commission, postal inspectors, and the Bureau of Customs play important roles.

Only a few of the many local, state, and federal agencies which have enforcement responsibilities are mentioned here, but even this short list should include the Internal Revenue Service and the state and local tax offices.

TYPES OF ARREST

Over one-third of the arrests are for drunkenness, with disorderly conduct being second at about 12 percent of the most frequent offenses. The three property crimes of burglary, auto theft, and larceny amount to about 14 percent of the crimes committed. Seven or eight of every ten arrests are made for misdemeanors as compared to two or three felony arrests.

DEGREE OF UNIFORMITY BETWEEN STATES

A high degree of uniformity exists between the states in the enforcement and arrest policies for serious felonies and serious breaches of the peace offenses. This high degree of uniformity also exists in the laws granting arrest power where probable cause exists to believe that the person to be arrested has committed a serious offense. However, this uniformity does not exist for less serious offenses and misdemeanors. Gambling laws and their enforcement, for example, vary considerably from state to state. Not only do the state criminal codes vary, but also the statutes of the states which vest the authority to arrest for misdemeanors vary. Not only do enforcement and arrest policies vary from state to state, but they also vary somewhat from community to community within states.

Because of this lack of uniformity, it is impossible to state specific rules applicable to each situation in every state.

CONSTITUTIONAL REQUIREMENTS FOR AN ARREST

The famous English lawyer and writer, Sir William Blackstone, defined the legal term "arrest" in his *Commentaries*, which were published in the 1760s, as:

> ...the apprehending or restraining of one's person, in order to be forthcoming to answer an alleged or suspected crime.

This and the many similar definitions of arrest originate from court decisions where the question of arrest was at issue. The court decisions, in turn, define the constitutional requirements of a valid arrest. From these decisions and definitions concerning arrest, four distinct and required elements necessary for a valid arrest have emerged. They are:

1. The authority to arrest must exist (that is, the person making the arrest must have the authority to do so by power vested in him by statutory or common law).
2. There must be an intent to use this authority by the person making the arrest (for citizen's arrest, see Chap. 3).
3. There must be an actual or constructive seizure of the person who is to be arrested.
4. There must be an understanding and comprehension by the arrested person of the fact that he is being arrested and why he is being arrested.

AUTHORITY TO MAKE AN ARREST

With an Arrest Warrant

An officer making an arrest with an arrest warrant receives his authority from the warrant and is merely obeying the command in the arrest warrant to arrest the person named in the warrant. To make a valid arrest, the officer should:

Identify himself.
Inform the person that he has a warrant for his arrest (or that a warrant for his arrest exists).
Inform the person of his intention to arrest him.
Inform the person of the offense upon which the warrant was issued.

Without an Arrest Warrant

If the state criminal code (or municipal ordinance) forbids a certain act (or requires that an act be done),
And the state statute or common law of his jurisdiction gives the officer (or citizen) the authority to make an arrest for this offense,
And the officer has probable cause to believe that such person has committed such an act (or failed to do a required act) under the circumstances which exist,
Then the officer has the authority to make an arrest.

INTENT TO USE THE AUTHORITY TO MAKE AN ARREST

If the officer intends to make an arrest and the detention is for the purposes of making an arrest, then it will be held that there was an arrest and the question usually before the court is whether authority existed to make the arrest. If the authority existed and the other elements are present, then it will be held that there was a valid arrest.

If there was no intent to make an arrest and the detention was incidental to the proper exercise of a valid function or duty which the officer was exercising in his official capacity as an agent of the state, then it is not an arrest.

Example: Detentions to issue traffic citations are not arrests because there is no intent to take the motorist into custody and deprive him of his liberty. It has also been held that road checks for the good-faith purpose of inspecting motor vehicle licenses, registration certificates, or the mechanical fitness of the vehicle when authorized by statutes are not arrests.

The question of intent to make an arrest can come before a court when a defense attorney or a state prosecutor asks the officer whether he intended to make an arrest. If the officer answers "yes," the question then before the court is whether the authority to arrest existed. If the officer answers "no," this statement would be evidence that no intent to arrest existed. However, intent to arrest may be shown by the actions of the officer even though no formal announcement of intent was made.

Example: An officer places a person in handcuffs and takes him into the station. Unless other reasons for detaining the person can be shown, this would be held to be evidence of an intent to arrest.

There have been cases where law enforcement officers have physically removed persons from political meetings or sporting events because of their conduct. Once the officer had the person outside the building, however, the officer released him and told him to go home. Although authority to make arrests could exist in these cases, the courts have held that there was no arrest if the officer did not intend to make an arrest.

UNDERSTANDING AND COMPREHENSION BY THE ARRESTED PERSON THAT HE IS BEING ARRESTED

Section 3.08 of the American Law Institute's *Model Code of Pre-Arraignment Procedure* suggests the following procedure on making an arrest:

Upon making any arrest, a law enforcement officer shall
   (a) identify himself as such unless his identity is otherwise apparent;

(b) inform the arrested person that he is under arrest

(c) as promptly as is reasonable under the circumstances, inform the arrested person of the cause of the arrest, unless the cause appears to be evident . . . .

and for (d) the ALI *Model Code* suggests that the Miranda-type warnings be given all arrested persons. These warnings, at the present time, are generally not required by statute or decisions unless the person is being asked accusatorial questions (see Chap. 6 on the law on interrogation of an arrested person).

It is necessary that the arrested person understand that he is being arrested and taken into custody. It is also necessary that he understand the cause of his arrest. There are, however, exceptions to this requirement:

1. If the officer reasonably believes that by giving such notice of arrest, he would endanger himself or others; or if he reasonably believes that by making such an announcement of his intentions, he would jeopardize the opportunity to make a peaceful arrest, he may then delay for a reasonable time the giving of the notice of arrest.

> *Example:* Two officers enter a crowded tavern for the purpose of making an arrest. Fearing that the people in the tavern might react adversely to having their fellow patron arrested, the officers ask the man to step outside for a few minutes to answer questions. Once outside the tavern, they inform the man of his arrest.

2. When the person being arrested cannot understand that he is being arrested because of drunkenness, a drugged condition, mental incapacity, etc., and if the other necessary elements are present, then the arrest is valid even though the person arrested does not understand that he is being arrested.

3. If the reason for the arrest is very obvious to a person arrested after a pursuit or the suspect is arrested during the commission of a crime, many states do not require him to be formally told that he is under arrest and formally told the reason for the arrest.

ACTUAL OR CONSTRUCTIVE SEIZURE OF THE PERSON BEING ARRESTED

In the great majority of arrests, the authority to make the arrest is apparent to all parties concerned, and when the officer expresses his intent to make the arrest, most arrested persons peacefully submit themselves to the control and the authority of the officer. Although touching the person is not necessary to make an arrest valid, many law enforcement agencies recommend a symbolic touching. This can be done by the officer placing his hand on the person or by the officer taking the arm of the person he has arrested and gently guiding him in the direction the officer wants him to move.

Should force be needed to effect an arrest, the officer may use the necessary reasonable force within the limits prescribed within his jurisdiction (see Chap. 4, "The Use of Force").

The ability to make an actual or constructive seizure is a necessary element of an arrest.

Example: The FBI cannot declare the ten most-wanted men arrested. The authority exists along with the intent to make the arrest. The ten most-wanted men understand that they are being sought. But until these wanted persons are located and actual or constructive seizure can be made, no arrest can be made.

Prudence demands that officers not make an arrest when they do not have the necessary force to effect it. One officer telling a large angry crowd that they are all under arrest could bring about unpleasant or tragic results. The 1967 Detroit police raid on a "blind pig" where the Detroit police encountered and arrested more people than the equipment immediately at hand could convey triggered off the Detroit riots of that year.

WHO CAN BE ARRESTED?

Anyone subject to the laws may be arrested, and this is practically everyone. One exception is foreign nationals traveling on a diplomatic passport. Practically all other people—citizens and noncitizens alike—upon entering a state are subject not only to the laws of that state but also to the laws of the United States. Foreign consuls are commercial agents and are also subject to the laws and can be arrested.

The U.S. State Department in Washington, D.C., will provide the names of foreign nationals privileged from arrest. Should a question come up, these lists are available to law enforcement agencies along with advice on how best to handle situations which may confront the agency.

Article I, section 6, of the U.S. Constitution provides that U.S. senators and representatives ". . . shall in all cases except treason, felony and breach of the peace, be privileged from arrest during their attendance at the session of their respective houses, and in going to and returning from the same. . . ." Most state constitutions extend the same or similar privileges to state legislators while the legislature is in session.

PURPOSE OF AN ARREST

Many departments inform their officers that there can be only one purpose for a law enforcement officer to make an arrest and that is to cause the arrested person to be brought before a court or public official (district attorney or city attorney). These departments warn their men that taking a person into custody for any other purpose is invalid and could be false imprisonment.

This is the general rule, and it is the best rule for a law enforcement officer to follow. However, the 1965 American Bar Foundation book, *Arrest: The Decision to Take a Suspect into Custody* by Wayne R. LaFave (published by Little, Brown and Company), states on page 437 that "arrests for purposes other than prosecution are common." Their studies showed that drunks are commonly taken into custody for their own safety and released without a court appearance. They point out that prostitutes are sometimes arrested for the purpose of giving them a medical examination. Transvestites, gamblers, and liquor law violators are sometimes taken into custody just to keep them "on the run" and to discourage their activity in a community.

The book devotes five chapters to the subject of arrests for purposes other than prosecution. It is recommended reading for students, particularly chapter 25, which discusses possible civil suits and departmental discipline against the officer.

TIME LIMITS ON ARRESTS AND THE ISSUANCE
OF ARREST WARRANTS AND SUMMONSES

All states and the federal government have enacted statutes of limitations which set time limitations for the arrest and prosecution of crimes. California statutes limit the time to one year for misdemeanors and three years for felonies. Wisconsin has a three-year statute for misdemeanors and a six-year statute for felonies. Arrest and prosecution for murder may ordinarily be made at any time without any time limit. Crimes of theft are designated separately in some states because a theft is not always discovered immediately by the victim.

The running of the statute of limitations is stopped by the issuance of a warrant or summons, and many states do not include the time in which the wanted person was not a public resident of that state.

The time at which the victim reports the crime has a considerable effect. The credibility of a woman reporting a rape three months after it occurred would be questioned not only by the law enforcement agency but also by the prosecuting attorney, the court, and the jury.

Studies and surveys show that less than half of the crimes committed in the United States are reported. Only one-third of the forcible rapes and burglaries and only one-half of the robberies and aggravated assaults were reported. The reason most frequently given was that the police could not do anything. Another reason was that the offense was a private matter or that the victim did not want to harm the offender. Fear of reprisal was strongest in cases of assault and family crimes.

DOES A SUSPECT HAVE A RIGHT TO BE ARRESTED?

This question came before the U.S. Supreme Court in the 1966 case of *Hoffa v. United States* (see Chap. 19). The defendant argued that when the police had probable cause to arrest him, they were obligated to do so and that evidence obtained after that time was inadmissible because he was not given the Fifth and Sixth Amendment warnings. The Court in rejecting the argument stated:

> ...There is no constitutional right to be arrested. The police are not required to guess at their peril the precise moment at which they have probable cause to arrest a suspect, risking a violation of the Fourth Amendment if they act too soon and a violation of the Sixth Amendment if they wait too long. Law enforcement officers are under no constitutional duty to call a halt to a criminal investigation the moment they have the minimum evidence to establish probable cause, a quantum of evidence which may fall far short of the amount necessary to support a criminal conviction.

This question has come before lower courts many times, and they have consistently held that *if* the law enforcement officer has good reason, he need not make an arrest when a crime is committed in his presence.

Example: An undercover police officer witnesses a narcotics transaction, but because he wants to continue the investigation to determine the identity of the suppliers, he does not arrest the pushers. The authority to arrest exists but the intent to arrest does not (at that time).

The question of whether the officer used proper judgment in not making an arrest is subject to review by his superiors in his department. Failure to take proper action could result in disciplinary proceedings by the department.

WHERE AND WHEN CAN AN ARREST BE MADE?

There are no sanctuaries in the United States, such as there are in some Latin countries, where a person to be arrested would be immune from arrest. An arrest can be made anywhere and anytime, with the limited exceptions of a witness extradited to another state to testify, a speedy trial conveyance, or a person in court in response to a subpoena. See your legal adviser for the law in your state in regard to these exceptions.

The general rule is that if the officer (1) has the authority to make an arrest either as a law enforcement officer or as a citizen, (2) has the intent to make the arrest, and (3) is legally where he has a right to be, then he may make the arrest.

Arrests have been made in courtrooms and on the floors of legislative bodies. These governmental units have contempt and arrest power of their own. Whether an officer should come in from the outside to make an arrest in a courtroom or on the floor of a legislature without prior consent not only is a matter of discretion but could also be determined by the constitution and law of the state. Another important factor would be the seriousness of the offense for which the arrest is being made.

ALTERNATIVES TO ARREST

A number of alternatives to arrest are available to the law enforcement officer. Instead of making an arrest, the officer could:

1. Release the person with a warning
2. Invite the person to come down to police headquarters to discuss the incident
3. Release the person and report the incident to the parents, or school authorities, or the probation officer, or the employer, or military officials if the matter was of concern to any of these
4. "Order the person in" (that is, order the person to appear at the prosecuting attorney's office at a given time and date)

Many factors could be considered by the officer in determining what course of action should be taken. Some of those factors are:

1. The seriousness of the offense involved
2. Whether there is danger of harm to persons or property if an arrest is not immediately made
3. Whether the defendant will flee and not appear before the prosecuting attorney as ordered
4. The amount and the strength of the evidence against the offender

5. The age, identity, and past record of the offender
6. Whether the person is a resident of the community and whether he is employed in the community
7. The written or informal policy of the officer's department for the handling of the type of offense involved

On page 21 of the *Task Force Report: The Police*, the President's Commission on Law Enforcement states:

> Whether a criminal prosecution is initiated against an individual depends, in most instances, upon a police judgment. Theoretically, this judgment is based upon the statutory definition of the crime, but it is abundantly clear that there are many situations in which a violation has in fact occurred and is known to the police, but where there is no effort by the police to make an arrest. Among the factors accounting for this exercise of discretion are the volume of violations, the limited resources of the police, the overgeneralization of legislative enactments defining criminal conduct, and the various local pressures reflecting community values and attitudes.
>
> Social gambling affords a good example of the dilemma which police face. In most jurisdictions, all forms of gambling are illegal. Yet it is apparent that legislatures neither intend nor expect that such statute be fully enforced. The consequence is that police are left with the responsibility for developing an enforcement policy for the particular community....

WHEN IS AN ARREST MADE?

The point and time at which an arrest is made do not depend upon the presence or absence of any formal announcement by an officer that he is making an arrest but are an issue of fact to be determined by the court.

If the actions of the officer are such as to amount to an arrest, then the court will hold that an arrest was made even though the officer did not verbally announce his intention to make an arrest. Pointing a gun or putting handcuffs on a person could be facts which would cause a court to hold that an arrest was made.

See the Sibron case in Chap. 11, where the U.S. Supreme Court stated, "It is a question of fact precisely when in each case, the arrest took place." In Sibron, the Court held that the arrest took place when the officer grabbed the defendant (Peters) by the collar after chasing him downstairs. The Court stated:

> ... By the time Officer Lasky caught up with Peters on the stairway between the fourth and fifth floors of the apartment building, he had probable cause to arrest him for attempted burglary. The officer heard strange noises at his door which apparently led him to believe that

someone sought to force entry. When he investigated these noises he saw two men, whom he had never seen before in his 12 years in the building, tiptoeing furtively about the hallway. They were still engaged in these maneuvers after he called the police and dressed hurriedly. And when Officer Lasky entered the hallway, the men fled down the stairs. It is difficult to conceive of stronger grounds for an arrest, short of actual eyewitness observation of criminal activity. As the trial court explicitly recognized, deliberately furtive actions and flight at the approach of strangers or law officers are strong indicia of mens rea, and when coupled with specific knowledge on the part of the officer relating the suspect to the evidence of crime, they are proper factors to be considered in the decision to make an arrest.

The Court of Appeals of New York stated in *People v. Butterly*, 250 N.E.2d 340 (1969), that:

> The question of precisely when an arrest occurred is one of fact ... there must be a determination (in the case before the Court) of whether the conduct of the officers amounted to an arrest or was only a routine surveillance of the defendant but grounded on more than baseless suspicion.

See *Rios v. United States* in the case section of this chapter, where the U.S. Supreme Court held that the validity of the search "turns on the narrow question of when the arrest occurred."

FEDERAL DISTRICT OF COLUMBIA COURT REFORM AND CRIMINAL PROCEDURE ACT OF 1970

Subchapter V—Arrest without Warrant

§ 23–581. Arrests without warrant by law enforcement officers

(a) (1) A law enforcement officer may arrest, without a warrant having previously been issued therefor—

(A) a person whom he has probable cause to believe has committed or is committing a felony;

(B) a person whom he has probable cause to believe has committed or is committing an offense in his presence;

(C) a person whom he has probable cause to believe has committed or is about to commit any offense listed in paragraph (2) and, unless immediately arrested, may not be apprehended, may cause injury to others, or may tamper with, dispose of, or destroy evidence.

(2) The offenses referred to in subparagraph (C) of paragraph (1) are the following:

(A) The following offenses specified in the Act entitled "An Act to establish a code of law for the District of Columbia," approved March 3, 1901, and listed in the following table:

Offense:	Specified in—
Assault	section 806 (D.C. Code, sec. 22–504).
Petit larceny	section 827 (D.C. Code, sec. 22–2202).

Receiving stolen goods .... section 829 (D.C. Code, sec. 22–2205).

Unlawful entry .... section 824 (D.C. Code, sec. 22–3102).

(B) Attempts to commit the following offenses specified in such Act and listed in the following table:

Offense: Specified in—

Burglary .... section 823 (D.C. Code, sec. 22–1801).

Grand larceny .... section 826 (D.C. Code, sec. 22–2201).

Unauthorized use of vehicles .. section 826b (D.C. Code, sec. 22–2204).

(b) A law enforcement officer may, even if his jurisdiction does not extend beyond the District of Columbia, continue beyond the District, if necessary, a pursuit commenced within the District of a person who has committed an offense or whom he has probable cause to believe has committed or is committing a felony, and may arrest that person in any State the laws of which contain provisions equivalent to those of section 23–901.

THE PROBABLE-CAUSE REQUIREMENT

Law enforcement officers *must* know the laws and the ordinances which they are enforcing. They *must* know what arrest authority is vested in them by state statute (or by common law). They also *must* know what "probable cause" is and whether it exists in the situation in which the officer is considering making an arrest.

The requirement that probable cause must exist before an arrest can be made is a requirement of the Fourth Amendment of the U.S. Constitution. State statutes granting arrest authority to law enforcement officers in their states must be written in harmony with the Fourth Amendment and also other sections of the U.S. Constitution.

Many state statutes use the term "reasonable ground to believe" instead of the term "probable cause." As both terms mean the same, they may be used interchangeably. Both terms mean exactly what they say. The law requires no more and will accept no less than reasonable and probable grounds to believe that the person who is to be arrested has committed the crime he is being arrested for. It is not necessary that the evidence be sufficient to prove ultimate guilt beyond a reasonable doubt or even that it be sufficient to prove that guilt is more probable than not. In order to make an arrest, the officer must reasonably believe that guilt is more than a possibility.

The most common legal attack on the authority of a law enforcement officer to make an arrest is that "probable cause" did not exist and therefore the arrest is invalid. An arrest with less than probable cause deprives the person of his Fourth Amendment rights and leaves the arresting officer vulnerable to civil suit. If the arrest is held invalid and a search was made incident to the arrest, then the search was also improper and the motion to suppress the evidence thereby obtained would be sustained.

It is impossible to draw up a list that would include all the possible factors that could add up to probable cause. The following is an attempt to illustrate some of the most common situations.

INCIDENTS WHICH ALONE AND IN THEMSELVES WOULD AMOUNT TO PROBABLE CAUSE.	KNOWLEDGE THAT A CRIME WAS COMMITTED PLUS ONE OR MORE OF THE FOLLOWING WOULD IN MOST CASES AMOUNT TO PROBABLE CAUSE.	SUSPICION THAT A CRIME HAS BEEN COMMITTED OR IS BEING COMMITTED PLUS TWO OR MORE OF THE FOLLOWING MIGHT AMOUNT TO PROBABLE CAUSE.
A crime is committed in the presence of the officer.	Fingerprints which put the suspect at the scene of the crime.	Flight or attempt to hide.
Admissions or a confession is made to the commission of a crime.	Identification by the victim or a witness (by photograph, lineup, for instance).	Evasive or inconsistent answers. A suspect's refusal to identify himself or refusal to explain the circumstances surrounding his presence in the area or refusal to be detained under circumstances where the state statute requires the suspect to stay in the presence of the officer for questioning.
Circumstances where the officer can reasonably conclude that only X could have committed the crime although the officer did not see the crime committed.	Identification by unusual characteristics (a one-armed man with red hair, for instance).	
A reasonable belief that one of a small group of persons must have committed the crime. (The mass arrest of 142 people in Detroit in April of 1969 was held illegal although it was reasonable to believe that one of them killed the police officer whose death was being investigated.) The authority for such a multiple arrest can be found in *Restatement (second) of Torts*, sec. 119, illustration 2 (1965): "A sees B and C bending over a dead man D. B and C each accuse the other of murdering D. A is not sure that either B or C did the killing, but he has a reasonable suspicion that either B or C killed D. A is privileged to arrest either or both."	Information from a reliable informer. Flight from the crime zone...or attempt to hide. Attempt to destroy evidence. Photograph of the crime being committed (bank camera).	Hearsay information from the general public, another police officer, or an informant. Knowledge of the suspect's past criminal record, weaknesses, or reputation (drug addiction, alcohol, gambling, etc.). These may not ordinarily be used in a criminal trial against him but may be considered in determining probable cause.

BURDENS OF PROOF AND QUANTUMS (AMOUNTS) OF EVIDENCE AS THEY
(The Block Building of Evidence)

REASONABLE SUSPICION

"A police officer may stop any person abroad in a public place whom he reasonably suspects is committing, has committed or is about to commit a felony or any of the crimes specified in section 552 of this chapter, and may demand of him, his name, address and explanation of his actions." New York Code Criminal Pro. Sec. 180a(1)

EVIDENCE WITHOUT LEGAL SIGNIFICANCE

Quantum of evidence which does not rise to the dignity of either reasonable suspicion or probable cause such as a hunch or intuition or mere suspicion and therefore does not have the legal significance which probable cause or reasonable suspicion has.

Gives the officer no authority

Gives the officer authority to question and investigate (see Chap. 11)

RELATE TO ONE ANOTHER

PROBABLE CAUSE

Quantum of evidence needed to make an arrest or to obtain a search warrant.

"The substance of all definitions of probable cause is a reasonable ground for belief of guilt.... And this means less than evidence which would justify condemnation or conviction.... Probable cause exists where the facts and circumstances within their [the officers'] knowledge and of which they had reasonably trustworthy information [are] sufficient in themselves to warrant a man of reasonable caution in the belief that an offense has been or is being committed." U.S. Supreme Court in *Brinegar v. United States* (1949)

Gives the officer authority to arrest; to obtain a search warrant, or to make a search under the Carroll rule (see Chap. 10)

GUILT BEYOND A REASONABLE DOUBT

"The law presumes every person charged with the commission of an offense to be innocent. This presumption attends the defendant throughout the trial and prevails at its close unless overcome by evidence which satisfies the jury of his guilt beyond a reasonable doubt. The defendant is not required to prove his innocence.

"The burden of proving the defendant guilty of every element of the crime charged is upon the State. Before you can return a verdict of guilt the State must prove to your satisfaction beyond a reasonable doubt that the defendant is guilty.

The term 'reasonable doubt' means a doubt based upon reason and common sense. It is a doubt for which a reason can be given, arising from a fair and rational consideration of the evidence or want of evidence. It means such doubt as would cause a man of ordinary prudence to pause or hesitate when called upon to act in the most important affairs of life."

See *Wisconsin Jury Instruction No. 140*

Amount of evidence necessary to convict a person of a crime.

In a 1963 false arrest and imprisonment suit against Wisconsin police officers of the Milwaukee and West Allis Police Departments, Justice E. Harold Hallows of the Wisconsin Supreme Court defined "reasonable grounds to believe" and "probable cause" in the following manner:

> "An arrest without a warrant for a felony is valid if there is reasonable and probable grounds of suspicion or to suspect that the person arrested has committed a felony. Reasonable grounds to believe means 'a reasonable ground of suspicion supported by circumstances sufficiently strong in themselves to warrant a cautious man in believing the accused guilty.' The word 'suspicion' does not mean mere suspicion. Nor does probable cause, or as sometimes stated, 'reasonable grounds to believe', depend upon the outcome of the subsequent prosecution resulting from the arrest. Probable and reasonable cause in this case depended upon the fact information given to the police and its sufficiency and the reliability of the informants." *Stelloh v. Liban*, 21 Wis. (2d), 119 (1963). (The court in its definition quoted *State v. Cox* [1952], 262 Wis. 303.)

This case, like most false arrest and false imprisonment suits, resulted from a situation where the accused was not convicted in the trial which followed the arrest. The Wisconsin Supreme Court held that there was probable cause to sustain the arrest, and sustained the use of an undisclosed reliable informer's statements to establish probable cause if it is in the best public interest.

As stated in the quoted section of *Stelloh v. Liban*, a conviction does not have to follow every arrest. Probable cause can exist to arrest a person who, when the investigation is completed and all the facts are in, is shown to be innocent.

Example: A police officer directing traffic at a busy intersection is told by an excited well-dressed man that a liquor store a block away is being robbed by a red-headed man wearing yellow shoes. The police officer immediately starts toward the liquor store without getting the well-dressed man's name. On the way, the officer hears what he thinks to be a gunshot. As he approaches the liquor store, a red-headed man with yellow shoes runs out of the store and down the street away from the officer. After a 50-yard chase, the officer stops the man with a football tackle and tells the man that he is under arrest. When they return to the store, the officer is told that there has been no robbery and that the noise that he thought was a shot instead was a car engine backfiring. The officer had probable cause to make an arrest but the man arrested was innocent and immediately released.

It is most important that the officer be able to recall and to describe the information which was made available to him. He has to be able to explain why he acted as he did. He could draw wrong conclusions from the facts made available to him or he even could be wrong about the facts, but as long as he accepts the information made available to him in good faith and believes that guilt is more than a possibility, he is justified in making an arrest. The Fourth Amendment test is that of reasonability—a reasonable man acting in a reasonable manner in view of the circumstances which confront him.

Before every arrest, the officer must ask himself whether he has probable cause, and in most situations the answer is an easy one to give.

The officer must not only make the value judgment as to what the quantum of evidence available to him is, but he must also be prepared "... to articulate this [information] because in determining the existence of probable cause, the law is concerned with the knowledge of the law enforcement officer and, also, his motives before he: 1) makes an arrest; or 2) makes a search subsequent to the arrest or 3) petitions a court for a search warrant. Because probable cause is determined by the knowledge of the police officer and his motives, hearsay evidence may be considered by the officer, in part, in determining whether he has probable cause and the officer may testify to and repeat hearsay evidence in court in sustaining and showing that he did have probable cause when he acted so long as there ... [is] a substantial basis for crediting the hearsay." U.S. Supreme Court in *Brinegar v. United States*, 1949 (case section of this chapter).

Today, hearsay evidence *alone* will support a conclusion by an officer that probable cause exists. See Chap. 19 for the tests which are used to determine whether hearsay evidence may be used as an essential element in the determination of probable cause. However, good motives alone will *not* sustain the finding that probable cause existed.

The law enforcement officer may use all of his senses to receive information and relate not only what he heard or saw but also what his sense of smell, touch, or taste reasonably led him to conclude.

MODEL CODE OF PRE-ARRAIGNMENT PROCEDURE

The American Law Institute's *Model Code of Pre-Arraignment Procedure* defines and explains probable cause as follows under article, 3, "Arrest":

> (2) *Reasonable Cause.* Reasonable cause exists under this section where there is a substantial objective basis for believing that the person to be arrested has committed a crime. An arrest shall not be deemed to have been made on insufficient cause hereunder

solely on the ground that the officer is unable to determine the particular crime which may have been committed.

(3) *Determining Reasonable Cause.* In determining whether reasonable cause exists to justify an arrest under this section, a law enforcement officer may take into account all facts, including those based upon any expert knowledge which the officer in fact possesses, which a prudent officer would judge relevant to the likelihood that a crime has been committed and that the person to be arrested has committed it, including any failure to comply with an obligation imposed by this Code or with a lawful request for cooperation; *provided* that no such failure shall alone be deemed sufficient to justify an arrest in any case where such failure does not itself constitute a crime.

WHEN THE OFFICER HAS LESS THAN PROBABLE CAUSE

An arrest *cannot* be made if the quantum of evidence is less than probable cause or reasonable grounds to believe. If less than probable cause exists, the officer should continue the investigation in the legal manners available to him.

The U.S. Supreme Court decisions in the Terry, Peters, and Sibron cases (see Chap. 11) have laid down guidelines which have been of great assistance to law enforcement officers. These specific guidelines cover situations where the quantum of evidence available is less than probable cause but sufficient to amount to reasonable suspicion. Ordinarily the officer should be able either to resolve and clear the suspicion he has or to add enough information to what he already has to have the total add up to probable cause. However, if after the questioning, the quantum of knowledge available to the officer is still less than probable cause, then no arrest can be made. The officer has the name and address of the person (or persons) in addition to the other information which he has received, and this information might prove helpful to his department at a later date.

DOES PROBABLE CAUSE VARY TO SOME EXTENT WITH THE SERIOUSNESS OF THE CRIME?

The question can be asked: Do the objective standards for determining probable cause remain constant in all cases? Is a police department which is seeking a psychopath who has killed five times and threatens to kill again bound by the same standards as a police department routinely cracking down on the numbers racket or prostitution (the so-called "victimless" crimes)?

If the psychopath walks into a police station and gives himself up, or if he is caught in the act of killing, there is no question that probable cause exists. When a law enforcement officer finds himself in a situation similar to the situation in which a sheriff in northern New York State found himself in 1967, should he act otherwise than the sheriff did?

The sheriff received a radio message about 9:00 A.M. on a January morning that a bank 18 miles away had been robbed by two men wearing business suits with silk stockings over their faces. They drove away from the bank in a 1965 brown Chevrolet with license plate number FG-759.

With only this to go on, the sheriff and another officer, both of them armed with loaded shotguns, took station at the main intersection of their town and began checking operator's licenses and vehicle registrations.

At 9:20 A.M. an Alfa Romeo sports car with one man in it drove up. The man was dressed in a cowboy outfit and had his driver's license but no current registration for the Alfa Romeo. He also had three other registration cards, two for pickup trucks and one for an automobile, none of which were in his name.

The sheriff said that he became suspicious about the registration cards and also because the driver was a little overpolite and a little too cooperative. The sheriff then demanded to see what was in the suitcase on the floor of the front seat of the car. Consent was not given, but the sheriff opened the suitcase and found the $99,000 taken from the bank. The other bank robber was found hidden in the trunk of the car.

In a motion to suppress, the U.S. District Court held that the sheriff had probable cause under the circumstances which existed. The court said in *United States v. Kuntz*, 265 F. Supp. 543 (1967),

> If probable cause, an elusive concept, must be determined here, I think the fact of armed robbery, itself, known to the police officers as having occurred in the near vicinity, the alarm to the police with descriptions and warnings, the obvious conclusion the robbers would be fleeing the scene of the crime and the area, the specific acts and conduct of Kuntz and his resemblance somewhat to the broadcast physical description of one of the robbers, and his failure to produce the proper registration give adequate support for probable cause to arrest lawfully and search. None know how the other minds work, particularly when the other is differently trained, but these factors are reasonable, in my judgment, to accept as a proper base for the quick conclusion that had to be made by police officers who knew they might at any moment be exposed to the danger of being shot.

Professor Fred E. Inbau, in his text *Criminal Justice, Cases and Comments*, puts the Kuntz case in a subsection entitled "The Outer Limits of Probable Cause."

The type of case and the gravity of the offense which is before the court will undoubtedly have an effect upon the attitude of the court in determining the question of whether probable cause exists or not. Nationally known police officers and law professors have urged that more specific guidelines be developed for law enforcement officers in determining probable cause. It seems unlikely that state legislatures are going to tackle this very difficult job, and officers will have to continue to rely on present legislation and the case-to-case guidelines laid down by the courts plus their own good common sense and judgment in reacting to unusual situations.

PREVENTIVE ARREST

The question of whether an arrest can be made to prevent a crime *or to prevent a riot* is similar to the question of whether a material witness can be arrested (see Chap. 2 on detention of material witnesses). In all cases, the constitutional requirement that probable cause exist in order to make an arrest must be complied with and observed. If the officer has probable cause to believe that a crime *has been* or *is being* committed, then an arrest may be made. If probable cause does not exist, then an arrest should not and cannot be made.

Example: A man states, "I am going home and will kill my wife." He has not committed a crime as yet. He has not conspired to commit a crime, nor has he solicited to commit a crime, nor has he attempted to commit a crime. Can a preventive arrest be made? The answer is "no" unless the requirement of probable cause is met. Under this situation, it would be best to detain him and take him into custody under the emergency detention statutes of the state because he threatens violence and appears irresponsible and dangerous. This is not an arrest but a detention (see page 40 on emergency detention).

The above example has a fairly easy solution for the law enforcement officer. Officers are sometimes confronted with much more difficult problems. In 1968 the comedian Dick Gregory led a group of civil rights marchers in a peaceful and orderly march from downtown Chicago to the home of the Chicago mayor, Richard Daley. They were accompanied by Chicago police and an assistant city attorney. The marchers were orderly and peaceful and cooperated with police requests, such as to cease singing at 8:30 P.M.

They marched in the vicinity of the mayor's home for some time, during which the crowd of onlookers and spectators from the neighborhood grew and the language and the conduct of the spectators became rougher and tougher. The police feared that the situation could no longer be contained.

The problem which faced the police was how to prevent an ugly situation from erupting. Should they order the thousand or so bystanders to disperse and leave the immediate area? The bystanders were from the neighborhood and far outnumbered the forty-five policemen at the scene. Or should the police order the demonstrators, who were marching in a completely orderly fashion, to disperse?

The Chicago police demanded that the demonstrators disperse, and when they refused, Dick Gregory and some of his demonstrators were arrested for disorderly conduct. Following a conviction in the trial court, the Illinois Supreme Court sustained the conviction. On appeal to the U.S. Supreme Court, the court held in *Gregory v. City of Chicago*, 394 U.S. 111 (1969), that there was no evidence on the record that the conduct of the demonstrators was disorderly and therefore probable cause for the arrest did not exist. The U.S. Supreme Court reversed the convictions.

To avoid this type of dangerous situation, many municipalities have enacted statutes forbidding the picketing of private homes. There has also been a tightening up of the issuance of parade permits by municipalities on the grounds that police forces just don't have the manpower to prevent ugly situations from erupting.

THE IN-PRESENCE REQUIREMENT
FOR A MISDEMEANOR ARREST

The old English and American common law permitted an officer to make a warrantless arrest for a misdemeanor *only if* (1) the misdemeanor was committed in his presence (giving the officer probable cause) and (2) the offense was one which constituted a disturbance of the public peace. Communities were small and practically everyone was known by name. Travel was slow and the misdemeanant was unlikely to flee or leave the area. Should the need arise, an arrest warrant could easily be obtained from a magistrate.

Over the years as communities became urbanized, the disturbance of the peace or "breach-of-the-peace" requirement was abolished by most states as a requirement to make a misdemeanor arrest. The "in-presence" requirement has been maintained by most states.

However, some jurisdictions have abolished both common-law requirements (Wisconsin in 1971) and broadened the police officer's power to authorize an arrest when the officer has reasonable ground to believe that a crime (either felony or misdemeanor) has been committed.

In jurisdictions using the in-presence requirement (which apparently are most of the states at the present time), an officer must have probable cause to believe that a misdemeanor was (or is being) committed in his presence. The officer may become aware of the misdemeanor by any one of his five senses (sight, hearing, smell, feel, or taste).

Sight is the most common way an officer becomes aware that a misdemeanor has been or is being committed in his presence. Binoculars, telescopes, flashlights, and in some instances searchlights may be used to increase the range of sight and to illuminate at night (see the section on plain view in Chap. 16 for examples).

Hearing evidence indicating that a crime is being committed has also uniformly been held to satisfy the in-presence requirement. In *People v. Goldberg*, 227 N.E.2d 575 (1967), *cert. denied*, 390 U.S. 909 (1968), a New York officer who was standing in a public hall overheard bets being placed and other conversations indicating that gambling was being conducted. The New York Court of Appeals sustained the conviction, stating that the "officer acted on the evidence he perceived by means of his own senses, without any artificial aids. He relied on his own sight (when the door was opened) and hearing, and not on any information supplied to him. To limit the meaning of 'presence' to observation perceived through one sense, sight, seems unsupportable."

Hearing through telephones, radio receivers, or electronic means has been held to place the officer constructively at the scene of the conversation and to satisfy the in-presence requirement. A California appellate court stated in *People v. Burgess*, 388 P.2d 524 (1963), that "presence is liberally construed . . . a public offense may be committed in an officer's presence when his auditory perception is effected by an electronic device." See Chap. 15 and the U.S. Supreme Court cases of On Lee and White in that chapter.

Smell. Cases of smell usually have to do with the smell of marijuana, opium (see *Johnson v. United States*, Chap. 12, p. 285 and Chap. 17, p. 403), and illegal moonshine. If the officer's sense of smell reasonably leads him to conclude that a crime is being committed in his presence, he is then authorized to make further investigation, if necessary, and an arrest if the evidence points to a single person.

Touch or feel. If, during a pat-down during a temporary detention for questioning (see Chap. 11), the officer feels a gun or dangerous weapon and reasonably believes that the possession of the object is a crime, he may make an immediate arrest.

Taste. While cases of satisfying the in-presence requirement through taste are probably rare, there is no reason for an officer to ignore what his sense of taste tells him.

Example: An officer purchased a cup of coffee in an espresso coffee shop. His sense of taste told him that there was probably whiskey in the coffee. The coffee was placed in a container and examined in a laboratory. Tests showed that the coffee contained whiskey. The owner of the shop was charged with selling liquor without a license.

CIRCUMSTANCES OF NECESSITY

States using the in-presence requirement for warrantless misdemeanor arrests frequently include exceptions for circumstances of necessity. In those states, in-presence is not required if the officer has reasonable cause to believe that a person has committed a misdemeanor and also reasonable cause to believe that such person will not be apprehended unless immediately arrested, or may cause injury to himself or others or damage to property unless immediately arrested.

Example: A battered and bruised wife reports to an officer that her husband has been beating her. The offense has not been committed in the presence of the officer, but if there is reasonable cause to believe that the husband will cause additional injury to the wife, the officer may make an immediate arrest of the husband.

MAY AN ARREST BE MADE FOR AN OFFENSE WHICH IS NOT A CRIME?

States and municipalities have enacted many offenses which ordinarily are not considered crimes because they are not punishable by imprisonment. These offenses are often referred to as civil offenses as distinguished from criminal offenses. Most traffic offenses are not crimes and can be classified as civil offenses along with such offenses as jaywalking and overtime or illegal parking.

An arrest may *not* be made for a civil offense unless the statutes of the state specifically authorize the officer to make such an arrest. However, an arrest may be made for failure to obey an officer who has ordered a person to discontinue or cease the activity which amounts to a civil offense under the statutes of the state.

Example: An officer observes a person deliberately littering a public street (assume that littering is a civil offense in that state). The officer orders the person to stop littering, but the person continues to litter and will not obey the officer. Depending upon the statutes of his state, the officer may arrest the person for failure to obey an officer, disorderly conduct, or obstructing.

Example: In *City of Wauwatosa v. King*, 49 Wis.2d 398 (1970), the defendants were notified that picketing a private home was forbidden by ordinance in Wauwatosa. The police arrested five persons who were ordered to stop but continued to picket after they had been given a reasonable time to disperse. The Supreme Court of Wisconsin sustained the arrest.

Detentions (as distinguished from arrests) are sometimes made for civil offenses to ensure the payment of a fine or penalty.

Example: An out-of-state motorist may be detained until he appears before a local court or until he pays the fine or posts a bond for the civil offense of speeding.

CASES FOR CHAPTER ONE

BRINEGAR v. UNITED STATES
SUPREME COURT OF THE UNITED STATES
338 U.S. 160 (1949)

The defendant was convicted of importing liquor from Missouri (a wet state) into Oklahoma (a dry state) in violation of a federal statute forbidding such importation. A federal agent who had arrested the defendant previous to this incident on the same charge, also knew that the defendant had a reputation for hauling liquor. The federal agent saw the defendant driving on a highway coming from Missouri to Oklahoma. The agent testified that the defendant's car appeared to be "heavily loaded" and "weighed with something."

When the federal agent and his partner stopped the defendant's car, the agent said, "Hello Brinegar, how much liquor have you got in the car?" The defendant replied, "Not too much" or "Not so much." After further questioning, the defendant admitted that he had 12 cases. The federal agent testified that one case which was on the front seat was visible from outside the car but the defendant testified that it was covered by a lap robe.

The defendant was arrested and tried by a federal court and found guilty. On the issue of whether the federal agent had probable cause, the court allowed testimony of:

(1) the prior arrest
(2) the knowledge by the agent of the defendant's reputation for hauling liquor (some of which was hearsay).

The trial court held that this knowledge by the officer, and the facts taking place before the defendant made the incriminating statements, gave the officer probable cause for the search and the evidence of the liquor was admitted against the defendant at the trial.

On the issue of guilt, (1) and (2) of the above, were not admitted into evidence.

THE COURT. The court's ruling, one admitting, the other excluding the identical testimony were neither inconsistent nor improper. They illustrate the difference in standards and latitude allowed in passing upon the distinct issues of probable cause and guilt. Guilt in a criminal case must be proved beyond a reasonable doubt and by evidence confined to that which long experience in the common-law tradition, to some extent embodied in the Constitution, has crystallized into rules of evidence consistent with that standard. These rules are historically grounded rights of our system, developed to safeguard men from dubious and unjust convictions, with resulting forfeitures of life, liberty and property.

However, if those standards were to be made applicable in determining probable cause for an arrest or for search and seizure, more especially in cases such as this involving moving vehicles used in the commission of crime, few indeed would be the situations in which an officer charged with protecting the public interest by enforcing the law could take effective action toward that end. Those standards have seldom been so applied.

In dealing with probable cause, however, as the very name implies, we deal with probabilities. These are not technical; they are the factual and practical considerations of everyday life on which reasonable and prudent men, not legal technicians, act. The standard of proof is accordingly correlative to what must be proved.

"The substance of all the definitions" of probable cause "is a reasonable ground for belief of guilt." *McCarthy v. DeArmit* 99 Pa. St. 63. . . . And this "means less than evidence which would justify condemnation or conviction," as Marshall C.J. said for the Court more than a century ago in *Locke v. United States* 7 Cranch 339. Since Marshall's time, at any rate, it has come to mean more than bare suspicion. Probable cause exists where "the facts and circumstances within their [the officers'] knowledge and of which they had reasonably trustworthy information [are] sufficient in themselves to warrant a man of reasonable caution in the belief that" an offense has been or is being committed. *Carroll v. United States* 267 U.S. 267. . . .

These long-prevailing standards seek to safeguard citizens from rash and unreasonable interferences with privacy and from unfounded charges of crime. They also seek to give fair leeway for enforcing the law in the community's protection. Because many situations which confront officers in the course of executing their duties are more or less ambiguous, room must be allowed for some mistakes on their part. But the mistakes must be those of reasonable men, acting on facts leading sensibly to their conclusions of probability. The rule of probable cause is a practical, nontechnical conception affording the best compromise that has been found for accommodating these often opposing interests. Requiring more would unduly hamper law enforcement. To allow less would be to leave law-abiding citizens at the mercy of the officers' whim or caprice.

The troublesome line posed by the facts in the *Carroll* case and this case is one between suspicion and probable cause. That line necessarily must be drawn by an act of judgment formed in the light of the particular situation and with account taken of all circumstances. No problem of searching the home or any other place of privacy was presented either in *Carroll* or here. Both cases involve freedom to use public highways in swiftly moving vehicles for dealing in contraband, and to be unmolested by investigation and search in those movements. In such a case the citizen who has given no good cause for believing he is engaged in that sort of activity is entitled to proceed on his way without interference. But one who recently and repeatedly has given substantial ground for believing that he is engaging in the forbidden transportation in the area of his usual operations has no such immunity, if the officer who intercepts him in that region knows that fact at the time he makes the interception and the circumstances under which it is made are not such as to indicate the suspect is going about legitimate affairs.

This does not mean, as seems to be assumed, that every traveler along the public highways may be stopped and searched at the officers' whim, caprice, or mere suspicion. The question presented in the *Carroll* case lay on the border between suspicion and probable cause. But the Court carefully considered that problem and resolved it by concluding that the facts within the officers' knowledge when they intercepted the *Carroll* defendants amounted to more than mere suspicion and constituted probable cause for their action. We cannot say this conclusion was wrong or was so lacking in reason and consistency with the Fourth Amendment purpose that it should now be overridden. Nor, as we have said, can we find in the present facts any substantial basis for distinguishing this case from the *Carroll* case.

Judgment affirmed.

JACKSON, J., DISSENTING. . . . With this prologue, I come to the case of Brinegar. His automobile was one of his "effects" and hence within the express protection of the Fourth Amendment. Undoubtedly the automobile presents peculiar problems for enforcement agencies, is frequently a facility for the perpetration of crime and an aid in the escape of criminals. But if we are to make judicial exceptions to the Fourth Amendment for these reasons, it seems to me they should depend somewhat upon the gravity of the offense. If we assume, for example, that a child is kidnaped and the officers throw a roadblock about the neighborhood and search each outgoing car, it would be a drastic and undiscriminating use of the search. The officers might be unable to show probable cause for searching any particular car. However, I should candidly strive hard to sustain such an action, executed fairly and in good faith, because it might be reasonable to subject travelers to that indignity if it was the only way to save a threatened life and detect a vicious crime. But I should not strain to sustain such a roadblock and universal search to salvage a few bottles of bourbon and catch a bootlegger. . . .

RIOS v. UNITED STATES
SUPREME COURT OF THE UNITED STATES
364 U.S. 253 (1959)

MR. JUSTICE STEWART. At about ten o'clock on the night of February 18, 1957, two Los Angeles police officers, dressed in plain clothes and riding in an unmarked car, observed a taxicab standing in a parking lot next to an apartment house at the corner of First and Flower Streets in Los Angeles. The neighborhood had a reputation for "narcotics activity." The officers saw the petitioner look up and down the street, walk across the lot, and get into the cab. Neither officer had ever before seen the petitioner, and neither of them had any idea of his identity. Except for the reputation of the neighborhood, neither officer had received information of any kind to suggest that someone might be engaged in criminal activity at that time and place. They were not searching for a participant in any previous crime. They were in possession of no arrest or search warrants.

The taxicab drove away, and the officers followed it in their car for a distance of about two miles through the city. At the intersection of First and State Streets the cab stopped for a traffic light. The two officers alighted from their car and approached on foot to opposite sides of the cab. One of the officers identified himself as a policeman. In the next minute there occurred a rapid succession of events. The cab door was opened; the petitioner dropped a recognizable package of narcotics to the floor of the vehicle; one of the officers grabbed the petitioner as he alighted from the cab; the other officer retrieved the package; and the first officer drew his revolver.[1]

The precise chronology of all that happened is not clear in the record. In their original arrest report the police stated that the petitioner dropped the package only after one of the officers had opened the cab door. In testifying later, this officer said that he saw the defendant drop the package before the door of the cab was opened. The taxi driver gave a substantially different version of what occurred. He stated that one of the officers drew his revolver and "took hold of the defendant's arm while he was still in the cab."

A state criminal prosecution was instituted against the petitioner, charging him with possession of narcotics, a felony under California law. Cal. Health and Safety Code, § 11500. At a preliminary hearing the two Los Angeles officers testified as to the circumstances surrounding the arrest and seizure. When the case came on for trial in the Superior Court of Los Angeles County, the petitioner moved to suppress as evidence the package of heroin which the police had seized. On the basis of the transcript of the preliminary hearing, and after brief argument by counsel, the court granted the motion and entered a judgment of acquittal.

Thereafter, one of the Los Angeles officers who had arrested the petitioner discussed the case with his superiors and suggested giving the evidence to United States authorities. He then got in touch with federal narcotics agents and told them about the petitioner's case. This led to the federal prosecution we now review.

. . . .

. . . we have concluded that the interests of justice will best be served by remanding the case to the District Court. There, free from the entanglement of other issues that have now become irrelevant, the lawfulness of the policemen's conduct can be determined in accord with the basic principles governing the validity of searches and seizures by federal officers under the Fourth Amendment.

Under these principles the inquiry in the present case will be narrowly oriented. The seizure can survive constitutional inhibition only upon a showing that the surrounding facts brought it within one of the exceptions to the rule that a search must rest upon a search warrant. Here justification is primarily sought upon the claim that the search was an incident to a lawful arrest. Yet upon no possible view of the circumstances revealed in the testimony of the Los Angeles officers could it be said that there existed probable cause for an arrest at the time the officers decided to alight from their car and approach the taxi in which the petitioner was riding. This the Government concedes.

If, therefore, the arrest occurred when the officers took their positions at the doors of the taxicab, then nothing that happened thereafter could make that arrest lawful, or justify a search as its incident. But the Government argues that the policemen approached the standing taxi only for the purpose of routine interrogation, and that they had no intent to detain the petitioner beyond the momentary requirements of such a mission. If the petitioner thereafter voluntarily revealed the package of narcotics to the officers' view, a lawful arrest could then have been supported by their reasonable cause to believe that a felony was being committed in their presence. The validity of the search thus turns upon the narrow question of when the arrest occurred, and the answer to that question depends upon an evaluation of the conflicting testimony of those who were there that night.

---

[1] The petitioner later broke free from the policeman's grasp and ran into an alley. There the officer apprehended him after shooting him in the back.

The judgment is vacated, and the case is remanded to the District Court for further proceedings consistent with this opinion.

Vacated and remanded.

QUESTIONS AND PROBLEMS

1. In the United States, thousands of motorists are stopped every day for traffic violations. Would most of these "stops" be arrests? Give the reason for your answer.
2. Could you, as a law enforcement officer, issue a ticket to or arrest the following persons (assume that the way they were handling their vehicles would justify a ticket or an arrest)?
   a. The driver of a U.S. mail truck
   b. The driver of a U.S. Army vehicle who is in full uniform
   c. An attorney (who is an officer of a court) and is very late for a divorce case
   d. A state legislator hurrying to get to the state capital
   e. A Canadian visitor to the United States
   f. A German merchant seaman off a foreign merchant vessel
3. Indicate the *minimum* quantum of evidence:
   a. To make a valid arrest
   b. To stop a vehicle and ask the motorist to display his driver's license
   c. To stop a pedestrian and request information on a voluntary basis
   d. To stop a pedestrian and demand that he identify himself and give an explanation of his conduct
   e. To make a weapons search (frisk) of the person stopped in 3d
   f. To issue a search or arrest warrant
   g. To determine, at a preliminary hearing, whether the defendant will be bound over for trial
   h. To determine guilt or innocence at a criminal trial

   Available Answers for Question 3
   1. Proof beyond a reasonable doubt
   2. Preponderance of the evidence
   3. Probable cause or reasonable grounds to believe
   4. Reasonable suspicion
   5. A hunch or mere suspicion

4. Name some of the 2,072 federal bureaus, agencies, departments, offices, etc., which are enforcing criminal law in your jurisdiction.
5. What are some of the state and local agencies enforcing criminal law in your jurisdiction?

6. The Sixth Amendment of the U.S. Constitution provides for a "speedy" trial for the accused. Could a police officer who saw a person commit a misdemeanor hold this crime over the person's head until just before the statute of limitation expired and then charge him successfully?

Local Law

1. In your state, are there any differences in the arrest power of:
   a. Municipal police officers
   b. County deputy sheriffs
   c. State police officers
   d. State highway officers (highway patrol)
   e. State officers from state offices such as the department of justice, revenue, alcohol, tax enforcement, etc.
2. Can all the officers of question 1 arrest for felonies not committed in their presence? for misdemeanors committed in their presence? for misdemeanors not committed in their presence?
3. What privilege from arrest does your state constitution or state law extend to state legislators?
4. What are the statutes of limitation in your state in regard to: (a) misdemeanors, (b) felonies, (c) thefts, (d) murders and homicides?
5. What actions stop the statute of limitations from running in your state?

2

DETENTION AS RELATED TO ARREST

Detention, like arrest, search, and seizure, is a use of the police power of the state. Detention is a restraint of freedom of movement which might be for a few minutes or for a lifetime. The legality of the detention is determined by its purpose and the length of time that the person was detained.

The forms of detention in our modern society vary from the temporary detention while an officer is checking a driver's license to a situation where a person is held indefinitely because he is found to have such physical and mental aberrations that if released, he is likely to burn down buildings for sexual excitement (sex-deviate laws).

Detention must be used if public order and safety are to be maintained. Therefore, democracies seek to establish safeguards to ensure that detention is used only for the overall public good.

An arrest must include a detention, but many detentions are used in situations where there is no arrest. Arrest is the legalized procedure in which detention is used to bring the person arrested before a court to face a charge. If convicted, the defendant can face prolonged detention by judgment of the court. Search and seizure pertain to the seeking and obtaining of evidence or contraband. Seizure can also be construed to include the seizure of the person.

A government which may use detention without any legal or constitutional restraints has a formidable and terrible power at its disposal. The practice of putting people in jail without stating the nature of their alleged crimes or ever bringing them to trial has always been considered one of the worst abuses by government. Most authoritarian and totalitarian governments have used this power of detention, not only to eliminate political opposition but also to terrorize their subjects into submission. The slave-labor camps of Stalin and Hitler illustrate what a terrible weapon detention can be in the hands of a ruthless government.

Visitors to George Washington's home at Mount Vernon can observe the key to the Bastille, which Lafayette gave to Washington in 1790, with the statement that this was "the main key to the fortress of despotism." In order to ensure against such unlawful detention as was practiced in the Bastille, the founding fathers not only defined the rights of the individual in the U.S. Constitution but also provided in article I, section 9, that "the privilege of the writ of habeas corpus shall not be suspended unless when in cases of rebellion or invasion the public safety may require it."

HABEAS CORPUS

The sole function of the writ of habeas corpus is to bring the issue of the lawfulness of a detention before a court of competent jurisdiction. Blackstone refers to habeas corpus as "the most celebrated writ in the English law." Chief Justice John Marshall of the U.S. Supreme Court called it a "great constitutional privilege," and the Supreme Court has stated a number of times that "there is no higher duty than to maintain it unimpaired."

The writ owes its origin to English common law, and its present form probably came into existence through an act of Parliament of 1679. Although it was included in the U.S. Constitution, all the original thirteen states placed the guarantee of the right to habeas corpus in their constitutions. Many states strengthen the constitutional guarantee by statutory provisions such as that used in the Wisconsin statutes. Section 292.09 states, "If any judge shall wilfully refuse to grant such writ, when legally applied for, he shall be liable to the prisoner in the sum of one thousand dollars."

The present federal habeas corpus statute (28 U.S.C. § 2243) remains substantially unchanged since the original enactment of 1867. This law reinstated what apparently was the common-law understanding in regard to the power of the federal courts on habeas corpus hearings. The act provides that the federal courts can take testimony and determine the facts de novo in the largest terms. In *Townsend v. Sain*, 372 U.S. 293 (1963), the U.S. Supreme Court, in ruling on the power and obligation of the federal courts to hear habeas corpus petitions, stated:

> ... In construing the mandate of Congress, so plainly designed to afford a trial-type proceeding in federal court for state prisoners aggrieved by unconstitutional detentions, this Court has consistently upheld the power of the federal courts on habeas corpus to take evidence relevant to claims of such detention....
>
> The rule could not be otherwise. The whole history of the writ—its unique development—refutes a construction of the federal courts'

habeas corpus powers that would assimilate their task to that of courts of appellate review. The function on habeas is different. It is to test by way of an original civil proceeding, independent of the normal channels of review of criminal judgments, the very gravest allegations. State prisoners are entitled to relief on federal habeas corpus only upon proving that their detention violates the fundamental liberties of the person, safeguarded against state action by the Federal Constitution. Simply because detention so obtained is intolerable, the opportunity for redress, which presupposes the opportunity to be heard, to argue and present evidence, must never be totally foreclosed.

A habeas corpus hearing determines not whether the prisoner is guilty or innocent, but only whether his detention is lawful. The writ is served upon the authority holding the person, whether this authority is a sheriff, the U.S. Army, a mental institution, or a children's detention center. The writ orders that authority or institution to appear before the court issuing the writ with the person and to show lawful reasons for his detention.

WHEN MAY A DETENTION OR A RESTRAINT ON PERSONAL LIBERTY BE MADE?

A detention or a restraint of personal liberty may be made:

1. In order to effect an arrest and to enforce laws and ordinances
2. When necessary for the protection of the public and in the interest of public safety

   Example: A person who threatens violence and who appears irresponsible and dangerous may be taken into temporary custody under the emergency detention statute of that state.

3. When necessary for investigation purposes by a law enforcement officer; examples of investigative detention are:
   a. The temporary detention of material witnesses to a crime which the officer is investigating
   b. The temporary detention of a person when an officer reasonably suspects that the person has committed or is committing a crime (see Chap. 11)
   c. Temporary detention for the purpose of enforcing such laws as the motor vehicle code of the state

DETENTION WITHOUT ARREST TO INVESTIGATE A SUSPECTED OR KNOWN CRIME

Detention on the street or at the scene of an accident or a crime may be used to investigate a suspected or a known crime.

Example: An officer is called to the scene of an automobile accident where a person was injured. Caring for the injured person, investigating the accident, and questioning the witnesses takes three hours.

Example: An officer is called to the scene of a homicide. Witnesses are detained for four hours for investigative and questioning purposes.

Example: A shop owner calls the police to report that he is holding a person whom he saw take merchandise and attempt to leave without paying. The investigation and questioning take an hour.

Detentions without arrest may be made in all the above examples in order to investigate the incidents and to determine whether a crime has been committed and an arrest should be made. The test for determining the legality of detentions is (1) whether the reason for the detention is reasonable and (2) whether the length of time that the person was detained is reasonable.

The authority to search a person during an investigative detention is presented in Chap. 11. That chapter also contains the 1968 Terry, Peters, and Sibron cases, in which the U.S. Supreme Court lays down the guidelines for temporary detentions for questioning without arrest and the searches which may be made during such detentions.

DETENTION BETWEEN ARREST AND THE INITIAL APPEARANCE BEFORE A JUDGE (STATION-HOUSE DETENTION)

After a suspect has been lawfully arrested and probable cause exists to sustain the arrest, uncertainty may still exist as to whether there is sufficient evidence to charge the individual.

Example: A liquor store has been robbed by two men. The owner of the store was slugged and is unconscious in the hospital. The only other witness saw the men getting into a 1969 green Ford but did not get a good look at the men. Twenty minutes later, a car matching the description given for the holdup car is stopped by the police 3 miles away from the holdup scene. The two men say that they have been just driving around for the last hour.

Example: A woman reports that she has been raped and describes the man who assaulted her as being about 5 feet 10 inches, weighing 150 pounds, wearing a blue sweater and black pants. Two hours later, officers in a squad car observe a man fitting this vague description on a street in the neighborhood of the assault. When the man sees the squad, he ducks into an alley and runs. When he is caught, he refuses to respond to questions.

On the basis of the new rules of lineup and identification, should the men in both examples be released on the street and asked to appear voluntarily? Should they be brought in and immediately charged with the crimes they are suspected of committing? Or should they be brought in and held pending the outcome of further investigation?

In testifying before a U.S. Senate committee in 1963, the former superintendent of the Chicago Police Department, O. W. Wilson, pointed out that "bringing a suspect to a police station affords the police an opportunity to discharge six important obligations."*

1. Checking out the suspect's story
2. Checking the identity of the suspect
3. Getting statements from victims and witnesses (in the first example, the victim is unconscious in the hospital)
4. Making laboratory analysis of physical evidence
5. Searching for weapons which were used and the loot obtained in the crime
6. A lineup for victims and witnesses

In-custody investigation can resolve doubts one way or another, and, if innocent, the subject may be immediately released without being charged with a crime. On the other hand, the investigation can build a better case for the state.

However, it is important that officers have a clear understanding of the time which is available to them for any in-custody investigation they seek to make before charging the person before a judge or magistrate. This time period is determined by the laws of their state or the court decisions of their state.

State statutes either require that the person arrested be taken before a magistrate or judge within a specific period of time or "without unreasonable delay." Failure to comply with the time requirement of the jurisdiction could have a number of effects:

1. It could cast doubt upon the voluntariness of any admissions or confessions obtained from the suspect during that period.
2. If the detention were unreasonable or unlawful, the delay could be held to be a violation of the Fourteenth Amendment due process of the law clause. A confession obtained during a period of unlawful detention, even though a voluntary confession, would probably not be accepted by the court.

Another effect of unreasonable delay in bringing the suspect before a magistrate or judge is that the officers involved become more

* *Hearing on H.R. 7525 and S. 486 before the Senate Committee on the District of Columbia,* 88th Cong., 1st Sess., pt. 1, at 310–11 (1963).

vulnerable to a false imprisonment suit. As a judge cannot ordinarily be successfully sued for false imprisonment or false arrest, the general practice is to take the suspect before a magistrate or judge as soon as possible.

The authorization (either by statute or court decisions) of a short period of station-house detention is proposed by the American Law Institute in *Model Code of Pre-Arraignment Procedure*, article 4, and a discussion of the justification of station-house detention is on pages 137–150 of the proposed draft. The practical necessity of institutionalizing "a period of screening prior to the decision whether and with what to charge a person arrested without a warrant" is urged because of the incomplete information available to the officer at the time of the encounter and also because in many situations the officer is operating under emergency circumstances in an atmosphere of confusion and alarm.

STATION-HOUSE DETENTION AS DISTINGUISHED FROM THE EUROPEAN INVESTIGATIVE ARREST

In the United States, in order to sustain any prolonged station-house detention, there would have to be probable cause to hold the person. "Investigative arrest" is commonly used and legalized by European countries and is an arrest on suspicion or any other standard less than probable cause or reasonable cause. The use of station-house detention or investigative arrest without probable cause would be seriously challenged in American courts, as the Fourth Amendment requires probable cause in order to make an arrest.

Another procedure which has been denounced by American courts occurs when the suspect is charged with a misdemeanor (disorderly conduct, vagrancy, etc.) in order to hold him while an investigation for a felony is taking place. If the investigation provides sufficient evidence, the suspect is then charged with the felony which he was suspected of committing.

DETENTION OF MATERIAL WITNESSES

While material witnesses cannot be arrested unless probable cause exists, material witnesses can be reasonably detained until the investigating officer has obtained the necessary information to fulfill his duty and obligation to investigate the criminal incident. When the state is concerned with the safety of a material witness, various arrangements can be made if the witness is cooperative.

The witness who identified James Earl Ray as the man rushing down the rooming house steps immediately after the shooting of the Rev. Martin Luther King, Jr., was cooperative and moved into the county jail in Memphis. He was free to come and go but was provided with a bodyguard when he left the jail. This was agreeable to all concerned for a while until the police thought that he was jeopardizing his own safety by leaving too often.

Most states have statutes providing that bail may be set for the appearance of witnesses; the state of Tennessee went into court and asked that bail be set to ensure the appearance of this witness at the trial of James Earl Ray. Bail was set at $10,000, but as the witness was living on a small pension, he could not meet the bail and was detained in jail.

His attorneys went back into court on a writ of habeas corpus and argued that the witness had been denied due process and that his bail was excessive. The outcome was an arrangement whereby the witness spent the remaining time before trial in a police-protected apartment.

Other means which can be used to preserve and safeguard the testimony of important witnesses are:

1. Having the witness appear and testify under oath and be subject to cross-examination at the preliminary examination. Should the witness be unavailable at the trial because of death or because the state could not find him, his former testimony could be used. This is a practical answer unless the defense waives their right to a preliminary examination.
2. If there is no preliminary examination and the state is concerned about the appearance of an important material witness, another safeguard might be a deposition. About a third of the states have statutes permitting the use of depositions in criminal cases. However, the constitutional requirement of confrontation would still have to be complied with.

CIVIL DETENTIONS

Mental illness is the greatest health problem in the United States. There are more mental patients in mental hospitals than patients with all other diseases in all other hospitals combined. More than half a million patients are being detained in mental hospitals in the United States, and most of these patients are hospitalized by court action.

All the states have statutes providing for commitment procedure and usually define mental illness as insanity, mental infirmity as mental senility, and mental deficiency as feeblemindedness; a fourth disability, alcoholism, is also recognized. The writ of habeas corpus can be used to question the legality of the detention of a person in a mental hospital or asylum.

EMERGENCY DETENTION

State statutes contain emergency detention provisions providing that law enforcement officers *may* take into temporary custody persons who are violent or who threaten violence and appear irresponsible and dangerous. These statutes are intended to be used for the protection of persons and property.

Example: Police officers are called to a home by a wife. The husband has not beaten the wife and is not drunk but threatens to kill the wife and the children that night. There are no grounds to arrest the husband, but if the threats are made in the presence of the officers, he could be (and should be) taken into temporary custody under the emergency detention statutes of that state.

The same emergency detention statute usually also provides that law enforcement officers *shall* take into temporary custody a person when certified by written application and signed by a number of persons (usually three) that such person either has a mental illness or is in need of hospitalization and is irresponsible and dangerous to himself or others. State statutes require that one of the persons be a physician licensed to practice medicine in that state.

Police stations and the county sheriff's office have these applications available, and it is usually the wife, husband, or a member of the family who initiates the process. State statutes provide that such persons may be kept in custody until regular proceedings are instituted to cope with the case. The statutes set a maximum number of days in which the emergency detention is applicable.

Law enforcement officials and other persons using such emergency detention statutes are not liable in civil actions as long as they stay within the scope of the authority granted by the statutes. In 1968, a dean in a midwestern university, the school doctor, and another person filled out an application for emergency detention when a girl student insisted that she was going to drop out of school. The coed spent one night in detention at the county sanitarium. In the subsequent civil suit for false imprisonment, she recovered a total of $45,000 in damages.

DETENTION OF CHILDREN

Parents, guardians, and those who act in the place of the parent or guardian (*in loco parentis*) have the duty to provide food, clothing, shelter, medical care, education, and discipline for a child within their care. They have the right to the care, custody, and control of the child. Law enforcement officers occasionally find that they are called into a home and confronted with a situation similar to this example, which actually happened not long ago.

Example: A sixteen-year-old girl dressed up and started to leave the house. When asked where she was going, she told her father that she was going to a movie. As it was a weekday night, her father told her "no" and took her by the arm, telling her to get up to her room and study. She phoned the police complaining that her father was unlawfully detaining her and had assaulted her. When the police arrived, the girl again stated her complaint. As there was no evidence of physical abuse and it was apparent that the father was reasonably exercising the duties and rights vested in him as a parent, the officers told the girl that her father had the responsibility to impose such restraints upon her.

The question of reasonable restraint also comes up when an eighth-grade student wants to leave the school at 2 P.M. and go to a movie. The school is acting *in loco parentis* and not only has the right to custody and control of the child but also has the duty of imposing reasonable discipline and restraints upon the child.

Children's codes have been enacted by all the states. These codes provide that a child who violates the law is treated in a different manner from an adult (a person over eighteen). The child is not arrested but is taken into custody and detained in the manner prescribed by the code. Unfortunately, sixteen-year-old children violate more criminal laws than any other age bracket. The seventeen-year-old age bracket follows close behind the record set by the sixteen-year-olds. Law enforcement officers' problems (and those of society) are compounded by the fact that most states have facilities to institutionalize *only* an estimated 20 percent of the children who should be institutionalized. Because of the lack of room in children's institutions, the child who has been taken into custody is soon released and too many times returns to a broken home and an environment likely to cause him to get into trouble again.

DETENTION FOR SHOPLIFTING

Shoplifting is one of the more perplexing problems confronting law enforcement officers and merchants. The loss from shoplifting runs into millions of dollars per year in the United States, and many small merchants have been forced out of business because of shoplifting losses. A merchant's loss from shoplifting is a cost of doing business and must, of necessity, be passed on to the consumer in the form of increased prices.

Because of the increased losses in merchandise year after year, chambers of commerce and retail merchant associations have petitioned state legislatures for shoplifting statutes. Some merchants would like legislation which would authorize them to search anyone they *suspect* of shoplifting, but such legislation would violate the Fourth Amendment. Signs are sometimes seen in stores stating that the store reserves the right to search handbags, parcels, and packages. What if the customer still refuses to allow himself to be searched? A consent search is always valid, and many times quickly clears up the situation one way or the other. State legislatures have been very reluctant to authorize nonconsent searches by merchants, and most shoplifting statutes provide authority *only* for the merchant and/or his adult employee to detain a person in a reasonable manner for a reasonable length of time when the merchant or his employee has *probable cause* to believe that the person has violated the shoplifting statute or the theft statute.

The law enforcement officer, when called by a merchant on a shoplifting complaint, may find himself confronted by any one of various situations which we categorize as follows:

1. The most common, and the easiest one for the officer, is the situation where the merchant or his employee states that he has seen the person take an item and the merchandise is already recovered. The officer may then order the person and the merchant to appear at a given date before the district attorney or the city attorney unless the replacement value to the merchant makes the incident a felony and the officer, because of this, makes the decision to arrest and takes the person to the station.

2. A more difficult situation arises when the merchant says that he has seen the person take the item but the item has not been recovered. It is recommended that the officer try to persuade the person being detained to produce the item voluntarily or to persuade him to consent to search by the officer. If the item is recovered, the person can be ordered in, but if the item is not recovered after a *consent* search, the decision to order in would in most instances depend upon the merchant's insistence on having the parties appear before the prosecuting attorney.

3. If the person will not give his permission for a *consent* search and protests his innocence, the officer must then decide whether he can and should make an arrest and make a search subsequent to the arrest. When the merchant states, "I saw him take the item," the

officer has probable cause to make an arrest in some jurisdictions. (What is the law in your state on this?) But if the merchant indicates only suspicion of the person, then the officer does not have probable cause and the merchant should not have made the detention.

4. The most difficult situation confronting the merchant is one where on the merchant's complaint, the officer has made an arrest and made a search but no stolen merchandise is recovered. Whether to proceed or whether to drop the matter is a decision for the officer and/or the merchant. The value of the merchandise involved might be the deciding factor.

The officer making an arrest in a shoplifting case is ordinarily immune in a civil suit if he has acted within the scope of his authority and in good faith. This would necessarily require a showing of probable cause. Because state statutes differ in the authority granted to merchants and to officers, no definite general rule can be laid down covering situations arising in the many jurisdictions of the United States.

Officers should not mistake their power to make a search under the so-called "stop-and-frisk" statutes in a shoplifting confrontation. The frisk authorized by the stop-and-frisk doctrine (see Chap. 11) is a weapons search, and the officer may make such a frisk *only* when he has reasonable grounds to believe that the person he is questioning is armed and dangerous.

OTHER DETENTIONS OR RESTRAINTS
UNDER THE POLICE POWER OF THE STATE

Highways

Highways are built and owned by the state. To use the public highway, one must not only have a valid driver's license but also be operating a properly licensed vehicle which is in good mechanical condition. Road checks for the good-faith purpose of inspecting motor vehicle licenses and registration certificates have been held to be a constitutionally valid method of enforcing public safety as long as the road check is not used as a subterfuge for uncovering evidence of other crimes.

> If stopping motorists indiscriminately by police officers for the good faith purpose of inspecting or asking for the exhibition of a driver's license was not permitted, the licensing law would break down and become a nullity, and the objective for promoting public safety from irresponsible automobile drivers would be seriously impeded. There

would be but few occasions where an officer could otherwise learn that the law was being violated. *Commonwealth v. Mitchell*, 355 S.W.2d 688 (Ky. 1962)

Curfews

Curfews have been used by cities and states during emergency situations. This form of detention to the residence and exclusion from the public streets (or other areas) has been held to be a valid use of the police power of the state when reasonably used.

Sex-deviate Laws

States have provided by statute that if a person is found to have mental or physical aberrations, he shall be detained as long as such control is necessary for the protection of the public. The type of person detained might be one who would commit arson because of the desire for sexual excitement furnished by such an incident. These laws have been sustained as being a proper use of the police power of the state as long as the detention is not for punishment but for the public safety and the treatment of the individual.

CASES FOR CHAPTER TWO

MORALES v. NEW YORK
SUPREME COURT OF THE UNITED STATES
396 U.S. 102, 90 S. CT. 291 (1969)

PER CURIAM.* On October 4, 1964, a murder by stabbing took place in an elevator of an apartment building where petitioner Morales' mother lived and where Morales frequently visited. On October 13, his mother informed Morales by telephone that the police wished to talk with him; petitioner said that he would come that evening to his mother's place of business. This he did. He was apprehended by police officers and taken to the police station, arriving at 8:30 P.M. Within 15 minutes he had confessed to the crime and by 9:05 P.M. he had written and signed a statement. In response to subsequent questioning by police officers, Morales later repeated the substance of this confession. At the trial, the court held a separate hearing on the voluntariness of the confessions, found them voluntary and admitted them over Morales' objection. Morales was convicted, the jury apparently rejecting his alibi defense that he was with his mother at the time of the murder. The Appellate Division of the New York Supreme Court affirmed without opinion.... In the New York Court of Appeals, Morales for the first time raised a Fourth Amendment issue, claiming that there was no probable cause for his detention at the time of his confession and that the confessions, even if voluntary

---

* *Per curiam* means "by the court." The term is used to distinguish an opinion of the whole court from one written by any one judge.

were inadmissible fruits of the illegal detention. The State asserted that the issue had not been decided below and that there had hence been no opportunity to make a record of the relevant facts; moreover, the State claimed that Morales had voluntarily surrendered himself for questioning and that in any event the voluntary confessions were the result of an independent choice by Morales such that the legality of the detention was irrelevant to the admissibility of the confessions.

The Court of Appeals affirmed, accepting without discussion the trial court's finding as to the voluntariness of Morales' confession.... The court dealt with and rejected the Fourth Amendment claim not on the ground that there was probable cause to arrest but rather on the ground that the police conduct involved was reasonable under the circumstances of the case. Although Morales was not free to leave at the time he was apprehended and would have been restrained had he attempted to flee, the Court of Appeals stated that his detention was not a formal arrest under New York law and that had he refused to answer questions in the police station (where he was entitled to have a lawyer if he desired one) he would have been free to leave. The Court of Appeals held that the State had authority under the Fourth Amendment to conduct brief custodial interrogation of "those persons reasonably suspected of possessing knowledge of the crime under investigation in circumstances involving crimes presenting a high degree of public concern affecting the public safety." We granted certiorari....

After considering the full record, we do not disturb the determination of the trial court, affirmed by the New York appellate courts, that Morales' confessions were voluntarily given. The trial occurred prior to *Miranda v. Arizona* 384 US 436 ... (1966), and the totality of the circumstances surrounding the confessions shows that the confessions were voluntary, not coerced.

We should not, however, decide on the record before us whether Morales' conviction, should otherwise be affirmed. The ruling below, that the State may detain for custodial questioning on less than probable cause for a traditional arrest, is manifestly important, goes beyond our subsequent decisions in Terry v. Ohio 392 U.S. 1 ... and Sibron v. New York 392 U.S. 40 (1968) ... [see Chap. 11] and is claimed by petitioner to be at odds with Davis v. Mississippi 394 U.S. 721 ... (1969). But we have concluded after considering the parties' briefs and hearing oral argument that there is merit in the State's position that the record does not permit a satisfactory evaluation of the facts surrounding the apprehension and detention of Morales. A lengthy hearing was held on the question of the voluntariness of the confessions, but the basis for the apprehension of Morales does not appear to have been fully explored since no challenge to the lawfulness of the apprehension was raised until the case came to the Court of Appeals. Although that court stated that "[i]t may be conceded that the apprehending detectives did not have probable cause to justify an arrest of defendant at the time they took him into custody" ... the court later said that "[t]he checkerboard square of the police investigation, although resting upon circumstantial evidence, pointed only to defendant.... In fact, defendant was the only person the police could have reasonably detained for questioning based upon the instant record."...

Given an opportunity to develop in an evidentiary hearing the circumstances leading to the detention of Morales and his confessions, the State may be able to show that there was probable cause for an arrest or that Morales' confrontation with the police was voluntarily undertaken by him or that the confessions were not the product of illegal detention. In any event, in the absence of a record which squarely and necessarily presents the issue and fully illuminates the factual context in which the question arises, we choose not to grapple with the question of the legality of custodial questioning on less than probable cause for a full-fledged arrest.

We accordingly vacate the judgment below and remand the case for further proceedings not inconsistent with this opinion.

It is so ordered.

Mr. Justice Black dissents.

DAVIS v. MISSISSIPPI
SUPREME COURT OF THE UNITED STATES
394 U.S. 721 (1969)

Mr. Justice Brennan delivered the opinion of the Court.

Petitioner was convicted of rape and sentenced to life imprisonment by a jury.... The only issue before us is whether fingerprints obtained from petitioner should have been excluded from evidence as the product of a detention which was illegal under the 4th and 14th Amendments.

The rape occurred on the evening of December 2, 1965 at the victim's home in Meridian, Mississippi. The victim could give no better description of her assailant than that he was a Negro youth. Finger and palm prints found on the sill and border of the window through which the assailant apparently entered the victim's home constituted the only other lead available at the outset of the police investigation. Beginning on Dec. 3 and for a period of about 10 days the Meridian police without warrants took at least 24 Negro youths to police headquarters where they were questioned briefly, fingerprinted and then released without charge. The police also interrogated 40 or 50 other Negro youths either at police headquarters, at school or on the street. Petitioner, a 14-year-old youth who had occasionally worked for the victim as a yardboy was brought in on Dec. 3 and released after being fingerprinted and routinely questioned. Between Dec. 3 and Dec. 7, he was interrogated by the police on several occasions—sometimes at home or in a car, other times at police headquarters. This questioning apparently related primarily to investigation of other potential suspects. Several times during this period petitioner was exhibited to the victim in her hospital room. A police officer testified that 3 confrontations were for the purpose of sharpening the victim's description of her assailant by providing a "gauge to go by on size and color." The victim did not identify petitioner as her assailant at any of these confrontations.

On Dec. 12, the police drove petitioner 90 miles to the city of Jackson and confined him overnight in the Jackson jail. The State conceded on oral argument in this Court that there was neither a warrant or probable cause for this arrest. The next day, petitioner who had not yet been afforded counsel, took a lie detector test and signed a statement. He was then returned to and confined in the Meridian jail. On Dec. 14, while so confined, petitioner was fingerprinted a second time. That same day, the December 14 prints together with the fingerprints of 23 other Negro youths apparently still under suspicion were sent to the FBI in Washington D.C. for comparison with the latent prints taken from the window of the victim's house. The FBI reported that petitioner's prints matched those taken from the window. Petitioner was subsequently indicted and tried for the rape and the fingerprint evidence was admitted in evidence at trial over petitioner's timely objections that the fingerprints should be excluded as the product of an unlawful detention....

...We turn then to the question whether the detention of petitioner during which the fingerprints used at trial were taken constituted an unreasonable seizure of his person in violation of the 4th Amendment. The opinion of the Mississippi Supreme Court proceeded on the mistaken premise that petitioner's prints introduced at trial were taken during his brief detention on Dec. 3. In fact, as both parties before us agree, the fingerprint evidence used at trial was obtained on Dec. 14 while petitioner was still in detention following his Dec. 12th arrest. The legality of his arrest was not determined by the Mississippi Supreme Court. However, on oral argument here, the State conceded that the arrest on Dec. 12 and the ensuing detention through Dec. 14 were based on neither a warrant or probable cause and were therefore constitutionally invalid. . . .

The State makes no claim that petitioner voluntarily accompanied the police officers to headquarters on Dec. 3 and willingly submitted to fingerprinting. The State's brief also candidly admits that "[a]ll that the Meridian Police could possible have known about petitioner at the time . . . would not amount to probable cause for his arrest." The State argues, however that the Dec. 3 detention was of a type which does not require probable cause. Two rationales for this position are suggested. First, it is argued that the detention occurred during the investigative rather than accusatory stage and thus was not a seizure requiring probable cause. The second and related argument is that, at the least, detention for the sole purpose of obtaining fingerprints does not require probable cause.

It is true that at the time of the Dec. 3 detention the police had no intention of charging petitioner with the crime and were far from making him the primary focus of their investigation. But to argue that the 4th Amendment does not apply to the investigatory stage is fundamentally to misconceive the purposes of the 4th Amendment. Investigatory seizures would subject unlimited numbers of innocent persons to the harassment and ignominy incident to involuntary detention. Nothing is more clear than that the 4th Amendment was meant to prevent wholesale intrusions upon the personal security of our citizenry, whether these intrusions be termed "arrests" or "investigatory detentions." We made this explicit only last term in *Terry v. Ohio* 392 US 1 (1968) when we rejected "the notions that the 4th Amendment does not come into play at all as a limitation upon police conduct if the officers stop short of something called a "technical arrest" or a "full-blown search."

Detention for the sole purpose of obtaining fingerprints are no less subject to the constraints of the 4th Amendment. It is arguable, however, that because of the unique nature of the fingerprint process, such detentions might, under narrowly defined circumstances, be found to comply with the 4th Amendment even though there was no probable cause in the traditional sense. See *Camara v. Municipal Court* 387 U.S. 523 (1967) Detention for fingerprinting may constitute a much less serious intrusion upon personal security than other types of police searches and detentions. Fingerprinting involves none of the probing into an individual's private life and thoughts that mark an interrogation or search. Nor can fingerprint detention be employed repeatly to harass any individual, since the police need only one set of each person's prints. Furthermore, fingerprinting is an inherently more reliable and effective crime-solving tool, than eyewitness identification or confessions and is not subject to such abuses as the improper lineup and the "third degree." Finally because there is no danger of destruction of fingerprints, the limited detention need not come unexpectedly or at an inconvenient time. For this same reason, the general requirement that the authorization of a judicial officer be obtained in advance of detention would seem not to admit of any exception in the fingerprinting context.

We have no occasion in this case, however, to determine whether the requirements of the 4th Amendment could be met by narrowly circumscribed procedures for obtaining, during the course of a criminal investigation, the fingerprints of individuals for whom there is no probable cause to arrest. For it is clear that no attempt was made here to employ procedures which might comply with the requirements of the 4th Amendment; the detention at police headquarters of petitioner and the other Negroes was not authorized by a judicial officer; petitioner was unnecessarily required to undergo two fingerprinting sessions; and petitioner was not merely fingerprinted during the December 3 detention but was also subjected to interrogation.

Conviction reversed.

MR. JUSTICE HARLAN, CONCURRING. I join the opinion of the Court, with one reservation. The Court states in dictum that, because fingerprinting may be scheduled for a time convenient to the citizen, "the general requirement that the authorization of a judicial officer be obtained in advance of detection would seem not to admit of any exception in the fingerprinting context." Ante, this page. I cannot concur in so sweeping a proposition. There may be circumstances, falling short of the "dragnet" procedures employed in this case, where compelled submission to fingerprinting would not amount to a violation of the 4th Amendment even in the absence of a warrant. . . .

[Dissent by Mr. Justice Black is omitted.]

PROBLEMS AND QUESTIONS

1. Suppose that the confession in the Morales case was suppressed (excluded from use in evidence) and the state did not have probable cause to charge. Would the defendant be a free man or would the state of New York have other alternative actions which they could bring against him?

    See *United States ex rel. Williams v. Fay*, 323 F.2d 69 (7th Cir. 1964), where a confession was excluded in a brutal murder case when the police held the defendant in detention for eighteen or nineteen hours of continuous questioning until he confessed. The Court reminded the state that although the confession could not be used in a criminal case, it could be used in a civil sanity hearing.

2. In determining whether the detention was lawful, would the following variable factors have any effect upon the court's decision?

    a. The gravity of the offense which is being investigated

    b. The degree of certainty that an offense has been committed (a child is missing and it is not known whether he is lost or kidnapped, as distinguished from a situation where the officer has specific information showing that the child has been kidnapped)

    c. The need for immediate action by the officers

3. In the following situations, what quantum of evidence is necessary

to make the detention, what length of time may the person be detained, and in what place may the detention be made?

    a. A person is suspected of a crime such as burglary.

    b. A person is suspected of a crime "presenting a high degree of public concern affecting the public safety," such as the brutal murder in the Morales case.

    c. A suspect has been arrested but not charged.

    d. *After* the arrest and charging but *before* appearance before a judge or court.

4. At midnight on New Year's Eve, police officers set up a road check a short way down the road from a popular nightclub. They stop all cars coming from the direction of the club and request the drivers to show their driver's licenses. The defendant is stopped at the road check and then arrested and convicted of a charge of driving a motor vehicle while under the influence of alcohol. Is the stop and detention at the road check a valid procedure? (See *State v. Severance*, 237 A.2d 683, where a similar situation was appealed to the Supreme Court of New Hampshire in 1968.)

5. A man is murdered in a tavern. The twenty patrons who witnessed the incident will not provide any information to the police when questioned. The owner and license holder of the tavern claims that he was in the basement when the incident occurred and that he knows nothing of what happened. What can and should the investigating officers do in this case?

6. In the Morales case, the New York court limited their ruling to "crimes presenting a high degree of public concern affecting the public safety." What types of crimes would fit this description?

7. List the possible defense attacks on a detention made by the police.

Local Law

1. What are the constitutional and statutory provisions in your state on habeas corpus?

2. Does your state have a statute providing for:

    a. The setting of bail for a material witness in a criminal case?

    b. The granting of immunity to witnesses or suspects?

    c. The taking of depositions from witnesses in criminal cases?

3. What are the emergency detention statutes in your state? Are these statutes part of the state mental health laws?

3
THE CITIZEN'S ROLE

The burden of maintaining public order and safety rests primarily upon law enforcement agencies appointed and paid for by the community to accomplish this task. Good cooperation and coordination between municipal, county, state, and national agencies ordinarily can do the job when the great majority of the people morally or ethically comply with and support the rule of law.

In the United States, there is an average of two law enforcement officers per 1,000 people. Larger cities have a higher ratio of officers than smaller cities or rural areas. Washington, D.C., has the highest police ratio in the United States with over four officers per 1,000 people. In using these ratios, it is necessary to keep in mind that law enforcement agencies assign their men on a three-shift basis to operate twenty-four hours per day and that men are not available to them at times because of vacation, illness, court appearances, etc. So that at any given time in the United States, the average number of officers available immediately is far less than two per 1,000 inhabitants.

From the above, it is easy to conclude that public order and safety cannot be maintained without the cooperation of the people within the community. This cooperation primarily consists of people conducting themselves in a law-abiding manner, but cooperation also takes other forms. This chapter presents some of the aspects of the citizen's role in the maintenance of public order and safety.

HISTORICAL DEVELOPMENTS

Before the development of organized law enforcement agencies, the task of maintaining order in the community rested upon the citizens themselves. The ancient "hue and cry" was a call for community response to stop a crime or prevent a breach of the public peace. Law enforcement agencies did not exist and the citizens had to do the job themselves.

As cities grew in size and industries and commerce began to grow, it became apparent that trained bodies of organized citizens were needed. The City of London had no police force before 1827, and the organization of a force in that year by Sir Robert Peel met surprising resistance from the citizens of London.

In the United States, settlers opened up territories, and communities came into existence before law enforcement agencies were established. Sheriffs, marshals, and police officers usually followed and agencies came into existence as the need for them became apparent. It was different in Canada, where the Mounties arrived before the settlers; as the settlers arrived, they were advised as to the existing rule of law which was being enforced by the Northwestern Mounted Police.

In 1908, the Federal Bureau of Investigation (FBI) was organized, but it was not until 1924, after reorganization and the appointment of a new director named J. Edgar Hoover, that the FBI became important and famous as it combated criminals who had begun using automobiles and the newly built highways to commit crimes more effectively.

Even with the organization of law enforcement agencies, the opportunity for a person to request immediate assistance did not exist in many instances until the installation of the modern American telephone system was begun in the 1930s. This was followed by the installation of radio equipment in police and sheriff cars in the 1940s and 1950s. As America was a frontier nation until seventy years ago and an agricultural society until fifty years ago, many people living in the United States had to rely upon themselves for the protection of their families and their property. As a result of this heritage, American citizens have more guns and rifles in their possession than are possessed by the U.S. Armed Forces and American law enforcement agencies combined. Efforts to pass legislation for the registration of weapons in the hands of private citizens are countered with such slogans as "If guns are outlawed, only outlaws will have guns."

CITIZEN'S ARREST

The power and the authority of the private citizen to make an arrest came into existence in the days when officers of the law were practically unknown. Little change in this power of the private citizen to make an arrest has occurred in the years since unless the statutes of his state have either modified or enlarged this power. The following important differences exist between a law enforcement officer's power to arrest and the power of a private citizen to make an arrest.

1. The law enforcement officer has broader and greater powers of arrest than a private citizen.
2. The law enforcement officer receives his power to make an arrest from the statutes of his state, but in most instances the private citizen's power to make an arrest is based upon common law. There is not always the conciseness and clarity in applying ancient common law to our modern society that should exist in the law of arrest.
3. The law enforcement officer ordinarily has a duty to make an arrest; a citizen can use his own discretion as to whether he will use his power of arrest or not.

As most states have not statutorized this common-law power of citizen's arrest, more than just a little confusion exists in the mind of the average citizen as to the scope, use, and limitations of the power of citizen's arrest. The question of whether citizens should be encouraged to make arrests in this day and age is debatable. One side argues that the situation should be left just as it is while the other side urges that citizens should be encouraged to use their power to arrest more frequently and to assist more actively in the enforcement of criminal laws. To do this, they point out that the scope of the citizen's power to make an arrest could be adapted by statutes in the states to the conditions and problems of modern society. The clarification achieved by statutorizing the power would alone encourage more citizen's arrests.

In many states, a citizen has the power to make a citizen's arrest only for a felony committed in his presence. Other states authorize a citizen to make an arrest not only for a felony committed in his presence but also for a breach of the peace committed in his presence. Jurisdictions which have statutorized citizen's arrest specify the crimes in which an arrest can be made. Section 23-582(b) of the Federal District of Columbia Court Reform and Criminal Procedure Act of 1970 is as follows:

> (b) A private person may arrest another—
>   (1) whom he has probable cause to believe is committing in his presence—
>   (A) a felony, or
>   (B) an offense enumerated in section 23–581(a)(2);* or

* Authors' note: Section 23–581(a)(2) includes the crimes of assault, petty larceny, receiving stolen goods, unlawful entry.

(2)   in aid of a law enforcement officer or special policeman, or other person authorized by law to make an arrest

(c)   Any person making an arrest pursuant to this section shall deliver the person arrested to a law enforcement officer without unreasonable delay

THE LAW ENFORCEMENT OFFICER'S USE OF CITIZEN'S ARREST POWER

The statutory power of a law enforcement officer to make an arrest is ordinarily limited to the jurisdiction which has appointed him and granted him the authority to arrest. This may be a city, a county, a state, or the United States (i.e., city or village police; county sheriff; state patrol or state troopers; FBI, Treasury agents, etc.).

However, the statutes of the state could extend the power of a city police force to arrest to include the county or to extend throughout the entire state.

If a law enforcement officer is outside of his arrest jurisdiction (whether city, county, or state), one of the following two procedures could be used, depending upon the circumstances:

1.   A city police officer or deputy sheriff who is sent to another city (or county) in the same state to make an arrest would request the assistance of the police (or sheriff) of that area. The local police or sheriff would actually make the arrest. This could be done with or without the authority of an arrest warrant (and is not meant to include hot-pursuit situations).

2.   An off-duty officer who is outside of his arrest jurisdiction has the power to make a citizen's arrest as authorized by the state he is in at the time the citizen's arrest is made.

ENLISTING AID FROM CITIZENS

Law enforcement officers may call upon private citizens to assist them, and most states have statutes imposing a legal duty upon persons to assist officers unless they have a reasonable excuse. Some states require that the person must be a male and at least eighteen years of age.

If there is a clear identification that a law enforcement officer is commanding and requesting assistance, failure to render assistance or aid may be punished as a misdemeanor unless circumstances existed which would excuse the person.

Example: A police officer who has arrested a drunk is having a difficult time because the drunk is resisting the arrest. He requests the assistance of two young men who only laugh and continue to watch the officer in his difficulty without rendering assistance. When the paddy wagon arrives, not only is the drunk taken to the station, but also the two men who refused to aid the officer.

This example is typical of the request for physical assistance made to a citizen from a police officer or sheriff. The Kagel case at the end of this chapter concerns the commandeering of the property of citizens and also involves the interesting question of the civil liability of a citizen who parked his truck across a highway as ordered by a deputy sheriff.

DUTY OF CITIZENS TO PROVIDE INFORMATION

It is one of the duties of citizenship that persons assist government in its law enforcement function. In areas where law enforcement agencies receive information and the wholehearted cooperation of the people, they are able to operate more effectively and efficiently than in areas where the police are told little and no one wants "to get involved."

When a citizen provides information to the police or sheriff, a reciprocal duty then arises on the part of that law enforcement agency to protect him. The position of the person who has provided information can sometimes become hazardous. A person noted an FBI flier on a notorious fugitive named Willie Sutton and informed the police of the whereabouts of Sutton. With this information, the police were able to capture Sutton, and the incident was given a great deal of publicity in the newspapers. When the citizen received threats on his life, he requested and received protection from the police. When the police protection was withdrawn, the citizen protested in vain and a short time later was slain in gangland fashion. *Shuster v. The City of New York,* 5 N.Y. (2d) 75 (1958), was a civil suit by the estate for the wrongful death of the citizen. The courts of New York held for the plaintiffs and ruled that where a person has aided in the apprehension or the prosecution of the enemies of society, a reciprocal duty arises on the part of society to use reasonable care to provide for his protection.

GIVING FALSE INFORMATION OR OBSTRUCTING AN OFFICER

All states have statutes making it a crime to *knowingly* give false information to a law enforcement officer with the intent to mislead him in the performance of his duty.

PRIVILEGES AGAINST DISCLOSURES

Doctors, lawyers, and clergymen are obligated to maintain in confidence information which they receive in their professional relations with patients, clients, and penitents. Therefore, law enforcement officers investigating a criminal incident are required to respect this privilege against disclosure which is given by the statutes of their state. All states have statutes which extend this privilege to wives; about sixteen states extend the privilege to newspapermen, and some states extend it to school and university deans and counselors.

However, the state statutes providing for such privileges against disclosure *limit* the privilege to very *specific* relations (unusually confidential professional relations) which are deemed to be in the best public interest. If the disclosure does not fall within the area specified as being privileged by the state statute, then the doctor, lawyer, clergyman, and wife are like all other citizens and have a duty to assist government in its law enforcement functions.

Example: John Smith goes into a bank to rob it and by coincidence his wife, his doctor, his attorney, and his clergyman are all in the bank at the time. They all recognize him and in most states (if not all states) are all obligated to provide the investigating officers with this information, as it is not privileged information.

For more specific information on this subject, see your state statutes as to the laws concerning privilege against disclosure in your state, and also read discussions in Stuckey's *Evidence for the Law Enforcement Officer* or *McCormick on Evidence*.

DOES THE EXCLUSIONARY RULE APPLY AGAINST PERSONS WHO ARE NOT LAW ENFORCEMENT OFFICERS?

The protection of the Fourth Amendment applies only to government intrusions. It is the government acting through its agents who are prohibited from making unreasonable searches and seizures. This distinction was clearly made in the 1921 case before the United States Supreme Court of *Burdeau v. McDowell*, 256 U.S. 465, 65 L. Ed. 1048, 41 S. Ct. 574.

In that case, Joseph Burdeau, as Assistant United States Attorney General, intended to present "certain private books, papers, memoranda, etc.," to a grand jury in an effort to obtain an indictment against J. C. McDowell for an alleged violation of the United States criminal code for the fraudulent use of the mails. McDowell complained that the evidence intended to be used by the government was taken from

McDowell's office by unknown persons who "drilled the petitioner's private safes, broke the locks upon his private desks and broke into and abstracted from the files in his offices his private papers."

McDowell filed a petition in court asking for the return of his property, claiming that the government's use of the books, papers, memoranda, etc., either directly or indirectly, was a violation of his Fourth Amendment rights. The Supreme Court held:

> The Fourth Amendment gives protection against unlawful searches and seizures, and, as shown in the previous cases, its protection applies to government action. Its origin and history clearly show that it was intended as a restraint upon the activities of sovereign authority, and was not intended to be a limitation upon other than governmental agencies; as against such authorities it was the purpose of Fourth Amendment to secure the citizen in the right of unmolested occupation of his dwelling and the possession of his property, subject to the right of seizure by process duly issued.
>
> In the present case the record clearly shows that no official of the Federal Government had anything to do with the wrongful seizure of the petitioner's property, or any knowledge thereof until several months after the property had been taken from him and was in the possession of the Cities Service Co. It is manifest that there was no invasion of the security afforded by the Fourth Amendment against unreasonable search and seizure, as whatever wrong was done was the act of individuals in taking the property of another. A portion of the property so taken and held was turned over to the prosecuting officers of the Federal Government. We assume that petitioner has an unquestionable right of redress against those who illegally and wrongfully took his private property under the circumstances herein disclosed, but with such remedies we are not now concerned.

In *Irvine v. California*, 374 U.S. 126, 98 L. Ed. 561, 74 S. Ct. 381 (1954), the U.S. Supreme Court reiterated the principle that the Fourth Amendment was a restriction upon the government and that its restrictions did not apply to others.

CASE FOR CHAPTER THREE

KAGEL v. BRUGGER
SUPREME COURT OF WISCONSIN
19 WIS. 2d 1 (1962)

FACTS. About midnight on April 30, 1956, deputy sheriffs were ordered to set up a roadblock to stop a fleeing motorist. The deputies stopped two semitrailers belonging to Mr. Nead and ordered that the semitrailers be used along with their squad car to block the highway.

The fleeing motorist was injured when he ran into one of the semitrailers and this civil action by him is against the sheriff, the deputy sheriffs, the county and

Mr. Nead. They are charged with negligence in setting up the "illegal" roadblock and for not adequately and properly lighting the roadblock and the equipment.

All of the defendants demur on the grounds that the complaint does not state a cause of action and ask that the suit be dismissed. The demurrers were over-ruled by the trial court. Only Nead appeals on this point.

The question before the Supreme Court of Wisconsin is whether Nead should have to defend himself in a civil suit for acts which he did in obeying the orders of the deputy sheriff.

HALLOWS, J. This is a case of first impression and presents the novel question whether a private citizen whose vehicle has been commandeered by a police officer and who has been directed to park his vehicle across a public highway can be held negligent in creating a roadblock or in failing to have his vehicle adequately lighted for such use. . . .

Sheriffs and other law enforcement officers possess authority to set up road-blocks in a reasonable manner for the apprehension of fleeing violators. Such authority is inherent in the power and the duties of law enforcement officers if those duties are to be effectively discharged. The right to set up roadblocks to appre-hend violators has been tacitly acknowledged in *Freedom v. State* (1950), 195 Md. 275, 73. The use of the roadblock device is recognized as a specialized technique in the apprehension of violators by law-enforcement officers. See FBI Law En-forcement Bulletins, June, 1952, Vol 21. The responsibility for the use of the road-block and for the type used, whether blocking the entire highway or only one lane of traffic or of using lights and signs or a squad car at the side of the highway leaving all lanes open or any other device for stopping traffic upon the highway, is upon the law-enforcement officer or agency establishing the road-block.

In using the roadblock for the apprehension of law violators, a peace officer has the power to commandeer a motor vehicle. Its use is the modern outgrowth of the ancient hue and cry and of the power to call up a posse comitatus. We have said there is a duty resting on all citizens who know of the call to go to the relief of an officer even though the failure to perform such duty does not constitute an offense. It is a moral duty incident to citizenship. *Krueger v. State* (1920). 171 Wis. 566, 177 N.W. 917. The duty of a citizen to respond to a request or direction is even greater than to a call for assistance, which frequently was not addressed to specific individuals but a general call for help to those who may hear or learn of it. Can the duty of citizenship be any less upon a citizen who has specifically been commanded by an officer to furnish help, not only of himself, but of his vehicle and directed to use his vehicle in a particular way? It is true, in *Randles v. Waukesha County* (1897), 96 Wis. 629, 71 N.W. 1034, we held although the sheriff had the power to call up a posse, he did not have the power to call up for his use a horse belonging to a private citizen because in those days the sheriff was required to perform his duties by furnishing his own horse. The prin-ciple is not applicable to modern times when counties furnish police cars to sheriffs to perform their duties. The right to commandeer an automobile by a police officer to be used in hot pursuit of a law violator was recognized in *Babing-ton v. Yellow Taxi Corp.* (1928), 250 N.Y. 14, 164 N.E. 726. Public policy has recog-nized the duty of a citizen to aid the law-enforcement officer in arresting a fugitive or suppressing a disturbance of the peace, clothing him with the immunities and rights of a deputy. If injured in performing such duty and obeying the call or command of the police officer, the citizen is entitled to workmen's compensation as a deputy. *West Salem v. Industrial Comm.* (1916), 162 Wis. 57, 155 N.W. 929.

There is statutory authority for the power of the sheriff to call to his aid such persons as he deems necessary for prescribed purposes. Sec. 59.24, Stats. The duty of a citizen to obey the lawful orders of the traffic police is found in sec. 85.12 (2), Stats 1955 (now sec. 346.04). While this section is probably intended only to apply to the direction of traffic by police officers, it is a recognition of the duty of the citizen under those circumstances. Likewise, sec. 946.40 makes it a crime for one without reasonable excuse to refuse or fail upon command to aid a police officer if he is authorized under the circumstances to command such assistance.

When a police officer commandeers a motor vehicle to aid him in creating a roadblock, the citizen has no duty to argue about the officer's right, the need for the roadblock, or the details of creating it. When performing his duties as a citizen in acting under the direction of the law-enforcement officer, the private citizen is not a volunteer acting on his own initiative and such duty as he has not to block or park on a public highway is suspended under such circumstances. Whether the roadblock was adequate or inadequate, or whether it was negligently established and maintained, is not the concern or the responsibility of the private citizen. This is not to say if a sheriff should commandeer a private vehicle in the hot pursuit of a criminal that the private citizen using his own judgment in the management and speed of his car could not be negligent. However, when a law enforcement officer commands the private citizen to do what would otherwise be a negligent act, the private citizen ought not be held to be negligent. The claimed illegality and negligence in establishing and maintaining the roadblock is an issue between the plaintiff and the defendant sheriffs but is not pertinent to the question of the defendant Nead's duty or liability.

It is contended even though the defendant might not be negligent in parking his semitrailer across the highway to form the roadblock as directed by the deputy sheriff, Nead was negligent in not having his semitrailer adequately lighted under the circumstances. The argument assumes an absolute duty on the defendant Nead to set out flares or other warning devices or have his semitrailer equipped as an emergency vehicle. Secs. 85.06 (18) and 85.12 (5), Stats. 1955. It is not to be expected or required that the private citizen whose vehicle is commandeered to establish a roadblock must use his individual judgment and initiative as to the adequacy of the lighting of his vehicle. The defendant's duty in regard to lights on his semitrailer must be considered from the viewpoint that the semitrailer was part and parcel of the roadblock established under direction of a law-enforcement officer and not from the viewpoint of a truck which was placed in that position by choice or negligence of its driver. Since the responsibility for the truck being across the highway was that of the law-enforcement agency, it was its duty to adequately light the truck and roadblock or to warn the traveling public of the danger. Nead had no such duty unless he had been directed by the police officer in charge and failed to carry out such direction. No such allegation is made in the complaint.

We cannot reach the opposite conclusion on the theory the private citizen while in the course of assisting a police officer is considered deputized for the purpose of workmen's compensation. See Anno. Workmen's Compensation—Public Emergency, 142 A.L.R. 657; Anderson v. Bituminous Casualty Co., supra and cases therein cited. It is true, a police officer may be held liable for his negligent acts. 43 Am. Jur., Public Officers, p. 92, sec. 279; 47 Am. Jur. Apart from any privilege or immunity, failure to properly light a roadblock may constitute negligence on the part of a police officer. However, not every police officer aiding in the establishment of a roadblock could be charged with negligence but only those who have the responsibility for the establishment and the manner in which it is established. Such duty in this case did not rest upon the defendant Nead while aiding the deputy sheriff under his direction. Private citizens are not to interfere with police methods of apprehending law violators. The law holds police officers accountable for the reasonableness and the validity of their methods. A citizen answering the cry of help or despair of a police officer or his commands should be given reasonable protection in furnishing assistance if we expect citizens to fulfill their duties of citizenship. If the citizen refuses the command of the officer, he runs the risk of the criminal sanction of sec. 946.40, Stats. Must a citizen choose between the risk of Scylla and the risk of Charybdis at his peril? The complaint states no cause of action against the defendant Nead.

BY THE COURT. The order overruling the demurrer is reversed. [Nead does not have to defend himself in this suit. He is excused.]

QUESTIONS AND PROBLEMS

1. Would the ruling in the Burdeau case apply to the following situations?
    a. An attorney throws copies of letters to a client who is under investigation by a law enforcement agency into a wastebasket. The investigating officers have requested the cleaning woman to turn the contents of the lawyer's wastebasket over to them. She cooperates and the officers receive the information.
    b. A policewoman takes a job as a maid in a hotel in order to gain access to a hotel room used by a suspect.
    c. Officers request trash and garbage men to keep material collected from X's home separate from other trash and turned over to them so that it can be searched for evidence and information. (See Chap. 16 for cases on this procedure.)
2. An employee of a corporation bugs the office of his boss and obtains evidence showing violations of the Sherman Antitrust law (price fixing). The employee has embezzled a considerable sum of money from the corporation and flees to a foreign country. He telephones his boss and tells him what he has done. He tells his boss that if his embezzlement is reported to the prosecuting attorney, he will turn over the tapes which he has obtained to the U.S. attorney. The corporation officials report the embezzlement, and the employee turns the tapes over to a U.S. attorney. May the tapes be used in a criminal antitrust suit against the corporation and the officers involved? [See *United States v. American Radiator Corp. and Standard San. Corp.*, 272 F. Supp. 691 (1967).]
3. A woman was raped after she got off a bus late at night. She went to the nearest house for assistance. While the woman in the house called the police, the husband took his gun and cruised in his car

with the rape victim looking for the assailant. When the rape victim identified a man on the street as her assailant, a citizen's arrest was made and the assailant was turned over to the police. Who can make a citizen's arrest under these circumstances? Should the husband be commended for what he did? Were his actions lawful?

4. Smith (a citizen) sees a car going 40 mph in a 25-mile zone. He chases the speeder in his car and makes a citizen's arrest. How would you handle this situation if you were the sergeant at the desk when Smith brought the speeder into the police station?

5. Assuming that *probable cause* exists in all the following cases, indicate who can make the arrest.

   a. For a felony committed in his presence
   b. For a felony *not* committed in his presence
   c. For a misdemeanor committed in his presence which is not a breach of the peace
   d. For a misdemeanor *not* committed in his presence
   e. For a breach of the peace committed in his presence
   f. For shoplifting a $10 item in his presence
   g. For a misdemeanor theft committed in his presence
   h. For conduct punishable only by forfeiture and not by imprisonment
   i. For exceeding the speed limit by 8 mph

   Available Answers for Question 5
   1. *Only* a law enforcement officer may make an arrest.
   2. *Only* a citizen may make an arrest.
   3. *Both* the citizen and the law enforcement officer may make an arrest.
   4. *Neither* the citizen nor the officer may make an arrest.

6. An officer is writing out a speeding ticket for a motorist when a piece of paper slips out of his hand and flies away. Because of the heavy traffic, the officer does not attempt to recover the paper. The motorist then tells the officer that he is arresting the officer (citizen's arrest) for littering. How would you handle this situation if you were the officer?

7. What are possible areas of attack by a defense attorney whose client was brought into custody by means of a citizen's arrest?

8. Should citizens be encouraged to make more citizen's arrests? Should citizen's arrest power be broadened to include more misdemeanors which are not breaches of the peace?

Local Law

1. What power of arrest does a citizen have in your state? Is this statutory law or common law?
2. Is the statutory power of a law enforcement officer to arrest limited in your state to:
    a. his municipality?
    b. his county?
    c. The entire state?
3. What are the hot-pursuit or close-pursuit statutes in your state:
    a. From county to county?
    b. From your state into the neighboring states?
4. What are the statutes of your state imposing a legal duty upon private persons to render assistance and aid to law enforcement officers when requested?
5. What is the common law or statutory law in your state in regard to the commandeering of private property by a law enforcement officer?
6. What is the statutory law in your state concerning the giving of false information to an officer or obstructing an officer in the performance of his duty?

4
THE USE
OF
FORCE

Law enforcement officers and their departments are the front line of our domestic security and sometimes the thin blue line between order and chaos. Most states authorize law enforcement departments either by statute or by common law to have available and to use any weapons which are necessary to perform their functions. In addition to automatic and semiautomatic weapons, other sophisticated equipment is available to support the law enforcement officer.

If an officer seeks to make an arrest and cannot effect it alone, he may call for assistance. The department can, if necessary, deploy all the men available to handle the situation. If the department cannot handle the problem, assistance can be requested from other departments and from the state. If this is not enough, the state legislature or the state governor (when the legislature cannot be convened) can request assistance from the federal government. The federal government is obligated under article IV, section 4, of the U.S. Constitution to commit such forces as may be needed to restore public order.

Behind every arrest, and also other government action, there must exist a position of strength. Not only must force be available to use, if necessary, but there must also be a realization that at times force must be used. Unfortunately, it is a fact of life that in order for a democracy to continue to exist, force must sometimes be used to maintain public order and to enforce the law. Taxes must be collected; laws must be enforced; public order and safety must be maintained. President Washington found that he had to use force in 1792 to enforce a tax law passed by the First Congress. Force has had to be used to enforce draft laws, court desegregation orders, and practically all our criminal laws.

The armed law enforcement officer carries with him an awesome power not only to enforce the law but also for his own protection. He may have to decide in a split second whether he should use the weapons his department has ordered him to carry and how they should be used. The responsibility for such action as he may take is his, but he uses such force on behalf of the state because he represents the authority of the state at that place and time. The state and the law impose conditions and limitations upon the use of force, and he must know and comply with these limitations. His department must instruct and train him, and he must train himself to use force with restraint and within the limits imposed by law.

The weapons carried by a law enforcement officer have not changed much over the last hundred years. He has the strength and use of his arms and legs, his nightstick, and his handcuffs. The most deadly of the weapons available for his use is the gun he carries. Other than tear gas or chemical mace, few new alternatives have been made available to solve his problem of subduing resistance and bringing an offender before a court of law.

The use of weapons which fire rubber or wooden bullets, foam, or water under high pressure are used from time to time for crowd control. These tools are limited to unique situations. Their use on a routine or daily basis is impractical and ineffective.

WHEN MAY FORCE BE USED?

The indiscriminate use of force is prohibited. Law enforcement officers may use force only to protect themselves and others or to make an arrest and to detain a person, lawfully arrested, in custody.

The use of force, alone, may be construed by a court as such a seizure and restraint of the person as to amount to an arrest. Certainly placing handcuffs on a person against his will is such a detention as to amount to an arrest, unless there is other justification for placing the handcuffs on the person.

WHAT DEGREE OF FORCE MAY BE USED?

The officer (or citizen) making an arrest may use only such force as he reasonably believes is necessary to:

1. Detain the offender and to make the arrest and sustain the detention
2. Overcome resistance
3. Prevent escape and retake the person if he escapes
4. Protect himself, others, and his prisoner, if necessary

This is the basic rule used throughout the United States, but it is only part of the total rule. The law divides force into (1) *deadly force:* that force which is likely or intended to cause death or great bodily injury and (2) *less than deadly force:* use of means not intended or likely to cause death or great bodily injury.

THE USE OF DEADLY FORCE

The law and instructions to law enforcement officers on the use of deadly force vary somewhat in detail and in language from state to state and from department to department. The universal police designation for remembering the types of offenses in which deadly force may be employed, with modifications from jurisdiction to jurisdiction as a result of different titles for the offenses involved, is the name MAM BARKER.

*M*urder
*A*rmed robbery
*M*ayhem

*B*urglary of a dwelling
*A*rson of a building where lives are involved
*R*ape
*K*idnapping
*E*ndangering safety or injury by conduct regardless of life
*R*iots that endanger lives or bodily security

An offender attempting to escape after committing one of the named offenses is also considered to be in that category where deadly force may be used. As it is obvious that each of the named offenses involves danger to lives or serious bodily injury, it can be stated that the common denominator for the use of deadly force is that it may be used as a last resort to save a life or to prevent serious bodily harm.

Deadly force may not be used in most felonies and all misdemeanors because there is not threat to life or serious bodily injury. An officer would not reasonably use deadly force to capture an embezzler or an offender who had written a bad check.

Many states forbid the use of deadly force merely to protect property. Although some states do allow it for that purpose, many law enforcement agencies within those states discourage the use of deadly force by their officers under such circumstances, the reasoning being that the value of human life outweighs the gravity of a property offense.

REASONABLENESS IN THE USE OF DEADLY FORCE

The officer's conduct in the use of deadly force must always be governed by the criterion of reasonableness. Deadly force should be employed only as a last resort when all else fails.

Example: An officer, hearing screams, runs to the scene and observes a man raping a woman while holding a knife to her throat. The officer, fearing that the woman may be killed if he is observed by the rapist, fires his pistol and strikes the rapist.

In the same situation, the rapist observes the officer, jumps to his feet, and flees. The officer observes that the man's wallet has fallen out of his trousers. The woman cries, "Sam! Why did you do this terrible thing?" The officer, realizing that the offender's identity is known or ascertainable, does not fire his pistol.

It is not reasonable to use deadly force to prevent another from committing suicide unless his act will result in death or serious bodily injury to another.

Example: A man stands on the window ledge on the twentieth floor of a building and threatens to jump. The officer should merely attempt to persuade the would-be suicide not to jump.

A man walks into a crowded office carrying a briefcase which he claims is a bomb and announces that he is going to detonate the bomb and kill himself. Before he can pull a cord attached to the case, an officer shoots the man.

LIABILITY

An officer is not liable for injuries caused to an innocent third party if his use of deadly force is:

1. Proper
2. Justified
3. Non-negligent
4. Within the scope of his skill and training

Example: An officer, 200 yards away at night, observes an armed holdup in progress under a streetlight. He fires his handgun from that distance with the intention of shooting the gun out of the robber's hand. His bullet strikes the victim of the robbery. Under such conditions the officer's conduct would be considered negligent and outside the scope of his skill and training.

Before using deadly force, the officer should consider:

1. Whether the information in his possession is positive that the offender is in fact committing an offense dangerous to life
2. Whether the use of deadly force is reasonably necessary
3. Whether the use of deadly force is a last resort
4. The possibility of summoning aid
5. The danger to innocent bystanders
6. His skill and training in the use of the weapon he chooses to employ

THE USE OF FORCE IN SELF-DEFENSE

Not only law enforcement officers, but all persons may threaten to use force and may, if necessary, use deadly force to protect themselves or others if they reasonably believe that this is the only means of preventing death or great bodily harm. All states have statutes concerning homicide in self-defense, and the question of whether the use of deadly force was reasonable is one which can be presented to a jury or a judge by the prosecuting attorney.

THE USE OF LESS THAN DEADLY FORCE

In making an arrest for a misdemeanor or a felony which is not a "serious" felony, the officer is privileged to use a reasonable amount of force but it must be less than deadly force. What is reasonable force depends upon all the facts and circumstances as they appear at the time. The officer is not required to gauge the exact amount of force necessary because this would be very difficult, if not impossible, to do. He cannot use unreasonably excessive force or if there is no resistance, he cannot use force at all. He may use only such amount of force as he reasonably believes necessary to accomplish his legal purpose.

Under no circumstances may he use deadly force to make an arrest for a misdemeanor or for a felony which is not a serious felony. The basis for this rule is the respect for human life and the value which we place upon it in our society. Human life is valued too highly to allow deadly force to be used in such cases.

If an eighteen-year-old man is taking a $105 bike (which is a felony in most states), should deadly force be used to stop him as he rapidly moves away from the officer who is standing and calling for him to stop? Factors which the officer should consider are:

1. The eighteen-year-old will probably be apprehended at a later time.
2. There may be a mix-up on bikes.

3. The bike may be worth only $90, which would make the theft a misdemeanor and not a felony.
4. The person fleeing may be hard of hearing and is not hearing the calls to stop.

HANDCUFFING AS A FORM OF RESTRAINT

Depending upon the facts and circumstances in each particular case, if an officer believes and has reasonable grounds for believing that such precaution is necessary, he may handcuff or otherwise manacle his prisoner. This precaution may be taken to protect the officer, or to protect other prisoners or other persons and also to prevent the escape of the prisoner.

If the officer is alone, there is greater justification in using handcuffs. If the arrest is for a major crime, or if the prisoner has resisted the arrest, or if there is reason to believe that he will resist or will attempt an escape, the precaution of using handcuffs is justified.

In addition to considering the crime for which the arrest was made, and the number of prisoners in relation to the number of officers, other factors in making the decision whether or not to use handcuffs are:

1. The distance which the prisoner will have to be transported and the time which this will take
2. The possibility of the prisoner's attempting to commit suicide (a man who has just murdered his wife and is suffering terribly)

Male police officers will usually handcuff a woman they have arrested for a serious crime because they cannot make a thorough weapons search of her person to determine whether she is carrying a dangerous weapon.

FORCE WHICH MAY BE USED TO PREVENT AN ESCAPE

The same rules that are used in making an arrest apply to preventing an attempted escape. Deadly force should be used only on a serious felony case and in self-protection when needed. Otherwise the officer may use only such amount of force as he reasonably believes necessary to prevent the escape. The officer may not use unreasonably excessive force, nor may he punish the person for attempting the escape. An attempt to escape from lawful custody and arrest is a crime in itself, and an additional charge can be brought against the person. If handcuffs have not been used, an attempted escape justifies the use of handcuffs.

Example: An officer has arrested two men who are excessively drunk. While the officer is telephoning for assistance, one of the drunks runs off. The officer may handcuff the drunk in custody to a light pole, if he wishes, and attempt to recapture the other drunk. He cannot use deadly force in recapturing or to prevent another escape. However, if the escaped drunk were to obtain a gun and indicated that he would use it to free his friend, the situation would change from a misdemeanor to a serious felony.

SUMMONING OF OTHERS FOR ASSISTANCE

In many situations, the officer may summon other officers or citizens to assist him. The expectation of such assistance might have some effect on the degree of force which would be necessary to effect the arrest or prevent an escape.

DOES A RIGHT TO RESIST AN ARREST EXIST?

If the officer has identified himself as a law enforcement officer and the arrest is a *lawful* arrest, then there is clearly no right to resist the arrest. To resist is a violation of the law, and the resistance itself is another crime.

Under common law, if the arrest is *not a lawful arrest*, the citizen has a right to resist the arrest. This rule developed hundreds of years ago in England when the life expectancy of a person was under thirty years and the jails were dreaded because of the many diseases which could quickly kill a person. The person could be held for a long time before he was brought before a judge and had no opportunity for bail and had no right to counsel. There was a good possibility of his dying before trial or release.

The old common law that a person could resist an unlawful arrest is being changed by state statutes (*California Penal Code*, section 834a, prohibits a person from resisting an arrest which he believes is unlawful) and by court decisions. Following are excerpts from two such cases.

> "... In this era of constantly expanding legal protection of the rights of the accused in criminal proceedings, one deeming himself illegally arrested can reasonably be asked to submit peaceably to arrest by a police officer and to take recourse in his legal remedies for regaining his liberty and defending the ensuing prosecution against him. At the same time, police officers attempting, in good faith, although mistakenly, to perform their duties in effecting an arrest should be relieved of the threat of physical harm at the hands of the arrestee." *State v. Koonce,* 214 A.2d 429, 89 N.J. S. Ct. 169 (1965)

"... The question of whether one may resist an unlawful arrest is apparently a new one in Wisconsin, since we have found and been cited to no Wisconsin law on the subject.... If an arrest is unlawful, the place to argue about it is in the court, not in the street, and, if the arrest was without probable cause, defendant has civil remedies open to him. We do not pay the police enough to ask them to endanger their lives or health to have to fight every person arrested who may feel that his arrest is unlawful. We do not accept any rule which permits a defendant to resist arrest by officers in uniform acting in their official capacity. The time is here to discourage, not to incite violence." *State of Wisconsin v. Conjurske*, Circuit Court of Dane County (Madison), Sept. 1969.

CIVIL REMEDIES AVAILABLE TO OFFICERS

A surprising number of officers are under the impression that it is part of their job to take a certain amount of physical abuse in the form of blows, bruises, torn uniforms, and having teeth knocked out when making an arrest. Drunks, especially, can be very difficult to handle. Many criminal judges attempt to provide restitution to the officer when such cases come before them, but the officer should be also aware that a civil tort action is available to him. He must show injury (missing tooth, scar, injured back, etc.), and in addition to receiving damages for the injury which he sustained, he can receive punitive damages from the violator. From a practical point of view, such suits are started when the defendant has the means to pay the judgment.

Ten and twenty years ago, law enforcement agencies tended to discourage such civil suits by their officers and were reluctant to give permission to officers to start such an action. Today, departments readily give permission on the theory that there will be fewer illegal resistances to arrest if more irresponsible persons have civil actions brought against them. Many departments leave this matter entirely up to the officers.

RIOTS

Because of the increases in civil disorders and riots, law enforcement agencies have placed more emphasis on the training of their men to handle such situations. Departmental policies must be made on the use of force within the limits authorized by law.

Riots are defined by the American Law Institute in the *Restatement (Second) of Torts*, sec. 142, and by *Black's Law Dictionary* as an assemblage of three or more persons in a public place for the purpose of either (1) accomplishing an unlawful act or (2) together doing a lawful act in an unlawful, violent, or tumultuous manner to the disturbance of others.

Therefore, not all assemblages are riots or unlawful assemblies. Groups of people may assemble under their First Amendment right "*peacefully* to assemble and to petition the government for a redress of grievances."

Most states make the participation in a riot a misdemeanor in itself, but other states require that the "riot act be read." By this is meant that the unlawful assembly or the riot is ordered dispersed by a public official (a police officer or mayor), and the intentional failure or refusal to withdraw from a riot or unlawful assembly is a misdemeanor.

Ordinarily, only one or more of the following misdemeanors are committed and are charged: participation in a riot, disorderly conduct, refusal to disperse from an unlawful assembly. If the unlawful act or means of attempting to do a lawful act by unlawful means is not felonious, then the rule is that only reasonable force which is less than deadly force may be used.

If the obvious purpose of the riot is to do a serious unlawful act such as the destruction of draft records or widespread damage to property, and if such actions create the possibility or the probability that persons in the vicinity will be harmed seriously, then the officers may use whatever force they reasonably believe necessary to restore public order, including the use of deadly force.

Section 142 of the *Restatement of Torts* (American Law Institute) states:

> If the riot itself threatens death or serious bodily harm, it is sufficiently serious to justify the use of deadly means to suppress it. It is not necessary that the avowed purpose of the riot be to inflict such harm. It is enough that the conduct of the rioters is such as to create the probability or even the possibility of such consequences.

The American Law Institute expressed no opinion on the use of force where there was destruction of property but no threat to life or possibility of serious bodily injury. It is hard to imagine widespread destruction of property without threat to life and bodily injury unless there were two or three abandoned farm houses which no one was interested in. With the destruction of any other property, the owner is likely to attempt to defend it or will be in the property, and therefore immediately life is endangered.

It is said that most riots are made up of the following groups of people:

1. Those actively involved in a conspiracy to do an unlawful act or to do a lawful act in an unlawful manner
2. Those who are participating in the group action and are probably sympathetic with the activists but are not part of the conspiracy to riot and do not have criminal intent
3. Innocent bystanders and people attracted to the area out of curiosity

If this mixture exists, the task of the law enforcement officer is complicated. However, in the use of force under such circumstances, the American Law Institute states in section 142 of the *Restatement of Torts* that

> It is enough that the circumstances are such as would lead a reasonable person to believe that the other is participating or is immediately about to participate therein (in the riot actually in progress).

Example:

> While a riot is in progress, A uses force against B in the reasonable belief that B is participating in the riot. B is, in fact, himself endeavoring to suppress the riot. If A's use of force is reasonable under the circumstances, he is not liable to B.

CASES FOR CHAPTER FOUR

SAULS v. HUTTO AND RUPPERT
U.S. DISTRICT COURT FOR THE EASTERN DISTRICT OF LOUISIANA
CIVIL ACTION NO. 16409 DECIDED ON JULY 23, 1969

RUBIN, DISTRICT JUDGE. A police officer who shot and killed a fleeing seventeen-year-old suspected of committing a felony is here sued for damages. The suit raises the question of justification for the use of deadly force in contemporary society.

I. FACTS

On March 21, 1965, at about 10:00 p.m., two police officers, James Hutto and Frederick C. Ruppert, Jr., were operating Patrol Car 54. They drove to an ice cream parlor to investigate a complaint. While they were there, a Mustang automobile was driven recklessly past them at a high rate of speed. They jumped in the patrol car and, with Hutto driving, pursued the Mustang. Hutto turned on the blue police warning light and sounded the siren. But the driver of the Mustang continued to flee, driving through the streets of New Orleans at a high rate of speed. The defendants therefore suspected the speeding car was stolen.

There were four young men in the car. Philip Paul Barlett, also known as Philip Sauls, was driving. According to the testimony of the three passengers, he had invited them for a ride. They also testified that Barlett had told them the automobile belonged to his brother. In fact Barlett had stolen the car by putting a jumper wire on the ignition circuit.

Four pistol shots were fired by Officer Ruppert at the racing car in an effort to bring it to a halt. One shot missed completely; two struck the car but did not penetrate it; and the last shot, which was fired at the car as it careened to its right around a corner on Esplanade Street, penetrated the right front door, ricocheted off the dashboard and fell spent inside the vehicle.

When the passengers heard Ruppert's shots and realized that the police were after them, one of them urged Barlett to stop. Barlett, however, said that the car was stolen, and that he couldn't afford to stop.

Barlett lost control of the Mustang, and it crashed into a parked car. The police car also stopped, and the two policemen ran up, guns in hand. Three of the juveniles surrendered and Ruppert took them into custody. Barlett, however, tried to escape, crouching as he ran away. Officer Hutto ran after him. He shot once at the fleeing boy, and his shot struck Barlett in the back. Because Barlett was bent over, the bullet went through his body at an angle, penetrated his liver, spleen, stomach and heart, and he fell dead in the street.

Shortly thereafter, Hutto said that he had not intended to kill Barlett, but being excited, he was not entirely certain what had happened. One of the other occupants of the car was later found to be carrying a weapon. Some also had prior police records. All of them were hardened youths, and all later were convicted and sentenced for theft.

Defendants contend they had probable cause to arrest Barlett for theft, and they are correct. Barlett not only drove past them recklessly and wildly at a high rate of speed, but continued to race away when he knew the police were attempting to stop him. The defendants testified that it had been their experience that cars driven in such a manner late at night often are stolen and they suspected theft. Probable cause exists "if the facts and circumstances known to the officer warrant a prudent man in believing that the offense has been committed." *Henry v. United States*, 1959, 361 U.S. 98, 102. Police officers often must make immediate judgments and the circumstances the court must consider "are those of the moment." *Dixon v. United States*, D.C. Cir., 1961, 296 F.2d 427, 428. In suspecting theft in these circumstances the defendants did not act imprudently, and they had probable cause to arrest the plaintiff for that offense.

Suit is brought by the natural mother of the deceased (an illegitimate child) for damages under the Civil Rights Act, 42 U.S.C. 1983 and under Louisiana law, LSA-C.C. Art. 2315, 2316, under the doctrine of pendant jurisdiction. The police officers are no longer with the New Orleans police force and are presently unemployed. Therefore, should the plaintiff prevail, there is scant likelihood that any recovery can be effected, but the plaintiff seeks vindication for her son.

II. CIVIL RIGHTS ACT

Plaintiff bases her claim under 42 U.S.C. 1983 on two grounds. (1) The defendant police officers violated Louisiana law in shooting her son and thereby deprived him of life without due process of law; (2) regardless of state law, the killing violated substantive due process and was therefore unconstitutional.

"[The] right to have state law obeyed is not a federal right protected by Section 1983," the Fifth Circuit recently held in *Dorsey v. National Association for the Advancement of Colored People*, 5 Cir. 1969,—F.2d—. Section 1983 protects only *federal* rights that are violated under color of state law. The Fourteenth Amendment does not import an overriding requirement that state officials obey state laws in every regard. "Mere violation of a state statute does not infringe the federal Constitution.... It was not intended by the Fourteenth Amendment and the Civil Rights Acts that all matters formerly within the exclusive cognizance of the states should become matters of national concern." *Snowden v. Hughes,* 321 U.S. 1 (1944). If this were not so, virtually any suit for a tort committed by any state employee could be brought in federal court.

The second basis for plaintiff's claim under Section 1983 is in effect that any time a person is killed by a law enforcement officer merely to protect property, he has been deprived of his life without due process of law, and, consequently, his federal constitutional rights have been violated. Since plaintiff is entitled to recover damages for her son's death under state law, determination of her federal constitutional claim is pretermitted because it would afford her no additional relief. In Justice Peckham's words:

> "Where a case in this court can be decided without reference to questions arising under the Federal Constitution, that course is usually pursued and is not departed from without important reasons. In this case we think it much better to decide it with regard to the question of a local nature, involving the construction of the state statute ... rather than to unnecessarily decide the ... constitutional question appearing in the record." *Siler v. Louisville and Nashville Railroad Co.,* 1909, 213 U.S. 175.

. . . .

V. USE OF DEADLY FORCE

Officer Hutto had probable cause to arrest Barlett for theft, a felony not involving danger to life or person, and he reasonably believed that the suspect could not be immediately apprehended without the use of deadly force. In these circumstances, was he legally justified in shooting at the deceased? There has been a spate of literature dealing with this problem, and various state legislatures have recently been reconsidering their laws to reflect current attitudes on it.

At common law, any person, whether policeman or private citizen, was privileged to use *any* force necessary, albeit deadly, to apprehend a fleeing felon if he had cause to believe a felony had been committed. Deadly force, however, was never permissible to apprehend misdemeanants. To a great extent, this view was based on the fact that, at common law, felonies were punishable by death.

Louisiana has not followed the common law approach. The provisions of the Louisiana Criminal Code and Code of Criminal Procedure when read together limit the use of deadly force even by police officers to situations involving danger to life or person.

Article 220 of the Code of Criminal Procedure provides:

> "A person shall submit peaceably to a lawful arrest. The person making a lawful arrest may use reasonable force to effect the arrest and detention, and also to overcome any resistance or threatened resistance of the person being arrested or detained."

The draftsmen of the Code pointed out in the Official Comment to Article 220 that the "requirement of reasonableness would preclude the use of clearly inappropriate force." More significant assistance in determining what is reasonable force on the part of police officers is provided by the definition of justifiable homicide in the Louisiana Criminal Code:

"A homicide is justifiable:

(1)   When committed in self-defense. . . .

(2)   When committed, for the purpose of preventing a violent or forcible felony involving danger to life or of great bodily harm, by one who reasonably believes that such an offense is about to be committed and that such action is necessary for its prevention. . . ."
LSA—R.S. 14:20.

Thus, deadly force may not be used to prevent the commission of a felony involving only property, a marked departure from the common law rule.

Since it is illegal for one to use deadly force to *prevent* the commission of a felony involving only property, it is unreasonable (and inappropriate) for a policeman to use deadly force to *arrest* a man suspected of committing such a crime.

The current Regulations on Firearms of the New Orleans Police Department also limit the use of deadly force in felony cases. They provide:

"The use of deadly force shall be restricted to the apprehension of perpetrators, who in the course of their criminal actions threaten the use of deadly force or apprehensions when officers believe that the person whose arrest is sought will cause death or serious bodily harm if his apprehension is delayed."

The use of deadly force in apprehending persons suspected of committing felonies not involving danger to life or person has never been specifically considered by Louisiana's appellate courts. However, three cases have held that deadly force may not lawfully be used to arrest a misdemeanant or prevent the commission of a misdemeanor. *State v. Turner*, 1938, 190 La. 198, 182 So. 325; *State v. Plumlee*, 1933, 177 La. 687, 149 So. 425; *Graham v. Ogden*, 3d La. App., 1963, 157 So.2d 365. And two of them, *State v. Turner, supra*, and *State v. Plumlee, supra*, indicate that deadly force can be used only to prevent "a great crime." Both LSA-R.S. 14:20, which does not permit the use of deadly force in crimes not involving danger to life or person, and LSA-R.S. 14:67, which provides for a 10 year maximum sentence for theft, suggest that Barlett had not committed "a great crime," and that Officer Hutto acted unlawfully in using deadly force in an attempt to apprehend him.

The Model Penal Code of the American Law Institute has followed the same approach as Louisiana and does not permit the use of deadly force to make an arrest for a crime involving only property. The various interests at stake have been balanced; the felon's life may be taken only if his escape would provide a threat to the life or personal safety of his fellow citizens.

Our society does not lightly forfeit human life. No longer is there a host of felonies punishable by death. Indeed, since June, 1967, no one has been executed in the United States for a criminal offense. Fifteen states have entirely eliminated the death penalty. Elsewhere capital punishment may be decreed only after due process of law has been afforded.

Hence a man's life may not be taken on the spot by a police officer without substantial justification. Barlett, a theft suspect and reckless driver, was not killed by officer Hutto in self defense; nor was he slain to prevent a crime involving danger to life or person, or even to property, from being completed. Both his theft offense and his reckless driving had been completed long before his death; the car and its passengers were in custody. He was shot only to prevent his escape.

If Barlett had been arrested, fairly tried, and convicted for theft, he could have been sentenced to "not more than 10 years with or without hard labor." He would have been eligible for parole after serving one-third of his sentence. If he had in addition been tried and convicted of resisting arrest, his maximum sentence on that charge would have been six months and a $500 fine.

Professor Mikell puts the question bluntly:

> "It has been said, 'Why should not this man be shot down, the man who is running away with an automobile?' . . . May I ask what we are killing him for when he steals an automobile and runs off with it? Are we killing him for stealing the automobile? If we catch him and try him we throw every protection around him. We say he cannot be tried until 12 men of the grand jury indict him, and then he cannot be convicted until 12 men of the petit jury have proved him guilty beyond a reasonable doubt, and then when we have done all that, what do we do to him? Put him before a policeman and have a policeman shoot him? Of course not. We give him three years in a penitentiary. It cannot be then that we allow the officer to kill him because he stole the automobile, because the statute provides only three years in a penitentiary for that. Is it then for fleeing? . . . Is it for fleeing that we kill him? Fleeing from arrest is also a common-law offense and is punishable by a light penalty, a penalty much less than that for stealing the automobile. If we are not killing him for stealing the automobile and not killing him for fleeing, what are we killing him for?" Michael & Wechsler, Criminal Law and Its Administration, p. 82, n. 3 (1940).

Louisiana's courts likely would take this view: a police officer is not justified in shooting at a man who is suspected of stealing an automobile in order to apprehend him. A bullet in the back is not Louisiana's penalty for fleeing to escape arrest. Deadly force may be used only when life itself is endangered or great bodily harm is threatened.

Under LSA-R.S. C.C. Art. 2315, plaintiff is entitled to recover damages from Officer Hutto for the wrongful death of her son. A hearing will be held to determine damages. Officer Ruppert did not participate in Barlett's killing, and judgment is rendered dismissing the suit as to him.

KATKO v. BRINEY
SUPREME COURT OF IOWA
183 N.W. 2d 657 (1971)

MOORE, CHIEF JUSTICE. The primary issue presented here is whether an owner may protect personal property in an unoccupied boarded-up farm house against trespassers and thieves by a spring gun capable of inflicting death or serious injury.

We are not here concerned with a man's right to protect his home and members of his family. Defendants' home was several miles from the scene of the incident to which we refer infra.

Plaintiff's action is for damages resulting from serious injury caused by a shot from a 20-gauge spring shotgun set by defendants in a bedroom of an old farm house which had been uninhabited for several years. Plaintiff and his companion,

Marvin McDonough, had broken and entered the house to find and steal old bottles and dated fruit jars which they considered antiques.

At defendants' request plaintiff's action was tried to a jury consisting of residents of the community where defendants' property was located. The jury returned a verdict for plaintiff and against defendants for $20,000 actual and $10,000 punitive damages.

. . . .

II. Most of the facts are not disputed. In 1957 defendant Bertha L. Briney inherited her parents' farm land in Mahaska and Monroe Counties. Included was an 80-acre tract in southwest Mahaska County where her grandparents and parents had lived. No one occupied the house thereafter. Her husband, Edward, attempted to care for the land. He kept no farm machinery thereon. The outbuildings became dilapidated.

For about 10 years, 1957 to 1967, there occurred a series of trespassing and house-breaking events with loss of some household items, the breaking of windows and "messing up of the property in general." The latest occurred June 8, 1967, prior to the event on July 16, 1967 herein involved.

Defendants through the years boarded up the windows and doors in an attempt to stop the intrusions. They had posted "no trespass" signs on the land several years before 1967. The nearest one was 35 feet from the house. On June 11, 1967 defendants set "a shotgun trap" in the north bedroom. After Mr. Briney cleaned and oiled his 20-gauge shotgun, the power of which he was well aware, defendants took it to the old house where they secured it to an iron bed with the barrel pointed at the bedroom door. It was rigged with wire from the doorknob to the gun's trigger so it would fire when the door was opened. Briney first pointed the gun so an intruder would be hit in the stomach but at Mrs. Briney's suggestion it was lowered to hit the legs. He admitted he did so "because I was mad and tired of being tormented" but "he did not intend to injure anyone." He gave no explanation of why he used a loaded shell and set it to hit a person already in the house. Tin was nailed over the bedroom window. The spring gun could not be seen from the outside. No warning of its presence was posted.

Plaintiff lived with his wife and worked regularly as a gasoline station attendant in Eddyville, seven miles from the old house. He had observed it for several years while hunting in the area and considered it as being abandoned. He knew it had long been uninhabited. In 1967 the area around the house was covered with high weeds. Prior to July 16, 1967 plaintiff and McDonough had been to the premises and found several old bottles and fruit jars which they took and added to their collection of antiques. On the latter date about 9:30 p. m. they made a second trip to the Briney property. They entered the old house by removing a board from a porch window which was without glass. While McDonough was looking around the kitchen area plaintiff went to another part of the house. As he started to open the north bedroom door the shotgun went off striking him in the right leg above the ankle bone. Much of his leg, including part of the tibia, was blown away. Only by McDonough's assistance was plaintiff able to get out of the house and after crawling some distance was put in his vehicle and rushed to a doctor and then to a hospital. He remained in the hospital 40 days.

Plaintiff's doctor testified he seriously considered amputation but eventually the healing process was successful. Some weeks after his release from the hospital plaintiff returned to work on crutches. He was required to keep the injured leg in a cast for approximately a year and wear a special brace for another year. He continued to suffer pain during this period.

There was undenied medical testimony plaintiff had a permanent deformity, a loss of tissue, and a shortening of the leg.

. . . .

Plaintiff testified he knew he had no right to break and enter the house with intent to steal bottles and fruit jars therefrom. He further testified he had entered a plea of guilty to larceny in the nighttime of property of less than $20 value from a private building. He stated he had been fined $50 and costs and paroled during good behavior from a 60-day jail sentence. Other than minor traffic charges this was plaintiff's first brush with the law. On this civil case appeal it is not our prerogative to review the disposition made of the criminal charge against him.

. . . .

The overwhelming weight of authority, both textbook and case law, supports the trial court's statement of the applicable principles of law.

. . . .

Restatement of Torts, section 85, page 180, states: "The value of human life and limb, not only to the individual concerned but also to society, so outweighs the interest of a possessor of land in excluding from it those whom he is not willing to admit thereto that a possessor of land has, as is stated in § 79, no privilege to use force intended or likely to cause death or serious harm against another whom the possessor sees about to enter his premises or meddle with his chattel, unless the intrusion threatens death or serious bodily harm to the occupiers or users of the premises. . . . A possessor of land cannot do indirectly and by a mechanical device that which, were he present, he could not do immediately and in person. Therefore, he cannot gain a privilege to install, for the purpose of protecting his land from intrusions harmless to the lives and limbs of the occupiers or users of it, a mechanical device whose only purpose is to inflict death or serious harm upon such as may intrude, by giving notice of his intention to inflict, by mechanical means and indirectly, harm which he could not, even after request, inflict directly were he present."

Similar statements are found in 38 Am. Jur., Negligence, section 114, pages 776, 777, and 65 C.J.S. Negligence § 62(23), pages 678, 679; Anno. 44 A.L.R.2d 383, entitled "Trap to protect property."

In Hooker v. Miller, 37 Iowa 613, we held defendant vineyard owner liable for damages resulting from a spring gun shot although plaintiff was a trespasser and there to steal grapes. At pages 614, 615, this statement is made: "This court has held that a mere trespass against property other than a dwelling is not a sufficient justification to authorize the use of a deadly weapon by the owner in its defense; and that if death results in such a case it will be murder, though the killing be actually necessary to prevent the trespass. The State v. Vance, 17 Iowa 138." At page 617 this court said: "[T]respassers and other inconsiderable violators of the law are not to be visited by barbarous punishments or prevented by inhuman inflictions of bodily injuries."

The facts in Allison v. Fiscus, 156 Ohio 120, 100 N.E.2d 237, 44 A.L.R.2d 369, decided in 1951, are very similar to the case at bar. There plaintiff's right to damages was recognized for injuries received when he feloniously broke a door latch and started to enter defendant's warehouse with intent to steal. As he entered a trap of two sticks of dynamite buried under the doorway by defendant owner was set off and plaintiff seriously injured. The court held the question whether a particular trap was justified as a use of reasonable and necessary force against a trespasser engaged in the commission of a felony should have been submitted to the jury. The Ohio Supreme Court recognized plaintiff's right to recover punitive or exemplary damages in addition to compensatory damages.

In Starkey v. Dameron, 96 Colo. 459, 45 P.2d 172, plaintiff was allowed to recover compensatory and punitive damages for injuries received from a spring gun which defendant filling station operator had concealed in an automatic gasoline pump as protection against thieves.

In Wilder v. Gardner, 39 Ga.App. 608, 147 S.E. 911, judgment for plaintiff for injuries received from a spring gun which defendant had set, the court said: "A person in control of premises may be responsible even to a trespasser for injuries caused by pitfalls, mantraps, or other like contrivances so dangerous in character as to imply a disregard of consequences or a willingness to inflict injury."

In Phelps v. Hamlett, Tex.Civ.App., 207 S.W. 425, defendant rigged a bomb inside his outdoor theater so that if anyone came through the door the bomb would explode. The court reversed plaintiff's recovery because of an incorrect instruction but at page 426 said: "While the law authorizes an owner to protect his property by such reasonable means as he may find to be necessary, yet considerations of humanity preclude him from setting out, even on his own property, traps and devices dangerous to the life and limb of those whose appearance and presence may be reasonably anticipated, even though they may be trespassers."

In United Zinc & Chemical Co. v. Britt, 258 U.S. 268, 275, 42 S.Ct. 299, 66 L.Ed. 615, 617, the court states: "The liability for spring guns and mantraps arises from the fact that the defendant has . . . expected the trespasser and prepared an injury that is no more justified than if he had held the gun and fired it."

In addition to civil liability many jurisdictions hold a land owner criminally liable for serious injuries or homicide caused by spring guns or other set devices. See State v. Childers, 133 Ohio 508, 14 N.E.2d 767 (melon thief shot by spring gun); Pierce v. Commonwealth, 135 Va. 635, 115 S.E. 686 (policeman killed by spring gun when he opened unlocked front door of defendant's shoe repair shop); State v. Marfaudille, 48 Wash. 117, 92 P. 939 (murder conviction for death from spring gun set in a trunk); State v. Beckham, 306 Mo. 566, 267 S.W. 817 (boy killed by spring gun attached to window of defendant's chili stand); State v. Green, 118 S.C. 279, 110 S.E. 145, 19 A.L.R. 1431 (intruder shot by spring gun when he broke and entered vacant house. Manslaughter conviction of owner-affirmed); State v. Barr, 11 Wash. 481, 39 P. 1080 (murder conviction affirmed for death of an intruder into a boarded up cabin in which owner had set a spring gun).

In Wisconsin, Oregon and England the use of spring guns and similar devices is specifically made unlawful by statute.

Judgment affirmed.

QUESTIONS AND PROBLEMS

1. Smith and his wife are returning home from vacation. As they are unlocking and entering their front door, they hear a noise from the rear of the house. Smith gets his gun, which he keeps in a front bedroom, and as he enters the kitchen, he sees someone running down the back steps and into the Smith backyard. Smith fires his gun from the back door and hits the figure, who is now in the

alley. Upon investigation, it is determined that Smith has killed a sixteen-year-old boy who was burglarizing the Smith home. Was this a lawful use of deadly force?

2. A police officer is on duty in a residential neighborhood on a hot summer night. Shortly after midnight, he hears a woman scream. The officer runs in the direction of the scream. A man runs out from between two houses ahead of the officer and down the street away from the officer. He does not stop when the officer yells to him to stop and the officer cannot catch him.

    a. Should the officer shoot at the fleeing suspect?

    b. Would the officer be civilly liable if he shot and wounded the fleeing suspect and investigation showed that the suspect was a windowpeeper?

3. Indicate the degree of force which may be used in the following situations:

    a. The person arrested offers no resistance and obeys the orders given to him.

    b. The person being arrested pulls a gun and fires at the officer.

    c. A shoplifter has taken a $500 watch from a store and is running away with it. It appears that the shoplifter cannot be caught. What force may a police officer use? Would the answer be different for a store security man?

    d. A police officer is writing out a ticket for a jaywalker when the person runs off. The officer cannot catch the person.

    e. Small boys are stealing apples from a prize apple tree belonging to X. X complains to you and asks you as a law enforcement officer what degree of force he may legally use to protect his apples. What should your advice be to X?

    f. Officers see X, who has committed a serious felony, escaping but they know that he cannot go far and will be apprehended shortly by other officers. What force may they use?

    g. In a high-speed chase, officers are following men in a vehicle which they believe to be stolen. The chase started when the men ran a red light. May the officers fire their guns at the fleeing car and the men in the car?

    h. A windowpeeper will not stop when ordered to stop by an officer.

Available Answers for Question 3

1. Deadly force may be used.

2. Reasonable force *less than* deadly force may be used.

3. No force may be (or should be) used.

Local Law

1. In your state, when may:
   a. Deadly force be used?
   b. Reasonable force but *less than* deadly force be used?
2. What are the laws in your state in regard to:
   a. The use of force to protect property?
   b. The use of force in self-defense or the defense of others?
3. In making a citizen's arrest, may the citizen use the same amount of force as a law enforcement officer could use if he were making the arrest?

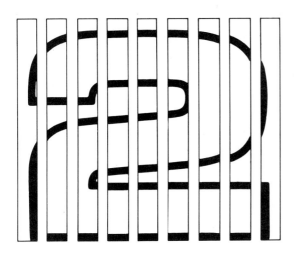

THE EXCLUSIONARY RULES

In prosecuting for a crime, the state must present evidence in court which proves beyond a reasonable doubt that the defendant has committed the crime with which he is charged. The exclusionary rules (or the Suppression doctrine) concern themselves with the methods and procedures used by the government in obtaining the evidence which the state seeks to use in court. If the evidence was obtained by procedures forbidden by the U.S. Constitution, by statute, or by court rule, it is excluded (or suppressed) from use in the trial. This is done regardless of the probative value or the reliability of the evidence, and even if such suppression means that a guilty suspect will be turned free. The reason most frequently given by the courts for excluding such evidence is that this action, although drastic, is necessary to deter illegal police practices.

The U.S. Supreme Court currently enforces an exclusionary rule in both state and federal criminal courts in regard to:

1. Searches and seizures which violate the Fourth Amendment (see Chap. 5)
2. Confessions or admissions which were obtained in violation of the Fifth and Sixth Amendments (see Chap. 6)
3. Identification testimony obtained in an improper manner (see Chap. 7)

Wiretapping and electronic surveillance evidence and testimony can also be excluded and suppressed under the exclusionary rule. This law, discussed in Chap. 15, is primarily governed today by federal and state statutes passed in the last few years.

The controversy over how best to protect the constitutional rights of suspects and persons under investigation while at the same time permitting the government to fulfill its obligation and responsibility to provide for public order and domestic tranquillity has been debated for years. Justice Benjamin Cardozo and Dean John Henry Wigmore (author of Wigmore on Evidence) were among those who opposed the original federal rule before World War I. Justices Frankfurter, Harlan, and Whittaker opposed imposing the federal Weeks rule on all the states in 1961. At that time, only about half the states had adapted exclusionary rules while the remaining half were using other means to protect the rights of defendants.

Extension and expansion of the exclusionary rules throughout the 1960s brought further disagreement (for example, adoption of the Miranda rule in 1965 was made in a 5-4 decision). The Suppression doctrine became a complex doctrine by the late 1960s with technicalities and ramifications which are understood by only a small percentage of law enforcement officers. While some of the exclusionary rules have almost unanimous acceptance by citizens and officers alike, other rules are highly controversial. Some of the central issues of the debate concerning the exclusionary rules and their expansion are:

While restraints are necessary on police in democratic countries because of the nature of their power and the possible abuses which can result from the misuse of such power, what type of restraints should be used?

Who should "police the police"? Is this an executive function, a legislative function, or a judicial function? Or is this a collective responsibility of all branches of government?

What should be the role of the federal courts in regard to state courts and state enforcement procedures? Should there be more or less activism on the part of federal judges? Has the federal judiciary usurped state prerogatives?

How effective are the other traditional safeguards which are available in our system? Could they be improved to do the task which the exclusionary rules seek to accomplish? The safeguards which democratic countries use to "police the police" include:

1. *Criminal actions against law enforcement officers if they violate federal or state criminal laws*
2. *Civil suits against transgressing officers brought in state or*

federal courts by parties who allege that their rights have been violated (the number of such suits has increased substantially in the United States in the 1960s)

3. Departmental insistence that proper procedures be used by officers and departmental discipline against offending officers

4. The democratic processes of putting additional statutory restraints on law enforcement agencies, if necessary, or through the power of the ballot box, changing the membership of police and fire commissions

In what percentage of cases do law enforcement officers violate the rights of suspects? Do these violations occur in an insignificant number of cases or in a substantial number of cases?

Have the exclusionary rules been an effective tool to upgrade procedural practices used by American police, or have they unnecessarily hampered effective law enforcement in the United States? (As the Suppression doctrine is uniquely American, it is not possible to observe its use in other countries to determine how successfully they have used it.)

Should the Fourth, Fifth, and Sixth Amendments of the United States Constitution be rewritten in concise, clear language specifically defining the rights of suspects and defendants?

Are other alternatives available? Some prominent Americans think so. See the article "Who Will Watch the Watchman" by Judge Warren E. Burger (now Chief Justice of the U.S. Supreme Court) in 14 Am. U.L. Rev. 1 (1964), where Judge Burger explores the use of a "possible tool to improve the administration of justice at its first point of contact with offenders."

ALI RECOMMENDED REFORM

In May of 1971, the America Law Institute (ALI) recommended that the present exclusionary rules in the United States be modified. Instead of automatically suppressing evidence when there is a violation, as is now required under the present exclusionary rule, the trial judge could admit the evidence (1) if the trial judge found that the violation was less than flagrant, and (2) that excluding the evidence would not deter police from similar invasions of privacy in the future, (3) unless the defendant could prove that the police violation of the constitutional or legal rights of the defendant was "willful."

If these changes were made through legislation and court decisions, the American exclusionary rule would then more closely follow the rules and practices which are now used in countries such as England, where the trial judge may exercise such discretion.

Example: *If the police were to beat a suspect or not feed a prisoner until he confessed, the confession would be suppressed in both England and in the United States.*

However, if the officer inadvertently omitted part of the four-part warning (officers are required to "caution" the suspect in England) or if the officer failed to obtain a clear, expressed waiver from the suspect that he understood his rights and waived them, the English trial judge could admit the resulting statement or confession while the American judge would have to suppress the evidence.

While law enforcement officers, as citizens, may exercise their rights to urge changes of the law and the Constitution through the political processes, they must obey the existing law. The present requirements of the exclusionary rules are now the law of the land and must be observed and complied with by all governmental officials.

The following three chapters seek to present the important principles and cases of the exclusionary rules which are now in effect in the United States. These rules apply only to governments and their agents and have, generally, not been held to be applicable to private persons.

(Authors' note: See the Dombrowski case on p. 242 (Prob. 4). This case is pending before the U.S. Supreme Court as this text is going to press and may become a very important search and seizure case.)

THE EXCLUSIONARY RULES (THE AMERICAN SUPPRESSION DOCTRINE)

TYPE OF EVIDENCE	CONTROLLING AMENDMENT OR STATUTE	TEST OF ADMISSIBILITY	
Physical evidence (weapons, finger-prints, clothing, contraband, etc. On blood see the Schmerber case in Chap. 8.)	*Fourth Amendment* "The right of the people to be secure ... against unreasonable searches and seizures shall not be violated."	The officer must show authority to make the search and seizure. (See Chap. 8 through 14.) The test is whether the search and seizure was reasonable. Plain view is not a search.	See Chap. 5
Oral admissions or statements; written admissions or confessions	*Fifth Amendment* "No person ... shall be compelled ... to be a witness against himself." *Sixth Amendment* "In all criminal prosecutions, the accused shall enjoy the right ... to have the assistance of Counsel for his defense."	1. Voluntariness test in view of the totality of the circumstances 2. Miranda test and requirements 3. Massiah test	See Chap. 6
Eyewitness and voice identification	*Fifth and Fourteenth Amendments* "No person shall be ... deprived of life, liberty, or property, without due process of law." *Sixth Amendment* "In all criminal prosecutions, the accused shall enjoy the right ... to have the assistance of Counsel for his defense."	1. Were the procedures used so unnecessarily suggestive and conducive to irreparable mistaken identification as to be a denial of due process of law? 2. Was the accused denied the assistance of counsel at an important and critical stage of the criminal proceedings?	See Chap. 7
Evidence obtained as a result of wire-tapping or electronic surveillance	Title III of the 1968 Federal Omnibus Crime Control and Safe Streets Act (see Chap. 15) and applicable state statutes	Was the evidence obtained in conformity with the applicable statute (or statutes)?	See Chap. 15

5

THE FOURTH AMENDMENT SEARCH AND SEIZURE EXCLUSIONARY RULE

"The right of the people to be secure in their persons, houses, papers, and effects, against *unreasonable* searches and seizures, shall not be violated, and no Warrants shall issue, but upon *probable cause*, supported by Oath or affirmation, and *particularly* describing the place to be searched, and the persons or things to be seized." Fourth Amendment of the U.S. Constitution (emphasis added to designate key words)

The Fourth Amendment to the U.S. Constitution was ratified in 1791 as part of the Bill of Rights. A strong national government had just been created by the Constitution proposed by the Philadelphia Convention of 1787, and the Bill of Rights was added to this Constitution to define and protect the rights of the people against this newly formed government.

In tracing the history of the Fourth Amendment, the U.S. Supreme Court stated in *Stanford v. Texas*, 379 U.S. 476, 85 S. Ct. 506 (1965):

... Vivid in the memory of the newly formed independent Americans were those general warrants known as writs of assistance under which officers of the Crown had so bedeviled the Colonists. The hated writs of assistance had given customs officials blanket authority to search where they pleased for goods imported in violation of British tax laws. They were denounced by James Otis as "the worst instrument of arbitrary power, the most destructive of English liberty, and the fundamental principles of law, that ever was found in an English law book" because they placed "the liberty of every man in the hands of every petty officer." The historic occasion of that denunciation in 1761 at Boston, has been characterized as "perhaps the most prominent event which inaugurated the resistance of the colonies to the oppressions of the mother country." "Then and there" said John Adams, "Then and there was the first scene of the first act of opposition to the arbitrary claims of Great Britain. Then and there the child Independence was born."

But while the Fourth Amendment was most immediately the product of contemporary revulsion against a regime of writs of assistance, its roots go far deeper. Its adoption in the Constitution of this new Nation reflected the culmination in England a few years earlier of a struggle against oppression which had endured for centuries. The story of that struggle has been fully chronicled in the pages of this Court's reports, and it would be a needless exercise in pedantry to review again the detailed history of the use of general warrants as instruments of oppression from the time of the Tudors, through the Star Chamber, the Long Parliament, the Restoration and beyond.

THE FEDERAL EXCLUSIONARY RULE

Before 1914, no exclusionary rules existed in the United States, either in federal or in state criminal courts. Evidence was admitted for use if it passed the relevancy and materiality tests, and conformed to other court requirements. Courts would not question where and how the evidence was obtained. A defendant who complained in a criminal case that the evidence being used against him was obtained by governmental trespass or by other illegal governmental means was told that his remedy was by suit in civil court.

In 1914, the United States Supreme Court held in *Weeks v. United States*, 232 U.S. 383, that any evidence which was unlawfully obtained by federal officers would be excluded from use in federal criminal trials. The Weeks rule did not apply to states. In the years which followed, some of the individual states did adopt their own exclusionary rules, and when *Wolf v. Colorado*, 338 U.S. 25, was heard in 1949, the U.S. Supreme Court noted that seventeen states had adopted the Weeks rule.

REQUIREMENT THAT STATES USE
THE FEDERAL EXCLUSIONARY RULE

By 1961, approximately half the states had adopted exclusionary rules. In that year, a criminal conviction in the Ohio courts was appealed to the U.S. Supreme Court and in a 5-4 decision, the Supreme Court reversed the Ohio trial court and stated in *Mapp v. Ohio* (see cases, this chapter):

... Today we once again examine ... the right to privacy free from unreasonable state intrusion ... by official lawlessness in flagrant abuse of that basic right, reserved to all persons as a specific guarantee against that very same unlawful conduct. We hold that all evidence by searches and seizure in violation of the Constitution is, by the same authority, inadmissible in a State court.

The Mapp ruling requires all states to conform to the Federal exclusionary rule.

THE RIGHT OF PRIVACY

The right to privacy and the expectation of privacy are rights vested in each person in the United States. The Fourth Amendment protects this right of privacy against unreasonable governmental intrusion. In *Miller v. United States* (see cases, Chap. 17), the United States Supreme Court quoted from the *Oxford Dictionary of Quotations* (2d ed., 1953), attributing the following remark to William Pitt in 1763:

> The poorest man may in his cottage bid defiance to all the forces of the Crown. It may be frail—its roof may shake—the wind may blow through it—the storm may enter—the rain may enter—but the King of England cannot enter—all his force dares not cross the threshold of the ruined tenement!

ARE ALL GOVERNMENTAL SEARCHES PROHIBITED BY THE FOURTH AMENDMENT?

The framers of the Constitution did not intend that a man's home, papers, or effects become a legal sanctuary against any and all government intrusions. They recognized, and so have the courts, that the right of the individual to privacy must sometimes give way to the needs of society. Hence, it has been determined that *not all* searches and seizures are forbidden, but only those which are *unreasonable*. In *Harris v. United States*, 331 U.S. 145, 67 S. Ct. 1098 (1947), the Court stated:

> This Court has also pointed out that it is only unreasonable searches and seizures which come within the constitutional interdict. The test of reasonableness cannot be stated in rigid and absolute terms. Each case is to be decided on its own facts and circumstances.

And in *Go-Bart Importing Co. v. United States*, 282 U.S. 344, 51 S. Ct. 153 (1931), the Court stated:

> The first clause of the Fourth Amendment declares: "The right of the people to be secure in their persons, houses, papers and effects against unreasonable searches and seizures shall not be violated." It is general and forbids every search that is unreasonable; it protects all, those suspected or known to be offenders as well as the innocent, and unquestionably extends to the premises where the search was made and papers taken....

WHAT IS A SEARCH?

A search was described by the United States Supreme Court in *Weeks v. United States*, 232 U.S. 383, as "a quest by an officer of the law, and a seizure contemplates a forcible dispossession of the owner." A search can be further described as a looking into; a seeking; a prying into, under, around, over, or behind to find that which has been concealed.

Wiretapping and electronic surveillance are also searches within the meaning of the Fourth Amendment (see the Katz case in Chap. 15). In *Davis v. Mississippi* (see Chap. 2), the U.S. Supreme Court held that detention under the conditions which existed in that case for the purposes of obtaining fingerprints violated the Fourth Amendment.

PLAIN VIEW OR OPEN VIEW IS NOT A SEARCH

If the officer is lawfully where he has a right to be, whatever he observes in the open, where it can be observed by anyone who cares to look, is plain view and is *not* a search. In *Ker v. California* (see Chap. 8) the U.S. Supreme Court held that

> ... the discovery of the brick of marijuana did not constitute a search, since the officer merely saw what was placed before him in full view.

In *Harris v. United States*, 331 U.S. 145, 67 S. Ct. 1098 (1947), the Supreme Court stated:

> It has long been settled that objects falling in the plain view of an officer who has a right to be in the position to have that view are subject to seizure and may be introduced in evidence.

Thus an officer who has a right to be where he is and views contraband or a criminal act through the open door of an apartment or hotel room, or views contraband through the window of an automobile or home, has not made a search and does not have to ignore what he has seen. This is open view or plain view. This subject is discussed in greater detail in Chap. 16.

WHO AND WHAT ARE PROTECTED?

When the founding fathers drafted the Fourth Amendment over 180 years ago, they specifically listed "persons, houses, papers, and effects" as being constitutionally protected. Although the U.S. Supreme Court stated in the Katz case (see Chap. 15) that "... the correct solution of Fourth Amendment problems is not necessarily promoted by incantation of the phrase 'constitutionally protected area'...," the Court has before and after the Katz case indicated areas in addition to those listed in the Fourth Amendment as being constitutionally protected.

In addition to "persons, houses, papers, and effects," the following have been held to fall under the protection of the Fourth Amendment:

Offices, hotel rooms, motor vehicles, etc. (see *Hoffa v. United States*, Chap. 19)
Business places and businessmen going about their business (*Colonnade Catering Corp. v. United States*, Chap. 14)
Private conversations and communications (see Chap. 15)
Garages (*Taylor v. United States*, 286 U.S. 1 [1932])
First-class mail (*Ex parte Jackson*, 1878, 96 U.S. 727)
Fingerprints (*Davis v. Mississippi*, see Chap. 2)

For a discussion of areas not protected by the Fourth Amendment, see Chap. 16 of this text.

WHAT IS SUBJECT TO SEIZURE?

All states probably have statutes defining what may be seized under the authority of a search warrant in that jurisdiction. With few exceptions, the same property may be searched for and seized by an officer having the authority to make a warrantless search.

Title II, section 23-521(d), of the Federal Criminal Procedure Act of 1970 provides:

> Property is subject to seizure pursuant to a search warrant if there is probable cause to believe that it—
> 1) is stolen or embezzled;
> 2) is contraband or otherwise illegally possessed;
> 3) has been used or is possessed for the purpose of being used, or is designed or intended to be used, to commit or conceal the commission of a criminal offense; or
> 4) constitutes evidence of or tends to demonstrate the commission of an offense or the identity of a person participating in the commission of an offense.

An officer may seize contraband or any property illegally possessed anytime he sees such property in plain view. This includes

PROPERTY WHICH MAY BE SEIZED

Property which a person has *no* right to possess may be seized *at any time.* *Examples:* narcotics concealed weapons stolen property burglary tools any contraband or items declared illegal by the state	Property in which the person has either the right of ownership or the right of possession may not be seized *unless* the officer has reasonable grounds to believe that a crime has been committed or is being committed *and* reasonable grounds to believe that the property is: an instrument or implement used to commit the crime a fruit of the crime evidence of the crime (shoes, clothing, masks, etc., which will link the suspect to the crime)

property which the officer has probable cause to believe has been stolen or embezzled.

Example: An officer is talking to a man on the street. The nervous suspect is taking something out of his pocket and opens his coat enough for the officer to see part of a gun. The officer may seize the gun and arrest the man for carrying a concealed weapon.
(What if, instead of a gun, the man had a package of fresh $1,000 bills?)

Not only may physical or tangible articles be seized, but also in a proper situation, an officer may "seize" conversations or statements or may record and testify as to his observations of what he saw and heard. This aspect of "seizing" is further discussed in Chap. 15.

SCOPE OF THE SEARCH

The scope of the search depends upon either the authority granted in the search warrant (see Chap. 13) or the authority which justifies the officer to make a warrantless search. See Part 3 for a discussion and cases on warrantless searches and searches made under the authority of a search warrant.

Depending on the circumstances of the case, the warrantless search of a three-floor house and the basement may be reasonable (see *Warden v. Hayden*, Chap. 8), but in another case the warrantless search of a single room may be held unreasonable (see *Chimel v. California*, in Chap. 9).

THE DERIVATIVE EVIDENCE RULE
(FRUIT OF THE POISONOUS TREE)

The exclusionary rule not only prohibits *direct* use of unlawfully obtained evidence but also prohibits its use *indirectly.* Unlawfully obtained information cannot be the lead or the basis for further investigation which then develops other evidence. The new evidence is said to be tainted or the "fruit of the poisonous tree" (this phrase was first used in a 1939 U.S. Supreme Court eavesdropping case by Mr. Justice Frankfurter (*Nardone v. United States,* 308 U.S. 338).

Example: Smith is arrested for murder. Officer Able, without consent and without a warrant, breaks into Smith's house. The officer finds Smith's diary in his desk. An entry states that Smith hid the murder weapon under a tree in the backyard. A warrant is obtained to dig under the tree and the weapon is found. It cannot be used in evidence because it is tainted by the illegality of the breakin.

The "fruit of the poisonous tree" doctrine is applicable if illegally obtained evidence is the basis for the discovery of:

1. Other evidence which otherwise would not have been found
2. A witness who otherwise might not have been found
3. A confession or admission which would not have been made if the suspect or defendant were not confronted with tainted evidence

The trial court, upon proper motion, would have to determine whether the witness, the confession, or the new evidence was tainted (and to what extent it was tainted) by the illegally seized evidence.

On occasion, officers uncover critical evidence which positively connects a suspect to a crime. But if the evidence is obtained by means considered to be in violation of the suspect's Fourth Amendment rights, the evidence cannot be used.

THE WARRANT REQUIREMENT

Except in certain well-defined areas, police *must* obtain a search warrant prior to conducting any search. The U.S. Supreme Court has been emphatic and consistent in requiring that a magistrate or judicial officer intervene between the police and the accused before the accused's constitutional rights are intruded upon. In *McDonald v. United States,* 355 U.S. 451, 69 S. Ct. 191, the Court stated:

We are not dealing with formalities. The presence of a search warrant serves a high function. Absent some grave emergency, the Fourth Amendment has interposed a magistrate between the citizen and the

> police. This was done not to shield criminals nor to make the home a safe haven for illegal activities. It was done so that an objective mind might determine the need to invade that privacy in order to enforce the law. The right of privacy was deemed too precious to entrust to the discretion of those whose job is the detection of crime and the arrest of criminals.
>
> ... And so the Constitution requires a magistrate to pass on the desires of the police before they violate the privacy of the home. We cannot be true to that constitutional requirement and excuse the absence of a search warrant without a showing by those who seek exemption from the constitutional mandate that the exigencies of the situation made that course imperative.

In *Vale v. Louisiana* (cases, Chap. 9) the U.S. Supreme Court stated in 1970:

> ... our past decisions make clear that only in a few specifically established and well delineated situations, may a warrantless search of a dwelling withstand constitutional scrutiny, even though the authorities have probable cause to conduct it. The burden rests on the State to show the existence of such an exceptional situation. ...

In reviewing a search and seizure, the courts generally give the officers the benefit of the doubt if they were acting under the authority of a search warrant. A warrant should be obtained:

1. If there is time to get a search warrant
2. If the officer *cannot* clearly show his authority to make a warrantless search (the burden is on the state to show this authority)
3. If there is any doubt whether a search warrant is necessary

Situations where searches and seizures can be made without a search warrant are discussed in Chaps. 8 through 14.

MOTION TO SUPPRESS

"Motion" means an application for a court order. A motion to suppress is an application to the trial court for an order to suppress evidence which the state plans to use against the defendant in a forthcoming criminal trial. The defense, in this manner, can challenge the evidence and is alleging and asserting that the evidence was obtained in violation of the exclusionary rules. The allegation that the property was illegally seized without a warrant is the most frequent grounds for a motion to suppress evidence.

A date for hearing the motion is set by the trial court; at this time arguments are heard by the defense and the state as to the admissibility of the evidence. The hearing is before the court (usually before the trial) and without the jury being present. Officers who were involved in the investigation may be subpoenaed to testify in regard to the manner in which the evidence was obtained.

The motion to suppress is not only a procedure in which the defendant can challenge the admissibility of evidence which is going to be used against him but it can also be a discovery device for the defense. The defense attorney is able to gauge the strength and weaknesses of the state's case before going to trial and before the case is presented to a jury. For this reason prosecutors urge officers to avoid, if possible, situations where they can be challenged on a motion to suppress.

STANDING TO MAKE THE MOTION TO SUPPRESS EVIDENCE

"Standing" is the right to challenge the legality and admissibility of the evidence in question. The challenge is usually made by a motion to suppress. In the case of a homeowner who is arrested and tried on the basis of evidence seized during an unlawful search of his home, the question is not difficult to resolve. The evidence may not be used against him. He may object to the use of the evidence at the trial on the basis of the Fourth Amendment protection of ". . . houses, papers, and effects. . . ."

But what of a guest in the home? If the evidence which was obtained is not being used against the homeowner but instead is being used against a guest in the house, he cannot claim that *his* "house" was unlawfully searched. The same problems have risen for invitees, licensees, etc., who were present lawfully on the premises but had no property interest in the premises which were searched. Under the old rules, one had to have a "property interest" in the premises or the unlawfully seized articles before one could complain, or have standing to object to, its use in evidence. These strict rules of property law gave way slowly to a concept of "possessory interest" in the articles seized. If the accused had a possessory interest in the articles, he was thereupon imbued with standing to object to its introduction into evidence against him in court.

Possessory interest, however, created a new problem. What happens in a case where mere possession of the article or substance is itself a crime, e.g., heroin? In order to complain that it was unlawfully seized, the defendant has to allege that the heroin was taken from his possession. But the defendant in admitting possession is also convicting himself. The lower courts resolved this dilemma by, in effect, telling the defendants in such cases that it was their problem. They could not have their cake and eat it too. The U.S. Supreme Court resolved the issue in another manner in *Jones v. United States*, 362 U.S. 257, 4 L. Ed. 2d 697, 80 S. Ct. 725 (1960). In this case, the U.S. Supreme Court interpreted standing "... by recognizing that anyone legitimately on the premises where a search occurs may challenge by way of a motion to suppress, when its fruits are proposed to be used against him."

DO THE EXCLUSIONARY RULES APPLY TO EVIDENCE ILLEGALLY OBTAINED BY PRIVATE PERSONS?

If the private citizen is acting as an agent of the police, the exclusionary rules would apply. But if the private person is acting independently, the exclusionary rules generally would not apply. See Chap. 3 on this subject.

DO OTHER DEMOCRATIC COUNTRIES USE THESE EXCLUSIONARY RULES?

In other democratic countries such as England and Canada, the manner in which evidence is obtained is not an issue in a criminal trial. If the evidence is relevant and passes other tests of admissibility within that jurisdiction, it is admitted into evidence even if it has been illegally obtained. However, if the manner of obtaining the evidence is so unfair when balancing the good of the community against the rights of the accused, the trial judge does have the power to exclude it. Therefore, it can be stated that only in the United States are fixed and rigid exclusionary rules used.

CASES FOR CHAPTER FIVE

MAPP v. OHIO
SUPREME COURT OF THE UNITED STATES
367 U.S. 643, 6 L. ED. 2d 1081, 81 S. CT. 1684 (1961)

OPINION OF THE COURT

Mr. Justice Clark delivered the opinion of the Court.

Appellant stands convicted of knowingly having had in her possession and under her control certain lewd and lascivious books, pictures, and photographs in violation of § 2905.34 of Ohio's Revised Code. As officially stated in the syllabus to its opinion, the Supreme Court of Ohio found that her conviction was valid though "based primarily upon the introduction in evidence of lewd and lascivious books and pictures unlawfully seized during an unlawful search of defendant's home..."

On May 23, 1957, three Cleveland police officers arrived at appellant's residence in that city pursuant to information that "a person [was] hiding out in the home, who was wanted for questioning in connection with a recent bombing, and that there was a large amount of policy paraphernalia being hidden in the home." Miss Mapp and her daughter by a former marriage lived on the top floor of the two-family dwelling. Upon their arrival at that house, the officers knocked on the door and demanded entrance but appellant, after telephoning her attorney, refused to admit them without a search warrant. They advised their headquarters of the situation and undertook a surveillance of the house.

The officers again sought entrance some three hours later when four or more additional officers arrived on the scene. When Miss Mapp did not come to the door immediately, at least one of the several doors to the house was forcibly opened and the policemen gained admittance. Meanwhile Miss Mapp's attorney arrived, but the officers, having secured their own entry, and continuing in their defiance of the law, would permit him neither to see Miss Mapp nor to enter the house. It appears that Miss Mapp was halfway down the stairs from the upper floor to the front door when the officers, in this highhanded manner, broke into the hall. She demanded to see the search warrant. A paper, claimed to be a warrant, was held up by one of the officers. She grabbed the "warrant" and placed it in her bosom. A struggle ensued in which the officers recovered the piece of paper and as a result of which they handcuffed appellant because she had been "belligerent" in resisting their official rescue of the "warrant" from her person. Running roughshod over appellant, a policeman "grabbed" her, "twisted [her] hand," and she "yelled [and] pleaded with him" because "it was hurting." Appellant, in handcuffs, was then forcibly taken upstairs to her bedroom where the officers searched a dresser, a chest of drawers, a closet and some suitcases. They also looked into a photo album and through personal papers belonging to the appellant. The search spread to the rest of the second floor including the child's bedroom, the living room, the kitchen and a dinette. The basement of the building and a trunk found therein were also searched. The obscene materials for possession of which she was ultimately convicted were discovered in the course of that widespread search.

At the trial no search warrant was produced by the prosecution, nor was the failure to produce one explained or accounted for. At best, "There is, in the record, considerable doubt as to whether there ever was any warrant for the search of defendant's home." The Ohio Supreme Court believed a "reasonable argument" could be made that the conviction should be reversed "because the 'methods' employed to obtain the [evidence] ... were such as to 'offend "a sense of justice,"'" but the court found determinative the fact that the evidence had not been taken "from defendant's person by the use of brutal or offensive physical force against defendant."

The State says that even if the search were made without authority, or otherwise unreasonably, it is not prevented from using the unconstitutionally seized evidence at trial, citing Wolf v Colorado, 338 US 25 (1949), in which this Court did indeed hold "that in a prosecution in a State court for a State crime the Fourteenth Amendment does not forbid the admission of evidence obtained by an unreasonable search and seizure." On this appeal, of which we have noted probable jurisdiction, it is urged once again that we review that holding.

I.

Seventy-five years ago, in Boyd v United States, 116 US 616 (1886), considering the Fourth and Fifth Amendments as running "almost into each other" on the facts before it, this Court held that the doctrines of those Amendments "apply to all invasions on the part of the government and its employes of the sanctity of a man's home and the privacies of life. It is not the breaking of his doors, and the rummaging of his drawers, that constitutes the essence of the offence; but it is the invasion of his indefeasible right of personal security, personal liberty and private property.... Breaking into a house and opening boxes and drawers are circumstances of aggravation; but any forcible and compulsory extortion of a man's own testimony or of his private papers to be used as evidence to convict him of crime or to forfeit his goods, is within the condemnation ... [of those Amendments]."

The Court noted that "constitutional provisions for the security of person and property should be liberally construed.... It is the duty of courts to be watchful for the constitutional rights of the citizen, and against any stealthy encroachments thereon."

In this jealous regard for maintaining the integrity of individual rights, the Court gave life to Madison's prediction that "independent tribunals of justice ... will be naturally led to resist every encroachment upon rights expressly stipulated for in the Constitution by the declaration of rights." Concluding, the Court specifically referred to the use of the evidence there seized as "unconstitutional."

Less than 30 years after Boyd, this Court, in Weeks v United States, 232 US 383 (1914), stated that "the Fourth Amendment ... put the courts of the United States and Federal officials, in the exercise of their power and authority, under limitations and restraints [and] ... forever secure[d] the people, their persons, houses, papers and effects against all unreasonable searches and seizures under the guise of law ... and the duty of giving to it force and effect is obligatory upon all entrusted under our Federal system with the enforcement of the laws."

Specifically dealing with the use of the evidence unconstitutionally seized, the Court concluded:

> "If letters and private documents can thus be seized and held and used in evidence against a citizen accused of an offense, the protection of the Fourth Amendment declaring his right to be secure against such searches and seizures is of no value, and, so far as those thus placed are concerned, might as well be stricken from the Constitution. The efforts of the courts and their officials to bring the guilty to punishment, praiseworthy as they are, are not to be aided by the sacrifice of those great principles established by years of endeavor and suffering which have resulted in their embodiment in the fundamental law of the land."

Finally, the Court in that case clearly stated that use of the seized evidence involved "a denial of the constitutional rights of the accused." Thus, in the year 1914, in the Weeks Case, this Court "for the first time" held that "in a federal prosecution the Fourth Amendment barred the use of evidence secured through an illegal search and seizure." This Court has ever since required of federal law officers a strict adherence to that command which this Court has held to be a clear, specific, and constitutionally required—even if judicially implied—deterrent safeguard without insistence upon which the Fourth Amendment would have been reduced to "a form of words." Silverthorne Lumber Co. v United States, 251 US 385 (1920). It meant, quite simply, that "conviction by means of unlawful seizures and enforced confessions ... should find no sanction in the judgments of the courts ...," Weeks v United States, supra, and that such evidence "shall not be used at all." Silverthorne Lumber Co. v United States, supra.

There are in the cases of this Court some passing references to the Weeks rule as being one of evidence. But the plain and unequivocal language of Weeks —and its later paraphrase in Wolf—to the effect that the Weeks rule is of constitutional origin, remains entirely undisturbed. In Byars v United States, 273 US

28 (1927), a unanimous Court declared that "the doctrine [cannot] . . . be tolerated *under our constitutional system*, that evidences of crime discovered by a federal officer in making a search without lawful warrant may be used against the victim of the unlawful search where a timely challenge has been interposed." The Court, in Olmstead v United States, 277 US 438, 72 L ed 944, 48 C Ct 564, 66 ALR 376 (1928), in unmistakable language restated the Weeks rule:

> "The striking outcome of the Weeks case and those which fol-
> lowed it was the sweeping declaration that the Fourth Amendment,
> although not referring to or limiting the use of evidence in courts,
> really forbade its introduction if obtained by government officers
> through a violation of the Amendment."

In McNabb v United States, 318 US 332 (1943), we note this statement:

> "[A] conviction in the federal courts, the foundation of which is
> evidence obtained in disregard of liberties deemed fundamental by
> the Constitution, cannot stand. . . . And this Court has, on Constitutional
> grounds, set aside convictions, both in the federal and state courts,
> which were based upon confessions 'secured by protracted and re-
> peated questioning of ignorant and untutored persons, in whose minds
> the power of officers was greatly magnified' . . . or 'who have been un-
> lawfully held incommunicado without advice of friends or counsel' . . . ."

Significantly, in McNabb, the Court did then pass on to formulate a rule of evidence, saying, "[i]n the view we take of the case, however, it becomes un-necessary to reach the Constitutional issue [for] . . . [t]he principles governing the admissibility of evidence in federal criminal trials have not been restricted . . . to those derived solely from the Constitution."

II.

In 1949, 35 years after Weeks was announced, this Court, in Wolf v Colorado (US) supra, again for the first time, discussed the effect of the Fourth Amendment upon the States through the operation of the Due Process Clause of the Fourteenth Amendment. It said:

> "[W]e have no hesitation in saying that were a State affirmatively
> to sanction such police incursion into privacy it would run counter to
> the guaranty of the Fourteenth Amendment."

Nevertheless, after declaring that the "security of one's privacy against ar-bitrary intrusion by the police" is "implicit in 'the concept of ordered liberty' and as such enforceable against the States through the Due Process Clause," and an-nouncing that it "stoutly adhere[d]" to the Weeks decision, the Court decided that the Weeks exclusionary rule would not then be imposed upon the States as "an essential ingredient of the right." The Court's reasons for not considering essen-tial to the right to privacy, as a curb imposed upon the States by the Due Process Clause, that which decades before had been posited as part and parcel of the Fourth Amendment's limitation upon federal encroachment of individual privacy, were bottomed on factual considerations.

While they are not basically relevant to a decision that the exclusionary rule is an essential ingredient of the Fourth Amendment as the right it embodies is vouchsafed against the States by the Due Process Clause, we will consider the current validity of the factual grounds upon which Wolf was based.

The Court in Wolf first stated that "[t]he contrariety of views of the States" on the adoption of the exclusionary rule of Weeks was "particularly impressive" and, in this connection, that it could not "brush aside the experience of States which deem the incidence of such conduct by the police too slight to call for a deterrent remedy . . . by overriding the [States'] relevant rules of evidence." While in 1949, prior to the Wolf Case, almost two-thirds of the States were opposed to the use of the exclusionary rule, now, despite the Wolf Case, more than half of those since passing upon it, by their own legislative or judicial decision, have wholly or partly adopted or adhered to the Weeks rule. See Elkins v United States, 364 US 206 (1960). Significantly, among those now following the rule is California, which, according to its highest court, was "compelled to reach that conclusion because other remedies have completely failed to secure compliance with the constitutional provisions. . . ." In connection with this California case, we note that the second basis elaborated in Wolf in support of its failure to enforce the exclusionary doctrine against the States was that "other means of protection" have been afforded "the right to privacy." The experience of California that such other remedies have been worthless and futile is buttressed by the experience of other States. The obvious futility of relegating the Fourth Amendment to the protection of other remedies has, moreover, been recognized by this Court since Wolf. See Irvine v California, 347 US 128 (1954).

Likewise, time has set its face against what Wolf called the "weighty testimony" of People v Defore, 242 NY 13 (1926). There Justice (then Judge) Cardozo, rejecting adoption of the Weeks exclusionary rule in New York, had said that "[t]he Federal rule as it stands is either too strict or too lax." However, the force of that reasoning has been largely vitiated by later decisions of this Court. These include the recent discarding of the "silver platter" doctrine which allowed federal judicial use of evidence seized in violation of the Constitution by state agents, Elkins v United States, 364 US 206, 4 L ed 2d 1669, 80 S Ct 1437, supra; the relaxation of the formerly strict requirements as to standing to challenge the use of evidence thus seized, so that now the procedure of exclusion, "ultimately referable to constitutional safeguards," is available to anyone even "legitimately on [the] premises" unlawfully searched, Jones v United States, 362 US 257 (1960); and, finally, the formulation of a method to prevent state use of evidence unconstitutionally seized by federal agents, Rea v United States, 350 US 214 (1956). Because there can be no fixed formula, we are admittedly met with "recurring questions of the reasonableness of searches," but less is not to be expected when dealing with a Constitution, and, at any rate, "[r]easonableness is in the first instance for the [trial court] . . . to determine." United States v Rabinowitz, 339 US 56 (1950).

It, therefore, plainly appears that the factual considerations supporting the failure of the Wolf Court to include the Weeks exclusionary rule when it recognized the enforceability of the right to privacy against the States in 1949, while not basically relevant to the constitutional consideration, could not, in any analysis, now be deemed controlling.

III.

Some five years after Wolf, in answer to a plea made here Term after Term that we overturn its doctrine on applicability of the Weeks exclusionary rule, this Court indicated that such should not be done until the States had "adequate opportunity to adopt or reject the [Weeks] rule." Irvine v California, supra (347 US, at 134). There again it was said:

> "Never until June of 1949 did this Court hold the basic search-and-seizure prohibition in any way applicable to the states under the Fourteenth Amendment." Ibid.

And only last Term, after again carefully re-examining the Wolf doctrine in Elkins v United States (US) supra, the Court pointed out that "the controlling principles" as to search and seizure and the problem of admissibility "seemed clear" until the announcement in Wolf "that the Due Process Clause of the Fourteenth Amendment does not itself require state courts to adopt the exclusionary rule" of the Weeks Case. At the same time, the Court pointed out, "the underlying constitutional doctrine which Wolf established . . . that the Federal Constitution . . . prohibits unreasonable searches and seizures by state officers" had undermined the "foundation upon which the admissibility of state-seized evidence in a federal trial originally rested. . . ." Ibid. The Court concluded that it was therefore obliged to hold, although it chose the narrower ground on which to do so, that all evidence obtained by an unconstitutional search and seizure was inadmissible in a federal court regardless of its source. Today we once again examine Wolf's constitutional documentation of the right to privacy free from unreasonable state intrusion, and, after its dozen years on our books, are led by it to close the only courtroom door remaining open to evidence secured by official lawlessness in flagrant abuse of that basic right, reserved to all persons as a specific guarantee against that very same unlawful conduct. We hold that all evidence obtained by searches and seizures in violation of the Constitution is, by that same authority, inadmissible in a state court.

IV.

. Since the Fourth Amendment's right of privacy has been declared enforceable against the States through the Due Process Clause of the Fourteenth, it is enforceable against them by the same sanction of exclusion as is used against the Federal Government. Were it otherwise, then just as without the Weeks rule the assurance against unreasonable federal searches and seizures would be "a form of words," valueless and undeserving of mention in a perpetual charter of inestimable human liberties, so too, without that rule the freedom from state invasions of privacy would be so ephemeral and so neatly severed from its conceptual nexus with the freedom from all brutish means of coercing evidence as not to merit this Court's high regard as a freedom "implicit in the concept of ordered liberty." At the time that the Court held in Wolf that the Amendment was applicable to the States through the Due Process Clause, the cases of this Court, as we have seen, had steadfastly held that as to federal officers the Fourth Amendment included the exclusion of the evidence seized in violation of its provisions. Even Wolf "stoutly adhered" to that proposition. The right to privacy, when conceded operatively enforceable against the States, was not susceptible of destruction by avulsion of the sanction upon which its protection and enjoyment had always been deemed dependent under the Boyd, Weeks and Silverthorne Cases. Therefore, in extending the substantive protections of due process to all constitutionally unreasonable searches—state or federal—it was logically and constitutionally necessary that the exclusion doctrine—an essential part of the right to privacy—be also insisted upon as an essential ingredient of the right newly recognized by the Wolf Case. In short, the admission of the new constitutional right by Wolf could not consistently tolerate denial of its most important constitutional privilege, namely, the exclusion of the evidence which an accused had been forced to give by reason of the unlawful seizure. To hold otherwise is to grant the right but in reality to withhold its privilege and enjoyment. Only last year the Court itself recognized that the purpose of the exclusionary rule "is to deter—to compel respect for the constitutional guaranty in the only effectively available way—by removing the incentive to disregard it." Elkins v United States, supra.

Indeed, we are aware of no restraint, similar to that rejected today, conditioning the enforcement of any other basic constitutional right. The right to privacy, no less important than any other right carefully and particularly reserved to the people, would stand in marked contrast to all other rights declared as "basic to a free society." Wolf v Colorado, supra. This Court has not hesitated to enforce as strictly against the States as it does against the Federal Government the rights of free speech and of a free press, the rights to notice and to a fair, public trial, including, as it does, the right not to be convicted by use of a coerced confession, however logically relevant it be, and without regard to its reliability.

And nothing could be more certain than that when a coerced confession is involved, "the relevant rules of evidence" are overridden without regard to "the incidence of such conduct by the police," slight or frequent. Why should not the same rule apply to what is tantamount to coerced testimony by way of unconstitutional seizure of goods, papers, effects, documents, etc.? We find that, as to the Federal Government, the Fourth and Fifth Amendments and, as to the States, the freedom from unconscionable invasions of privacy and the freedom from convictions based upon coerced confessions do enjoy an "intimate relation" in their perpetuation of "principles of humanity and civil liberty [secured] ... only after years of struggle."

They express "supplementing phases of the same constitutional purpose—to maintain inviolate large areas of personal privacy."

The philosophy of each Amendment and of each freedom is complementary to, although not dependent upon, that of the other in its sphere of influence—the very least that together they assure in either sphere is that no man is to be convicted on unconstitutional evidence.

V.

Moreover, our holding that the exclusionary rule is an essential part of both the Fourth and Fourteenth Amendments is not only the logical dictate of prior cases, but it also makes very good sense. There is no war between the Constitution and common sense. Presently, a federal prosecutor may make no use of evidence illegally seized, but a State's attorney across the street may, although he supposedly is operating under the enforceable prohibitions of the same Amendment. Thus the State, by admitting evidence unlawfully seized, serves to encourage disobedience to the Federal Constitution which it is bound to uphold. Moreover, as was said in Elkins, "[t]he very essence of a healthy federalism depends upon the avoidance of needless conflict between state and federal courts." Such a conflict, hereafter needless, arose this very Term, in Wilson v Schnettler, 365 US 381 (1961), in which, and in spite of the promise made by Rea, we gave full recognition to our practice in this regard by refusing to restrain a federal officer from testifying in a state court as to evidence unconstitutionally seized by him in the performance of his duties. Yet the double standard recognized until today hardly put such a thesis into practice. In nonexclusionary States, federal officers, being human, were by it invited to and did, as our cases indicate, step across the street to the State's attorney with their unconstitutionally seized evidence. Prosecution on the basis of that evidence was then had in a state court in utter disregard of the enforceable Fourth Amendment. If the fruits of an unconstitutional search had been inadmissible in both state and federal courts, this inducement to evasion would have been sooner eliminated. There would be no need to reconcile such cases as Rea and Schnettler, each pointing up the hazardous uncertainties of our heretofore ambivalent approach.

Federal-state cooperation in the solution of crime under constitutional standards will be promoted, if only by recognition of their now mutual obligation to respect the same fundamental criteria in their approaches. "However much in a particular case insistence upon such rules may appear as a technicality that inures to the benefit of a guilty person, the history of the criminal law proves that tolerance of shortcut methods in law enforcement impairs its enduring effectiveness."

Denying shortcuts to only one of two cooperating law enforcement agencies tends naturally to breed legitimate suspicion of "working arrangements" whose results are equally tainted.

There are those who say, as did Justice (then Judge) Cardozo, that under our constitutional exclusionary doctrine "[t]he criminal is to go free because the constable has blundered." In some cases this will undoubtedly be the result. But, as was said in Elkins, "there is another consideration—the imperative of judicial integrity." The criminal goes free, if he must, but it is the law that sets him free. Nothing can destroy a government more quickly than its failure to observe its own laws, or worse, its disregard of the charter of its own existence. As Mr. Justice Brandeis, dissenting, said in Olmstead v United States, 277 US 438 (1928): "Our Government is the potent, the omnipresent teacher. For good or for ill, it teaches the whole people by its example.... If the Government becomes a lawbreaker, it breeds contempt for law; it invites every man to become a law unto himself; it invites anarchy." Nor can it lightly be assumed that, as a practical matter, adoption of the exclusionary rule fetters law enforcement. Only last year this Court expressly considered that contention and found that "pragmatic evidence of a sort" to the contrary was not wanting. Elkins v United States, supra.

The Court noted that

> "The federal courts themselves have operated under the exclusionary rule of Weeks for almost half a century; yet it has not been suggested either that the Federal Bureau of Investigation has thereby been rendered ineffective, or that the administration of criminal justice in the federal courts has thereby been disrupted. Moreover, the experience of the states is impressive.... The movement towards the rule of exclusion has been halting but seemingly inexorable."

The ignoble shortcut to conviction left open to the State tends to destroy the entire system of constitutional restraints on which the liberties of the people rest. Having once recognized that the right to privacy embodied in the Fourth Amendment is enforceable against the States, and that the right to be secure against rude invasions of privacy by state officers is, therefore, constitutional in origin, we can no longer permit that right to remain an empty promise. Because it is enforceable in the same manner and to like effect as other basic rights secured by the Due Process Clause, we can no longer permit it to be revocable at the whim of any police officer who, in the name of law enforcement itself, chooses to suspend its enjoyment. Our decision, founded on reason and truth, gives to the individual no more than that which the Constitution guarantees him, to the police officer no less than that to which honest law enforcement is entitled, and, to the courts, that judicial integrity so necessary in the true administration of justice.

The judgment of the Supreme Court of Ohio is reversed and the cause remanded for further proceedings not inconsistent with this opinion.

Reversed and remanded.

[Authors' note: A UPI newspaper article of November 3, 1970, reported that the New York police searched Mrs. Dollree Mapp's home in New York under the authority of a search warrant. Mrs. Mapp was the defendant in the Mapp case. The police reported that they found more than 50,000 envelopes of heroin with a street value of $150,000 and stolen property worth more than $850,000. Mrs. Mapp was alleged to have been in the business of trading the heroin for shoplifted and burglarized merchandise. Mrs. Mapp's home was reported to be equipped with two burglar alarms, heavy steel fire doors on all entrances, and bars on the windows.]

WONG SUN v. UNITED STATES
SUPREME COURT OF THE UNITED STATES
371 U.S. 471, 83 S. CT. 407, 9 L. ED. 2d 441 (1963)

OPINION OF THE COURT

Mr. Justice Brennan delivered the opinion of the Court

The petitioners were tried without a jury in the District Court for the Northern District of California under a two-count indictment for violation of the Federal Narcotics Laws, 21 USC § 174. They were acquitted under the first count which charged a conspiracy, but convicted under the second count which charged the substantive offense of fraudulent and knowing transportation and concealment of illegally imported heroin. The Court of Appeals for the Ninth Circuit, one judge dissenting, affirmed the convictions. We granted certiorari.

About 2 a. m. on the morning of June 4, 1959, federal narcotics agents in San Francisco, after having had one Hom Way under surveillance for six weeks, arrested him and found heroin in his possession. Hom Way, who had not before been an informant, stated after his arrest that he had bought an ounce of heroin the night before from one known to him only as "Blackie Toy," proprietor of a laundry on Leavenworth Street.

About 6 a. m. that morning six or seven federal agents went to a laundry at 1733 Leavenworth Street. The sign above the door of this establishment said "Oye's Laundry." It was operated by the petitioner James Wah Toy. There is, however, nothing in the record which identifies James Wah Toy and "Blackie Toy" as the same person. The other federal officers remained nearby out of sight while Agent Alton Wong, who was of Chinese ancestry, rang the bell. When petitioner Toy appeared and opened the door, Agent Wong told him that he was calling for laundry and dry cleaning. Toy replied that he didn't open until 8 o''clock and told the agent to come back at that time. Toy started to close the door. Agent Wong thereupon took his badge from his pocket and said, "I am a federal narcotics agent." Toy immediately "slammed the door and started running" down the hallway through the laundry to his living quarters at the back where his wife and child were sleeping in a bedroom. Agent Wong and the other federal officers broke down the door and followed Toy down the hallway to the living quarters and into the bedroom. Toy reached into a nightstand drawer. Agent Wong thereupon drew his pistol, pulled Toy's hand out of the drawer, placed him under arrest and handcuffed him. There was nothing in the drawer and a search of the premises uncovered no narcotics.

One of the agents said to Toy "... [Hom Way] says he got narcotics from you." Toy responded, "No, I haven't been selling any narcotics at all. However, I do know somebody who has." When asked who that was, Toy said, "I only know him as Johnny. I don't know his last name." However, Toy described a house on Eleventh Avenue where he said Johnny lived; he also described a bedroom in the house where he said "Johnny kept about a piece"[1] of heroin, and where he and Johnny had smoked some of the drug the night before. The agents left immediately for Eleventh Avenue and located the house. They entered and found one Johnny Yee in the bedroom. After a discussion with the agents, Yee took from a bureau drawer several tubes containing in all just less than one ounce of heroin, and surrendered them. Within the hour Yee and Toy were taken to the Office of the Bureau of Narcotics. Yee there stated that the heroin had been brought to him some four days earlier by petitioner Toy and another Chinese known to him only as "Sea Dog."

Toy was questioned as to the identity of "Sea Dog" and said that "Sea Dog" was Wong Sun. Some agents, including Agent Alton Wong, took Toy to Wong Sun's neighborhood where Toy pointed out a multifamily dwelling where he said Wong Sun lived. Agent Wong rang a downstairs door bell and a buzzer sounded, opening the door. The officer identified himself as a narcotics agent to a woman on the landing and asked "for Mr. Wong." The woman was the wife of petitioner Wong Sun. She said that Wong Sun was "in the back room sleeping." Alton Wong and some six other officers climbed the stairs and entered the apartment. One of the officers went into the back room and brought petitioner Wong Sun from the bedroom in handcuffs. A thorough search of the apartment followed, but no narcotics were discovered.

Petitioner Toy and Johnny Yee were arraigned before a United States Commissioner on June 4 on a complaint charging a violation of 21 USC § 174. Later that day, each was released on his own recognizance. Petitioner Wong Sun was arraigned on a similar complaint filed the next day and was also released on his own recognizance. Within a few days, both petitioners and Yee were interrogated at the office of the Narcotics Bureau by Agent William Wong, also of Chinese ancestry.[2] The agent advised each of the three of his right to withhold information which might be used against him, and stated to each that he was entitled to the advice of counsel, though it does not appear that any attorney was present during the questioning of any of the three. The officer also explained to each that no promises or offers of immunity or leniency were being or could be made.

The agent interrogated each of the three separately. After each had been in-

---

[1] A "piece" is approximately one ounce.

[2] Because neither statement was ever signed, the blanks in which the dates were to have been inserted were never filled in. The heading of Toy's statement suggests that it was made on June 5, although Agent William Wong at the trial suggested he had only talked informally with Toy on that date, the formal statement not being made until June 9. The agent also testified that Wong Sun's statement was made June 9, although a rubber-stamp date beneath the agent's own signature at the foot of the statement reads, "June 15, 1959."

terrogated the agent prepared a statement in English from rough notes. The agent read petitioner Toy's statement to him in English and interpreted certain portions of it for him in Chinese. Toy also read the statement in English aloud to the agent, said there were corrections to be made, and made the corrections in his own hand. Toy would not sign the statement, however; in the agent's words "he wanted to know first if the other persons involved in the case had signed theirs." Wong Sun had considerable difficulty understanding the statement in English and the agent restated its substance in Chinese. Wong Sun refused to sign the statement although he admitted the accuracy of its contents.

Hom Way did not testify at petitioners' trial. The Government offered Johnny Yee as its principal witness but excused him after he invoked the privilege against self-incrimination and flatly repudiated the statement he had given to Agent William Wong. That statement was not offered in evidence nor was any testimony elicited from him identifying either petitioner as the source of the heroin in his possession, or otherwise tending to support the charges against the petitioners.

The statute expressly provides that proof of the accused's possession of the drug will support a conviction under the statute unless the accused satisfactorily explains the possession. The Government's evidence tending to prove the petitioners' possession (the petitioners offered no exculpatory testimony) consisted of four items which the trial court admitted over timely objections that they were inadmissible as "fruits" of unlawful arrests or of attendant searches: (1) the statements made orally by petitioner Toy in his bedroom at the time of his arrest; (2) the heroin surrendered to the agents by Johnny Yee; (3) petitioner Toy's pretrial unsigned statement; and (4) petitioner Wong Sun's similar statement. The dispute below and here has centered around the correctness of the rulings of the trial judge allowing these items in evidence.

The Court of Appeals held that the arrests of both petitioners were illegal because not based on " 'probable cause' within the meaning of the Fourth Amendment" nor "reasonable grounds" within the meaning of the Narcotic Control Act of 1956. The court said as to Toy's arrest, "There is no showing in this case that the agent knew Hom Way to be reliable," and, furthermore, found "nothing in the circumstances occurring at Toy's premises that would provide sufficient justification for his arrest without a warrant." As to Wong Sun's arrest, the court said "there is no showing that Johnnie Yee was a reliable informer." The Court of Appeals nevertheless held that the four items of proof were not the "fruits" of the illegal arrests and that they were therefore properly admitted in evidence.

The Court of Appeals rejected two additional contentions of the petitioners. The first was that there was insufficient evidence to corroborate the petitioners' unsigned admissions of possession of narcotics. The court held that the narcotics in evidence surrendered by Johnny Yee, together with Toy's statements in his bedroom at the time of arrest, corroborated petitioners' admissions. The second contention was that the confessions were inadmissible because they were not signed. The Court of Appeals held on this point that the petitioners were not prejudiced, since the agent might properly have testified to the substance of the conversations which produced the statements.

We believe that significant differences between the cases of the two petitioners require separate discussion of each. We shall first consider the case of petitioner Toy.

I.

The Court of Appeals found there was neither reasonable grounds nor probable cause for Toy's arrest. Giving due weight to that finding, we think it is amply justified by the facts clearly shown on this record. It is basic that an arrest with or without a warrant must stand upon firmer ground than mere suspicion, see Henry v United States, 361 US 98, though the arresting officer need not have in hand evidence which would suffice to convict. The quantum of information which constitutes probable cause—evidence which would "warrant a man of reasonable caution in the belief" that a felony has been committed, Carroll v United States, 267 US 132,—must be measured by the facts of the particular case. The history of the use, and not infrequent abuse, of the power to arrest cautions that a relaxation of the fundamental requirements of probable cause would "leave law-abiding citizens at the mercy of the officers' whim or caprice." Brinegar v United States, 338 US 160.

Whether or not the requirements of reliability and particularity of the information on which an officer may act are more stringent where an arrest warrant is absent, they surely cannot be less stringent than where an arrest warrant is obtained. Otherwise, a principal incentive now existing for the procurement of arrest warrants would be destroyed. The threshold question in this case, therefore, is whether the officers could, on the information which impelled them to act, have procured a warrant for the arrest of Toy. We think that no warrant would have issued on evidence then available.

The narcotics agents had no basis in experience for confidence in the reliability of Hom Way's information; he had never before given information. And yet they acted upon his imprecise suggestion that a person described only as "Blackie Toy," the proprietor of a laundry somewhere on Leavenworth Street, had sold one ounce of heroin. We have held that identification of the suspect by a reliable informant may constitute probable cause for arrest where the information given is sufficiently accurate to lead the officers directly to the suspect. Draper v United States, 358 US 307. That rule does not, however, fit this case. For aught that the record discloses, Hom Way's accusation merely invited the officers to roam the length of Leavenworth Street (some 30 blocks) in search of one "Blackie Toy's" laundry—and whether by chance or other means (the record does not say) they came upon petitioner Toy's laundry, which bore not his name over the door, but the unrevealing label "Oye's." Not the slightest intimation appears on the record, or was made on oral argument, to suggest that the agents had information giving them reason to equate "Blackie" Toy and James Wah Toy—e. g., that they had the criminal record of a Toy, or that they had consulted some other kind of official record or list, or had some information of some kind which had narrowed the scope of their search to this particular Toy.

It is conceded that the officers made no attempt to obtain a warrant for Toy's arrest. The simple fact is that on the sparse information at the officers' command, no arrest warrant could have issued consistently with Rules 3 and 4 of the Federal Rules of Criminal Procedure. Giordenello v United States, 357 US 480. The arrest warrant procedure serves to insure that the deliberate, impartial judgment of a judicial officer will be interposed between the citizen and the police, to assess the weight and credibility of the information which the complaining officer adduces as probable cause. To hold that an officer may act in his own, unchecked discretion upon information too vague and from too untested a source to permit a judicial officer to accept it as probable cause for an arrest warrant, would subvert this fundamental policy.

The Government contends, however, that any defects in the information which somehow took the officers to petitioner Toy's laundry were remedied by events which occurred after they arrived. Specifically, it is urged that Toy's flight down the hall when the supposed customer at the door revealed that he was a narcotics agent adequately corroborates the suspicion generated by Hom Way's accusation. Our holding in Miller v United States, 357 US 301, is relevant here, and exposes the fallacy of this contention. We noted in that case that the lawfulness of an officer's entry to arrest without a warrant "must be tested by criteria identical with those embodied in 18 USC § 3109, which deals with entry to execute a search warrant."

That statute requires that an officer must state his authority and his purpose at the threshold, and be refused admittance, before he may break open the door. We held that when an officer insufficiently or unclearly identifies his office or his mission, the occupant's flight from the door must be regarded as ambiguous conduct. We expressly reserved the question "whether the unqualified requirements of the rule admit of an exception justifying noncompliance in exigent circumstances." In the instant case, Toy's flight from the door afforded no surer an inference of guilty knowledge than did the suspect's conduct in the Miller Case. Agent Wong did eventually disclose that he was a narcotics officer. However, he affirmatively misrepresented his mission at the outset, by stating that he had come for laundry and dry cleaning. And before Toy fled, the officer never adequately dispelled the misimpression engendered by his own ruse.

Moreover, he made no effort at that time, nor indeed at any time thereafter, to ascertain whether the man at the door was the "Blackie Toy" named by Hom Way. Therefore, this is not the case we hypothesized in Miller where "without an express announcement of purpose, the facts known to officers would justify them in being virtually certain" that the person at the door knows their purpose.

Toy's refusal to admit the officers and his flight down the hallway thus signified a guilty knowledge no more clearly than it did a natural desire to repel an apparently unauthorized intrusion. Here, as in Miller, the Government claims no extraordinary circumstances—such as the imminent destruction of vital evidence, or the need to rescue a victim in peril—which excused the officer's failure truthfully to state his mission before he broke in.

A contrary holding here would mean that a vague suspicion could be transformed into probable cause for arrest by reason of ambiguous conduct which the arresting officers themselves have provoked. That result would have the same essential vice as a proposition we have consistently rejected—that a search unlawful at its inception may be validated by what it turns up. Thus we conclude that the Court of Appeals' finding that the officers' uninvited entry into Toy's living quarters was unlawful and that the bedroom arrest which followed was likewise unlawful, was fully justified on the evidence. It remains to be seen what consequences flow from this conclusion.

II.

It is conceded that Toy's declarations in his bedroom are to be excluded if they are held to be "fruits" of the agents' unlawful action.

In order to make effective the fundamental constitutional guarantees of sanctity of the home and inviolability of the person, this Court held nearly half a century ago that evidence seized during an unlawful search could not constitute proof against the victim of the search. The exclusionary prohibition extends as well to the indirect as the direct products of such invasions. Mr. Justice Holmes, speaking for the Court in that case (Silverthorne Lumber Co. v United States 251 US 385) in holding that the Government might not make use of information obtained during an unlawful search to subpoena from the victims the very documents illegally viewed, expressed succinctly the policy of the broad exclusionary rule:

"The essence of a provision forbidding the acquisition of evidence in a certain way is that not merely evidence so acquired shall not be used before the Court but that it shall not be used at all. Of course this does not mean that the facts thus obtained become sacred and inaccessible. If knowledge of them is gained from an independent source they may be proved like any others, but the knowledge gained by the Government's own wrong cannot be used by it in the way proposed."

The exclusionary rule has traditionally barred from trial physical, tangible materials obtained either during or as a direct result of an unlawful invasion. It follows from our holding in Silverman v United States, 365 US 505, that the Fourth Amendment may protect against the overhearing of verbal statements as well as against the more traditional seizure of "papers and effects." Similarly, testimony as to matters observed during an unlawful invasion has been excluded in order to enforce the basic constitutional policies.

Thus, verbal evidence which derives so immediately from an unlawful entry and an unauthorized arrest as the officers' action in the present case is no less the "fruit" of official illegality than the more common tangible fruits of the unwarranted intrusion. Nor do the policies underlying the exclusionary rule invite any logical distinction between physical and verbal evidence. Either in terms of deterring lawless conduct by federal officers, or of closing the doors of the federal courts to any use of evidence unconstitutionally obtained, the danger in relaxing the exclusionary rules in the case of verbal evidence would seem too great to warrant introducing such a distinction.

The Government argues that Toy's statements to the officers in his bedroom, although closely consequent upon the invasion which we hold unlawful, were nevertheless admissible because they resulted from "an intervening independent act of a free will." This contention, however, takes insufficient account of the circumstances. Six or seven officers had broken the door and followed on Toy's heels into the bedroom where his wife and child were sleeping. He had been almost immediately handcuffed and arrested. Under such circumstances it is unreasonable to infer that Toy's response was sufficiently an act of free will to purge the primary taint of the unlawful invasion.

The Government also contends that Toy's declarations should be admissible because they were ostensibly exculpatory rather than incriminating. There are two answers to this argument. First, the statements soon turned out to be incriminating, for they led directly to the evidence which implicated Toy. Second, when circumstances are shown such as those which induced these declarations, it is immaterial whether the declarations be termed "exculpatory." Thus we find no substantial reason to omit Toy's declarations from the protection of the exclusionary rule.

III.

We now consider whether the exclusion of Toy's declarations requires also the exclusion of the narcotics taken from Yee, to which those declarations led the police. The prosecutor candidly told the trial court that "we wouldn't have found those drugs except that Mr. Toy helped us to." Hence this is not the case envisioned by this Court where the exclusionary rule has no application because the Government learned of the evidence "from an independent source," Silverthorne Lumber Co. v United States, 251 US 385; nor is this a case in which the connection between the lawless conduct of the police and the discovery of the challenged evidence has "become so attenuated as to dissipate the taint." We need not hold that all evidence is "fruit of the poisonous tree" simply because it would not have come to light but for the illegal actions of the police. Rather, the more apt question in such a case is "whether, granting establishment of the primary illegality, the evidence to which instant objection is made has been come at by exploitation of that illegality or instead by means sufficiently distinguishable to be purged of the primary taint." ... We think it clear that the narcotics were "come at by the exploitation of that illegality" and hence that they may not be used against Toy.

IV.

It remains only to consider Toy's unsigned statement. We need not decide whether, in light of the fact that Toy was free on his own recognizance when he made the statement, that statement was a fruit of the illegal arrest. Since we have concluded that his declarations in the bedroom and the narcotics surrendered by Yee should not have been admitted in evidence against him, the only proofs remaining to sustain his conviction are his and Wong Sun's unsigned statements. Without scrutinizing the contents of Toy's ambiguous recitals, we conclude that no reference to Toy in Wong Sun's statement constitutes admissible evidence corroborating any admission by Toy. We arrive at this conclusion upon two clear lines of decisions which converge to require it. One line of our decisions establishes that criminal confessions and admissions of guilt require extrinsic corroboration; the other line of precedents holds that an out-of-court declaration made after arrest may not be used at trial against one of the declarant's partners in crime.

It is a settled principle of the administration of criminal justice in the federal courts that a conviction must rest upon firmer ground than the uncorroborated admission or confession of the accused. We observed in Smith v United States, 348 US 147, that the requirement of corroboration is rooted in "a long history of judicial experience with confessions and in the realization that sound law enforcement requires police investigations which extend beyond the words of the accused." In Opper v United States, 348 US 84, we elaborated the reasons for the requirement:

> "In our country the doubt persists that the zeal of the agencies of prosecution to protect the peace, the self-interest of the accomplice, the maliciousness of an enemy or the aberration or weakness of the accused under the strain of suspicion may tinge or warp the facts of the confession. Admissions, retold at a trial, are much like hearsay, that is, statements not made at the pending trial. They had neither the compulsion of the oath nor the test of cross-examination."

It is true that in Smith v United States, 348 US 147 supra, we held that although "corroboration is necessary for all elements of the offense established by admissions alone," extrinsic proof was sufficient which "merely fortifies the truth of the confession, without independently establishing the crime charged...."

However, Wong Sun's unsigned confession does not furnish competent corroborative evidence. The second governing principle, likewise well settled in our decisions, is that an out-of-court declaration made after arrest may not be used at trial against one of the declarant's partners in crime. While such a statement is "admissible against the others where it is in furtherance of the criminal undertaking... all such responsibility is at an end when the conspiracy ends." We have consistently refused to broaden that very narrow exception to the traditional hearsay rule which admits statements of a codefendant made in furtherance of a conspiracy or joint undertaking.

And where post-conspiracy declarations have been admitted, we have carefully ascertained that limiting instructions kept the jury from considering the contents with respect to the guilt of anyone but the declarant.

We have never ruled squarely on the question presented here, whether a codefendant's statement might serve to corroborate even where it will not suffice to convict. We see no warrant for a different result so long as the rule which regulates the use of out-of-court statements is one of admissibility, rather than simply of weight, of the evidence. The import of our previous holdings is that a co-conspirator's hearsay statements may be admitted against the accused for no purpose whatever, unless made during and in furtherance of the conspiracy. Thus as to Toy the only possible source of corroboration is removed and his conviction must be set aside for lack of competent evidence to support it.

V.

We turn now to the case of the other petitioner, Wong Sun. We have no occasion to disagree with the finding of the Court of Appeals that his arrest, also, was without probable cause or reasonable grounds. At all events no evidentiary consequences turn upon that question. For Wong Sun's unsigned confession was not the fruit of that arrest, and was therefore properly admitted at trial. On the evidence that Wong Sun had been released on his own recognizance after a lawful arraignment, and had returned voluntarily several days later to make the statement, we hold that the connection between the arrest and the statement had "become so attenuated as to dissipate the taint." Nardone v United States, 308 US 338. The fact that the statement was unsigned, whatever bearing this may have upon its weight and credibility, does not render it inadmissible; Wong Sun understood and adopted its substance, though he could not comprehend the English words. The petitioner has never suggested any impropriety in the interrogation itself which would require the exclusion of this statement.

We must then consider the admissibility of the narcotics surrendered by Yee. Our holding, supra, that this ounce of heroin was inadmissible against Toy does not compel a like result with respect to Wong Sun. The exclusion of the narcotics as to Toy was required solely by their tainted relationship to information unlawfully obtained from Toy, and not by any official impropriety connected with their surrender by Yee. The seizure of this heroin invaded no right of privacy of person or premises which would entitle Wong Sun to object to its use at his trial.

However, for the reasons that Wong Sun's statement was incompetent to corroborate Toy's admissions contained in Toy's own statement, any references to Wong Sun in Toy's statement were incompetent to corroborate Wong Sun's admissions. Thus, the only competent source of corroboration for Wong Sun's statement was the heroin itself. We cannot be certain, however, on this state of the record, that the trial judge may not also have considered the contents of Toy's statement as a source of corroboration. Petitioners raised as one ground of objection to the introduction of the statements the claim that each statement, "even if it were a purported admission or confession or declaration against interest of a defendant . . . would not be binding upon the other defendant." The trial judge, in allowing the statements in, apparently overruled all of petitioners' objections, including this one. Thus we presume that he considered all portions of both statements as bearing upon the guilt of both petitioners.

We intimate no view one way or the other as to whether the trial judge might have found in the narcotics alone sufficient evidence to corroborate Wong Sun's admissions that he delivered heroin to Yee and smoked heroin at Yee's house around the date in question. But because he might, as the factfinder, have found insufficient corroboration from the narcotics alone, we cannot be sure that the scales were not tipped in favor of conviction by reliance upon the inadmissible Toy statement. This is particularly important because of the nature of the offense involved here.

Surely, under the narcotics statute, the discovery of heroin raises a presumption that someone—generally the possessor—violated the law. As to him, once possession alone is proved, the other elements of the offense—transportation and concealment with knowledge of the illegal importation of the drug—need not be separately demonstrated, much less corroborated. 21 USC § 174. Thus particular care ought to be taken in this area, when the crucial element of the accused's possession is proved solely by his own admissions, that the requisite corroboration be found among the evidence which is properly before the trier of facts. We therefore hold that petitioner Wong Sun is also entitled to a new trial.

The judgment of the Court of Appeals is reversed and the case is remanded to the District Court for further proceedings consistent with this opinion.

It is so ordered.

Mr. Justice Clark, with whom Mr. Justice Harlan, Mr. Justice Stewart and Mr. Justice White join, dissenting.

The Court has made a Chinese puzzle out of this simple case involving four participants: Hom Way, Blackie Toy, Johnny Yee and "Sea Dog" Sun. In setting aside the convictions of Toy and Sun it has dashed to pieces the heretofore recognized standards of probable cause necessary to secure an arrest warrant or to make an arrest without one. Instead of dealing with probable cause as involving "probabilities," "the factual and practical considerations of everyday life on which reasonable and prudent men, not legal technicians, act," Brinegar v United States, 338 US 160 (1949), the Court sets up rigid, mechanical standards, applying the 20–20 vision of hindsight in an area where the ambiguity and immediacy inherent in unexpected arrest are present. While probable cause must be based on more than mere suspicion, it does not require proof sufficient to establish guilt. The sole requirement heretofore has been that the knowledge in the hands of the officers at the time of arrest must support a "man of reasonable caution in the belief" that the subject had committed narcotic offenses. That decision is faced initially not in the courtroom but at the scene of arrest where the totality of the circumstances facing the officer is weighed against his split-second decision to make the arrest. This is an everyday occurrence facing law enforcement officers, and the unrealistic, enlarged standards announced here place an unnecessarily heavy hand upon them. I therefore dissent.

I.

The first character in this affair is Hom Way, who was arrested in possession of narcotics and told the officers early that morning that he had purchased an ounce of heroin on the previous night from Blackie Toy, who operated a laundry on Leavenworth Street. Narcotics agents, armed with this information from a person they had known for six weeks and who was under arrest for possession of narcotics, immediately sought out Blackie Toy, the second character. The laundry was located without difficulty (as far as the record shows) from the information furnished by Hom Way. The Court gratuitously reads into the record its supposition that How Way "merely invited the officers to roam the length of Leavenworth Street (some 30 blocks) in search of one 'Blackie Toy's' laundry...." On the contrary, the identification of "Blackie" and the directions to his laundry were sufficiently accurate for the officers—two of whom were of Chinese ancestry—to find Blackie at his laundry within an hour. I cannot say in the face of this record that this was a "roaming" performance up and down Leavenworth Street. To me it was efficient police work by officers familiar with San Francisco and the habits and practices of its Chinese-American inhabitants. Indeed, the information was much more explicit than that approved by this Court in Draper v United States, 358 US 307.

There are other indicia of reliability, however. Here the informer believed by the officers to be reliable, was under arrest when he implicated himself in the purchase of an ounce of heroin the previous night. Since he was in possession of narcotics and his information related to a narcotics sale in which he was the buyer, the officers had good reason to rely on Hom Way's knowledge. As to his credibility, he was confronted with prosecution for possession of narcotics and well knew that any discrepancies in his story might go hard with him. Furthermore, the statement was a declaration against interest which stripped Hom Way of any explanation for his possession of narcotics and made certain the presumption of 21 USC § 174. I do not see what stronger and more reliable information one could have to establish probable cause for the arrest without warrant of Blackie Toy.

But even assuming there was no probable cause at this point, the Government produced additional evidence to support the lawfulness of Blackie's arrest. In broad daylight, about 6:30 on the same morning that Hom Way was arrested, one of the officers of Chinese ancestry, Agent Alton Wong, knocked on Blackie Toy's laundry door. When Wong told him that he wanted laundry, Blackie opened the door and advised him to return at 8 a. m. Wong testified that he then "pulled out [his] badge" and announced that he was a narcotics agent. Blackie slammed the door in Wong's face and ran down the hall of the laundry. Wong broke through the door after him—calling again that he was "a narcotics Treasury agent." Only when Blackie reached the family bedroom was Wong able to arrest him, as he reached into a nightstand drawer, apparently looking for narcotics. Agent Wong immediately confronted him with Hom Way's accusation that Blackie Toy had sold him narcotics. Blackie denied selling narcotics, but he did not deny knowing Hom Way and later admitted knowing him. There is no basis in Miller v United States, 357 US 301 (1958), for the Court's conclusion that Blackie's flight "signified . . . a natural desire [by Toy] to repel an apparently unauthorized intrusion. . . ." As I see it this is incredible in the light of the record. Nor is there any support in the record that "before Toy fled, the officer never adequately dispelled the misimpression engendered by his own ruse." On the contrary the officer's showing of his badge and announcement that he was a narcotics agent immediately put Blackie in flight behind the slamming door. To conclude otherwise takes all prizes as a non sequitur. As he pursued, Wong continued to identify himself as a narcotics agent. I ask, how could he more clearly announce himself and his purpose?

This Court has often held unexplained flight—as here—from an officer to be strong evidence of guilt. . . . See Henry v United States, 361 US 98, where the Court was careful to distinguish its facts from those of "fleeing men or men acting furtively." Moreover, as the Government has always emphasized, this is particularly true in narcotics cases where delay may have serious consequences, i. e., the hiding or destruction of the drugs. This Court noted without disapproval in Miller v United States, 357 US 301, the state decisions holding that "justification for noncompliance [with the rule] exists in exigent circumstances, as, for example, when the officers may in good faith believe . . . that the person to be arrested is fleeing or attempting to destroy evidence. People v. Maddox, 357 US, at 309." And the Court continued, "It may be that, without an express announcement of purpose, the facts known to officers would justify them in being virtually certain that the petitioner already knows their purpose so that an announcement would be a useless gesture."

The Court places entire reliance on the decision in Miller. I submit that it is inapposite. That case involved interpretation of the law of the District of Columbia. The arrest was at night, and the door was broken in just as the defendant began to close it. Thus there was no flight but only what the officers believed to be an attempt to bar their entrance. The only identification given by the officers occurred before the defendant opened the door, when "in a low voice" through the closed door they answered the defendant's query as to who was there by saying, "Police." The facts in Miller differ significantly from this case both in the clarity of identification by the officers and in the character and extent of the defendant's conduct. For that reason, the conclusions that Blackie's flight is evidence to support probable cause and that the officers gave sufficient notice to permit lawful entry are supported rather than weakened by the Court's decision in Miller.

The information from Hom Way and Blackie Toy's unexplained flight cannot be viewed "in two separate, logic-tight compartments.... [T]ogether they composed a picture meaningful to a trained, experienced observer." Christensen v United States, 104 App DC 35, 36, 259 F2d 192, 193 (1958). I submit that the officers as reasonable men properly concluded that the petitioner was the "Blackie Toy" who Hom Way informed them had committed a felony and that his immediate arrest—as he ran through his hall—was lawful and was imperative in order to prevent his escape. In view of this there is no "poisonous tree" whose fruits we must evaluate, and Blackie's declaration at the time of the arrest and the narcotics found in Yee's possession are admissible in evidence. The trial court found that evidence sufficiently corroborative of Toy's confession, and the Court of Appeals affirmed. For the same reasons discussed, infra, as to Wong Sun, I see no occasion to overturn these consistent findings of two courts.

II.

As to "Sea Dog," Wong Sun, there is no disagreement that his confession and the narcotics found in Yee's possession were admissible in evidence against him. The question remains as to whether there was sufficient independent evidence to corroborate the confession. Such evidence "does not have to prove the offense beyond a reasonable doubt, or even by a preponderance...." Smith v United States, 348 US 147 (1954). The requirement is satisfied "if the corroboration merely fortifies the truth of the confession, without independently establishing the crime charged...." Ibid.; see also Opper v United States, 348 US 84 (1954). Wong Sun's confession stated in part that about four days before his arrest he and Toy delivered an ounce of heroin to Yee and that on the night before his arrest—the night of June 3, 1959—he and Toy smoked some heroin at Yee's house. On June 4, 1959, the officers found at Yee's residence quantities of heroin totaling "just less than one ounce." In light of this evidence, I am unable to say that the trial court and the Court of Appeals erred in holding that Wong Sun's confession was sufficiently corroborated.

The Court does not reach a contrary conclusion as to corroboration but it grants Wong Sun a new trial on the ground that the trial court "may" also "have considered the contents of Toy's statement as a source of corroboration" of it. This point was not raised as a question here nor was it discussed in the briefs. Despite this the Court goes to some lengths to develop a chain of inferences in finding prejudicial error. This might be plausible where the case was tried to a jury, as were all the cases cited by the Court. Indeed, I find no case where such presumption of error was applied, as here, to a trial before a judge. The Court admits that the heroin found in Johnny Yee's possession might itself be sufficient corroboration, but it reverses on the excuse that the judge "may" have considered Toy's confession as well. I see no reason for this assumption where a federal judge is the trier of the fact, and I would therefore affirm the judgment as to both petitioners.

FAHY v. CONNECTICUT
SUPREME COURT OF THE UNITED STATES
375 U.S. 85, 11 L. ED. 2d 171, 84 S. CT. 229 (1963)

OPINION OF THE COURT

Mr. Chief Justice Warren delivered the opinion of the Court.

Petitioner waived trial by jury and was convicted in a Connecticut state court of wilfully injuring a public building in violation of Connecticut General Statutes § 53–45(a). Specifically, petitioner and his codefendant Arnold were found guilty of having painted swastikas on a Norwalk, Connecticut, synagogue. The trial took place before our decision in Mapp v Ohio, 367 US 643, but the conviction was affirmed on appeal after that decision.

At the trial of the case, a can of black paint and a paint brush were admitted into evidence over petitioner's objection. On appeal, the Connecticut Supreme Court of Errors held that the paint and brush had been obtained by means of an illegal search and seizure. It further held that the Mapp decision applies to cases pending on appeal in Connecticut courts at the time that decision was rendered, and, therefore, the trial court erred in admitting the paint and brush into evidence. However, the court affirmed petitioner's conviction because it found the admission of the unconstitutionally obtained evidence to have been harmless error. We granted certiorari.

On the facts of this case, it is not now necessary for us to decide whether the erroneous admission of evidence obtained by an illegal search and seizure can ever be subject to the normal rules of "harmless error" under the federal standard of what constitutes harmless error. We find that the erroneous admission of this unconstitutionally obtained evidence at this petitioner's trial was prejudicial; therefore, the error was not harmless, and the conviction must be reversed. We are not concerned here with whether there was sufficient evidence on which the petitioner could have been convicted without the evidence complained of. The question is whether there is a reasonable possibility that the evidence complained of might have contributed to the conviction. To decide this question, it is necessary to review the facts of the case and the evidence adduced at trial.

On February 1, 1960, between the hours of 4 and 5 a. m., swastikas were painted with black paint on the steps and walls of a Norwalk synagogue. At about 4:40 a. m., Officer Lindwall of the Norwalk police saw an automobile being operated without lights about a block from the synagogue. Upon stopping the car, Lindwall questioned Fahy and Arnold about their reason for being out at that hour, and they told him they had been to a diner for coffee and were going home. Lindwall also checked the car and found a can of black paint and a paint brush under the front seat. Having no reason to do otherwise, Lindwall released Fahy and Arnold. He followed the car to Fahy's home. Later the same morning, Lindwall learned of the painting of the swastikas. Thereupon, he went to Fahy's home and —without having applied for or obtained an arrest or search warrant—entered the garage under the house and removed from Fahy's car the can of paint and the brush. About two hours later, Lindwall returned to the Fahy home, this time in the company of two other Norwalk policemen. Pursuant to a valid arrest warrant, the officers arrested Fahy and Arnold.

At the trial, the court admitted the paint and brush into evidence over petitioner's objection. We assume, as did the Connecticut Supreme Court of Errors, that doing so was error because this evidence was obtained by an illegal search and seizure and was thus inadmissible under the rule of Mapp v Ohio. Examining the effect of this evidence upon the other evidence adduced at trial and upon the conduct of the defense, we find inescapable the conclusion that the trial court's error was prejudicial and cannot be called harmless.

Obviously, the tangible evidence of the paint and brush was itself incriminating. In addition, it was used to corroborate the testimony of Officer Lindwall as to the presence of petitioner near the scene of the crime at about the time it was committed and as to the presence of a can of paint and a brush in petitioner's car at that time. When Officer Lindwall testified at trial concerning that incident, the following transpired:

"Q. Will you tell the Court what you found in the car?
. . . .
"A. Checking on the passengers' side, under the front seat I found a small jar of paint and a paint brush.
"Q. Are you able to identify this object I show you?
"A. Yes.
"Q. What is it?
"A. A jar of paint I found in the motor vehicle.
. . . .
"Q. I show you this object and ask you if you can identify that.
"A. Yes, sir.
"Q. What is it?
"A. A paint brush.
"Q. Where did you first see this paint brush?
"A. Under the front seat of Mr. Fahy's car."

The brush and paint were offered in evidence and were received over petitioner's objection. The trial court found: "13. The police found the same can of black paint and the brush in the car which the defendants had been operating when stopped by Officer Lindwall earlier in the morning." It can be inferred from this that the admission of the illegally seized evidence made Lindwall's testimony far more damaging than it would otherwise have been.

In addition, the illegally obtained evidence was used as the basis of opinion testimony to the effect that the paint and brush matched the markings on the synagogue, thus forging another link between the accused and the crime charged. At trial, Norwalk Police Officer Tigano testified that he had examined the markings on the synagogue and had determined that they were put on with black paint. He further testified that he had examined the contents of the can illegally seized from Fahy's car and had determined that it contained black paint. Even more damaging was Tigano's testimony that he had taken the illegally seized brush to the synagogue "to measure the width of the brush with the width of the paintings of the swastikas." Over objection, Tigano then testified that the brush "fitted the same as the paint brush in some drawings of the lines and some it did not due to the fact the paint dripped." Thus the trial court found: "14. The two-inch paint brush matched the markings made with black paint upon the synagogue." In relation to this testimony, the prejudiced effect of admitting the illegally obtained evidence is obvious.

Other incriminating evidence admitted at trial concerned admissions petitioner made when he was arrested and a full confession made at the police station later. Testifying at trial, Norwalk Police Lieutenant Virgulak recounted what took place when Fahy, who was just waking up at the time, was arrested:

> "I told him I [sic, he] was under arrest for painting swastikas on the synagogue. He said, 'Oh, that?' and he appeared to lay back in bed.
>
> . . . .
>
> "Q. Did you have any further conversation with Fahy before you reached the police station that you remember?
> "A. I asked him what the reason was for painting the swastikas and he said it was only a prank and I asked him why and he said for kicks."

At the police station, there was further questioning, and Fahy told Lieutenant Virgulak that he, Fahy, would take the responsibility for painting the swastikas. In addition, some hours after the arrest Arnold was asked to give a statement of the events, and he complied, dictating a complete confession of two typewritten pages. After this confession was admitted against Arnold at trial, Lieutenant Virgulak testified that he had read the confession to Fahy and:

> "Q. After you finished reading it, will you tell us whether or not he [Fahy] made any comment?
> "A. I asked him what his version was and he said the story was as I had it from Mr. Arnold. I asked him if he would like to give a written statement and he declined."

The record does not show whether Fahy knew that the police had seized the paint and brush before he made his admissions at the time of arrest and en route to the police station. In oral argument, however, counsel for the State told the Court that Fahy "probably" had been told of the search and seizure by then. Of course, the full confession was more damaging to the defendants, and unquestionably the defendants knew the police had obtained the paint and brush by the time they confessed. But the defendants were not allowed to pursue the illegal search and seizure inquiry at trial, because, at the time of trial, the exclusionary rule was not applied in Connecticut state courts. Thus petitioner was unable to claim at trial that the illegally seized evidence induced his admissions and confession. Petitioner has told the Court that he would so claim were he allowed to challenge the search and seizure as illegal at a new trial. And we think that such a line of inquiry is permissible. As the Court has noted in the past: "The essence of a provision forbidding the acquisition of evidence in a certain way is that not merely evidence so acquired shall not be used before the Court but that it shall not be used at all." See Silverthorne Lumber Co. v United States, 251 US 385. Thus petitioner should have had a chance to show that his admissions were induced by being confronted with the illegally seized evidence.

Nor can we ignore the cumulative prejudicial effect of this evidence upon the conduct of the defense at trial. It was only after admission of the paint and brush and only after their subsequent use to corroborate other state's evidence and only after introduction of the confession that the defendants took the stand, admitted their acts, and tried to establish that the nature of those acts was not within the scope of the felony statute under which the defendants had been charged. We do not mean to suggest that petitioner has presented any valid claim based on the privilege against self-incrimination. We merely note this course of events as another indication of the prejudicial effect of the erroneously admitted evidence.

From the foregoing it clearly appears that the erroneous admission of this illegally obtained evidence was prejudicial to petitioner and hence it cannot be called harmless error. Therefore, the conviction is reversed, and the cause is remanded for proceedings not inconsistent with this opinion.

It is so ordered.

QUESTIONS AND PROBLEMS

1. Who and what are protected by the Fourth Amendment?
2. Does the Fourth Amendment protection against unreasonable intrusions apply against representatives of the federal government? against representatives of state and local government? against private persons and citizens?
3. What is the "exclusionary rule" or the "American Suppression doctrine?
4. What is a search? What is a seizure?
5. What is subject to search? What is subject to seizure?
6. What is meant by "probable cause" (or reasonable grounds to believe)?
7. What is meant by "judicial intercession" (the need to obtain a search warrant)? Why is it desirable? May it be dispensed with?
8. How does the derivative evidence rule ("fruit of the poisonous tree" doctrine) apply to the collection and use of evidence?
9. What is meant by "standing"? How does standing relate to a motion to suppress evidence?
10. What is meant by "plain view"? Is plain view a search?
11. Can the results of a search ever justify the search?
12. Why is it necessary for the officer to be prepared to "articulate" the facts and observations made by him prior to a search?
13. Late at night, a police department receives a call that a noisy marijuana party is going on at an apartment at a given address. Two officers are sent to investigate. A person in the apartment opens the apartment door in response to the knock of the officers. The officers can smell the marijuana, and they can see through the open door bottles of hard liquor on a table in the apartment. The officers can also see that a number of girls in the apartment are obviously minors. May the officers go into the apartment without consent? If you answer "yes," under what authority may they enter the apartment without consent? Would they need a search warrant to enter the apartment? If arrests were made, what offenses could be charged from the facts given?

6

THE EXCLUSIONARY RULES APPLICABLE TO POLICE AND GOVERNMENT INTERROGATION

Law enforcement officers very seldom witness the commission of major crimes and therefore in fulfilling their responsibility to investigate reported crime, they must interrogate and question victims, eyewitnesses, and suspects. Questioning and interrogation always have been and always will be a very vital part of criminal investigation. In order to protect the constitutional rights of suspects and those accused of crimes, interrogation exclusionary rules have been developed in the United States which are binding upon officers who represent federal, state, or local governments.

THE PRIVILEGE AGAINST SELF-INCRIMINATION

The Fifth Amendment requirement that "No person . . . shall be required in any criminal case to be a witness against himself . . ." has a long history which goes back to the thirteenth century. At that time, medieval torture devices such as the rack and the screw, the pillory, the use of chains and beatings, and confinement in filthy, disease-ridden jails were common. Following conviction, punishment for minor offenses was often some form of mutilation, such as branding, blinding, cropping (clipping the ears), while most major offenses were punished by hanging, drawing and quartering, or death by burning. The English Black Act of 1722 made offenses against public order, against the administration of justice, against property and persons, all punishable by death. Public group hangings were considered in those days to be an event of boisterous entertainment.

The practice of picking up a person and torturing him while conducting a "fishing" interrogation about his conduct and possible crimes was not uncommon. The suspect could then be charged on the basis of the information which he provided to his torturers.

McCormick on Evidence (chap. 13) and *Wigmore on Evidence* present scholarly reviews of the historical background of the Fifth Amendment privilege against self-incrimination. They trace the history of the heresy hunts, the high-handed methods used by the English Star Chamber, and the reforms which slowly came about in England.

McCormick and Wigmore state that it was a common practice of common-law judges to question the accused in a criminal case and to bully him into admitting his guilt. By the early 1700s, the general principle had become accepted that the accused was not to be badgered in this way by the judge who had sentencing power over him. This was the evolution of the principle that defendants and witnesses did not have to testify in court as to facts which could incriminate them and assist the state in proving their guilt.

The American founding fathers were understandably concerned with the possibility of such abuses by the newly formed central government and therefore wrote the Fifth Amendment to provide the safeguards which they considered necessary.

Interpretation of the Fifth Amendment has been the issue of debate for years. McCormick asks how "the maxim which once meant that no man shall be questioned until he has been first accused comes to mean that no man shall ever be required to answer about his crimes." His answer to this question is that "the hatred of the end is visited upon the means."

The notion of the privilege against self-incrimination was not included in any of the great English charters (Magna Charta, Petition of Right, or the Bill of Rights of 1689). The privilege against self-incrimination evolved from the concept that no man shall be compelled to make the first charge against himself.

THE TEST OF VOLUNTARINESS
FOR STATEMENTS AND CONFESSIONS

Prior to 1964, the principal test for the admissibility of a defendant's statement or confession was its "voluntariness." In order to determine voluntariness, the courts looked at the "totality of the circumstances." This means that the courts would consider all the facts of the case to determine whether the statement or confession was voluntary. Significant facts for consideration could be:

Was there coercion? What was the nature of the coercion?
    Physical torture
    Denial of food
    Solitary confinement
    Prolonged detention

Denial of sleep, denial of normal facilities
Clothing taken away
Were inherent weaknesses of the accused taken advantage of?
Age of accused (very young or very old?)
Education of the accused
Was accused a narcotic addict or alcoholic?
Intelligence of the accused
Physical condition and sickness of accused
Language barrier
Mental condition or insanity
Did the interrogating officers:
Fail to bring the accused before a magistrate within a reasonable period of time?
Hold the person incommunicado and not permit him to call an attorney or his family?
Take statement or question the accused after an attorney was appointed or hired and bail set? (see *Massiah v. United States* in this chapter)
Make promises to the accused—as to leniency—not to arrest a friend?
Trick or mislead the accused?
Threaten the accused?
Prepare the confession for the accused to sign or did he write out the confession himself?
Was the questioning:
Extended and done by relay teams?
Done in the early morning hours?
Conducted against the will of the accused?
Conducted by more than one or two interrogators?
Conducted with the assistance or cooperation of friends or relatives of the defendant?
Conducted with the assistance of a psychiatrist?
Conducted in a place other than an interrogation room?
Were unusual procedures used?
Taking a woman suspected of killing her child or lover or husband down to the morgue to view the body when the body has already been properly identified
Use of truth serum
Use of a lie detector

If, in view of the "totality of the circumstances," the statement or confession of the accused is ruled not to be voluntary, then the statement or confession is suppressed and not allowed in evidence.

The test of "voluntariness" continues to be used by the courts, but since 1964 more challenges are made under the new rule and requirements laid down by the 1964 case of *Escobedo v. Illinois*, 378 U.S. 478, 84 S. Ct. 1758, 12 L. Ed. 2d 246, and the 1966 case of *Miranda v. Arizona* (see cases). Speculations as to the reason for this change are:

1. It is simpler and easier to claim that the Miranda requirements have not been complied with than to claim and prove coercion or involuntariness.
2. Law enforcement officers, in attempting to comply with Miranda, have eliminated the opportunity for coercion (or the opportunity to claim coercion or involuntariness).

RIGHT TO COUNSEL

The Sixth Amendment of the U.S. Constitution provides that "In all criminal prosecutions, the accused shall enjoy the right . . . to have the assistance of counsel for his defense." By 1963, most states were providing the services of lawyers to indigent persons charged with serious crimes. Florida was one of the few states providing the services of an attorney *only* in cases where the defendant was charged with a capital offense. In 1963, the U.S. Supreme Court in the Florida case of *Gideon v. Wainright*, 372 U.S. 335, held that all states must provide counsel if the person is indigent and is charged with a serious offense. Twenty-two states filed briefs, as friends of the court, urging this change while only Florida and two other states resisted and opposed the change.

In June of 1972, the U.S. Supreme Court held in *Argersinger v. Hamlin*, 407 U.S. 25, that a trial judge may not imprison an indigent person for any length of time unless the indigent defendant is offered the services of a lawyer appointed by the court and paid by the state or local government.

In the 1964 case of *Massiah v. United States* (see cases), it was held that statements and confessions obtained after indictment and the appointment or retention of counsel violated the Sixth Amendment right to counsel unless the right was waived or counsel was present at the time of questioning.

The 1964 case of *Escobedo v. Illinois*, 378 U.S. 478, and the 1966 case of *Miranda v. Arizona* (see cases) establish the principle that the Sixth Amendment right to counsel and the Fifth Amendment privilege against self-incrimination exist *not only* at the time of arrest *but also* during "custodial interrogation" of a person who has been ". . . deprived of his freedom of action in any significant way. . . ."

THE MIRANDA EXCLUSIONARY RULE

"...the prosecution may not use statements, whether exculpatory or inculpatory, stemming from custodial interrogation of the defendant unless it demonstrates the use of procedural safeguards effective to secure the privilege against self-incrimination. By custodial interrogation, we mean questioning initiated by law enforcement officers after a person has been taken into custody or otherwise deprived of his freedom of action in any significant way...." U.S. Supreme Court in *Miranda v. Arizona*

Before the Miranda rule was established by the U.S. Supreme Court, a suspect could be questioned over his objections. No warnings were required and a statement or confession obtained under these circumstances was admissible if the totality of circumstances indicated that the confession or statement had been made voluntarily. The Court in *Miranda v. Arizona* took the position that custodial interrogations are inherently coercive and it is now mandatory for all police officers who wish to question a suspect without his lawyer being present and after the person has been "...deprived of his freedom of action in any significant way..." to first warn him.*

* The Los Angeles Police Department advises its officers to give the following admonition and ask the following questions:

Admonition of Rights. When a suspect in custody is to be interrogated regarding his possible participation in the commission of a criminal offense, he shall be 'warned' exactly as follows:

1. You have the right to remain silent.
2. If you give up the right to remain silent, anything you say will be used against you in a court of law.
3. You have the right to speak with an attorney and to have the attorney present during questioning.
4. If you so desire and cannot afford one, an attorney will be appointed for you without charge before questioning.

After the admonition has been given, the following questions shall be asked:

1. Do you understand each of these rights I have explained to you?
2. Do you wish to give up the right to remain silent?
3. Do you wish to give up the right to speak to an attorney and have him present during questioning?

Include in any resulting report or recording of the interview:

1. The admonition of rights in its entirety, AND
2. Statements indicating the subject's understanding of the admonition, AND
3. Statements indicating whether the suspect waived his rights to remain silent and to have an attorney present, and how he waived them.

The Miranda rule then imposes the requirement that:

> After such warnings have been given, and such opportunity afforded him, the individual may knowingly and intelligently waive these rights and agree to answer questions or make a statement. But unless and until such warnings and waiver are demonstrated by the prosecution at trial, no evidence obtained as a result of interrogation can be used against him.

Miranda also requires:

> Likewise, if the individual is alone and indicates in any manner that he does not wish to be interrogated, the police may not question him. The mere fact that he may have answered some questions or volunteered some statements on his own does not deprive him of the right to refrain from answering any further inquiries until he has consulted with an attorney and thereafter consents to be questioned.

WHEN ARE THE MIRANDA WARNINGS NOT REQUIRED?

1. The warnings are *not* required when a person volunteers information or without being questioned seeks to make a statement or confession.

   Example: A man walks into a police station and states that he has just killed his wife. The Court in Miranda stated, "There is no requirement that police stop a person who enters a police station and states that he wishes to confess a crime, or a person who calls the police to offer a confession or any other statement he desires to make."

2. The warnings are *not* required when an officer is *not* asking a person or prisoner for incriminating testimony (that is, a question which might produce an answer which might be incriminating). Warnings are not required for questions such as: What is your name? Where do you live?

3. The warnings do *not* have to be given if the person is *not* in custody or has *not* been deprived of his freedom of action in any significant way.

   Example: An officer comes up to a crowd of people gathered on the street and says, "What's going on here?" No one is in custody and the officer is asking a general investigative question.

   Example: An officer called to investigate an automobile accident or a drugstore robbery does not have to give the warnings when asking questions of a general investigative nature while no one is in custody.

IMPORTANT U.S. SUPREME COURT CASES INTERPRETING THE FIFTH AMENDMENT PRIVILEGE AGAINST SELF-INCRIMINATION AND THE SIXTH AMENDMENT RIGHT TO THE ASSISTANCE OF COUNSEL

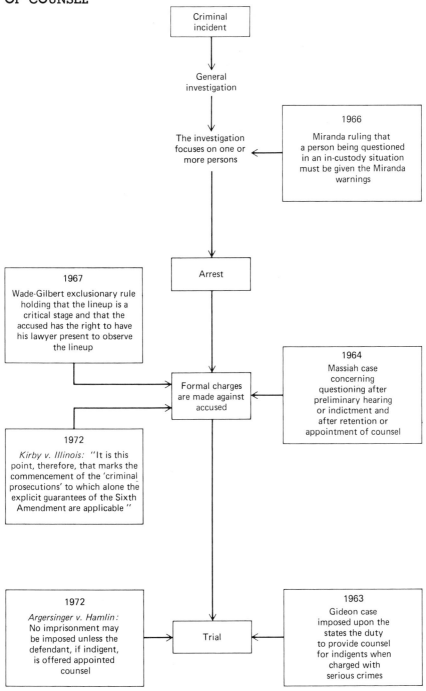

4. The warnings do *not* have to be given to persons stopped on the street or in cars because of suspicious circumstances surrounding their activity or their presence. (See Chap. 11 for a further discussion of this authority.)

> *Example:*   A man running down an alley at three o'clock in the morning may be stopped and asked who he is and what he is doing there without being given the warnings.

5. If the police have arrested a man but do not intend to question him, the warnings need not be given unless the statutes of the state require that warnings be given after all arrests.

> *Example:*   A man is arrested for being drunk in a public place. Except for identification purposes, the police have no intentions of questioning the drunk.

6. In interpreting Miranda, some courts have held that warnings do not have to be given when lives are at stake in emergency situations (see *People v. Modesto*, 62 Cal. 2d 436).

> *Example:*   In attempting to save the life of a kidnapped victim, officers would not be required to give Miranda warnings while seeking vital information regarding him.

WHAT IS AN IN-CUSTODY SITUATION?

Court decisions since Miranda have shown that the place of interrogation is a *vital factor* in determining custody. However, the place of interrogation is *not a conclusive factor*. The following material is extracted from *Confessions and Interrogations after Miranda (A Comprehensive Guideline of the Law)* with the permission of the National District Attorneys' Association (publishers of the material).

> *Police stations and sheriff's offices*   There are numerous cases holding the presence of a suspect in "building housing law enforcement personnel" must be considered custodial.
> However, this is not conclusive and if unusual circumstances exist, courts have held that it was not custodial.
> *Police vehicles and sheriff vehicles*   Such questioning has also been frequently characterized as essentially custodial under the particular facts.
> However, situations such as the person being there because of an invitation or because of weather conditions have caused courts to hold that the questioning was non-custodial.
> *Jails and prisons*   The general rule is that if the suspect is in jail, he is in custody for the purposes of any interrogations.

Homes and residencies   Most of the cases have held that questioning at the suspect's home is non-custodial. The cases which have held that it was custodial usually rely on the focussing of suspicion on the suspect alone. Also, if the officer went to the home to make an arrest or admits that he would not have allowed the suspect to leave his presence, it would be held to be custodial.

Places of business   As in the case of the home, the place of business represents a familiar surrounding and interrogation in a man's place of business is usually held to be non-custodial.

Motor vehicles   Most cases where a suspect is questioned in his car are usually resolved on the theory that traffic stop does not in itself constitute an "in-custody" situation.

Crime scenes   "Generally speaking, questioning prior to arrest near the scene of the crime is not custodial interrogation."

ACTIONS OF THE OFFICER AS INDICATIVE OF "IN-CUSTODY"

Statement by an officer   "You are under arrest"—this is "in-custody." "Get into the squad car"—this is "in-custody." "You are coming with us"—this is "in-custody."

Physical restraint   "The existence of physical restraint has almost invariably led to a finding of custody." Thus putting handcuffs on a man or holding his arm is indicative of "in-custody" unless there are other reasons for the detention.

Use of weapons   "Holding a gun on a suspect creates a clearly custodial situation." *However, if the suspect is also armed*, this "should be weighed strongly against a finding of custody."

Admissions by the officer that he intended to arrest the suspect and would not have permitted him to leave his presence have led courts to hold that an "in-custody" situation existed.

OTHER ASPECTS OF MIRANDA

"Generally speaking, questioning of a suspect prior to arrest near the scene of a crime is not custodial interrogation." The NDA refers to the *Miranda* decision (page 477–78) which states "General on-the-scene questioning as to facts surrounding a crime or other general questioning of citizens in the fact finding process is not affected by our holding. It is an act of responsible citizenship for individuals to give whatever information they may have to aid in law-enforcement."

"The officer who tells a suspect that he is not under arrest and is free to leave at any time has fairly definitely established that the interview is non-custodial."

"The length and nature of the interrogation is of considerable significance. Almost all of the cases approving crime scene and street interrogations conducted without warnings rely upon the additional fact that questioning was brief—consuming little time and involving a few, very general inquiries."

"The fact that a suspect summons the police and/or initiates the interview supports the premise that the interview was non-custodial."

"The fact that a suspect was arrested immediately following an interview does not mean the interview was necessarily custodial. In nearly every case dealing with non-custodial interviews the suspect was, in fact, promptly arrested afterwards. However, the case where a suspect is allowed to go free after the interview is almost certainly one in which the interrogation is non-custodial."

"If a suspect does not know he is speaking to a policeman he can hardly be said to have a reasonable belief that he is in custody." [See *Hoffa v. United States*, Chap. 19.]

"Generally speaking, it is proper to confront a suspect with the evidence against him, or with other facts of the case. This has been approved even when the police misstate or falsely represent the state of the evidence, i.e., that an accomplice has confessed."

"It is invariably held that a suspect who makes damaging admissions in response to interrogation by private citizens need not have been warned of his rights."

"The most common error in giving warnings relates to the right of counsel. Either the officer merely says the suspect has a right to counsel, or he says counsel will be appointed by the Court, or he informs the suspect that the police have no way of getting counsel for him immediately. To say any of these things is to mandate reversal in most cases."

"*Miranda* warnings must be given in a clear, unhurried manner; in such a way that the individual would feel free to claim his rights without fear. The warnings should not be given in a perfunctory fashion."

"The testimony of an officer that he gave the warnings is sufficient. It need not be corroborated even if contradicted by defendant."

"The issue of waiver under *Miranda* will, in time, become the most dominant issue.... The *Miranda* opinion says two things about waiver. First, it says that waiver cannot be inferred from silence. Second, *Miranda* noted that an express statement of the suspect that he is willing to make a statement and does not want an attorney followed closely by a statement might constitute a waiver."

"The courts have rarely dealt with a model *Miranda* waiver.... The area of waiver is one where problems do exist.... Not the least problem is the indecisive suspect who seems never to quite get to the point of waiving or claiming his rights."

"*Miranda* is usually thought not to apply to civil commitments involving narcotic addict, mentally ill, sexually dangerous or delinquent persons.... Nor does *Miranda* apply to customs procedures at international borders.... Its application to juvenile proceedings is still in doubt.... But some state jurisdictions have required all or part of the warnings in juvenile cases." (California Welfare and Institutions Code Section 625 requires officers to advise juveniles of their constitutional rights before questioning.)

"*Miranda* is inapplicable to an interview by a probation officer with his probationer.... *Miranda* has no application to extradition proceedings."

Are the Miranda warnings required prior to a consent to search?
"The majority rule is that warnings are not required but that the absence of warnings will be considered on the issue of the voluntariness

of the consent. . . . A minority of jurisdictions have held that warnings are required."

MASSIAH AND MIRANDA

"Massiah and Miranda doctrines become intertwined when, prior to indictment, a suspect, who is represented by counsel, is questioned. . . . The majority rule in both pre and post *Miranda* cases is that a voluntary statement made by one who has retained counsel is admissible if he voluntarily elects to speak in the absence of that counsel or waives the right to have counsel present. These holdings are scattered with dissents. In a few cases the courts have alluded to canons of ethics (of the bar association) to conclude that such practices (by attorneys) are not favored. . . . Other jurisdictions have banned such interrogation outright, or, at least, when it is initiated by police (New York in 234 N.E.2d 422, Missouri in 422 S.W. 2d 304, California in 464 P 2d 114, Kansas in 421 P2d 170).

"Where defense counsel has instructed the police not to question his client or asks to be present during interrogation or instructs the police to notify him if they want to question his client—it is doubtful that any Court would allow in evidence statements taken when these instructions of defense counsel were ignored."

RESTRICTIVE AND BROAD INTERPRETATION OF MASSIAH

State and lower federal courts vary in the interpretation and application of the Massiah rule. The issue before the courts is the admissibility of statements or confessions made by the defendant after he was charged and without the presence or consent of the defendant's lawyer.

Broad Interpretation

All statements or confessions are inadmissible when obtained from a defendant who has been charged and obtained without the presence and the consent of his attorney. This applies to situations where the interrogation was initiated by the police and where the Miranda warnings were given and the defendant waived these rights.

Restricted Interpretation

Examples of the restricted rule can be found in *United States v. De Loy*, 421 F.2d 900 (1970), where the Fifth Circuit Court of Appeals stated:

... We do not comprehend *Massiah* as a sweeping mandate tainting all post-indictment statements made by a defendant without the presence of his counsel. Police officers are not made constitutionally deaf

> to the uncoerced, insistent and untricked statement of a properly warned defendant.

and in *Davis v. State*, 148 N.W.2d 53 (1967), where the Supreme Court of Wisconsin interpreted Massiah to be applicable only to situations where the accused was "... tricked or misled into confessing...."

DO OTHER DEMOCRACIES USE A MIRANDA RULE?

The answer is no—not as such. England, for example, has the "Judges rules," which require that British officers "caution" suspects of their rights before asking accusatory questions. The "Judges rules" are only guides, and even if they are broken, the statement may be admitted in evidence. However, the trial judge does have the power to exclude the statement if it is in the best interest of justice.

CAN STATEMENTS OR CONFESSIONS WHICH HAVE BEEN SUPPRESSED BE USED FOR IMPEACHMENT PURPOSES?

This question came before the U.S. Supreme Court in *Harris v. New York*, 28 L. Ed. 2d 1 (Feb. 1971). The defendant was arrested for illegally selling narcotics in New York State. Harris made statements after his arrest in response to questions from an officer. Because he had not been properly warned, the statements were suppressed and could not be introduced into evidence against him.

However, Harris took the stand in his own defense and denied selling heroin. On cross-examination, the prosecutor sought to impeach Harris (show that the witness is unworthy of belief) by asking him questions about the statements he made after his arrest. The trial judge allowed the prosecutor to paraphrase the statements for impeachment purposes. The actual statements were not disclosed to the jury. The jury found Harris guilty and the case was appealed to the U.S. Supreme Court. In a 5-4 decision, the conviction was affirmed. Chief Justice Warren Burger, writing for the majority, stated:

> The shield provided by Miranda cannot be perverted into a license to use perjury by way of a defense, free from the risk of confrontation with prior inconsistent utterances.

Justice Brennan, writing for the minority, stated:

> The court today tells police that they may freely interrogate an accused incommunicado and without counsel and know that although

any statement they obtain in violation of Miranda can't be used on the state's direct case, it may be introduced if the defendant has the temerity to testify in his own defense. . . .

USE OF THE POLYGRAPH (LIE DETECTOR)

The polygraph, or lie detector, is a device which simultaneously records changes in heartbeat, blood pressure, respiration rate and depth as well as psychogalvanic skin reflex. The purpose is to determine whether or not the person being questioned is lying or withholding the truth.

A witness, suspect, or defendant *cannot* be compelled to take this test (or any similar test), as this would violate his Fifth Amendment privilege not to be a witness against himself. However, this test and others may be used in the following manners:

Where a witness, suspect, or defendant *voluntarily* agrees to take the test under any of the following circumstances:

In agreement with or upon the request of the investigating law enforcement officers who seek to determine the credibility of statements which have been made.

In agreement with or upon the request of the prosecuting attorney, who could use the results of such test in determining whether to charge and also what charges would be made. The results of tests taken pursuant to stipulated agreements are generally admissible in evidence in the United States. (See *State v. Valdez*, 371 P.2d 894 (Ariz. 1962) for a review of the history of the polygraph.)

Occasionally, a trial judge will offer a defendant the opportunity to prove himself innocent by taking a polygraph test. Most appellate courts would hold this to be in error if the case were appealed.

As a condition of employment, an employer may request that the employee take the test. Many law enforcement agencies use the polygraph test to screen applicants for positions in their departments. During the course of the employment, the employer (whether in a police department or a bank) may for good reason request that the employee take a polygraph test as a condition of the employment. Failure to take the test could result in the dismissal of the employee. To prevent the results of such a test from being used in a civil or criminal action against the employee, the use of the suggested form in Chap. 21 is recommended. (Twelve states have legislation which would forbid in many instances the use of the polygraph as a condition of employment or for preemployment screening.)

Sections 3501 and 3502 of Title II of the Federal Omnibus Crime Control and Safe Streets Act of 1968

§ 3501. Admissibility of confessions.

(a) In any criminal prosecution brought by the United States or by the District of Columbia, a confession, as defined in subsection (e) hereof, shall be admissible in evidence if it is voluntarily given. Before such confession is received in evidence, the trial judge shall, out of the presence of the jury, determine any issue as to voluntariness. If the trial judge determines that the confession was voluntarily made it shall be admitted in evidence and the trial judge shall permit the jury to hear relevant evidence on the issue of voluntariness and shall instruct the jury to give such weight to the confession as the jury feels it deserves under all the circumstances.

(b) The trial judge in determining the issue of voluntariness shall take into consideration all the circumstances surrounding the giving of the confession, including (1) the time elapsing between arrest and arraignment of the defendant making the confession, if it was made after arrest and before arraignment, (2) whether such defendant knew the nature of the offense with which he was charged or of which he was suspected at the time of making the confession, (3) whether or not such defendant was advised or knew that he was not required to make any statement and that any such statement could be used against him, (4) whether or not such defendant had been advised prior to questioning of his right to the assistance of counsel; and (5) whether or not such defendant was without the assistance of counsel when questioned and when giving such confession.

The presence or absence of any of the above-mentioned factors to be taken into consideration by the judge need not be conclusive on the issue of voluntariness of the confession.

(c) In any criminal prosecution by the United States or by the District of Columbia, a confession made or given by a person who is a defendant therein, while such person was under arrest or other detention in the custody of any law-enforcement officer or law-enforcement agency, shall not be inadmissible solely because of delay in bringing such persons before a magistrate or other officer empowered to commit persons charged with offenses against the laws of the United States or of the District of Columbia if such confession is found by the trial judge to have been made voluntarily and if the weight to be given the confession is left to the jury and if such confession was made or given by such person within six hours immediately following his arrest or other detention: *Provided*, That the time limitation contained in this subsection shall not apply in any case in which the delay in bringing such person before such magistrate or other officer beyond such six-hour period is found by the trial judge to be reasonable considering the means of transportation and the distance to be traveled to the nearest available such magistrate or other officer.

(d) Nothing contained in this section shall bar the admission in evidence of any confession made or given voluntarily by any person to any other person without interrogation by anyone, or at any time at which the person who made or gave such confession was not under arrest or other detention.

(e) As used in this section, the term "confession" means any confession of guilt of any criminal offense or any self-incriminating statement made or given orally or in writing.

§ 3502. Admissibility in evidence of eye witness testimony.

The testimony of a witness that he saw the accused commit or participate in the commission of the crime for which the accused is being tried shall be admissible in evidence in a criminal prosecution in any trial court ordained and established under article III of the Constitution of the United States.

CASES FOR CHAPTER SIX

MASSIAH v. UNITED STATES
SUPREME COURT OF THE UNITED STATES
377 U.S. 201, 12 L. ED. 2d 246, 84 S. CT. 1199 (1964)

Mr. Justice Stewart delivered the opinion of the Court.

The petitioner was indicted for violating the federal narcotics laws. He retained a lawyer, pleaded not guilty, and was released on bail. While he was free on bail a federal agent succeeded by surreptitious means in listening to incriminating statements made by him. Evidence of these statements was introduced against the petitioner at his trial over his objection. He was convicted, and the Court of Appeals affirmed. We granted certiorari to consider whether, under the circumstances here presented, the prosecution's use at the trial of evidence of the petitioner's own incriminating statements deprived him of any right secured to him under the Federal Constitution.

The petitioner, a merchant seaman, was in 1958 a member of the crew of the SS Santa Maria. In April of that year federal customs officials in New York received information that he was going to transport a quantity of narcotics aboard that ship from South America to the United States. As a result of this and other information, the agents searched the Santa Maria upon its arrival in New York and found in the afterpeak of the vessel five packages containing about three and a half pounds of cocaine. They also learned of circumstances, not here relevant, tending to connect the petitioner with the cocaine. He was arrested, promptly arraigned, and subsequently indicted for possession of narcotics aboard a United States vessel. In July a superseding indictment was returned, charging the petitioner and a man named Colson with the same substantive offense, and in separate counts charging the petitioner, Colson, and others with having conspired to possess narcotics aboard a United States vessel, and to import, conceal, and facilitate the sale of narcotics. The petitioner, who had retained a lawyer, pleaded not guilty and was released on bail, along with Colson.

A few days later, and quite without the petitioner's knowledge, Colson decided to cooperate with the government agents in their continuing investigation of the narcotics activities in which the petitioner, Colson and others had allegedly been engaged. Colson permitted an agent named Murphy to install a Schmidt radio transmitter under the front seat of Colson's automobile, by means of which Murphy, equipped with an appropriate receiving device, could overhear from some distance away conversations carried on in Colson's car.

On the evening of November 19, 1959, Colson and the petitioner held a lengthy conversation while sitting in Colson's automobile, parked on a New York street. By prearrangement with Colson, and totally unbeknown to the petitioner, the agent Murphy sat in a car parked out of sight down the street and listened over the radio to the entire conversation. The petitioner made several incriminating statements during the course of this conversation. At the petitioner's trial these incriminating statements were brought before the jury through Murphy's testimony, despite the insistent objection of defense counsel. The jury convicted the petitioner of several related narcotics offenses, and the convictions were affirmed by the Court of Appeals.

The petitioner argues that it was an error of constitutional dimensions to permit the agent Murphy at the trial to testify to the petitioner's incriminating statements which Murphy had overheard under the circumstances disclosed by this record. This argument is based upon two distinct and independent grounds. First, we are told that Murphy's use of the radio equipment violated the petitioner's rights under the Fourth Amendment, and consequently, that all evidence which Murphy thereby obtained was, under the rule of *Weeks v. United States*, inadmissible against the petitioner at the trial. Secondly, it is said that the petitioner's Fifth and Sixth Amendment rights were violated by the use in evidence against him of incriminating statements which government agents had deliberately elicited from him after he had been indicted and in the absence of his retained counsel. Because of the way we dispose of the case, we do not reach the Fourth Amendment issue.

In *Spano v. New York*, this Court reversed a state criminal conviction because a confession had been wrongly admitted into evidence against the defendant at his trial. In that case the defendant had already been indicted for first degree murder at the time he confessed. The Court held that the defendant's conviction could not stand under the Fourteenth Amendment. While the Court's opinion relied upon the totality of the circumstances under which the confession had been obtained, four concurring Justices pointed out that the Constitution required reversal of the conviction upon the sole and specific ground that the confession had been deliberately elicited by the police after the defendant had been indicted, and therefore at a time when he was clearly entitled to a lawyer's help. It was pointed out that under our system of justice the most elemental concepts of due process of law contemplate that an indictment be followed by a trial, "in an orderly courtroom, presided over by a judge, open to the public, and protected by all the procedural safeguards of the law." It was said that a Constitution which guarantees a defendant the aid of counsel at such trial could surely vouchsafe no less to an indicted defendant under interrogation by the police in a completely extrajudicial proceeding. Anything less, it was said, might deny a defendant "effective representation by counsel at the only stage when legal aid and advice would help him."

Ever since this Court's decision in the *Spano* case, the New York courts have unequivocally followed this constitutional rule. "Any secret interrogation of the defendant, from and after the finding of the indictment, without the protection afforded by the presence of counsel, contravenes the basic dictates of fairness in the conduct of criminal causes and the fundamental rights of persons charged with crime." *People v. Waterman.*

This view no more than reflects a constitutional principle established as long ago as *Powell v. Alabama*, where the Court noted that "... during perhaps the most critical period of the proceedings ... that is to say, from the time of their arraignment until the beginning of their trial, when consultation, thorough-going investigation and preparation [are] vitally important, the defendants ... [are] as much entitled to such aid [of counsel] during that period as at the trial itself." And since the *Spano* decision the same basic constitutional principle has been broadly reaffirmed by this Court. See *Gideon v. Wainwright*.

Here we deal not with a state court conviction, but with a federal case, where the specific guarantee of the Sixth Amendment directly applies. *Johnson v. Zerbst.* We hold that the petitioner was denied the basic protections of that guarantee when there was used against him at his trial evidence of his own incriminating words, which federal agents had deliberately elicited from him after he had been indicted and in the absence of his counsel. It is true that in the *Spano* case the defendant was interrogated in a police station, while here the damaging testimony was elicited from the defendant without his knowledge while he was free on bail. But, as Judge Hays pointed out in his dissent in the Court of Appeals, "if such a rule is to have any efficacy it must apply to indirect and surreptitious interrogations as well as those conducted in the jailhouse. In this case, Massiah was more seriously imposed upon . . . because he did not even know that he was under interrogation by a government agent.

The Solicitor General, in his brief and oral argument, has strenuously contended that the federal law enforcement agents had the right, if not indeed the duty, to continue their investigation of the petitioner and his alleged criminal associates even though the petitioner had been indicted. He points out that the Governmen was continuing its investigation in order to uncover not only the source of narcotics found on the SS Santa Maria, but also their intended buyer. He says that the quantity of narcotics involved was such as to suggest that the petitioner was part of a large and well-organized ring, and indeed that the continuing investigation confirmed this suspicion, since it resulted in criminal charges against many defendants. Under these circumstances the Solicitor General concludes that the government agents were completely "justified in making use of Colson's cooperation by having Colson continue his normal associations and by surveilling them."

We may accept and, at least for present purposes, completely approve all that this argument implies, Fourth Amendment problems to one side. We do not question that in this case, as in many cases, it was entirely proper to continue an investigation of the suspected criminal activities of the defendant and his alleged confederates, even though the defendant had already been indicted. All that we hold is that the defendant's incriminating statements, obtained by federal agents under the circumstances here disclosed, could not constitutionally be used by the prosecution as evidence against *him* at his trial.

Reversed.

[Dissenting opinion of three justices is omitted.]

MIRANDA v. ARIZONA
SUPREME COURT OF THE UNITED STATES
394 U.S. 436, 86 S. CT. 1602, 16 L. ED. 2d 694 (1965)*

Mr. Chief Justice Warren delivered the opinion of the Court.

The cases before us raise questions which go to the roots of our concepts of American criminal jurisprudence: the restraints society must observe consistent with the Federal Constitution in prosecuting individuals for crime. More specifically, we deal with the admissibility of statements obtained from an individual who is subjected to custodial police interrogation and the necessity for procedures which assure that the individual is accorded his privilege under the Fifth Amendment to the Constitution not to be compelled to incriminate himself.

* Authors' note: Because the Miranda decision is over 100 pages long, only a small part of that decision can be presented.

We dealt with certain phases of this problem recently in *Escobedo v. Illinois*, 378 U. S. 478 (1964). There, as in the four cases before us, law enforcement officials took the defendant into custody and interrogated him in a police station for the purpose of obtaining a confession. The police did not effectively advise him of his right to remain silent or of his right to consult with his attorney. Rather, they confronted him with an alleged accomplice who accused him of having perpetrated a murder. When the defendant denied the accusation and said "I didn't shoot Manuel, you did it," they handcuffed him and took him to an interrogation room. There, while handcuffed and standing, he was questioned for four hours until he confessed. During this interrogation, the police denied his request to speak to his attorney, and they prevented his retained attorney, who had come to the police station, from consulting with him. At his trial, the State, over his objection, introduced the confession against him. We held that the statements thus made were constitutionally inadmissible.

This case has been the subject of judicial interpretation and spirited legal debate since it was decided two years ago. Both state and federal courts, in assessing its implications, have arrived at varying conclusions. A wealth of scholarly material has been written tracing its ramifications and underpinnings. Police and prosecutor have speculated on its range and desirability. We granted certiorari in these cases, 382 U. S. 924, 925, 937, in order further to explore some facets of the problems thus exposed, of applying the privilege against self-incrimination to in-custody interrogation. . . .

. . . .

Our holding will be spelled out with some specificity in the pages which follow but briefly stated it is this: the prosecution may not use statements, whether exculpatory or inculpatory, stemming from custodial interrogation of the defendant unless it demonstrates the use of procedural safeguards effective to secure the privilege against self-incrimination. By custodial interrogation, we mean questioning initiated by law enforcement officers after a person has been taken into custody or otherwise deprived of his freedom of action in any significant way. As for the procedural safeguards to be employed, unless other fully effective means are devised to inform accused persons of their right of silence and to assure a continuous opportunity to exercise it, the following measures are required. Prior to any questioning, the person must be warned that he has a right to remain silent, that any statement he does make may be used as evidence against him, and that he has a right to the presence of an attorney, either retained or appointed. The defendant may waive effectuation of these rights, provided the waiver is made voluntarily, knowingly and intelligently. If, however, he indicates in any manner and at any stage of the process that he wishes to consult with an attorney before speaking there can be no questioning. Likewise, if the individual is alone and indicates in any manner that he does not wish to be interrogated, the police may not question him. The mere fact that he may have answered some questions or volunteered some statements on his own does not deprive him of the right to refrain from answering any further inquiries until he has conulted with an attorney and thereafter consents to be questioned.

I.

The constitutional issue we decide in each of these cases is the admissibility of statements obtained from a defendant questioned while in custody or otherwise deprived of his freedom of action in any significant way. In each, the defendant was questioned by police officers, detectives, or a prosecuting attorney in a room in which he was cut off from the outside world. In none of these cases was the defendant given a full and effective warning of his rights at the outset of the interrogation process. In all the cases, the questioning elicited oral admissions, and in three of them, signed statements as well which were admitted at their trials. They all thus share salient features—incommunicado interrogation of individuals in a police-dominated atmosphere, resulting in self-incriminating statements without full warnings of constitutional rights.

. . . .

In dealing with statements obtained through interrogation, we do not purport to find all confessions inadmissible. Confessions remain a proper element in law enforcement. Any statement given freely and voluntarily without any compelling influences is, of course, admissible in evidence. The fundamental import of the privilege while an individual is in custody is not whether he is allowed to talk to the police without the benefit of warnings and counsel, but whether he can be interrogated. There is no requirement that police stop a person who enters a police station and states that he wishes to confess to a crime, or a person who calls the police to offer a confession or any other statement he desires to make. Volunteered statements of any kind are not barred by the Fifth Amendment and their admissibility is not affected by our holding today.

To summarize, we hold that when an individual is taken into custody or otherwise deprived of his freedom by the authorities in any significant way and is subjected to questioning, the privilege against self-incrimination is jeopardized. Procedural safeguards must be employed to protect the privilege, and unless other fully effective means are adopted to notify the person of his right of silence and to assure that the exercise of the right will be scrupulously honored, the following measures are required. He must be warned prior to any questioning that he has the right to remain silent, that anything he says can be used against him in a court of law, that he has the right to the presence of an attorney, and that if he cannot afford an attorney one will be appointed for him prior to any questioning if he so desires. Opportunity to exercise these rights must be afforded to him throughout the interrogation. After such warnings have been given, and such opportunity afforded him, the individual may knowingly and intelligently waive these rights and agree to answer questions or make a statement. But unless and until such warnings and waiver are demonstrated by the prosecution at trial, no evidence obtained as a result of interrogation can be used against him.

. . . .

At the top of the statement was a typed paragraph stating that the confession was made voluntarily, without threats or promises of immunity and "with full knowledge of my legal rights, understanding any statement I make may be used against me."[1]

At his trial before a jury, the written confession was admitted into evidence over the objection of defense counsel, and the officers testified to the prior oral confession made by Miranda during the interrogation. Miranda was found guilty of kidnapping and rape. He was sentenced to 20 to 30 years' imprisonment on each count, the sentences to run concurrently. On appeal, the Supreme Court of Arizona held that Miranda's constitutional rights were not violated in obtaining the confession and affirmed the conviction. 98 Ariz. 18, 401 P. 2d 721. In reaching its decision, the court emphasized heavily the fact that Miranda did not specifically request counsel.

We reverse. From the testimony of the officers and by the admission of respondent, it is clear that Miranda was not in any way apprised of his right to

---

[1] One of the officers testified that he read this paragraph to Miranda. Apparently, however, he did not do so until after Miranda had confessed orally.

consult with an attorney and to have one present during the interrogation, nor was his right not to be compelled to incriminate himself effectively protected in any other manner. Without these warnings the statements were inadmissible. The mere fact that he signed a statement which contained a typed-in clause stating that he had "full knowledge" of his "legal rights" does not approach the knowing and intelligent waiver required to relinquish constitutional rights.

QUESTIONS AND PROBLEMS

Available Answers for Questions 1 to 9

1. Violates the voluntariness test in view of the totality of the circumstances.
2. The Miranda requirements were not complied with.
3. Violates the Massiah rule.
4. The evidence would be admitted as there were no violations of the exclusionary rules.

1. Y, who is in jail, prior to his trial is told that until he "cooperates," he will receive only bread and water for his meals. After three days, Y agrees to "cooperate." After being given the Miranda warnings and waiving his constitutional rights in writing, Y signs a confession. Is the confession admissible?

2. An officer asks an arrested person, "What is your name?" The suspect answers, "I am sorry I killed her." No Miranda warnings were given. (See *Parson v. United States*, 387 F.2d 944.)

3. The defendant interrupted the officer as he was giving the Miranda warnings and stated, "I don't need a damm [*sic*] lawyer. I done it." (See *State v. Wilson*, 268 N.E.2d 814.)

4. The suspect was questioned on Tuesday after being given the Miranda warnings. No significant information was obtained. On Wednesday, the suspect was questioned again because the investigation had revealed additional facts. The Miranda warnings were not given on Wednesday. Would the Wednesday confession be admissible?

5. After being advised of his rights, the defendant who was in custody refused to talk with the investigating officers. Without putting any pressure on the defendant, the officers asked a second time if the defendant would waive his constitutional rights. The defendant then waived his rights and confessed. Is the confession admissible? (See *People v. Rice*, 94 Cal. Rptr. 4.)

6. An arrested person being taken to the jail asks an officer, "How much time can I get for this?" The officer answers, "For what?" The arrested person says, "For robbing the drugstore." Is this statement admissible in evidence? (See *Campbell v. State*, 243 A.2d 642.)

7. A defendant who was freed on bail started an argument with a police officer in the halls of the courthouse. The defendant stated,

"You can be killed too." The officer responded, "You're not dealing with any little old lady now—you weren't so brave when you killed that little old lady." The defendant said, "Sure I did it, but you guys can't prove it." Is this statement admissible in evidence? (See *People v. McKie*, 210 N.E.2d 36 [N.Y. 1969].)

8. Although the body of the victim has been properly identified, police take a suspect down to the morgue to view the body of his former friend. While there, the suspect breaks down and states that he wants to confess. He is given the Miranda warnings and signs a confession after signing a waiver of his rights. Is the confession admissible?

9. A defendant who confessed after being given the four Miranda warnings and waiving his rights argues that he was not advised that he could terminate the interrogation whenever he requested that the questioning cease. Would this confession be admissible? (See *State v. Harper*, 465 S.W.2d 547.)

Available Answers for Questions 10 to 23

1. The Miranda warnings should be given if the statement (or evidence) is to be introduced in evidence.

2. The Miranda warnings need *not* be given and the statement (or evidence) may be introduced in evidence.

10. In an armed robbery case, the suspect is questioned as to the location of the gun used in the robbery.

11. A bank employee is questioned by his boss in regard to funds which are missing from the bank. He admits taking the money.

12. An officer stops a person for temporary questioning without arrest (a "stop" under the statutes of your state) and asks the person to identify himself and explain the circumstances surrounding his presence in that area.

13. The police officer asks a drunken driver whom he plans to arrest how many drinks he had.

14. A man walks into a police station stating that he has just killed his wife and begins telling the details. Should the officer stop him and give him the warnings?

15. *Question 14 continued:* In order to help the woman if she can be helped, the officer asks where the incident occurred and whether the woman is dead.

16. *Question 14 continued:* The officer questions the man as to what he did with the murder weapon.

17. *Question 14 continued:* The officer questions the man as to whether he had an accomplice. The man states that he and X became drunk and together they murdered the woman.

18. Y is suspected of armed robbery. Y and X share an apartment. X is questioned as to Y's activity and X shows the officers where the loot and the gun are hidden in the apartment.

19. A drunk is arrested on the street and is questioned as to his name, address, and place of employment. Should the warnings be given?

20. Officers see a large crowd of people on a street corner. They walk up to the crowd and ask, "What is going on here?"

21. An officer asks an arrested person, "Why did you do it?"

22. A department store employee signs a confession drawn up by the store attorney which summarizes oral statements which he made to the store security officer.

23. An officer tells a suspect that he is not under arrest and that he is free to leave the presence of the officer anytime he wants to leave. The officer then asks questions to which the suspect gives incriminating answers and the officer then arrests him.

24. Can you stand up in class and give the Miranda warnings?

25. Describe the waiver which must be given if the oral answers or statements are to be admitted in evidence.

26. In what situations should the warnings be given?

27. Under what situations may officers ask questions without giving the warnings:
    a. Of persons at the scene of a crime?
    b. Of suspects of a crime?
    c. Of persons arrested for a crime?

28. What is the most common mistake officers make in giving the Miranda warnings?

29. What are some other mistakes?

30. Which of the following would be a sufficient waiver of Fifth and Sixth Amendment rights when followed by incriminating statements?
    a. Nodding the head
    b. Mumbling "okay"
    c. Silence

31. What are the possible defense attacks which may be made in a motion to oral statements or written confessions?

32. Which of the following would make the best evidence?
    a. Oral statements which are repeated by an officer in court
    b. A typewritten statement prepared by a police officer and signed by the defendant
    c. A statement written by the defendant

7

THE EXCLUSIONARY RULES APPLICABLE TO EYEWITNESS IDENTIFICATION

Eyewitness identification is often an important and critical phase of the investigation of crimes of violence such as rape, homicide, assault and battery, mugging, robbery, and other theft crimes. Identification by victims or witnesses is sometimes the only evidence available to investigating officers, and therefore the whole case may rest upon the identification.

The following observations can be generally made in regard to eyewitness identification:

1. Witnesses vary:
   a. In their ability to observe and in the accuracy of their observations.
   b. In their ability to retain what they have observed and make an identification days, weeks, or months after the criminal incident.
   c. In their ability to express themselves verbally as to what they have observed.

   Some victims and witnesses are very good observers and can retain and express themselves well; other witnesses are not as good and some are very poor. Police officers who have acted as "fillers" in a lineup are sometimes identified by the latter group as the assailant.
2. Many witnesses are influenced by the statements and observations of other witnesses. If, in a savings and loan robbery, the boss states that the robber had red hair and was 6 feet tall, other employees are not likely to disagree with him (at least not in his presence). Therefore it is important that eyewitnesses be questioned separately and apart from one another.
3. Officers should be careful to ascertain whether the witness is speaking from his own knowledge and observations. The witness

might, either consciously or unconsciously, fill in gaps in his own observations with hearsay from other witnesses or opinions which he heard expressed. Witnesses have been known to form answers based on what they thought the stereotype of a criminal should be.

4. Many witnesses will recall specific characteristics and details of the assailant, such as a gold tooth, an unusual manner of speech or walk, a mole on his cheek, or a tattoo on his arm or chest. Women may take particular note of the type of clothing the assailant wore, and men may recall in detail the type of weapon and equipment used. Although the officer should not use leading or suggestive questions, he should question witnesses and victims in detail to bring out exact and accurate information.

5. Memory or recall is best immediately after the criminal incident and tends to fade as the days and weeks go by. Therefore, it is important that every available witness be carefully questioned as soon after the incident as possible. In serious cases, the information given by the witness or victim should be reduced to writing and, if possible, signed by the victim or witness.

6. The investigating officer should determine whether the witness was in a position to observe the assailant, considering the distance from the criminal incident, the lighting, the length of time in which he could observe, and his position relative to the assailant. The officer should also determine whether the witness has any obvious defects in sight, hearing, or smell which would bear upon the accuracy of the statements given. Fear, anger, excitement, and other emotions might seriously affect the ability of some witnesses to observe and report accurately what they have seen. Such emotions have been known to have the opposite effect on other victims and witnesses.

IDENTIFICATION PRIOR TO ARREST OR DETENTION OF THE SUBJECT

Identification *before* arrest is usually made by using photographs. In some instances, artist's drawings are used. Occasionally, the victim or witness is taken by the police to a place where the suspect is likely to be and identification can be made in this manner.

Photographic Identification

The following statement by the United States Supreme Court was made in *Simmons v. United States*, 390 U.S. 377 (1968):

Despite the hazards of initial identification by photograph, this procedure has been used widely and effectively in criminal law enforcement, from the standpoint both of apprehending offenders and of sparing innocent suspects the ignominy of arrest by allowing eyewitnesses to exonerate them through scrutiny of photographs. The danger that use of the technique may result in convictions based on misidentification may be substantially lessened by a course of cross-examination at trial which exposes to the jury the method's potential for error. We are unwilling to prohibit its employment, either in the exercise of our supervisory power or, still less, as a matter of constitutional requirement. Instead, we hold that each case must be considered on its own facts and that convictions based on eyewitness identification at trial following a pretrial identification by photograph will be set aside on that ground only if the photographic identification procedure was so impermissibly suggestive as to give rise to a very substantial likelihood of irreparable misidentification. . . .

The U.S. Supreme Court concluded in the Simmons case that while ". . . the identification procedure employed may have in some respects fallen short of the ideal . . .," it did not violate the defendant's due process rights so as to call for a reversal.

While victims and witnesses may view as many as 500 photographs, a few cases where the court used the test that "each case must be considered on its own facts" have held that the showing of only one photograph before arrest or detention was not in itself impermissibly suggestive. Such procedures may be considered by a jury in determining the weight that will be given to the identification.

Officers should make every effort to show more than a few photographs and should do the best they can under the circumstances in which they are working to ensure that the witnesses' opportunity to identify or reject is as free from suggestiveness as is possible.

Artist's Sketches

Many large departments have staff artists available to make composites, sketches, and drawings of assailants based upon descriptions given to them by victims and witnesses. Commercial kits are also available for this type of work.

Taking a Witness to a Place Where the Suspect Is Likely to Be

This procedure is practical and acceptable if done in a manner free of excessive suggestiveness. A crowded courtroom, a busy shopping center, a factory gate as a shift is changing are all areas where the witness could view many people.

An example of the successful use of this procedure is *Dozie v. State*, 49 Wis.2d 209 (1970). The Milwaukee police had arrested Dozie for the robbery of a gasoline station and suspected on the basis of the type of the crime and a description given by another victim that he had robbed other stations. The police asked a victim to appear in a courtroom where they knew that Dozie would appear for the charge for which he was arrested. The witnesse sat by himself for an hour and a half during which time over a hundred people came and went. When Dozie appeared, the witness immediately identified him and informed a police officer of the positive identification. In sustaining the identification and the conviction, the Supreme Court of Wisconsin stated:

> ... The defendant was in custody, but on another criminal charge, not related to the offense here involved.... The identifications here, we conclude, were made at a purely investigatory, not accusatory, stage of the proceedings....

However, to have the witness sit in front of the suspect's house in an automobile or to send the witness to a gasoline station where the suspect worked may be held to be impermissibly suggestive.

IDENTIFICATION AFTER ARREST BUT BEFORE INDICTMENT

In June 1972, the U.S. Supreme Court handed down the decision in the case of *Kirby v. Illinois* (see case, this chapter). The Court affirmed a Chicago conviction where the victim of a robbery which had occurred two days before was brought into the police station and identified the defendant as one of the robbers. The defendant was not advised of his right to counsel, nor was he offered nor did he receive legal assistance.

Scene-of-the-Crime Identification

Before the Kirby case, many states had adopted the "scene of the crime," "on-the-spot confrontation," or the "short detour" rule in regard to identification. These states held that the police may bring a suspect who has been apprehended back to the scene of a recently committed crime for identification by the victim or a witness to the crime. In some of the cases, the victim or witness is brought to the place where the suspect is being held.

The U.S. Supreme Court denied certiorari (393 U.S. 1034) and also a rehearing (393 U.S. 1112) in the 1966 scene-of-the-crime identification case of *Commonwealth v. Bumpus*. The defendant in that case was apprehended immediately after the crime was committed and taken back to the scene of the crime, where he was identified by the victim of the crime. The reasoning used by the state courts in sustaining this procedure is:

The memory of the witness is very fresh.

If the suspect is not the person who committed the crime, he may be immediately released and is not inconvenienced or embarrassed any further.

If identification is made, officers and the department may discontinue their efforts, but if they have the wrong person, they may resume their efforts and their search.

IDENTIFICATION AFTER ARREST AND AFTER INDICTMENT

After the arrest and indictment of the suspect, the pressing need to determine whether the police have the right suspect in custody no longer exists. The possibility of inconveniencing and embarrassing innocent suspects by further detention has been minimized. The matter has moved from the investigatory stage to the accusatorial stage, and the government has committed itself to prosecute. The U.S. Supreme Court in the Kirby case stated that "It is this point, therefore, that marks the commencement of the 'criminal prosecutions' to which alone the explicit guarantees of the Sixth Amendment are applicable."

In 1967, the U.S. Supreme Court handed down the three cases of Wade, Gilbert, and Stovall in one day. The exclusionary rule contained in these cases is known as the Wade-Gilbert-Stovall rule. The rule holds that an identification confrontation after arrest and indictment is an important and critical stage of the criminal proceedings and that the accused is entitled to have his lawyer present to observe on a firsthand basis whether there was improper influence, suggestions, or mistakes made. The new exclusionary rule was imposed because the Court concluded that a witness who identifies a suspect to the police will seldom change his mind and admit later that he is uncertain or was wrong.

In *United States v. Wade*, 388 U.S. 218 (1967), the lineup was conducted in the absence of Wade's attorney and without prior notice to Wade or his lawyer. As a result, the question of whether the in-court identification had an independent source was remanded and the identification was probably suppressed.

In *Gilbert v. California*, 388 U.S. 263 (1967), the lineup was conducted before some 100 witnesses to the many robberies which Gilbert was alleged to have committed. Not only did witnesses make identifications in each other's presence, but the lineup was conducted without the presence of Gilbert's lawyer. The situation was held to be so *unnecessarily suggestive* and conducive to *irreparable mistaken identification* as to violate Gilbert's rights.

Lineups must now be conducted in the manner detailed in Rule 10 of the Council of Judges, which can be found at the end of this chapter. The Wade-Gilbert-Stovall rule holds that the defendant's constitutional right to due process and his right to have the assistance of counsel for his defense must be observed.

In *Stovall v. Denno*, 388 U.S. 293 (1967), the only living witness to the crime in which her husband was killed was herself in critical condition, as she had been stabbed eleven times. The suspect was taken in handcuffs into the hospital room and identified by the witness. No other persons were brought in to make up a lineup and the identification took place two days after the assault. The witness did live and identified the defendant at the trial. The U.S. Supreme Court held that "immediate hospital confrontation was imperative" and quoted the Court of Appeal in the decision: "Here was the only person in the world who could possible exonerate Stovall. Her words and only her words, 'He is not the man' could have resulted in freedom for Stovall. . . ."

WILL IMPROPER PROCEDURE BY THE INVESTIGATING OFFICER CAUSE SUPPRESSION OF AN IN-COURT IDENTIFICATION?

Yes, if the court rules that the procedure was so *unnecessarily suggestive* and conducive to *irreparable mistaken identification*. However, if it can be shown that the in-court identification had an independent source free from the improper procedure used, then the in-court identification will ordinarily be admissible.

Example: A drugstore is robbed by a man whom the druggist has seen frequently in the store for some months before the robbery. However, the druggist does not know his name. Five days after the robbery a suspect is brought into the store in handcuffs. When one of the officers asks, "Is this the man?" the druggist answers, "Yes."

In the example given, the identification has an independent source (the fact that the druggist had seen the suspect frequently before the crime). This independent source for the in-court identification is free from the taint of the improper procedure. Other independent sources might be unusual tattoos, scars, speech, etc., or a combination of such characteristics which clearly identify the suspect as the assailant.

ANTICIPATING A CHALLENGE

Officers should make every reasonable effort to observe the constitutional rights of suspects in identification procedures. The officer should avoid, if possible, any procedure which is unnecessarily suggestive. He should also, if possible, preserve and file the evidence and notes showing that the method used was fair. In this way, if the identification procedure is challenged, the evidence which he has preserved and filed can be used by the state to show that proper procedures were used.

REENACTMENT OF THE CRIME

As part of the investigation of major crimes, the French and some of the other European countries routinely reenact the crimes. This procedure is used:

1. Because of the possibility that facts will emerge which were not previously disclosed.
2. To bring out discrepancies in the stories given to the police. Even accomplished liars sometimes find that their verbal accounts do not correspond with the physical reenactment of what happened.
3. Photographs and movies can be made of the reenactment which in some instances could be very helpful to the court and jury in visualizing the criminal incident.

Occasionally, law enforcement officers in the United States will make arrangements for the reenactment of a criminal incident. If the reenactment is done with only the victim (and witnesses), no Sixth Amendment obligation to provide for the notice and presence of the defense attorney exists.

A defendant could not be compelled to participate in the reenactment because this would violate his Fifth Amendment rights. Should a defendant or suspect volunteer to participate in the reenactment of a crime, it would be advisable to inform him that he could have his attorney or a friend present during the reenactment.

OPEN-CRIME LINEUP

An investigative procedure which is sometimes used is the "open-crime" lineup. When the *modus operandi* of the crime for which the suspect has been arrested is similar to unsolved crimes, an open-crime lineup may be considered by the law enforcement agency. Victims or witnesses to other unsolved similar crimes may in this manner view the suspect and others in a lineup showing.

The defendant in *United States v. Allen*, 408 F.2d 1287 (1969), objected to this procedure, but the District of Columbia Circuit Court stated that "the inherent suggestibility of a lineup is outweighed in this case by the reasonable suspicion that the appellant may indeed be responsible for the open crimes."

The identification procedures stated in rule 10 of the *Model Rules* should be complied with by the law enforcement agency conducting the lineup.

VIDEOTAPE RECORDING

In 1937 Dean Wigmore suggested the use of talking movies as a "scientific method" of pretrial identification. The U.S. Supreme Court refers to these suggestions in footnote 30 of the Wade case.

This idea is more practical and workable today than it was thirty years ago. Today videotaping equipment is readily available and simple to operate. It not only presents a workable alternative to the cumbersome and time-consuming task of preparing and staging a lineup, but it also would "eliminate the risks of abuse and unintentional suggestion at lineup proceedings and the impediments to meaningful confrontation at trial may also remove the basis for regarding the stage as 'critical'." (The U.S. Supreme Court in *United States v. Wade*)

IDENTIFICATION BY VOICEPRINT (SPECTROGRAM)

Just after midnight on May 22, 1970, the St. Paul Police Department received an anonymous telephone call requesting assistance for a woman about to give birth. The two officers sent to the address found a darkened house. One officer went around to the back of the house, and the other officer suddenly found himself under fire from a sniper. The officer was killed in what seemed to be a random attack on "police in general."

The only clue available was the telephone call, which had been routinely taped. Police interviewed women in the neighborhood and made voiceprints of the voices of the women interviewed. When a voiceprint was found to match the voiceprint of the taped call, police obtained an arrest warrant and a search warrant for an eighteen-year-old woman, Caroline Trimble.

In *Trimble v. Hedman*, 192 N.W.2d 432 (1971), the Supreme Court of Minnesota became the first American civilian appellate court to hold that voiceprints, or spectrograms, may be used in criminal cases to aid in voice identification. The court stated:

> Identification of a person by recognition of his voice from hearing it at different times is generally upheld as admissible.... We have followed this general rule for many years....
>
> While most of the cases dealing with the subject relate to conversations over the telephone or to one listening to a person speak and comparing the voice with that heard prior thereof, the rule has been applied to evidence of conversations received by other mechanical means....
>
> It would seem to follow that if identification can be made by comparing a voice over a telephone or by requiring an accused to speak certain words in the presence of an accuser in a lineup or by means of other mechanical recording, the two tapes involved in this case, one of the voice of a known person and the other an unknown, should be admissible for the purpose of comparison aurally, the same as if the words were spoken in some other manner, assuming that a foundation is laid showing that there has been no alteration of the tape and that the tape is mechanically perfected to the point where voices can be identified from it....
>
> In view of the fact that identification by aural voice comparison, either respecting telephone conversations or words spoken at a lineup, or recorded by other mechanical means is admissible, and the admission that voice comparisons by spectrograms corroborate identification by means of ear, we are convinced that spectrograms ought to be admissible at least for the purpose of corroborating opinions as to identification by means of ear alone. They ought also to be admissible for the purpose of impeachment. The weight and credibility of such evidence lie with the finder of facts, but that does not involve the question of admissibility. In this case, the information submitted to the magistrate for the purpose of determining probable cause was sufficient to justify the issuance of a warrant for arrest and a search warrant.

Model Rules of Court for Police Action from Arrest to Arraignment by the Council of Judges of the National Council on Crime and Delinquency

RULE 10. IDENTIFICATION PROCEDURES

Where identification of a suspect or a defendant is made by a victim or a witness at the scene of a crime or in the vicinity, or from photographs, any procedure may be used that fairly tests recognition and is devoid of suggestion to the person making the identification, and if the line-up procedure specified below cannot be followed.

In all other situations, an out-of-court identification of a suspect or a defendant in custody shall be by a line-up conducted as follows:

(a) Reasonable notice of the proposed line-up shall be given to the suspect and his counsel, and both shall be informed that the suspect may have his attorney present at the line-up. If the suspect is not represented by counsel, he shall be advised of his right to have counsel assigned without charge. He may waive in writing the presence of his attorney.

(b) The line-up should consist of at least six persons, approximately alike in age, size, color, and dress, and none of them other than possibly the suspect shall be known to the witness.

(c) Persons in the line-up may be requested to speak certain words, identical for each person, for purposes of voice identification.

(d) Neither directly nor indirectly shall any police officer indicate or allow anyone but the witness to indicate in any way any person in the line-up as the suspect or defendant. Any instructions shall be given to all as a group, not individually.

(e) The line-up shall be viewed by only one witness at a time, others being excluded from the room and not permitted to discuss the line-up or descriptions of the suspect.

In an emergency, such as where it is reasonably feared that the witness may die before making an identification as required by this rule, those provisions that are impractical under the circumstances may be disregarded. However, any disregard of the provisions will be subject to scrutiny to determine whether the identification was valid.

CASE FOR CHAPTER SEVEN

KIRBY v. ILLINOIS
SUPREME COURT OF THE UNITED STATES
406 U.S. 682, 92 S. CT. 1877, 32 L. ED. 2d 411 (JUNE 1972)

Mr. Justice Stewart. . . . On February 21, 1968, a man named Willie Shard reported to the Chicago police that the previous day two men had robbed him on a Chicago street of a wallet containing, among other things, travellers checks and a Social Security card. On February 22, two police officers stopped the petitioner and a companion, Ralph Bean, on West Madison Street in Chicago.[1] When asked for identification, the petitioner produced a wallet that contained three travellers checks and a Social Security card, all bearing the name of Willie Shard. Papers with Shard's name on them were also found in Bean's possession. When asked to explain his possession of Shard's property, the petitioner first said that the travellers checks were "play money," and then told the officers that he had won them in a crap game. The officers then arrested the petitioner and Bean and took them to a police station.

Only after arriving at the police station, and checking the records there, did the arresting officers learn of the Shard robbery. A police car was then dispatched to Shard's place of employment, where it picked up Shard and brought him to the

---

[1] The officers stopped the petitioner and his companion because they thought the petitioner was a man named Hampton, who was "wanted" in connection with an unrelated criminal offense. The legitimacy of this stop and the subsequent arrest is not before us.

police station. Immediately upon entering the room in the police station where the petitioner and Bean were seated at a table, Shard positively identified them as the men who had robbed him two days earlier. No lawyer was present in the room, and neither the petitioner nor Bean had asked for legal assistance, or been advised of any right to the presence of counsel.

More than six weeks later, the petitioner and Bean were indicted for the robbery of Willie Shard. Upon arraignment, counsel was appointed to represent them, and they pleaded not guilty. A pretrial motion to suppress Shard's identification testimony was denied, and at the trial Shard testified as a witness for the prosecution. In his testimony he described his identification of the two men at the police station on February 22, and identified them again in the courtroom as the men who had robbed him on February 20. He was cross-examined at length regarding the circumstances of his identification of the two defendants. The jury found both defendants guilty, and the petitioner's conviction was affirmed on appeal. The Illinois appellate court held that the admission of Shard's testimony was not error, relying upon an earlier decision of the Illinois Supreme Court holding that the *Wade-Gilbert per se* exclusionary rule is not applicable to pre-indictment confrontations. We granted certiorari, limited to this question.

I

. . . .

The initiation of judicial criminal proceedings is far from a mere formalism. It is the starting point of our whole system of adversary criminal justice. For it is only then that the Government has committed itself to prosecute, and only then that the adverse positions of Government and defendant have solidified. It is then that a defendant finds himself faced with the prosecutorial forces of organized society, and immersed in the intricacies of substantive and procedural criminal law. It is this point, therefore, that marks the commencement of the "criminal prosecutions" to which alone the explicit guarantees of the Sixth Amendment are applicable.

In this case we are asked to import into a routine police investigation an absolute constitutional guarantee historically and rationally applicable only after the onset of formal prosecutorial proceedings. We decline to do so. Less than a year after *Wade* and *Gilbert* were decided, the Court explained the rule of those decisions as follows: "The rationale of those cases was that an accused is entitled to counsel at any 'critical stage of the *prosecution*,' and that a post-indictment lineup is such a 'critical stage.'" (Emphasis supplied.) *Simmons v. United States*, 390 U. S. 377, 382–383. We decline to depart from that rationale today by imposing a per se exclusionary rule upon testimony concerning an identification that took place long before the commencement of any prosecution whatever.

II

What has been said is not to suggest that there may not be occasions during the course of a criminal investigation when the police do abuse identification procedures. Such abuses are not beyond the reach of the Constitution. As the Court pointed out in *Wade* itself, it is always necessary to "scrutinize *any* pretrial confrontation. . . ." 388 U. S., at 227. The Due Process Clause of the Fifth and Fourteenth Amendments forbids a lineup that is unnecessarily suggestive and conducive to irreparable mistaken identification. When a person has not been formally charged with a criminal offense, *Stovall* strikes the appropriate constitutional balance between the right of a suspect to be protected from prejudicial procedures and the interest of society in the prompt and purposeful investigation of an unsolved crime.

The judgment is affirmed.

QUESTIONS AND PROBLEMS

Available Answers for Questions 1 to 15
Choose the answer which best fits the situation.

1. The procedure is (or was) so unnecessarily suggestive and conducive to irreparable mistaken identification as to be a *denial of due process* of law.

2. The procedure denied the suspect (or defendant) his Sixth Amendment right to an attorney.

3. The procedure was in violation of another constitutional right (other than those in answers 1 and 2).

4. There was *no substantial* violation of the defendant's or suspect's rights.

1. In order to narrow the focus of suspicion, a general street roundup is made for the purpose of questioning and lineups.
2. Weekly lineups are used to familiarize police personnel with known gamblers, pickpockets, prostitutes, etc., who are being held in custody. The lineups are *not* held for identification purposes.
3. A lineup was conducted before some 100 witnesses to the many robberies which the suspect is believed to have committed.
4. A suspect who has not been arrested volunteers to come in and appear in a lineup. He is told that he may bring his attorney, but he waives this right. A positive identification is made, and the suspect is arrested and charged.
5. Officers have reasonable suspicion to believe that X has committed a crime. They pick him up for lineup showing, and his attorney is present at the lineup. The attorney protests the holding of his client without probable cause. An identification is made, and X is charged with a crime.
6. A rape victim views persons coming in and out of a sheriff's office through one-way glass. Some persons come in voluntarily while others are brought in for other offenses. After an hour of watching, she identifies a man as her assailant.
7. The victim of a robbery is allowed to view two suspects being held in a jail cell. The victim identifies one of the men. (See *In re Hill*, 458 P.2d 449, Cal.)
8. A suspect who is arrested five minutes after a holdup is taken back to the scene of the crime and is identified.
9. A suspect who is arrested *five hours* after a holdup is taken back to the scene of the crime and is identified.
10. While the victim is waiting for the lineup to start, he sees the

suspect being brought in handcuffed. The victim identifies this person as the assailant.

11. A suspect is taken to the victim's home one hour after the rape occurred there. The victim has known the defendant for twenty years and identifies him as her assailant. (See *State v. Lewis*, 229 So. 2d 726, La.)

12. The men in the lineup are requested to try on a hat found at the scene of the crime and known to belong to the assailant. The hat fits *only* the suspect. An identification is made.

13. The victim identifies the defendant in court during the trial. The defendant is sitting at the defense table next to his attorney. There has been no lineup and no photographs have been shown to the victim.

14. An officer who is showing eight photographs to a crime victim comments, "Take a good look at this picture." The victim identifies that one as a picture of her assailant.

15. A police officer telephones a victim, saying, "We have the guys that did it, come down and identify them." Identification is made. (See *People v. Lee*, 254 N.E.2d 469, Ill.)

16. Explain how the following identification procedures may be *properly* used:
    a. *Before* arrest and with *less* than probable cause:
    Photographs
    Artist's sketches or composites
    Taking the witness to a place where the suspect is likely to be
    Lineup where the suspect volunteers to appear
    b. *After* arrest *but before* the defendant has been formally charged by the state:
    Photographs
    Lineups
    A confrontation as in the Kirby case
    c. *After* arrest *and after* the defendant has been formally charged by the state:
    Photographs
    Lineups

17. What attacks could be made by the defense in an attempt to suppress identification when much of the state's case rests upon identification by a witness or a victim?

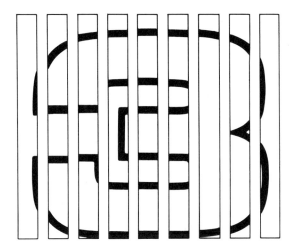

SEARCH
AND
SEIZURE

Search warrants provide the authority for only a small percentage of the searches which are made every year in the United States. The authority for the great majority of the searches is other than that of a search warrant. To make a search, the officer must have authority and the burden is upon him and the state to show that this authority did exist and therefore the search was reasonable under the Fourth Amendment.

Over the years, the United States Supreme Court has consistently reaffirmed the search warrant requirements of the Fourth Amendment. The following are a few of the instances:

In 1948
The "... guarantee of protection against unreasonable search and seizure extends to the innocent and guilty alike. It marks the right of privacy as one of the unique values of our civilization and, with few exceptions, stays the hands of the police unless they have a search warrant issued by a magistrate on probable cause supported by oath or affirmation...." McDonald v. United States, 335 U.S. 451.

In 1967
"... We do not retreat from our holdings that the police must, whenever practicable, obtain advance judicial approval of searches and seizure through the warrant procedure, or that in most instances fail-

ure to comply with the warrant requirements can only be excused by exigent circumstances. . . ." Terry v. Ohio, 392 U.S. 1

In 1970

". . . our past decisions make clear that only in a few specifically established and well delineated situations may a warrantless search of a dwelling withstand constitutional scrutiny, even though the authorities have probable cause to conduct it. The burden rests on the State to show the existence of such an exceptional situation. . . ." Vale v. Louisiana, 399 U.S. 30

In reviewing a search and seizure, the courts generally give the officer the benefit of the doubt if he was acting under the authority of a search warrant. A search warrant should be obtained:

1. If there is time to get a search warrant
2. If the officer can not clearly show his authority to make a warrantless search (the burden is on the state to show the authority for a warrantless search)
3. If there is any doubt as to whether a search warrant is necessary

Part 3 of this text presents the "well delineated situations" when warrantless searches may be made. Chapter 13 presents the law in regard to search warrants. The Fourth Amendment forbids not all searches but only unreasonable searches; the following seven chapters present the law of reasonable searches.

The law pertaining to search and seizure is often presented in three units dealing in turn with (1) search of the person, (2) search of the premises, and (3) search of motor vehicles. We have chosen instead to present the law of search and seizure in chapters identifying the authority by which officers may make a search and seizure. The charts on the following pages are intended to assist in summarizing and in cross-referencing.

AUTHORITY FOR ARREST, SEARCH, SEIZURE, AND DETENTION

TO MAKE:	THE OFFICER MUST BE ABLE TO SHOW AUTHORITY FROM:
AN ARREST	1. The fact that the officer has reasonable grounds to believe that the person is committing or has committed a crime (as defined by the statutes in his jurisdiction), or
	2. The existence of a valid arrest warrant (requirement as to where the warrant is at the time of the arrest is determined by the statutes of his jurisdiction)
A SEARCH	*The fact that the search is made:*
	1. Incident to a lawful arrest
	2. With consent
	3. Pursuant to a valid search warrant
	4. When an exigency exists where a life might be endangered or there is hot pursuit of a person who has committed a crime
	5. During an authorized temporary questioning when the officer reasonably suspects that he or another is in danger of physical injury (stop and frisk)
	6. When there exists probable cause arising out of circumstances known to the officer that an automobile (or any mobile object such as an airplane or boat) contains that which is subject to seizure by the officer. The Carroll Rule 267 U.S. 132 (1926)
	7. With the authority and within the scope of a right of lawful inspection
A SEIZURE	1. The fact that the valid search revealed that which could be seized by the officer, or
	2. The fact that contraband (or that which could be seized) was seen in plain view
A DETENTION	Statutory or common-law authority to make a reasonable detention

SEARCH OF THE PERSON

AUTHORITY FOR SEARCH	EVIDENCE NECESSARY TO JUSTIFY SEARCH	REASON AND PURPOSE FOR SEARCH	ALLOWABLE SCOPE OF SEARCH	TIME OF SEARCH	AUTHORITY OR REFERENCE
Incident to a lawful arrest	The arrest must be lawful and not a pretext to make such a search.	Officer's safety; to prevent escape; to obtain fruits of the crime; to preserve evidence of crime	The person and the area within his immediate control to accomplish the purpose of search	At the time and place of the arrest	See *Chimel v. California*
Search during temporary detention for questioning (stop and frisk)	Officer's reasonable fear for his safety	Self-protection of officer	A weapons search of the person	At the time of such detention	See Terry, Peters, and Sibron cases; see Chap. 11
Consent search	Voluntary, express consent of person	Search for weapons, contraband, or evidence	Area allowed by consent	Within a reasonable time and before revocation	See Chap. 12
Search warrant	Existence of a valid warrant	As stated in the warrant	Reasonable area necessary to comply with search required by warrant	Within time limit set by warrant or by statute	See Chap. 13
Within scope of lawful inspection	Lawful statute or authority to make inspection or search (customs search)	To comply with statute	Reasonabe area necessary to comply with inspection requirement	Within time limit set by statute or a reasonable time	See Chap. 14

SEARCH OF PRIVATE PREMISES

AUTHORITY FOR SEARCH	EVIDENCE NECESSARY TO JUSTIFY SEARCH	REASON AND PURPOSE FOR SEARCH	ALLOWABLE SCOPE OF SEARCH	TIME OF SEARCH	AUTHORITY OR REFERENCE
Exigency search	Existence of an exigency	To save lives; to prevent public disaster and hot pursuit	Reasonable area necessary to cope with exigency	During existence of exigency (*Davidson v. State*)	See *Ker v. California*, *Warden v. Hayden*
Incident to a lawful arrest	There must be a lawful arrest.	Officer's safety; to prevent escape; to obtain fruits of crime; to preserve evidence	The person and the area within his immediate control to accomplish the purpose of search	At the time of the arrest	See *Chimel v. California*
Consent search	Voluntary, express consent by person with authority to give consent	Search and seize evidence or contraband	Area allowed by consent	Within a reasonable time after consent	See *Bumper v. North Carolina*, *Stoner v. California*
Search warrant	Existence of a valid warrant	As stated in the warrant	Reasonable area necessary to comply with warrant	Within time limit set by warrant or statute	See Chap. 13
Within scope of lawful inspection	Lawful statute or authority to make inspection (licensed premises, for example)	To comply with statute	Reasonable area necessary to comply with inspection requirement	Within time limit set by statute	See Chap. 14

SEARCH OF MOTOR VEHICLES

AUTHORITY FOR SEARCH	EVIDENCE NECESSARY TO JUSTIFY SEARCH	REASON AND PURPOSE FOR SEARCH	ALLOWABLE SCOPE OF SEARCH	TIME OF SEARCH	AUTHORITY OR REFERENCE
Incident to a lawful arrest	Probable cause to arrest someone in the motor vehicle (pretext arrest will not justify search)	Officer's safety; to prevent escape; to obtain fruits of the crime; to preserve evidence of crime	The person and the area within his immediate control to accomplish the purpose of search	At the time and place of the arrest	See *Preston v. United States* *Chimel v. California*
Search during temporary detention for questioning (stop and frisk)	Officer's reasonable fear for his safety	Self-protection of officer	A weapons search of the person and area of car in his control	At the time of such detention	See *Terry, Peters, and Sibron* cases; see Chap. 11
Consent search	Voluntary, express consent by person with authority to give consent	To search for weapons, contraband, evidence, or hidden persons	Area allowed by consent	Within a reasonable time and before revocation	See Chap. 12
Probable-cause search under the Carroll rule	Officer has probable cause to believe that the vehicle contains that which is subject to seizure by the officer.	To find and preserve contraband or evidence	Area of vehicle where contraband or evidence could be hidden	Within a reasonable time	See *Chambers v. Maroney;* see Chap. 10
Search warrant	Existence of a valid warrant	As stated in the warrant	Reasonable area necessary to comply with search required by warrant	Within time limit set by warrant or by statute	See Chap. 13

| Within scope of lawful inspection | Lawful statute or authority to make inspection or search (customs search) | To comply with statute | Reasonable area necessary to comply with inspection requirement | Within time limit set by statute or a reasonable time | See Chap. 14 |
| Custodial search of impounded vehicle | Police regulation to inventory and protect property in their custody | To inventory and to protect property in police custody | Reasonable area to comply with regulations | Anytime | See Chap. 14 |

8

AUTHORITY TO SEARCH BECAUSE OF EXIGENCY

Law enforcement officers and other government officials have always been called upon to respond to exigencies or emergencies. Life has always been endangered by accidents, sudden illnesses, or criminal assault. The authority given to government officials to make entrances into private premises because of emergencies or exigencies is one of the doctrines of law which has existed since government has existed.

The authority for the entrance is the existence of an emergency or an exigency demanding immediate action by the officer with insufficient time for the officer to obtain a search warrant or court order to enter the premises. The officer must have reasonable grounds to believe that such emergency does exist in order to act. The types of emergencies which are discussed in this chapter do not include all the emergencies which could authorize the officer to act without prior judicial approval.

TO MAKE THE ENTRANCE OR THE SEARCH

In order to have reasonable grounds to believe that an emergency exists, the officer must have heard, seen, felt, tasted, or smelled something which led him to reasonably conclude that the exigency does exist. In some instances, the information which the officer receives could cause him to act immediately (a child or adult screaming). However, in other situations the information which the officer receives would cause him to investigate and seek facts to determine whether an exigency does exist.

Example: Neighbors call the police to report that they have not seen a seventy-year-old man in or around his home for the last two days. The neighbors are worried because he lives alone and had a heart attack a few years previously. The man did not mention that he was leaving on a

> trip. When the officers approach the house, they see the newspapers for the last two days at the front door.

Further investigation could consist in obtaining more detailed information and further pertinent facts from the reporting party. In the example given, after ringing and knocking at the front and back doors, the officers could look in and knock on the windows (if the person lives at the first-floor level). They could also telephone relatives and friends of the person to determine whether anything is known of his whereabouts.

After a reasonable effort is made to determine whether an emergency exists, thought can then be given as to how to make an entry into the premises. Entry would be easiest by obtaining a key or seeking an open window or an open door.

FORCED ENTRY

Before an entry is forced into private premises, the common-law requirements or the statutory requirements of the jurisdiction must be complied with. In federal jurisdictions, the 1970 federal "knock or no-knock" statute (see Chap. 17) must be complied with.

The common-law requirements are that the officer knock and identify himself, state his purpose, and await a refusal or silence before entering. These common-law requirements do not have to be observed if:

1. The officer has reasonable grounds to believe such notice is likely to endanger the life or the safety of the officer or another person
2. The officer has reasonable grounds to believe that such notice is likely to result in the evidence subject to seizure being easily and quickly destroyed or disposed of (this was the justification in the Ker case; see cases)
3. Such notice is likely to enable the party to be arrested to escape (hot pursuit of a dangerous felon)
4. Such notice would be a useless gesture (there has been a large explosion in the premises or there is a serious fire burning)

There are two good reasons for imposing such requirements on unannounced police entries into private premises:

1. Possibility of mistake:

> "... cases of mistaken identity are surely not novel in the investigation of crime. The possibility is very real that the police may be misinformed as to the name or address of a suspect, or as to other ma-

terial information.... Innocent citizens should not suffer the shock, fright or embarrassment attendant upon an unannounced police intrusion." U.S. Supreme Court in the Ker case (see cases; see also *Wayne v. United States*, 318 F.2d 205 (1963), where the investigating officers were given the wrong apartment number)

2. Protection of the officers:

"(it) ... is also a safeguard for the police themselves who might be mistaken for prowlers and be shot down by a fearful householder." U.S. Supreme Court in the Miller case (cases, Chap. 17)

In an exigency entrance such as looking for the seventy-year-old man, the officers should make an effort to minimize the damage to the premises. The apartment superintendent has a key, or a small panel of glass can be broken so that a door or window can be opened. The problem of repair and locking up will confront the officer when he is ready to leave. In some cases, the situation turns out not to be an emergency.

Example: A suburban police department received a telephone call from a mental institution. It was a Sunday night and one of the elderly patients from the institution had not returned after being given a weekend leave. The institution asked if the police would check the home of the elderly patient. When officers arrived, the house was dark and no one answered the doorbell. After knocking at the back door, the officers shined their flashlights into the windows of the house. When they came to a bedroom window, they could see that a person was in the bed. They knocked on the window but received no response. The person did not move. They called in to the station and were told to force an entry with minimum damage to the house. Once in the house, they went to the bedroom and turned on the light. The elderly man immediately sat up in bed and put on his hearing aid. He had lain down for a nap but instead had slept over five hours, causing the institution to become concerned about him.

WHEN THE EXIGENT ENTRY REVEALS A CRIME SCENE

Exigent entries are made every day in all large American cities. Nothing is found in some of the entries, but other entries reveal persons who have died of heart attacks or other physical causes. In some entries, officers arrive in time to save persons through first aid and immediate medical attention.

In most exigency entrances and searches, there is no intention on the part of the police officers either to arrest or to search and seize contraband or criminal evidence. The officers are performing their duty, and when they enter premises under exigency circumstances, they are legally where they have a right to be. Therefore, if while in and on the premises, they see contraband in plain view or uncover it in a reasonable exigency search, the evidence may be lawfully seized and will not be suppressed under the exclusionary rule.

In some instances, the exigency entrance reveals a crime scene. The officer may take any reasonable action to cope with the situation. His presence on the premises is lawful, and anything which he sees, hears, or uncovers in the reasonable performance of his duty can be lawfully seized and used as evidence. His obligation and duty consist of:

1. Rendering any assistance possible to the victim of the crime.
2. Determining, if possible, who the perpetrator of the crime is and whether the perpetrator is hiding or lurking on or near the crime scene. This would entail a search of the whole premises.
3. Preserving and collecting any evidence of the crime. This could include not only evidence from within the premises but also evidence found or obtained in or on the curtilage (the open space surrounding a dwelling which an average person would consider a part of the dwelling). This could include footprints from soft ground or, as in the Davidson case, the defendant's eyeglasses, which were found on the lawn.

SCOPE OF THE SEARCH

The scope of the search is any reasonable area necessary to cope with and handle the emergency. It could include the whole premises as in the Hayden case, and also the curtilage, as in the Davidson case; or depending on the type of emergency, it could be limited to a single room. The test which would be used would be the reasonableness test of the Fourth Amendment.

DURATION OF THE EXIGENCY AND AUTHORITY TO SEARCH

The authority to enter exists as long as the exigency or emergency exists and for a reasonable time after the exigency has ceased to exist, to conclude the necessary investigation of the incident. The authority to enter the premises the next day or several days after the exigency has ceased for further investigation is not authorized. The police would then have to obtain authority to enter by consent of persons in control of the premises or would have to obtain a search warrant in order to enter the premises lawfully.

Example: In *State v. Davidson*, 44 Wis.2d 177 (1969), the body of the deceased was found on October 14. On October 17, the police again entered the premises. As they had no authority for the October 17 entry (no search warrant or consent to enter), the search was held to be illegal. However, as the evidence obtained on October 17 was much the same as the evidence they had obtained on October 14, it was held not to be prejudicial error.

STANDING TO CHALLENGE OR OBJECT

In order to challenge the authority of the police to enter the premises, the defendant must have standing. To have standing, the defendant must be either the owner of the premises, a tenant, an invited guest, or lawfully on the premises in some way. A trespasser does not have standing to challenge the authority of the police to enter.

Example: X breaks into a home and kills the occupant and then burglarizes the home. X is a trespasser and does not have standing in court to challenge the authority of the police to enter the premises and investigate the crime.

Example: In the Davidson case, the defendant owned the home as a tenant in common with his deceased wife. At her death, he became the sole owner of the home and as· such he had standing to challenge the authority of the police to enter the second time on October 17.

EXIGENT SEARCHES OF THE PERSON
OR OF MOTOR VEHICLES

While most exigent searches are of premises, it is possible to make exigency searches of motor vehicles or of a person. The authority to make such a search would be the reasonable conclusion of the officer that an emergency exists. The test would be the need to make such a search, the reasonableness of the officer's action, and whether there was time to obtain a search warrant.

Examples of exigency searches of the person are:

PEOPLE v. SMITH, 265 N.E.2d 139 (1970)

The Supreme Court of Illinois sustained a conviction for the possession of marijuana, stating, "Here the officers were summoned to investigate the circumstances involving a distressed person. They found him in a stupor, not intoxicated apparently, for there was no odor of alcohol. But he was totally disoriented and incoherent, unable to answer their questions as to his condition or identity. For all they knew he may have been a diabetic in shock or a distressed cardiac patient. The officers were faced with an entirely different set of facts requiring different guide lines. This was an emergency situation where the welfare of the individual was at stake . . . we find that the search of defendant and the seizure of narcotics from his person were reasonable and lawful and not a violation of his constitutional rights."

PEOPLE v. SMITH, 254 N.E.2d 492 (1969)

In this case, the police found damaging evidence when they searched the wallet of a seriously wounded and semiconscious person. The Supreme Court of Illinois held that it was reasonable to ". . . consider that the wallet might provide information of value in the handling of the wounded man e.g. information concerning his blood type, being a diabetic, being unable to tolerate certain medications or anesthetics, religious affiliation, and that, in fact, had the officer failed to secure the wallet, a criticism of his professional conduct could not be lightly dismissed."

PEOPLE v. GONZALES, 5 CAL. RPTR. 920 (1960)

The court held that where the defendant was found either unconscious or nearly so with a knife wound, a search made for identification of the defendant was reasonable and lawful and the seizure of a package of marijuana from his pants pocket was not a violation of his constitutional rights.

UNITED STATES v. HICKEY, 247 F. SUPP. 621 (1965)

It was held that where an accused was so drunk when found in an alley that it was impossible for the police to be certain that he had given them his correct name and address, a search of defendant to obtain his wallet was justified. The court stated that it was not only the right but the duty of the arresting officer to search an arrested person if necessary to determine his true identity and that where evidence of a greater offense is uncovered in such a search incident to his arrest for intoxication such evidence is admissible against him in his trial on the greater offense.

INVASION OF THE BODY; SCHMERBER v. CALIFORNIA

Invasion of a person's body is probably the most severe form of interference with the person's right of privacy. In some limited instances, however, it is necessary to invade the suspect's body surface to extract evidence which would otherwise be lost. Operating a motor vehicle under the influence of an intoxicant is the leading example of such a situation which up to now has been decided by the Supreme Court of the United States.

The amount of alcohol in the blood can, through analysis, be reduced to evidence for presentation in court. In *Schmerber v. California* (see cases), the Court carefully described the limits to which the police could invade the body surface in securing evidence without a warrant and without consent. Such evidence, the Court explained, is not of a testimonial nature—not evidence extracted from the defendant's own lips—and therefore not within the protection afforded by the Fifth Amendment of the U.S. Constitution.

The Fourth Amendment, the Court explained, protects a person from searches "not justified under the circumstances." Probing beyond the body surface is certainly a search. It can *only* be made where the officers have a "clear indication" that the evidence they are searching for is there and that the evidence may disappear unless there is an immediate search.

Practically all states have adopted "implied-consent" laws which govern situations where the officer has reasonable grounds to believe that the driver of a vehicle is operating the vehicle while under the influence of intoxicants or narcotics. These laws do *not* nullify the principles enunciated in the Schmerber case. The state implied-consent laws prescribe procedures which officers must follow in that state. Some of the implied-consent laws are very effective and tough while other laws are not.

The principle of the exigency rule of the Schmerber case is that if the officer has reasonable grounds to believe that the evidence is in the body and may (or will) disappear before the officer can obtain a search warrant to extract the evidence, then he can act immediately, as in other emergency situations.

If the evidence will *not* be destroyed or disappear in a short time because of the body functions, or if the officer has other pieces of the same evidence, then there is no exigency and there is time for the officer to obtain a search warrant or a court order.

In *Rochin v. California*, 342 U.S. 165 (1952), the U.S. Supreme Court was confronted with a case where police officers had a doctor pump out the stomach of a narcotics peddler who had swallowed his narcotics. This was done without a search warrant or a court order. The Court held that the action was "conduct that shocks the conscience" and "methods too close to the rack and screw to permit constitutional differentiation." The Court overturned the state conviction allowing the evidence to be received.

However, in 1966 the Ninth Circuit Court of Appeals held that vomiting which was induced by allowing fluids to flow into the stomach through a tube inserted through the nose of the defendant did not violate the defendant's constitutional rights. *Blefare v. United States*, 362 F.2d 870 (9th Cir. 1966). The packets of heroin discovered were held to be admissible over the objection that they constituted illegally acquired evidence.

HOT PURSUIT OR CLOSE PURSUIT

Hot pursuit or close pursuit is another example of a type of exigent circumstance which justifies entry without a warrant to apprehend and arrest a suspect. The search justified in a hot-pursuit situation must always be supported by probable cause. The information within the officer's knowledge must be such as would convince a magistrate to issue a warrant otherwise. The officer must be prepared to articulate his information as well as his own personal observation in a detailed, professional manner so that the reviewing court may make a determination as to whether or not the situation presented was of such character as to justify the hot-pursuit search.

FIRE EMERGENCIES

Many states have statutorized the common-law right of fire officers to go upon and enter any property or premises and do whatever may reasonably be necessary in the performance of their duties of putting out fires, aiding persons, or minimizing the loss of property. If, in the performance of such duty, they come upon contraband or evidence of a crime, they may seize such evidence or call in law enforcement officers to handle the investigation.

In order to make such an exigency entry, the fire officer must have reasonable ground to believe that such an emergency exists. Thus, the firemen arriving at a city home out of which smoke and fire are pouring cannot be denied entry to the home by the owner, who may be attempting to destroy evidence of a crime which he has committed.

CAMPUS PROBLEMS OF THE 1970S

New types of problems have arisen as a result of campus disorders in recent years. An example of the problems confronting law enforcement officers occurred in 1970, when students seized and occupied a chapel building in a large midwestern university. When university officials found that they could not get in and could not get the students out of the chapel, they called the police.

When the students would not leave the chapel for the police, the university officials asked the police to break the door down and arrest the students. As the police could see no emergency, they told the university officials to have their people break the door down and they would then make the arrests. The university officials would not order this done, and so everybody sat down and waited.

After a few hours, city fire trucks and firemen arrived at the scene. Someone had telephoned that there was a bomb in the chapel. The door was then broken down, and the students were arrested.

At the trial, the charges against the students were dismissed when the trial judge ruled that the police should have announced their intention to break down the door just before it was broken down, giving the students one last chance to come out of the chapel.

CASES FOR CHAPTER EIGHT

SCHMERBER v. CALIFORNIA
SUPREME COURT OF THE UNITED STATES
384 U.S. 757, 16 L. ED. 2d 908, 86 S. CT. 1826 (1965)

Petitioner was convicted in Los Angeles Municipal Court of the criminal offense of driving an automobile while under the influence of intoxicating liquor.[1] He had been arrested at a hospital while receiving treatment for injuries suffered in an accident involving the automobile that he had apparently been driving.[2] At the direction of a police officer, a blood sample was then withdrawn from petitioner's body by a physician at the hospital. The chemical analysis of this sample revealed a percent by weight of alcohol in his blood at the time of the offense which indicated intoxication, and the report of this analysis was admitted in evidence at the trial. Petitioner objected to receipt of this evidence of the analysis on the ground that the blood had been withdrawn despite his refusal, on the advice of his counsel, to consent to the test. He contended that in that circumstance the withdrawal of the blood and the admission of the analysis in evidence denied him due process of law under the Fourteenth Amendment, as well as specific guarantees of the Bill of Rights secured against the States by that Amendment: his privilege against self-incrimination under the Fifth Amendment; his right to counsel under the Sixth Amendment; and his right not to be subjected to unreasonable searches and seizures in violation of the Fourth Amendment. The Appellate Department of the California Superior Court rejected these contentions and affirmed the conviction. In view of constitutional decisions since we last considered these issues in Breithaupt v Abram, 352 US 432, we granted certiorari. We affirm.

I. THE DUE PROCESS CLAUSE CLAIM.

Breithaupt was also a case in which police officers caused blood to be withdrawn from the driver of an automobile involved in an accident, and in which there was ample justification for the officer's conclusion that the driver was under the influence of alcohol. There, as here, the extraction was made by a physician in a simple, medically acceptable manner in a hospital environment. There, however, the driver was unconscious at the time the blood was withdrawn and hence had no opportunity to object to the procedure. We affirmed the conviction there

---

[1] California Vehicle Code § 23102 (a) provides, in pertinent part, "it is unlawful for any person who is under the influence of intoxicating liquor ... to drive a vehicle upon any highway...." The offense is a misdemeanor.

[2] Petitioner and a companion had been drinking at a tavern and bowling alley. There was evidence showing that petitioner was driving from the bowling alley about midnight November 12, 1964, when the car skidded, crossed the road and struck a tree. Both petitioner and his companion were injured and taken to a hospital for treatment.

resulting from the use of the test in evidence, holding that under such circumstances the withdrawal did not offend "that 'sense of justice' of which we spoke in Rochin v California, 342 US 165." Breithaupt thus requires the rejection of petitioner's due process argument, and nothing in the circumstances of this case or in supervening events persuades us that this aspect of Breithaupt should be overruled.

II. THE PRIVILEGE AGAINST SELF-INCRIMINATION CLAIM.

Breithaupt summarily rejected an argument that the withdrawal of blood and the admission of the analysis report involved in that state case violated the Fifth Amendment privilege of any person not to "be compelled in any criminal case to be a witness against himself," citing Twining v New Jersey, 211 US 78, 53 L ed 97, 29 S Ct 14. But that case, holding that the protections of the Fourteenth Amendment do not embrace this Fifth Amendment privilege, has been succeeded by Malloy v Hogan, 378 US 1, 8. We there held that "[t]he Fourteenth Amendment secures against state invasion the same privilege that the Fifth Amendment guarantees against federal infringement—the right of a person to remain silent unless he chooses to speak in the unfettered exercise of his own will, and to suffer no penalty . . . for such silence." We therefore must now decide whether the withdrawal of the blood and admission in evidence of the analysis involved in this case violated petitioner's privilege. We hold that the privilege protects an accused only from being compelled to testify against himself, or otherwise provide the State with evidence of a testimonial or communicative nature,[3] and that the withdrawal of blood and use of the analysis in question in this case did not involve compulsion to these ends.

It could not be denied that in requiring petitioner to submit to the withdrawal and chemical analysis of his blood the State compelled him to submit to an attempt to discover evidence that might be used to prosecute him for a criminal offense. He submitted only after the police officer rejected his objection and directed the physician to proceed. The officer's direction to the physician to administer the test over petitioner's objection constituted compulsion for the purposes of the privilege. The critical question, then, is whether petitioner was thus compelled "to be a witness against himself."[4]

---

[3] A dissent suggests that the report of the blood test was "testimonial" or "communicative," because the test was performed in order to obtain the testimony of others, communicating to the jury facts about petitioner's condition. Of course, all evidence received in court is "testimonial" or "communicative" if these words are thus used. But the Fifth Amendment relates only to acts on the part of the person to whom the privilege applies, and we use these words subject to the same limitations. A nod or head-shake is as much a "testimonial" or "communicative" act in this sense as are spoken words. But the terms as we use them do not apply to evidence of acts noncommunicative in nature as to the person asserting the privilege, even though, as here, such acts are compelled to obtain the testimony of others.
[4] Many state constitutions, including those of most of the original Colonies, phrase the privilege in terms of compelling a person to give "evidence" against himself. But our decision cannot turn on the Fifth Amendment's use of the word "witness." "[A]s the manifest purpose of the constitutional provisions, both of the States and of the United States, is to prohibit the compelling of testimony of a self-incriminating kind from a party or a witness, the liberal construction which must be placed upon constitutional provisions for the protection of personal rights would seem to require that the constitutional guaranties, however differently worded, should have as far as possible the same interpretation. . . ."

If the scope of the privilege coincided with the complex of values it helps to protect, we might be obliged to conclude that the privilege was violated. In Miranda v Arizona, 384 US 436, the Court said of the interests protected by the privilege: "All these policies point to one overriding thought: the constitutional foundation underlying the privilege is the respect a government—state or federal—must accord to the dignity and integrity of its citizens. To maintain a 'fair state-individual balance,' to require the government 'to shoulder the entire load' ... to respect the inviolability of the human personality, our accusatory system of criminal justice demands that the government seeking to punish an individual produce the evidence against him by its own independent labors, rather than by the cruel, simple expedient of compelling it from his own mouth." The withdrawal of blood necessarily involves puncturing the skin for extraction, and the percent by weight of alcohol in that blood, as established by chemical analysis, is evidence of criminal guilt. Compelled submission fails on one view to respect the "inviolability of the human personality." Moreover, since it enables the State to rely on evidence forced from the accused, the compulsion violates at least one meaning of the requirement that the State procure the evidence against an accused "by its own independent labors."

As the passage in Miranda implicitly recognizes, however, the privilege has never been given the full scope which the values it helps to protect suggest. History and a long line of authorities in lower courts have consistently limited its protection to situations in which the State seeks to submerge those values by obtaining the evidence against an accused through "the cruel, simple expedient of compelling it from his own mouth. ... In sum, the privilege is fulfilled only when the person is guaranteed the right 'to remain silent unless he chooses to speak in the unfettered exercise of his own will.'" Ibid. The leading case in this Court is Holt v United States, 218 US 245. There the question was whether evidence was admissible that the accused, prior to trial and over his protest, put on a blouse that fitted him. It was contended that compelling the accused to submit to the demand that he model the blouse violated the privilege. Mr. Justice Holmes, speaking for the Court, rejected the argument as "based upon an extravagant extension of the Fifth Amendment," and went on to say: "[T]he prohibition of compelling a man in a criminal court to be witness against himself is a prohibition of the use of physical or moral compulsion to extort communications from him, not an exclusion of his body as evidence when it may be material. The objection in principle would forbid a jury to look at a prisoner and compare his features with a photograph in proof."

It is clear that the protection of the privilege reaches an accused's communications, whatever form they might take, and the compulsion of responses which are also communications, for example, compliance with a subpoena to produce one's papers.

On the other hand, both federal and state courts have usually held that it offers no protection against compulsion to submit to fingerprinting, photographing, or measurements, to write or speak for identification, to appear in court, to stand, to assume a stance, to walk, or to make a particular gesture. The distinction which has emerged, often expressed in different ways, is that the privilege is a bar against compelling "communications" or "testimony," but that compulsion which makes a suspect or accused the source of "real or physical evidence" does not violate it.

Although we agree that this distinction is a helpful framework for analysis, we are not to be understood to agree with past applications in all instances.

There will be many cases in which such a distinction is not readily drawn. Some tests seemingly directed to obtain "physical evidence," for example, lie detector tests measuring changes in body function during interrogation, may actually be directed to eliciting responses which are essentially testimonial. To compel a person to submit to testing in which an effort will be made to determine his guilt or innocence on the basis of physiological responses, whether willed or not, is to evoke the spirit and history of the Fifth Amendment. Such situations call to mind the principle that the protection of the privilege "is as broad as the mischief against which it seeks to guard."

In the present case, however, no such problem of application is presented. Not even a shadow of testimonial compulsion upon or enforced communication by the accused was involved either in the extraction or in the chemical analysis. Petitioner's testimonial capacities were in no way implicated; indeed, his participation, except as a donor, was irrelevant to the results of the test, which depend on chemical analysis and on that alone. Since the blood test evidence, although an incriminating product of compulsion, was neither petitioner's testimony nor evidence relating to some communicative act or writing by the petitioner, it was not inadmissible on privilege grounds.

III. THE RIGHT TO COUNSEL CLAIM.

This conclusion also answers petitioner's claim that in compelling him to submit to the test in face of the fact that his objection was made on the advice of counsel, he was denied his Sixth Amendment right to the assistance of counsel. Since petitioner was not entitled to assert the privilege, he has no greater right because counsel erroneously advised him that he could assert it. His claim is strictly limited to the failure of the police to respect his wish, reinforced by counsel's advice, to be left inviolate. No issue of counsel's ability to assist petitioner in respect of any rights he did possess is presented. The limited claim thus made must be rejected.

IV. THE SEARCH AND SEIZURE CLAIM.

In Breithaupt, as here, it was also contended that the chemical analysis should be excluded from evidence as the product of an unlawful search and seizure in violation of the Fourth and Fourteenth Amendments. The Court did not decide whether the extraction of blood in that case was unlawful, but rejected the claim on the basis of Wolf v Colorado, 338 US 25. That case had held that the Constitution did not require, in state prosecutions for state crimes, the exclusion of evidence obtained in violation of the Fourth Amendment's provisions. We have since overruled Wolf in that respect, holding in Mapp v Ohio, 367 US 643, that the exclusionary rule adopted for federal prosecutions in Weeks v United States 232 US 383, must also be applied in criminal prosecutions in state courts. The question is squarely presented therefore, whether the chemical analysis introduced in evidence in this case should have been excluded as the product of an unconstitutional search and seizure.

The overriding function of the Fourth Amendment is to protect personal privacy and dignity against unwarranted intrusion by the State. In Wolf we recognized "[t]he security of one's privacy against arbitrary intrusion by the police" as being "at the core of the Fourth Amendment" and "basic to a free society." We reaffirmed that broad view of the Amendment's purpose in applying the federal exclusionary rule to the States in Mapp.

The values protected by the Fourth Amendment thus substantially overlap those the Fifth Amendment helps to protect. History and precedent have required that we today reject the claim that the Self-Incrimination Clause of the Fifth

Amendment requires the human body in all circumstances to be held inviolate against state expeditions seeking evidence of crime. But if compulsory administration of a blood test does not implicate the Fifth Amendment, it plainly involves the broadly conceived reach of a search and seizure under the Fourth Amendment. That Amendment expressly provides that "[t]he right of the people to be secure in their *persons*, houses, papers, and effects, against unreasonable searches and seizures, shall not be violated...." (Emphasis added.) It could not reasonably be argued, and indeed respondent does not argue, that the administration of the blood test in this case was free of the constraints of the Fourth Amendment. Such testing procedures plainly constitute searches of "persons," and depend antecedently upon seizures of "persons," within the meaning of that Amendment.

Because we are dealing with intrusions into the human body rather than with state interferences with property relationships or private papers—"houses, papers, and effects"—we write on a clean slate. Limitations on the kinds of property which may be seized under warrant, as distinct from the procedures for search and the permissible scope of search, are not instructive in this context. We begin with the assumption that once the privilege against self-incrimination has been found not to bar compelled intrusions into the body for blood to be analyzed for alcohol content, the Fourth Amendment's proper function is to constrain, not against all intrusions as such, but against intrusions which are not justified in the circumstances, or which are made in an improper manner. In other words, the questions we must decide in this case are whether the police were justified in requiring petitioner to submit to the blood test, and whether the means and procedures employed in taking his blood respected relevant Fourth Amendment standards of reasonableness.

In this case, as will often be true when charges of driving under the influence of alcohol are pressed, these questions arise in the context of an arrest made by an officer without a warrant. Here, there was plainly probable cause for the officer to arrest petitioner and charge him with driving an automobile while under the influence of intoxicating liquor.[5] The police officer who arrived at the scene shortly after the accident smelled liquor on petitioner's breath, and testified that petitioner's eyes were "bloodshot, watery, sort of a glassy appearance." The officer saw petitioner again at the hospital, within two hours of the accident. There he noticed similar symptoms of drunkenness. He thereupon informed petitioner "that he was under arrest and that he was entitled to the services of an attorney, and that he could remain silent, and that anything that he told me would be used against him in evidence."

While early cases suggest that there is an unrestricted "right on the part of the Government, always recognized under English and American law, to search the person of the accused when legally arrested to discover and seize the fruits or evidences of crime," Weeks v United States, 232 US 383, the mere fact of a lawful arrest does not end our inquiry. The suggestion of these cases apparently rests on two factors—first, there may be more immediate danger of concealed weapons or

---

[5] California law authorizes a peace officer to arrest "without a warrant ... [w]henever he has reasonable cause to believe that the person to be arrested has committed a felony, whether or not a felony has in fact been committed." Cal Penal Code § 836.3. Although petitioner was ultimately prosecuted for a misdemeanor, he was subject to prosecution for the felony since a companion in his car was injured in the accident, which apparently was the result of traffic law violations. Cal Vehicle Code § 23101. California's test of probable cause follows the federal standard. People v Cockrell, 63 Cal 2d 659, 408 P2d 116 (1965).

of destruction of evidence under the direct control of the accused, second, once a search of the arrested person for weapons is permitted, it would be both impractical and unnecessary to enforcement of the Fourth Amendment's purpose to attempt to confine the search to those objects alone. Whatever the validity of these considerations in general, they have little applicability with respect to searches involving intrusions beyond the body's surface. The interests in human dignity and privacy which the Fourth Amendment protects forbid any such intrusions on the mere chance that desired evidence might be obtained. In the absence of a clear indication that in fact such evidence will be found, these fundamental human interests require law officers to suffer the risk that such evidence may disappear unless there is an immediate search.

Although the facts which established probable cause to arrest in this case also suggested the required relevance and likely success of a test of petitioner's blood for alcohol, the question remains whether the arresting officer was permitted to draw these inferences himself, or was required instead to procure a warrant before proceeding with the test. Search warrants are ordinarily required for searches of dwellings, and, absent an emergency, no less could be required where intrusions into the human body are concerned. The requirement that a warrant be obtained is a requirement that the inferences to support the search "be drawn by a neutral and detached magistrate instead of being judged by the officer engaged in the often competitive enterprise of ferreting out crime."

The importance of informed, detached and deliberate determinations of the issue whether or not to invade another's body in search of evidence of guilt is indisputable and great.

The officer in the present case, however, might reasonably have believed that he was confronted with an emergency, in which the delay necessary to obtain a warrant, under the circumstances, threatened "the destruction of evidence."

We are told that the percentage of alcohol in the blood begins to diminish shortly after drinking stops, as the body functions to eliminate it from the system. Particularly in a case such as this, where time had to be taken to bring the accused to a hospital and to investigate the scene of the accident, there was no time to seek out a magistrate and secure a warrant. Given these special facts, we conclude that the attempt to secure evidence of blood-alcohol content in this case was an appropriate incident to petitioner's arrest.

Similarly, we are satisfied that the test chosen to measure petitioner's blood-alcohol level was a reasonable one. Extraction of blood samples for testing is a highly effective means of determining the degree to which a person is under the influence of alcohol. Such tests are a commonplace in these days of periodic physical examinations [6] and experience with them teaches that the quantity of blood extracted is minimal, and that for most people the procedure involves virtually no risk, trauma, or pain. Petitioner is not one of the few who on grounds of fear, concern for health, or religious scruple might prefer some other means of testing, such as the "breathalyzer" test petitioner refused. We need not decide whether such wishes would have to be respected.

Finally, the record shows that the test was performed in a reasonable manner. Petitioner's blood was taken by a physician in a hospital environment according

---

[6] "The blood test procedure has become routine in our everyday life. It is a ritual for those going into the military service as well as those applying for marriage licenses. Many colleges require such tests before permitting entrance and literally millions of us have voluntarily gone through the same, though a longer, routine in becoming blood donors." Breithaupt v Abram, 352 US at 436, 1 L ed 2d at 451.

to accepted medical practices. We are thus not presented with the serious questions which would arise if a search involving use of medical technique, even of the most rudimentary sort, were made by other than medical personnel or in other than a medical environment—for example, if it were administered by police in the privacy of the stationhouse. To tolerate searches under these conditions might be to invite an unjustified element of personal risk of infection and pain.

We thus conclude that the present record shows no violation of petitioner's right under the Fourth and Fourteenth Amendments to be free of unreasonable searches and seizures. It bears repeating, however, that we reach this judgment only on the facts of the present record. The integrity of an individual's person is a cherished value of our society. That we today hold that the Constitution does not forbid the States minor intrusions into an individual's body under stringently limited conditions in no way indicates that it permits more substantial intrusions, or intrusions under other conditions.

Affirmed.

KER v. CALIFORNIA
SUPREME COURT OF THE UNITED STATES
374 U.S. 23 (1963)

Mr. Justice Clark delivered the opinion of the Court with reference to the standard by which state searches and seizures must be evaluated (Part I), together with an opinion applying that standard, in which Mr. Justice Black, Mr. Justice Stewart and Mr. Justice White join (Parts II–V), and announced the judgment of the Court.

This case raises search and seizure questions under the rule of *Mapp v. Ohio.* Petitioners, husband and wife, were convicted of possession of marijuana in violation of § 11530 of the California Health and Safety Code. The California District Court of Appeal affirmed despite the contention of petitioners that their arrests in their apartment without warrants lacked probable cause and the evidence seized incident thereto and introduced at their trial was therefore inadmissible. The California Supreme Court denied without opinion a petition for hearing. This being the first case arriving here since our opinion in *Mapp* which would afford suitable opportunity for further explication of that holding in the light of intervening experience, we granted certiorari. We affirm the judgment before us.

The state courts' conviction and affirmance are based on these events, which culminated in the petitioners' arrests. Sergeant Cook of the Los Angeles County Sheriff's Office, in negotiating the purchase of marijuana, from one Terrhagen, accompanied him to a bowling alley about 7 p. m. on July 26, 1960, where they were to meet Terrhagen's "connection." Terrhagen went inside and returned shortly, pointing to a 1946 DeSoto as his "connection's" automobile and explaining that they were to meet him "up by the oil fields" near Fairfax and Slauson Avenues in Los Angeles. As they neared that location, Terrhagen again pointed out the DeSoto traveling ahead of them, stating that the "connection" kept his supply of narcotics "somewhere up in the hills." They parked near some vacant fields in the vicinity of the intersection of Fairfax and Slauson, and, shortly thereafter, the DeSoto reappeared and pulled up beside them. The deputy then recognized the driver as one Roland Murphy, whose "mug" photograph he had seen and whom he knew from other narcotics officers to be a large-scale seller of marijuana currently out on bail in connection with narcotics charges.

Terrhagen entered the DeSoto and drove off toward the oil fields with Murphy, while the Sergeant waited. They returned shortly, Terrhagen left Murphy's car carrying a package of marijuana and entered his own vehicle, and they drove to Terrhagen's residence. There Terrhagen cut one pound of marijuana and gave it to Sergeant Cook, who had previously paid him. The Sergeant later reported this occurrence to Los Angeles County Officers Berman and Warthen, the latter of whom had observed the occurrences as well.

On the following day, July 27, Murphy was placed under surveillance. Officer Warthen, who had observed the Terrhagen-Murphy episode the previous night, and Officer Markman were assigned this duty. At about 7 p. m. that evening they followed Murphy's DeSoto as he drove to the same bowling alley in which he had met Terrhagen on the previous evening. Murphy went inside, emerged in about 10 minutes and drove to a house where he made a brief visit. The officers continued to follow him but, upon losing sight of his vehicle, proceeded to the vicinity of Fairfax and Slauson Avenues where they parked. There, immediately across the street from the location at which Terrhagen and Sergeant Cook had met Murphy on the previous evening, the officers observed a parked automobile whose lone occupant they later determined to be the petitioner George Douglas Ker.

The officers then saw Murphy drive past them. They followed but lost sight of him when he extinguished his lights and entered the oil fields. The officers returned to their vantage point and, shortly thereafter, observed Murphy return and park behind Ker. From their location approximately 1,000 feet from the two vehicles, they watched through field glasses. Murphy was seen leaving his DeSoto and walking up to the driver's side of Ker's car, where he "appeared to have conversation with him." It was shortly before 9 p. m. and the distance in the twilight was too great for the officers to see anything pass between Murphy and Ker or whether the former had anything in his hands as he approached.

While Murphy and Ker were talking, the officers had driven past them in order to see their faces closely and in order to take the license number from Ker's vehicle. Soon thereafter Ker drove away and the officers followed him but lost him when he made a U-turn in the middle of the block and drove in the opposite direction. Now, having lost contact with Ker, they checked the registration with the Department of Motor Vehicles and ascertained that the automobile was registered to Douglas Ker at 4801 Slauson. They then communicated this information to Officer Berman, within 15 to 30 minutes after observing the meeting between Ker and Murphy. The officers Warthen and Markman had no previous knowledge of Ker. Berman had received information at various times beginning in November of 1959 that Ker was selling marijuana from his apartment and that "he was possibly securing this Marijuana from Ronnie Murphy who is the alias of Roland Murphy." In early 1960 Officer Berman had received a "mug" photograph of Ker from the Inglewood Police Department. He further testified that between May and July 27, 1960, he had received information as to Ker from one Robert Black, who had previously given information leading to at least three arrests and whose information was believed by Berman to be reliable. According to Officer Berman, Black had told him on four or five occasions after May 1960 that Ker and others, including himself, had purchased marijuana from Murphy.

Armed with the knowledge of the meeting between Ker and Murphy and with Berman's information as to Ker's dealings with Murphy, the three officers and a fourth, Officer Love, proceeded immediately to the address which they had obtained through Ker's license number. They found the automobile which they had been following—and which they had learned was Ker's—in the parking lot of the multiple-apartment building and also ascertained that there was someone in the Kers' apartment. They then went to the office of the building manager and obtained from him a passkey to the apartment. Officer Markman was stationed outside the window to intercept any evidence which might be ejected, and the other three officers entered the apartment. Officer Berman unlocked and opened the door, proceeding quietly, he testified, in order to prevent the destruction of evidence, and found petitioner George Ker sitting in the living room. Just as he identified himself, stating that "We are Sheriff's Narcotics Officers, conducting a narcotics investigation," petitioner Diane Ker emerged from the kitchen. Berman testified that he repeated his identification to her and immediately walked to the kitchen. Without entering, he observed through the open doorway a small scale atop the kitchen sink, upon which lay a "brick-like—brick-shaped package containing the green leafy substance" which he recognized as marijuana. He beckoned the petitioners into the kitchen where, following their denial of knowledge of the contents of the two-and-two-tenths-pound package and failure to answer a question as to its ownership, he placed them under arrest for suspicion of violating the State Narcotic Law. Officer Markman testified that he entered the apartment approximately "a minute, a minute and a half" after the other officers, at which time Officer Berman was placing the petitioners under arrest. As to this sequence of events, petitioner George Ker testified that his arrest took place immediately upon the officers' entry and before they saw the brick of marijuana in the kitchen.

Subsequent to the arrest and the petitioners' denial of possession of any other narcotics, the officers, proceeding without search warrants, found a half-ounce package of marijuana in the kitchen cupboard and another atop the bedroom dresser. Petitioners were asked if they had any other automobile other than the one observed by the officers, and George Ker replied in the negative, while Diane remained silent. On the next day, having learned that an automobile was registered in the name of Diane Ker, Officer Warthen searched this car without a warrant, finding marijuana and marijuana seeds in the glove compartment and under the rear seat. The marijuana found on the kitchen scale, that found in the kitchen cupboard and in the bedroom, and that found in Diane Ker's automobile were all introduced into evidence against the petitioners.

The California District Court of Appeal in affirming the convictions found that there was probable cause for the arrests; that the entry into the apartment was for the purpose of arrest and was not unlawful; and that the search being incident to the arrest was likewise lawful and its fruits admissible in evidence against petitioners. These conclusions were essential to the affirmance, since the California Supreme Court in 1955 had held that evidence obtained by means of unlawful searches and seizures was inadmissible in criminal trials. The court concluded that in view of its findings and the implied findings of the trial court, this Court's intervening decision in *Mapp v. Ohio*, did "not justify a change in our original conclusion."

I.

In *Mapp v. Ohio*, we followed *Boyd v. United States*, which held that the Fourth Amendment implemented by the self-incrimination clause of the Fifth, forbids the Federal Government to convict a man of crime by using testimony or papers obtained from him by unreasonable searches and seizures as defined in the Fourth Amendment. We specifically held in *Mapp* that this constitutional prohibition is enforceable against the States through the Fourteenth Amendment. This means, as we said in *Mapp*, that the Fourth Amendment "is enforceable against them [the states] by the same sanction of exclusion as is used against the Federal

Government," by the application of the same constitutional standard prohibiting "unreasonable searches and seizures." We now face the specific question as to whether *Mapp* requires the exclusion of evidence in this case which the California District Court of Appeal has held to be lawfully seized. It is perhaps ironic that the initial test under the *Mapp* holding comes from California, whose decision voluntarily to adopt the exclusionary rule in 1955 has been commended by us previously. See *Mapp v. Ohio; Elkins v. United States.*

Preliminary to our examination of the search and seizures involved here, it might be helpful for us to indicate what was not decided in *Mapp.* First, it must be recognized that the "principles governing the admissibility of evidence in federal criminal trials have not been restricted . . . to those derived solely from the Constitution. In the exercise of its supervisory authority over the administration of criminal justice in the federal courts . . . this Court has . . . formulated rules of evidence to be applied in federal criminal prosecutions." *McNabb v. United States. Mapp,* however, established no assumption by this Court of supervisory authority over state courts, cf. *Cleary v. Bolger,* and, consequently, it implied no total obliteration of state laws relating to arrest and searches in favor of federal law. *Mapp* sounded no death knell for our federalism; rather, it echoed the sentiment of *Elkins v. United States* that "a healthy federalism depends upon the avoidance of needless conflict between state and federal courts" by itself urging that "[f]ederal-state cooperation in the solution of crime under constitutional standards will be promoted, if only by recognition of their now mutual obligation to respect *the same fundamental criteria* in their approaches. Second, *Mapp* did not attempt the impossible task of laying down a "fixed formula" for the application in specific cases of the constitutional prohibition against unreasonable searches and seizures; it recognized that we would be "met with 'recurring questions of the reasonableness of searches'" and that "at any rate, '[r]easonableness is in the first instance for the [trial court] . . . to determine,'" thus indicating that the usual weight be given to findings of trial courts.

Mapp, of course, did not lend itself to a detailed explication of standards, since the search involved there was clearly unreasonable and bore no stamp of legality even from the Ohio Supreme Court. This is true also of *Elkins v. United States,* where all of the courts assumed the unreasonableness of the search in question and this Court "invoked" its "supervisory power over the administration of criminal justice in the federal courts," in declaring that the evidence so seized by state officers was inadmissible in a federal prosecution. The prosecution being in a federal court, this Court of course announced that "[t]he test is one of federal law, neither enlarged by what one state court may have countenanced, nor diminished by what another may have colorably suppressed." Significantly in the *Elkins* holding is the statement, apposite here, that "it can fairly be said that in applying the Fourth Amendment this Court has seldom shown itself unaware of the practical demands of effective criminal investigation and law enforcement."

Implicit in the Fourth Amendment's protection from unreasonable searches and seizures is its recognition of individual freedom. That safeguard has been declared to be "as of the very essence of constitutional liberty" the guaranty of which "is as important and as imperative as are the guaranties of the other fundamental rights of the individual citizen. . . ." *Gouled v. United States.* While the language of the Amendment is "general," it "forbids every search that is unreasonable; it protects all, those suspected or known to be offenders as well as the innocent, and unquestionably extends to the premises where the search was made. . . ." *Go-Bart Importing Co. v. United States.* Mr. Justice Butler there stated for the Court that "[t]he Amendment is to be liberally construed and all owe the duty of vigilance for its effective enforcement lest there shall be impairment of the rights for the protection of which it was adopted." He also recognized that "[t]here is no formula for the determination of reasonableness. Each case is to be decided on its own facts and circumstances."

This Court's long-established recognition that standards of reasonableness under the Fourth Amendment are not susceptible of Procrustean application is carried forward when that Amendment's proscriptions are enforced against the States through the Fourteenth Amendment. And, although the standard of reasonableness is the same under the Fourth and Fourteenth Amendments, the demands of our federal system compel us to distinguish between evidence held inadmissible because of our supervisory powers over federal courts and that held inadmissible because prohibited by the United States Constitution. We reiterate that the reasonableness of a search is in the first instance a substantive determination to be made by the trial court from the facts and circumstances of the case and in the light of the "fundamental criteria" laid down by the Fourth Amendment and in opinions of this Court applying that Amendment. Findings of reasonableness, of course, are respected only insofar as consistent with federal constitutional guarantees. As we have stated above and in other cases involving federal constitutional rights, findings of state courts are by no means insulated against examination here. While this Court does not sit as in *nisi prius* to appraise contradictory factual questions, it will, where necessary to the determination of constitutional rights, make an independent examination of the facts, the findings, and the record so that it can determine for itself whether in the decision as to reasonableness the fundamental—i.e., constitutional—criteria established by this Court have been respected. The States are not thereby precluded from developing workable rules governing arrests, searches and seizures to meet "the practical demands of effective criminal investigation and law enforcement" in the States, provided that those rules do not violate the constitutional proscription of unreasonable searches and seizures and the concomitant command that evidence so seized is inadmissible against one who has standing to complain. See *Jones v. United States.* Such a standard implies no derogation of uniformity in applying federal constitutional guarantees but is only a recognition that conditions and circumstances vary just as do investigative and enforcement techniques.

Applying this federal constitutional standard we proceed to examine the entire record including the findings of California's courts to determine whether the evidence seized from petitioners was constitutionally admissible under the circumstances of this case.

II.

The evidence at issue, in order to be admissible, must be the product of a search incident to a lawful arrest, since the officers had no search warrant. The lawfulness of the arrest without warrant, in turn, must be based upon probable cause, which exists "where 'the facts and circumstances within their [the officers'] knowledge and of which they had reasonably trustworthy information [are] sufficient in themselves to warrant a man of reasonable caution in the belief that' an offense has been or is being committed." *Brinegar v. United States.* The information within the knowledge of the officers at the time they arrived at the Kers' apartment, as California's courts specifically found, clearly furnished grounds for a reasonable belief that petitioner George Ker had committed and was committing the offense of possession of marijuana. Officers Markman and Warthen observed a rendezvous between Murphy and Ker on the evening of the arrest which was a virtual reenactment of the previous night's encounter between Murphy, Terrhagen and Sergeant Cook, which concluded in the sale by Murphy to Terrhagen and the Sergeant of a package of marijuana of which the latter had paid Terrhagen for one pound which he received from Terrhagen after the encounter with Murphy. To be sure, the distance and lack of light prevented the officers from seeing and they did not see any substance pass between the two men, but the virtual identity of the surrounding circumstances warranted a strong suspicion that the one remaining element—a sale of narcotics—was a part of this encounter as it was the previous night. But Ker's arrest does not depend upon this single episode with Murphy. When Ker's U-turn thwarted the officer's pursuit, they learned his name and address from the Department of Motor Vehicles and reported the occurrence to Officer Berman. Berman, in turn, revealed information from an informer whose reliability had been tested previously, as well as from other sources, not only that Ker had been selling marijuana from his apartment but also that his likely supply was Murphy himself. That this information was hearsay does not destroy its role in establishing probable cause. *Brinegar v. United States.* In *Draper v. United States,* we held that information from a reliable informer, corroborated by the agents' observations as to the accuracy of the informer's description of the accused and of his presence at a particular place, was sufficient to establish probable cause for an arrest without warrant. The corroborative elements in *Draper* were innocuous in themselves, but here both the informer's tip and the personal observations connected Ker with specific illegal activities involving the same man, Murphy, a known marijuana dealer. To say that this coincidence of information was sufficient to support a reasonable belief of the officers that Ker was illegally in possession of marijuana is to indulge in understatement.

Probable cause for the arrest of petitioner Diane Ker, while not present at the time the officers entered the apartment to arrest her husband, was nevertheless present at the time of her arrest. Upon their entry and announcement of their identity, the officers were met not only by George Ker, but also by Diane Ker, who was emerging from the kitchen. Officer Berman immediately walked to the doorway from which she emerged and, without entering, observed the brick-shaped package of marijuana in plain view. Even assuming that her presence in a small room with the contraband in a prominent position on the kitchen sink would not alone establish a reasonable ground for the officers' belief that she was in joint possession with her husband, that fact was accompanied by the officers' information that Ker had been using his apartment as a base of operations for his narcotics activities. Therefore, we cannot say that at the time of her arrest there were not sufficient grounds for reasonable belief that Diane Ker, as well as her husband, was committing the offense of possession of marijuana in the presence of the officers.

III.

It is contended that the lawfulness of the petitioners' arrest, even if they were based upon probable cause, was vitiated by the method of entry. This Court, in cases under the Fourth Amendment, has long recognized that the lawfulness of arrests for federal offenses is to be determined by reference to state law insofar as it is not violative of the Federal Constitution. *A fortiori,* the lawfulness of these arrests by state officers for state offenses is to be determined by California law. California Penal Code, § 844, permits peace officers to break into a dwelling place for the purpose of arrest after demanding admittance and explaining their purpose. Admittedly the officers did not comply with the terms of this statute since they entered quietly and without announcement, in order to prevent the destruction of contraband. The California District Court of Appeal, however, held that the circumstances here came within a judicial exception which had been engrafted upon the statute by a series of decisions, and that the noncompliance was therefore lawful.

Since the petitioners' federal constitutional protection from unreasonable searches and seizures by police officers is here to be determined by whether the search was incident to a lawful arrest, we are warranted in examining that arrest to determine whether, notwithstanding its legality under state law, the method of entering the home may offend federal constitutional standards of reasonableness and therefore vitiate the legality of an accompanying search. We find no such offensiveness on the facts here. Assuming that the officers' entry by use of a key obtained from the manager is the legal equivalent of a "breaking," see *Keiningham v. United States*, it has been recognized from the early common law that such breaking is permissible in executing an arrest under certain circumstances. Indeed, 18 U. S. C. § 3109, dealing with the execution of search warrants by federal officers, authorizes breaking of doors in words very similar to those of the California statute, both statutes including a requirement of notice of authority and purpose. In *Miller v. United States*, this Court held unlawful an arrest, and therefore its accompanying search, on the ground that the District of Columbia officers before entering a dwelling did not fully satisfy the requirement of disclosing their identity and purpose. The Court stated that "the lawfulness of the arrest without warrant is to be determined by reference to state law. . . . By like reasoning the validity of the arrest of petitioner is to be determined by reference to the law of the District of Columbia." The parties there conceded and the Court accepted that the criteria for testing the arrest under District of Columbia law were "substantially identical" to the requirements of § 3109. Here, however, the criteria under California law clearly include an exception to the notice requirement where exigent circumstances are present. Moreover, insofar as violation of a federal statute required the exclusion of evidence in *Miller*, the case is inapposite for state prosecutions, where admissibility is governed by constitutional standards. Finally, the basis of the judicial exception to the California statute, as expressed by Justice Traynor in *People v. Maddox*, effectively answers the petitioners' contention:

> "It must be borne in mind that the primary purpose of the constitutional guarantees is to prevent unreasonable invasions of the security of the people in their persons, houses, papers, and effects, and when an officer has reasonable cause to enter a dwelling to make an arrest and as an incident to that arrest is authorized to make a reasonable search, his entry and his search are not unreasonable. Suspects have no constitutional right to destroy or dispose of evidence, and no basic constitutional guarantees are violated because an officer succeeds in getting to a place where he is entitled to be more quickly than he would, had he complied with section 844. Moreover, since the demand and explanation requirements of section 844 are a codification of the common law, they may reasonably be interpreted as limited by the common law rules that compliance is not required if the officer's peril would have been increased or the arrest frustrated had he demanded entrance and stated his purpose. Without the benefit of hindsight and ordinarily on the spur of the moment, the officer must decide these questions in the first instance."

No such exigent circumstances as would authorize noncompliance with the California statute were argued in *Miller*, and the Court expressly refrained from discussing the question, citing the *Maddox* case without disapproval. Here justification for the officers' failure to give notice is uniquely present. In addition to the officers' belief that Ker was in possession of narcotics, which could be quickly and easily destroyed, Ker's furtive conduct in eluding them shortly before the arrest was ground for the belief that he might well have been expecting the police. We therefore hold that in the particular circumstances of this case the officers' method of entry, sanctioned by the law of California, was not unreasonable under the standards of the Fourth Amendment as applied to the States through the Fourteenth Amendment.

IV.

Having held the petitioners' arrest lawful, it remains only to consider whether the search which produced the evidence leading to their convictions was lawful as incident to those arrests. The doctrine that a search without warrant may be lawfully conducted if incident to a lawful arrest has long been recognized as consistent with the Fourth Amendment's protection against unreasonable searches and seizures. The cases have imposed no requirement that the arrest be under authority of an arrest warrant, but only that it be lawful. The question remains whether the officers' action here exceeded the recognized bounds of an incidental search.

Petitioners contend that the search was unreasonable in that the officers could practicably have obtained a search warrant. The practicability of obtaining a warrant is not the controlling factor when a search is sought to be justified as incident to arrest, *United States v. Rabinowitz*; but we need not rest the validity of the search here on *Rabinowitz*, since we agree with the California court that time clearly was of the essence. The officers' observations and their corroboration, which furnished probable cause for George Ker's arrest, occurred at about 9 p. m., approximately one hour before the time of arrest. The officers had reason to act quickly because of Ker's furtive conduct and the likelihood that the marijuana would be distributed or hidden before a warrant could be obtained at that time of night. Thus the facts bear no resemblance to those in *Trupiano v. United States*, where federal agents for three weeks had been in possession of knowledge sufficient to secure a search warrant.

The search of the petitioners' apartment was well within the limits upheld in *Harris v. United States*, which also concerned a private apartment dwelling. The evidence here, unlike that in *Harris*, was the instrumentality of the very crime for which petitioners were arrested, and the record does not indicate that the search here was as extensive in time or in area as that upheld in *Harris*.

The petitioners' only remaining contention is that the discovery of the brick of marijuana cannot be justified as incidental to arrest since it preceded the arrest. This contention is of course contrary to George Ker's testimony, but we reject it in any event. While an arrest may not be used merely as the pretext for a search without warrant, the California court specifically found and the record supports both that the officers entered the apartment for the purpose of arresting George Ker and that they had probable cause to make that arrest prior to the entry. We cannot say that it was unreasonable for Officer Berman, upon seeing Diane Ker emerge from the kitchen, merely to walk to the doorway of that adjacent room. We thus agree with the California court's holding that the discovery of the brick of marijuana did not constitute a search, since the officer merely saw what was placed before him in full view. Therefore, while California law does not require that an arrest precede an incidental search as long as probable cause exists at the onset, *Willson v. Superior Court*, the California court did not rely on that rule and we need not reach the question of its status under the Federal Constitution.

V.

The petitioners state and the record bears out that the officers searched Diane Ker's automobile on the day subsequent to her arrest. The reasonableness of that search, however, was not raised in the petition for certiorari, nor was it discussed in the brief here. Ordinarily, "[w]e do not reach for constitutional questions not raised by the parties," *Mazer v. Stein*, nor extend our review beyond those specific federal questions properly raised in the state court. The record gives no indication that the issue was raised in the trial court or in the District Court of Appeal, the latter court did not adjudicate it and we therefore find no reason to reach it on the record.

For these reasons the judgment of the California District Court of Appeal is affirmed.

[The dissenting opinion in which four justices joined is omitted.]

WARDEN, MARYLAND PENITENTIARY v. HAYDEN
SUPREME COURT OF THE UNITED STATES
387 U.S. 294, 87 S. CT. 1642, 18 L. ED. 2d 782 (1967)

MR. JUSTICE BRENNAN. About 8 a. m. on March 17, 1962, an armed robber entered the business premises of the Diamond Cab Company in Baltimore, Maryland. He took some $363 and ran. Two cab drivers in the vicinity, attracted by shouts of "Holdup," followed the man to 2111 Cocoa Lane. One driver notified the company dispatcher by radio that the man was a Negro about 5'8" tall, wearing a light cap and dark jacket, and that he had entered the house on Cocoa Lane. The dispatcher relayed the information to police who were proceeding to the scene of the robbery. Within minutes, police arrived at the house in a number of patrol cars. An officer knocked and announced their presence. Mrs. Hayden answered, and the officers told her they believed that a robber had entered the house and asked to search the house. She offered no objection.[1]

The officers spread out through the first and second floors and the cellar in search of the robber. Hayden was found in an upstairs bedroom feigning sleep. He was arrested when the officers on the first floor and in the cellar reported that no other man was in the house. Meanwhile an officer was attracted to an adjoining bathroom by the noise of running water, and discovered a shotgun and a pistol in a flush tank; another officer who, according to the District Court, "was searching the cellar for a man or the money" found in a washing machine a jacket and trousers of the type the fleeing man was said to have worn. A clip of

---

[1] The state postconviction court found that Mrs. Hayden "gave the policeman permission to enter the home." The federal habeas corpus court stated it "would be justified in accepting the findings of historical fact made by Judge Sodaro on that issue . . . ," but concluded that resolution of the issue would be unnecessary, because the officers were "justified in entering and searching the house for the felon, for his weapons and for the fruits of the robbery."

ammunition for the pistol and a cap were found under the mattress of Hayden's bed, and ammunition for the shotgun was found in a bureau drawer in Hayden's room. All these items of evidence were introduced against respondent at his trial.

II.

We agree with the Court of Appeals that neither the entry without warrant to search for the robber, nor the search for him without warrant was invalid. Under the circumstances of this case, "the exigencies of the situation made that course imperative." *McDonald* v. *United States*, 335 U. S. 451, 456. The police were informed that an armed robbery had taken place, and that the suspect had entered 2111 Cocoa Lane less than five minutes before they reached it. They acted reasonably when they entered the house and began to search for a man of the description they had been given and for weapons which he had used in the robbery or might use against them. The Fourth Amendment does not require police officers to delay in the course of an investigation if to do so would gravely endanger their lives or the lives of others. Speed here was essential, and only a thorough search of the house for persons and weapons could have insured that Hayden was the only man present and that the police had control of all weapons which could be used against them or to effect an escape.

We do not rely upon *Harris* v. *United States* in sustaining the validity of the search. The principal issue in *Harris* was whether the search there could properly be regarded as incident to the lawful arrest, since Harris was in custody before the search was made and the evidence seized. Here, the seizures occurred prior to or immediately contemporaneous with Hayden's arrest, as part of an effort to find a suspected felon, armed, within the house into which he had run only minutes before the police arrived. The permissible scope of search must, therefore, at the least, be as broad as may reasonably be necessary to prevent the dangers that the suspect at large in the house may resist or escape.

It is argued that, while the weapons, ammunition, and cap may have been seized in the course of a search for weapons, the officer who seized the clothing was searching neither for the suspect nor for weapons when he looked into the washing machine in which he found the clothing. But even if we assume, although we do not decide, that the exigent circumstances in this case made lawful a search without warrant only for the suspect or his weapons, it cannot be said on this record that the officer who found the clothes in the washing machine was not searching for weapons. He testified that he was searching for the man or the money, but his failure to state explicitly that he was searching for weapons, in the absence of a specific question to that effect, can hardly be accorded controlling weight. He knew that the robber was armed and he did not know that some weapons had been found at the time he opened the machine.[2] In these circumstances the inference that he was in fact also looking for weapons is fully justified.

[The Court held that the entry and the search was valid.]

---

[2] The officer was asked in the District Court whether he found the money. He answered that he did not, and stated: "By the time I had gotten down into the basement I heard someone say upstairs, 'There's a man up here.'" He was asked: "What did you do then?" and answered: "By this time I had already discovered some clothing which fit the description of the clothing worn by the subject that we were looking for. . . ." It is clear from the record and from the findings that the weapons were found after or at the same time the police found Hayden.

DORMAN v. UNITED STATES
CIRCUIT COURT OF APPEALS, D.C.
435 F.2d 385 (1970)

LEVENTHAL, CIRCUIT JUDGE. These are the pertinent facts as they appear from the transcript of the trial and Dorman's motion to suppress the suit of clothes, supplemented by the remand proceedings.

Shortly after 6 p.m. on a Friday evening, four armed men entered Carl's Men's Shop. In the store were three salesmen, two customers, a man and his wife, and a co-owner of the shop. The men entered in pairs. Dorman, one of the first two in the store, and wearing blue-black corduroy pants, asked salesman Holmes if he could see a size 38 blue sharkskin suit similar to one in the window. By the time Holmes returned with such a suit from the stock room the other two men had entered the store, drawn a gun, and announced, "This is it." Dorman, who had also drawn a gun, relieved Holmes of the suit. Holmes and the other five victims were herded into the stock room while the weapons were freely brandished. Jones pointed a gun at the head of another salesman and poked him with it a couple of times. One of the robbers put a gun to the chin of the male customer, Richards, and said, "Do not look," and put the gun to his chin to move his head up so he would not observe them.

The gunmen ushered the six persons into the stock room, stripped them of their billfolds, watches and rings, bound them around the ankles and wrists with neckties taken from a nearby rack, and made them lie on the floor. Two of the robbers remained in the stock room, pointed guns at the victims and made threats. The other two rummaged about the store, looking for money and clothes of certain sizes. During this period a shot was fired in the back room "when they were passing the gun from one to another."

An officer on traffic duty across from the store saw three men emerge with their arms full of clothes. He pursued one of them, but was unsuccessful. Police were swiftly called to the scene, and they investigated the premises from 7:00 to 7:45 p. m. Detective Blancato found on the floor of a changing room a pair of dark corduroy pants, and copies of a monthly probation report showing the name and address of defendant Dorman. Apparently Dorman left the store wearing the blue sharkskin suit.

Detective Blancato phoned the Identification Bureau and shortly after 8:00 p. m. he learned that the files contained Dorman's photograph. He drove three victims to headquarters, arriving at 8:30 p. m., and the victims made a photographic identification of Dorman.

. . . .

[The police attempted to get a search warrant that night but could not get one. About 10 P.M. they left to arrest Dorman at his home.]

About 10:20 p.m. the police arrived at Dorman's home, knocked twice and announced their identity. Dorman's mother answered the door, in her nightgown. When the police said they were looking for her son, she told them that he had been there but had left some minutes earlier, and suggested that if they did not believe her, they could come in and look for themselves. At that point, "We heard a noise from one of the back bedrooms." In the belief that Dorman was hiding within, the police brushed past Mrs. Dorman and encountered one Allen, a man friend of Mrs. Dorman who lived in the apartment, coming out of a bedroom.

Blancato and the officers continued their search for Dorman. Some policemen looked in the other rooms, and behind a sofa pulled far enough away from the wall to conceal a man. Blancato pushed open the slightly-ajar door of a walk-in closet with the barrel of his shotgun. Inside the closet, "right in front of us," was a blue suit. The unhemmed cuffs were visible beneath the suit jacket. The suit bore the label of Carl's Men's Shop.

Blancato left two of his men in the apartment to apprehend Dorman if he returned. The District Court credited his statement that this was with the acquiescence of Mrs. Dorman because it lessened the danger of a shoot-out and for that reason was preferable to a stakeout.

[Dorman was arrested the next day in an automobile.]

. . . .

Terms like "exigent circumstances" or "urgent need" are useful in underscoring the heavy burden on the police to show that there was a need that could not brook the delay incident to obtaining a warrant, and that it is only in the light of those circumstances and that need that the warrantless search meets the ultimate test of avoiding condemnation under the Fourth Amendment as "unreasonable." While the numerous and varied street fact situations do not permit a comprehensive catalog of the cases covered by these terms, it may be useful to refer to a number of considerations that are material, and have particular pertinence in the case at bar.

First, that a grave offense is involved, particularly one that is a crime of violence. Contrariwise the restrictive requirement for a warrant is more likely to be retained, and the need for proceeding without a warrant found lacking, when the offense is what has been sometimes referred to as one of the "complacent" crimes, like gambling.

Second, and obviously inter-related, that the suspect is reasonably believed to be armed. Delay in arrest of an armed felon may well increase danger to the community meanwhile, or to the officers at a time of arrest. This consideration bears materially on the justification for a warrantless entry.

Third, that there exists not merely the minimum of probable cause, that is requisite even when a warrant has been issued, but beyond that a clear showing of probable cause, including "reasonably trustworthy information," to believe that the suspect committed the crime involved.

Fourth, strong reason to believe that the suspect is in the premises being entered.

Fifth, a likelihood that the suspect will escape if not swiftly apprehended.

Sixth, the circumstance that the entry, though not consented, is made peaceably. Forcible entry may in some instances be justified. But the fact that entry was not forcible aids in showing reasonableness of police attitude and conduct. The police, by identifying their mission, give the person an opportunity to surrender himself without a struggle and thus to avoid the invasion of privacy involved in entry into the home.

Another factor to be taken into account, though it works in more than one direction, relates to time of entry—whether it is made at night. On the one hand, as we shall later develop, the late hour may underscore the delay (and perhaps impracticability of) obtaining a warrant, and hence serve to justify proceeding without one. On the other hand, the fact that an entry is made at night raises particular concern over its reasonableness, as indicated in Justice Harlan's opinion in Jones v. United States, 357 U.S. 493 (1958) and may elevate the degree of probable cause required, both as implicating the suspect, and as showing that he is in the place entered.

We see no basis for disturbing the judgment of the District Court that the case at bar presented the kind of exigent circumstances and urgent need that justified an entry into Dorman's home without the delay incident to a warrant. Dorman had been positively identified as one who had committed a crime of violence. He and his associates had been armed and abused their victims. There was no special knowledge that he was home, but concepts of probable cause and reasonableness prima facie justify looking for a man at home after 10 p. m.

There was at least a possibility that delay might permit escape, when and if the suspect came to realize his papers had been left behind. These factors are offset somewhat, but not decisively, by the circumstance that the entry after 10 p. m. came some four hours after the offense. This was not a case of hot pursuit, unless that term is to be stretched beyond all reasonable meaning. But the ultimate underlying factors were similar to those involved in a case of hot pursuit. The police were still dealing with a relatively recent crime, and prompt arrest might locate and recover the instrumentalities and fruits of the crime before otherwise disposed of. And the delay was not of their own making, which might undercut the showing of reasonableness. The courts have respect for the intelligent law enforcement activities of the police, situated as they are in the front line of the campaign for law and order, and this case plainly depicts police officers engaged steadily and systematically in the identification and pursuit of the criminal suspects. Last, but not least, the entry was made peacefully, and after announcement of purpose.

The search made upon peaceable entry was only to locate the person of the suspect, on suspicion that the noise heard was made by the suspect in hiding. If the entry to make an arrest was lawful, the police acted reasonably in looking behind sofas and in closets to locate the suspect. There was no rummaging of drawers, etc., to cloud the purpose of the police. Since we hold that the police acted reasonably and lawfully when they took the action without a warrant of entering the house and searching for Dorman in appropriate places, no valid objection can be made to their conduct, when in the course of the search in the closet for Dorman they saw the uncuffed trousers readily identifiable as coming from the store that had been robbed, in seizing this clothing notwithstanding the absence of a warrant.

. . . .

Conviction affirmed.

QUESTIONS AND PROBLEMS

1. Firemen and police officers are called to a building which obviously has an uncontrolled fire burning in it. However, the occupant or owner of the building stops them, saying that he does not want them in the building and that he can handle the fire. What can and should be done? Does your jurisdiction have any statutes regarding such situations?

2. Neighbors (or relatives) telephone and state:
   a. That terrible noises of a fight and struggle can be heard from a home (address given) and that they believe that a man is beating his wife

    b. That there is a seriously injured person in a home (address given) in your city

    c. That there is a bomb planted to go off in a home (address given)

When you arrive at the above addresses, no one answers the door and there does not seem to be anyone in the house. What should and can be done?

3. As an officer, you are in hot pursuit of a person when he runs into a house. Would you enter and how would you enter if the person had done the following?

    a. Committed an armed robbery as in the Hayden case

    b. Shoplifted a $250 watch

    c. Shoplifted a 39-cent item

    d. Jaywalked (crossed a street against the lights, causing traffic to stop to avoid hitting him)

4. A telephone call is received, stating, "I am having a heart attack. I am Mrs. X in Apartment 310 at 610 W. Main St." When the rescue breathing squad and police officers arrive, no one answers the bell and the door is locked at Apartment 310. What should be done?

5. List possible defense attacks when the state cites an exigency as the authority to search and seize.

9
AUTHORITY TO SEARCH INCIDENT TO A LAWFUL ARREST

The search incident to a lawful arrest is the most frequent type of search conducted by law enforcement officers. The history of the right to make this type of search finds its origin in ancient common law. In 1914, the U.S. Supreme Court observed that there has been a "right on the part of the Government, always recognized under the English and American law, to search the person of the accused when legally arrested to discover and seize the fruits or evidence of the crime." *Weeks v. United States*, 232 U.S. 383. In 1923, Justice Cardozo stated that the basis for the rule was "a shrewd appreciation for the necessities of government." *People v. Chicagles*, 237 N.Y. 193, 142 N.E. 583, 584.

THE ARREST REQUIREMENT

The authority for the search is that it is incident to a lawful arrest. The arrest requirements are:

1. *The arrest must be lawful.* It can be a valid arrest
   a. Based on probable cause (without an arrest warrant)
   b. Made under the authority of an arrest warrant
2. *The arrest must be made in good faith.* The arrest of a person on some pretext or subterfuge merely for the purpose of searching him or the area within his immediate control will not withstand the scrutiny of the courts. Evidence obtained under such circumstances would be suppressed under the exclusionary rule.
3. *The search and the arrest must be contemporaneous.* The courts have uniformly held that a search is reasonable if it is made immediately upon arrest and at the same time and place as the arrest. If it is impractical to make the search of the person of the arrestee immediately at the scene of the arrest because of some

emergency situation, i.e., fire, explosion, snipers, riot, etc., the officer should make the search as soon as it may be done with safety. In such a case, the officer should also make careful note of the reason for the removal of the arrestee or the delay of the search. His reasons may bear heavily at a later judicial determination of the reasonableness of the search.

> *Example:* If the officer determines for good reason that some or all of the arrestee's clothing must be removed in order to make an effective search, the arrestee would have to be removed to a private place to make the necessary strip search. The officer must be prepared to show that the search and methods used were reasonable.

WHAT MAY BE SEARCHED FOR

If the search is to be deemed reasonable, it must bear some relation to the offense for which the arrest was made.

> *Example:* Giving a motorist a citation for having a burned-out tail lamp does not justify a minute search with a flashlight into the linings of the motorist's pockets for marijuana.

Once the right to search is given, the search may be as extensive and intensive as required to effectuate the purpose of the search, whether the arrest is for a felony or a misdemeanor.

> *Example:* An arrest for shoplifting may require a strip search in an effort to recover the stolen article, but a search incident to an arrest for bigamy may require only a cursory search for weapons.

The objects of a search pursuant to a lawful arrest include:

Weapons. In all arrests, a search of the person of the arrestee is considered a necessary precaution, primarily for the protection of the officer. This is to prevent the possible use of concealed weapons which could injure or kill the officer and could effect an escape. The search is also justified as a precaution against a suicide attempt.

Fruits of the crime. In a narcotics arrest, the officer may search for narcotics. In a bribery arrest, the officer would probably be searching for money (which may have been marked). In a robbery or theft arrest, the officer may search for the loot. If the theft was of truck tires or TV sets, the officer could not justify a detailed search of the arrestee's pockets. Some crimes do not have fruits of the crime. Therefore, in these instances the search would be limited to a weapons search and evidence or instrumentalities of the crime. Examples of crimes where there usually are not fruits of the crime are battery, rape, disorderly conduct, homicide, and most traffic offenses.

Example: In an arrest for attempted rape, the officer came upon five small sealed envelopes in the defendant's pocket. Although an envelope could not have contained a weapon, the officer opened the envelopes and found narcotics. The court held that "There was no danger that the contents of the envelope would be used to effectuate an escape . . . or that the evidence would be destroyed (they were in the officer's possession). Under these circumstances, the police officers should have secured a search warrant prior to opening the sealed envelopes." *Caver v. Kropp*, 306 F. Supp. 1329 (Mich. 1969)

Instrumentalities of the crime which are tools and devices used to commit the crime. Examples are burglary tools, lock-picking equipment, weapons, and other items necessary for the perpetration of the crime. A motor vehicle could be an instrumentality of a crime.

Evidence of the crime. This is evidence which tends to show that the arrestee committed the crime for which he is being arrested. Such evidence is known as "mere evidence." Examples would be face masks, clothing fitting the description of the person wanted, clothing with blood or semen stains, clothing with tears or other readily identifying characteristics.

WHAT MAY BE SEIZED

Any item which may be searched for may be seized when seen in plain view or when uncovered in a reasonable search. Also, any other contraband which the officer sees in plain view or uncovers within the scope of his lawful search may be seized.

Example: If the officer in the Caver case (above example) were to come upon a hand-rolled cigarette during a lawful search, and by reason of his experience, training, and prior observations he recognized the substance as marijuana, he might seize the cigarette. If subsequent scientific analysis confirmed what the officer believed, the cigarette might then be used as evidence against the arrestee on a separate charge of possession of marijuana.

WHO MAY MAKE THE SEARCH

The authority to search derives from the lawful arrest. Therefore, the officer or officers making the arrest have the authority to make the search incident to the arrest. Should federal and state officers be working together and the arrest is made by the state officers, the authority to make the search is vested in the state officers. The same procedure should be observed if county and municipal officers or officers from two different municipalities are working together. Search by an officer who was not immediately involved in the arrest or who was not at the scene of the arrest is not prohibited. Multiple searches, however, must not be used as harassment or coercion. The search after the initial search by the arresting officer must be a valid exercise of a legitimate police function.

Example: Uniformed officers apprehend a burglar at the scene of the burglary. They make a cursory search of the arrestee and hold him for interrogation at the scene for detectives. Before interrogation, the detectives may search the arrestee even though he has been previously searched for weapons or fruits or instrumentalities of the offense. After the interrogation, the detectives may turn over custody of the arrestee to the wagon officers for conveyance to the station. The wagon men, immediately upon receiving custody of the prisoner, may search the prisoner to make certain that he is not armed. Similarly, in the station, the booking officer will conduct a station-house search during the booking process.

When the arrestee is received by the jailer to be held until the legal process begins, the jailer will also conduct a search of the arrestee's person prior to placing him in a cell.

Any contraband or evidence uncovered during any of the custodial searches may be used against the arrestee.

Most police department regulations require that when an officer takes custody of a police prisoner, the prisoner must be searched. It is the responsibility of the custodial officer to ensure that the arrestee does not possess a weapon or implement of escape.

WHEN MAY THE SEARCH BE MADE?

The results of a search can never be used to justify the search or to justify the arrest. Probable cause, independent of the results of the search, must exist to justify the authority to make the arrest. The search must be *contemporaneously* made with the arrest. The general rule requires that the arrest precede the search in order to be valid.

There are some notable exceptions. If an emergency situation presents itself, the evidence which may be in danger of loss or destruction may be seized before the arrest is made. The arrest, however, in those cases will be made immediately upon the seizure of the evidence so that the seizure and the arrest are substantially *contemporaneous.* An officer witnessing the sale of heroin may step in, seize the heroin, and then place the parties under arrest. So long as the officer had probable cause to make the arrest prior to the seizure and the arrest immediately followed the seizure, the seizure is valid. In *Holt v. Simpson*, 340 F.2d 853 (1965), and *Tinny v. Wilson*, 408 F.2d 912 (1969), the court held:

> When probable cause for an arrest exists independently of what the search produces, the fact that the search precedes the formal arrest is immaterial when the search and seizure are nearly simultaneous and constitute for all practical purposes but one transaction. To hold differently would be to allow a technical formality of time to control when there has been no real interferences with the substantive right of a defendant.

Unless the officer can justify the exception, the general rule followed in most jurisdictions is that search and seizure must follow the arrest unless they are nearly simultaneous.

SCOPE OF THE SEARCH

The U.S. Supreme Court has consistently held that the scope of a search based on a valid arrest is limited. In 1969, the U.S. Supreme Court narrowly restricted the scope of a search incident to a lawful arrest in *Chimel v. California* (see cases). In the Chimel case, the Court held that a search incident to an arrest must be limited to the arrestee's person or the area from within which he might obtain either a weapon or something that can be used as evidence against him.

A general, unrestrained, exploratory search has always been condemned by the Court. The Court in *Go-Bart Importing Co. v. United States*, 282 U.S. 344, held that the police cannot use the arrest as a pretext to conduct a general search and rummage or ransack an office or residence in an indiscriminate manner looking for whatever might turn up in such a search. Again, in *United States v. Lefkowitz*, 285 U.S. 452, the Court held that exploratory searches are invalid. The police must have reasonable knowledge of what they are searching for. They cannot proceed to examine everything in the premises in an unrestrained manner, hoping that evidence of some crime will be uncovered.

Like exploratory searches, mass seizure of property cannot be sustained as an incident to an arrest unless it can be shown that such seizure was reasonable. In *Kremen v. United States*, 353 U.S. 346, it was held that the seizure of the entire contents of a cabin which were then transported 200 miles away for examination and inventory was unreasonable. The arrest was for harboring fugitives.

NEED FOR A SEARCH WARRANT

The search incident to a lawful arrest is limited in scope to the person of the arrestee and the area within his immediate control. If officers who have made an arrest have reason to believe that evidence, contraband, or fruits of a crime are located outside the permissible area of search, they must obtain a search warrant to search that area. It may be possible to leave officers on guard while a search warrant is being obtained. The requirement for a search warrant is rested upon the desirability of having magistrates rather than police officers determine when searches and seizures are permissible and what limitation should be placed upon such activity.

SEARCH OF THE PERSON INCIDENT TO A LAWFUL ARREST

Arrests of persons are made under an endless variety of circumstances. Three different types of searches of an arrested person are made, depending upon the reason for the arrest and the circumstances:

1. *The weapons search* (frisk or pat-down), which is made to determine whether the arrestee has a weapon on his person.
2. *The field search*, which is a search not only for weapons but also for fruits of the crime and for evidence of the crime which the person has been arrested for.
3. *The station-house* or *jail search*, which in most cases is the most thorough search. This search is made prior to incarceration of the person.

The Chimel rule applies to the first two of the above searches.

RESTRAINT OF THE ARRESTED PERSON

Defense lawyers have argued that if the arrested person is restrained by handcuffs, then the permissible area of the search should be further limited. The California court in *Pugh v. Superior Court*, 91 Cal. Rptr. 168 (1970), held that "... [t]he fact that the driver was manacled and outside the vehicle and could neither destroy evidence in the vehicle nor seize a weapon is immaterial."

WHEN MAY PURSES, WALLETS, BILLFOLDS, OR BRIEFCASES AND PACKAGES BE SEARCHED?

Weapons searches may be made incident to all arrests of the person and the area under his immediate control. If the purse, wallet, briefcase, or package is large enough to hold a weapon, then it may be searched if the container is under the control of the arrestee.

If the officer has reason to look for fruits of the crime, evidence of the crime or instrumentalities of the crime and such evidence could reasonably be found in any of the containers listed; then a search of these containers would be justified. (See *People v. Belvin*, 80 Cal. Rptr. 382 (1969), where the court held that the arrestee's purse amounted to an extension of her person and could be searched upon her arrest.)

CONSTRUCTIVE POSSESSION

The term "constructive possession" is used to indicate control over property which the arrestee does not have in his actual possession. The property is elsewhere, but the arrestee has such control over the property that he usually can obtain possession of it when he wishes.

The problem of constructive possession arises in a search incident to a lawful arrest when the arresting and searching officer:

1. In his search of the arrested person comes upon a baggage claim check, a locker key, a parking lot check, a receipt for the storage of goods, etc.
2. Has knowledge or receives information which leads him to believe that the property exists and is "constructively possessed" by the arrestee

When the officer has reason to believe that contraband or evidence of the crime may be found in the property which is in the constructive possession of the arrestee, his problem is how to obtain or search the property.

The rule laid down in the 1969 case of *Chimel v. California* (see cases) severely limits the search of such constructively possessed property by limiting the permissible area of the search incident to a lawful arrest to the area under the immediate control of the arrestee.

Search warrants would have to be obtained if the property is in the custody of a common carrier or in a public storage locker, or to search a vehicle remote from the place of arrest.

There is always the possibility that consent to search may be given by a wife or bailee. This, of course, would depend upon the nature and extent of control which the person in possession of the property has (see Chap. 12, "Authority to Search with Consent").

If there is danger of destruction of the property or if the police have reasonable grounds to believe that the property would be removed by an associate or friends of the arrestee before a search warrant could be obtained, an immediate seizure of the property would be justified. The following case is an example of such justified seizure.

PARISH v. PEYTON, 408 F.2d 60 (4th CIR. 1969), CERT. DENIED, 395 U.S. 984 (1969)

> Officers observed a person known to be a "fence" (dealer in stolen property) make an inquiry of a baggage agent as to the arrival of certain packages. Upon the arrival of the packages at the terminal, officers could see, through a tear in one of the packages, suits which they thought to be stolen. After keeping the packages under surveillance for several hours, the officers then took them to the police station, where they obtained a warrant before searching them. The Court sustained the seizure of packages stating, "the police could reasonably have believed that the . . . carton might be claimed by the thieves or their collaborators and removed beyond retrieval. In response to the obvious necessity for swift action, they proceeded without a warrant, but limited themselves to securing possession of the articles. Exercising restraint, they deferred the search until after they had obtained search warrants from a magistrate."

Delaying a search of the seized property until after a search warrant has been obtained is probably the more prudent procedure. However, recent California cases have sustained the search of such seized property in that state without a search warrant in the cases of *People v. Gordon*, 89 Cal. Rptr. 214 (Ct. App. 1970), and *People v. Temple*, 82 Cal. Rptr. 885 (Ct. App. 1969).

Information or reason to believe that a bomb or incendiary device is in a package or a storage locker would always justify an emergency entry into such container in the interest of public safety.

THE STATION-HOUSE OR JAIL SEARCH

It is a common-law right of a jailer to search the person who is being processsed for incarceration. The purpose of the search is to find and seize:

1. Articles which might be used in escaping, such as weapons, keys, etc.
2. Evidence which would tend to show that the arrestee committed the crime which he is charged with

The common-law authority for this search is derived from the need to maintain the security of the jail and to maintain the safekeeping of the prisoners. This search is not related to or dependent upon the search incident to a lawful arrest but is a lawful, customary and routine search, which is conducted in jails or police stations prior to incarceration.

For obvious reasons, a jail cannot be equated with a man's home and for this reason the custodian of a jail can search prisoners and their cells without a search warrant and without probable cause. The United States Supreme Court stated in *Lanza v. New York*, 370 U.S. 139:

> ...[T]o say that a public jail is the equivalent of a man's house or that it is a place where he can claim constitutional immunity from search or seizure of his person, his papers, or his effects, is at best a novel argument.

Therefore, if within the permissible scope of any of these lawful searches, the officers uncover evidence of another crime or uncover contraband, this evidence may be seized and used against the person in court. Recent cases resulting from jail searches include:

STATE v. PIETRASZEWSKI, 172 N.W.2d 758 (MINN. 1969)

Defendant was arrested for the rape-murder of a baby-sitter. While in jail, he became involved in a disturbance with one of the jailers and was moved to another cell. After he was moved, a jailer found that the defendant had left a thick sheaf of papers with incriminating statements in his first cell. These papers were turned over to the prosecutor and were introduced into evidence. The court held that the seizure was reasonable and was not a violation of the Fourth Amendment rights of the defendant.

UNITED STATES v. JONES, 317 F. SUPP. 856 (TENN. 1970)

A counterfeit $20 bill was found in the side compartment of the defendant's billfold after the billfold was taken from him and he was jailed for failure to pay a fine for an unspecified misdemeanor. When a motion to suppress was made to the counterfeiting charge, the court held that the search which revealed the $20 bill was not related to the gathering of evidence in the original charge and evidence was suppressed.

BRETT v. UNITED STATES, 412 F.2d 401 (5th CIR. 1969)

The defendant was jailed for a narcotics violation. He was not searched thoroughly. His clothes were taken from him and put into a bag which was stored in the prisoners' property room. After the defendant was in jail three days, a narcotics officer requested a jailer to search the defendant's clothing. Narcotics were found in the watch pocket of the defendant's trousers. The Fifth Circuit Court of Appeals held that the search was illegal, stating that there was no authority for the search and that there was ample opportunity to obtain a search warrant.

PEOPLE v. TRUDEAU, 177 N.W.2d 171 (MICH. APP., 1970)

> The defendant was arrested and held in jail on a charge of burglary
> of a United States post office in Detroit. In the investigation of a
> murder in a synagogue, the police had reason to include the defend-
> ant as a suspect. They requested and obtained his shoes to compare
> the heel imprint found at the scene of the crime. No search warrant
> was obtained for the shoes. The court pointed out that the shoes were
> in open view and that no thorough search of his effects took place.
> The shoes were used as evidence in the trial which resulted in a
> second-degree murder conviction. The appellate court held that there
> was no Fourth Amendment violation and the conviction was affirmed.

SEARCH OF THE PREMISES INCIDENT TO A VALID ARREST

The term "premises" generally refers to immovable real property, i.e.,
buildings, structures, etc. The curtilage is the area immediately surrounding such a building or structure which may be considered a part
of or belonging to the structure, such as the lawn or area between
buildings.

The search of the premises has had considerable judicial attention
over the years. The limitation placed upon the police in searching the
premises has had an accordionlike expansion and contraction over the
years. The history of the swinging pendulum of cases is traced in
Chimel v. California (see cases) by the U.S. Supreme Court. This case
now rules as to the permissible limits of the search incident to the
lawful arrest.

The search of the premises, whether a dwelling or a place of
business, can be justified as incident to a valid arrest only if it is
reasonable. What is unreasonable, the Supreme Court has held, depends upon the circumstances of each case.

It has been held that a warrantless search of premises incident to
a valid arrest under appropriate circumstances does not violate the
protection afforded by the Fourth Amendment. The mere fact that there
was a valid arrest, however, does not by itself make a subsequent
search and seizure reasonable. In *Trupiano v. United States*, 334 U.S.
699, it was held that unless there is an apparent need for summary
seizure, even if probable cause is present, the officer *must* obtain a
search warrant. A lawful arrest, in and of itself, does not ipso facto
dispense with the need for a search warrant. Inconvenience to the
officer or some slight delay does not justify a search without a warrant.

Unless the prosecution can demonstrate impracticability to obtain
a search warrant such as exigent circumstances, consent, response to
an emergency, or hot pursuit of a fleeing felon, or that the evidence

was in the process of destruction or removal from the jurisdiction, the officer must obtain a search warrant.

Example: Assuming probable cause, police officers obtain a valid arrest warrant charging the arrestee with theft of twenty truck tires. The officers arrest the suspect on the second floor of his residence. They do not see the tires in the residence where the arrest took place, but have reason to believe that the tires are in the closed and locked garage of the home. The arrestee refuses to give consent to a search of the garage. The officers must obtain a search warrant before searching for the tires.

THE ARREST AND SEARCH MUST BE CONTEMPORANEOUS IN TIME AND PLACE

The search of the premises can be justified *only* if the search was substantially contemporaneous with the arrest. The arrest can be made pursuant to a warrant of arrest or on the basis of probable cause without a warrant. The arrest must take place *within* the premises to be searched to form the basis of the search. If a valid arrest occurs in one place, the police cannot use that arrest to justify the search of premises which are elsewhere. An arrest two blocks away from the place to be searched as in *James v. Louisiana*, 382 U.S. 36 (1965), or 15 feet away as in *Shipley v. California*, 395 U.S. 818 (1969), or on the doorstep as in *Vale v. Louisiana* (see cases) did not justify the search of premises on the basis of being incident to the arrest. The Supreme Court has held that a search must be limited to the immediate vicinity of the arrest.

Even if the arrest results in probable cause to believe that evidence, contraband, or weapons are located in another place, the search of the other place may be made *only* with a search warrant or with valid consent or if some exigent circumstance would make such a search reasonable.

PERMISSIBLE SCOPE OF THE SEARCH

If the arrest takes place *within* the premises, then a search of *the premises* may be made incident to the arrest. The rule laid down in the Chimel case will govern the scope and method of the warrantless search incident to a lawful arrest. The officers may:

1. Search the arrestee and the area under his immediate control for weapons, fruits of the crime, and evidence of the crime.
2. Make a check of other rooms and parts of the premises for other

persons wanted in connection with the crime, or to protect themselves from attack if there is any reason to suspect violence or the presence of other wanted persons.

3.   While making this check of other parts of the house, seize evidence or contraband seen in plain view. The officers may not search drawers, cabinets, etc., for evidence because this is beyond the permissible scope of a search incident to a lawful arrest.

Unless consent is given or a search warrant is obtained, the search may not exceed the permissible scope as laid down in the Chimel doctrine. If the arrest is made outside the premises, the arrestee may not be taken into the premises for the sole purpose of searching the premises.

ALLOWING THE ARRESTEE TO GO INTO AN AREA OF THE PREMISES WHICH HAS NOT BEEN SEARCHED

After the arrest and search, the arrested person may state that he has to go to the bathroom, or that he needs additional clothing, or that the oven has to be turned off. If the request seems valid to the officer, does this extend the permissible area which may be searched? The answer is yes. The police should not allow the arrestee to go into unsearched areas of the premises where a weapon may be obtained or evidence destroyed. The police may conduct a search of any additional area that necessarily must be placed under the arrestee's control in order to remove him from the place of the arrest. Precautions must be taken to prevent the arrestee from obtaining weapons or destroying evidence.

Example: The person who has been arrested for burglary states that he must go to the bathroom immediately. A search of the bathroom reveals narcotics and a gun. Both items may be lawfully seized.

EXCEPTIONS TO CHIMEL AND THE SEARCH-WARRANT REQUIREMENT

In the 1969 Chimel case, the Supreme Court stated that there were "well recognized" exceptions to this new rule. The Chimel rule does not apply to:

Plain view. What is in plain view is not a search. Officers lawfully on the premises, conducting a reasonable search, need not close their eyes to what they see in plain view or open view *even if it is outside of the permissible area of search.*

> *Example:*   Officers see contraband or a criminal act being committed through an open door. If they are legally where they have a right or duty to be, they may act on what they have seen.

Exigent circumstances. If lives are endangered or evidence is being destroyed or, as in the Ker case (see cases Chap. 8), there is a likelihood that evidence will be destroyed, then officers may respond to the emergency and act immediately without a warrant. See *United States v. Pino*, 431 F.2d 1043 (1970).

Hot pursuit. Such as in the case of *Warden v. Hayden* (see cases Chap. 8). Incriminating evidence obtained under such circumstances is admissible in evidence.

Motor vehicles. Because of their mobility, motor vehicles come under exceptions to the Chimel rule and since 1925 have special rules applicable to them. See Chap. 10.

SEARCH OF MOTOR VEHICLE INCIDENT TO LAWFUL ARRESTS

It has been suggested that the ideal situation would be one where all searches were authorized by search warrants. All agree that this would be not only impractical but also impossible. Most searches are, out of necessity, made without search warrants, and the law of warrantless searches has become complex because of the varieties of situations which confront law enforcement officers.

Since the wide use of the motor vehicle began in the 1920s, the law has treated searches of motor vehicles differently from searches of premises and searches of the person. A man can carry only a limited amount of contraband or fruits of a crime on his person without having the fact become obvious. And he cannot travel fast and far on foot.

Premises are permanently located in one place, and the apartment or house will be there tomorrow for a search under the authority of a search warrant, if necessary. Also, most persons have a residence and have accumulated more personal belongings than can be quickly thrown into one or two suitcases.

The motor vehicle, however, can be moved very rapidly to unknown places out of a jurisdiction and can conceal considerable amounts of contraband and fruits of a crime without the fact becoming obvious. The motor vehicle can be an instrument of the crime. Crimes can also be committed in motor vehicles, and the motor vehicle can be the object of a theft or taking. For these reasons, the motor vehicle must be treated differently from the person or premises in the law of warrantless searches.

THE REQUIREMENT THAT THE ARREST BE MADE IN OR NEAR THE VEHICLE AND THAT THE SEARCH BE MADE A REASONABLE TIME AFTER THE ARREST

The general rule is that if a person has been arrested for a crime and the arrest takes place in or near the motor vehicle which he was driving or was a passenger in, then the vehicle (or parts thereof) may be searched as an incident to the lawful arrest. Stated in another way, the rule is that a search incident to a lawful arrest may be made if:

1. The motor vehicle is the place where the arrest was made.
2. The vehicle is under the arrestee's immediate control.
3. The vehicle is located within the "immediate vicinity of the arrest" as distinguished from a situation where the arrest is made in a place "substantially removed geographically" from the motor vehicle. Stoner v. California, 376 U.S. 483

However, not all courts will approve of a search of the vehicle when the arrestee is not in the vehicle at the time of the arrest. Local law should be checked on this point.

Not only must the arrest be made within the immediate vicinity of the vehicle, but the search must be made within a reasonable time after the arrest to be authorized as a search incident to a lawful arrest.

Cases Illustrating the Rule Allowing Contemporaneous Searches

PRESTON v. UNITED STATES (SEE CASES)

> The court held the search unreasonable, stating, "[o]nce an accused is under arrest and in custody, then a search made at another place, without a warrant, is simply not incident to the arrest." (Note that the defendants were arrested for vagrancy and were in jail at the time the search was made.)

DYKE v. TAYLOR IMPLEMENT MFG. CO., 391 U.S. 216 (1968)

> This case is to the same effect and follows Preston.

UNITED STATES v. DOYLE, 373 F.2d 875 (1967)

> The search was declared reasonable where "the car was in Doyle's immediate presence and but a few feet from him when he was handcuffed and taken into custody."

PEOPLE v. BROWN, 84 CAL. RPTR. 390 (1970)

> Defendant was arrested in the act of robbing a service station. The arresting officer suspected that he had come to the scene of the rob-

bery by automobile. The officer walked in the direction that the defendant was seen coming from and saw only one car on the street. The doors of the automobile were unlocked; the ignition key was in place, and the hood of the car was still warm. The court held that the vehicle was a getaway car and therefore an instrumentality of the crime. The search of the vehicle was held to be reasonable.

KATZ v. PEYTON, 334 F.2d 77 (1964)

The defendant walked away when he saw the police officer and was arrested one block away for shoplifting. He was taken back to the store and his car was searched in the parking lot of the store. Several cartons of stolen cigarettes were recovered. The search of the vehicle was held to be a reasonable incident of the arrest.

ALVEY v. STATE, 443 S.W.2d 518 (1969)

Officers responding to a burglar alarm report pursued a vehicle which they had seen parked in front of a drugstore. They stopped the fleeing vehicle four blocks away and searched the two persons in the car. The defendants were placed in the police car and taken back to the drugstore. The front door of the drugstore was open with evidence of a forced entry. Twenty-five minutes after the arrest, the defendants were taken back to their vehicle. A search of the vehicle produced items which were taken from the drugstore. The search was held reasonable.

LIAKAS v. STATE, 199 TENN. 298, 286 S.W.2d 856 (1956)

Officers arrested the defendants on the street for stealing two suits of men's clothes. One of the defendants attempted to swallow a parking lot ticket but was stopped. Upon finding the car, the officers could see uncuffed men's suits and other new clothes lying on the seat of the car. The search of the car was held to be reasonable.

The arresting officers may for a good reason postpone the search and move the motor vehicle. The safety of the officers certainly would justify such action. If the vehicle to be searched was stopped on a busy expressway with little room to conduct the search, it could be moved to a more appropriate place. Extremely bad weather would seem to justify postponing the search. In the following cases, the defendants were taken to a police station (or hospital) before the search of the motor vehicle was made.

STATE v. THOMPSON, 173 N.W.2d 459 (MINN. 1970)

When the police attempted to arrest the two defendants for armed robbery, one broke away and started to run. The fleeing felon was shot in the leg, and the two defendants were then arrested. When they were safely in custody, their automobile (the getaway vehicle) was searched and evidence was obtained. The Supreme Court of Minnesota held that the warrantless search was valid.

PEOPLE v. FOSTER, 169 N.W.2d 648 (MICH. APP. 1969)
STATE v. CARTER, 225 A.2d 746 (N.J. 1969)
GASTON v. STATE, 457 P.2d 807 (OKLA. 1969)

In all three of these cases, the police concluded that it was not advisable to make a search of the vehicles at the scene of the arrest because crowds of people had gathered. In the Foster case, the defendant attempted to incite the crowd and the crowd appeared hostile. The defendants were taken to the station, and the cars were towed in. While the defendants were in custody in the station, the vehicles were searched. All were held to be valid searches incident to lawful arrests.

THE REQUIREMENT THAT THE SEARCH BE REASONABLY RELATED TO THE ARREST

While a weapons search is justified after all arrests, a search for evidence of the crime or fruits of the crime is not justified after all arrests. Some crimes do not have fruits of the crime which might be searched for and there may not be evidence of the crime which might be searched for.

WILLETT v. SUPERIOR COURT, SAN DIEGO COUNTY, 83 CAL RPTR. 22 (CAL. APP. 1969)

The arrest was for failure to notify authorities of his change of address as a registered narcotics offender. The arrest was made after the defendant's car was stopped for a traffic violation. The court held that arrest did not support and provide a basis for the search of the car.

DOES A STOP FOR A TRAFFIC VIOLATION JUSTIFY A SEARCH?

Most traffic violations are *not* crimes, and therefore stops for traffic violations do *not* in and of themselves justify a search. However, if the traffic violation is a crime and the officer is making an arrest, then a search for the fruits of the crime or evidence of the crime is justified in addition to the weapons search.

If in any type of traffic stop the officer has any reason to fear for his safety, he may make a weapons search of the person or the persons and the area under their immediate control. The authority for this search is discussed in Chap. 11.

THE IMPOUNDED OR SEIZED MOTOR VEHICLE

The federal government and many of the states have statutes which provide for the seizure and impounding of motor vehicles that are used in the commission of certain crimes. Vehicles are sometimes also seized as evidence of the crime and as an instrumentality of the crime for which the person has been arrested. In other situations, the vehicle is taken into custody (police or private garage) because the owner has been arrested and the vehicle cannot be left on the street or highway (a drunken-driving arrest would be an example of this). The following cases illustrate the law of warrantless searches of such vehicles.

COOPER v. CALIFORNIA, 386 U.S. 58, 87 S. CT. 788 (1967)

The defendant was arrested for a narcotics violation and his car was impounded pursuant to a California statute. The statute (sec. 11611) provides that the officer making an arrest for narcotics violations shall seize and deliver the vehicle to the State Division of Narcotics and that such vehicle shall be held as evidence until a forfeiture has been declared or a release ordered. A week after the arrest, the vehicle was searched without a warrant and evidence found in the glove compartment of the car was used to convict the defendant. The majority of the U.S. Supreme Court in a 5-4 decision distinguished this case from Preston, where they pointed out the search was totally unrelated to the vagrancy arrest which had been made. In affirming the California conviction, the Court stated:

"This case is not *Preston* nor is it controlled by it. Here the officers seized the petitioner's car because they were required to do so by state law. They seized it because of the crime for which they arrested petitioner. They seized it to impound it and they had to keep it until forfeiture proceedings were concluded. Their subsequent search of the car—whether the State had 'legal title' to it or not—was closely related to the reason petitioner was arrested, the reason his car had been impounded, and the reason it was being retained. The forfeiture of petitioner's car did not take place until over four months after it was lawfully seized. It would be unreasonable to hold that the police, having to retain the car in their custody for such a length of time, had no right, even for their own protection, to search it. It is no answer to say that the police could have obtained a search warrant . . . we cannot hold unreasonable under the Fourth Amendment the examination or search of a car validly held by officers for use as evidence in a forfeiture proceeding."

HARRIS v. UNITED STATES, 390 U.S. 234, 88 S. CT. 992 (1968)

The defendant was arrested in Washington, D.C., for robbery, and his car was seized as evidence of the crime. After the car was towed in, the arresting officer went to the car and opened a door to roll up a window because it was raining. On the floor, he saw a card which was used as incriminating evidence against the defendant. A unanimous court held that the officer had a right to seize that which was in plain or open view. The Court stated:

> "A regulation of the Metropolitan Police Dept. requires the officer who takes an impounded vehicle in charge to search the vehicle thoroughly, to remove all valuables from it, and to attach to the vehicle a property tag listing certain information about the circumstances of the impounding. Pursuant to this regulation, and without a warrant, the arresting officer proceeded to the lot to which the petitioner's car had been towed, in order to search the vehicle, to place a property tag on it, to roll up the windows and to lock the doors."

HEFFLEY v. STATE, 423 P.2d 666 (NEV. 1967)

It was held that if the police activity is motivated by a desire to safeguard the car and its contents against loss or to safeguard the police against false claims of loss, the examination of the car is valid and permissible.

STATE v. MILLER, 206 A.2d 835 (CONN. 1965)

The defendant attacked a mother and daughter in Connecticut. He killed the mother and took the daughter in his car. After driving several hours, he again attacked the girl in his car. The girl subsequently escaped. Several days later, the defendant was arrested by the FBI and the car was seized in Georgia. Connecticut police searched the car in Georgia without a search warrant and again in Connecticut, taking evidence of the crime from the car. When the issue of admissibility of this evidence came before the Supreme Court of Connecticut, it was held that the warrantless search of the car was illegal.

PEOPLE v. MOZZETTI, 94 CAL. RPTR. 412 (APRIL 1971)

Officers searched a suitcase within an impounded vehicle. Marijuana found in the suitcase was suppressed because the search was made without a search warrant.

INSPECTION TO DETERMINE OWNERSHIP
OF THE MOTOR VEHICLE

As over a half million motor vehicles are stolen every year in the United States, officers are constantly alert to identify motor vehicles as stolen. Many states require that the license registration be affixed in the vehicle so that it can be read from the outside of the vehicle. The

Fifth Circuit Court of Appeals held as follows in regard to inspection to determine ownership of vehicles:

> "The Court en banc is the opinion that the panel correctly decided that inspection of motor vehicles performed by police officers, who were entitled to be on the property where the vehicles were located, which in no way damaged the vehicles and were limited to determining the correct identification numbers thereof were not searches within the meaning of the 4th Amendment and that alternatively, if either of such inspections constituted a 4th Amendment search, then no search warrant was necessary because such inspections were reasonable and did not violate the right of the people to be secure in their persons, houses, papers, or effects." *United States v. Johnson*, 431 F.2d 441 (1970).

AFFIRMED IN UNITED STATES v. JONES, 432 F.2d 773 (1970)

> An FBI agent inspected a car which was impounded by a Georgia sheriff and recorded the car's license number and vehicle identification number to determine that the vehicle was stolen.

PEOPLE v. BROWN, 84 CAL. RPTR. 390 (CAL. 1970)

> The court held that "... officers finding an unlocked car with its ignition key in place, are reasonably permitted to investigate its ownership. Its registration certificate might lead to a disclosure that the vehicle was stolen; in any event it would enable the officers to advise the owner that the key was left in the vehicle thus decreasing the likelihood of its later theft."

STATE v. WOODS, 475 P.2d 573 (WASH. 1970)

> Police investigating a burglary saw an illegally parked car nearby. The ignition key was in the car, and the required registration certificate was not displayed. The limited search of the glove compartment which produced evidence which was used to convict the defendant was held to be valid.

PEOPLE v. FRANK, 305 N.Y.S.2d 940 (S. CT., QUEENS CO., N.Y., 1969)

> The court held that raising the hood of an automobile "... to ascertain whether it was stolen—particularly where, as here, there was probable cause to believe that it was in fact a stolen car—does not constitute a search in violation of the Fourth Amendment. Therefore, such action did not require, as does a search which comes under the Fourth Amendment, a search warrant or an arrest incident thereto. Particularly is this so where none of the contents of the automobile was taken as evidence to be used against the defendant."

GENERAL RULES GOVERNING SEARCHES INCIDENT TO LAWFUL ARREST

"Searches . . . are to be judged by whether they are reasonable . . . and common sense dictates that reasonableness varies with the circumstances of the search." (Justice Black in the Preston and Vale cases)

	TYPE OF SEARCH	WHEN SEARCH CAN BE MADE	JUSTIFICATION AND REASON FOR SEARCH	SCOPE AND EXTENT OF SEARCH	TIME AND PLACE SEARCH MAY BE MADE
SEARCHES OF THE PERSON	Weapons search	After every arrest	For the protection of the officer and other persons and to prevent escape	Limited to search for weapons or objects readily capable of causing physical injury	Contemporaneous in time and place with the arrest
	Evidence search	When necessary to search for fruits and evidence of the crime charged	To seize and preserve the fruits and evidence of the crime for which the arrest was made	Reasonable area (search may be intense in narcotics arrest while little or no search would be justified for stealing truck tires)	Contemporaneous in time and place with the arrest
	Station-house or jail search	If the person is to be booked or jailed	For the protection of officers and to prevent escape; also to obtain evidence of the crime for which the person was arrested	Intensive search of the person, his clothing, and personal effects; also to inventory valuables	At the time of booking and incarceration
SEARCHES OF PRIVATE PREMISES	Weapons search	After every arrest when the arrest occurs within the premises	For the protection of the officer and other persons and to prevent escape	Reasonable area of the arrestee's person and the premises within the immediate control of the arrestee	Contemporaneous in time and place with the arrest

Evidence search	When necessary to search for fruits and/or evidence of crime charged. Arrest must occur within premises	To seize and preserve the fruits and/or evidence of the crime charged	Reasonable area of the arrestee's person and the premises within the immediate control of the arrestee	Contemporaneous in time and place with the arrest
Search for other wanted persons	When officer has reason to suspect that another person (or persons) wanted for the same crime may also be present in the premises		Any part of the private premises where the wanted person or persons could be hiding	Contemporaneous in time and place with the arrest
SEARCHES OF MOTOR VEHICLES				
Weapons search	After every arrest when the arrestee is in the vehicle	For the protection of the officer and other persons and to prevent escape	Reasonable area within the immediate control of the arrestee	Contemporaneous in time and place with the arrest
Evidence search	When the arrestee is in the vehicle at the time of arrest. In some instances a search of the vehicle will be sustained if the vehicle is within the immediate area.	When necessary to seize and preserve the fruits and/or evidence of the crime for which the arrest was made	Any place in the motor vehicle where the fruits and/or evidence of the crime could reasonably be hidden	Reasonably contemporaneous in time and place with the arrest
*Search of seized or impounded vehicle**	When a motor vehicle is seized or impounded by a law enforcement agency	To inventory and take custody of valuables; for the protection of officers; to search for evidence and fruits of crime	See *Harris v. United States* for the custodial and inventory search; see *Cooper v. California* for other searches of seized vehicles	While the motor vehicle is within the custody of the law enforcement agency
*Inspection to determine ownership of vehicle**	While the vehicle is in a public place	To determine whether the vehicle is stolen and ownership	Limited to the determination of the ownership of the vehicle	Anytime the vehicle is in a public place

* These searches (or inspections) do not necessarily have to be related to a lawful arrest. The above are *general* rules which may vary in some states.

SEARCH OF MOTOR VEHICLES
(Also applicable to mobile aircraft and watercraft)

A search warrant *must* be obtained unless:
1. The search is made as incident to an arrest which requires:
   a. That there must be a lawful arrest made in good faith
   b. That the arrest was made in the vehicle
      (some courts will sustain searches where the arrest was made *near* the vehicle)
   c. That the search was made a reasonable time after the arrest
   d. That the search was reasonably related to the arrest
      Exceptions to b and c: if there are compelling circumstances which delay the search or force the vehicle to be moved
2. The search is made under the Carroll rule (see Chap. 10), which requires:
   a. That the officer has *probable cause* to believe that the vehicle contains that which is subject to seizure by the officer
   b. That the vehicle is in a mobile condition and has not been immobilized by police seizure of the vehicle
   c. That there is not the time to obtain a search warrant
3. Valid consent has been given to search the vehicle by a person authorized to give such consent (see Chap. 12)
4. Objects which may be seized are seen in plain view or open view
5. a. The motor vehicle is "validly held by officers for use as evidence in a forfeiture proceeding" (*Cooper v. California*)
   b. While in the process of safeguarding the car and its contents against loss, the officer sees evidence or contraband in plain view or open view (*Harris v. United States*)
   c. The officer has valid reason to make an inspection to determine ownership (the vehicle appears to have been abandoned or there is reason to believe that it is a stolen vehicle)

STANDING OF THE DEFENDANT TO CHALLENGE THE SEARCH OF THE MOTOR VEHICLE HE IS CHARGED WITH STEALING

A trespasser upon premises does not have standing to challenge the search of the premises by officers (a burglar cannot challenge evidence being used against him which was obtained in the home he burglarized). The question of whether a defendant can challenge evidence obtained from a car which he illegally possessed confronted a federal district court in Virginia.

MEADE v. COX, 310 F. SUPP. 233 (VA. 1970)

> The defendant was charged with murder and taking the murder victim's car. The court held he lacked standing to challenge the search of the car at the police station while he was held in custody.

SEARCH OF MOBILE HOMES

With the increased use of mobile homes in the United States, the question of searches of mobile homes may come up from time to time. While some mobile homes are very mobile, others are not and would be treated as premises. Mobility is the factor which causes motor vehicles to be treated differently in the law of warrantless searches. The fact that the mobile home is a home should also cause the officer to be more cautious and careful in making a warrantless search.

CASES FOR CHAPTER NINE

CHIMEL v. CALIFORNIA
SUPREME COURT OF THE UNITED STATES
395 U.S. 752, 23 L. ED. 2685, 89 S. CT. 2043 (1969)

Mr. Justice Stewart delivered the opinion of the Court.

This case raises basic questions concerning the permissible scope under the Fourth Amendment of a search incident to a lawful arrest.

The relevant facts are essentially undisputed. Late in the afternoon of September 13, 1965, three police officers arrived at the Santa Ana, California, home of the petitioner with a warrant authorizing his arrest for the burglary of a coin shop. The officers knocked on the door, identified themselves to the petitioner's wife, and asked if they might come inside. She ushered them into the house, where they waited 10 or 15 minutes until the petitioner returned home from work. When the petitioner entered the house, one of the officers handed him the arrest warrant and asked for permission to "look around." The petitioner objected, but was advised that "on the basis of the lawful arrest," the officers would nonetheless conduct a search. No search warrant had been issued.

Accompanied by the petitioner's wife, the officers then looked through the entire three-bedroom house, including the attic, the garage, and a small workshop. In some rooms the search was relatively cursory. In the master bedroom and sewing room, however, the officers directed the petitioner's wife to open drawers and "to physically move contents of the drawers from side to side so that [they] might view any items that would have come from [the] burglary." After completing the search, they seized numerous items—primarily coins, but also several medals, tokens, and a few other objects. The entire search took between 45 minutes and an hour.

At the petitioner's subsequent state trial on two charges of burglary, the items taken from his house were admitted into evidence against him, over his objection that they had been unconstitutionally seized. He was convicted, and the judgments of conviction were affirmed by both the California Court of Appeal and the California Supreme Court. Both courts accepted the petitioner's contention that the arrest warrant was invalid because the supporting affidavit was set out in conclusory terms, but held that since the arresting officers had procured the warrant "in good faith," and since in any event they had had sufficient information to constitute probable cause for the petitioner's arrest, that arrest had been lawful. From this conclusion the appellate courts went on to hold that the search of the petitioner's home had been justified, despite the absence of a search warrant, on the ground that it had been incident to a valid arrest. We granted certiorari in order to consider the petitioner's substantial constitutional claims.

Without deciding the question, we proceed on the hypothesis that the California courts were correct in holding that the arrest of the petitioner was valid under the Constitution. This brings us directly to the question whether the warrantless search of the petitioner's entire house can be constitutionally justified as incident to that arrest. The decisions of this Court bearing upon that question have been far from consistent, as even the most cursory review makes evident.

Approval of a warrantless search incident to a lawful arrest seems first to have been articulated by the Court in 1914 as dictum in Weeks v. United States, 232 US 383, in which the Court stated:

> "What then is the present case? Before answering that inquiry specifically, it may be well by a process of exclusion to state what it is not. It is not an assertion of the right on the part of the Government, always recognized under English and American law, to search the person of the accused when legally arrested to discover and seize the fruits or evidences of crime."

That statement made no reference to any right to search the *place* where an arrest occurs, but was limited to a right to search the "person." Eleven years later the case of Carroll v United States, 267 US 132, 69 L Ed 543, 45 S Ct 280, 39 ALR 790, brought the following embellishment of the Weeks statement:

> "When a man is legally arrested for an offense, whatever is found upon his person or *in his control* which it is unlawful for him to have and which may be used to prove the offense may be seized and held as evidence in the prosecution." (Emphasis added.)

Still, that assertion too was far from a claim that the "place" where one is arrested may be searched so long as the arrest is valid. Without explanation, however, the principle emerged in expanded form a few months later in Agnello v United States, 269 US 20—although still by way of dictum:

> "The right without a search warrant contemporaneously to search persons lawfully arrested while committing crime and to search the place where the arrest is made in order to find and seize things connected with the crime as its fruits or as the means by which it was committed as well as weapons and other things to effect an escape from custody, is not to be doubted."

And in Marron v United States, 275 US 192, 72 L Ed 231, 48 S Ct 74, two years later, the dictum of Agnello appeared to be the foundation of the Court's decision. In that case federal agents had secured a search warrant authorizing the seizure of liquor and certain articles used in its manufacture. When they arrived at the premises to be searched, they saw "that the place was used for retailing and drinking intoxicating liquors." They proceeded to arrest the person in charge and to execute the warrant. In searching a closet for the items listed in the warrant they came across an incriminating ledger, concededly not covered by the warrant, which they also seized. The Court upheld the seizure of the ledger by holding that since the agents had made a lawful arrest, "[t]hey had a right without a warrant contemporaneously to search the place in order to find and seize the things used to carry on the criminal enterprise."

That the Marron opinion did not mean all that it seemed to say became evident, however, a few years later in Go-Bart Importing Co. v United States, 282 US 344, and the United States v Lefkowitz, 285 US 452. In each of those cases the opinion of the Court was written by Mr. Justice Butler, the author of the opinion in Marron. In Go-Bart, agents had searched the office of persons whom they had lawfully arrested, and had taken several papers from a desk, a safe, and other parts of the office. The Court noted that no crime had been committed in the agents' presence, and that although the agent in charge "had an abundance of information and time to swear out a valid [search] warrant, he failed to do so." In holding the search and seizure unlawful, the Court stated:

> "Plainly the case before us is essentially different from Marron v United States, 275 US 192. There, officers executing a valid search warrant for intoxicating liquors found and arrested one Birdsall who in pursuance of a conspiracy was actually engaged in running a saloon. As an incident to the arrest they seized a ledger in a closet where the liquor or some of it was kept and some bills beside the cash register. These things were visible and accessible and in the offender's immediate custody. There was no threat of force or general search or rummaging of the place."

This limited characterization of Marron was reiterated in Lefkowitz, a case in which the Court held unlawful a search of desk drawers and a cabinet despite the fact that the search had accompanied a lawful arrest.

The limiting views expressed in Go-Bart and Lefkowitz were thrown to the winds, however, in Harris v United States, 331 US 145, decided in 1947. In that case, officers had obtained a warrant for Harris' arrest on the basis of his alleged involvement with the cashing and interstate transportation of a forged check. He was arrested in the living room of his four-room apartment, and in an attempt to recover two canceled checks thought to have been used in effecting the forgery, the officers undertook a thorough search of the entire apartment. Inside a desk drawer they found a sealed envelope marked "George Harris, personal papers." The envelope, which was then torn open, was found to contain altered Selective Service documents, and those documents were used to secure Harris' conviction for violating the Selective Training and Service Act of 1940. The Court rejected Harris' Fourth Amendment claim, sustaining the search as "incident to arrest."

Only a year after Harris, however, the pendulum swung again. In Trupiano v United States, 334 US 699, 92 L Ed 1663, 68 S Ct 1229, agents raided the site of an illicit distillery, saw one of several conspirators operating the still, and arrested him, contemporaneously "seiz[ing] the illicit distillery." The Court held that the arrest and others made subsequently had been valid, but that the unexplained failure of the agents to procure a search warrant—in spite of the fact that they had had more than enough time before the raid to do so—rendered the search unlawful. The opinion stated:

> "It is a cardinal rule that, in seizing goods and articles, law enforcement agents must secure and use search warrants wherever reasonably practicable.... This rule rests upon the desirability of having magistrates rather than police officers determine when searches and

seizures are permissible and what limitations should be placed upon such activities.... To provide the necessary security against unreasonable intrusions upon the private lives of individuals, the framers of the Fourth Amendment required adherence to judicial processes wherever possible. And subsequent history has confirmed the wisdom of that requirement.

....

"A search or seizure without a warrant as an incident to a lawful arrest has always been considered to be a strictly limited right. It grows out of the inherent necessities of the situation at the time of the arrest. But there must be something more in the way of necessity than merely a lawful arrest."

In 1950, two years after Trupiano, came United States v Rabinowitz, 339 US 56, 94 L Ed 653, 70 S Ct 430, the decision upon which California primarily relies in the case now before us. In Rabinowitz, federal authorities had been informed that the defendant was dealing in stamps bearing forged overprints. On the basis of that information they secured a warrant for his arrest, which they executed at his one-room business office. At the time of the arrest, the officers "searched the desk, safe, and file cabinets in the office for about an hour and a half," and seized 573 stamps with forged overprints. The stamps were admitted into evidence at the defendant's trial, and this Court affirmed his conviction, rejecting the contention that the warrantless search had been unlawful. The Court held that the search in its entirety fell within the principle giving law enforcement authorities "[t]he right 'to search the place where the arrest is made in order to find and seize things connected with the crime....'" Harris was regarded as "ample authority" for that conclusion. The opinion rejected the rule of Trupiano that "in seizing goods and articles, law enforcement agents must secure and use search warrants wherever reasonably practicable." The test, said the Court, "is not whether it is reasonable to procure a search warrant, but whether the search was reasonable."

Rabinowitz has come to stand for the proposition, inter alia, that a warrantless search "incident to a lawful arrest" may generally extend to the area that is considered to be in the "possession" or under the "control" of the person arrested. And it was on the basis of that proposition that the California courts upheld the search of the petitioner's entire house in this case. That doctrine, however, at least in the broad sense in which it was applied by the California courts in this case, can withstand neither historical nor rational analysis.

Even limited to its own facts, the Rabinowitz decision was, as we have seen, hardly founded on an unimpeachable line of authority. As Mr. Justice Frankfurter commented in dissent in that case, the "hint" contained in Weeks was, without persuasive justification, "loosely turned into dictum and finally elevated to a decision." And the approach taken in cases such as Go-Bart, Lefkowitz, and Trupiano was essentially disregarded by the Rabinowitz Court.

Nor is the rationale by which the State seeks here to sustain the search of the petitioner's house supported by a reasoned view of the background and purpose of the Fourth Amendment. Mr. Justice Frankfurter wisely pointed out in his Rabinowitz dissent that the Amendment's proscription of "unreasonable searches and seizures" must be read in light of "the history that gave rise to the words"—a history of "abuses so deeply felt by the Colonies as to be one of the potent causes of the Revolution.... The Amendment was in large part a reaction to the general warrants and warrantless searches that had so alienated the colonists and had helped speed the movement for independence. In the scheme of the Amendment, therefore, the requirement that "no Warrants shall issue, but upon probable cause," plays a crucial part. As the Court put it in McDonald v United States, 335 US 451:

> "We are not dealing with formalities. The presence of a search warrant serves a high function. Absent some grave emergency, the Fourth Amendment has interposed a magistrate between the citizen and the police. This was done not to shield criminals nor to make the home a safe haven for illegal activities. It was done so that an objective mind might weigh the need to invade that privacy in order to enforce the law. The right of privacy was deemed too precious to entrust to the discretion of those whose job is the detection of crime and the arrest of criminals.... And so the Constitution requires a magistrate to pass on the desires of the police before they violate the privacy of the home. We cannot be true to that constitutional requirement and excuse the absence of a search warrant without a showing by those who seek exemption from the constitutional mandate that the exigencies of the situation made that course imperative."

Even in the Agnello case the Court relied upon the rule that "[b]elief, however well founded, that an article sought is concealed in a dwelling house furnishes no justification for a search of that place without a warrant. And such searches are held unlawful notwithstanding facts unquestionably showing probable cause." Clearly, the general requirement that a search warrant be obtained is not lightly to be dispensed with, and "the burden is on those seeking [an] exemption [from the requirement] to show the need for it...." United States v Jeffers, 342 US 48, 51, 96 L Ed 59, 64, 72 S Ct 93.

Only last Term in Terry v Ohio, 392 US 1, we emphasized that "the police must, whenever practicable, obtain advance judicial approval of searches and seizures through the warrant procedure," and that "[t]he scope of [a] search must be 'strictly tied to and justified by' the circumstances which rendered its initiation permissible." The search undertaken by the officer in that "stop and frisk" case was sustained under that test, because it was no more than a "protective... search for weapons." But in a companion case, Sibron v New York, 392 US 40, we applied the same standard to another set of facts and reached a contrary result, holding that a policeman's action in thrusting his hand into a suspect's pocket had been neither motivated by nor limited to the objective of protection. Rather, the search had been made in order to find narcotics, which were in fact found.

A similar analysis underlies the "search incident to arrest" principle, and marks its proper extent. When an arrest is made, it is reasonable for the arresting officer to search the person arrested in order to remove any weapons that the latter might seek to use in order to resist arrest or effect his escape. Otherwise, the officer's safety might well be endangered, and the arrest itself frustrated. In addition, it is entirely reasonable for the arresting officer to search for and seize any evidence on the arrestee's person in order to prevent its concealment or destruction. And the area into which an arrestee might reach in order to grab a weapon or evidentiary items must, of course, be governed by a like rule. A gun on a table or in a drawer in front of one who is arrested can be as dangerous to the arresting officer as one concealed in the clothing of the person arrested. There is ample justification, therefore, for a search of the arrestee's person and the area "within his immediate control"—construing that phrase to mean the area from within which he might gain possession of a weapon or destructible evidence.

There is no comparable justification, however, for routinely searching any room other than that in which an arrest occurs—or, for that matter, for searching through all the desk drawers or other closed or concealed areas in that room itself. Such searches, in the absence of well-recognized exceptions, may be made only under the authority of a search warrant.[1] The "adherence to judicial processes" mandated by the Fourth Amendment requires no less.

This is the principle that underlay our decision in Preston v United States, 376 US 364, 11 L Ed 2d 777, 84 S Ct 881. In that case three men had been arrested in a parked car, which had later been towed to a garage and searched by police. We held the search to have been unlawful under the Fourth Amendment, despite the contention that it had been incidental to a valid arrest. Our reasoning was straightforward:

> "The rule allowing contemporaneous searches is justified, for example, by the need to seize weapons and other things which might be used to assault an officer or effect an escape, as well as by the need to prevent the destruction of evidence of the crime—things which might easily happen where the weapon or evidence is on the accused's person or under his immediate control. But these justifications are absent where a search is remote in time or place from the arrest."

The same basic principle was reflected in our opinion last Term in Sibron. That opinion dealt with Peters v New York, 392 US 40, 20 L Ed 2d 917, 88 S Ct 1889, as well as with Sibron's case, and Peters involved a search that we upheld as incident to a proper arrest. We sustained the search, however, only because its scope had been "reasonably limited" by the "need to seize weapons" and "to prevent the destruction of evidence," to which Preston had referred. We emphasized that the arresting officer "did not engage in an unrestrained and thoroughgoing examination of Peters and his personal effects. He seized him to cut short his flight, and he searched him primarily for weapons." 392 U. S., at 67.

. . . .

Rabinowitz and Harris have been the subject of critical commentary for many years, and have been relied upon less and less in our own decisions. It is time, for the reasons we have stated, to hold that on their own facts, and insofar as the principles they stand for are inconsistent with those that we have endorsed today, they are no longer to be followed.

Application of sound Fourth Amendment principles to the facts of this case produces a clear result. The search here went far beyond the petitioner's person and the area from within which he might have obtained either a weapon or something that could have been used as evidence against him. There was no constitutional justification, in the absence of a search warrant, for extending the search beyond that area. The scope of the search was, therefore, "unreasonable" under the Fourth and Fourteenth Amendments, and the petitioner's conviction cannot stand.

Reversed.

[Separate opinions omitted.]

[1] Our holding today is of course entirely consistent with the recognized principle that, assuming the existence of probable cause, automobiles and other vehicles may be searched without warrants "where it is not practicable to secure a warrant because the vehicle can be quickly moved out of the locality or jurisdiction in which the warrant must be sought." Carroll v United States, 267 US 132; see Brinegar v United States, 338 US 160.

VALE v. LOUISIANA
SUPREME COURT OF THE UNITED STATES
399 U.S. 30, 90 S. CT. 1969, 26 L. ED. 2d 409 (1970)

MR. JUSTICE STEWART.   . . . The evidence of what then took place was summarized by the Louisiana Supreme Court as follows:

> "After approximately 15 minutes the officers observed a green 1958 Chevrolet drive up and sound the horn and after backing into a parking place, again blew the horn. At this juncture Donald Vale, who was well known to Officer Brady having [sic] arrested him twice in the previous month, was seen coming out of the house and walk [sic] up to the passenger side of the Chevrolet where he had a close brief conversation with the driver; and after looking up and down the street returned inside of the house. Within a few minutes he reappeared on the porch, and again cautiously looked up and down the street before proceeding to the passenger side of the Chevrolet, leaning through the window. From this the officers were convinced a narcotics sale had taken place. They returned to their car and immediately drove toward Donald Vale, and as they reached within approximately three cars [sic] lengths from the accused, (Donald Vale) he looked up and, obviously recognizing the officers, turned around, walking quickly toward the house. At the same time the driver of the Chevrolet started to make his get away when the car was blocked by the police vehicle. The three officers promptly alighted from the car, whereupon Officers Soule and Laumann called to Donald Vale to stop as he reached the front steps of the house, telling him he was under arrest. Officer Brady at the same time, seeing the driver of the Chevrolet, Arizzio Saucier, whom the officers knew to be a narcotic addict, place something hurriedly in his mouth, immediately placed him under arrest and joined his co-officers. Because of the transaction they had just observed they informed Donald Vale they were going to search the house, and thereupon advised him of his constitutional rights. After they all entered the front room, Officer Laumann made a cursory inspection of the house to ascertain if anyone else was present and within about three minutes Mrs. Vale and James Vale, mother and brother of Donald Vale, returned home carrying groceries and were informed of the arrest and impending search."

The search of a rear bedroom revealed a quantity of narcotics.

The Louisiana Supreme Court held that the search of the house did not violate the Fourth Amendment because it occurred "in the immediate vicinity of the arrest" of Donald Vale and was "substantially contemporaneous therewith. . . ." We cannot agree. Last Term in Chimel v. California, 395 U. S. 752, we held that when the search of a dwelling is sought to be justified as incident to a lawful arrest, it must constitutionally be confined to the area within the arrestee's reach at the time of his arrest—"the area from within which he might gain possession of a weapon or destructible evidence." 395 U. S., at 763. But even if Chimel is not accorded retroactive effect—a question on which we do not now express an opinion—no precedent of this Court can sustain the constitutional validity of the search in the case before us.

A search may be incident to an arrest " 'only if it is substantially contemporaneous with the arrest and is confined to the *immediate* vicinity of the arrest.' " *Shipley v. California,* 395 U. S. 818, 819; *Stoner v. California,* 376 U. S. 483, 486. If a search of a house is to be upheld as incident to an arrest, that arrest must take place *inside* the house, not somewhere outside—whether two blocks away, *James v. Louisiana,* 382 U. S. 36, twenty feet away, *Shipley v. California, supra,* or on the sidewalk near the front steps. "Belief, however well founded, that an article sought is concealed in a dwelling house furnishes no justification for a search of that place without a warrant." *Agnello v. United States* 269 U. S. 20. That basic rule "has never been questioned in this Court." *Stoner v. California, supra,* at 487 n. 5.

The Louisiana Supreme Court thought the search independently supportable because it involved narcotics, which are easily removed, hidden, or destroyed. It would be unreasonable, the Louisiana court concluded, "to require the officers under the facts of the case to first secure a search warrant before searching the premises, as time is of the essence inasmuch as the officers never know whether there is anyone on the premises to be searched who could very easily destroy the evidence." 252 La., at 1070, 215 So. 2d, at 816. Such a rationale could not apply to the present case, since by their own account the arresting officers satisfied themselves that no one else was in the house when they first entered the premises. But entirely apart from that point, our past decisions make clear that only in "a few specifically established and well-delineated" situations may a warrantless search of a dwelling withstand constitutional scrutiny, even though the authorities have probable cause to conduct it. The burden rests on the State to show the existence of such an exceptional situation. And the record before us discloses none.

There is no suggestion that anyone consented to the search. The officers were not responding to an emergency. They were not in hot pursuit of a fleeing felon. The goods ultimately seized were not in the process of destruction. *Schmerber v. California,* 384 U. S. 757, 770–771. Nor were they about to be removed from the jurisdiction. *Chapman v. United States,* 365 U. S. 610.

The officers were able to procure two warrants for Vale's arrest. They also had information that he was residing at the address where they found him. There is thus no reason, so far as anything before us appears, to suppose that it was impracticable for them to obtain a search warrant as well. We decline to hold that an arrest on the street can provide its own "exigent circumstance" so as to justify a warrantless search of the arrestee's house.

The Louisiana courts committed constitutional error in admitting into evidence the fruits of the illegal search. Accordingly, the judgment is reversed and the case is remanded to the Louisiana Supreme Court for further proceedings not inconsistent with this opinion.

It is so ordered.

Mr. Justice Blackmun took no part in the consideration or decision of this case.

Mr. Justice Black, with whom the Chief Justice joins, dissenting.

The Fourth Amendment to the United States Constitution prohibits only "unreasonable searches." A warrant has never been thought to be an absolute requirement for a constitutionally proper search. Searches, whether with or without a warrant, are to be judged by whether they are reasonable, and, as I said, speaking for the Court in *Preston v. United States,* 376 U. S. 364, 366–367 (1964), common sense dictates that reasonableness varies with the circumstances of the search. The Louisiana Supreme Court held not only that the police action here was reasonable but also that failure to conduct an immediate search would have been unreasonable. With that view I am in complete agreement, for the following reasons.

The police had probable cause to believe that Vale was engaged in a narcotics transfer, and that a supply of narcotics would be found in the house, to which Vale had returned after his first conversation, from which he had emerged furtively bearing what the police could readily deduce was a supply of narcotics, and toward which he hurried after seeing the police. But the police did not know then who else might be in the house. Vale's arrest took place near the house, and anyone observing from inside would surely have been alerted to destroy the stocks of contraband which the police believed Vale had left there. The police had already seen Saucier, the narcotics addict, apparently swallow what Vale had given him. Believing that some evidence had already been destroyed and that other evidence might well be, the police were faced with the choice of risking the immediate destruction of evidence or entering the house and conducting a search. I cannot say that their decision to search was unreasonable. Delay in order to obtain a warrant would have given an accomplice just the time he needed.

That the arresting officers did, in fact, believe that others might be in the house is attested to by their actions upon entering the door left open by Vale. The police at once checked the small house to determine if anyone else was present. Just as they discovered the house was empty, however, Vale's mother and brother arrived. Now what had been a suspicion became a certainty: Vale's relatives were in possession and knew of his arrest. To have abandoned the search at this point, and left the house with Vale, would not have been the action of reasonable police officers.... For reasons given above I am convinced that the search here was reasonable, even though Vale had not yet crossed the threshold of the house toward which he was headed.

. . . .

PRESTON v. UNITED STATES
SUPREME COURT OF THE UNITED STATES
376 U.S. 364, 84 S. CT. 881 (1964)

Mr. Justice Black delivered the opinion of the Court.

Petitioner and three others were convicted in the United States District Court for the Eastern District of Kentucky on a charge of conspiracy to rob a federally insured bank in violation of 18 U. S. C. § 2113, the conviction having been based largely on evidence obtained by the search of a motorcar. The Court of Appeals for the Sixth Circuit affirmed, rejecting the contentions, timely made in the trial and appellate courts, that both the original arrest, on a charge of vagrancy, and the subsequent search and seizure had violated the Fourth Amendment. 305 F. 2d 172. We granted certiorari. 373 U. S. 931. In the view we take of the case, we need not decide whether the arrest was valid, since we hold that the search and seizure was not.

The police of Newport, Kentucky, received a telephone complaint at 3 o'clock one morning that "three suspicious men acting suspiciously" had been seated in a motorcar parked in a business district since 10 o'clock the evening before. Four policemen straightaway went to the place where the car was parked and found petitioner and two companions. The officers asked the three men why they were parked there, but the men gave answers which the officers testified were unsatisfactory and evasive. All three men admitted that they were unemployed; all of them together had only 25 cents. One of the men said that he had bought the car the day before (which later turned out to be true), but he could not produce any title. They said that their reason for being there was to meet a truck driver who would pass through Newport that night, but they could not identify the company he worked for, could not say what his truck looked like, and did not know what time he would arrive. The officers arrested the three men for vagrancy, searched them for weapons, and took them to police headquarters. The car, which had not been searched at the time of the arrest, was driven by an officer to the station, from which it was towed to a garage. Soon after the men had been booked at the station, some of the police officers went to the garage to search the car and found two loaded revolvers in the glove compartment. They were unable to open the trunk and returned to the station, where a detective told one of the officers to go back and try to get into the trunk. The officer did so, was able to enter the trunk through the back seat of the car, and in the trunk found caps, women's stockings (one with mouth and eye holes), rope, pillow slips, an illegally manufactured license plate equipped to be snapped over another plate, and other items. After the search, one of petitioner's companions confessed that he and two others —he did not name petitioner—intended to rob a bank in Berry, Kentucky, a town about 51 miles from Newport. At this, the police called the Federal Bureau of Investigation into the case and turned over to the Bureau the articles found in the car. It was the use of these articles, over timely objections, which raised the Fourth Amendment question we here consider.

The Amendment provides:

> "The right of the people to be secure in their persons, houses, papers, and effects, against unreasonable searches and seizures, shall not be violated, and no Warrants shall issue, but upon probable cause, supported by Oath or affirmation, and particularly describing the place to be searched, and the persons or things to be seized."

The question whether evidence obtained by state officers and used against a defendant in a federal trial was obtained by unreasonable search and seizure is to be judged as if the search and seizure had been made by federal officers. *Elkins* v. *United States*, 364 U. S. 206 (1960). Our cases make it clear that searches of motorcars must meet the test of reasonableness under the Fourth Amendment before evidence obtained as a result of such searches is admissible. *E. g., Carroll* v. *United States*, 267 U. S. 132 (1925); *Brinegar* v. *United States*, 338 U. S. 160 (1949). Common sense dictates, of course, that questions involving searches of motorcars or other things readily moved cannot be treated as identical to questions arising out of searches of fixed structures like houses. For this reason, what may be an unreasonable search of a house may be reasonable in the case of a motorcar. See *Carroll* v. *United States, supra,* 267 U. S., at 153. But even in the case of motorcars, the test still is, was the search unreasonable. Therefore we must inquire whether the facts of this case are such as to fall within any of the exceptions to the constitutional rule that a search warrant must be had before a search may be made.

It is argued that the search and seizure was justified as incidental to a lawful arrest. Unquestionably, when a person is lawfully arrested, the police have the right, without a search warrant, to make a contemporaneous search of the person of the accused for weapons or for the fruits of or implements used to commit the crime. This right to search and seize without a search warrant extends to things under the accused's immediate control, and, to an extent depending on the circumstances of the case, to the place where he is arrested.

The rule allowing contemporaneous searches is justified, for example, by the need to seize weapons and other things which might be used to assault an officer or effect an escape, as well as by the need to prevent the destruction of evidence of the crime—things which might easily happen where the weapon or evidence is on the accused's person or under his immediate control. But these justifications are absent where a search is remote in time or place from the arrest. Once an accused is under arrest and in custody, then a search made at another place, without a warrant, is simply not incident to the arrest. Here, we may assume, as the Government urges, that, either because the arrests were valid or because the police had probable cause to think the car stolen, the police had the right to search the car when they first came on the scene. But this does not decide the question of the reasonableness of a search at a later time and at another place. See *Stoner* v. *California, post,* p. 483. The search of the car was not undertaken until petitioner and his companions had been arrested and taken in custody to the police station and the car had been towed to the garage. At this point there was no danger that any of the men arrested could have used any weapons in the car or could have destroyed any evidence of a crime—assuming that there are articles which can be the "fruits" or "implements" of the crime of vagrancy. Cf. *United States* v. *Jeffers,* 342 U. S. 48, 51–52 (1951). Nor, since the men were under arrest at the police station and the car was in police custody at a garage, was there any danger that the car would be moved out of the locality or jurisdiction. See *Carroll* v. *United States, supra,* 267 U. S., at 153. We think that the search was too remote in time or place to have been made as incidental to the arrest and conclude, therefore, that the search of the car without a warrant failed to meet the test of reasonableness under the Fourth Amendment, rendering the evidence obtained as a result of the search inadmissible.

Reversed and remanded.

PEOPLE v. MANN
SUPREME COURT, BRONX COUNTY
305 N.Y.S.2d 226 (1969)

Police were looking for the defendant and another man to arrest them. They knocked at the defendant's door and the defendant opened the door dressed only in his underwear. They arrested the defendant and ordered him to get dressed. The police accompanied the defendant down a hall to his bedroom where he was to dress. En route, they saw the accomplice whom they also arrested. They also observed stolen property on a dresser which they seized. The defense argues that the seizure violated the rule of law laid down in *Chimel v. California.*

THE COURT. Certainly it was reasonable for the police who arrested defendant Mann in a state of undress, to accompany him to the bedroom and keep him under continuous surveillance while he was putting on his clothing. This is not only common sense, it is mandated by the Code of Criminal Procedure (Sections 171, 172). Secondly, even if Mann had been fully dressed, it was equally reasonable for the police officers, as a matter of self-protection and as a safeguard against any attempt to escape, knowing Mann had not acted alone and knowing another person might be present in the apartment, to check the adjacent rooms for the presence of any potential accomplice. In one such room they found co-defendant Ferguson and some of the fruits of the crime. Under those circumstances, they were not obliged to disregard what they saw, for practical necessity conferred the mantle of legitimacy on their presence in the other room to see and to seize the evidence in question. Reasonableness of the search is the key, and what the police did here was pre-eminently reasonable. Arrest gives the police the right to search the person and the immediate surroundings of the arrestee; surveillance of a prisoner and the right to check for confederates or accomplices extends that right to permit the police an over-all view of the other rooms in the premises, with the concomitant right to seize evidence or weapons in plain view. "When the things received in evidence are the fruits of *lawful* search, the claim of privilege is hollow." *People v. Chiagles,* 237 N.Y. 193, 142 N.E. 583, 32 A.L.R. 676.*

QUESTIONS AND PROBLEMS

Answer questions 1 through 4 indicating the scope and the extent of the search when the arrest is for:

a. Drunkenness	g. Assault and battery
b. Disorderly conduct	h. Homicide
c. Parole violations	i. Burglary
d. Shoplifting	j. Drug or narcotics charge
e. Stolen-vehicle charge	
f. Driving a vehicle while drugged or intoxicated	

When a traffic stop is made for:

k. Exceeding the speed limit	l. One headlight being out

1. *In a field search:* Indicate what may be searched for *on the person* of the arrestee and the permissible scope of the search.

   When may a search of the following objects be made: purse? briefcase? box or bag? wallet? sealed envelope?

   If the arrest was made *inside* the premises, what area of the premises may be searched and what may be searched for?

   What area may be searched if the arrest was made in or near the vehicle which the arrestee was driving?

   What area may be searched when the arrestee is a passenger in the vehicle?

   When may the trunk of the vehicle be opened and searched?

   When may contraband not related to the crime for which the arrest was made be searched for?
2. What procedure would be used in searching a woman arrested for the crimes listed?

---

* For similar cases and rulings, see *United States v. Broomfield,* 336 F. Supp. 179 (U.S.D.C. for E. Mich. 1972), and the California Supreme Court case of *People v. Block,* 93 Cal. Rptr. 779 (1971). The federal court in the Broomfield case held that "exigent circumstances" justified the precautionary sweep through the house to determine whether other fugitives were present. While making the sweep, contraband was seen in plain view.

3. What would be the scope of the station-house or jail search made prior to jailing a person for the crimes listed?

4. X is arrested *in his home*, without a search warrant, for the armed robbery of a service station. X is one of three men at large wanted for this robbery. Describe in detail the permissible scope of the search of X's premises.

   a. X's car is parked in his driveway. The car is thought to be the vehicle used in the crime. Can the car be searched without consent and without a search warrant?

In questions 5 to 8, indicate which of the following answers are correct.

5. The warrantless search of parts of premises incident to a lawful arrest may be made:

   a. Regardless of where the arrest was made
   b. If the arrest was made near but outside the premises
   c. If the arrest was made inside the premises
   d. Under none of the above conditions

6. The permissible area of search in question 5:

   a. Includes the entire dwelling or premises
   b. Is limited to the area within the immediate control of the person being arrested
   c. Varies, depending upon the crime for which the arrest was made

7. If the arresting officers have reasonable grounds to believe that objects which may be seized are located *in the premises* beyond the permissible area of the search:

   a. They may search for these objects and seize them.
   b. They may go into these areas to determine whether the objects are in plain view and then seize them.
   c. And if the objects are seized under condition 1 or 2, the exclusionary rule would not permit the use of such items as evidence.

8. Entry into the premises *after* the arrest is made *outside* the premises would be authorized:

   a. If the officer had a search warrant to search the premises
   b. If the officer had reasonable grounds to believe that the evidence or contraband was being destroyed or removed
   c. If an emergency justified such entry into the premises
   d. Under all of the above conditions
   e. Under none of the above conditions

9. At 3:18 A.M. a Phoenix police officer received a radio bulletin that three men in a gray Cadillac had just robbed a man. A few minutes later, the officer saw a gray 1960 Cadillac with three men in it. The officer stopped the car and after checking the driver's license, the officer radioed for help. When additional officers arrived, the men in the Cadillac were placed under arrest and were taken to the police station in a police car. The Cadillac was then moved off the highway to a parking lot of a nearby garage. It was then searched (about 30 minutes after the stop). Items taken from the robbery victim were found in the car. *State v. Madden,* 465 P.2d 363 (Ariz. 1970)

   a. Did the officer have probable cause to arrest the three men?

   b. Was the search of the vehicle a proper search incident to a lawful arrest?

10. An officer stopped a car when he saw a large number of rifles on the back seat. He asked the driver for his identification and his driver's license. As the driver was getting his wallet out of his pocket, the officer saw the butt end of a gun protruding from under the driver's seat. The driver was asked to get out of the car and the officer placed him under arrest. Another squad was called and took the defendant to the police station. The arresting officer then drove the defendant's car to the station, and after he parked the car at the station, he searched it. Two passports and two motor vehicle registration certificates were found which investigation showed to be items taken in a burglary. *Heffley v. Hocker,* 420 F.2d 881 (1969). Which of the search and seizures would be held valid?

   a. *Both* the gun from under the front seat and the documents (passports and registration certificates)

   b. *Only* the gun from under the front seat

   c. Only the documents

   d. *None* of the above objects

11. In most searches incident to a lawful arrest, the *arrest* is made first and is followed by the *search,* which is then followed by the *seizure.*

   a. Would a *search* followed by a *seizure* and then the *arrest* be valid?

   b. Would a *seizure* followed by an *arrest* and then a *search* be valid in any instances?

12. What are possible defense attacks on evidence which the state alleges was obtained as the result of a search incident to an arrest?

10
AUTHORITY TO SEARCH UNDER THE CARROLL RULE

Surveys show that motor vehicles are involved in some manner in over 75 percent of the crimes committed today in the United States. This problem was recognized years ago by Dean Roscoe Pound when he wrote that "the coming of the automobile has begun to make new chapters both in the civil and in the criminal law, and is making over other chapters. Indeed, the general use of motor vehicles is affecting the conditions that make for crime, the difficulties of preventing and detecting crimes, and the administration of punitive justice." Pound, *Criminal Justice in America* (1929).

The United States Supreme Court responded early to the use of the motor vehicle by criminals and adopted in 1925 one of the few exceptions to the warrant requirements of the Fourth Amendment. In the landmark case of *Carroll v. United States*, the Court held that if an officer has probable cause to believe that a motor vehicle contains that which "offend[s] against the law," he may make a warrantless search of the vehicle.

Over the years, the U.S. Supreme Court has time and again reaffirmed the Carroll rule or doctrine. In 1949, it was affirmed in *Brinegar v. United States* (see cases, Chap. 1). In 1968, in the important case of *Chimel v. California* (see cases, Chap. 9), the Court stated in a footnote of that case:

> Our holding today is of course entirely consistent with the recognized principle that, assuming the existence of probable cause, automobiles and other vehicles may be searched without warrants "where it is not practicable to secure a warrant because the vehicle can be quickly moved out of the locality or jurisdiction in which the warrant must be sought." *Carroll v. United States*, 267 U.S. 132, 153; see *Brinegar v. United States*, 338 U.S. 160.

Again, in June of 1970 the Carroll rule was reaffirmed in *Chambers v. Maroney* (see cases, this chapter) by the Supreme Court.

The Carroll rule is a federal rule and vests in federal officers authority for a warrantless search under the circumstances described for federal offenses. Most (and probably all) states have adopted the rule, although a state could impose limitations within its own jurisdiction which are not found in the federal rule. Most states have adopted the Carroll rule by court decisions, and a few have adopted it by statute.

THE CARROLL RULE (SEARCH ON PROBABLE CAUSE)

The Carroll rule is applicable to motor vehicles, aircraft, and water craft. According to the rule, an officer may make a warrantless search of a vehicle for the objects which he has probable cause to believe that the vehicle contains:

1. If the officer has *probable cause* to believe that the vehicle contains that which is subject to seizure by the officer.
2. And if the vehicle is in a *mobile* condition and has not been immobilized by police seizure or by damage to the vehicle, etc.
3. And if "it is not practicable to secure a warrant because the vehicle can be quickly moved out of the locality or jurisdiction in which the warrant must be sought." *Carroll v. United States*, 267 U.S. 132 (1925).

If the objects are found, the officer may seize them. If he did not have probable cause to arrest prior to the search, finding the objects may give him probable cause to arrest.

Example: A reliable informant telephones a sheriff's department with information that merchandise which was burglarized in that city recently is now on a truck and leaving for another state. (1) The officers have probable cause to believe that the truck contains that which they may lawfully seize; (2) the truck is mobile; and (3) they do not have time to obtain a search warrant.

WHAT "OFFEND[S] AGAINST THE LAW"?

In most jurisdictions, the Carroll rule is applicable to all criminal offenses—both felony and misdemeanor. This would mean that the Carroll rule would apply to a misdemeanor shoplifting situation as well as to a felonious drug case. The officer may use the probable-cause search for contraband, fruits of a crime (stolen objects), or instrumentalities of a crime (such as burglary tools). If the officer has probable cause to believe that the vehicle itself is stolen, this gives him the authority to search the vehicle as long as the vehicle is mobile.

IS IT NECESSARY TO HAVE PROBABLE CAUSE TO ARREST SOMEONE IN THE VEHICLE?

The officer does *not* have to have probable cause to arrest the driver or a passenger in the vehicle. The authority to make a search under the Carroll rule is a separate and distinct authority. It is not related to or dependent upon the arrest of anyone in the vehicle. However, situations do occur where the officer has both probable cause to arrest an occupant of the vehicle and probable cause to make a search under the Carroll rule.

Example: An officer sees X, who is wanted for parole violation, in a moving vehicle. When he stops the car, a strong smell of marijuana comes out to him from the car. A California court held in *People v. Fitzpatrick*, 84 Cal. Rptr. 78, that it is reasonable to believe that one who has recently smoked a marijuana cigarette has others in his possession. The officer has probable cause to believe that a person within the vehicle has marijuana in his possession or that the vehicle contains marijuana.

If probable cause to arrest and probable cause to search both exist, there is then an overlapping of the two separate authorities. Parts of the search could then be justified by either of the two authorities.

WHEN IS A VEHICLE MOBILE OR MOVABLE?

The Carroll rule (or the "mobility doctrine," as it is sometimes called) requires that the vehicle be in running order and capable of being driven away. If the vehicle has been damaged so badly that it cannot be driven or if the vehicle is in police custody, then the vehicle is no longer considered mobile by the courts.

In *Preston v. United States* (see cases, Chap. 9) the United States Supreme Court unanimously held, in 1964:

> Here, we may assume, as the Government urges, that, either because the arrests were valid or because the police had probable cause to think the car stolen, the police had the right to search the car when they first came on the scene. But this does not decide the question of the reasonableness of a search at a later time and another place. The search of the car was not undertaken until petitioner and his com-

panions had been arrested and taken in custody to the police station and the car had been towed to the garage. At this point there was no danger that any of the men arrested could have used any weapons in the car or could have destroyed any evidence of a crime—assuming that there are articles which can be the "fruits" or "implements" of the crime of vagrancy. Nor, since the men were under arrest at the police station and the car was in police custody at a garage, was there any danger that the car would be moved out of the locality or jurisdiction. See *Carroll v. United States* 267 U.S. at 153.

In comparing the 1970 U.S. Supreme Court ruling in *Chambers v. Maroney* (see cases, this chapter), keep in mind that the arrest in Chambers was not for vagrancy but for armed robbery. The Court stated in footnote 25 in Chambers:

> It was not unreasonable in this case to take the car to the station house. All occupants in the car were arrested in a dark parking lot in the middle of the night. A careful search at that point was impractical and perhaps not safe for the officers....

A parked vehicle is mobile. It is not moving at the time, but it can be moved by the owner or others who have keys. Nor does the arrest of the owner or the driver of the vehicle make it immobile. Others may move the vehicle. Additional cases where the mobility of the vehicle was in issue are:

HUSTY v. UNITED STATES, 282 U.S. 132 (U.S. S. CT. 1930)

Officers had probable cause to believe that the car contained contraband. When they stopped the car, two of the three occupants fled. The Court held that the "... arrest of the transportation or possession need not precede the search. We think the testimony which we have summarized is ample to establish the lawfulness of the present search. To show probable cause it is not necessary that the arresting officer should have had before him legal evidence of the suspected illegal act. It is enough if the apparent facts which have come to his attention are sufficient, in the circumstances, to lead a reasonably discreet and prudent man to believe that liquor is illegally possessed in the automobile to be searched." The fact that the vehicle had come to a temporary halt did not cause it to lose its mobility.

UNITED STATES v. WALKER, 307 F.2d 250 (4th CIR. 1962)

"Appellant would limit Carroll to those cases where the vehicle is in transit on a public road or highway. However, this argument ignores the basic reason for the Carroll doctrine—that a vehicle by its very nature can be quickly moved out of the locality or jurisdiction in which the warrant might be sought and law enforcement thereby frus-

trated. This very practical consideration is present whether the vehicle
is in transit on the open road or parked."

ARMADA v. UNITED STATES, 319 F.2d 793 (1963)

The vehicle was unoccupied and the officers had probable cause to
believe that it contained cocaine. The defendant was standing nearby
and had the car keys in his possession. The court held that, "Unless
Armada was arrested or the car was seized, the automobile could
readily be moved." The court stated that "the search of the automobile
and its contents was reasonable."

UNITED STATES v. HAITH, 297 F.2d 65 (4th CIR. 1961),
CERT. DENIED, 369 U.S. 804 (U.S. S. CT. 1962)

Officers were seeking to arrest the defendant under the authority of an
arrest warrant for liquor violations. They observed him park a Pontiac
in front of his house and then go into the residence.

"The agents observed that the rear of the Pontiac was very low,
although its rear springs were reinforced with air lift devices. Along
the crack between the lid of the trunk and the body of the Pontiac
automobile they recognized the odor of moonshine whisky, from which
the agents concluded that the load in the trunk of the car was illicit
whisky."

The officers arrested the defendant when they were admitted to
the home. They asked him for the keys to the Pontiac and the defendant gave them the key to the ignition but denied having a key to
the trunk. One of the agents removed the rear seat and was able to
remove a half-gallon jar from the trunk. From the odor of the contents
of the jar, the officers concluded it contained moonshine whisky. The
defendant then produced the key to the trunk and 90 gallons of illicit
whisky were found.

The court held that "The case is within the well-established rule
that a warrant is not required for the search of a movable vehicle if
the officers have reasonable cause to believe that it contains contraband. . . . In all of the automobile cases, once the officers have seized
the vehicle, and obtained exclusive possession of it, it becomes practical, in a sense, to postpone the search until a warrant has been obtained. Probable cause being present, however, the cases unanimously
sustain the legality of an undelayed search, and none suggest the distinction the defendant urges."

RENT v. UNITED STATES, 209 F.2d 893 (5th CIR. 1954)

The defendant was arrested on a narcotics charge. His car was driven
to the police station, where it was parked and locked. After booking,
the arresting officers went home and the next day (ten hours after the
arrest), they searched the car without a warrant. The court suppressed
the evidence obtained from the car, stating, "The automobile was at
rest, was actually in the custody of the officers, locked, and not likely
to be disturbed."

WHEN IS IT POSSIBLE AND PRACTICAL TO OBTAIN A SEARCH WARRANT?

If the vehicle is mobile, there are very few situations where it is practical and possible to obtain a search warrant. One of these situations occurred in the case of *Clay v. United States*, 239 F.2d 196 (1956). The court, in this case, held that the defendant's fixed pattern of activity allowed time for a warrant to be obtained. The defendant was the pickup man for a numbers racket and made daily rounds to collect betting slips. He was under surveillance for a number of days before he was stopped. A probable-cause search of the automobile was made under the Carroll rule. There was no question that probable cause existed to believe that the car contained that which could be seized and that the car was mobile. But the court held that in this case it was practical and possible to obtain a search warrant.

POSSIBLE DEFENSE ATTACKS ON A PROBABLE-CAUSE SEARCH

That there was no probable cause to believe that the vehicle did not contain something subject to seizure by the officer

That the vehicle was no longer mobile

That it was practical to obtain a search warrant and the officer failed to obtain one

CASES FOR CHAPTER TEN

CHAMBERS v. MARONEY
SUPREME COURT OF THE UNITED STATES
399 U.S. 42, 90 S. CT. 1975, 26 L. ED. 2d 419 (1970)

Mr. Justice White delivered the opinion of the Court.

The principal question in this case concerns the admissibility of evidence seized from an automobile, in which petitioner was riding at the time of his arrest, after the automobile was taken to a police station and was there thoroughly searched without a warrant. The Court of Appeals for the Third Circuit found no violation of petitioner's Fourth Amendment rights. We affirm.

I

During the night of May 20, 1963, a Gulf service station in North Braddock, Pennsylvania, was robbed by two men, each of whom carried and displayed a gun. The robbers took the currency from the cash register; the service station attendant, one Stephen Kovacich, was directed to place the coins in his right-hand glove, which was then taken by the robbers. Two teen-agers, who had earlier noticed a blue compact station wagon circling the block in the vicinity of the Gulf station, then saw the station wagon speed away from a parking lot close to the Gulf station. About the same time, they learned that the Gulf station had been robbed. They reported to police, who arrived immediately, that four men were in the station wagon and one was wearing a green sweater. Kovacich told the police that one of the men who robbed him was wearing a green sweater and the other was wearing a trench coat. A description of the car and the two robbers was broadcast over the police radio. Within an hour, a light blue compact station wagon answering the description and carrying four men was stopped by the police about two miles from the Gulf Station. Petitioner was one of the men in the station wagon. He was wearing a green sweater and there was a trench coat in the car. The occupants were arrested and the car was driven to the police station. In the course of a thorough search of the car at the station, the police found concealed in a compartment under the dashboard two .38-caliber revolvers (one loaded with dumdum bullets), a right-hand glove containing small change, and certain cards bearing the name of Raymond Havicon, the attendant at a Boron service station in McKeesport, Pennsylvania, who had been robbed at gunpoint on May 13, 1963. In the course of a warrant-authorized search of petitioner's home the day after petitioner's arrest, police found and seized certain .38-caliber ammunition, including some dumdum bullets similar to those found in one of the guns taken from the station wagon.

Petitioner was indicted for both robberies. His first trial ended in a mistrial but he was convicted of both robberies at the second trial. Both Kovacich and Havicon identified petitioner as one of the robbers. The materials taken from the station wagon were introduced into evidence, Kovacich identifying his glove and Havicon the cards taken in the May 13 robbery. The bullets seized at petitioner's house were also introduced over objections of petitioner's counsel. Petitioner was sentenced to a term of four to eight years' imprisonment for the May 13 robbery and to a term of two to seven years' imprisonment for the May 20 robbery, the sentences to run consecutively. Petitioner did not take a direct appeal from these convictions. In 1965, petitioner sought a writ of habeas corpus in the state court, which denied the writ after a brief evidentiary hearing; the denial of the writ was affirmed on appeal in the Pennsylvania appellate courts. Habeas corpus proceedings were then commenced in the United States District Court for the Western District of Pennsylvania. An order to show cause was issued. Based on the State's response and the state court record, the petition for habeas corpus was denied without a hearing. The Court of Appeals for the Third Circuit affirmed, 408 F. 2d 1186, and we granted certiorari, 396 U. S. 900 (1969).

II

We pass quickly the claim that the search of the automobile was the fruit of an unlawful arrest. Both the courts below thought the arresting officers had probable cause to make the arrest. We agree. Having talked to the teen-age observers and to the victim Kovacich, the police had ample cause to stop a light blue compact station wagon carrying four men and to arrest the occupants, one of whom was wearing a green sweater and one of whom had a trench coat with him in the car.[1]

Even so, the search that produced the incriminating evidence was made at the police station some time after the arrest and cannot be justified as a search incident to an arrest: "Once an accused is under arrest and in custody, then a search made at another place, without a warrant, is simply not incident to the arrest."

---

[1] In any event, as we point out below, the validity of an arrest is not necessarily determinative of the right to search a car if there is probable cause to make the search. Here, as will be true in many cases, the circumstances justifying the arrest are also those furnishing probable cause for the search.

Preston v. *United States,* 376 U. S. 364, 367 (1964). *Dyke* v. *Taylor Implement Mfg. Co.,* 391 U. S. 216 (1968), is to the same effect; the reasons that have been thought sufficient to justify warrantless searches carried out in connection with an arrest no longer obtain when the accused is safely in custody at the station house.

There are, however, alternative grounds arguably justifying the search of the car in this case. In *Preston, supra,* the arrest was for vagrancy; it was apparent that the officers had no cause to believe that evidence of crime was concealed in the auto. In *Dyke, supra,* the Court expressly rejected the suggestion that there was probable cause to search the car, 391 U. S., at 221–222. Here the situation is different, for the police had probable cause to believe that the robbers, carrying guns and the fruits of the crime, had fled the scene in a light blue compact station wagon which would be carrying four men, one wearing a green sweater and another wearing a trench coat. As the state courts correctly held, there was probable cause to arrest the occupants of the station wagon that the officers stopped; just as obviously was there probable cause to search the car for guns and stolen money.

In terms of the circumstances justifying a warrantless search, the Court has long distinguished between an automobile and a home or office. In *Carroll* v. *United States,* 267 U. S. 132 (1925), the issue was the admissibility in evidence of contraband liquor seized in a warrantless search of a car on the highway. After surveying the law from the time of the adoption of the Fourth Amendment onward, the Court held that automobiles and other conveyances may be searched without a warrant in circumstances that would not justify the search without a warrant of a house or an office, provided that there is probable cause to believe that the car contains articles that the officers are entitled to seize. The Court expressed its holding as follows:

> "We have made a somewhat extended reference to these statutes to show that the guaranty of freedom from unreasonable searches and seizures by the Fourth Amendment has been construed, practically since the beginning of the Government, as recognizing a necessary difference between a search of a store, dwelling house or other structure in respect of which a proper official warrant readily may be obtained, and a search of a ship, motor boat, wagon or automobile, for contraband goods, where it is not practicable to secure a warrant because the vehicle can be quickly moved out of the locality or jurisdiction in which the warrant must be sought.
>
> "Having thus established that contraband goods concealed and illegally transported in an automobile or other vehicle may be searched for without a warrant, we come now to consider under what circumstances such search may be made.... [T]hose lawfully within the country, entitled to use the public highways, have a right to free passage without interruption or search unless there is known to a competent official authorized to search, probable cause for believing that their vehicles are carrying contraband or illegal merchandise....
>
> . . . .
>
> "The measure of legality of such a seizure is, therefore, that the seizing officer shall have reasonable or probable cause for believing that the automobile which he stops and seizes has contraband liquor therein which is being illegally transported." 267 U. S., at 153–154, 155–156.

The Court also noted that the search of an auto on probable cause proceeds on a theory wholly different from that justifying the search incident to an arrest:

> "The right to search and the validity of the seizure are not dependent on the right to arrest. They are dependent on the reasonable cause the seizing officer has for belief that the contents of the automobile offend against the law." 267 U. S., at 158, 159.

Finding that there was probable cause for the search and seizure at issue before it, the Court affirmed the convictions.

Carroll was followed and applied in *Husty* v. *United States*, 282 U. S. 694 (1931), and *Scher* v. *United States*, 305 U. S. 251 (1938). It was reaffirmed and followed in *Brinegar* v. *United States*, 338 U. S. 160 (1949). In 1964, the opinion in *Preston, supra*, cited both *Brinegar* and *Carroll* with approval, 376 U. S., at 366–367. In *Cooper* v. *California*, 386 U. S. 58 (1967),[2] the Court read *Preston* as dealing primarily with a search incident to arrest and cited that case for the proposition that the mobility of a car may make the search of a car without a warrant reasonable "although the result might be the opposite in a search of a home, a store, or other fixed piece of property." 386 U. S., at 59. The Court's opinion in *Dyke*, 391 U. S., at 221, recognized that "[a]utomobiles, because of their mobility, may be searched without a warrant upon facts not justifying a warrantless search of a residence or office," citing *Brinegar* and *Carroll, supra*. However, because there was insufficient reason to search the car involved in the *Dyke* case, the Court did not reach the question of whether those cases "extend to a warrantless search, based upon probable cause, of an automobile which, having been stopped originally on a highway, is parked outside a courthouse." 391 U. S., at 222.

Neither *Carroll, supra*, nor other cases in this Court require or suggest that in every conceivable circumstance the search of an auto even with probable cause may be made without the extra protection for privacy that a warrant affords. But the circumstances that furnish probable cause to search a particular auto for particular articles are most often unforeseeable; moreover, the opportunity to search is fleeting since a car is readily movable. Where this is true, as in *Carroll* and the case before us now, if an effective search is to be made at any time, either the search must be made immediately without a warrant or the car itself must be seized and held without a warrant for whatever period is necessary to obtain a warrant for the search.[3]

In enforcing the Fourth Amendment's prohibition against unreasonable searches and seizures, the Court has insisted upon probable cause as a minimum requirement for a reasonable search permitted by the Constitution. As a general rule, it has also required the judgment of a magistrate on the probable-cause issue

---

[2] *Cooper* involved the warrantless search of a car held for forfeiture under state law. Evidence seized from the car in that search was held admissible. In the case before us no claim is made that state law authorized that the station wagon be held as evidence or as an instrumentality of the crime; nor was the station wagon an abandoned or stolen vehicle. The question here is whether probable cause justifies a warrantless search in the circumstances presented.

[3] Following the car until a warrant can be obtained seems an impractical alternative since, among other things, the car may be taken out of the jurisdiction. Tracing the car and searching it hours or days later would of course permit instruments or fruits of crime to be removed from the car before the search.

and the issuance of a warrant before a search is made. Only in exigent circumstances will the judgment of the police as to probable cause serve as a sufficient authorization for a search. *Carroll, supra*, holds a search warrant unnecessary where there is probable cause to search an automobile stopped on the highway; the car is movable, the occupants are alerted, and the car's contents may never be found again if a warrant must be obtained. Hence an immediate search is constitutionally permissible.

Arguably, because of the preference for a magistrate's judgment, only the immobilization of the car should be permitted until a search warrant is obtained; arguably, only the "lesser" intrusion is permissible until the magistrate authorizes the "greater." But which is the "greater" and which the "lesser" intrusion is itself a debatable question and the answer may depend on a variety of circumstances. For constitutional purposes, we see no difference between on the one hand seizing and holding a car before presenting the probable-cause issue to a magistrate and on the other hand carrying out an immediate search without a warrant. Given probable cause to search, either course is reasonable under the Fourth Amendment.

On the facts before us, the blue station wagon could have been searched on the spot when it was stopped since there was probable cause to search and it was a fleeting target for a search. The probable-cause factor still obtained at the station house and so did the mobility of the car unless the Fourth Amendment permits a warrantless seizure of the car and the denial of its use to anyone until a warrant is secured. In that event there is little to choose in terms of practical consequences between an immediate search without a warrant and the car's immobilization until a warrant is obtained.[4] The same consequences may not follow where there is unforeseeable cause to search a house. Compare *Vale v. Louisiana*. But as *Carroll, supra*, held, for the purposes of the Fourth Amendment there is a constitutional difference between houses and cars.

. . . .

Affirmed.

LEDERER v. TEHAN
CIRCUIT COURT OF APPEALS, 6th DISTRICT
441 F.2d 295 (1971)

On an April evening, a Cincinnati park patrolman saw a U-Haul truck parked in a parking lot of one of the city parks. As this was a violation of an ordinance, the officer approached the truck. The rear sliding door of the truck was raised about a foot and the officer could see that an individual was inside the truck in tennis shoes.

When the officer reached the rear of the truck, the sliding door was opened completely by the person inside and the officer could then see a crate in the truck with its top and one side removed. The crate contained a partially broken plaster statue. Knives, guns, vases, a hammer, other tools and a suitcase were on the floor

---

[4] It was not unreasonable in this case to take the car to the station house. All occupants in the car were arrested in a dark parking lot in the middle of the night. A careful search at that point was impractical and perhaps not safe for the officers, and it would serve the owner's convenience and the safety of his car to have the vehicle and the keys together at the station house.

of the truck near the crate and the officer could see some small white packets protruding from the broken part of the statute.

The officer entered the van and examined the packets more closely. He then placed the defendant under arrest. Tests showed that the packets contained hashish. The estimated value of the hashish found in the truck was $300,000.

The defendant appeals from his conviction alleging an illegal search and seizure. In affirming the conviction the Court stated:

THE COURT "Like the District Judge, we are of the opinion that while the park policeman was looking in the truck, and before he interfered with appellant Lederer's freedom in any way, he had probable cause to believe the narcotics laws were being violated. The subsequent seizure was justified by what the officer had in ''plain view.''

. . . .

The impossibility of following search warrant procedures under the facts of this case is obvious. So is the hazard that the evidence of the crime would have been rapidly removed from the scene unless the police officer acted with dispatch. Such considerations have provided an historic differentiation between search and seizure cases involving houses and those involving moving vehicles.

As long ago as 1925 the Supreme Court said: [The court quoted the U.S. Supreme Court case of *Carroll v. United States.*]

As is obvious from what has been said earlier, we believe that the officer in this case did have probable cause to believe the van contained ''contraband or illegal merchandise,'' as of the moment he determined upon the search and seizure.

The last issue in this case which we feel needs specific comment arises from a portion of the cross-examination of the police officer at the state court trial:

> ''Question: For what crime did you arrest him?
> Answer: I suspected that the substance was some type of narcotics.
> Question: You arrested this man then on your suspicion, is that correct?
> Answer: Yes.''

As to this issue, we accept fully Judge Porter's decision and reasoning:

> ''[W]e have not overlooked the fact that petitioner places considerable reliance upon Officer Depenbrock's testimony to the effect that he arrested petitioner on suspicion. As we stated earlier, suspicion does not suffice as a basis to arrest. Of course, in certain situations there is a nebulous line between suspicion and probable cause, but it is recognized that the ultimate determination as to the existence or nonexistence of probable cause always rests with the courts. In other words, based upon the facts within his personal knowledge, what an officer might say was his suspicion might well be ample, when considered by a judge, to fulfill the probable cause standard. The point is that the controlling test is not dependent upon how the particular officer describes his feelings or the choice of words which he may select. After all, police officers, in testifying, are only expected to honestly relate the facts as they transpired, and we do not expect them to be legal linguists who express themselves in terms of legal jargon, such as 'probable cause,' 'reasonable grounds to believe,' etc.

Instead, as stated above, the controlling test is based upon the facts possessed by the officer as applied, by a judge, against the hypothetical reasonable man standard (i.e., whether the facts and circumstances within the officer's knowledge are sufficient to warrant a man of reasonable caution in the belief that an offense has been or is being committed).

"In short, because Officer Depenbrock answered 'Yes' in response to the question: 'You arrested this man then on your suspicion, is that correct?' is not determinative of the matter. What is decisive is, as we in the exercise of our judicial responsibilities have held above, that when Officer Depenbrock entered the rear of the truck he possessed facts which would have warranted a reasonable man in believing that a crime had been or was being committed."

For these reasons and those set out more fully in the District Judge's opinion, dated May 13, 1970, the judgment of the District Court is affirmed.

QUESTIONS AND PROBLEMS

After reading the following cases, indicate whether the *searches* were:

    a.   valid as an incident to a lawful arrest;
    b.   valid probable-cause searches under the Carroll rule;
    c.   valid under an authority other than a or b; or
    d.   *invalid.* If invalid, indicate the procedure the officer should have used.

1.   Men in a control tower at the Cleveland airport observed conduct by the defendant which made it quite clear that the defendant was stealing from cars parked at the airport. The defendant was arrested by officers sent to the scene. He was searched, but nothing was found and the keys to his car were not found. After the defendant was taken to the police station in a squad car, a key was discovered in the back seat of the police car. The defendant denied owning the key. One of the arresting officers returned to the airport parking lot, where another police officer had remained to watch the car thought to be owned by the defendant. The key which was found matched the numbers on the trunk lock and the officer opened the car trunk. The evidence seized in the trunk is contested as being obtained by an unlawful search and seizure. *Colosimo v. Perini,* 415 F.2d 804 (6th Cir. 1969)

2.   A police officer on duty on the Ohio State Turnpike received a radio message that there had been an armed robbery at the exit 6 motel and that it was believed that the suspect entered the turnpike at exit 6. A short time later, the officer saw a car and a man matching the description given to him. After radioing for assistance,

COMPARISON OF RULING AUTO SEARCH CASES

U.S. SUPREME COURT CASE	STATUS OF VEHICLE WHEN POLICE APPROACHED	WAS SEARCH MADE BEFORE OR AFTER ARREST?	WAS SEARCH MADE AT THE TIME AND PLACE OF ARREST OR STOP?	AUTHORITY GIVEN BY THE STATE (AND THE POLICE) FOR SEARCH	WAS SEARCH HELD VALID AND LEGAL?
Carroll v. U.S., 267 U.S. 132 (1925)	Moving on highway	The search was made before the arrest. After finding the contraband, the arrest was made	Yes	Reasonable grounds to believe that the mobile vehicle contained contraband	Yes
Preston v. U.S. 376 U.S. 364 (1964)	Vehicle was parked	The search was made after the arrest for vagrancy	No, the search was made at another time and place and no compelling reason was given for the delay	Search incident to the arrest	No
Chambers v. Maroney 399 U.S. 42 (1970)	Vehicle was moving	The search was made after the arrest for armed robbery	No, the search was made at another time and place but the Court held that this was not unreasonable (see footnote 3 of the case)	Reasonable grounds to believe that the vehicle contained that which could be seized by the police (could also be sustained as a lawful search incident to the arrest)	Yes
Collidge v. New Hampshire 403 U.S. 443 (1971)	The car was parked on the driveway of the home when the defendant was arrested in the house for the murder of a 14-year-old girl	The car was searched and vacuumed on three different occasions after the arrest	No, the car was impounded at the time of the arrest. It was towed away 2½ hours after the arrest and searched 2 days after the arrest, a year after the arrest, and 14 months after the arrest	Search incident to the valid arrest, probable-cause search under the Carroll rule, and a "plain view" exception to the search warrant requirement as the car was seized as an "instrumentality of the crime" (see this case in Chap. 16)	No, all three arguments were rejected by the Court

the officer stopped the car and asked to see the defendant's toll ticket. The ticket showed that the defendant entered the turnpike at exit 6. The man was then arrested and a search produced a tear-gas gun. When other officers arrived, a search of the car was conducted. In addition to items taken from the motel, the officers found a checkbook taken in a robbery in Indiana. The issue before the court is whether the evidence obtained in the search of the car was lawful. *Patterson v. State*, 255 N.E. 520, (S. Ct. Indiana 1970)

3. The arresting officers were members of the gambling detail. They knew the defendant because they had arrested him for gambling previously. The officers saw the defendant park his car and go into a building. He also saw them at that time. Twenty minutes later, the defendant came out of the building but when he saw the officers again, he ran back into the building. The officers pursued him and arrested him for parking his car too close to a crosswalk. They searched his person and found policy tickets. The defendant was charged with violating Illinois gambling laws. Would the arrest and search be valid and reasonable in your jurisdiction? *People v. Watkins*, 19 Ill.2d 11 (S. Ct. Ill. 1960)

4. A sheriff's department received a telephone call from a man who stated that he smashed his car into a bridge abutment. When officers arrived at the scene, they arrested the man for drunkenness. The car, which was rented, was towed to a garage and the defendant was taken to the sheriff's office. One of the arresting officers then went to the garage to which the car had been towed and with some effort opened the trunk. He obtained thirteen objects which tests showed to be covered with type O human blood. The next day, a murder victim was found on a farm owned by the man arrested. He was charged with first-degree murder. The thirteen items taken from the trunk of the car are the basis for much of the state's case against the defendant. The officers had no knowledge of the murder at the time they investigated the accident. *State v. Dombrowski*, 44 Wis.2d 486 (S. Ct. Wis. 1970)

[*Authors' note as text is going to press:* The U.S. Supreme Court has agreed to hear the Dombrowski case after Dombrowski's conviction was reversed by the U.S. Court of Appeals for the 7th Circuit (11 Crim. L. R. 2289). In oral arguments which will be heard in March 1973, the State of Wisconsin will argue that the exclusionary rule should be modified.]

11

AUTHORITY TO SEARCH DURING TEMPORARY DETENTION FOR QUESTIONING (STOP AND FRISK)

Experienced law enforcement officers are well aware that they can be confronted with situations where there is insufficient evidence to justify an arrest. But because of suspicious or unusual activities which they have observed, they know that an inquiry should be made.

If an officer determines that the facts which are available to him amount to "reasonable suspicion," then under the statutory or common law of his jurisdiction, he has the authority to make a temporary detention for questioning. The usual statutory definition of reasonable suspicion is that there is sufficient ground to reasonably suspect that the person being detained has committed, is committing, or is about to commit a crime.

If reasonable suspicion does not exist, then the officer has the alternative of continuing his investigation (or his surveillance) or engaging the person in a voluntary conversation. Either of these alternatives may clear the doubt in the officer's mind, or they may provide additional information to justify a temporary detention for questioning or an arrest.

THE TERRY, SIBRON, AND PETERS CASES

It was not until 1968 that the U.S. Supreme Court ruled on the question of temporary street detention for questioning and the possible weapons search for the officer's protection during this detention. The Court states in the Terry case that this "... sensitive area of police activity [raises] issues which have never before been squarely presented to this Court."

The authority of the police to make reasonable inquiry always existed in English and American law, but it was never seriously challenged until the early 1960s. See the article "Demanding Name and Address," 66 L. Q Rev. 465, where the author stated in 1950 that "[t]he

DEGREE OF POLICE CONTACT	EVIDENCE NECESSARY TO JUSTIFY THE POLICE ACTION	THE DEGREE OF FORCE WHICH MAY BE USED	WARNINGS NECESSARY PRIOR TO QUESTIONING	SEARCH THAT MAY ACCOMPANY THE POLICE ACTION
The "voluntary conversation"	None	None	None	None
Temporary questioning without arrest (the "stop")	Reasonable suspicion, based on objective circumstances, that the person stopped has committed, is committing, or is about to commit a crime	Reasonable force not likely to cause death or serious bodily injury	None (unless the question is accusatory: "Did you rob Smith's bakery?")	See *Search during Temporary Questioning* below
Search during temporary questioning (the "frisk")	The officer has reason to conclude that the suspect may be armed and dangerous, or the officer reasonably suspects that he or another is in danger of physical injury	Reasonable force not likely to cause death or serious bodily injury	None	*A pat-down for weapons:* "...where nothing in the initial stages of the encounter serves to dispel his reasonable fear for his own or others' safety, he is entitled for the protection of himself and others in the area to conduct a carefully limited search of the outer clothing of such persons in an attempt to discover weapons which might be used to assault him." U.S. Supreme Court in *Terry v. Ohio* (see cases)

The "arrest"	Probable cause to believe that the suspect is guilty of a specific crime	Reasonable force not likely to cause death or serious bodily injury unless the arrest is for a serious felony, when deadly force may be use	If the officer is questioning the arrested person, the Miranda warnings must be given	A full search designed to protect the officer and to prevent the destruction of evidence of the crime

This chart is adapted from material from the FBI National Academy.

law works as well as it does chiefly because the moral authority of the police enables them to get on without powers."

In 1968, the United States Supreme Court established the common law guideline for the authority to search during a temporary detention for questioning by stating:

> We merely hold today that where a police officer observes un-usual conduct which leads him reasonably to conclude in light of his experience that criminal activity may be afoot and that the person with whom he is dealing may be armed and presently dangerous, where in the course of investigating this behavior he identifies himself as a policeman and makes reasonable inquiries, and where nothing in the initial stages of the encounter serves to dispel his reasonable fear for his own or others' safety, he is entitled for the protection of himself and others in the area to conduct a carefully limited search of the outer clothing of such persons in an attempt to discover weapons which might be used to assault him.

STATUTORY AUTHORITY TO SEARCH
DURING TEMPORARY DETENTION FOR QUESTIONING

Probably all states now have passed statutes establishing the authority of law enforcement officers to make weapons searches during tempo-rary detention for questioning when the officer reasonably suspects that he or another is in danger of physical injury. A few states passed their statutes before the Terry, Sibron, and Peters cases of 1968. New York passed such a statute in 1964.

Probably all or most of the state statutes give officers a *narrower* scope of authority than the common-law authority established in Terry, Sibron, and Peters. In 1970, the New York Court of Appeals held in *People v. Rosemond*, 257 N.E.2d 23 (1970), that officers may rely upon their common-law authority to stop persons and make reasonable inquiry concerning their unusual activities. The court held that the New York statute does *not* ". . . prescribe the full scope of police activity."

AUTHORITY TO MAKE THE STOP

Neither the statutes nor the common law gives officers the authority to stop just any passerby. A mere hunch or intuition is not sufficient. Nor should a person be stopped *only* because he is found near the scene of a crime. A past criminal record *alone* is not sufficient to justify a stop.

Most state statutes require that the officer have reasonable suspicion to believe that the subject is committing, has committed, or is about to commit a felony or a misdemeanor included in the "stop" statute.

Reasonable suspicion is more than unsupported suspicion but less than evidence that amounts to probable cause or reasonable belief that the suspect has committed, is committing, or is about to commit a crime.

There must be adequate observation or investigation by the police officer or information in his possession before any stop of a suspect can be made upon reasonable suspicion. Such information or observation should, as the Supreme Court stated in the Terry case, lead the officer "reasonably to conclude in light of his experience that criminal activity may be afoot...." Some of the factors which may be considered by the officer in determining whether reasonable suspicion exists are:

The appearance and/or the manner of the suspect
His activity at the time the officer observes him
The time of the day or night the suspect is observed
The particular streets and area involved
The type of clothing the suspect is wearing and whether there are
    bulges which suggest a concealed weapon
Whether the suspect is carrying anything and, if so, the nature thereof
Prior knowledge which the officer has of the suspect
    a. Suspect's past record
    b. Information from an informant or third party
    c. Any overheard conversation known to the officer
The proximity to a known crime scene. Is the area known for its high
    crime rate?

(This listing is not meant to be all-inclusive.)

REQUIREMENT OF PUBLIC PLACE

Statutes authorizing officers to detain a person temporarily for questioning generally require that it be in a "public place." In the Peters case, the court held that the sixth-floor hall of an apartment building was a public place within the meaning of the statute.

A public place is generally described as any place where the public has a right to go. It may be privately owned or controlled, as a shopping center. The public may have to pay to go into the public place, as in the case of a football game or theater, or they may have to be adults, as in the case of a tavern.

THE AUTHORITY TO QUESTION

The New York State Combined Council of Law Enforcement Officials define the right to "question" as follows (on page 40 of *The Challenge of Crime in a Free Society, Task Force Report: The Police*):

1. No questions are to be asked until the officer has, either by being in uniform or by showing his shield and stating he is a police officer, identified himself.
2. Promptly thereafter, the suspect should be questioned (and "frisked," when appropriate) in the immediate area in which he was stopped.
3. Should the suspect refuse to answer the officer's questions, the officer cannot compel an answer and should not attempt to do so. The suspect's refusal to answer shall not be considered as an element by the officer in determining whether or not there is a basis for an arrest.

   [*Authors' note:* In other jurisdictions such as Wisconsin, if the suspect refuses to identify himself or refuses to explain his conduct or refuses to stay in the presence of the officer, this may be construed to be a violation of the "obstruction of an officer" statute and an arrest may be made. The temporary detention statute would have to give the officer the authority to demand the name and address of the suspect and an explanation of his conduct. Convictions have been obtained where there is a firm basis of reasonable suspicion and the suspect does not comply with the officer's demand.]

4. In ascertaining "his name" from the suspect, the officer may request to see verification of his identity, but a person shall not be compelled to produce such verification.
5. If the suspect does answer, and his answers appear to be false or unsatisfactory, the officer may question further. Answers of this nature may serve as an element in determining whether a basis for arrest exists. (But if an officer determines that an answer is "unsatisfactory" and relies upon this in part to sustain his arrest, he should be able to explain with particularity the manner in which it is "unsatisfactory.")

ARE THE MIRANDA WARNINGS NECESSARY PRIOR TO QUESTIONING IN A TEMPORARY DETENTION?

The Miranda warnings are *not* necessary prior to asking a suspect for his name, address, and an explanation of his conduct. However, if in the course of the conversation the officer were to ask a question which specifically could produce an incriminating answer, then the Miranda warnings should be given prior to the question. An example of this would be, "Did you burglarize the drugstore on the corner?"

THE AUTHORITY TO SEARCH

The New York State Combined Council of Law Enforcement Officials define the right to "search" as follows (also see the cases in this chapter for court determination as to method and scope of the search):

1. Clearly no right to search exists unless there is a right to stop.
2. Nor is a search lawful in every case in which a right to stop exists. A search is only justified under the new law when the officer reasonably suspects he is in danger. This claim is not to be used as a pretext for obtaining evidence. In instances in which evidence is produced as a result of search, the superior officers, the prosecutors and—it is anticipated—the courts, will scrutinize particularly closely all the circumstances relied upon for justifying the stopping and searching.
3. No search is appropriate unless the officer "reasonably suspects that he is in danger." Among the factors that may be considered in determining whether to search are:
    a. Nature of the suspected crime, and whether it involved the use of a weapon or violence.
    b. The presence or absence of assistance to the officer, and the number of suspects being stopped.
    c. The time of the day or night.
    d. Prior knowledge of the suspect's record and reputation.
    e. The sex of the suspect.
    f. The demeanor and seeming agility of the suspect, and whether his clothes so bulge as to be indicative of concealed weapons.
    (This list is not all-inclusive)
4. Initially, once the determination has been made that the officer may be in danger, all that is necessary is a frisk—an external feeling of clothing—such as would reveal a weapon of immediate danger to the officer.
5. A search of the suspect's clothing and pockets should not be made unless something is felt by this frisk—such as a hard object that feels as if it may be a weapon. In such event, the officer may search that portion of the suspect's clothing to uncover the article that was felt.
6. If the suspect is carrying an object such as a handbag, suitcase, sack, etc. which may conceal a weapon, the officer should not open that item, but should see that it is placed out of reach of the suspect so that its presence will not represent any immediate danger to the officer.
    An example may help to illustrate. Assume that a mugging has just occurred. The officer questions the victim. She says that her pocket book was taken and she gives a description of the suspect stating, among other things, that he is about six feet tall and was wearing a brown leather windbreaker. While the victim is receiving medical treatment, the officer starts a search of the area. He sees a man hurrying down a dark street. The man's hand is clutching

at a bulge under his brown windbreaker, and he glances back at the officer repeatedly. The suspect meets the description of the perpetrator except for one discrepancy—he is about five feet tall. The officer does not have reasonable grounds to arrest the suspect for his description is clearly inconsistent with the victim's estimate for the perpetrator's height. However, from the officer's experience he realizes that victims of crime, in an excited condition, often give descriptions which are not correct in every detail. Although he lacks reasonable grounds to make an arrest, from all of the circumstances the officer "reasonably suspects" that the man he has spotted has committed the crime. Under the new law, the officer may stop this person and may ask for his identification and an explanation of his actions. And because the crime involved violence and the suspect's windbreaker seems to conceal unnatural bulges, a frisk may be in order.

MOTOR VEHICLES AND THEIR OCCUPANTS

The law and authority to temporarily detain for questioning applies to the occupants of motor vehicles. In 1960, the court in *United States v. Bonanno*, 180 F. SUPP. 71 (D.C. S.D. N.Y.), stated, "Courts have recognized the right of law enforcement agents reasonably and temporarily to stop vehicles and question occupants on grounds that might not amount to a basis for arrest or search."

In addition to obtaining information as to the identity of the suspect and an explanation of his conduct, the officer may make a driver's license check and may inquire as to the ownership of the vehicle. If the evidence does not amount to probable cause and the driver has a license and proof of ownership, the officer must release the vehicle and person detained.

EXTENT OF THE PROTECTIVE SEARCH

The question of the extent of the use of the protective search has not as yet been fully determined by the courts. Courts will give great consideration to the testimony of an officer that he made the frisk because he feared for his own safety. The courts will, however, look at the circumstances in each case to determine whether the officer was justified in making the protective search. Also, the burden is on the state to show that the circumstances warranted the use of the protective search.

UNITED STATES v. GONZALES, 319 F. SUPP. 563 (CONN. 1970)

The court held that the officer was justified in frisking the companion of the person who was arrested. But when the officer felt a soft bulge, he reached into the pocket and pulled out a cigarette pack containing marijuana. It was held that the second search into the pocket was not justified.

968.16 OF THE WISCONSIN STATUTES

This provides that "The person executing the search warrant may reasonably detain and search any person on the premises at the time to protect himself from attack or to prevent the disposal or concealment of any item particularly described in the search warrant." (This statute was enacted in 1970.)

TEMPORARY AND BRIEF DETENTION ON LESS THAN PROBABLE CAUSE AT THE STATION HOUSE

In *Davis v. Mississippi* (see cases Chap. 2), the question as to whether a person could be detained for a short period of time on less than probable cause in order to obtain evidence such as fingerprints came before the United States Supreme Court. The Court did not rule on the question but stated in dictum (with Justice Harlan dissenting on the point) that such detention would have to be authorized by a judicial officer. Colorado Supreme Court rule 41.1 and the proposed 18 U.S.C. 3507 would authorize such brief detention under the supervision of judicial officers in order to obtain evidence which could not be obtained from other sources and there is reasonable grounds to believe such evidence will identify the person who had committed a specific crime.

CASES FOR CHAPTER ELEVEN

TERRY v. OHIO
SUPREME COURT OF THE UNITED STATES
392 U.S. 1, 20 L. ED. 2d 889, 88 S. CT. 1868 (1968)

Mr. Chief Justice Warren delivered the opinion of the Court.

This case presents serious questions concerning the role of the Fourth Amendment in the confrontation on the street between the citizen and the policeman investigating suspicious circumstances.

Petitioner Terry was convicted of carrying a concealed weapon and sentenced to the statutorily prescribed term of one to three years in the penitentiary.[1] Following the denial of a pretrial motion to suppress, the prosecution introduced in evidence two revolvers and a number of bullets seized from Terry and a codefendant,

---

[1] Ohio Rev. Code § 2923.01 (1953) provides in part that "no person shall carry a pistol, bowie knife, dirk, or other dangerous weapon concealed on or about his person." An exception is made for properly authorized law enforcement officers.

Richard Chilton,[2] by Cleveland Police Detective Martin McFadden. At the hearing on the motion to suppress this evidence, [Officer McFadden testified that while he was patrolling in plain clothes in downtown Cleveland at approximately 2:30 in the afternoon of October 31, 1963, his attention was attracted by two men, Chilton and Terry, standing on the corner of Huron Road and Euclid Avenue. He had never seen the two men before, and he was unable to say precisely what first drew his eye to them. However, he testified that he had been a policeman for 39 years and a detective for 35 and that he had been assigned to patrol this vicinity of downtown Cleveland for shoplifters and pickpockets for 30 years. He explained that he had developed routine habits of observation over the years and that he would "stand and watch people or walk and watch people at many intervals of the day." He added: "Now, in this case when I looked over they didn't look right at me at the time."

His interest aroused, Officer McFadden took up a post of observation in the entrance to a store 300 to 400 feet away from the two men. "I get more purpose to watch them when I seen their movements," he testified. He saw one of the men leave the other one and walk southwest on Huron Road, past some stores. The man paused for a moment and looked in a store window, then walked on a short distance, turned around and walked back toward the corner, pausing once again to look in the same store window. He rejoined his companion at the corner, and the two conferred briefly. Then the second man went through the same series of motions, strolling down Huron Road, looking in the same window, walking on a short distance, turning back, peering in the store window again, and returning to confer with the first man at the corner. The two men repeated this ritual alternately between five and six times apiece—in all roughly a dozen trips. At one point, while the two were standing together on the corner, a third man approached them and engaged them briefly in conversation. This man then left the two others and walked west on Euclid Avenue. Chilton and Terry resumed their measured pacing, peering, and conferring. After this had gone on for 10 to 12 minutes, the two men walked off together, heading west on Euclid Avenue, following the path taken earlier by the third man.

By this time Officer McFadden had become thoroughly suspicious. He testified that after observing their elaborately casual and oft-repeated reconnaissance of the store window on Huron Road, he suspected the two men of "casing a job, a stick-up," and that he considered it his duty as a police officer to investigate further. He added that he feared "they may have a gun." Thus, Officer McFadden followed Chilton and Terry and saw them stop in front of Zucker's store to talk to the same man who had conferred with them earlier on the street corner. Deciding that the situation was ripe for direct action, Officer McFadden approached the three men, identified himself as a police officer and asked for their names. At this

---

[2] Terry and Chilton were arrested, indicted, tried, and convicted together. They were represented by the same attorney, and they made a joint motion to suppress the guns. After the motion was denied, evidence was taken in the case against Chilton. This evidence consisted of the testimony of the arresting officer and of Chilton. It was then stipulated that this testimony would be applied to the case against Terry, and no further evidence was introduced in that case. The trial judge considered the two cases together, rendered the decisions at the same time and sentenced the two men at the same time. They prosecuted their state court appeals together through the same attorney, and they petitioned this Court for certiorari together. Following the grant of the writ upon this joint petition, Chilton died. Thus, only Terry's conviction is here for review.

point his knowledge was confined to what he had observed. He was not acquainted with any of the three men by name or by sight, and he had received no information concerning them from any other source. When the men "mumbled something" in response to his inquiries, Officer McFadden grabbed petitioner Terry, spun him around so that they were facing the other two, with Terry between McFadden and the others, and patted down the outside of his clothing. In the left breast pocket of Terry's overcoat Officer McFadden felt a pistol. He reached inside the overcoat pocket, but was unable to remove the gun. At this point, keeping Terry between himself and the others, the officer ordered all three men to enter Zucker's store. As they went in, he removed Terry's overcoat completely, removed a .38-caliber revolver from the pocket and ordered all three men to face the wall with their hands raised. Officer McFadden proceeded to pat down the outer clothing of Chilton and the third man, Katz. He discovered another revolver in the outer pocket of Chilton's overcoat, but no weapons were found on Katz. The officer testified that he only patted the men down to see whether they had weapons, and that he did not put his hands beneath the outer garments of either Terry or Chilton until he felt their guns. So far as appears from the record, he never placed his hands beneath Katz' outer garments. Officer McFadden seized Chilton's gun, asked the proprietor of the store to call a police wagon, and took all three men to the station, where Chilton and Terry were formally charged with carrying concealed weapons.

On the motion to suppress the guns the prosecution took the position that they had been seized following a search incident to a lawful arrest. The trial court rejected this theory, stating that it "would be stretching the facts beyond reasonable comprehension" to find that Officer McFadden had had probable cause to arrest the men before he patted them down for weapons. However, the court denied the defendants' motion on the ground that Officer McFadden, on the basis of his experience, "had reasonable cause to believe . . . that the defendants were conducting themselves suspiciously, and some interrogation should be made of their action." Purely for his own protection, the court held, the officer had the right to pat down the outer clothing of these men, who he had reasonable cause to believe might be armed. The court distinguished between an investigatory "stop" and an arrest, and between a "frisk" of the outer clothing for weapons and a full-blown search for evidence of crime. The frisk, it held, was essential to the proper performance of the officer's investigatory duties, for without it "the answer to the police officer may be a bullet, and a loaded pistol discovered during the frisk is admissible."

After the court denied their motion to suppress, Chilton and Terry waived jury trial and pleaded not guilty. The court adjudged them guilty, and the Court of Appeals for the Eighth Judicial District, Cuyahoga County, affirmed. The Supreme Court of Ohio dismissed their appeal on the ground that no "substantial constitutional question" was involved. We granted certiorari, to determine whether the admission of the revolvers in evidence violated petitioner's rights under the Fourth Amendment, made applicable to the States by the Fourteenth. We affirm the conviction.

I.

The Fourth Amendment provides that "the right of the people to be secure in their persons, houses, papers, and effects, against unreasonable searches and seizures, shall not be violated. . . ." This inestimable right of personal security belongs as much to the citizen on the streets of our cities as to the homeowner closeted in his study to dispose of his secret affairs. For, as this Court has always recognized,

"No right is held more sacred, or is more carefully guarded, by the common law, than the right of every individual to the possession and control of his own person, free from all restraint or interference of others, unless by clear and unquestionable authority of law."

We have recently held that "the Fourth Amendment protects people, not places," Katz v United States, 389 US 347, 351, 19 L Ed 2d 576, 582, 88 S Ct 507 (1967), and wherever an individual may harbor a reasonable "expectation of privacy," he is entitled to be free from unreasonable governmental intrusion. Of course, the specific content and incidents of this right must be shaped by the context in which it is asserted. For "what the Constitution forbids is not all searches and seizures, but unreasonable searches and seizures." Unquestionably petitioner was entitled to the protection of the Fourth Amendment as he walked down the street in Cleveland. The question is whether in all the circumstances of this on-the-street encounter, his right to personal security was violated by an unreasonable search and seizure.

We would be less than candid if we did not acknowledge that this question thrusts to the fore difficult and troublesome issues regarding a sensitive area of police activity—issues which have never before been squarely presented to this Court. Reflective of the tensions involved are the practical and constitutional arguments pressed with great vigor on both sides of the public debate over the power of the police to "stop and frisk"—as it is sometimes euphemistically termed—suspicious persons.

On the one hand, it is frequently argued that in dealing with the rapidly unfolding and often dangerous situations on city streets the police are in need of an escalating set of flexible responses, graduated in relation to the amount of information they possess. For this purpose it is urged that distinctions should be made between a "stop" and an "arrest" (or a "seizure" of a person), and between a "frisk" and a "search." Thus, it is argued, the police should be allowed to "stop" a person and detain him briefly for questioning upon suspicion that he may be connected with criminal activity. Upon suspicion that the person may be armed, the police should have the power to "frisk" him for weapons. If the "stop" and the "frisk" give rise to probable cause to believe that the suspect has committed a crime, then the police should be empowered to make a formal "arrest," and a full incident "search" of the person. This scheme is justified in part upon the notion that a "stop" and a "frisk" amount to a mere "minor inconvenience and petty indignity,"[3] which can properly be imposed upon the citizen in the interest of effective law enforcement on the basis of a police officer's suspicion.[4]

[3] People v Rivera, n. 3, at 447, 201 NE2d, at 36, 252 NYS2d, at 464.
[4] The theory is well laid out in the Rivera opinion:
"[T]he evidence needed to make the inquiry is not of the same degree of conclusiveness as that required for an arrest. The stopping of the individual to inquire is not an arrest and the ground upon which the police may make the inquiry may be less incriminating than the ground for an arrest for a crime known to have been committed....
. . . .
"And as the right to stop and inquire is to be justified for a cause less conclusive than that which would sustain an arrest, so the right to frisk may be justified as an incident to inquiry upon grounds of elemental safety and precaution which might not initially sustain a search. Ultimately the validity of the frisk narrows down to whether there is or is not a right by the police to touch the person ques-

On the other side the argument is made that the authority of the police must be strictly circumscribed by the law of arrest and search as it has developed to date in the traditional jurisprudence of the Fourth Amendment. It is contended with some force that there is not—and cannot be—a variety of police activity which does not depend solely upon the voluntary cooperation of the citizen and yet which stops short of an arrest based upon probable cause to make such an arrest. The heart of the Fourth Amendment, the argument runs, is a severe requirement of specific justification for any intrusion upon protected personal security, coupled with a highly developed system of judicial controls to enforce upon the agents of the State the commands of the Constitution. Acquiescence by the courts in the compulsion inherent in the field interrogation practices at issue here, it is urged, would constitute an abdication of judicial control over, and indeed an encouragement of, substantial interference with liberty and personal security by police officers whose judgment is necessarily colored by their primary involvement in "the often competitive enterprise of ferreting out crime." This, it is argued, can only serve to exacerbate police-community tensions in the crowded centers of our Nation's cities.

In this context we approach the issues in this case mindful of the limitations of the judicial function in controlling the myriad daily situations in which policemen and citizens confront each other on the street. The State has characterized the issue here as "the right of a police officer . . . to make an on-the-street stop, interrogate and pat down for weapons (known in street vernacular as 'stop and frisk')." But this is only partly accurate. For the issue is not the abstract propriety of the police conduct, but the admissibility against petitioner of the evidence uncovered by the search and seizure. Ever since its inception, the rule excluding evidence seized in violations of the Fourth Amendment has been recognized as a principal mode of discouraging lawless police conduct. Thus its major thrust is a deterrent one, and experience has taught that it is the only effective deterrent to police misconduct in the criminal context, and that without it the constitutional guarantee against unreasonable searches and seizures would be a mere "form of words." The rule also serves another vital function—"the imperative of judicial integrity." Courts which sit under our Constitution cannot and will not be made party to lawless invasions of the constitutional rights of citizens by permitting unhindered governmental use of the fruits of such invasions. Thus in our system evidentiary rulings provide the context in which the judicial process of inclusion and exclusion approves some conduct as comporting with constitutional guarantees and disapproves other actions by state agents. A ruling admitting evidence in a criminal trial, we recognize, has the necessary effect of legitimizing the conduct which produced the evidence, while an application of the exclusionary rule withholds the constitutional imprimatur.

The exclusionary rule has its limitations, however, as a tool of judicial control. It cannot properly be invoked to exclude the products of legitimate police investigative techniques on the ground that much conduct which is closely similar involves unwarranted intrusions upon constitutional protections. Moreover, in some contexts the rule is ineffective as a deterrent. Street encounters between citizens

---

tioned. The sense of exterior touch here involved is not very far different from the sense of sight or hearing—senses upon which police customarily act." People v Rivera, 14 NY2d 441, 445, 447, 201 NE2d 32, 34, 35, 252 NYS2d 458, 461, 463 (1964), cert denied, 379 US 978, 13 L Ed 2d 568, 85 S Ct 679 (1965).

and police officers are incredibly rich in diversity. They range from wholly friendly exchanges of pleasantries or mutually useful information to hostile confrontations of armed men involving arrests, or injuries, or loss of life. Moreover, hostile confrontations are not all of a piece. Some of them begin in a friendly enough manner, only to take a different turn upon the injection of some unexpected element into the conversation. Encounters are initiated by the police for a wide variety of purposes, some of which are wholly unrelated to a desire to prosecute for crime.[5] Doubtless some police "field interrogation" conduct violates the Fourth Amendment. But a stern refusal by this Court to condone such activity does not necessarily render it responsive to the exclusionary rule. Regardless of how effective the rule may be where obtaining convictions is an important objective of the police, it is powerless to deter invasions of constitutionally guaranteed rights where the police either have no interest in prosecuting or are willing to forgo successful prosecution in the interest of serving some other goal.

Proper adjudication of cases in which the exclusionary rule is invoked demands a constant awareness of these limitations. The wholesale harassment by certain elements of the police community, of which minority groups, particularly Negroes, frequently complain, will not be stopped by the exclusion of any evidence from any criminal trial. Yet a rigid and unthinking application of the exclusionary rule, in futile protest against practices which it can never be used effectively to control, may exact a high toll in human injury and frustration of efforts to prevent crime. No judicial opinion can comprehend the protean variety of the street encounter, and we can only judge the facts of the case before us. Nothing we say today is to be taken as indicating approval of police conduct outside the legitimate investigative sphere. Under our decision, courts still retain their traditional responsibility to guard against police conduct which is overbearing or harassing, or which trenches upon personal security without the objective evidentiary justification which the Constitution requires. When such conduct is identified, it must be condemned by the judiciary and its fruits must be excluded from evidence in criminal trials. And, of course, our approval of legitimate and restrained investigative conduct undertaken on the basis of ample factual justification should in no way discourage the employment of other remedies than the exclusionary rule to curtail abuses for which that sanction may prove inappropriate.

Having thus roughly sketched the perimeters of the constitutional debate over the limits on police investigative conduct in general and the background against which this case presents itself, we turn our attention to the quite narrow question posed by the facts before us: whether it is always unreasonable for a policeman to seize a person and subject him to a limited search for weapons unless there is probable cause for an arrest. Given the narrowness of this question, we have no occasion to canvass in detail the constitutional limitations upon the scope of a policeman's power when he confronts a citizen without probable cause to arrest him.

---

[5] This sort of police conduct may, for example, be designed simply to help an intoxicated person find his way home, with no intention of arresting him unless he becomes obstreperous. Or the police may be seeking to mediate a domestic quarrel which threatens to erupt into violence. They may accost a woman in an area known for prostitution as part of a harassment campaign designed to drive prostitutes away without the considerable difficulty involved in prosecuting them. Or they may be conducting a dragnet search of all teenagers in a particular section of the city for weapons because they have heard rumors of an impending gang fight.

II.

Our first task is to establish at what point in this encounter the Fourth Amendment becomes relevant. That is, we must decide whether and when Officer McFadden "seized" Terry and whether and when he conducted a "search." There is some suggestion in the use of such terms as "stop" and "frisk" that such police conduct is outside the purview of the Fourth Amendment because neither action rises to the level of a "search" or "seizure" within the meaning of the Constitution. We emphatically reject this notion. It is quite plain that the Fourth Amendment governs "seizures" of person which do not eventuate in a trip to the station house and prosecution for crime—"arrests" in traditional terminology. It must be recognized that whenever a police officer accosts an individual and restrains his freedom to walk away, he has "seized" that person. And it is nothing less than sheer torture of the English language to suggest that a careful exploration of the outer surfaces of a person's clothing all over his or her body in an attempt to find weapons is not a "search." Moreover, it is simply fantastic to urge that such a procedure performed in public by a policeman while the citizen stands helpless, perhaps facing a wall with his hands raised, is a "petty indignity." It is a serious intrusion upon the sanctity of the person, which may inflict great indignity and arouse strong resentment, and it is not to be undertaken lightly.

The danger in the logic which proceeds upon distinctions between a "stop" and an "arrest," or "seizure" of the person, and between a "frisk" and a "search" is twofold. It seeks to isolate from constitutional scrutiny the initial stages of the contact between the policeman and the citizen. And by suggesting a rigid all-or-nothing model of justification and regulation under the Amendment, it obscures the utility of limitations upon the scope, as well as the initiation, of police action as a means of constitutional regulation. This Court has held in the past that a search which is reasonable at its inception may violate the Fourth Amendment by virtue of its intolerable intensity and scope. The scope of the search must be "strictly tied to and justified by" the circumstances which rendered its initiation permissible.

The distinctions of classical "stop-and-frisk" theory thus serve to divert attention from the central inquiry under the Fourth Amendment—the reasonableness in all the circumstances of the particular governmental invasion of a citizen's personal security. "Search" and "seizure" are not talismans. We therefore reject the notions that the Fourth Amendment does not come into play at all as a limitation upon police conduct if the officers stop short of something called a "technical arrest" or a "full-blown search."

In this case there can be no question, then, that Officer McFadden "seized" petitioner and subjected him to a "search" when he took hold of him and patted down the outer surfaces of his clothing. We must decide whether at that point it was reasonable for Officer McFadden to have interfered with petitioner's personal security as he did.[6] And in determining whether the seizure and search were

---

[6] We thus decide nothing today concerning the constitutional propriety of an investigative "seizure" upon less than probable cause for purposes of "detention" and/or interrogation. Obviously, not all personal intercourse between policemen and citizens involves "seizures" of persons. Only when the officer, by means of physical force or show of authority, has in some way restrained the liberty of a citizen may we conclude that a "seizure" has occurred. We cannot tell with any certainty upon this record whether any such "seizure" took place here prior to Officer McFadden's initiation of physical contact for purposes of searching Terry for weapons, and we thus may assume that up to that point no intrusion upon constitutionally protected rights had occurred.

"unreasonable" our inquiry is a dual one—whether the officer's action was justified at its inception, and whether it was reasonably related in scope to the circumstances which justified the interference in the first place.

If this case involved police conduct subject to the Warrant Clause of the Fourth Amendment, we would have to ascertain whether "probable cause" existed to justify the search and seizure which took place. However, that is not the case. We do not retreat from our holdings that the police must, whenever practicable, obtain advance judicial approval of searches and seizures through the warrant procedure, or that in most instances failure to comply with the warrant requirement can only be excused by exigent circumstances. But we deal here with an entire rubric of police conduct—necessarily swift action predicated upon the on-the-spot observations of the officer on the beat—which historically has not been, and as a practical matter could not be, subjected to the warrant procedure. Instead, the conduct involved in this case must be tested by the Fourth Amendment's general proscription against unreasonable searches and seizures. Nonetheless, the notions which underlie both the warrant procedure and the requirement of probable cause remain fully relevant in this context. In order to assess the reasonableness of Officer McFadden's conduct as a general proposition, it is necessary "first to focus upon the governmental interest which allegedly justifies official intrusion upon the constitutionally protected interests of the private citizen," for there is "no ready test for determining reasonableness other than by balancing the need to search [or seize] against the invasion which the search [or seizure] entails." And in justifying the particular intrusion the police officer must be able to point to specfiic and articulable facts which, taken together with rational inferences from those facts, reasonably warrant that intrusion. The scheme of the Fourth Amendment becomes meaningful only when it is assured that at some point the conduct of those charged with enforcing the laws can be subjected to the more detached, neutral scrutiny of a judge who must evaluate the reasonableness of a particular search or seizure in light of the particular circumstances. And in making that assessment it is imperative that the facts be judged against an objective standard: would the facts available to the officer at the moment of the seizure or the search "warrant a man of reasonable caution in the belief" that the action taken was appropriate? Anything less would invite intrusions upon constitutionally guaranteed rights based on nothing more substantial than inarticulate hunches, a result this Court has consistently refused to sanction. And simple " 'good faith on the part of the arresting officer is not enough.'... If subjective good faith alone were the test, the protections of the Fourth Amendment would evaporate, and the people would be 'secure in their persons, houses, papers, and effects,' only in the discretion of the police."

Applying these principles to this case, we consider first the nature and extent of the governmental interests involved. One general interest is of course that of effective crime prevention and detection; it is this interest which underlies the recognition that a police officer may in appropriate circumstances and in an appropriate manner approach a person for purposes of investigating possibly criminal behavior even though there is no probable cause to make an arrest. It was this legitimate investigative function Officer McFadden was discharging when he decided to approach petitioner and his companions. He had observed Terry, Chilton, and Katz go through a series of acts, each of them perhaps innocent in itself, but which taken together warranted further investigation. There is nothing unusual in two men standing together on a street corner, perhaps waiting for someone. Nor is there anything suspicious about people in such circumstances strolling up and down the street, singly or in pairs. Store windows, moreover, are made to be looked in. But the story is quite different where, as here, two men hover about a street corner for an extended period of time, at the end of which it becomes apparent that they are not waiting for anyone or anything; where these men pace alternately along an identical route, pausing to stare in the same store window roughly 24 times; where each completion of this route is followed immediately by a conference between the two men on the corner; where they are joined in one of these conferences by a third man who leaves swiftly; and where the two men finally follow the third and rejoin him a couple of blocks away. It would have been poor police work indeed for an officer of 30 years' experience in the detection of thievery from stores in this same neighborhood to have failed to investigate this behavior further. The crux of this case, however, is not the propriety of Officer McFadden's taking steps to investigate petitioner's suspicious behavior, but rather, whether there was justification for McFadden's invasion of Terry's personal security by searching him for weapons in the course of that investigation. We are now concerned with more than the governmental interest in investigating crime; in addition, there is the more immediate interest of the police officer in taking steps to assure himself that the person with whom he is dealing is not armed with a weapon that could unexpectedly and fatally be used against him. Certainly it would be unreasonable to require that police officers take unnecessary risks in the performance of their duties. American criminals have a long tradition of armed violence, and every year in this country many law enforcement officers are killed in the line of duty, and thousands more are wounded. Virtually all of these deaths and a substantial portion of the injuries are inflicted with guns and knives.[7]

In view of these facts, we cannot blind ourselves to the need for law enforcement officers to protect themselves and other prospective victims of violence in situations where they may lack probable cause for an arrest. When an officer is justified in believing that the individual whose suspicious behavior he is investigating at close range is armed and presently dangerous to the officer or to others, it would appear to be clearly unreasonable to deny the officer the power to take necessary measures to determine whether the person is in fact carrying a weapon and to neutralize the threat of physical harm.

We must still consider, however, the nature and quality of the intrusion on individual rights which must be accepted if police officers are to be conceded the right to search for weapons in situations where probable cause to arrest for crime is lacking. Even a limited search of the outer clothing for weapons constitutes a severe, though brief, intrusion upon cherished personal security, and it must surely be an annoying, frightening, and perhaps humiliating experience. Petitioner contends that such an intrusion is permissible only incident to a lawful arrest, either

[7] Fifty-seven law enforcement officers were killed in the line of duty in this country in 1966, bringing the total to 335 for the seven-year period beginning with 1960. Also in 1966, there were 23,851 assaults on police officers, 9,113 of which resulted in injuries to the policemen. Fifty-five of the 57 officers killed in 1966 died from gunshot wounds, 41 of them inflicted by handguns easily secreted about the person. The remaining two murders were perpetrated by knives. See Federal Bureau of Investigation, Uniform Crime Reports for the United States—1966, at 45–48, 152 and Table 51.

The easy availability of firearms to potential criminals in this country is well known and has provoked much debate. See e. g., President's Commission on Law Enforment and Administration of Justice, The Challenge of Crime in a Free Society 239–243 (1967). Whatever the merits of gun-control proposals, this fact is relevant to an assessment of the need for some form of self-protective search power.

for a crime involving the possession of weapons or for a crime the commission of which led the officer to investigate in the first place. However, this argument must be closely examined.

Petitioner does not argue that a police officer should refrain from making any investigation of suspicious circumstances until such time as he has probable cause to make an arrest; nor does he deny that police officers in properly discharging their investigative function may find themselves confronting persons who might well be armed and dangerous. Moreover, he does not say that an officer is always unjustified in searching a suspect to discover weapons. Rather, he says it is unreasonable for the policeman to take that step until such time as the situation evolves to a point where there is probable cause to make an arrest. When that point has been reached, petitioner would concede the officer's right to conduct a search of the suspect for weapons, fruits or instrumentalities of the crime, or "mere" evidence, incident to the arrest.

There are two weaknesses in this line of reasoning, however. First, it fails to take account of traditional limitations upon the scope of searches, and thus recognizes no distinction in purpose, character, and extent between a search incident to an arrest and a limited search for weapons. The former, although justified in part by the acknowledged necessity to protect the arresting officer from assault with a concealed weapon, is also justified on other grounds, and can therefore involve a relatively extensive exploration of the person. A search for weapons in the absence of probable cause to arrest, however, must, like any other search, be strictly circumscribed by the exigencies which justify its initiation. Thus it must be limited to that which is necessary for the discovery of weapons which might be used to harm the officer or others nearby, and may realistically be characterized as something less than a "full" search, even though it remains a serious intrusion.

A second, and related, objection to petitioner's argument is that it assumes that the law of arrest has already worked out the balance between the particular interests involved here—the neutralization of danger to the policeman in the investigative circumstance and the sanctity of the individual. But this is not so. An arrest is a wholly different kind of intrusion upon individual freedom from a limited search for weapons, and the interests each is designed to serve are likewise quite different. An arrest is the initial stage of a criminal prosecution. It is intended to vindicate society's interest in having its laws obeyed, and it is inevitably accompanied by future interference with the individual's freedom of movement, whether or not trial or conviction ultimately follows. The protective search for weapons, on the other hand, constitutes a brief, though far from inconsiderable, intrusion upon the sanctity of the person. It does not follow that because an officer may lawfully arrest a person only when he is apprised of facts sufficient to warrant a belief that the person has committed or is committing a crime, the officer is equally unjustified, absent that kind of evidence, in making any intrusions short of an arrest. Moreover, a perfectly reasonable apprehension of danger may arise long before the officer is possessed of adequate information to justify taking a person into custody for the purpose of prosecuting him for a crime. Petitioner's reliance on cases which have worked out standards of reasonableness with regard to "seizures" constituting arrests and searches incident thereto is thus misplaced. It assumes that the interests sought to be vindicated and the invasions of personal security may be equated in the two cases, and thereby ignores a vital aspect of the analysis of the reasonableness of particular types of conduct under the Fourth Amendment. See Camara v Municipal Court.

Our evaluation of the proper balance that has to be struck in this type of case leads us to conclude that there must be a narrowly drawn authority to permit a reasonable search for weapons for the protection of the police officer, where he has reason to believe that he is dealing with an armed and dangerous individual, regardless of whether he has probable cause to arrest the individual for a crime. The officer need not be absolutely certain that the individual is armed; the issue is whether a reasonably prudent man in the circumstances would be warranted in the belief that his safety or that of others was in danger. And in determining whether the officer acted reasonably in such circumstances, due weight must be given, not to his inchoate and unparticularized suspicion or "hunch," but to the specific reasonable inferences which he is entitled to draw from the facts in light of his experience.

We must now examine the conduct of Officer McFadden in this case to determine whether his search and seizure of petitioner were reasonable, both at their inception and as conducted. He had observed Terry, together with Chilton and another man, acting in a manner he took to be preface to a "stick-up." We think on the facts and circumstances Officer McFadden detailed before the trial judge a reasonably prudent man would have been warranted in believing petitioner was armed and thus presented a threat to the officer's safety while he was investigating his suspicious behavior. The actions of Terry and Chilton were consistent with McFadden's hypothesis that these men were contemplating a daylight robbery—which, it is reasonable to assume, would be likely to involve the use of weapons—and nothing in their conduct from the time he first noticed them until the time he confronted them and identified himself as a police officer gave him sufficient reason to negate that hypothesis. Although the trio had departed the original scene, there was nothing to indicate abandonment of an intent to commit a robbery at some point. Thus, when Officer McFadden approached the three men gathered before the display window at Zucker's store he had observed enough to make it quite reasonable to fear that they were armed; and nothing in their response to his hailing them, identifying himself as a police officer, and asking their names served to dispel that reasonable belief. We cannot say his decision at that point to seize Terry and pat his clothing for weapons was the product of a volatile or inventive imagination, or was undertaken simply as an act of harassment; the record evidences the tempered act of a policeman who in the course of an investigation had to make a quick decision as to how to protect himself and others from possible danger, and took limited steps to do so.

The manner in which the seizure and search were conducted is, of course, as vital a part of the inquiry as whether they were warranted at all. The Fourth Amendment proceeds as much by limitations upon the scope of governmental action as by imposing preconditions upon its initiation. The entire deterrent purpose of the rule excluding evidence seized in violation of the Fourth Amendment rests on the assumption that "limitations upon the fruit to be gathered tend to limit the quest itself." Thus, evidence may not be introduced if it was discovered by means of a seizure and search which were not reasonably related in scope to the justification for their initiation.

We need not develop at length in this case, however, the limitations which the Fourth Amendment places upon a protective seizure and search for weapons. These limitations will have to be developed in the concrete factual circumstances of individual cases. Suffice it to note that such a search, unlike a search without a warrant incident to a lawful arrest, is not justified by any need to prevent the disappearance or destruction of evidence of crime. The sole justification of the search in the present situation is the protection of the police officer and others nearby, and it must therefore be confined in scope to an intrusion reasonably designed to discover guns, knives, clubs, or other hidden instruments for the assault of the police officer. The scope of the search in this case presents no serious problem in light of these standards. Officer McFadden patted down the outer clothing of petitioner and his two companions. He did not place his hands in their pockets or under the outer surface of their garments until he had felt weapons, and then he merely reached for and removed the guns. He never did invade Katz' person beyond the outer surfaces of his clothes, since he discovered nothing in his pat-down which might have been a weapon. Officer McFadden confined his search strictly to what was minimally necessary to learn whether the men were armed and to disarm them once he discovered the weapons. He did not conduct a general exploratory search for whatever evidence of criminal activity he might find.

We conclude that the revolver seized from Terry was properly admitted in evidence against him. At the time he seized petitioner and searched him for weapons, Officer McFadden had reasonable grounds to believe that petitioner was armed and dangerous, and it was necessary for the protection of himself and others to take swift measures to discover the true facts and neutralize the threat of harm if it materialized. The policeman carefully restricted his search to what was appropriate to the discovery of the particular items which he sought. Each case of this sort will, of course, have to be decided on its own facts. We merely hold today that where a police officer observes unusual conduct which leads him reasonably to conclude in light of his experience that criminal activity may be afoot and that the persons with whom he is dealing may be armed and presently dangerous, where in the course of investigating this behavior he identifies himself as a policeman and makes reasonable inquiries, and where nothing in the initial stages of the encounter serves to dispel his reasonable fear for his own or others' safety, he is entitled for the protection of himself and others in the area to conduct a carefully limited search of the outer clothing of such persons in an attempt to discover weapons which might be used to assault him. Such a search is a reasonable search under the Fourth Amendment, and any weapons seized may properly be introduced in evidence against the person from whom they were taken.

Affirmed.

SIBRON/PETERS v. NEW YORK
SUPREME COURT OF THE UNITED STATES
392 U.S. 40, 20 L. ED. 2d 917, 88 S. CT. 1899 (1968)

OPINION OF THE COURT

Mr. Chief Justice Warren delivered the opinion of the Court.

These are companion cases to Terry v Ohio, 392 US 1, 20 L Ed 2d 889, 88 S Ct 1868, decided today. They present related questions under the Fourth and Fourteenth Amendments, but the cases arise in the context of New York's "stop-and-frisk" law, NY Code Crim Proc § 180–a. This statute provides:

"1. A police officer may stop any person abroad in a public place whom he reasonably suspects is committing, has committed or is about to commit a felony or any of the offenses specified in section five hundred fifty-two of this chapter, and may demand of him his name, address and an explanation of his actions.

"2. When a police officer has stopped a person for questioning pursuant to this section and reasonably suspects that he is in danger of life or limb, he may search such person for a dangerous weapon. If the police officer finds such a weapon or any other thing the possession of which may constitute a crime, he may take and keep it until the completion of the questioning, at which time he shall either return it, if lawfully possessed, or arrest such person."

The appellants, Sibron and Peters, were both convicted of crimes in New York state courts on the basis of evidence seized from their persons by police officers. The Court of Appeals of New York held that the evidence was properly admitted, on the ground that the searches which uncovered it were authorized by the statute. Sibron and Peters have appealed their convictions to this Court, claiming that § 180–a is unconstitutional on its face and as construed and applied, because the searches and seizures which it was held to have authorized violated their rights under the Fourth Amendment, made applicable to the States by the Fourteenth. We noted probable jurisdiction, and consolidated the two cases for argument with No. 67.

The facts in these cases may be stated briefly. Sibron, the appellant in No. 63, was convicted of the unlawful possession of heroin. He moved before trial to suppress the heroin seized from his person by the arresting officer, Brooklyn Patrolman Anthony Martin. After the trial court denied his motion, Sibron pleaded guilty to the charge, preserving his right to appeal the evidentiary ruling. At the hearing on the motion to suppress, Officer Martin testified that while he was patrolling his beat in uniform on March 9, 1965, he observed Sibron "continually from the hours of 4:00 P.M. to 12:00, midnight ... in the vicinity of 642 Broadway." He stated that during this period of time he saw Sibron in conversation with six or eight persons whom he (Patrolman Martin) knew from past experience to be narcotics addicts. The officer testified that he did not overhear any of these conversations, and that he did not see anything pass between Sibron and any of the others. Later in the evening Sibron entered a restaurant. Patrolman Martin saw Sibron speak with three more known addicts inside the restaurant. Once again, nothing was overheard and nothing was seen to pass between Sibron and the addicts. Sibron sat down and ordered pie and coffee, and, as he was eating, Patrolman Martin approached him and told him to come outside. Once outside, the officer said to Sibron, "You know what I am after." According to the officer, Sibron "mumbled something and reached into his pocket." Simultaneously, Patrolman Martin thrust his hand into the same pocket, discovering several glassine envelopes, which, it turned out, contained heroin.

The State has had some difficulty in settling upon a theory for the admissibility of these envelopes of heroin. In his sworn complaint Patrolman Martin stated:

> "As the officer approached the defendant, the latter being in the direction of the officer and seeing him, he did put his hand in his left jacket pocket and pulled out a tinfoil envelope and did attempt to throw same to the ground. The officer never losing sight of the said envelope seized it from the def[endan]t's left hand, examined it and found it to contain ten glascine [sic] envelopes with a white substance alleged to be Heroin."

This version of the encounter, however, bears very little resemblance to Patrolman Martin's testimony at the hearing on the motion to suppress. In fact, he discarded the abandonment theory at the hearing.[1] Nor did the officer ever seriously suggest that he was in fear of bodily harm and that he searched Sibron in self-protection to find weapons.[2]

The prosecutor's theory at the hearing was that Patrolman Martin had probable cause to believe that Sibron was in possession of narcotics because he had seen him conversing with a number of known addicts over an eight-hour period. In the absence of any knowledge on Patrolman Martin's part concerning the nature of the intercourse between Sibron and the addicts, however, the trial court was inclined to grant the motion to suppress. As the judge stated, "All he knows about the unknown men: They are narcotics addicts. They might have been talking about the World Series. They might have been talking about prize fights." The prosecutor, however, reminded the judge that Sibron had admitted on the stand, in Patrolman Martin's absence, that he had been talking to the addicts about narcotics. Thereupon, the trial judge changed his mind and ruled that the officer had probable cause for an arrest.

Section 180-a, the "stop-and-frisk" statute, was not mentioned at any point in the trial court. The Appellate Term of the Supreme Court affirmed the conviction without opinion. In the Court of Appeals of New York, Sibron's case was consolidated with the Peters case, No. 74. The Court of Appeals held that the search in Peters was justified under the statute, but it wrote no opinion in Sibron's case. The dissents of Judges Fuld and Van Voorhis, however, indicate that the court rested its holding on § 180-a. At any rate, in its Brief in Opposition to the Jurisdictional Statement in this Court, the State sought to justify the search on the basis of the statute. After we noted probable jurisdiction, the District Attorney for Kings County confessed error.

Peters, the appellant in No. 74, was convicted of possessing burglary tools under circumstances evincing an intent to employ them in the commission of a crime.[3] The tools were seized from his person at the time of his arrest, and like

---

[1] Patrolman Martin stated several times that he put his hand into Sibron's pocket and seized the heroin before Sibron had any opportunity to remove his own hand from the pocket. The trial court questioned him on this point:

"Q. Would you say at that time that he reached into his pocket and handed the packets to you? Is that what he did or did he drop the packets?

"A. He did not drop them. *I do not know what his intentions were.* He pushed his hand into his pocket.

"Mr. Joseph [Prosecutor]: You intercepted it; didn't you, Officer?

"The Witness: Yes." (Emphasis added.)

It is of course highly unlikely that Sibron, facing the officer at such close quarters, would have tried to remove the heroin from his pocket and throw it to the ground in the hope that he could escape responsibility for it.

[2] The possibility that Sibron, who never, so far as appears from the record, offered any resistance, might have posed a danger to Patrolman Martin's safety was never even discussed as a potential justification for the search. The only mention of weapons by the officer in his entire testimony came in response to a leading question by Sibron's counsel, when Martin stated that he "thought he [Sibron] might have been" reaching for a gun. Even so, Patrolman Martin did not accept this suggestion by the opposition regarding the reason for his action; the discussion continued upon the plain premise that he had been looking for narcotics all the time.

[3] N. Y. Pen. Law of 1909 § 408, made the possession of such tools under such circumstances a misdemeanor for first offenders and a felony for all those who have "been previously convicted of any crime." Peters was convicted of a felony under this section.

Sibron he made a pretrial motion to suppress them. When the trial court denied the motion, he too pleaded guilty, preserving his right to appeal. Officer Samuel Lasky of the New York City Police Department testified at the hearing on the motion that he was at home in his apartment in Mount Vernon, New York, at about 1 p. m. on July 10, 1964. He had just finished taking a shower and was drying himself when he heard a noise at his door. His attempt to investigate was interrupted by a telephone call, but when he returned and looked through the peephole into the hall, Officer Lasky saw "two men tiptoeing out of the alcove toward the stairway." He immediately called the police, put on some civilian clothes and armed himself with his service revolver. Returning to the peephole, he saw "a tall man tiptoeing away from the alcove and followed by this shorter man, Mr. Peters, toward the stairway." Officer Lasky testified that he had lived in the 120-unit building for 12 years and that he did not recognize either of the men as tenants. Believing that he had happened upon the two men in the course of an attempted burglary,[4] Officer Lasky opened his door, entered the hallway and slammed the door loudly behind him. This precipitated a flight down the stairs on the part of the two men,[5] and Officer Lasky gave chase. His apartment was located on the sixth floor, and he apprehended Peters between the fourth and fifth floors. Grabbing Peters by the collar, he continued down another flight in unsuccessful pursuit of the other man. Peters explained his presence in the building to Officer Lasky by saying that he was visiting a girl friend. However, he declined to reveal the girl friend's name, on the ground that she was a married woman. Officer Lasky patted Peters down for weapons, and discovered a hard object in his pocket. He stated at the hearing that the object did not feel like a gun, but that it might have been a knife. He removed the object from Peters' pocket. It was an opaque plastic envelope, containing burglar's tools.

The trial court explicitly refused to credit Peters' testimony that he was merely in the building to visit his girl friend. It found that Officer Lasky had the requisite "reasonable suspicion" of Peters under § 180–a to stop him and question him. It also found that Peters' response was "clearly unsatisfactory," and that "under the circumstances Lasky's action in frisking Peters for a dangerous weapon was reasonable, even though Lasky was himself armed." It held that the hallway of the apartment building was a "public place" within the meaning of the statute. The Appellate Division of the Supreme Court affirmed without opinion. The Court of Appeals also affirmed, essentially adopting the reasoning of the trial judge, with Judges Fuld and Van Voorhis dissenting separately.

At the outset we must deal with the question whether we have jurisdiction in

---

[4] Officer Lasky testified that when he called the police immediately before leaving his apartment, he "told the Sergeant at the desk that two burglars were on my floor."

[5] Officer Lasky testified that when he emerged from his apartment, "I slammed the door, I had my gun and I ran down the stairs after them." A sworn affidavit of the Assistant District Attorney, which was before the trial court when it ruled on the motion to suppress, stated that when apprehended Peters was "fleeing down the steps of the building." The trial court explicitly took note of the flight of Peters and his companion as a factor contributing to Officer Lasky's "reasonable suspicion" of them:

"We think the testimony at the hearing does not require further laboring of this aspect of the matter, unless one is to believe that it is legitimately normal for a man to tip-toe about in the public hall of an apartment house while on a visit to his unidentified girl-friend, and, when observed by another tenant, to rapidly descend by stairway in the presence of elevators."

No. 63. It is asserted that because Sibron has completed service of the six-month sentence imposed upon him as a result of his conviction, the case has become moot under St. Pierre v United States, 319 US 41, 87 L Ed 1199, 63 S Ct 910 (1943). We have concluded that the case is not moot.

In the first place, it is clear that the broad dictum with which the Court commenced its discussion in St. Pierre—that "the case is moot because, after petitioner's service of his sentence and its expiration, there was no longer a subject matter on which the judgment of this Court could operate"—fails to take account of significant qualifications recognized in St. Pierre and developed in later cases. Only a few days ago we held unanimously that the writ of habeas corpus was available to test the constitutionality of a state conviction where the petitioner had been in custody when he applied for the writ, but had been released before this Court could adjudicate his claims. On numerous occasions in the past this Court has proceeded to adjudicate the merits of criminal cases in which the sentence had been fully served or the probationary period during which a suspended sentence could be reimposed had terminated. Thus mere release of the prisoner does not mechanically foreclose consideration of the merits by this Court.

St. Pierre itself recognized two possible exceptions to its "doctrine" of mootness, and both of them appear to us to be applicable here. The Court stated that "[i]t does not appear that petitioner could not have brought his case to this Court for review before the expiration of his sentence," noting also that because the petitioner's conviction was for contempt and because his controversy with the Government was a continuing one, there was a good chance that there would be "ample opportunity to review" the important question presented on the merits in a future proceeding. This was a plain recognition of the vital importance of keeping open avenues of judicial review of deprivations of constitutional right. There was no way for Sibron to bring his case here before his six-month sentence expired. By statute he was precluded from obtaining bail pending appeal, and by virtue of the inevitable delays of the New York court system, he was released less than a month after his newly appointed appellate counsel had been supplied with a copy of the transcript and roughly two months before it was physically possible to present his case to the first tier in the state appellate court system. This was true despite the fact that he took all steps to perfect his appeal in a prompt, diligent, and timely manner.

Many deep and abiding constitutional problems are encountered primarily at a level of "low visibility" in the criminal process—in the context of prosecutions for "minor" offenses which carry only short sentences. We do not believe that the Constitution contemplates that people deprived of constitutional rights at this level should be left utterly remediless and defenseless against repetitions of unconstitutional conduct. A State may not cut off federal review of whole classes of such cases by the simple expedient of a blanket denial of bail pending appeal. As St. Pierre clearly recognized, a State may not effectively deny a convict access to its appellate courts until he has been released and then argue that his case has been mooted by his failure to do what it alone prevented him from doing.

The second exception recognized in St. Pierre permits adjudication of the merits of a criminal case where "under either state or federal law further penalties or disabilities can be imposed...as a result of the judgment which has...been satisfied." Subsequent cases have expanded this exception to the point where it may realistically be said that inroads have been made upon the principle itself. St. Pierre implied that the burden was upon the convict to show the existence of collateral legal consequences. Three years later in Fiswick v United States, 329 US 211, 91 L Ed 196, 67 S Ct 224 (1946), however, the Court held that a criminal case had not become moot upon release of the prisoner, noting that the convict, an alien, might be subject to deportation for having committed a crime of "moral turpitude"—even though it had never been held (and the Court refused to hold) that the crime of which he was convicted fell into this category. The Court also pointed to the fact that if the petitioner should in the future decide he wanted to become an American citizen, he might have difficulty proving that he was of "good moral character."

The next case which dealt with the problem of collateral consequences was United States v Morgan, 346 US 502 (1954). There the convict had probably been subjected to a higher sentence as a recidivist by a state court on account of the old federal conviction which he sought to attack. But as the dissent pointed out, there was no indication that the recidivist increment would be removed from his state sentence upon invalidation of the federal conviction, and the Court chose to rest its holding that the case was not moot upon a broader view of the matter. Without canvassing the possible disabilities which might be imposed upon Morgan or alluding specifically to the recidivist sentence, the Court stated:

> "Although the term has been served, the results of the conviction may persist. Subsequent convictions may carry heavier penalties, civil rights may be affected. As the power to remedy an invalid sentence exists, we think, respondent is entitled to an opportunity to attempt to show that his conviction was invalid."

Three years later, in Pollard v United States, 352 US 354, 1 L Ed 2d 393, 77 S Ct 481 (1957), the Court abandoned all inquiry into the actual existence of specific collateral consequences and in effect presumed that they existed. With nothing more than citations to Morgan and Fiswick, and a statement that "convictions may entail collateral legal disadvantages in the future," the Court concluded that "[t]he possibility of consequences collateral to the imposition of sentence is sufficiently substantial to justify our dealing with the merits." The Court thus acknowledged the obvious fact of life that most criminal convictions do in fact entail adverse collateral legal consequences. The mere "possibility" that this will be the case is enough to preserve a criminal case from ending "ignominiously in the limbo of mootness."

This case certainly meets that test for survival. Without pausing to canvass the possibilities in detail, we note that New York expressly provides by statute that Sibron's conviction may be used to impeach his character should he choose to put it in issue at any future criminal trial, NY Code Crim Proc § 393–c, and that it must be submitted to a trial judge for his consideration in sentencing should Sibron again be convicted of a crime, NY Code Crim Proc § 482. There are doubtless other collateral consequences. Moreover, we see no relevance in the fact that Sibron is a multiple offender. Morgan was a multiple offender. A judge or jury faced with a question of character, like a sentencing judge, may be inclined to forgive or at least discount a limited number of minor transgressions, particularly if they occurred at some time in the relatively distant past.[6] It is impossible for this Court to say at what point the number of convictions on a man's record

[6] We do not know from the record how many convictions Sibron had, for what crimes, or when they were rendered. At the hearing he admitted to a 1955 conviction for burglary and a 1957 misdemeanor conviction for possession of narcotics. He also admitted that he had other convictions, but none were specifically alluded to.

renders his reputation irredeemable.[7] And even if we believed that an individual had reached that point, it would be impossible for us to say that he had no interest in beginning the process of redemption with the particular case sought to be adjudicated. We cannot foretell what opportunities might present themselves in the future for the removal of other convictions from an individual's record. The question of the validity of a criminal conviction can arise in many contexts, and the sooner the issue is fully litigated the better for all concerned. It is always preferable to litigate a matter when it is directly and principally in dispute, rather than in a proceeding where it is collateral to the central controversy. Moreover, litigation is better conducted when the dispute is fresh and additional facts may, if necessary, be taken without a substantial risk that witnesses will die or memories fade. And it is far better to eliminate the source of a potential legal disability than to require the citizen to suffer the possibly unjustified consequences of the disability itself for an indefinite period of time before he can secure adjudication of the State's right to impose it on the basis of some past action.[8]

None of the concededly imperative policies behind the constitutional rule against entertaining moot controversies would be served by a dismissal in this case. There is nothing abstract, feigned, or hypothetical about Sibron's appeal. Nor is there any suggestion that either Sibron or the State has been wanting in diligence or fervor in the litigation. We have before us a fully developed record of testimony about contested historical facts, which reflects the "impact of actuality"[9] to a far greater degree than many controversies accepted for adjudication as a matter of course under the Federal Declaratory Judgment Act, 28 USC § 2201.

St. Pierre v United States, supra, must be read in light of later cases to mean that a criminal case is moot only if it is shown that there is no possibility that any collateral legal consequences will be imposed on the basis of the challenged conviction. That certainly is not the case here. Sibron "has a substantial stake in the judgment of conviction which survives the satisfaction of the sentence imposed on him." The case is not moot.

We deal next with the confession of error by the District Attorney for Kings County in No. 63. Confessions of error are, of course, entitled to and given great weight, but they do not "relieve this Court of the performance of the judicial function." It is the uniform practice of this Court to conduct its own examination of the record in all cases where the Federal Government or a State confesses that a conviction has been erroneously obtained. For one thing, as we noted in Young, "our judgments are precedents, and the proper administration of the criminal law cannot be left merely to the stipulation of parties." This consideration is entitled to special weight where, as in this case, we deal with a judgment of a State's highest court interpreting a state statute which is challenged on constitutional grounds. The need for such authoritative declarations of state law in sensitive

---

[7] We note that there is a clear distinction between a general impairment of credibility, to which the Court referred in St. Pierre, see 319 US, at 43, and New York's specific statutory authorization for use of the conviction to impeach the "character" of a defendant in a criminal proceeding. The latter is a clear legal disability deliberately and specifically imposed by the legislature.

[8] This factor has clearly been considered relevant by the Court in the past in determining the issue of mootness. See Fiswick v United States, 329 US 211, 221–222, 91 L Ed 196, 202, 203, 67 S Ct 224 (1946).

[9] Frankfurter, A Note on Advisory Opinions, 37 Harv L Rev 1002, 1006 (1924). See also Parker v Ellis, 362 US 574, 592–593, 4 L Ed 2d 963, 974, 975, 80 S Ct 909 (1960) (dissenting opinion).

constitutional contexts has been the very reason for the development of the abstention doctrine by this Court. Such a judgment is the final product of a sovereign judicial system, and is deserving of respectful treatment by this Court. Moreover, in this case the confession of error on behalf of the entire state executive and judicial branches is made, not by a state official, but by the elected legal officer of one political subdivision within the State. The District Attorney for Kings County seems to have come late to the opinion that this conviction violated Sibron's constitutional rights. For us to accept his view blindly in the circumstances, when a majority of the Court of Appeals of New York has expressed the contrary view, would be a disservice to the State of New York and an abdication of our obligation to lower courts to decide cases upon proper constitutional grounds in a manner which permits them to conform their future behavior to the demands of the Constitution. We turn to the merits.

The parties on both sides of these two cases have urged that the principal issue before us is the constitutionality of § 180-a "on its face." We decline, however, to be drawn into what we view as the abstract and unproductive exercise of laying the extraordinarily elastic categories of § 180-a next to the categories of the Fourth Amendment in an effort to determine whether the two are in some sense compatible. The constitutional validity of a warrantless search is preeminently the sort of question which can only be decided in the concrete factual context of the individual case. In this respect it is quite different from the question of the adequacy of the procedural safeguards written into a statute which purports to authorize the issuance of search warrants in certain circumstances. No search required to be made under a warrant is valid if the procedure for the issuance of the warrant is inadequate to ensure the sort of neutral contemplation by a magistrate of the grounds for the search and its proposed scope, which lies at the heart of the Fourth Amendment. This Court held last Term in Berger v New York, supra, that NY Code Crim Proc § 813-a, which established a procedure for the issuance of search warrants to permit electronic eavesdropping, failed to embody the safeguards demanded by the Fourth and Fourteenth Amendments.

Section 180-a, unlike § 813-a, deals with the substantive validity of certain types of seizures and searches without warrants. It purports to authorize police officers to "stop" people, "demand" explanation of them and "search [them] for dangerous weapon[s]" in certain circumstances upon "reasonable suspicion" that they are engaged in criminal activity and that they represent a danger to the policeman. The operative categories of § 180-a are not the categories of the Fourth Amendment, and they are susceptible of a wide variety of interpretations.[10] New

---

[10] It is not apparent, for example, whether the power to "stop" granted by the statute entails a power to "detain" for investigation or interrogation upon less than probable cause, or if so what sort of durational limitations upon such detention are contemplated. And while the statute's apparent grant of a power of compulsion indicates that many "stops" will constitute "seizures," it is not clear that all conduct analyzed under the rubric of the statute will either rise to the level of a "seizure" or be based upon less than probable cause. In No. 74, the Peters case, for example, the New York courts justified the seizure of appellant under § 180-a, but we have concluded that there was in fact probable cause for an arrest when Officer Lasky seized Peters on the stairway. See infra, at 66, 20 L Ed. 2d at 937. In any event, at pronouncement by this Court upon the abstract validity of § 180-a's "stop" category would be most inappropriate in these cases, since we have concluded that neither of them presents the question of the validity of a seizure of the person for purposes of interrogation upon less than probable cause.

The statute's other categories are equally elastic, and it was passed too re-

York is, of course, free to develop its own law of search and seizure to meet the needs of local law enforcement, and in the process it may call the standards it employs by any names it may choose. It may not, however, authorize police conduct which trenches upon Fourth Amendment rights, regardless of the labels which it attaches to such conduct. The question in this Court upon review of a state-approved search or seizure "is not whether the search [or seizure] was authorized by state law. The question is rather whether the search was reasonable under the Fourth Amendment. Just as a search authorized by state law may be an unreasonable one under that amendment, so may a search not expressly authorized by state law be justified as a constitutionally reasonable one." Accordingly, we make no pronouncement on the facial constitutionality of § 180-a. The constitutional point with respect to a statute of this peculiar sort, as the Court of Appeals of New York recognized, is "not so much . . . the language employed as . . . the conduct it authorizes."

We have held today in Terry v Ohio, 392 US 1, that police conduct of the sort with which § 180-a deals must be judged under the Reasonable Search and Seizure Clause of the Fourth Amendment. The inquiry under that clause may differ sharply from the inquiry set up by the categories of § 180-a. Our constitutional inquiry would not be furthered here by an attempt to pronounce judgment on the words of the statute. We must confine our review instead to the reasonableness of the searches and seizures which underlie these two convictions.

Turning to the facts of Sibron's case, it is clear that the heroin was inadmissible in evidence against him. The prosecution has quite properly abandoned the notion that there was probable cause to arrest Sibron for any crime at the time Patrolman Martin accosted him in the restaurant, took him outside and searched him. The officer was not acquainted with Sibron and had no information concerning him. He merely saw Sibron talking to a number of known narcotics addicts over a period of eight hours. It must be emphasized that Patrolman Martin was

---

cently for the State's highest court to have ruled upon many of the questions involving potential intersections with federal constitutional guarantees. We cannot tell, for example, whether the officer's power to "demand" of a person an "explanation of his actions" contemplates either an obligation on the part of the citizen to answer or some additional power on the part of the officer in the event of a refusal to answer, or even whether the interrogation following the "stop" is "custodial." Compare Miranda v Arizona, 384 US 436, 16 L Ed 2d 694, 86 S Ct 1602, 10 ALR3d 974 (1966). There are, moreover, substantial indications that the statutory category of a "search for a dangerous weapon" may encompass conduct considerably broader in scope than that which we approved in Terry v Ohio, 392 US 1, 20 L Ed 2d 889, 88 S Ct 1868. See infra, at 65–66, 20 L Ed 2d at 936. See also People v Taggart, 20 NY 2d 335, 229 NE2d 581, 282 NYS2d 1 (1967). At least some of the activity apparently permitted under the rubric of searching for dangerous weapons may thus be permissible under the Constitution only if the "reasonable suspicion" of criminal activity rises to the level of probable cause. Finally, it is impossible to tell whether the standard of "reasonable suspicion" connotes the same sort of specificity, reliability, and objectivity which is the touchstone of permissible governmental action under the Fourth Amendment. Compare Terry v Ohio, supra, with People v Taggart, supra. In this connection we note that the searches and seizures in both Sibron and Peters were upheld by the Court of Appeals of New York, as predicated upon "reasonable suspicion," whereas we have concluded that the officer in Peters had probable cause for an arrest, while the policeman in Sibron was not possessed of any information which would justify an intrusion upon rights protected by the Fourth Amendment.

completely ignorant regarding the content of these conversations, and that he saw nothing pass between Sibron and the addicts. So far as he knew, they might indeed "have been talking about the World Series." The inference that persons who talk to narcotics addicts are engaged in the criminal traffic in narcotics is simply not the sort of reasonable inference required to support an intrusion by the police upon an individual's personal security. Nothing resembling probable cause existed until after the search had turned up the envelopes of heroin. It is axiomatic that an incident search may not precede an arrest and serve as part of its justification. Thus the search cannot be justified as incident to a lawful arrest.

If Patrolman Martin lacked probable cause for an arrest, however, his seizure and search of Sibron might still have been justified at the outset if he had reasonable grounds to believe that Sibron was armed and dangerous. Terry v Ohio, 392 US 1, 20 L Ed 2d 889, 88 S Ct 1868. We are not called upon to decide in this case whether there was a "seizure" of Sibron inside the restaurant antecedent to the physical seizure which accompanied the search. The record is unclear with respect to what transpired between Sibron and the officer inside the restaurant. It is totally barren of any indication whether Sibron accompanied Patrolman Martin outside in submission to a show of force or authority which left him no choice, or whether he went voluntarily in a spirit of apparent cooperation with the officer's investigation. In any event, this deficiency in the record is immaterial, since Patrolman Martin obtained no new information in the interval between his initiation of the encounter in the restaurant and his physical seizure and search of Sibron outside.

Although the Court of Appeals of New York wrote no opinion in this case, it seems to have viewed the search here as a self-protective search for weapons and to have affirmed on the basis of § 180–a, which authorizes such a search when the officer "reasonably suspects that he is in danger of life or limb." The Court of Appeals has, at any rate, justified searches during field interrogation on the ground that "[t]he answer to the question propounded by the policeman may be a bullet; in any case the exposure to danger could be very great." But the application of this reasoning to the facts of this case proves too much. The police officer is not entitled to seize and search every person whom he sees on the street or of whom he makes inquiries. Before he places a hand on the person of a citizen in search of anything, he must have constitutionally adequate, reasonable grounds for doing so. In the case of the self-protective search for weapons, he must be able to point to particular facts from which he reasonably inferred that the individual was armed and dangerous. Terry v Ohio, supra. Patrolman Martin's testimony reveals no such facts. The suspect's mere act of talking with a number of known narcotics addicts over an eight-hour period no more gives rise to reasonable fear of life or limb on the part of the police officer than it justifies an arrest for committing a crime. Nor did Patrolman Martin urge that when Sibron put his hand in his pocket, he feared that he was going for a weapon and acted in self-defense. His opening statement to Sibron—"You know what I am after"—made it abundantly clear that he sought narcotics, and his testimony at the hearing left no doubt that he thought there were narcotics in Sibron's pocket.[11]

[11] It is argued in dissent that this Court has in effect overturned factual findings by the two courts below that the search in this case was a self-protective measure on the part of Patrolman Martin, who thought that Sibron might have been reaching for a gun. It is true, as we have noted, that the Court of Appeals of New York apparently rested its approval of the search on this view. The trial court, however, made no such finding of fact. The trial judge adopted the theory of the prosecu-

Even assuming arguendo that there were adequate grounds to search Sibron for weapons, the nature and scope of the search conducted by Patrolman Martin were so clearly unrelated to that justification as to render the heroin inadmissible. The search for weapons approved in Terry consisted solely of a limited patting of the outer clothing of the suspect for concealed objects which might be used as instruments of assault. Only when he discovered such objects did the officer in Terry place his hands in the pockets of the men he searched. In this case, with no attempt at an initial limited exploration for arms, Patrolman Martin thrust his hand in Sibron's pocket and took from him envelopes of heroin. His testimony shows that he was looking for narcotics, and he found them. The search was not reasonably limited in scope to the accomplishment of the only goal which might conceivably have justified its inception—the protection of the officer by disarming a potentially dangerous man. Such a search violates the guarantee of the Fourth Amendment, which protects the sanctity of the person against unreasonable intrusions on the part of all government agents.

We think it is equally clear that the search in Peter's case was wholly reasonable under the Constitution. The Court of Appeals of New York held that the search was made legal by § 180-a, since Peters was "abroad in a public place," and since Officer Lasky was reasonably suspicious of his activities and, once he had stopped Peters, reasonably suspected that he was in danger of life or limb, even though he held Peters at gun point. This may be the justification for the search under state law. We think, however, that for purposes of the Fourth Amendment the search was properly incident to a lawful arrest. By the time Officer Lasky caught up with Peters on the stairway between the fourth and fifth floors of the apartment building, he had probable cause to arrest him for attempted burglary. The officer heard strange noises at his door which apparently led him to believe that someone sought to force entry. When he investigated these noises he saw two men, whom he had never seen before in his 12 years in the building, tiptoeing furtively about the hallway. They were still engaged in these maneuvers after he called the police and dressed hurriedly. And when Officer Lasky entered the hallway, the men fled down the stairs. It is difficult to conceive of stronger grounds for an arrest, short of actual eyewitness observation of criminal activity. As the trial court explicitly recognized, deliberately furtive actions and flight at the approach of strangers or law officers are strong indicia of mens rea, and

---

tion at the hearing on the motion to suppress. This theory was that there was probable cause to arrest Sibron for some crime having to do with narcotics. The fact which tipped the scales for the trial court had nothing to do with danger to the policeman. The judge expressly changed his original view and held the heroin admissible upon being reminded that Sibron had admitted on the stand that he spoke to the addicts about narcotics. This admission was not relevant on the issue of probable cause, and we do not understand the dissent to take the position that prior to the discovery of heroin, there was probable cause for an arrest.

Moreover, Patrolman Martin himself never at any time put forth the notion that he acted to protect himself. As we have noted, this subject never came up, until on re-direct examination defense counsel raised the question whether Patrolman Martin thought Sibron was going for a gun. See n. 2, supra. This was the only reference to weapons at any point in the hearing, and the subject was swiftly dropped. In the circumstances an unarticulated "finding" by an appellate court which wrote no opinion, apparently to the effect that the officer's invasion of Sibron's person comported with the Constitution because of the need to protect himself, is not deserving of controlling deference.

when coupled with specific knowledge on the part of the officer relating the suspect to the evidence of crime, they are proper factors to be considered in the decision to make an arrest.

As we noted in Sibron's case, a search incident to a lawful arrest may not precede the arrest and serve as part of its justification. It is a question of fact precisely when, in each case, the arrest took place. And while there was some inconclusive discussion in the trial court concerning when Officer Lasky "arrested" Peters, it is clear that the arrest had, for purposes of constitutional justification, already taken place before the search commenced. When the policeman grabbed Peters by the collar, he abruptly "seized" him and curtailed his freedom of movement on the basis of probable cause to believe that he was engaged in criminal activity. At that point he had the authority to search Peters and the incident search was obviously justified "by the need to seize weapons and other things which might be used to assault an officer or effect an escape, as well as by the need to prevent the destruction of evidence of the crime." Moreover, it was reasonably limited in scope by these purposes. Officer Lasky did not engage in an unrestrained and thorough-going examination of Peters and his personal effects. He seized him to cut short his flight, and he searched him primarily for weapons. While patting down his outer clothing, Officer Lasky discovered an object in his pocket which might have been used as a weapon. He seized it and discovered it to be a potential instrument of the crime of burglary.

We have concluded that Peters' conviction fully comports with the commands of the Fourth and Fourteenth Amendments, and must be affirmed. The conviction in No. 63, however, must be reversed, on the ground that the heroin was unconstitutionally admitted in evidence against the appellant.

It is so ordered.

PEOPLE v. MANIS
CALIFORNIA COURT OF APPEAL (4th DISTRICT)
74 CAL. RPTR. 423 (1969)

. . . .

About noon on 24 January 1967 during a heavy rainstorm, Officer Gaines, a burglary investigator for the Los Angeles Police Department, saw appellant without a raincoat walk by his patrol car, heading west on Eighth Street and carrying what appeared to be a new portable typewriter case. Because many burglaries in that area involved stolen typewriters, and because appellant was apparently exposing a new portable typewriter to a heavy downpour (most typewriter cases are not waterproof), Officer Gaines and his partner followed. Appellant continued west on Eighth Street and then north on Alvarado Street toward an area of several pawnshops. From time to time he looked back in the officers' direction. After appellant crossed Seventh Street the officers drove past him, and when they did so appellant reversed his direction, returned to Seventh Street, and headed west. As the officers made a U-turn to go back to Seventh Street, appellant turned into MacArthur Park. At that point the officers left their car, and stopped appellant in the tunnel under Wilshire Boulevard.

Officer Gaines, after identifying himself, asked appellant where he was going. Santa Monica, the latter replied. How would he get there? Walk. What was in the case he had set down? Radios. Did he have a receipt for the radios? "No," said appellant, "I stole them." The police arrested appellant and advised him of his constitutional rights. Four radios with Bullock's department store tags were found in the case. Appellant told the officers he had spent the previous night in Bullock's and walked out of the store that morning with the radios in the case.

At the preliminary hearing a saleswoman for Bullock's testified the radios in appellant's possession were those missing from the store on the morning of 24 January. She had been the last person to leave the radio department the previous night and had forgotten to lock up. For reasons not apparent from the record, the court in the preliminary hearing ruled appellant's confession of burglary inadmissible and ordered it stricken, but did permit appellant's pre-arrest admission of theft, "I stole them," to stand.

The cause was submitted to the trial court on the transcript of the preliminary hearing, supplemented by appellant's testimony on the circumstances of his arrest. Appellant was convicted of second-degree burglary.

Appellant's first two claims are interrelated. Initially, he argues there was insufficient cause to detain him on the street and therefore all evidence resulting from that detention—the radios, the case, and his admission of theft—was illegally obtained and hence inadmissible. In the alternative, he argues that if sufficient cause for his detention existed, then his admission of theft was improperly elicited during a custodial interrogation because of the failure to give the warning required by Miranda v. Arizona, 384 U.S. 436.

. . . .

QUESTIONING DURING TEMPORARY DETENTION

The purpose of temporary detention is to enable the police to determine, with minimum intrusion into personal rights, whether they should arrest a suspect and charge him with crime, whether they should investigate further, or whether they should take no action because their initial suspicion proved groundless. What tools do we allow the police to use in making a decision which often calls for the employment of nice discrimination? Obviously, the police can use their sense of sight, hearing, and smell and thereby obtain a certain amount of information from the person's dress, appearance, physical condition, and demeanor. But where, as here, the circumstances which have induced the temporary detention suggest that stolen property is about to be pawned, the keenest personal observation is apt to prove uninformative and unenlightening. In this, as in many investigations, progress toward a rational decision about what to do next can only be made by asking questions. The information needed by the police to make an intelligent decision on street detention is ordinarily obtainable only from the suspect's answers. "Despite modern advances in the technology of crime detection, offenses frequently occur about which things cannot be made to speak. And where there cannot be found innocent human witnesses to such offenses, nothing remains—if police investigation is not to be balked before it has fairly begun—but to seek out possibly guilty witnesses and ask them questions, witnesses, that is, who are suspected of knowing something about the offense precisely because they are suspected of implication in it." (Culombe v. Connecticut, 367 U.S. 568.)

. . . .

Perhaps a few concrete examples of circumstances in which temporary detention is customarily used will give form and content to its general idea.

Item: A motorist driving in an eccentric manner on the freeway.
        The police suspect the possibility the driver may be intoxicated.

Item: A motorist driving without proper lighting on his license plates and with dirt obscuring the visibility of the numbers.
        The police suspect the possibility the car may be stolen.

Item: A driver sitting in an automobile with the motor racing at the side entrance of a suburban bank during banking hours.
The police suspect the possibility of a holdup.

Item: A motorist driving a truck without lights from a closed warehouse driveway at 2 a. m.
The police suspect the possibility of theft or commercial fraud.

Item: A man staggering on the street outside a bar at 11 p. m.
The police suspect the possibility of drunkenness in a public place.

Item: Two men parked in an automobile in lovers' lane at midnight with the lights out.
The police suspect the possibility of an attempt at robbery or rape.

Item: A man on the street at 11 p. m. in a high burglary area carrying several large bulky cardboard cartons.
The police suspect the possibility of burglary.

Item: An elderly man in a public park in the afternoon offering candy to young children and patting them on the arm.
The police suspect the possibility of child molestation.

Item: The appearance on the highway of three men in a grey Chevrolet after the police have received a report of a gas station stickup an hour ago in another part of the city by three men in a grey Chevrolet.
The police suspect the possibility the men are wanted for robbery.

In each of these instances police investigation is called for because there is some rational suspicion that the persons involved have committed, are committing, or are about to commit some crime. This suspicion, although rational, does not constitute probable cause to make an arrest and, as often as not, the suspicion may be quickly dissipated by an explanation from the actors involved.

When we reflect on the commonplaceness of such events and the frequency of their occurrence, it seems evident that temporary detention provides a legally useful procedure which the police should use on appropriate occasion for the benefit of the community. The stopping and questioning by police officers of persons whose conduct, although suspicious, does not give probable cause for arrest, essentially amounts to a halfway house between the station of arrest on probable cause and that of official inaction.

. . . .

Custody has become the critical element which triggers the necessity for warning against incrimination, and appellant argues we should equate temporary detention with custody for purposes of the required warning. But to classify temporary detention as a form of custody which thereby initiates the accusatory stage of a criminal proceeding would distort the accepted meaning of custody and ignore the legal formalities which attach to it.

. . . .

Temporary detention only slightly resembles custody, "as the mist resembles the rain."[1] True enough, a person temporarily detained has been subjected to some restraint and his freedom of movement has been temporarily restricted. But the person detained is in no sense an accused but rather one merely suspected of misconduct. Since the police can make no valid accusation against him, we do

[1] Longfellow: "The Day Is Done"

not think the process has shifted from investigatory to accusatory (Escobedo v. Illinois, supra, 378 U.S. at p. 492, 84 S.Ct. 1758), or that an investigation has "focused on an accused" (Miranda v. Arizona, supra, 384 U.S. at p. 444, fn. 4, 86 S.Ct. 1602). Only when suspicion focuses sharply enough to provide reasonable cause for arrest or charge does the relationship between the police and the person detained become that of accuser and accused.

The nature of the warning required by Miranda has itself become a significant factor in the process, for to properly deliver the warning consumes an appreciable amount of time, perhaps a minimum of 45 seconds. The length and formality of the warning and the somewhat detailed legal advice it imparts persuade us it need not be given in every transitory, informal or casual exchange between police and suspect, even those in which the suspect's presence has been compelled. To initiate each encounter between police and suspect with a 45-second warning on the perils of talking without counsel would, we believe, unnecessarily formalize the relationship between the two and unnecessarily inhibit the police from carrying out their traditional function of investigating crime. Until such time as the police have probable cause to make an accusation, the relationship between suspect and police remains that of citizen and peace officer rather than accused and accuser.

The distinction between transitory restraint and more permanent restraint has been preserved in the Miranda opinion itself, which defines custodial interrogation as questioning initiated by law enforcement officers while an individual is in custody or otherwise deprived of his freedom in any significant way. (Miranda v. Arizona, 384 U.S. 436).

. . . .

From another portion of the court's opinion we infer that general on-the-scene questioning does not fall within the category of legally significant restraint. The court said: "General on-the-scene questioning as to the facts surrounding a crime or other general questioning of citizens in the fact-finding process is not affected by our holding. It is an act of responsible citizenship for individuals to give whatever information they may have to aid law enforcement. In such situations the compelling atmosphere inherent in the process of in-custody interrogation is not necessarily present." (Pp. 477–478, 86 S.Ct. pp. 1629, 1630.)

We conclude that persons temporarily detained for brief questioning by police officers who lack probable cause to make an arrest or bring an accusation need not be warned about incrimination and their right to counsel, until such time as the point of arrest or accusation has been reached or the questioning has ceased to be brief and casual and become sustained and coercive.

QUESTIONS AND PROBLEMS

Indicate the correct answer for the following questions.

1. The U.S. Supreme Court in the Terry case:
   a. Approves and condones a frisk in every case following a stop
   b. Approves a frisk in almost every case
   c. Approves a frisk when the officer reasonably suspects that he or another is in danger of physical injury
   d. Approves a frisk only after a lawful arrest
2. The frisk approved in Terry is:
   a. A full search of the person

  b. A search for mere evidence

  c. A weapons search to determine whether the person is carrying an instrument or article or substance readily capable of
causing physical injury

3. It can be said that the Terry decision:

  a. Gives law enforcement officers a wide degree of latitude in
what they may do in such situations

  b. Has been interpreted very differently in each of the fifty states

  c. Gives the police a very narrow authority within the guidelines
set down

4. If during the pat-down the officer feels a piece of paper which
when removed from the person turns out to be a gambling policy
slip, the piece of paper:

  a. Is admissible in evidence on a gambling charge

  b. Is not admissible in evidence on a gambling charge

5. The frisk under the Terry and Peters cases:

  a. Is to confirm the suspect's story

  b. Is a general search

  c. Is only for the protection of the officer or others

6. If during the pat-down the officer feels a hard object which may
be a weapon and when removed is found to be a burglary tool:

  a. It may be introduced in evidence on a charge of possession
of burglary tools.

  b. It may not be introduced in evidence on such a charge.

7. A weapon such as a revolver which was obtained as the result of
a pat-down in a valid stop and frisk:

  a. Must be returned to the suspect immediately even though he
has no permit to carry the revolver

  b. May not be used in evidence against the suspect

  c. May be used in evidence in a carrying a concealed weapon
charge against the suspect

8. If such a weapon is used in evidence, the officer:

  a. Can justify the search in terms of the hunch which he had
and which proved to be correct

  b. Must be able to point to and express particular facts from
which he reasonably inferred that the suspect was armed and
dangerous

  c. Must be able to show that he had probable cause before he
stopped the person

9. When an officer has hard, cold facts to show that reasonable suspicion exists:

  a. He may make an arrest.

  b. He may only *ask* the person if he will give his name, address,
and an explanation of his conduct.

    c. He may *demand* the suspect's name, address, and an explation of his conduct.

10. If the person "stopped" in question 9 refuses to provide any information:

    a. The officer should immediately release the person.

    b. The officer may arrest the person for obstructing an officer.

    c. The officer may detain the person for further questioning at the station house.

11. If the person "stopped" in question 9 is obviously providing false information:

    a. The officer should take notes and then release the person.

    b. The officer may arrest the person for obstructing an officer.

    c. The officer may detain the person until truthful answers are given.

12. The purpose of the exclusionary rules is:

    a. To control the methods in which evidence is obtained by officers

    b. To preserve the dignity of the courts

    c. To provide the only practical way of enforcing constitutional and statutory requirements

    d. All the above are correct.

    e. None of the above are correct.

Available Answers for Questions 13 to 20

For each question, indicate the one that best describes each situation.

1. This *alone* would amount to reasonable suspicion so as to justify a stop.	2. This *alone* would *not* amount to reasonable suspicion.

13. The officer has a hunch and mere suspicion about the person.

14. An anonymous telephone caller states that a man (description given) on Fifth and Main Street has a concealed gun.

15. The officer sees a man whom he knows to have been previously convicted of a burglary talking on the street to a man with a narcotics record.

16. The officer tells the court that he made the stop on the sole grounds that the man was seen near the scene of the crime.

17. An officer approaches a man to talk to him on a "voluntary" basis, but the man turns and runs away from the officer.

18. A man is seen running in a residential neighborhood at 3 o'clock in the morning.

19. An officer sees a person who is obviously a stranger in the neighborhood.

20. An officer sees a person who is a hippie.

Available Answers for Questions 21 to 29
1. Would be an *important* factor in determining whether a stop or a frisk is justified
2. Would *not* be an important factor in determining whether a stop or a frisk is justified

21. The time of day or night
22. The type and the bulkiness of the clothing
23. The fact that the officer has not made an arrest in two months and a quota system is used in his department
24. The fact that a very serious murder-rape was committed and young males are seen near the scene of the crime
25. The fact that the area has a very high crime rate
26. The seriousness of the crime being investigated
27. The occurrence of prior acts of violence against officers and citizens in the area
28. The fact that the officer has nothing else to do
29. The fact that the officer is suspicious of hippies or college students

Available Answers for Questions 30 to 37
1. Probable cause to make an arrest exists.
2. Reasonable suspicion exists and the officer may detain the person for a reasonable period of time.
3. *No* arrest or *no* detention is authorized from the facts given.

30. An officer who is on a city bus sees a man who looks very similar to an artist's sketch of a man wanted for a very serious crime.
31. The victim states, "That is the man who robbed me."
32. The victim states, "He looks like the man who robbed me but I am not sure."
33. Reasonable suspicion exists to make the stop for questioning, but the suspect refuses to stay in the presence of the officer.
34. Reasonable suspicion exists to make the stop, but the suspect refuses to answer any questions.
35. Reasonable suspicion exists to make the stop, but the suspect answers every question with the statement that he has the Fifth Amendment right to remain silent.
36. Reasonable suspicion does *not* exist to make the stop and the suspect will *not* answer any questions asked him.

37. A man walks up to a police officer and states that he has just murdered his wife.

38. A very effective classroom demonstration is the acting out by students of the situations in Terry and Sibron. Do you know the cases well enough to act out one of the roles?

39. Assume that you are on duty in a squad car when a radio dispatch orders you to investigate three men sitting in a car parked in the business district of your town. It is three o'clock in the morning and the men have been sitting in the car for five hours (facts from the Preston case). You and your partner locate the car and question the men. The men state that they are waiting to meet a truck driver who will pass through the town that night. They cannot identify the company he works for, cannot say what his truck looks like, and do not know what time he will arrive. You order the men out of the car and make a weapons search of their persons and also the interior of the car. No weapons are found. You conclude that the men are not telling the truth as to why they are waiting for five hours at that place.

   a. What quantum of evidence did the officers have when they arrived at the scene (probable cause, reasonable suspicion, or less than reasonable suspicion)?

   b. Can the weapons search of the three men be justified? How?

   c. Can the weapons search of the interior of the car be justified? how?

   d. Which of the following courses of action would be justified in your state?

       Arresting the men for vagrancy (as was done in Preston)

       Arresting the men for obstructing (in that they failed to explain adequately their reason for being where they were for five hours)

       Inviting the men to come down to the station voluntarily for further questioning

       If a parking violation has occurred, issuing a parking ticket and holding the driver until payment was made (the men had only 25 cents between them)

       Discontinuing the interview as you have the names of the men and other information; advising the men, however, that they will be kept under surveillance

       Ordering the men to leave the area and town with a threat of arrest if they do not leave immediately

   e. Would it be good police practice to ask for permission to search the trunk of the car?

12
AUTHORITY
TO SEARCH
WITH
CONSENT

The Fourth Amendment of the U.S. Constitution forbids unreasonable searches and seizures. The Constitution and the law favor searches and seizures made under the authority of a search warrant, but in most situations it is either impossible or impractical to obtain a search warrant.

If the person lawfully entitled to possession of the property waives his Fourth Amendment rights and gives consent to the officer to search his property (or person), this is held to be a lawful and reasonable search if:

The consent is intelligently given (the person knows that he is waiving his constitutional rights and knows that he does not have to waive these rights).

The consent is freely and voluntarily given.

The consent is clear and explicit.

Constitutional rights are highly regarded and a person consenting to a search waives the rights given to him under the Constitution. The courts "... indulge every reasonable presumption against waiver of fundamental constitutional rights." *Johnson v. Zerbst*, 304 U.S. 458, 464 (1938). The government has the burden of showing by "clear and convincing" evidence that the consent was, in fact, freely and voluntarily given by a person who was aware of his right not to consent. *Bumper v. United States*, 391 U.S. 543 (1968).

MUST WARNINGS BE GIVEN BY THE OFFICER?

The question of whether the person must first be advised of his Fourth Amendment rights in a manner similar to advising a person of his Fifth and Sixth Amendment rights (Miranda warnings) has come before the lower courts many times. The lower courts are divided on the question, and this issue has not been decided by the United States Supreme Court since *Miranda v. Arizona* triggered off the controversy in 1966 as to whether warnings are necessary in order to obtain consent to search.

The National District Attorneys Association's publication *Confessions and Interrogations after Miranda* states on page 63:

> A minority of jurisdictions have held that warnings are required. . . .
> The majority rule is that warnings are not required but that the absence of warnings will be considered on the issue of the voluntariness of the consent.

An example of the majority ruling is the following case, which came before the Supreme Court of Missouri in 1970:

STATE v. WITHERSPOON, 460 S.W.2d 281 (MO. 1970)

> "We believe the better reasoned and balanced view to be that a consent or waiver of Fourth Amendment rights should not be automatically excluded because of failure to spell out the full rights in every detail; and neither should a waiver be exclusively presumed from a verbal expression of consent or acts tantamount thereto . . . we believe that all factors should be considered in a 'totality of circumstances' criterion."

Advising a person of his Fourth Amendment rights will in all situations increase the possibilities that any evidence seized will be admitted as evidence. Warnings which may be given are:

That the person need not give consent if he does not wish to
That a search will not be made if no consent is given
That if consent is given, any fruits of that search may be used against
him in a criminal prosecution

WRITTEN CONSENT

Officers are advised to obtain written consent, if at all possible. This would make the probability of admission into evidence even more certain. The advantages of obtaining written consent are:

1. It would eliminate the contest which would result if the defendant or a third party denied that consent was given.
2. If the warnings were incorporated into the written waiver, it would eliminate any contest as to whether the warnings were given.

3. A properly written waiver should in most cases eliminate any contest as to whether the consent was knowingly, voluntarily, and explicitly given.

If possible, the written consent should be witnessed. Many departments have forms of written consent available for their officers.

TEST OF VOLUNTARINESS

To be valid, the waiver of rights must be voluntary as well intelligent. The consent should almost amount to an invitation. The question of voluntariness is a difficult question for courts to decide because any coercion, actual or implied, will negate the voluntariness of the consent. The following cases illustrate the issue of voluntariness.

If the Consent Is Obtained by Threats
(Whether of Force or Otherwise)

WALDRON v. UNITED STATES, 219 F.2d 37 (D.C. CIR. 1955)

> Officers told the defendant's wife (eighteen years old and pregnant) that if they had to get a search warrant, they would not be responsible for what would happen to the contents of the apartment. If she would let them in of her own free will, they would then put everything back where they found it. It was held that the consent was involuntary and not intelligently given.

WEED v. UNITED STATES, 340 F.2d 827 (10th CIR. 1965)

> Officers who had their guns drawn told the defendant that they had no search warrant but could get a search warrant if he did not consent. It was held that the consent was involuntary and not intelligently given.

THURMAN v. STATE, 455 S.W.2d 177 (TENN. 1970)

> When asked for consent, the defendant said he did not have a key to the trunk of the car. The officer replied that he could obtain a warrant. The defendant then stated, "You got me." He picked up the key from the floor of the car, got out of the car, and opened the trunk. It was held that the defendant voluntarily waived the requirement of a warrant.

STATE v. DOUGLAS, 481 P.2d 653 (ORE. APP. 1971)

> The officer told the defendant several times in a twenty-minute period that if he did not consent to a search of his suitcase, they would get a search warrant. Held to be valid consent.

If Deception Is Used to Obtain Consent

UNITED STATES v. WALLACE, 160 F. SUPP. 859 (D.D.C. 1958)

> The defendant was under arrest and denied having any part in the burglary. The defendant did admit having a suitcase, a camera, and a coat in his home which the officer told him were part of the property stolen. The defendant claimed he obtained the items from the co-defendant. The officers told him that he had nothing to fear if he did not participate in the burglary and that there was no reason why he should not turn over the stolen property. The defendant then gave his consent to a search of his premises but was then charged with re-ceiving stolen property. The court held that the defendant was tricked or coerced into giving consent, stating "It would not be likely that defendant would understand that the exclusive possession of recently stolen property raises an inference that defendant was the thief and that such inference takes the case to the jury, which may be sufficient for a finding of guilt unless explained away."

However, a mistake or ignorance of the criminal law does not necessarily affect the voluntary nature of the consent.

HALL v. UNITED STATES, 418 F.2d 1230 (A.A.N.M. 1969)

> The court held that the fact that the defendant may be ignorant of the criminal law does not affect the voluntariness of the waiver. The suspect thought that carrying a gun in his valise was not a violation of the law when he consented. The police found the gun after being invited to search. Held to be a valid search.

GRAVES v. BETO, 424 F.2d 524 (5th CIR. 1970)

> The defendant consented to the taking of blood samples when it was intimated that the samples would be used for alcohol tests. Instead the blood was used to compare with samples found at the scene of a rape. The court held that the consent to the blood samples was not freely and intelligently given.

COMMONWEALTH v. BROWN, 261 A.2d 879 (PA. 1970)

> The officer advised the defendant of his rights and then questioned the defendant. Being informed that the defendant needed money and was selling personal items, the officer asked if the defendant had a handgun. The officer offered to sell the gun for him and the defendant agreed. The officer sold the gun but borrowed it back from the buyer to have ballistic tests run on the gun. The tests showed that the gun was used in the homicide the officer was investigating and was the most damaging evidence against the defendant in the trial. The majority on the court compared the deception with the gun to the decep-tion approved of by the United States Supreme Court in *Lewis v. United States, Hoffa v. United States,* and *Lopez v. United States.* The procedure was held valid.

If the Officers Have a Search Warrant (Valid or Invalid)
But Rely Instead on the Resulting Consent

BUMPER v. NORTH CAROLINA, 391 U.S. 543 (U.S. S. CT. 1968)

In investigating a rape case, four officers went to the defendant's home. The defendant was not home and his grandmother met the officers at the front door. One of the officers announced, "I have a search warrant to search your house." The grandmother responded, "Go ahead," and opened the door. The rifle which is in controversy was found in the kitchen. Instead of relying on the search warrant, which was never returned to the issuing court, the state relies on the consent of the grandmother. The Court held, "When a law enforcement officer claims authority to search a home under a warrant, he announces in effect that the occupant has no right to resist the search. The situation is instinct with coercion—albeit colorably lawful coercion. Where there is coercion there cannot be consent." Reversed.

UNITED STATES v. MORGAN, 306 F. Supp. 107 (D.C. CAL. 1969)

After agents arrested the defendant, they informed the defendant's wife that as soon as a search warrant arrived, they intended to search the home. She consented to a search of the home before the search warrant arrived. The search warrant, which arrived during the search, proved to be defective. The name of the commissioner executing the warrant was inserted in the blank in which the name of the officer to whom the warrant was directed should have been entered. The blank in which the name of the person making the affidavit should have been inserted contained only the words "special agent." The court held that the search was a valid consent search.

If the Authority of the Officer or Government Is Used to Obtain
Consent and the Person Is Complying with What Appears to Be the
Lawful Commands of Law Enforcement Officers

AMOS v. UNITED STATES, 255 U.S. 313 (U.S. S. CT. 1921)

The officers went to the defendant's home without a warrant and told his wife that they had come to search the premises "for violations of the revenue law" (bootlegging). The Court held that ". . . demanding admission to make a search of it under government authority, cannot be entertained . . . it is perfectly clear that under the implied coercion here presented, no such waiver was intended or effected."

JOHNSON v. UNITED STATES, 333 U.S. 10 (U.S. S. CT. 1948)

Information was obtained from an informant that an unknown person was smoking opium in a certain hotel. Seattle narcotics officers went there and smelled burning opium in the hallway. The odor led them to room 1. The officers did not know who was occupying the room. They knocked and a voice inside asked who was there. "Lieutenant Balland," was the reply. There was a slight delay, some "shuffling or noise" in the room, and then the defendant opened the door. The officer said, "I want to talk to you a little bit." She then, as he described it, "stepped back acquiescently and admitted us." He said, "I want to talk to you about this opium smell in the room here." She denied that there was such a smell. The officer said, "I want you to consider yourself under arrest because we are going to search the room." Opium was found in the search, and the defendant was convicted on a narcotics charge. The Supreme Court, although deciding the case on other grounds, reversed the conviction, stating, "Entry to defendant's living quarters, which was the beginning of the search, was demanded under color of office. It was granted in submission to authority rather than as an understanding and intentional waiver of a constitutional right." [This case was a 5-4 decision.]

If the Defendant, Who Denies His Guilt, Has Been Arrested and Is Being Held in Custody When Consent Is Obtained

Some courts hold almost regardless of the circumstances that such consent is void while other courts consider the circumstances under which consent was obtained.

Invalid consent cases:

UNITED STATES v. WALLACE, 160 F. SUPP. 859 (D.D.C. 1958)

"Where the defendant is under arrest the Government's burden is particularly heavy. Intimidation and duress are almost necessarily implicit in such situations, and if the Government alleges their absence it has the burden of convincing the Court that they are in fact absent. Paraphrasing this, the consent must be shown to be free, uncoerced and voluntary."

HIGGINS v. UNITED STATES, 209 F.2d 819 (CT. APP. D.C. CIR. 1954)

". . . no sane man who denies his guilt would actually be willing that policemen search his room for contraband which is certain to be discovered. It follows that when police identify themselves as such, search a room and find contraband in it, the occupant's words or signs of acquiescence in the search, accompanied by denial of guilt, do not show consent: at least in the absence of some extraordinary circumstance, such as ignorance that contraband is present. No such circumstance is shown here."

CHANNEL v. UNITED STATES, 285 F.2d 217 (9th CIR. 1960)

The defendant was arrested in Los Angeles by narcotics officers and taken to their office. The narcotics agents testified that the defendant stated during the questioning, "I have no stuff in my apartment and you are welcome to go search the whole place." The agents obtained the key and searched the apartment. It was held that the consent had been induced by inherently coercive circumstances.

JUDD v. UNITED STATES, 190 F.2d 649 (D.C. CIR. 1951)

Defendant was arrested at eleven o'clock at night. After being questioned for several hours, he was taken in handcuffs and with four officers to his apartment. The police obtained a shoe which matched a footprint found at the scene of the burglary. The court held that there was no consent and that the search and seizure were not permissible, stating, "Non-resistance to the orders or suggestions of the police is not infrequent . . . true consent, free of fear or pressure, is not so readily to be found."

Valid consent cases:

BURKE v. UNITED STATES, 328 F.2d 399 (1st CIR. 1964)

In the investigation of a mail robbery, Boston police arrested the defendant on a state charge. The arrest was held to be illegal. During the arrest, the defendant was asked to exchange two $20 bills which he had in his possession for two other $20 bills. The defendant was told that some of the bills taken in the mail robbery were marked and that postal officials could identify the markings and that if he gave the bills to the police, the money would be taken to the post office for identification. It was held that the defendant deliberately and voluntarily exchanged the bills and that the act was not under the compulsion of the illegal arrest.

UNITED STATES v. PEREZ, 242 F.2d 867 (2d CIR. 1957), CERT. DENIED, 354 U.S. 941

After the defendant was arrested, he requested to go up to his apartment to see his wife. The agents agreed if he would permit them to search the apartment. The court held that the defendant seemed to consent readily enough and that the search was legal.

ROBINSON v. UNITED STATES, 325 F.2d 880 (5th CIR. 1963)

The defendant was present when officers entered his home to search under the authority of a search warrant. After contraband was found, the defendant was arrested and his person was searched. The court stated, "As to the validity of the search of his automobile, parked in the yard (within the premises known as 2828 Screven Avenue described in the search warrant itself) we conclude that the automobile was sufficiently a part of the crime that was then in process as to warrant the officers in searching it. . . . Moreover, before searching the automobile, the Federal Agent asked Robinson for his automobile keys, told him he wanted to search it and Robinson gave him the keys without objection. The trial court, we think, was justified in finding that this amounted to consent."

If the Defendant Who Has Been Arrested Admits His Guilt and Consents to a Search

UNITED STATES v. MITCHELL, 322 U.S. 65 (U.S. S. CT. 1944)

> Immediately after the defendant was arrested and taken into custody, he admitted his guilt at the police station. He consented to the officers' recovering stolen property from his home. The Court held that the admission of guilt and the property recovered were admissible in evidence and that the admissibility of the evidence was not affected by the subsequent illegal detention of the suspect for eight days before arraignment.

> [Authors' Note: The fact that the defendant admitted his guilt and then gave consent to search presents a case entirely different from the cases where the defendant denies this guilt. A written waiver would almost certainly ensure the admissibility of any evidence found in the consent search.]

THE REQUIREMENT THAT THE CONSENT BE CLEAR AND EXPLICIT

In order to have consent to search, the waiver of the right of privacy must be clearly expressed. The state has the burden to show this and the officer's testimony must show that he was given consent to search in a clear and explicit manner. Some of the supporting facts which an officer might testify to in showing that consent was given are:

Evidence that the officer obtained written consent (either the form or a written statement)

Evidence that the defendant first suggested the search (*United States v. Simpson*, 353 F.2d 530 [1965], *cert. denied*, 383 U.S. 1971)

Evidence that the defendant specified the amount of money or the goods and told the officers exactly where they could be found (*United States v. Torres*, 354 F.2d 633 [1966])

Evidence that the defendant set the conditions under which the search would be conducted by stating "...I will take only two of you." (*United States v. Smith*, 308 F.2d 657 [1962], *cert. denied*, 372 U.S. 906)

CONSENT TO ENTER AS DISTINGUISHED FROM CONSENT TO SEARCH

Consent to enter premises is not consent to search the premises. But if there is consent to enter, what the officer sees in plain view or open view may be seized, as plain view is not a search.

DAVIS v. UNITED STATES, 327 F.2d 301 (9th CIR. 1964)

Two customs agents and two police officers went to the home of the defendant. All were dressed in plain clothes. They did not have sufficient probable cause to arrest the defendant, but went to his home at noontime to question him. Their knock was answered by the eight-year-old child of the defendant. The child, upon answering the door, stated, "Come in." Upon entering, the officers saw marijuana in plain view in a wastebasket. One of the agents asked the child if he could use the lavatory. The little girl pointed in the direction of the bathroom. While relieving himself, the agent observed more marijuana in a trash container in the bathroom. The defendant was then arrested in an upstairs bedroom, and more marijuana was found in the bedroom. The Court found that the officer's trip to the bathroom was prompted by necessity as testimony revealed that he had asked to stop at a service station before going to the defendant's home. Neither the child nor the defendant testified that the child's opening of the door and inviting the men into the house was unusual or unauthorized. Once the officers were inside pursuant to the valid entry, they were not required to remain blind to the obvious.

ROBBINS v. MACKENZIE, 364 F.2d 45 (1st CIR. 1966), CERT. DENIED, 87 S. CT. 215

The court held that where the police had reasonable suspicion but not probable cause and knocked on the door asking to talk and had no other purpose, they were entitled to treat an invitation to enter as voluntary consent. In this case, the officers saw the watch and a gold coin which had been stolen the night before in plain view. The court held that it was not a search because the watch and coin were in plain view.

COMMONWEALTH OF MASSACHUSETTS v. PAINTEN, 368 F.2d 142 (1st CIR. 1966)

The same court as in the Robbins case above distinguished that case from this case as follows: ". . . two policemen, knowing of a holdup but having no substantial clues, came across petitioner and one Ash, and followed them to petitioner's apartment. Their grounds for suspicion did not, even remotely, amount to probable cause for arresting either Ash or petitioner, either for the holdup or for any other crime. After arranging for plainclothesmen to station themselves at the back of the building, one of the uniformed officers then knocked on the door." The officers testified that they were admitted after first being asked to identify themselves through the partly opened door. In the ten seconds they were asked to wait, the officers heard what sounded "like a window opening and closing." When in the apartment, the officers noticed a bulge in Ash's pocket and removed some $200 in crumpled bills. They then checked the window and found a paper bag containing two pistols and some cartridges. Petitioner was thereupon arrested; the apartment was searched, and a large amount of currency was found under a mattress. One of the officers admitted with what the court called "commendable candor" that his purpose even before entering the apartment was to arrest the defendant. The court held, ". . . we distinguished cases where the purpose of the police was not merely to talk, but to make a search. . . . The Commonwealth's own evidence indicates that a search was in fact intended." In addition, the district court held that the police purpose was to arrest petitioner, although they had no warrant or ground for obtaining one.

UNITED STATES v. HORTON, 328 F.2d 132 (3rd CIR. 1964), CERT. DENIED SUB NOM.

"The householder may refuse admittance, but if he opens the door the visitor who is permitted to cross the threshold upon a lawful mission is in no sense a trespasser or wrongdoer, particularly when he properly identifies himself as he enters and does not push on beyond the entrance area where strangers on legitimate business missions are normally received. . . . We see no reason to discourage policemen from obtaining access, without trespass, to this entrance area to make proper inquiries, whether concerning suspected wrongdoing or for other official business. Such discouragement would be the only purpose served by excluding from evidence in subsequent litigation testimony based upon the observation of that which was in plain view, once the outer door of a residence was opened to the visitor."

WHO MAY CONSENT TO SEARCH

A valid consent to a search may be given *only* by a person who has a right to the lawful *use and control* of the property at the time consent to search is given. The words "use and control" (or "possession") do not necessarily imply ownership of the property.

Example: A man rents an automobile for a week from a car rental agency. During the week, he has the use, control, and possession of the car within the meaning of the contract which was signed with the car rental agency. The manager of the car rental agency could not give valid consent to the police to search the automobile while the person renting it had lawful possession.

Searches by the police based upon the consent of some person other than the suspect have been traditionally determined by resort to property law concepts. The theory used was that a person entitled to exercise a proprietary interest in the property could permit a search of the premises or property, at least to the area over which he exercised equal control. The cases in more recent times have begun to place the emphasis on the individual's right of privacy as protected by the Fourth Amendment rather than on strict property law.

Landlord and Tenant

A hotel clerk or manager cannot consent to the search of a room of a guest. Nor can a landlord or his employee consent to the search of a tenant's apartment or home.

CHAPMAN v. UNITED STATES, 365 U.S. 610, 5 L. ED. 2d 828 (U.S. S. CT. 1961)

The landlord discovered a strong "odor of mash" when he visited his rented house to invite the tenants to go to church. He called the sheriff and then made a forced entry through a window. The sheriff entered through the door with the landlord's "consent" after the landlord opened the door from the inside. The state argued that there is a common-law authority which allows a landlord to enter to "view waste." But it was held this does not allow forced entries through doors or windows and the landlord could not give consent for the sheriff to enter.

STONER v. CALIFORNIA, 376 U.S. 483, 11 L. ED. 2d 856 (U.S. S. CT. 1964)

A night clerk in a hotel took officers up to the defendant's room and gave "consent" to enter and search the room. The Court held that "...It is important to bear in mind that it was the petitioner's constitutional right which was at stake here, and not the night clerk's nor the hotel's. It was a right therefore, which only the petitioner could waive by word or deed...there is nothing in the record to indicate that the police had any basis whatsoever to believe that the night clerk had been authorized by the petitioner to permit the police to search the petitioner's room."

STATE v. COOK, 411 P.2d 78 (ORE. 1966)

The caretaker was authorized to live in the defendant's family farmhouse while the family was out of the state. He had a key and free access to the property. The court held that caretaker's voluntary admission of officers into the farmhouse made the search reasonable and the items found during the search, which included parts of clothing of a girl who was allegedly raped on the farm by the defendant, were admissible into evidence.

STATE v. WARFIELD, 198 N.W. 894 (WIS. 1924)

A landlady rented a room to the defendant and, under the terms of the tenancy, was to go into the room to clean and make the bed. It was held that the landlady had no right to search the room's repositories or rummage through the occupant's personal effects. The landlady could not give police officers authority to search without a search warrant.

GOODARD v. STATE, 481 P.2d 343 (WYO. 1971)

A landlord cannot consent to a search of the tenant's premises even after the tenant has been ordered to leave the premises but before he does. *After* the tenant has abandoned the premises or has been evicted, the landlord may consent to a search. (*Abel v. United States,* 362 U.S. 217, *Frank v. United States,* 347 F.2d 486, *Paroutian v. United States,* 299 F.2d 486).

Husband and Wife

Although there was some confusion in early decisions as to authority to consent to a search of the jointly occupied premises of one spouse in the absence of the other, the cases now seem to be uniform. *People v. Carter* has set out what now appears to be the general rule.

PEOPLE v. CARTER, 312 P.2d 655 (CAL. 1957)

When usual amicable relations exist between husband and wife and the property seized is of a kind over which the wife normally exercises as much control as the husband, the wife is in a position to consent to a search and seizure of property in their home.

ROBERTS v. UNITED STATES, 332 F.2d 892 (8th CIR. 1964)

The gun which was used in a murder was never found. During a conversation the wife of the defendant volunteered the information that the defendant had once fired a pistol into the ceiling of their home. The officers obtained written consent from the wife, who assisted the officers in locating the place where the bullet was still embedded in the ceiling and allowed the officers to remove it. The bullet was identified as having been fired from the same pistol as the bullet that killed the victim of the murder. The court held that the search and seizure were reasonable since the wife authorized entry into the premises where she lived and had control. There was nothing to support a charge that there was actual or implied coercion. The wife gave her consent voluntarily after being fully advised that the consent document was not a search warrant and that she did not have to sign it. The search did not extend to the personal effects of the defendant.

STATE v. EVANS, 372 P.2d 365 (HAWAII 1962)

The court after reviewing husband-wife consent stated, "Clearly, one in joint control of the premises, at least when no objection is made by the other occupant, may admit police officers to the house.... None of them [the cases] goes so far as to hold that a wife in joint occupancy of the home can permit a search of her husband's personal effects to discover jewelry hidden in a cuff link case in a bedroom bureau drawer. The wife has no such right." The court held that the search went beyond the bounds of any possible justification.

UNITED STATES EX REL. CABEY v. MAZURKIEWICZ, 431 F.2d 839 (PA. 1970)

> The court held that a wife could not consent to the search of a garage where the husband was the sole lessee and had the only key to the garage. The police were looking for a gun that her husband, then under arrest, may have used in a robbery. Some of their household furniture was stored in the garage. When questioned by the police, the wife stated, "If you care to look, here are the keys." A police officer asked, "Do I need a search warrant?" The wife replied, "No, I have nothing to hide." The court noted that either she did not understand the impact of the search as concerned her husband's interest, or that she was actually motivated by malice toward her husband. In either case, it was held that the consent was invalid.

COMMONWEALTH v. CONNOLLY, 255 N.E.2d 191 (MASS. 1970)

> "One having equal authority over premises may authorize a search of them."

Cotenants and Persons Living Together Who Are Not Married

These persons may consent for each other, and evidence found in the search may be used against the other. The scope of the search is limited to the area over which the consenting occupant has joint use or control. If there is personal property or private effects which the consenting party does not have equal rights to or control over, the consent to the personal property and private effects is invalid.

FRAZIER v. CUPP, 394 U.S. 731 (U.S. S. CT. 1969)

> "[The petitioner] argues that the trial judge erred in permitting some clothing seized from petitioner's duffel bag to be introduced into evidence. This duffel bag was being used jointly by petitioner and his cousin Rawls and it had been left in Rawls' home. The police, while arresting Rawls, asked him if they could have his clothing. They were directed to the duffel bag and both Rawls and his mother consented to its search. During this search, the officers came upon petitioner's clothing and it was seized as well. Since Rawls was a joint user of the bag, he clearly had authority to consent to its search. The officers therefore found evidence against petitioner while in the course of an otherwise lawful search. Under this Court's past decisions, they were clearly permitted to seize it. Harris v. United States 390 U.S. 234 (1968); Warden v. Hayden, 387 U.S. 294 (1967). Petitioner argues that Rawls only had actual permission to use one compartment of the bag and that he had no authority to consent to a search of the other compartments. We will not, however, engage in such metaphysical subtleties in judging the efficacy of Rawls' consent. Petitioner, in allowing Rawls to use the bag and in leaving it in his house, must be taken to have assumed the risk that Rawls would allow someone else to look inside. We find no valid search and seizure claim in this case."

COMMONWEALTH v. CONNOLLY, 255 N.E.2d. 191 (MASS. 1969)
DRUMMOND v. UNITED STATES, 350 F.2d 983 (8th CIR. 1969)

> In neither of these cases was the consenting party married to the other person, but they had equal authority over the premises with the person against whom the evidence was used. It was held to be valid consent.

UNITED STATES v. ELDRIDGE, 302 F.2d 463 (4th CIR. 1962)

> The person having custody and control of personal property may consent to a search. In this case, it was an automoblie.

Consent by the Bailee

The validity of consent in a bailment situation depends upon the bailment arrangement and the extent to which the bailee has control over the property.

VON EICHELBERGER v. UNITED STATES, 252 F.2d 184 (9th CIR. 1958)

> Contraband (guns) were stored "... in a garage belonging to and under the control of one Trost. Later, Trost summoned government investigating agents who entered Trost's garage at his request and opened the boxes in which the guns were contained. They had no search warrant. The premises were entirely under Trost's control. He alone had a key. He willingly and voluntarily granted permission for the agents to enter and search. This was a search with the consent of the person in charge of the premises.... We conclude ... that the search and seizure was a reasonable one."

Employment Situations

Courts have deemed searches reasonable if consented to by the person in lawful possession of the articles seized or the premises on which they are found.

UNITED STATES v. SFERAS, 210 F.2d 69 (7th CIR. 1954)

> The defendant's partner consented to the search. Held valid.

UNITED STATES v. ANTONELLI FIREWORKS CO., 155 F.2d 631 (2nd. 1946)

> An office manager in sole control of the office and the corporate records consented to the search and seizure. The Court commented that it was difficult to see how permission could have been obtained from a more proper person.

Consent by Parents

At the present time, the courts have held that a parent may consent to the search of a child's room or effects in the premises controlled by the parent and over which the parent may exercise dominion and control. The parents may consent to a search which extends in scope to the child's room, closet, and clothing. However, if the child pays rent, or room and board, a lessor-lessee relationship exists and this relationship would determine the validity of the consent.

STATE v. SCHOTT, 182 N.W.2d. 878 (MINN. 1971)

> The mother of a twenty-two-year-old son consented to the search of his room by the police. The court stated, "The record here establishes the mother's possessory interest in the house. At the time of the search and seizure, her control over the premises was apparently absolute. [The son had only once paid $100 to his mother for staying there].... Moreover, it does not appear that defendant had an exclusive right to possession of the room or that he used it regularly. There was testimony that the use of the room was shared with defendant's brother and sisters during his unexplained absences. Rather than establishing a landlord and tenant relationship, the record fairly establishes that other members of the family had equal access to, and use of, the room. Moreover, there was no evidence that any coercion was used in obtaining the mother's acquiescence in the search of the room."
>
> The Supreme Court of Minnesota stated in 136 N.W.2d 580, "...We cannot agree that a child, whether he be dependent or emancipated ...has the same constitutional rights of privacy in the family home which he might have in a rented hotel room. In considering the reasonableness of a search of a home when the search is consented to by the father, the protection afforded to the child must be viewed in light of the father's right to waive it."

REEVES v. WARDEN, MARYLAND PENITENTIARY, 346 F.2d 915 (4th CIR. 1965)

> The court held that a mother who was a guest or a tenant in the son's home did not have the authority to consent to a search of her son's room and a bureau in the room. The court held that the room and the bureau had been set aside exclusively for the son's regular use and only the son could give constitutionally effective permission for a search of the room and bureau without a warrant. The police discovered a note in the bureau which was used in the trial of the son.

CARR v. COMMONWEALTH, 463 S.W.2d 109 (KY. 1971)

> The defendant was one of ten children, of whom some lived with their parents regularly and others stayed at the residence from time to time. The defendant was permitted to sleep at the residence and made it his headquarters when he was around Lexington. In investigating a

rape-murder, a police detective went to the home about midnight on the day after the murder. The parents were not home, but the defendant's twenty-six-year-old sister (Mrs. Lyivers) admitted the officer and gave him information. She was the oldest person at the home that night. Upon the request of the detective, she accompanied the officer to the police station. When Mrs. Lyivers and the officer returned to the home, he requested permission to look around in the area where the defendant had changed clothes when coming in late the night before. Mrs. Lyivers granted the permission, and the officer found a pair of trousers and a pair of muddy work shoes belonging to the defendant. These items proved to be important evidence at the trial. The court held, "It is apparent from the evidence that the appellant [defendant] did not have exclusive possession or control of any portion of the dwelling house of his parents. It seems clear from the record that Mrs. Lyivers was at least temporarily in charge of the premises during the absence of her parents and had full authority to admit the officer and permit the search."

Consent by a Child

Generally, a child may not consent to the search of his parent's home without express authority of the parent. A child, however, may admit a police officer into the parent's home where such occurrence is not out of the ordinary behavior of the child. Once the officer is lawfully upon the premises, he may observe what is in plain view. If what he sees in plain view is contraband or otherwise lawfully seizable, he may seize the item immediately. [See *Davis v. United States* in this chapter (p. 289), where an eight-year-old child answered the door and admitted the officers. When in the house, the officers observed marijuana in plain view.]

Consent by University or School Officials to Search of Students' Dormitory Rooms by Police

COMMONWEALTH v. MCCLOSKEY, 272 A.271 (PA. APP. 1970)

". . . A dormitory room is analogous to an apartment or a hotel room. It certainly offers its occupant a more reasonable expectation of freedom from government intrusion than does a public telephone booth. The defendant rented the dormitory room for a certain period of time, agreeing to abide by the rules established by his lessor, the University. As in most rental situations, the lessor, Bucknell University, reserved the right to check the room for damages, wear and unauthorized appliances. Such right of the lessor, however, does not mean McCloskey was not entitled to have a 'reasonable expectation of freedom from government intrusion', or that he gave consent to the police search, or gave the University authority to consent to such search."

PIAZZOLA v. WATKINS, 442 F.2d 284 (5th CIR. 1971)

"...we must conclude that a student who occupies a college dormitory room enjoys the protection of the Fourth Amendment. True the University retains broad supervisory powers which permit it to adopt the regulation heretofore quoted, provided that regulation is reasonably construed and is limited in its application to further the University's function as an educational institution. The regulation cannot be construed or applied so as to give consent to a search for evidence for the primary purpose of a criminal prosecution. Otherwise, the regulation itself would constitute an unconstitutional attempt to require a student to waive his protection from unreasonable searches and seizures as a condition to his occupancy of a college dormitory room."

IF THE SUSPECT DENIES OWNERSHIP IN THE PROPERTY OR ANY INTEREST IN THE PREMISES

HAYES v. STATE, 158 N.W.2d 545 (WIS. 1967)

Wisconsin and Illinois police asked permission to search a room in a rooming house while investigating a murder and robbery. Oral and written consent was given by a man who stated he was a tenant in the room and was under arrest for another crime. This man was no longer a tenant in the room but did not tell this to the police. The landlady, who was also present, did not inform the police of this but ordered the man to get his property out of the room. The defendant, who was present and was the occupant of the room, denied any ownership in the room. Evidence was obtained in the search of the room which helped convict the defendant of murder and robbery. The Wisconsin Supreme Court held "...that there could be no unlawful search of premises in which the defendant disclaims any interest. See *Rossi v. U.S.* (7th Cir. 1932), 60 Fed. 2d 955, affirmed, 289 U.S. 89... *Creech v. U.S.* (5th Cir. 1938), 97 Fed 2d 390; *U.S. v. Eversole* (7th Cir., 1954), 209 Fed.2d 766."

LIMITATION AND REVOCATION OF CONSENT

If consent to search is given without any limitation ("You may search the house"), the officers may search until all areas under the control of consenter are searched. However, consent may be revoked or limited at any time before the completion of the search. Evidence obtained prior to revocation or limitation may be used as evidence or to sustain an arrest.

LUCERO v. DONOVAN, 354 F.2d 16 (9th CIR. 1965)

This is an action against police officers for unlawful arrest and search. Two Los Angeles police officers observed a man walking down a street and testified that his "eyes were in a fixed stare forward and he was shuffling along, dragging his feet, walking very slowly. And he appeared to be swaying from one side to the other as he was walking." The man denied being under the influence of narcotics but stated that he had just been released from jail that day. The man agreed to allow the officers to search his residence and took them to his sister's house. The sister denied that he lived there and said that he lived with another sister. Upon arriving at the second sister's apartment, the officers commenced a search. When the second sister discovered the presence of the officers, she demanded a search warrant and began calling the officers names. The sister was then arrested and handcuffed, and the search of the apartment continued. Pills were found which the officers believed to contain narcotics. The pills and the sister were taken to the police station, where it was found that the pills did not contain prohibited drugs. The trial court issued a directed verdict in favor of the police officers.

The Ninth Circuit held that "Assuming that [the brother] gave his own consent for search of the apartment, his authority, if any, to act for his sister was rescinded by her expressed protest and her demand for a search warrant.... If the protest occurred before the discovery of the bottle, the subsequent search for it and its seizure were unlawful. If the protest did not occur until after the pills were discovered, there would yet be the need to determine, in the light of the peculiar circumstances, the validity of any consent which [the brother] is claimed to have granted for the search of his sister's home." The case was remanded for these findings.

RESPONSIBILITY OF DETERMINING THE VALIDITY OF THE CONSENT

The responsibility of determining the validity of the waiver and consent rests upon the officer. Before making the search, he should determine that the right person is giving him consent to search.

Rather than asking the consenting person, "Do I need a search warrant?" the officer should determine from the consenting person the nature and the extent of the control which the person has over the property to be searched.

Should the evidence be very vital to the case, extra care (such as obtaining written consent) should be taken to make certain that the search for the evidence and the seizure are proper. It may not be necessary to take such extra precautions if the evidence is merely cumulative of evidence which the police have already seized.

Example: A narcotics arrest is made and a substantial amount of heroin is found on the person in the search after the arrest. The person admits that more heroin can be found in his apartment and that the police have his consent to search the apartment. The officers do not need the heroin as evidence but they are concerned with seizing the heroin as quickly as possible because of its danger.

POSSIBLE DEFENSE ATTACKS WHERE EVIDENCE WAS OBTAINED UNDER THE ALLEGED AUTHORITY OF CONSENT

That no consent was in fact given (the officer says it was and the
    defendant says that it was not)

That the consent is invalid because:

    The person did not know he was waiving his rights or knew that
      he did not have to waive these rights

    That the consent was not freely and voluntarily given

    That the language or action of the defendant did not amount to
      waiver of rights and consent

    That the officer did inform the defendant of his Fourth Amendment
      rights (in jurisdictions requiring this)

That the person giving consent did not have the authority to waive the
    rights of the defendant (the officer obtained consent from the
    wrong person)

CASE FOR CHAPTER TWELVE

GAUTREAUX v. STATE
SUPREME COURT OF WISCONSIN
52 WIS.2d 489 (1971)

. . . .

    It is argued by Gautreaux that when the consent was given at the police sta-
tion Charleston, along with the defendant and others, were under arrest and this
alone is sufficient to establish the consent was not voluntary but rather the product
of coercion and duress implied from the fact the defendants were subject to the
control of the officers. Although the state has the burden of proving by clear and
positive evidence the search was the result of a free, intelligent, unequivocal and
specific consent without any duress or coercion, actual or implied, *United States
v. Callahan* (2d Cir. 1971), 439 Fed. 2d 852; *United States v. Berkowitz* (1st Cir.
1970), 429 Fed. 2d 921, and its burden is more difficult when the consent is given
while the consenter is under arrest, *United States v. Page* (9th Cir. 1962), 302 Fed.
2d 81; *United States v. Jordan* (2d Cir. 1968), 399 Fed. 2d 610, there is no presumption a consent to a search given by a person under arrest is involuntary and
coerced as a matter of law.

    It is true the psychological effect of being in the custody of the police should
be taken into consideration and be given greater weight with first offenders than
with experienced criminals. Likewise, the time of day or night, the deprivation of
human comforts, the number of policemen interrogating the person are among the
factors to be considered in evaluating whether the consent was voluntary. However, the factors used in the evaluation do not differ essentially from those considered in determining voluntariness of an inculpatory statement or confession. In
terms of involuntariness and the freedom of choice, we see no legal difference
(same principles apply to search of a home and search of a person). We think
that even though the consent was given early in the morning while Charleston
was in custody and after he twice refused to give the consent, these factors are

not sufficient standing alone to render the consent involuntary in fact. Many courts have found a consent to be voluntarily given despite its "in custody" nature. . . . See Annot. (1966), *Validity of Consent to Search Given by One in Custody of Officers*, 9 A. L. R. 3d 858, 873.

But it is argued by Gautreaux the consent was obtained by coercion in that he was told he would be better off with reference to the charge if he consented to the search of the car and this was a veiled threat which implied he would face a more serious charge if he did not consent. We do not consider this statement of the police to contain an implied threat.

It is also argued an officer promised if nothing was found by the search the defendants could return to their homes in Illinois. We do not think this statement is tantamount to a threat or raises the implication that if Charleston did not let the police search the car they would hold the defendants. While the police cannot use deceit or trickery, they are entitled to make true statements and to interrogate one under arrest. A promise to let one go if a search does not result in incriminating evidence is not the type of promise which would vitiate the consent. The promise might constitute motivation or inducement for making a choice but its nature does not destroy the freedom of choice which is central to the concept of voluntariness.

Gautreaux relies for his argument of involuntariness in a constitutional sense on *People v. Parisi* (1964), 42 Misc. 2d 607, 249 N. Y. Supp. 2d 493, and *United States v. Wallace* (D. C. D. C. 1958), 160 Fed. Supp. 859. In *Parisi* the officer purposely misled the consenter as to the incriminating nature of the goods for which they wanted the search. In *Wallace* the officers searching for lottery printing presses lied to the consenter when they told him they knew the location of the presses and were about to get a search warrant. These cases hold what was psychologically a voluntary choice to be void because of trickery on the part of the police in obtaining the consent. Here, the police stated they intended to release the men if no incriminating evidence was found by the search and the trial court believed this testimony. The cases of *Dade v. State* (1941), 188 Okla. 677, 112 Pac. 2d 1102, and *United States v. Linderman* (E. D. N. Y. 1940), 32 Fed. Supp. 123, are not in point. They involve mere acquiescence or submission to the police rather than that degree of willingness which constitutes a free choice of consent in a constitutional sense.

The trial court found Charleston was aware no search could be conducted without his consent and concluded the consent was not a product of any coercion but rather Charleston chose to take a "calculated risk that the loot was well hidden and the possibility was the police would not find it by search of the vehicle." Taking a calculated risk its free choice and the circumstances of this case, especially the location where the loot was hidden, support the court's finding of the voluntariness of the consent and it will not be disturbed. . . .

QUESTIONS AND PROBLEMS

1.   Assume that you were the investigating officer in each of the cases in this chapter which were reversed. What procedure should have been used? Indicate when a search warrant could have been obtained. If a search would not be issued, what other alternatives were available to the investigating officers?

2. In 1971, suburban police officers were called by the parents of a fourteen-year-old girl at two o'clock in the morning. Their daughter was not home and they feared that she had been seduced by her dancing teacher. They knew that the dance instructor came to the suburb once a week from a nearby large city and usually stayed overnight at a motel in the suburb. Officers were sent to the motel and found that he was registered and that his car was in the parking lot. No one answered the door of the motel room when the officers knocked, and the room was dark. At the request of the officers, the motel manager opened the door of the motel room. The dance instructor and the fourteen-year-old girl were found inside the room. Can the entry and search be justified:

   a. By consent of the motel manager to the entry?
   b. Under the principle of "exigent circumstances" or "urgent need"?
   c. On the basis that the officers had reasonable grounds to believe that a felony was being committed in the room?

3. Two vice-squad officers in an unmarked police car stopped the defendant's car for a brake light violation. After the defendant was shown that the brake light did not work, he was told that the violation justified a search of his person and of his car. The defendant stated, "Go ahead. I'm clean." The search of the car revealed no incriminating evidence. After a pat-down for weapons, one of the officers looked into the defendant's pockets with a flashlight. The light disclosed a small quantity of green weed particles which tests showed to be marijuana. Defendant was tried and convicted on a charge of possession of marijuana. *Barnes v. State*, 130 N.W.2d 264 (Wis. 1964)

   a. Was the search authorized by the statement of the defendant, "Go ahead. I'm clean"?
   b. Could the search be justified as a search incident to a traffic arrest in your jurisdiction?

4. Indicate the extent of valid consent to search which ordinarily could be given by:

   A maid in a hotel as to:
   a. A guest's room
   b. Hotel property

   A wife as to:
   a. The home which she and her husband live in
   b. Her husband's office, which she visits once or twice a month
   c. Her husband's business car, which he alone drives and uses for business purposes

A divorced husband as to:

a. The apartment of his former wife

b. The bedroom and personal effects of his sixteen-year-old son who lives with him

A plant manager as to:

a. Corporation records in the plant

b. Another employee's desk

c. The locker of a man working in the plant

5. The state seeks to introduce evidence which it obtained as the result of a consent search. What possible attacks could the defense use in an attempt to have the evidence suppressed?

13
AUTHORITY TO SEARCH PURSUANT TO A VALID SEARCH WARRANT

WHAT IS A SEARCH WARRANT?

"A search warrant is an order signed by a judge directing a law enforcement officer to conduct a search of a designated person, a designated object or a designated place for the purpose of seizing designated property or kinds of property, and to deliver any property so seized to the Clerk designated in the warrant. A judge shall issue a search warrant if probable cause is shown. The warrant shall be based upon sworn complaint or affidavit, or testimony recorded by a phonographic reporter, showing probable cause therefor. The complaint, affidavit or testimony may be upon information and belief." *Wis. Stat.* 968.12. (Wiretapping and electronic surveillance are discussed later.)

PROTECTION AFFORDED

The predecessors of the search warrant as we know it today were the "general warrant" and "writ of assistance." Abuses were so common under the authority of such writs that the framers of the Bill of Rights wisely chose to abolish them. In seventeenth-century England, the general warrant was a common means of suppressing political dissent. These general warrants were what the name implies. No person was named, no place was named, and no time limit was prescribed on the execution of such warrants. The warrant was authorized by the Court of Star Chamber (a name which is now generally regarded as synonymous with disregard of judicial restraint and protection of individual rights), and the secretary of state, to a government official. The warrant gave the official his own discretion to seize material, books, pamphlets, printing equipment, etc., which was politically critical of the crown.

In pre-Revolution times in this country, and hence before the Constitution, writs of assistance were issued to officials of the government, usually revenue officers, to search for and seize smuggled goods. The time, place, scope of the search, and the person to be searched were left entirely to the discretion of the officer. Under such circumstances, with little, if any, limitation on the authority of the officer, no place or person was safe at any time from search founded on the mere whimsy of the officer.

It is with that background that the Constitution demands that before a search warrant may issue, it must be found (1) by a *magistrate* that there is (2) *probable cause* to believe that (3) a *particular place or person* has (4) *particular articles or things* for which a search may be authorized and which articles or things may be seized.

REQUIREMENT OF JUDICIAL INTERCESSION

The United States Supreme Court, speaking in *United States v. Ventresca*, 380 U.S. 102, 13 L. Ed. 2d 684, 85 S. Ct. 741 (1965), reiterated the requirement that before a search warrant is issued, some judicial officer must intervene and make the determination that probable cause exists. The Court stated:

> An evaluation of the Constitutionality of a search warrant should begin with the rule that the informed and deliberate determinations of magistrates empowered to issue warrants are to be preferred over the hurried action of officers who may happen to make arrests. . . . The reasons for this rule go to the foundations of the Fourth Amendment. . . . The point of the Fourth Amendment, which often is not grasped by zealous officers, is not that it denies law enforcement the support of the usual inferences which reasonable men draw from evidence. Its protection consists in requiring that those inferences be drawn by a neutral and detached magistrate instead of being judged by the officer engaged in the often competitive enterprise of ferreting out crime. Any assumption that evidence sufficient to support a magistrate's disinterested determination to issue a search warrant will justify the officers in making a search without a warrant would reduce the Amendment to a nullity and leave the people's homes secure only in the discretion of police officers.

THE PROBABLE-CAUSE REQUIREMENT

As previously discussed, probable cause for the issuance of a search warrant is that information in the officer's possession obtained by his own observations or through reliable and trustworthy sources, even unnamed informants, which would lead an ordinary, prudent person to conclude that what is sought is where it is claimed to be. The information may be presented to the magistrate, who may be a judge or court commissioner, or any judicial officer who has the authority of a judge *in camera*, i.e., the power of a judge in his chambers. The information may be presented in secret, sworn testimony directly to the magistrate and stenographically or mechanically recorded by stenotype (this is what is meant by "phonographically" recorded testimony, i.e., verbatim recordings), or by affidavit. The choice of which method is used is usually dictated by statute or local custom or the personal preference of the particular magistrate to whom the application is made. Many magistrates, because of the press of business, prefer not to take the time to listen to oral testimony. They feel that it is more convenient for the officer to submit his information in affidavit form which can be quickly read and which allows a more deliberate determination of probable cause.

ASSISTANCE OF PROSECUTOR

In either case, the officer should seek the assistance of the prosecuting attorney. Any prosecuting attorney would much prefer to spend the relatively brief time necessary to prepare a proper affidavit or make sure that sufficient oral testimony is provided to the magistrate than spend hours and perhaps days in court arguing whether or not the information was sufficient for a determination of probable cause. There is nothing more frustrating than seeing a big "bust" wasted because a motion to suppress is granted for some irregularity that could easily have been corrected if someone had taken the time to prepare the information for the search warrant properly.

SUFFICIENCY OF PROOF

Although the officer need not divulge all the evidence he has in order to obtain a search warrant, if what he has supplied is sufficient for a finding of probable cause, extreme care must be taken to be certain that there is sufficient information to sustain such finding. The determination by the magistrate does not resolve the issue of probable cause once and for all, nor does the finding by the magistrate insulate the search warrant against later attack. If the search warrant is attacked, usually in a motion to suppress the evidence found as a result of the execution of the search warrant, the reviewing judge may look *only* to the evidence presented to the magistrate at the time that the search warrant was issued. If the officer, for strategic reasons, held back information, he cannot use it at the later hearing to supplement the information given to the magistrate. The search warrant stands or falls on the affidavits or the oral testimony given to the magistrate *at the time the search warrant was issued*. If, because of lack of sufficient evidence to support a finding of probable cause, the motion to suppress is granted, the evidence cannot be used. The additional information in the possession of the officer can be used to paper the station-house walls for all its usefulness. (See *Aguilar v. Texas*, 378 U.S. 108, in cases, this chapter.)

THE MEASURES OF SUFFICIENCY FOR A FINDING OF PROBABLE CAUSE

In Ventresca the Supreme Court also outlined the standard or measure which will be used to determine what information is enough and what information may be used to supply the basis for a finding of probable cause. The Court stated:

> While a warrant may issue only upon a finding of "probable cause," this Court has long held that "the term 'probable cause' means less than evidence which would justify condemnation," and that a finding of "probable cause" may rest upon evidence which is not legally competent in a criminal trial. As the Court stated in *Brinegar v United States*, 338 US 160, 173, 93 L ed 1879, 1889. 69 S St 1302, "There is a large difference between the two things to be proved (guilt and probable cause), as well as between the tribunals which determine them, and therefore a like difference in the quanta and modes of proof required to establish them." Thus hearsay may be the basis for issuance of the warrant "so long as there ... [i]s a substantial basis for crediting the hearsay." And, in Aguilar we recognized that "an affidavit may be based on hearsay information and need not reflect the direct personal observations of the affiant," so long as the magistrate is "informed of some of the underlying circumstances" supporting the affiant's conclusions and his belief that any informant involved "whose identity need not be disclosed ... was 'credible' or his information 'reliable.'" *Aguilar v Texas*, supra 378 US at 114, 12 L ed 2d at 729.
>
> These decisions reflect the recognition that the Fourth Amendment's commands, like all constitutional requirements, are practical and not abstract. If the teachings of the Court's cases are to be followed and the constitutional policy served, affidavits for search warrants, such as the one involved here, must be tested and interpreted by magistrates and courts in a commonsense and realistic fashion.
>
> This is not to say that probable cause can be made out by affidavits which are purely conclusory, stating only the affiant's or an informer's belief that probable cause exists without detailing any of the "underlying circumstances" upon which that belief is based. See Aguilar v Texas, supra. Recital of some of the underlying circumstances in the affidavit is essential if the magistrate is to perform his

detached function and not serve merely as a rubber stamp for the police. However, where these circumstances are detailed, where reason for crediting the source of the information is given, and when a magistrate has found probable cause, the courts should not invalidate the warrant by interpreting the affidavit in a hypertechnical, rather than a commonsense, manner. Although in a particular case it may not be easy to determine when an affidavit demonstrates the existence of probable cause, the resolution of doubtful or marginal cases in this area should be largely determined by the preference to be accorded to warrants.

The affidavit of the officers which was held to be sufficient in the Ventresca case is as follows:

AFFIDAVIT IN SUPPORT OF SEARCH WARRANT.

Before W. Arthur Garrity, Worcester, Massachusetts

The undersigned being duly sworn deposes and says:

That he has reason to believe that on the premises known as a one-family light green wooden frame dwelling house located at 148½ Coburn Avenue, Worcester, occupied by Giacomo Ventresca and his family, together with all approaches and appurtenances thereto, in the District of Massachusetts, there is now being concealed certain property, namely an unknown quantity of material and certain apparatus, articles and devices, including a still and distilling apparatus setup with all attachments thereto, together with an unknown quantity of mash, an unknown quantity of distilled spirits, and other material used in the manufacture of non-tax-paid liquors; which are being held and possessed, and which have been used and are intended for use, in the distillation, manufacture, possession, and distribution of non-tax-paid liquors in violation of the provisions of 26 USC 5171(a), 5173, 5178, 5179(a), 5222(a), 5602, and 5686.

And that the facts tending to establish the foregoing grounds for issuance of a Search Warrant are as follows:

See Attached Sheet

/s/ Walter A. Mazaka

Investigator, Alcohol and Tobacco Tax Div.,
Internal Revenue Service

Sworn to before me, and subscribed in my presence, August 31st, 1961

/s/ W. Arthur Garrity

United States Commissioner

Based upon observations made by me, and based upon information received officially from other Investigators attached to the Alcohol and Tobacco Tax Division assigned to this investigation, and reports orally made to me describing the results of their observations and investigation, this request for the issuance of a search is made.

On or about July 28, 1961, about 6:45 P.M., an observation was made covering a Pontiac automobile owned by one Joseph Garry. Garry and one Joseph Incardone put thirteen bags of sugar into the car. These bags of sugar weighed sixty pounds each. Ten such bags were put into the trunk, and three were placed in the rear seat. Those in the rear seat were marked "Domino." The others appeared to have similar markings. After the sugar was loaded into the car, Garry together with Incardone drove it to the vicinity of 148 Coburn Avenue, Worcester, Massachusetts, where the car was parked. Sometime later, the car with its contents was driven into the yard to the rear of 148 and between the premises 148 and 148½ Coburn Avenue. After remaining there about twenty-five minutes, the same two men drove in the direction of Boston.

On August 2, 1961 a Pontiac car owned by Garry and driven by Garry with Incardone as a passenger, was followed from Boston to Worcester. The car appeared heavily laden. The car was again driven into the driveway at 148 and 148½ Coburn Avenue to the rear of the yard and between the above-numbered houses.

On August 7, 1961, at least six sixty-pound bags of Domino Sugar were loaded into the Pontiac owned by Garry. The loading was done by Garry and Incardone. The car traveled from Boston to Worcester, then to Holden, and returned with its contents and entered the driveway at 148 and 148½ Coburn Avenue, where the car was parked at the rear between two houses.

On August 11, 1961 new empty metal or tin cans were transferred from a car owned by Incardone to the Pontiac owned by Garry on Highland Street in Hyde Park. The Pontiac was driven by Garry with Incardone as a passenger to Worcester, and into the yard at 148 and 148½ Coburn Avenue to the rear and between the two numbered premises.

On August 16, 1961 the Pontiac was observed. In the back seat bags of sugar were observed covered with a cloth or tarpaulin. A sixty-pound bag of sugar was on the front seat. Garry was observed after loading the above-described sugar into the car placing a carton with various five-pound bags of sugar on the top of the tarpaulin. The car was then driven by Garry with Incardone as a passenger to Worcester together with its contents into the yard at 148 and 148½ Coburn Avenue to the rear of and between the two houses. About Midnight on the same night, the Pontiac driven by Garry with Incardone as a passenger was seen pulling up to the premises at 59 Highland Street, Hyde Park, where Garry lives. Garry opened the trunk of his car, and removed ten five-gallon cans therefrom, and placed them on the sidewalk. He then entered the house, and opened a door on the side. Incardone made five trips from the sidewalk to the side of the house carrying two five-gallon can on each such trip. It appeared that the cans were filled. On each of these trips, Incardone passed the two cans to someone standing in the doorway. Immediately after the first such trip, Garry came out of the door and joined Incardone. They walked to the sidewalk, and talked for a few minutes. Incardone then drove away, and Garry went into his home.

On August 18, 1961 Investigators smelled an odor of fermenting mash on two occasions between 4:00 A.M. and 5:00 A.M. The first such odor was detected as they walked along the sidewalk in front of 148 Coburn Avenue, and the second such odor was detected from the side of 148 Coburn Avenue. At or about the same time, the Investigators heard certain metallic noises which cannot be further identified by source or sound.

On August 24, 1961 the Pontiac was observed parked at a bowling alley and coffee shop off Route 9. The back of the car contained what appeared to be boxes covered by a cloth or tarpaulin, but which cannot be more specifically identified. On the front seat of the car was observed a sixty-pound bag of Revere Sugar. Garry and Incardone were observed in the restaurant or coffee shop eating. Later the car was seen driven to the rear of 148 between 148 and 148½ Coburn Avenue, Worcester.

About Midnight the Pontiac was observed pulling up in front of Garry's house at 59 Highland Street, Hyde Park. Garry was driving, and Incardone was a passenger. They both got out of the car. Garry opened the trunk, and then entered his house. From the trunk of the car there was removed eleven five-gallon cans which appeared to be filled. Incardone made six trips to a door on the side of the house. He carried two five-gallon cans on each trip, except the sixth trip. On that trip he carried one can, having passed the others to somebody in the doorway, and on the last trip he entered the house. He remained there at least forty-five minutes, and was not observed to leave.

On August 28, 1961 Garry drove Incardone in his car to Worcester. On Lake Ave. they met Giacomo Ventresca, who lives at 148½ Coburn Avenue, Worcester. Ventresca entered the car driven by Garry. The car was then driven into the yard to the rear of 148 and between 148 and 148½ Coburn Avenue. An observation was made that empty metal cans, five-gallon size, were being taken from the car owned by Garry, and brought into the premises at 148½ Coburn Avenue, which was occupied by Ventresca. Later new cans similar in size, shape and appearance were observed being placed into the trunk of Garry's car while parked at the rear of 148 and in front of 148½ Coburn Avenue. The manner in which the cans were handled, and the sounds which were heard during the handling of these cans, were consistent with that of cans containing liquid.

On August 30, 1961, at about 4:00 A.M., an odor of fermenting mash was detected while Investigators were walking on the sidewalk in front of 148 Coburn Avenue. At the same time, they heard sounds similar to that of a motor or a pump coming from the direction of 148½ Coburn Avenue.

The foregoing information is based upon personal knowledge and information which has been obtained from Investigators of the Alcohol and Tobacco Tax Division, Internal Revenue Service, who have been assigned to this investigation.

/s/ Walter A. Mazaka

TWO-PRONGED TEST

In *Aguilar v. Texas*, 378 U.S. 108, 12 L. Ed. 2d 723 (1964), the United States Supreme Court laid down a "two-pronged test" which determined whether or not the information supplied by the officers seeking the search warrant was sufficient when based on hearsay information:

1. Does the application set forth any of the underlying circumstances necessary to enable the magistrate *independently* to judge the validity of the informant's conclusion that the articles sought are where he says they are?
2. Have the affiant officers supported their claim that their informant is "credible" or his information "reliable"?

The majority of the court in Ventresca, Chief Justice Warren and Justice Douglas dissenting, held that the affidavit supplied by the officers in that case met the test.

The initial test for the magistrate's consideration is to determine whether the officers have supplied enough of the background information to answer the magistrate's question, "How does the informant know that the articles are where he says they are?" Usually the informant has relayed to the officer his personal observations. The officer then must state that the informant told him that he was personally present at the address in question and personally observed what it is that is being sought at that location.

In *Spinelli v. United States* (1969) the United States Supreme Court held that if it is not demonstrated in the affidavit or testimony in support of the application for the search warrant that the tip is trustworthy, it cannot pass the test of validity, even though parts of the tip are corroborated by independent sources. The following affidavit in Spinelli was found to be inadequate.

AFFIDAVIT IN SUPPORT OF SEARCH WARRANT.

I, Robert L. Bender, being duly sworn, depose and say that I am a Special Agent of the Federal Bureau of Investigation, and as such am authorized to make searches and seizures.

That on August 6, 1965, at approximately 11:44 a. m., William Spinelli was observed by an Agent of the Federal Bureau of Investigation driving a 1964 Ford Convertible, Missouri licence HC3–649, onto the Eastern approach of the Veterans Bridge leading from East St. Louis, Illinois, to St. Louis, Missouri.

That on August 11, 1965, at approximately 11:16 a. m., William Spinelli was observed by an Agent of the Federal Bureau of Investigation driving a 1964 Ford convertible, Missouri license HC3–649, onto the Eastern approach of the Eads Bridge leading from East St. Louis, Illinois, to St. Louis, Missouri.

Further, at approximately 11:18 a. m. on August 11, 1965, I observed William Spinelli driving the aforesaid Ford convertible from the Western approach of the Eads Bridge into St. Louis, Missouri.

Further, at approximately 4:40 p. m. on August 11, 1965, I observed the aforesaid Ford convertible, bearing Missouri license HC3–649, parked in a parking lot used by residents of The Chieftain Manor Apartments, approximately one block east of 1108 Indian Circle Drive.

On August 12, 1965, at approximately 12:07 p. m. William Spinelli was observed by an Agent of the Federal Bureau of Investigation driving the aforesaid 1964 Ford convertible onto the Eastern approach of the Veterans Bridge from East St. Louis, Illinois, in the direction of St. Louis, Missouri.

Further, on August 12, 1965, at approximately 3:46 p. m., I observed William Spinelli driving the aforesaid 1964 Ford convertible onto the parking lot used by the residents of The Chieftain Manor Apartments approximately one block east of 1108 Indian Circle Drive.

Further, on August 12, 1965, at approximately 3:49 p. m., William Spinelli was observed by an Agent of the Federal Bureau of Investigation entering the front entrance of the two-story apartment building located at 1108 Indian Circle Drive, this building being one of The Chieftain Manor Apartments.

On August 13, 1965, at approximately 11:08 a. m., William Spinelli was observed by an Agent of the Federal Bureau of Investigation driving the aforesaid Ford convertible onto the Eastern approach of the Eads Bridge from East St. Louis, Illinois, heading towards St. Louis, Missouri.

Further, on August 13, 1965, at approximately 11:11 a. m., I observed William Spinelli driving the aforesaid Ford convertible from the Western approach of the Eads Bridge into St. Louis, Missouri.

Further, on August 13, 1965, at approximately 3:45 p. m., I observed William Spinelli driving the aforesaid 1964 Ford convertible onto the parking area used by residents of The Chieftain Manor Apartments, said parking area being approximately one block from 1108 Indian Circle Drive.

Further, on August 13, 1965, at approximately 3:55 p. m., William Spinelli was observed by an Agent of the Federal Bureau of Investigation entering the corner apartment located on the second floor in the southwest corner, known as Apartment F, of the two-story apartment building known and numbered as 1108 Indian Circle Drive.

On August 16, 1965, at approximately 3:22 p. m., I observed William Spinelli driving the aforesaid Ford convertible onto the parking lot used by the residents of The Chieftain Manor Apartments approximately one block east of 1108 Indian Circle Drive.

Further, an Agent of the F. B. I. observed William Spinelli alight from the aforesaid Ford convertible and walk toward the apartment building located at 1108 Indian Circle Drive.

The records of the Southwestern Bell Telephone Company reflect that there are two telephones located in the southwest corner apartment on the second floor of the apartment building located at 1108 Indian Circle Drive under the name of Grace P. Hagen. The numbers listed in the Southwestern Bell Telephone Company records for the aforesaid telephones are WYdown 4–0029 and WYdown 4–0136.

William Spinelli is known to this affiant and to federal law enforcement agents and local law enforcement agents as a bookmaker, an associate of bookmakers, a gambler, and an associate of gamblers.

The Federal Bureau of Investigation has been informed by a confidential reliable informant that William Spinelli is operating a handbook and accepting wagers and disseminating wagering information

by means of the telephones which have been assigned the numbers
WYdown 4–0029 and WYdown 4–0136.
/s/ Robert L. Bender,
Robert L. Bender,
Special Agent Federal Bureau of Investigation.
Subscribed and sworn to before me this 18th day of August, 1965,
at St. Louis, Missouri.
/s/ William R. O'Toole.

The Court stated:

> Though the affiant swore that his confidant was "reliable" he offered
> the magistrate no reason in support of this conclusion. Perhaps even
> more important is the fact that *Aguilar's* other test has not been satis-
> fied. The tip does not contain a sufficient statement of the underlying
> circumstances from which the informer concluded that Spinelli was
> running a bookmaking operation. We are not told how the FBI's
> source received his information—it is not alleged that the informant
> personally observed Spinelli at work or that he had ever placed a bet
> with him. Moreover, if the informant came by the information in-
> directly, he did not explain why his sources were reliable. In the
> absence of a statement detailing the manner in which the information
> was gathered, it is especially important that the tip describe the
> accused's criminal activity in sufficient detail so that the magistrate
> may know that he is relying on something more substantial than a
> casual rumor circulating in the underworld or an accusation based
> merely on an individual's general reputation.

It appears that the Court is suggesting at least two ways in which
the validity of the informant's information may be established. (1) It
can be shown that there are sufficient underlying circumstances or
background information to convince the magistrate independently that
the informant does in fact know whereof he speaks. (2) Or the activities of the person against whom the search warrant is being sought
are in such detail that the magistrate is convinced that only a person
who has valid and trustworthy information would know them. The
Court in Spinelli used as an example the detail provided by an informant in *Draper v. United States*, 358 U.S. 307 (1959). Although
Draper did not involve a search warrant, the Court stated that such
information as was provided by the informant in that case would have
been sufficiently detailed to meet the test of Aguilar. In Draper, the
informant told the FBI that Draper had gone to Chicago the day before
by train and that he would return to Denver by train with 3 ounces
of heroin on one of two specified mornings. The informant went on to
describe, with minute particularity, the clothes that Draper would be
wearing upon his arrival in Denver. Although the informant did not
state the way in which he had obtained his information, the Court felt

that a magistrate, confronted with such detail, could reasonably infer that the informant had gained his information in a reliable way.

CREDIBILITY OF INFORMANT

The bald assertion by the affiant officer that he "believes" his informant to be reliable is not good enough. The following form of establishing such credibility of the informant has been successful: "Affiant further states that he is a Vice squad officer for said city particularly assigned to narcotics laws enforcement and has been so assigned for the last past four years; that during that period of time affiant has received information from informant on eight separate occasions, two of which were within the past four months; that on each of those occasions, your affiant has personally corroborated the information received from informant and found that it was accurate and correct in each instance; that as a direct result of the information received from said informant in the past, eight arrests for violations of the narcotic laws of this state have been made by affiant and other police officers of this city; that of the eight arrests so made, six have resulted in convictions of the persons arrested; that two of said cases are still pending in court." Of course such allegation may be made only in an appropriate case where such background is correct. The principle to be applied is merely to show to the magistrate that the informant is believable and that his information is trustworthy.

POOLING INFORMATION

It is not necessary that one officer have all the information in his personal possession to support the probable cause for the issuance of the search warrant. It is permissible for several officers to pool their information, both from their own observation and the information received from their respective informants, named or unnamed, as long as the requirements of validity and credibility are met. [Hood v. United States 422 F.2d 737 (7th Cir. 1970), cert. denied, 400 U.S. 820]

REVEALING IDENTITY OF UNNAMED INFORMANTS

The United States Supreme Court has held that it is in the public interest for police officers to develop confidential sources of information. The Court has recognized that without such citizen cooperation, many serious offenders would escape apprehension. In order to maintain this line of communication open and free from unnecessary harassment, the Court has ruled that the name and identity of such informant may remain secret. The officer, on the other hand, must be prepared to articulate to the magistrate or judge the reasons why he believes that the informant is reliable and trustworthy and that his information is probably correct.

If, at the trial, the nature of the circumstances makes the informer's identity obvious, there is no good reason to maintain the secrecy over his identity. Also, if the defense can show that the informer's identity is necessary for the defense of the defendant on the issue of guilt or innocence, the trial judge, in his discretion, may compel the officer to reveal the identity of the informant. If the officer feels that such revelation cannot be made and refuses to identify the informant, the judge is required to dismiss the case against the defendant.

PARTICULARITY

As has been previously discussed, one of the necessary requisites of a valid search warrant is that it particularly describe the place to be searched and the articles to be seized.

PLACE

The circumstances of the case will determine the degree of information necessary to particularize the place to be searched. A farm may not need to be described as intensively as an apartment in a multifamily dwelling unit. A general search warrant is illegal. The place must be described so that it is definitely ascertainable, *to the exclusion of all other places.* Although a legal description of the premises by metes and bounds is not necessary, a description is required sufficient to lead any person to the premises. A street address alone, depending on the type of structure, may be enough. If the street address encompasses several residences or businesses, or even two of them, it is not enough, because the description is not sufficient to exclude all other locations. A street address for a single-family residence where the warrant is for the entire premises would be enough.

The description may be by physical facts. It may describe the construction by size, color, location, particular distinguishing features, adjoining structures, or even the names of the occupants.

Describing the place as "occupied by John Doe, alias, in the City of Baraboo, or the surrounding County of Sauk," has been held to be too general.

The description of the place may be elicited from the informant and made a part of the affidavit of the officer, or described in his testimony, if that method is used. Often the officer affiant will have verified the information given by his informant so that he too can describe in detail the place to be searched.

Example 1: Apartment 4 located on the second floor, southeast portion thereof, of a four-family structure located at 1234 North East Street, City of Good Town, County of Ocean, State of New Paris, containing a living room, kitchen, two bedrooms and a bathroom, occupied by Helen W. Lawbreaker.

Example 2: 1234 North East Street in the City of Good Town, County of Ocean, State of New Paris, a four-family apartment.

Example 3: 1234 North East Street in the City of Ocean, County of Goodman, State of Paris, a single-family residence in its entirety.

Example 4: A green and white single-family frame dwelling with an attached one-car garage on the northeast corner of North 92d Street and West Thurston Avenue, Milwaukee, Wisconsin.

Example 1 is sufficient because it specifically describes the place to be searched. Example 2 is insufficient because it is vague and indefinite. Example 3 is sufficient because it specifically describes the place to be searched. Example 4 may be insufficient because it is too broad and does not specifically describe whether all or a part of the premises is to be searched.

LIMIT

The requirement of particularity not only requires the officer to describe the place to be searched, but limits him to the place described. The search warrant may not be used merely as a place to start and from which to wander about generally to search other places not described in the warrant. The warrant must leave the officer no doubt as to where he may search and no discretion to search elsewhere.

DESCRIPTION OF THINGS TO BE SEIZED

A search warrant may be issued for the seizure of:

1. Contraband, i.e., things which in themselves are illegal to possess, such as narcotic drugs, gambling machines, machine guns
2. Fruits of a crime, i.e., stolen goods
3. Instrumentalities, i.e., burglary tools, policy slips, bookmaker's "book"
4. Evidence of crimes or "mere evidence," i.e., books and records

Until *Warden v. Hayden,* 387 U.S. 294, 87 S. Ct. 1642 (1967), there was some confusion as to how far the officer could go in seizing mere evidence with a search warrant or pursuant to a search. It was generally held that mere evidence was outside the purview of a search warrant and could not be seized. Mere evidence may now be validly seized by officers. It must be noted, however, that the Court did not lift all limitation upon the seizing of mere evidence. Those Fifth Amendment restrictions on items of a "communicative" or "testimonial" nature are still protected. The Court stated:

> There must, of course, be a nexus—automatically provided in the case of fruits, instrumentalities or contraband—between the items to be seized and criminal behavior. Thus in the case of "mere evidence" probable cause must be examined in terms of cause to believe that the evidence sought will aid in a particular apprehension or conviction.

DEFINITENESS

General warrants for the purpose of looking indiscriminately for some evidence of some crime are strictly forbidden. The officer must be able to describe what evidence he is seeking and declare that he is seeking it because it is necessary to prove a particular crime, or to assist in the apprehension of a particular offender.

The degree of description of the property to be seized depends to some extent upon the type of article or property which is sought. Weapons or narcotics, or contraband, for instance, would not need the same detailed and precise description as books and documents would. In *Stanford v. Texas*, 379 U.S. 467 (1965), the warrant described the property sought as "books, records, pamphlets, cards, receipts, lists, memoranda, pictures, recordings and other written instruments concerning the communist party in Texas." The United States Supreme Court held:

> The indiscriminate sweep of that language is constitutionally intolerable. To hold otherwise would be false to the terms of the Fourth Amendment, false to its meaning and false to its history.

As early as 1927, the United States Supreme Court held in *Marron v. United States*, 275 U.S. 192:

> The requirement that warrants shall particularly describe the things to be seized makes general searches under them impossible and prevents the seizure of one thing under a warrant describing another. As to what is to be taken, nothing is left to the discretion of the officer executing the warrant.

TO WHOM DIRECTED

The search warrant is usually directed to the officer who has signed the complaint and supplied the information for the issuance of the warrant. Depending on local law, it may be directed to the sheriff, a peace officer, or a class of police officers, e.g., officers of the alcohol and beverage tax division of the state's attorney office. A private citizen is rarely permitted to serve a search warrant.

The common law and many jurisdictions restrict the execution of search warrants to daylight hours. Unless specifically provided for, the search warrant must be so executed. A general rule of thumb as to when it is daylight is when the features of a person can be clearly distinguished at 10 yards. An exception to the daylight execution may be made if specifically provided for in the warrant by the magistrate. This may occur when the officer is sure that the articles to be seized are where they are alleged to be and the magistrate is convinced that the articles will be moved or destroyed if not seized immediately. Local rules govern, however. Some states, like Wisconsin, make no provision for the time of day within which a search warrant may be executed.

REASON FOR DAYLIGHT LIMITATION

The courts in those jurisdictions limiting the time in which a search warrant may be executed have reasoned that if a person's constitutional protection against searches and seizures is to be invaded, it should be done with as little interference of his privacy as possible. Since the daylight hours will afford the least inconvenience, the search warrant is limited to those hours.

Other jurisdictions have reasoned that if there is probable cause to believe that a crime has been committed and that the fruits of that crime are in a particular place, the inconvenience to the person with such articles in his possession is relatively minor since the peace and dignity of the community have already been disturbed by the commission of the crime. In those cases, the courts have determined that the recovery of the articles should be made at the most expeditious time to ensure their recovery.

EXAMINATION OF THE PROCESS

The warrant and supporting affidavit and complaint are generally referred to as "process." Prior to executing the search warrant, the officer should carefully examine all the material to be certain that the information contained therein is accurate. Particularly the description and address of the place to be searched and the description of the things to be seized should be scrutinized very carefully. All names should be spelled correctly. The address of the place to be searched should be exactly correct. A typographical error in the address could invalidate the entire search, or at least require an unnecessary judicial proceeding and submission of evidence to prove that the error was simply mechanical. A typical checklist should make sure that the warrant:

1. Is properly executed (signed) by the magistrate
2. States who is directed to serve the search warrant
3. States what authority is granted under it
4. Shows clearly on its face the place to be searched and the articles to be seized

EXECUTION OF THE SEARCH WARRANT

Execution of the search warrant should be made promptly after it is issued. Execution simply refers to the act of conducting the search according to the authority of the warrant. The officer to whom the search warrant is directed should supervise the search and be present, even though he may be assisted by other officers.

TIME LIMIT ON EXECUTION

The search warrant must be executed within a reasonable time after it has been issued. As a general rule, it must be executed while it is still probable that the items to be sought are in the described premises. The officer cannot hold the search warrant and use it as a weapon or form of coercion upon the person or premises against which it is directed. Ten days is considered the limit in which a search pursuant to a search warrant may reasonably be made. Some jurisdictions have limited by statute the number of days which may elapse before a warrant automatically loses its validity. The magistrate may place a time limit within which the search may be conducted.

LENGTH OF SEARCH

The length of the search, once it is begun, depends upon the circumstances. The items sought and the type of place and its size will determine the reasonableness of the length of the search. The search must be made promptly and with dispatch. The officers may take as much time in conducting the search as is reasonably necessary, but cannot extend the search into a form of harassment. A search for a stolen 21-inch color TV and stereo set in a two-room apartment will take a short time. A search for a stolen TV set in a warehouse full of TV sets will take a long time and may extend into days.

NUMBER OF SEARCHERS

The number of officers who participate in the search will likewise be determined by what is sought and where the search takes place. There is no specific law on the subject except the ever-present requirement of reasonableness. The privacy of the occupant of the place searched is being lawfully interrupted. That interruption should take place with the minimum amount of inconvenience.

AMOUNT OF FORCE

An officer and anyone assisting him may use whatever force is necessary to execute the search warrant. After announcing his presence and purpose, the officer may take whatever reasonable action and use whatever reasonable force are required to search the premises and/or seize the property so found. The guiding principle is reasonableness. The use of force, where necessary, extends to the entry into the premises and any room, closet, trunk, drawer, compartment, cabinet, etc., within the premises. The force that is allowed may extend to persons on the premises who attempt to prevent the officer from entering the premises or to conduct a search therein. Such force may be used as will effectuate the search and seizure and no more. It is not reasonable to use deadly force except where death or great bodily harm is threatened.

DETENTION AND SEARCH OF PERSONS ON THE PREMISES

Since any person on the premises might be able to thwart the effectiveness of the search warrant by concealing the sought-after items on his person, and because the officer will want to protect himself from any attack by a concealed weapon, the search of such persons has generally been upheld. Wisconsin's *Code of Criminal Procedure*, enacted July 1, 1970, provides:

> "The person executing the search warrant may reasonably detain and search any person on the premises at the time to protect himself from attack or to prevent the disposal or concealment of any item particularly described in the search warrant." *Wis. Stat.* 968.16

If he has sufficient information, the officer may provide for the search of the occupant in the search warrant itself, thereby avoiding any question about his authority to do so if his state does not make provision by statute or case law for so doing.

MANNER OF EXECUTION

The Federal Rules and most states require that a copy of the search warrant and supporting affidavits be served upon the occupant as soon as practicable after entry is made into the premises. If the premises are unoccupied, the copy must be left in a conspicuous place within the premises. "As soon as practicable" means immediately upon entry. If the occupant is fighting, resisting, or attempting to flee, then such service must take place when it is safe to do so. Where such practice is not required by law, it is recommended that that practice be followed, for it will be an indication to the occupant that the officer is being as fair and reasonable as he may be under the circumstances. If no copy is available in those jurisdictions where service of a copy is not required, the supervising officer should at least read the search warrant to the occupant upon entry.

SEIZURE

The officer may seize the items or articles particularly described in the search warrant on the described premises. He may not use the search warrant premises as a launching pad to search indiscriminately places not described in the search warrant. If the warrant refers to the second-floor premises, the officer may not go next door and search, or go to a different level of the premises and search. He is confined to the place described in the warrant. It is therefore particularly important that the officer have sufficient information when applying for the warrant to cover all possibilities. It may be desirable, if the evidence supports it, to name and describe more than one location or premises in the same search warrant.

SEIZURE OF PROPERTY NOT DESCRIBED IN THE WARRANT

Although general searches are not allowed, an officer reasonably coming upon contraband, weapons, stolen property, evidence of crime other than the crime in which the warrant was issued, or other seizable items, need not stand helplessly and watch such items disappear merely because they were not named in the search warrant. The validity of the seizure of such articles is dependent upon the circumstances under which they were seized. If the officer is lawfully where he is and the seizure is reasonable, the seized articles will be admissible in evidence.

Example: An officer searching for heroin pursuant to a valid search warrant for heroin on the named premises comes across a stolen television set during the search; he may seize the television set.

An officer searching for a stolen 21-inch television set pursuant to a valid search warrant for that purpose finds a "dime bag" of heroin in the toe of a sock in a dresser drawer; he may not seize the heroin.

An officer searching for a stolen 21-inch television set pursuant to a valid search warrant for that purpose observes a "dime bag" of heroin lying on top of a dresser in the bedroom while searching for the television set; he may seize the heroin.

The scope of the search is determined by what is being sought. What is being sought will determine the reasonableness of the place it is sought and what other items are seized. What is seen in plain view is not a search and therefore may be seized, even if not described in the search warrant. Other articles may be seized although not described in the search warrant if reasonably related to the search for the named items; i.e., the search must be limited to the same extent and intensity as it would be in searching for the items described in the search warrant.

INVENTORY OF PROPERTY SEIZED

An itemized, correct, complete inventory of all property seized must be made by the officer. The Federal Rules and many jurisdictions require such inventory to be made in writing in the presence of the occupant right on the premises being searched and provide that a copy be left with the occupant or posted in a conspicuous place with a copy of the search warrant if the place is not occupied. Whether required by law or not, the better practice is for the officer to prepare such list, have it verified by the occupant by his signature if possible, or by the signature of a witness, and leave a receipt for the articles seized with the occupant. The property not needed for evidence should be promptly returned to the occupant, if he is the lawful owner. If the goods are stolen, or if there is a dispute over ownership of the property, the person claiming the property may be required to bring an action in the appropriate court for return of the property. The officer should not take it upon himself to settle disputes over claims of ownership.

RETURN OF THE WARRANT

The return of the warrant is literally what it implies: returning the warrant, with the results of its execution to the court, or a designated clerk of the court, that issued it. The return should list only those items particularly described in the search warrant. Although a return of the warrant has been held to be merely a ministerial act not affecting the validity of the search and seizure, proper care should be taken to fill out the return correctly. The return may be determinative in later proceedings as indicative of the legal basis and extent of the search and seizure. The return has been held, in some jurisdictions, to be conclusive upon the prosecution to that extent.

TIME LIMIT ON RETURN

If there is a time limit on the life of the warrant, then the warrant must be returned within that limit. The general rule is that the warrant must be returned within ten days of the issuance of the warrant if there is no other limitation. Some states provide that the warrant must be returned within forty-eight hours after its execution even if the life of the warrant has not lapsed. In Wisconsin, for instance, although a warrant may be executed anytime within five days after it is issued, if it is executed on the first day, the return must be made within forty-eight hours after the execution. The property itself is required to be kept in the custody of the officer in a safe place with proper evidentiary chain-of-custody precautions, "so long as necessary for the purpose of being produced as evidence on any trial."

SEARCH OF THE PERSON WITH A SEARCH WARRANT

If there is time, the officer must obtain a search warrant for the search of a person. The officer should not rely upon consent of the person to be searched, for the desired consent may not be forthcoming. The Terry, Sibron, and Peters cases have somewhat modified the law in this area, but the general principle remains the same. If there is time, get a search warrant. The requirement of judicial intercession is always preferable to the on-the-street decisions of the police officer whose zeal and involvement in the case may affect his objectivity. The same requirements of specificity in obtaining a search warrant for a place, with the necessary probable cause for its issuance, are present here. The person to be searched and the property sought must be described with the same degree of particularity as a place. If the person to be searched is not named, he must be described with the particularity necessary to exclude all other persons.

DEGREE OF FORCE IN SEARCH OF A PERSON

If the person named or described in the search warrant refuses to be searched, or if the search must be made to such a degree that it cannot be made in public, the officer may use that degree of force reasonably necessary to detain the person, or convey him to some convenient place or the station house to be searched. The degree of force to be used depends upon the circumstances. Deadly force is never reasonable unless the officer or another is threatened with death or great bodily harm. Obviously an officer would not shoot a person who was alleged to have forged checks in his possession if that person would not submit to a search. The officer would use whatever means were at his command, including physical force less than deadly, to persuade the offender to submit. If the offender, however, threatened deadly force, the officer could also use deadly force to apprehend and search the person.

The officer executing a search warrant for a person may use the same force and enter the same places in executing that warrant as he could if executing an arrest warrant.

MISCELLANEOUS RULES

The success of the search and seizure will not validate an otherwise invalid search warrant. Be sure that the warrant correctly and particularly describes the place to be searched and the things to be seized *before* the search is begun. The end does not justify the means.

The search warrant not only authorizes, but *limits* the officer in searching for those items particularly described in the particular place described, with the exceptions noted.

Other articles may be seized although not described in the search warrant if *reasonably related* to the search for the named items; i.e., the search must be limited to the same extent and intensity as it would be in searching for the items described in the search warrant. This exception usually applies only to contraband or stolen goods. The officer should always *announce his authority and his purpose* before attempting a forcible entry.

A search warrant is not required for *open fields*.

A place of business receives the same Fourth Amendment protection as a private residence, even though the Fifth Amendment self-incrimination rights do not apply to business corporations.

Most states provide for *criminal penalties* for violating the secrecy attendant upon execution and issuance of a search warrant.

What is discovered *in plain view* is not a search.

Fourth Amendment prohibitions apply *only* to law enforcement or government officers.

ORAL PROCEDURES FOR ISSUING SEARCH WARRANTS

Statutory authority for oral procedures in the issuing of search warrants began in California in 1970 and was followed by the enactment of Arizona legislation in 1971. Other states and perhaps the federal government may enact similar legislation.

The new procedure authorized by statute permits a magistrate to take an oral statement from an officer under oath which is recorded and later transcribed. The oral statement may be given in person, by telephone, or by radio.

If the magistrate finds that probable cause exists, a search warrant will be issued in the regular manner, or the magistrate may authorize the officer to complete a search warrant form at the scene and to sign the magistrate's name to the form. The form would be considered a duplicate to the original warrant which the magistrate would complete and issue in his office.

The officer could then make the necessary search under the authority of the duplicate warrant. The return of the warrant would be made in the normal manner.

The new oral procedures save considerable time and make search warrants readily available when probable cause exists. In cases of doubt, officers may quickly obtain warrants at any time of day or night.

CASES FOR CHAPTER THIRTEEN

AGUILAR v. TEXAS
SUPREME COURT OF THE UNITED STATES
378 U.S. 108, 12 L. ED. 2d 723, 84 S. CT. 1509 (1964)

This case presents questions concerning the constitutional requirements for obtaining a state search warrant.

Two Houston police officers applied to a local Justice of the Peace for a warrant to search for narcotics in petitioner's home. In support of their application, the officers submitted an affidavit which, in relevant part, recited that:

> "Affiants have received reliable information from a credible person and do believe that heroin, marijuana, barbiturates and other narcotics and narcotic paraphernalia are being kept at the above described premises for the purpose of sale and use contrary to the provisions of the law."[1]

---

[1] The record does not reveal, nor is it claimed, that any other information was brought to the attention of the Justice of the Peace. It is elementary that in passing on the validity of a warrant, the reviewing court may consider *only* information brought to the magistrate's attention.

The search warrant was issued.

In executing the warrant, the local police, along with federal officers, announced at petitioner's door that they were police with a warrant. Upon hearing a commotion within the house, the officers forced their way into the house and seized petitioner in the act of attempting to dispose of a packet of narcotics.

At his trial in the state court, petitioner, through his attorney, objected to the introduction of evidence obtained as a result of the execution of the warrant. The objections were overruled and the evidence admitted. Petitioner was convicted of illegal possession of heroin and sentenced to serve 20 years in the state penitentiary. On appeal to the Texas Court of Criminal Appeals, the conviction was affirmed. We granted a writ of certiorari to consider the important constitutional questions involved.

In Ker v California, 374 US 23, we held that the Fourth "Amendment's proscriptions are enforced against the States through the Fourteenth Amendment," and that "the standard of reasonableness is the same under the Fourth and Fourteenth Amendments."

Although Ker involved a search without a warrant, that case must certainly be read as holding that the standard for obtaining a search warrant is likewise "the same under the Fourth and Fourteenth Amendments."

An evaluation of the constitutionality of a search warrant should begin with the rule that "the informed and deliberate determinations of magistrates empowered to issue warrants . . . are to be preferred over the hurried action of officers . . .who may happen to make arrests." United States v Lefkowitz, 285 US 452. The reasons for this rule go to the foundations of the Fourth Amendment. A contrary rule "that evidence sufficient to support a magistrate's disinterested determination to issue a search warrant will justify the officers in making a search without a warrant would reduce the Amendment to a nullity and leave the people's homes secure only in the discretion of police officers." Johnson v United States, 333 US 10. Under such a rule "resort to [warrants] would ultimately be discouraged." Jones v United States, 362 US 257. Thus, when a search is based upon a magistrate's, rather than a police officer's, determination of probable cause, the reviewing courts will accept evidence of a less "judicially competent or persuasive character than would have justified an officer in acting on his own without a warrant," ibid., and will sustain the judicial determination so long as "there was substantial basis for [the magistrate] to conclude that narcotics were probable present. . . ." As so well stated by Mr. Justice Jackson:

> "The point of the Fourth Amendment, which often is not grasped by zealous officers, is not that it denies law enforcement the support of the usual inferences which reasonable men draw from evidence. Its protection consists in requiring that those inferences be drawn by a neutral and detached magistrate instead of being judged by the officer engaged in the often competitive enterprise of ferreting out crime." Johnson v United States, supra.

Although the reviewing court will pay substantial deference to judicial determinations of probable cause, the court must still insist that the magistrate perform his "neutral and detached" function and not serve merely as a rubber stamp for the police.

In Nathanson v United States, 290 US 41, a warrant was issued upon the sworn allegation that the affiant "has cause to suspect and does believe" that certain merchandise was in a specified location. The Court, noting that the affidavit "went upon a mere affirmation of suspicion and belief *without any statement of adequate supporting facts*," (emphasis added), announced the following rule:

> "Under the Fourth Amendment, an officer may not properly issue a warrant to search a private dwelling unless he can find probable cause therefor from *facts or circumstances* presented to him under oath or affirmation. Mere affirmance of belief or suspicion is not enough." (Emphasis added.)

The Court, in Giordenello v United States, 357 US 480, applied this rule to an affidavit similar to that relied upon here. Affiant in that case, swore that petitioner "did receive, conceal, etc., narcotic drugs ... with knowledge of unlawful importation...." The Court announced the guiding principles to be: "that the inferences from the facts which lead to the complaint '[must] be drawn by a neutral and detached magistrate instead of being judged by the officer engaged in the often competitive enterprise of ferreting out crime.' Johnson v. United States, 333 U. S. 10. The purpose of the complaint, then, is to enable the appropriate magistrate ... to determine whether the 'probable cause' required to support a warrant exists. The Commissioner must judge for himself the persuasiveness of the facts relied on by a complaining officer to show probable cause. He should not accept without question the complainant's mere conclusion...."

The Court, applying these principles to the complaint in that case, stated that: "it is clear that it does not pass muster because it does not provide any basis for the Commissioner's determination ... that probable cause existed. The complaint contains no affirmative allegation that the affiant spoke with personal knowledge of the matters contained therein; it does not indicate any sources for the complainant's belief; and it does not set forth any other sufficient basis upon which a finding of probable cause could be made."

The vice in the present affidavit is at least as great as in Nathanson and Giordenello. Here the "mere conclusion" that petitioner possessed narcotics was not even that of the affiant himself; it was that of an unidentified informant. The affidavit here not only "contains no affirmative allegation that the affiant spoke with personal knowledge of the matters contained therein," it does not even contain an "affirmative allegation" that the affiant's unidentified source "spoke with personal knowledge." For all that appears, the source here merely suspected, believed or concluded that there were narcotics in petitioner's possession.[2] The magistrate here certainly could not "judge for himself the persuasiveness of the facts relied on ... to show probable cause." He necessarily accepted "without question" the informant's "suspicion," "belief" or "mere conclusion."

Although an affidavit may be based on hearsay information and need not reflect the direct personal observations of the affiant, Jones v United States, 362 US 257, the magistrate must be informed of some of the underlying circumstances from which the informant concluded that the narcotics were where he claimed

---

[2] To approve this affidavit would open the door to easy circumvention of the rule announced in Nathanson and Giordenello. A police officer who arrived at the "suspicion," "belief" or "mere conclusion" that narcotics were in someone's possession could not obtain a warrant. But he could convey this conclusion to another police officer, who could then secure the warrant by swearing that he had "received reliable information from a credible person" that the narcotics were in someone's possession.

they were, and some of the underlying circumstances from which the officer concluded that the informant, whose identity need not be disclosed, see Rugendorf v United States, 376 US 528, 11 L ed 2d 887, 84 S Ct 825, was "credible" or his information "reliable." Otherwise, "the inferences from the facts which lead to the complaint" will be drawn not "by a neutral and detached magistrate," as the Constitution requires, but instead, by a police officer "engaged in the often competitive enterprise of ferreting out crime," or, as in this case, by an unidentified informant.

We conclude, therefore, that the search warrant should not have been issued because the affidavit did not provide a sufficient basis for a finding of probable cause and that the evidence obtained as a result of the search warrant was inadmissible in petitioner's trial.

The judgment of the Texas Court of Criminal Appeals is reversed and the case remanded for proceedings not inconsistent with this opinion.

Reversed and remanded.

SPINELLI v. UNITED STATES
SUPREME COURT OF THE UNITED STATES
393 U.S. 410, 21 L. ED. 2d 637, 89 S. CT. 584 (1969)

William Spinelli was convicted under 18 U. S. C. § 1952 of traveling to St. Louis, Missouri, from a nearby Illinois suburb with the intention of conducting gambling activities proscribed by Missouri law. See Mo. Rev. Stat § 563.360 (1959). At every appropriate stage in the proceedings in the lower courts, the petitioner challenged the constitutionality of the warrant which authorized the FBI search that uncovered the evidence necessary for his conviction. At each stage, Spinelli's challenge was treated in a different way. At a pretrial suppression hearing, the United States District Court for the Eastern District of Missouri held that Spinelli lacked standing to raise a Fourth Amendment objection. A unanimous panel of the Court of Appeals for the Eight Circuit rejected the District Court's ground, a majority holding further that the warrant was issued without probable cause. After an en banc rehearing, the Court of Appeals sustained the warrant and affirmed the conviction by a vote of six to two. Both the majority and dissenting en banc opinions reflect a most conscientious effort to apply the principles we announced in Aguilar v. Texas, 378 U. S. 108 (1964), to a factual situation whose basic characteristics have not been at all uncommon in recent search warrant cases. Believing it desirable that the principles of Aguilar should be further explicated, we granted certiorari, our writ being later limited to the question of the constitutional validity of the search and seizure.[1] For reasons that follow we reverse.

[1] We agree with the Court of Appeals that Spinelli has standing to raise his Fourth Amendment claim. The issue arises because at the time the FBI searched the apartment in which Spinelli was alleged to be conducting his bookmaking operation, the petitioner was not on the premises. Instead, the agents did not execute their search warrant until Spinelli was seen to leave the apartment, lock the door, and enter the hallway. At that point, petitioner was arrested; the key to the apartment was demanded of him, and the search commenced. Since petitioner would plainly have standing if he had been arrested inside the apartment, Jones v. United States, 362 U. S. 257, 267 (1960), it cannot matter that the agents preferred to delay the arrest until petitioner stepped into the hallway—especially when the FBI only managed to gain entry into the apartment by requiring petitioner to surrender his key.

In *Aguilar*, a search warrant had issued upon an affidavit of police officers who swore only that they had "received reliable information from a credible person and do believe" that narcotics were being illegally stored on the described premises. While recognizing that the constitutional requirement of probable cause can be satisfied by hearsay information, this Court held the affidavit inadequate for two reasons. First, the application failed to set forth any of the "underlying circumstances" necessary to enable the magistrate independently to judge of the validity of the informant's conclusion that the narcotics were where he said they were. Second, the affiant-officers did not attempt to support their claim that their informant was "'credible' or his information 'reliable.'" The Government is, however, quite right in saying that the FBI affidavit in the present case is more ample than that in *Aguilar*. Not only does it contain a report from an anonymous informant, but it also contains a report of an independent FBI investigation which is said to corroborate the informant's tip. We are, then, required to delineate the manner in which *Aguilar's* two-pronged test should be applied in these circumstances.

In essence, the affidavit, reproduced in full in the Appendix to this opinion, contained the following allegations:[2]

1. The FBI had kept track of Spinelli's movements on five days during the month of August 1965. On four of these occasions, Spinelli was seen crossing one of two bridges leading from Illinois into St. Louis, Missouri, between 11 a. m. and 12:15 p. m. On four of the five days, Spinelli was also seen parking his car in a lot used by residents of an apartment house at 1108 Indian Circle Drive in St. Louis, between 3:30 p. m. and 4:45 p. m.[3] On one day, Spinelli was followed further and seen to enter a particular apartment in the building.

2. An FBI check with the telephone company revealed that this apartment contained two telephones listed under the name of Grace P. Hagen, and carrying the numbers WYdown 4–0029 and WYdown 4–0136.

3. The application stated that "William Spinelli is known to this affiant and to federal law enforcement agents and local law enforcement agents as a bookmaker, an associate of bookmakers, a gambler, and an associate of gamblers."

4. Finally, it was stated that the FBI "has been informed by a confidential reliable informant that William Spinelli is operating a handbook and accepting wagers and disseminating wagering information by means of the telephones which have been assigned the numbers WYdown 4–0029 and WYdown 4–0136."

There can be no question that the last item mentioned, detailing the informant's tip, has a fundamental place in this warrant application. Without it, probable cause could not be established. The first two items reflect only innocent-seeming activity and data. Spinelli's travels to and from the apartment building and his entry into a particular apartment on one occasion could hardly be taken as be-

---

[2] It is, of course, of no consequence that the agents might have had additional information which could have been given to the Commissioner. "It is elementary that in passing on the validity of the warrant, the reviewing court may consider *only* information brought to the magistrate's attention." *Aguilar* v. *Texas*, 378 U. S. 108, 109, n. 1 (emphasis in original). Since the Government does not argue that whatever additional information the agents may have possessed was sufficient to provide probable cause for the arrest, thereby justifying the resultant search as well, we need not consider that question.

[3] No report was made as to Spinelli's movements during the period between his arrival in St. Louis at noon and his arrival at the parking lot in the late afternoon. In fact, the evidence at trial indicated that Spinelli frequented the offices of his stockbroker during this period.

speaking gambling activity; and there is surely nothing unusual about an apartment containing two separate telephones. Many a householder indulges himself in this petty luxury. Finally, the allegation that Spinelli was "known" to the affiant and to other federal and local law enforcement officers as a gambler and an associate of gamblers is but a bald and unilluminating assertion of suspicion that is entitled to no weight in appraising the magistrate's decision.

So much indeed the Government does not deny. Rather, following the reasoning of the Court of Appeals, the Government claims that the informant's tip gives a suspicious color to the FBI's reports detailing Spinelli's innocent-seeming conduct and that, conversely, the FBI's surveillance corroborates the informant's tip, thereby entitling it to more weight. It is true, of course, that the magistrate is obligated to render a judgment based upon a common-sense reading of the entire affidavit. United States v. Ventresca, 380 U. S. 102, 108 (1964). We believe, however, that the "totality of circumstances" approach taken by the Court of Appeals paints with too broad a brush. Where, as here, the informer's tip is a necessary element in a finding of probable cause, its proper weight must be determined by a more precise analysis.

The informer's report must first be measured against Aguilar's standards so that its probative value can be assessed. If the tip is found inadequate under Aguilar, the other allegations which corroborate the information contained in the hearsay report should then be considered. At this stage as well, however, the standards enunciated in Aguilar must inform the magistrate's decision. He must ask: Can it fairly be said that the tip, even when certain parts of it have been corroborated by independent sources, is as trustworthy as a tip which would pass Aguilar's tests without independent corroboration? Aguilar is relevant at this stage of the inquiry as well because the tests it establishes were designed to implement the long-standing principle that probable cause must be determined by a "neutral and detached magistrate," and not by "the officer engaged in the often competitive enterprise of ferreting out crime." Johnson v. United States, 333 U. S. 10, 14 (1948). A magistrate cannot be said to have properly discharged his constitutional duty if he relies on an informer's tip which—even when partially corroborated—is not as reliable as one which passes Aguilar's requirements when standing alone.

Applying these principles to the present case, we first consider the weight to be given the informer's tip when it is considered apart from the rest of the affidavit. It is clear that a Commissioner could not credit it without abdicating his constitutional function. Though the affiant swore that his confidant was "reliable," he offered the magistrate no reason in support of this conclusion. Perhaps even more important is the fact that Aguilar's other test has not been satisfied. The tip does not contain a sufficient statement of the underlying circumstances from which the informer concluded that Spinelli was running a bookmaking operation. We are not told how the FBI's source received his information—it is not alleged that the informant personally observed Spinelli at work or that he had ever placed a bet with him. Moreover, if the informant came by the information indirectly, he did not explain why his sources were reliable. Compare Jaben v. United States, 381 U. S. 214 (1965). In the absence of a statement detailing the manner in which the information was gathered, it is especially important that the tip describe the accused's criminal activity in sufficient detail so that the magistrate may know that he is relying on something more substantial than a casual rumor circulating in the underworld or an accusation based merely on an individual's general reputation.

The detail provided by the informant in Draper v. United States, 358 U. S. 307 (1959), provides a suitable benchmark. While Hereford, the FBI's informer in that case, did not state the way in which he had obtained his information, he reported that Draper had gone to Chicago the day before by train and that he would return to Denver by train with three ounces of heroin on one of two specified mornings. Moreover, Hereford went on to describe, with minute particularity, the clothes that Draper would be wearing upon his arrival at the Denver station. A magistrate, when confronted with such detail, could reasonably infer that the informant had gained his information in a reliable way.[4] Such an inference cannot be made in the present case. Here, the only facts supplied were that Spinelli was using two specified telephones and that these phones were being used in gambling operations. This meager report could easily have been obtained from an offhand remark heard at a neighborhood bar.

Nor do we believe that the patent doubts *Aguilar* raises as to the report's reliability are adequately resolved by a consideration of the allegations detailing the FBI's independent investigative efforts. At most, these allegations indicated that Spinelli could have used the telephones specified by the informant for some purpose. This cannot by itself be said to support both the inference that the informer was generally trustworthy and that he had made his charge against Spinelli on the basis of information obtained in a reliable way. Once again, *Draper* provides a relevant comparison. Independent police work in that case corroborated much more than one small detail that had been provided by the informant. There, the police, upon greeting the inbound Denver train on the second morning specified by informer Hereford, saw a man whose dress corresponded precisely to Hereford's detailed description. It was then apparent that the informant had not been fabricating his report out of whole cloth; since the report was of the sort which in common experience may be recognized as having been obtained in a reliable way, it was perfectly clear that probable cause had been established.

We conclude, then, that in the present case the informant's tip—even when corroborated to the extent indicated— was not sufficient to provide the basis for a finding of probable cause. This is not to say that the tip was so insubstantial that it could not properly have counted in the magistrate's determination. Rather, it needed some further support. When we look to the other parts of the application, however, we find nothing alleged which would permit the suspicions engendered by the informant's report to ripen into a judgment that a crime was probably being committed. As we have already seen, the allegations detailing the FBI's surveillance of Spinelli and its investigation of the telephone company records contain no suggestion of criminal conduct when taken by themselves— and they are not endowed with an aura of suspicion by virtue of the informer's tip. Nor do we find that the FBI's reports take on a sinister color when read in light of common knowledge that bookmaking is often carried on over the telephone and from premises ostensibly used by others for perfectly normal purposes. Such an argument would carry weight in a situation in which the premises contain an unusual number of telephones or abnormal activity is observed, cf. *McCray* v. *Illinois*, 386 U. S. 300, 302 (1967), but it does not fit this case where neither of these factors is present.[5] All that remains to be considered is the flat statement that Spinelli was "known" to the FBI and others as a gambler. But just as a sim-

---

[4] While *Draper* involved the question whether the police had probable cause for an arrest without a warrant, the analysis required for an answer to this question is basically similar to that demanded of a magistrate when he considers whether a search warrant should issue.

[5] A box containing three uninstalled telephones was found in the apartment, but only after execution of the search warrant.

ple assertion of police suspicion is not itself a sufficient basis for a magistrate's finding of probable cause, we do not believe it may be used to give additional weight to allegations that would otherwise be insufficient.

The affidavit, then, falls short of the standards set forth in *Aguilar*, *Draper*, and our other decisions that give content to the notion of probable cause. In holding as we have done, we do not retreat from the established propositions that only the probability, and not a prima facie showing, of criminal activity is the standard of probable cause, *Beck* v. *Ohio*, 379 U. S. 89, 96 (1964); that affidavits of probable cause are tested by much less rigorous standards than those governing the admissibility of evidence at trial, *McCray* v. *Illinois*, 386 U. S. 300, 311 (1967); that in judging probable cause issuing magistrates are not to be confined by niggardly limitations or by restrictions on the use of their common sense, *United States* v. *Ventresca*, 380 U. S. 102, 108 (1964); and that their determination of probable cause should be paid great deference by reviewing courts, *Jones* v. *United States*, 362 U. S. 257, 270-271 (1960). But we cannot sustain this warrant without diluting important safeguards that assure that the judgment of a disinterested judicial officer will interpose itself between the police and the citizenry.

The judgment of the Court of Appeals is reversed and the case is remanded to that court for further proceedings consistent with this opinion.

It is so ordered.

UNITED STATES v. HARRIS
SUPREME COURT OF THE UNITED STATES
403 U.S. 573, 91 S. CT. 2075, 29 L. ED. 2d 723 (1971)

Mr. Chief Justice Burger announced the judgment of the Court....

We granted certiorari in this case to consider the recurring question of what showing is constitutionally necessary to satisfy a magistrate that there is a substantial basis for crediting the report of an informant known to the police, but not identified to the magistrate, who purports to relate his personal knowledge of criminal activity.

In 1967 a federal tax investigator and a local constable entered the premises of respondent Harris, pursuant to a search warrant issued by a federal magistrate, and seized jugs of whiskey upon which the federal tax had not been paid. The warrant had been issued solely on the basis of the investigator's affidavit, which recited the following:

> "Roosevelt Harris has had a reputation with me for over four years as being a trafficker of nontaxpaid distilled spirits, and over this period I have received numerous information [sic] from all types of persons as to his activities. Constable Howard Johnson located a sizeable stash of illicit whiskey in an abandoned house under Harris' control during this period of time. This date, I have received information from a person who fears for their life [sic] and property should their name be revealed. I have interviewed this person, found this person to be a prudent person, and have, under a sworn verbal statement, gained the following information: This person has personal information of and has purchased illicit whiskey from within the residence described, for a period of more than 2 years, and most recently within the past 2 weeks, has knowledge of a person who purchased illicit whiskey

within the past two days from the house, has personal knowledge that the illicit whiskey is consumed by purchasers in the outbuilding known and utilized as the 'dance hall,' and has seen Roosevelt Harris go to the other outbuilding, located about 50 yards from the residence, on numerous occasions, to obtain whiskey for this person and other persons."

Respondent was subsequently charged with possession of nontaxpaid liquor, in violation of 26 U. S. C. § 5205(a)(2). His pretrial motion to suppress the seized evidence on the ground that the affidavit was insufficient to establish probable cause was overruled, and he was convicted after a jury trial and sentenced to two years' imprisonment. The Court of Appeals for the Sixth Circuit reversed the conviction, holding that the information in the affidavit was insufficient to enable the magistrate to assess the informant's reliability and trustworthiness.

. . . .

I

. . . .

The Court of Appeals seems to have believed, however, that there was no substantial basis for believing that the tip was truthful. Indeed, it emphasized that the affiant had never alleged that the informant was truthful, but only "prudent," a word that "signifies that he is circumspect in the conduct of his affairs, but reveals nothing about his credibility." Such a construction of the affidavit is the very sort of hypertechnicality—"the elaborate specificity once exacted under common law"—condemned by this Court in *Ventresca*. A policeman's affidavit "should not be judged as an entry in an essay contest," but rather must be judged by the facts it contains. While a bare statement by an affiant that he believed the informant to be truthful would not, in itself, provide a *factual* basis for crediting the report of an unnamed informant, we conclude that the affidavit in the present case contains an ample factual basis for believing the informant which, when coupled with his own knowledge of the respondent's background, afforded a basis upon which a magistrate could reasonably issue a warrant. The accusation by the informant was plainly a declaration against interest since it could readily warrant a prosecution and could sustain a conviction against the informant himself. This will be developed in Part III.

. . . .

We cannot conclude that a policeman's knowledge of a suspect's reputation—something that policemen frequently know and a factor that impressed such a "legal technician" as Justice Frankfurter—is not a "practical consideration of everyday life" upon which an officer (or a magistrate) may properly rely in assessing the reliability of an informant's tip. To the extent that *Spinelli* prohibits the use of such probative information, it has no support in our prior cases, logic, or experience and we decline to apply it to preclude a magistrate from relying on a law enforcement officer's knowledge of a suspect's reputation.

III

Quite apart from the affiant's own knowledge of respondent's activities, there was an additional reason for crediting the informant's tip. Here the warrant's affidavit recited extrajudicial statements of a declarant, who feared for his life and safety if his identity was revealed, that over the past two years he had many times and recently purchased "illicit whiskey." These statements were against the informant's penal interest, for he thereby admitted major elements of an offense under the Internal Revenue Code. Section 5205(a)(2), Title 26, United States Code, proscribes the sale, purchase or possession of unstamped liquor.

Common sense in the important daily affairs of life would induce a prudent and disinterested observer to credit these statements. People do not lightly admit a crime and place critical evidence in the hands of the police in the form of their own admissions. Admissions of crime, like admissions against proprietary interests, carry their own indicia of credibility—sufficient at least to support finding of probable cause to search. That the informant may be paid or promised a "break" does not eliminate the residual risk and opprobrium of having admitted criminal conduct. Concededly admissions of crime do not always lend credibility to contemporaneous or later accusations of another. But here the informant's admission that over a long period and currently he had been buying illicit liquor on a certain premise, itself and without more, implicated that property and furnished probable cause to search.

. . . .

It will not do to say that warrants may not issue on uncorroborated hearsay. This only avoids the issue of whether there is reason for crediting the out-of-court statement. Nor is it especially significant that neither the name nor the person of the informant was produced before the magistrate. The police themselves almost certainly knew his name, the truth of the affidavit is not in issue, and *McCray* v. *Illinois*, 386 U. S. 300 (1967), disposed of the claim that the informant must be produced whenever the defense so demands.

Reversed.

QUESTIONS AND PROBLEMS

1. In applying for a search warrant, the officer affiant submits the following affidavit to a judge:

   Based upon information from a confidential informant whom I consider to be reliable and further based upon my personal observations and the observations of other police officers, I believe there is now located on the premises of John Jones at 2367 N.W. Arlington Street, Chicago, Illinois, certain stolen merchandise such as television sets, radios, and other stolen articles.

   /s/ Joe Law

   Discuss the adequacy of the affidavit in light of the two-pronged test of Aguilar.

2. A court commissioner is contacted by the police for the purpose of applying for a search warrant. Because of the lateness of the hour, the court commissioner listens to the officer's evidence over the telephone. After satisfying himself that the officer has sufficient information to support a finding of probable cause, the court commissioner instructs the officer to type up the warrant and consents to have the officer sign the commissioner's name to the search warrant countersigned by the officer. The search reveals the articles described in the search warrant. Before trial, the defense

attorney brings a motion to suppress the evidence seized with the search warrant. Discuss fully.

3. Armed with a valid search warrant to search for heroin, officers approach the described premises. One of the officers knocks on the door and states in a loud, clear voice, "Police. We have a search warrant for these premises. Open the door." A voice from within says, "Just a minute." Immediately thereafter the officers hear the sound of footsteps moving rapidly and also hear the sound of a toilet flushing within the described premises. What, if anything, should the officers do? Why?

4. An officer executing a valid search warrant for heroin uncovers and recognizes a kilo of marijuana in the bottom of a dresser on the described premises. The officer should:

   a. Leave the marijuana where it is and obtain another search warrant

   b. Seize the marijuana as being a seizure reasonably related to the search for the named items

   c. Disregard the marijuana because it is not described in the search warrant

   d. Seize the marijuana because it is in plain view. Explain your answer fully.

14

AUTHORITY TO SEARCH WITHIN THE SCOPE OF LAWFUL INSPECTION

SANITATION, HEALTH, BUILDING, AND FIRE INSPECTIONS

Among the many problems of mass urban areas are those of ensuring against the infestation of rodents, insects, and disease; preventing fires; preventing the collapse of buildings; and ensuring that food products do not cause harmful effects. City, county, and state governments carry the primary obligation of maintaining safe and healthful conditions within their jurisdictions. To accomplish this task, local and state governments began long ago to enact ordinances and laws granting the power of inspection to health, sanitation, building, and fire departments. Most of the enacted ordinances and statutes punish the refusal to allow the inspectors entry by fines or imprisonment.

Inspection (or search) of private premises by a Baltimore health inspector who observed evidence of rat infestation was refused by the homeowner in *Frank v. Maryland*, 359 U.S. 360 (1958). The U.S. Supreme Court affirmed the conviction and $20 fine after reviewing the 200-year history of such inspections in Maryland. The Court stated:

> ... The need for preventive action is great and city after city has seen this need and granted the power of inspection to its health officials; and these inspections are apparently welcomed by all but an insignificant few. ...

In 1967, the U.S. Supreme Court reversed the decision of *Frank v. Maryland* in the two decisions of *Camara v. Municipal Court* (private premises), 387 U.S. 523, and *See v. Seattle* (commercial warehouse), 387 U.S. 541. The 1967 cases held that a homeowner or a business could refuse to allow an inspection of their premises and that such refusal could not be punished by fine or imprisonment. To make such an inspection, it is necessary for the inspector to obtain a search warrant.

The Court, however, made clear that in emergency situations such as seizure of unwholesome food, compulsory smallpox vaccination, health quarantine, or the summary destruction of tubercular cattle, it did not intend to foreclose prompt warrantless inspections.

LIQUOR CONTROL AND GUN CONTROL INSPECTIONS

In *Colonnade Catering Corp. v. United States*, 397 U.S. 72 (1970), the defendant was a commercial establishment operating under a liquor license issued by the government. In this case, federal inspectors without a warrant and without the owner's permission forcibly entered a locked storeroom and seized illegal liquor. The Court held that historically the government has broad authority to regulate the liquor industry and that Congress had ample power "to design such power of inspection under the liquor laws as it deems necessary to meet the evils at hand." The Court held, however, that Congress had not expressly provided for forcible entry in the absence of a warrant and has instead given government agents a remedy by making it a criminal offense to refuse admission to the inspectors under 26 U.S.C. § 7342.

In May 1972, the U.S. Supreme Court handed down the decision in *United States v. Biswell*, 406 U.S. 311. The defendant, who was federally licensed to deal in sporting weapons, was visited one afternoon by a federal Treasury agent who identified himself, inspected the defendant's books, and requested entry into a locked gun storeroom. The federal agent stated that he did not have a search warrant but that the federal law authorized such inspection. The defendant unlocked the storeroom after he saw a copy of the statute. The agent found two sawed-off rifles which the defendant was not licensed to possess and the defendant was charged with this offense. The Court held that the search and seizure was constitutional, stating:

> When the officers asked to inspect [defendant's] locked storeroom, they were merely asserting their statutory right, and [defendant] was on notice as to their identity and the legal basis for their action. [Defendant's] submission to lawful authority and his decision to step aside and permit the inspection rather than face a criminal prosecution is analogous to a householder's acquiescence in a search pursuant to a warrant when the alternative is a possible criminal prosecution for refusing entry or a forcible entry. In neither case does the lawfulness of the search depend on consent; in both, there is lawful authority independent of the will of the householder who might, other things being equal prefer no search at all.

CUSTOMS OR BORDER INSPECTION

Health, sanitation, building, and fire inspections were held to be an exception to Fourth Amendment requirements until *Frank v. Maryland* was reversed in 1967. The border or customs search is another exception well grounded in American law and practice. The present federal statute owes its origin to the law passed on July 18, 1866.

Title 19, United States Code, Sec. 482

Any of the officers or persons authorized to board or search vessels may stop, search and examine as well without as within their respective districts, any vehicles, beast, or person, on which or whom he or they shall suspect there is merchandise which is subject to duty, or shall have been introduced into the United States in any manner contrary to law, whether by the person in possession or charge, or by, in, or upon such vehicle or beast, or otherwise, and to search any trunk or envelope wherever found in which he may have a reasonable cause to suspect there is merchandise which was imported contrary to law; and if any such officer or other person so authorized shall find any merchandise on or about any such vehicle, beast, or person, or in any trunk or envelope, which he shall have reasonable cause to believe is subject to duty, or have been unlawfully introduced into the United States, whether by the person in possession or charge, or by, in, or upon such vehicle, beast or otherwise, he shall seize and secure the same for trial.

The Ninth Circuit Court of Appeals stated in *Alexander v. United States*, 362 F.2d 379 (1966), that:

Accordingly, it is well settled that a search by Customs officials of a vehicle, at the time and place of entering the jurisdiction of the United States, need not be based on probable cause; that "unsupported" or "mere" suspicion alone is sufficient to justify such a search for purposes of Customs law enforcement.

Must the Stop and Search Be Made at the Border or Point of Entry into the United States?

Although most stops and searches are made at the border or point of entry into the United States, a few are made a considerable distance away from the port of entry. The general rule of law concerning such searches was stated in *Alexander v. United States, supra:*

Where, however, a search for contraband by Customs officers is not made at or in the immediate vicinity of the point of the international border crossing, the legality of the search must be tested by a determination whether the totality of the surrounding circumstances, including the time and distance elapsed as well as the manner and extent of surveillance, are such as to convince the fact finder with reasonable certainty that any contraband which might be found in or on the vehicle at the time of search was aboard the vehicle at the time of entry into the jurisdiction of the United States. Any search by Customs officials which meets this test is properly called a "border search."

RODRIGUEZ-GONZALES v. UNITED STATES, 378 F.2d 256 (9th CIR. 1967)

Customs officials received information from an informant that a car with one of three license plates would enter the United States carrying marijuana. This car was allowed to pass through customs but was followed by officers. Fifteen hours later, they stopped the car and searched it. When they found the marijuana, they arrested the driver (not the same driver who drove the car across the border) although they did not have a search warrant to search the car. The court affirmed the conviction stating, "... there can be no doubt that the manner and extent of the surveillance of the car appellant was driving excluded the possibility that the marijuana found hidden in the rear door was placed there at any time following entry into the United States. From the time the car in question crossed the international border at San Ysidro until it stopped a few miles north of San Diego, it was under constant surveillance by a team of officers. Nothing occurred during that period of time which would suggest the marijuana (hidden behind a door panel secured with screws) might have been placed in the car after it crossed the border."

Strip Search and Search of Body Cavities

The courts have held that no person entering the United States should be subjected to the indignity of a strip search or a search of body cavities unless there are compelling reasons to do so. To make such searches, the customs officials must have "real suspicion" supported by objective, articulable facts that would reasonably lead experienced and prudent officers to suspect that the person is concealing something in his body in an attempt to transport it into the United States contrary to the laws of the United States.

MORALES v. UNITED STATES, 406 F.2d 1298 (9th CIR. 1969)

Because customs officials had been informed that the defendant's car was seen parked in the driveway of a narcotics dealer's home, they ordered a strip search. The physician found no indication that she was a narcotics user or was then under the influence of narcotics but did find three packets of heroin and one of cocaine in her vagina. The court held that the narcotics which were found were not admissible because there was not sufficiently clear indication of the possession of narcotics to justify a search of the defendant's vagina.

GUADALUPE-GARZA v. UNITED STATES, 421 F.2d 876 (9th CIR. 1970)

The defendant appeared nervous when a customs inspector asked him routine questions and "tilted his head" and "shied away." A strip search revealed nothing, but several emetics caused two balloons containing heroin to be disgorged from the defendant's stomach. It was held that the evidence obtained did not change the inspector's hunch into the real suspicion required to sustain a strip search.

SEARCHES AND INSPECTIONS BY PAROLE AND PROBATION OFFICERS

When authorized by state statute or by departmental regulations, parole and probation officers may permissibly enter a parolee's living quarters without a search warrant to determine whether there are any rule violations.

SMITH v. RHAY, 419 F.2d 160 (9th CIR. 1969)

[In this case, a sheriff who was investigating a burglary enlisted the aid of the defendant's parole officer. The sheriff and the parole officer located the defendant in a restaurant, and they all went to the defendant's hotel room, where in plain view they found items taken in the burglary.]

The court held, "We have assumed for the purposes of this opinion that a parole officer, in the performances of his duty as such, may permissibly enter a parolee's living quarters at any time and without the need for a search warrant. See generally Damiani, *Probation and Parole Under Recent Decisions*, 8 Trial Judges' J. 55 (1969). We also assume that the parole officer could report any incriminating evidence discovered by such entry to the proper law enforcement officials and that such evidence might be properly introduced in a subsequent criminal proceeding based upon it. We think it obvious, however, that a parole officer may *not* conduct a warrantless search of items in the parolee's possession while acting on the prior request of law enforcement officials and in concert with them. The parole officer is in such a case acting, not as the supervising guardian, so to speak, of the parolee, but as the agent of the very authority upon whom the requirement for a search warrant is constitutionally imposed. To permit concerted effort among officials in an attempt, such as is manifest here, to circumvent Smith's fourth amendment rights cannot be done...."

POSTAL INSPECTIONS

Postal officials may open mail other than first-class mail to determine whether postal laws have been complied with. The following two cases concern packages which were mailed first-class.

UNITED STATES v. VAN LEEUWEN, 397 U.S. 249 (U.S. S. CT. 1970)

Police had probable cause to believe that two first-class packages placed in the U.S. mail contained contraband (illegal coins). The packages were delayed twenty-nine hours in order to obtain a search warrant and to contact officials in the cities that the packages were sent to.

The Court of Appeals held that the coins were improperly admitted into evidence. The U.S. Supreme Court reversed holding that the evidence was properly admitted.

THE COURT. "It has long been held that first class mail such as letters and sealed packages subject to letter postage—as distinguished from newspapers, magazines, pamphlets, and other printed matter—is free from inspection by postal authorities, except in the manner provided by the Fourth Amendment.... Yet even first class mail is not beyond the reach of all inspection; and the sole question here is whether the condition for its detention and inspection had been satisfied. We think they had been....

"No interest protected by the Fourth Amendment was invaded by forwarding the packages the following day rather than the day when they were deposited. The significant Fourth Amendment interest was in the privacy of this first class mail; and that privacy was not disturbed or invaded until the approval of the magistrate was obtained.

"The rule of our decision certainly is not that first class mail can be detained 29 hours after mailing in order to obtain the search warrant needed for its inspection. We only hold that on the facts of this case—the nature of the mailings, their suspicious character, the fact that there were two packages going to separate destinations, the unavoidable delay in contacting the more distant of the two destinations, the distance between Mt. Vernon and Seattle—a 29 hour delay between the mailings and the service of the warrant cannot be said to be 'unreasonable' within the meaning of the Fourth Amendment. Detention for this limited time was indeed, the prudent act rather than letting the packages enter the mails and then, in case the initial suspicions were confirmed, trying to locate them enroute and enlisting the help of distant federal officials in serving the warrant. Reversed."

PEOPLE v. SUPERIOR COURT IN AND FOR THE COUNTY OF BUTTE, 79 CAL. RPTR. 904 (CAL. APP. 3d DIST. 1969)

A first-class package fell while being handled by a postman. The outside wrapping came apart and also the box inside of the wrapping. A brown paper bag which was not sealed fell out of the box. The postman opened the bag and when he looked inside "saw two plastic bags, each containing green leafy material which turned out to be marijuana." The postman removed some of the green leafy material and after he put the package together, he delivered it. The postman turned the marijuana over to the police, who on the basis of this information obtained a search warrant which resulted in the arrest and trial of the defendant. The trial court suppressed the evidence and this court affirmed the action of the trial court stating,

"...the postal employee, in possessing and handling the mail, is not acting as a private citizen; he is a government official deprived of any right to discover what is mailed in a first-class mail package except in limited cases."

The court stated that if the motive of the postman in opening the brown paper bag had been "...to see if the contents had been damaged, [or] to see if the repackaging contemplated and effected would cause further damage to the contents...there probably would have been no violation of law and we might not have been confronted with any problem. [However, the government] did not claim either motive, and it must therefore be taken as established for the purposes of this proceeding that he violated the law."

INSPECTIONS BY SCHOOL OFFICIALS

The U.S. Supreme Court stated in the 1969 case of *Tinker v. Des Moines Independent School District*, 390 U.S. 942, that students, like adults, have rights which "do not stop at the schoolhouse gate."

However, a special relationship continues to exist between school officials and students. This relationship is embodied in the doctrine of *in loco parentis* (the concept that school officials take the place of the parent while the student is in school) and the basic responsibility of school officials to maintain an educational atmosphere.

Changes have been made in the doctrine of *in loco parentis* which have weakened the supervisory role of school officials in such matters as clothing which must be worn, hair styles required, etc. But school authorities (particularly in the high schools and lower grades) continue to exercise a supervisory responsibility in determining whether drugs, weapons, and other undesirable and dangerous objects are being carried by students or are being stored in their lockers, desks, or rooms. Recent cases of inspection and searches by school officials are:

PEOPLE v. OVERTON, 283 N.Y.S. 2d 22 (N.Y. CT. APP. 1967)

A search of two high school students and their lockers by law enforcement officers produced marijuana. However, the search warrant authorizing the search was later proved to be defective. The trial court denied the motion to suppress the evidence on the grounds that the vice principal, Dr. Panitz, had consented to the search and that as a school official in the possession of the depository, he had the authority to consent to the search. The New York Court of Appeals sustained the search, stating:

"Dr. Panitz, in this case, gave his consent to the search of Overton's locker. The dissenting opinion suggests, however, that Dr. Panitz' consent was not freely given, because he acted under compulsion of the invalid search warrant. If this were the case, his consent might be rendered somewhat questionable. However, Dr. Panitz testified that:

'Being responsible for the order, assignment, and maintenance of the physical facilities, if *any* report were given to me by *anyone* of an article or item of the nature that does not belong there, or of an illegal nature, I would inspect the locker.' (Italics supplied.)

"This testimony demonstrates beyond doubt that Dr. Panitz would have consented as he did regardless of the presence of the invalid search warrant.

"The power of Dr. Panitz to give his consent to this search arises out of the distinct relationship between school authorities and students.

"The school authorities have an obligation to maintain discipline over the students. It is recognized that when large numbers of teen-agers are gathered together in such an environment, their inexperience and lack of mature judgment can often create hazards to each other. Parents, who surrender their children to this type of environment, in order that they may continue developing both intellectually and socially, have a right to expect certain safeguards.

"It is in the high school years particularly that parents are justifiably concerned that their children not become accustomed to antisocial behavior, such as the use of illegal drugs. The susceptibility to suggestion of students of high school age increases the danger. Thus, it is the affirmative obligation of the school authorities to investigate any charge that a student is using or possessing narcotics and to take appropriate steps, if the charge is substantiated.

"When Overton was assigned his locker, he, like all the other students at Mount Vernon High School, gave the combination to his home room teacher who, in turn, returned it to an office where it was kept on file. The students at Mount Vernon are well aware that the school authorities possess the combinations of their lockers. It appears understood that the lock and the combination are provided in order that each student may have exclusive possession of the locker vis-à-vis other students, but the student does not have such exclusivity over the locker as against the school authorities. In fact, the school issues regulations regarding what may and may not be kept in the lockers and presumably can spot check to insure compliance. The vice-principal testified that he had, on occasion, inspected the lockers of students.

"Indeed, it is doubtful if a school would be properly discharging its duty of supervision over the students, if it failed to retain control over the lockers. Not only have the school authorities a right to inspect but this right becomes a duty when suspicion arises that something of an illegal nature may be secreted there. When Dr. Panitz learned of the detectives' suspicion, he was obligated to inspect the locker. This interest, together with the nonexclusive nature of the locker, empowered him to consent to the search by the officers."

STATE v. STEIN, 456 P. 1 (KAN. 1967), CERT. DENIED, 397 U.S. 947

In the investigation of a burglary, two police officers went to a high school and talked to the principal. The defendant, who was a student in the high school, consented to the search of his school locker and the contents thereof. A key to a bus depot locker was found and the officers obtained a search warrant to search that locker. Property taken in the burglary was found in the bus depot locker. The defendant was convicted and challenges the search of his high school locker. The Supreme Court of Kansas sustained the search and the conviction, stating:

"Secondly, the defendant's argument must fail because of the nature of a high school locker. Its status in the law is somewhat anomalous; it does not possess all the attributes of a dwelling, a motor vehicle, or a private locker. As to the latter, the possessor's right of possession is exclusive; it is protected from unwarranted intrusion as against the world. The principal of the Ottawa High School testified that he has custody and control of, and access to, all lockers at the school; that he has a master list of all combinations to all combination padlocks, and a key which will open every locker. He testified also that he opened Stein's locker on his own judgment.

"Although a student may have control of his school locker as against fellow students, his possession is not exclusive against the school and its officials. A school does not supply its students with lockers for illicit use in harboring pilfered property or harmful substances. We deem it a proper function of school authorities to inspect the lockers under their control and to prevent their use in illicit ways or for illegal purposes. We believe this right of inspection is inherent in the authority vested in school administrators and that the same must be retained and exercised in the management of our schools if their educational functions are to be maintained and the welfare of the student bodies preserved."

IN RE DONALDSON 75 CAL. RPTR. 220 (CT. APP. 3d DIST. 1969)

When a high school student told the vice principal that she could purchase contraband in the high school, the vice principal told her to make a purchase. The vice principal then searched the locker of the fifteen-year-old boy who sold the marijuana. The Court of Appeals sustained the search, stating:

"We find the vice principal of the high school not to be a governmental official within the meaning of the Fourth Amendment so as to bring into play its prohibition against unreasonable searches and seizures. Such school official is one of the school authorities with an obligation to maintain discipline in the interest of a proper and orderly school operation, and the primary purpose of the school official's search was not to obtain convictions, but to secure evidence of student misconduct. That evidence of crime is uncovered and prosecution results therefrom should not of itself make the search and seizure unreasonable.

"The school stands in loco parentis and shares, in matters of school discipline, the parent's right to use moderate force to obtain obedience, and that right extends to the search of the appellant's locker under the factual situation herein related.

"The marijuana was not obtained by an unlawful search and seizure."

MERCER v. STATE, 450 S.W.2d 715 (CT. APP. 1970)

"We affirm the action of the trial court.

"Appellant was a student at Reagan High School in Austin. The dean of men received a 'tip' that appellant was in possession of marijuana at school and relayed the information to the principal. The principal caused appellant to be brought to his office where he directed the youth to empty his pockets. Appellant after some hesitation emptied his pockets upon being informed that his father would be called if he failed to comply with the principal's request. This procedure produced two marijuana cigarettes, marijuana, and marijuana seed.

"No force was used on appellant, nor was he searched or handled by the principal in the usual sense. The youth testified that if his father had been called, the father would have made appellant empty his pockets, and his father would not have used force to require the boy to empty his pockets. . . .

"Blackstone stated this authority of the school principal as one delegated by the parent. It was said that a parent may delegate part of parental authority to the schoolmaster '. . . who is then *in loco parentis*, and has such a portion of the power of the parent . . . as may be necessary to answer the purposes for which he is employed.' 1 W. Blackstone, Commentaries, 453.

"This principle has been recognized in Texas. Hailey v. Brooks, 191 S.W. 781 (Tex.Civ.App., Fort Worth, 1916, no writ). In Hailey the court asserted that

"Generally speaking . . . the . . . principal . . . of a public free school, to a limited extent at least, stand[s], as to pupils attending the school, in loco parentis, and . . . may exercise such powers of control, restraint, and correction over such pupils as may be reasonably necessary to enable the teachers to perform their duties and to effect the general purposes of education.'

"It does not seem to be outside the purposes of discipline in a system of education for the principal of a public school to discover and bring under control drugs considered dangerous under law and possession of which is made an offense by law. The same procedure employed by the principal, if used by the boy's father, would not violate security of appellant under the Fourth Amendment."

PEOPLE v. STEWART, 313 N.Y.S. 2d 253 (N.Y. CT. APP. 1970)

A high school dean of boys received information from student informants respecting the defendants. The dean had the defendants come into his office and empty their pockets. Narcotics were discovered. The Court of Appeals affirmed the action, stating:

"It is noted that, although the Dean admits the defendants remained with him in his office, he denied that he had made any citizen's arrest, or restrained them of their liberty as is inferred by the defense. Although that issue is not material here, it is true that the point at which an arrest is made does not depend upon the presence or absence of any formal words by the witness, but is an issue of fact to be determined by the Court. (People v. Butterly, 25 N.Y.2d 159, 303 N.Y.S.2d 57, 250 N.E.2d 340.) Therefore, upon a review of the circumstances of this case, I find as a fact that the defendants were not placed under arrest until the arrival of the policemen who took them into custody. There was no contention advanced at the hearing, and I find no suggestion from the records, that the Dean of Boys was either an agent of the police or in some fashion jointly endeavoring with them to uncover crime in his school. . . .

"Consequently, it may not be said that he was a law enforcement official. On the contrary, he, as an educator, being responsible for the safety and welfare of students at Brandeis High School, sought, not on his own whim or caprice, but on the information supplied by student-informers, to determine whether certain students were either using narcotics or were in possession of narcotics. Thus, when a reasonable suspicion should arise that something of an illegal nature may be occurring, the Dean was under an obligation to determine the validity of his information."

IN RE BOYKIN, 39 ILL. 2d 617 (S. CT. ILL. 1968)

An assistant high school principal told Chicago police that he had received anonymous information that a student in the school had a gun on his person. An officer searched the student and found the gun. The search was held to be valid.

MOORE v. STUDENT AFFAIRS COMMITTEE OF TROY STATE UNIVERSITY, 284 F. SUPP. 725 (D.C. ALA. 1968)

School officials and law enforcement officers searched Moore's room in the campus dormitory without his consent and without a warrant and found marijuana. Moore was indefinitely suspended from the university and brings this action to be reinstated. The suspension was sustained by the Court.

"College students who reside in dormitories have a special relationship with the college involved. Insofar as the Fourth Amendment affects that relationship, it does not depend on either a general theory of the right of privacy or on traditional property concepts. The college does not stand, strictly speaking, in loco parentis to its students, nor is their relationship purely contractual in the traditional sense. The relationship grows out of the peculiar and sometimes the seemingly competing interests of college and student. A student naturally has the right to be free of unreasonable search and seizures, and a tax-supported public college may not compel a 'waiver' of that right as a condition precedent to admission. The college, on the other hand, has an 'affirmative obligation' to promulgate and to enforce reasonable regulations designed to protect campus order and discipline and to promote an environment consistent with the educational process. The validity of the regulation authorizing search of dormitories thus does not depend on whether a student 'waives' his right to Fourth Amendment protection or on whether he has 'contracted' it away; rather, its validity is determined by whether the regulation is a reasonable exercise of the college's supervisory duty. In other words, if the regulation—or, in the absence of a regulation, the action of the college authorities—is necessary in aid of the basic responsibility of the institution regarding discipline and the maintenance of an 'educational atomosphere,' then it will be presumed facially reasonable despite the fact that it may infringe to some extent on the outer bounds of the Fourth Amendment rights of students."

[*Authors' Note:* The Moore case differs from other cases concerning the search of students' dormitory rooms in that the evidence obtained was used to suspend Moore from the school and was *not* used in a criminal action against him.]

AIRPORT INSPECTIONS

LINDSEY v. UNITED STATES, 451 F.2d 701 (3d CIR. 1971)

Two packages of heroin were found in a search of an "extremely nervous" passenger who was about to board a commercial airplane. The air marshal asked the defendant to identify himself and was shown identification using four different names. In holding that airport security personnel and sky marshals are subject to lower stop-and-frisk standards than required in the guidelines of the Terry, Peters, and Sibron cases (see Chap. 11) for other law enforcement officers, the Court stated:

"Applying *Terry* to the case at hand, we believe Marshal Brophy's reaction to the unusual behavior of the defendant were justified. In the context of a possible airplane highjacking with the enormous consequences which may flow therefrom, and in view of the limited time in which Marshal Brophy had to act, the level of suspicion required for a *Terry* investigative stop and protective search should be lowered. Therefore, despite the fact that it may be said that the level of suspicion present in the instant case is lower than in *Terry*, it was sufficiently high to justify Marshall Brophy's acting. . . ."

QUESTIONS AND PROBLEMS

1. A tavern keeper has patrons in his tavern during regular bar hours, but he has locked the doors and refuses admission to law enforcement officers. Does the tavern keeper have this right under recent case decisions?

2. Can a tavern keeper refuse to allow a liquor inspector to take an open bottle of liquor? The inspector would give the owner a receipt for the bottle and would have the contents of the bottle tested by

a chemist to determine whether cheap or bootlegged liquor had been substituted for the type of liquor which should be in the bottle.

3. Could a nursing home refuse permission to enter to a state inspector?
4. Could a meat-packing firm refuse to allow a meat inspector to inspect areas of their plant?
5. Could a restaurant owner refuse to allow a health inspector into the restaurant kitchen while the restaurant was open for business?
6. In the above cases:
   a. Could the business places be immediately closed and denied the right to do business by the government officials involved?
   b. Could the licensing board refuse to reissue (or immediately cancel) the license of businesses and persons who refused to cooperate with the inspections cited in the questions?

QUESTIONS FOR DISCUSSION—PART 3

1. What is a search?
2. What is a seizure?
3. What is subject to search?
4. What is subject to seizure?
5. What is meant by "probable cause"?
6. What is meant by "judicial intercession"? Why is it desirable? When may it be dispensed with?
7. Describe how a search warrant is obtained. What evidence is necessary? What must be shown if a confidential informant is the source of the information?
8. Can the information given to the magistrate later be supplemented if the search warrant is attacked in court?
9. What should be contained in a checklist of the search warrant?
10. How and when is a search warrant executed?
11. What is the limit of the search based on the authority of the search warrant?
12. What degree of force may be used in executing the search warrant?
13. Describe the "return" of the search warrant.
14. What is a "motion to suppress"?
15. Under what circumstances may the identity of an unnamed informer be required to be disclosed?

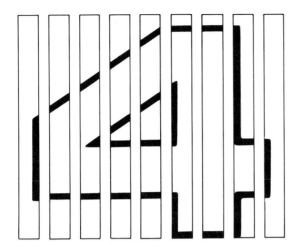

OTHER ASPECTS OF SEARCH AND SEIZURE

15

WIRETAPPING AND ELECTRONIC SURVEILLANCE

The first American president to have a telephone in his office was President Hoover. To use the telephone in 1928, the President had to leave his desk and go to a cumbersome contraption in another room. Six years later, in 1934, Congress passed the nation's first wiretapping law. This law did not make wiretapping a crime but forbade the interception and use of telephone and telegraph communications. As the telephone and telegraph system is interstate in nature, the laws of Congress preempt and control because the U.S. Constitution gives Congress the power to control interstate commerce in article I, section 8.

Remarkable advances were made during World War II (1939–1945) in the fields of communication and electronics. One of the developments was the parabolic mike. This was developed by the English to pick up the sounds of Nazi warplanes warming up on the airfields in France prior to air attacks on targets in England.

The advances in communication and electronics continued during the 1950s and the 1960s. Although the United States had entered the electronic age, it continued to use the 1934 law. This law was inadequate because it did not protect the right of privacy, nor did it have specific provisions authorizing and legalizing wiretapping by law enforcement agencies in the United States.

Wiretapping and bugging, however, were conducted by agencies of the federal government. This was done under the authority granted by American presidents beginning with President Roosevelt. The Department of Justice interpretation of the 1934 law was that interception (wiretapping and bugging) was permitted as long as no disclosure was made outside the department making the interception. Therefore, the results of the interceptions generally could not be used in court.

In 1966, the President's Commission noted the inadequacy of the

1934 wiretapping law on page 203 of *The Challenge of Crime in a Free Society* by commenting:

> The present status of the law with respect to wiretapping and bugging is intolerable. It serves the interest neither of privacy nor of law enforcement. One way or the other, the present controversy with respect to electronic surveillance must be resolved.

WIRETAPPING AND ELECTRONIC SURVEILLANCE AS A LAW ENFORCEMENT TOOL

The following quotation from *The Challenge of Crime in a Free Society* indicates the importance of wiretapping and electronic surveillance to law enforcement:

> *Significance to Law Enforcement.* The great majority of law enforcement officials believe that the evidence necessary to bring criminal sanctions to bear consistently on the higher echelons of organized crime will not be obtained without the aid of electronic surveillance techniques. They maintain these techniques are indispensable to develop adequate strategic intelligence concerning organized crime, to set up specific investigations, to develop witnesses, to corroborate their testimony, and to serve as substitutes for them—each a necessary step in the evidence-gathering process in organized crime investigations and prosecutions.
>
> . . . .
>
> District Attorney Frank S. Hogan, whose New York County office has been acknowledged for over 27 years as one of the country's most outstanding, has testified that electronic surveillance is:
>
> *the single most valuable weapon in law enforcement's fight against organized crime. . . . It has permitted us to undertake major investigations of organized crime. Without it, and I confine myself to top figures in the underworld, my own office could not have convicted Charles "Lucky" Luciano, Jimmy Hines, Louis "Lepke" Buchalter, Jacob "Gurrah" Shapiro, Joseph "Socks" Lanza, George Scalise, Frank Erickson, John "Dio" Dioguardi, and Frank Carbo. . . .*

Despite many pleas over the years, Congress did not enact legislation providing for legalized wiretapping. While law enforcement officers clearly saw the need to use wiretapping and electronic surveillance as a tool in their fight against crime, many civil libertarians looked upon such tactics as a gross infringement of the right of privacy.

In 1967, two events occurred which brought the debate over what type of legislation should be enacted to a point where something had to be done by the U.S. Congress. The two events were:

Katz v. United States (see case section) came before the United States Supreme Court. In this case, FBI agents placed a parabolic mike with a recording device on the top of a public telephone booth and obtained evidence that the defendant was engaged in transmitting wagering information across state lines in violation of a federal statute. The Court reversed previous rulings and held that "The Government's activities in electronically listening to and recording the petitioner's words violated the privacy upon which he justifiably relied while using the telephone booth and thus constituted a 'search and seizure' within the meaning of the Fourth Amendment. . . ."

The public became aware through U.S. Senate subcommittee hearings of the extent of wiretapping and electronic surveillance which governmental agencies were conducting. For example, in July of 1967 the Commissioner of the Internal Revenue Service admitted before a Senate subcommittee that in the eight years which ended in 1965, the IRS used wiretaps, electronic bugs, and other eavesdropping devices 1,010 times and made 723 uses of the pen register. The Commissioner admitted "improprieties" but stated such means were only used in criminal investigations of criminal violations by racketeers, gamblers, moonshiners, or persons attempting to bribe IRS agents.

TITLE III OF THE OMNIBUS CRIME CONTROL AND SAFE STREETS ACT OF 1968

In 1968, the U.S. Congress passed the Omnibus Crime Control and Safe Streets Act. This act provides for legalized wiretapping and electronic surveillance under the authority and supervision of a federal court. To protect the privacy of citizens, wiretapping and electronic surveillance conducted in violation of this act are made a felony. The act also makes the distribution, possession, and advertising of mechanical and electronic intercepting devices a felony, when done in violation of the provisions of the act.

Since 1968, many states have enacted state legislation to coordinate with Title III of the Crime Control Act. A few states had legislation prior to 1968 (New York for over twenty years because of its aggravated organized crime problems). In addition to controlling wiretapping, the state legislation would also regulate electronic surveillance and bugging, which are primarily under state control as they are intrastate.

Law enforcement officers in those states with such legislation now have specific legislation controlling and authorizing wiretapping and electronic surveillance procedures within their states. Cases which now come before the courts must be read in view of the new controlling legislation.

DEFINITION OF TERMS

The following terms are defined for use in this chapter:

eavesdropping Surreptitiously listening to, monitoring, transmitting, amplifying, or recording a private conversation.

wiretapping Eavesdropping and overhearing telephone conversations.

bugging The use of a planted or carried listening device.

pen register A device which records the telephone number which is dialed but not the conversation. Until 1966, this procedure was not considered an invasion of privacy, but in that year an appellate court ruled that it was. Pen registers are not mentioned specifically in Title III of the 1968 Crime Control Act, but it is thought that the provisions of that Act include their use.

electronic surveillance The use of any electronic device to intercept communications other than telephone or telegraph communications.

WIRETAPPING UNDER PRESENT STATUTES

With warrant See Sec. 2518 of the federal Crime Control Act of 1968 and the applicable state statute.

With consent of one of the parties to the conversation See Sec. 2511(2)(c)(d) of the federal Crime Control Act of 1968 and the applicable state statute.

Emergency provisions See Sec. 2518 (7) of the federal Crime Control Act of 1968 and the applicable state statute.

ELECTRONIC SURVEILLANCE OR BUGGING UNDER PRESENT STATUTES

As electronic surveillance or bugging is ordinarily not interstate in nature, the state statutes or the common law of the jurisdiction would ordinarily govern.

With warrant See the applicable state statutes.

With consent See the applicable state statutes or the general law of consent in the jurisdiction.

Emergency provisions See applicable state statutes (if any).

THE WALKING BUG

The term "walking bug" is used to describe a situation where a recording device is carried on the person, as in the 1963 *Lopez v. United States* case (see case section). The United States Supreme Court held that there had been "no act of any kind which could justify the creation of an exclusionary rule." The person (or officer) carrying the recording device is merely recording the conversation carried on in his presence. The rule of law laid down in the Lopez case has not been changed by the federal Crime Control Act of 1968. Another situation where this procedure has been used is in the following example:

Example: An officer on radar traffic duty found that he was occasionally subjected to some very abusive language from motorists receiving traffic tickets. He purchased a small recorder which he kept in his breast pocket and recorded the abusive remarks for replay before the court when the traffic charge was heard. The officer is doing the same thing which was done in the Lopez case and is accurately reproducing remarks made to him by motorists.

THE WALKING TRANSMITTER

The term "walking transmitter" is used to describe a situation where the person is carrying not a recording device, but a radio transmitter as in the On Lee and the White cases (see case section).

The procedure described in On Lee and White apparently is used with some frequency in narcotics investigations. The reason for this is probably that narcotics pushers and suppliers are aware that the danger of arrest is greater if they sell to unknown persons. Therefore, it is sometimes very difficult for undercover officers to work themselves into positions where they can make purchases of narcotics. An informant or person cooperating with the government may not have these problems and can act as a willing buyer.

The use of government informants carrying radio transmitters is a practical procedure in narcotics cases. However, the informant or the person cooperating with the government is frequently either a narcotics addict or a person with a previous narcotics conviction. The radio transmitter is used not only to ensure his safety but also as a manner of checking to ensure that the informant does not double-cross the government.

Another practical application of the radio transmitter is its use when carried by an undercover officer. Not only may he call for assistance if his safety is endangered, but he may also use the radio transmitter to coordinate a raid by signaling the proper time for the other officers to come in.

THE LIMITATION IMPOSED BY MASSIAH

The 1964 case of *Massiah v. United States* (see cases, Chap. 6) limits, in one way, the procedure used in On Lee and White. A radio transmitter was also used in Massiah, but the defendant in that case had already been indicted and was out on bail. The defendant was in effect being questioned by the government through his false friend. The Court held that the defendant had a right to have his lawyer present at any questioning after his indictment. Therefore this procedure may not be used to obtain further evidence of a crime for which the defendant has already been indicted.

THE OMNIBUS CRIME CONTROL AND SAFE STREETS ACT OF 1968

TITLE III WIRETAPPING AND ELECTRONIC SURVEILLANCE

The following are excerpts and summaries from Title 18, Chapter 119 of the above federal law.

SEC. 801. On the basis of its own investigations and of published studies, the Congress makes the following findings:

(a) Wire communications are normally conducted through the use of facilities which form part of an interstate network. The same facilities are used for interstate and intrastate communications. There has been extensive wiretapping carried on without legal sanctions, and without the consent of any of the parties to the conversation. Electronic, mechanical, and other intercepting devices are being used to overhear oral conversations made in private, without the consent of any of the parties to such communications. The contents of these communications and evidence derived therefrom are being used by public and private parties as evidence in court and administrative proceedings, and by persons whose activities affect interstate commerce. The possession, manufacture, distribution, advertising, and use of these devices are facilitated by interstate commerce.

(b) In order to protect effectively the privacy of wire and oral communications, to protect the integrity of court and administrative proceedings, and to prevent the obstruction of interstate commerce, it is necessary for Congress to define on a uniform basis the circumstances and conditions under which the interception of wire and oral communications may be authorized, to prohibit any unauthorized interception of such communications, and the use of the contents thereof in evidence in courts and administrative proceedings.

(c) Organized criminals make extensive use of wire and oral communications in their criminal activities. The interception of such communications to obtain evidence of the commission of crimes or to prevent their commission is an indispensable aid to law enforcement and the administration of justice.

(d) To safeguard the privacy of innocent persons, the interception of wire or oral communications where none of the parties to the communication has consented to the interception should be allowed only when authorized by a court of competent jurisdiction and should remain under the control and supervision of the authorizing court. Interception of wire and oral communications should further be limited to certain major types of offenses and specific categories of crime with assurances that the interception is justified and that the information obtained thereby will not be misused.

Sec. 2511 *Interception and disclosure of wire or oral communications prohibited*
   1) This section makes the following acts a felony:
      a) wilfully intercepting, attempting to intercept or procuring another person to intercept any wire or oral communication
      b) wilfully using, attempting to use or procuring another to use any electronic, mechanical or other device to intercept wire, cable or radio communication
      c) wilfully disclosing or attempting to disclose any wire or oral communication knowing or having reason to know that such communication was obtained in violation of this section
      d) wilfully using or attempting to use the contents of any wire or oral communication knowing or having reason to know that such communication was obtained in violation of this section
   2) This section is not applicable to:
      a) employees of communications firms who in the normal course of their employment are monitoring or observing the service for mechanical or service quality control checks
      b) employees of the Federal Communications Commission operating in the normal course of their employment
      c) a person acting under the color of law where such person is a party to the communication or has been given prior consent to intercept by one of the parties to the communication
      d) a person not acting under color of law where such person is a party to the communication or has been given prior consent to intercept by one of the parties to the communication and the interception is not for the purpose of committing a crime
   3) "Nothing contained in this chapter ... shall limit the constitutional power of the President to take such measures as he deems necessary to protect the Nation against actual or potential attack or other hostile acts of a foreign power to obtain foreign intelligence information deemed essential to the security of the United States or to protect national security information against foreign intelligence activities...."

Sec. 2512 Except as otherwise specifically provided in this section, the manufacture, distribution, possession and advertising of wire or oral communication intercepting devices is made a felony.

Sec. 2513 provides for the seizure and forfeiture of wire or oral communication interception devices which are used, possessed, sold or advertised in violation of section 2511 or section 2512.

Sec. 2514 provides for the application and granting of immunity to witnesses involving any violation enumerated in section 2516.

Sec. 2515 prohibits the use as evidence of intercepted wire or oral communications if the disclosure of that information would be in violation of this chapter.

Sec. 2516 An order authorizing the interception of wire or oral communication may be granted for the following crimes:

a) felonies relating to the Atomic Energy Act of 1954; espionage; sabotage; treason or riots

b) the crimes of kidnapping, robbery, murder, extortion and crimes dealing with restrictions on payments and loans to labor organizations

c) bribery of public officials and witnesses, transmission of wagering information, influencing or injuring an officer, juror or witness generally, Presidential assassinations, kidnapping and assault, interference with commerce by threats or violence, interstate and foreign travel or transportation in aid of racketeering enterprises, offer, acceptance or solicitation to influence operations of employee benefit plan, theft from interstate shipment, embezzlement from pension and welfare funds and interstate transportation of stolen property.

d) counterfeiting offenses

e) narcotic drugs, marijuana or other dangerous drugs offenses or bankruptcy frauds

f) extortionate credit transactions

g) conspiracy to commit any of the foregoing offenses

Sec. 2517 *Authorization for disclosure and use of intercepted wire or oral communications*

1) Disclosure may be made to another investigative or law enforcement officer to the extent that such disclosure is appropriate to the proper performance of the official duties of the officer making or receiving the disclosure. (The information must have been received in a lawful manner.)

2) Use of lawfully obtained information when appropriate to the proper performance of the official duties of a law enforcement officer.

3) Disclosure while giving testimony under oath or affirmation in any criminal proceeding in a court.

4) "No otherwise privileged wire or oral communication intercepted in accordance with, or in violation of, the provisions of this chapter shall lose its privileged character."

Sec. 2518 The procedure for obtaining a court order for the interception of wire or oral communication is detailed in this section.

7) "Notwithstanding any other provision of this chapter, any investigation or law enforcement officer, specially designated by the Attorney General or by the principal prosecuting attorney of any State or subdivision thereof acting pursuant to a statute of that State, who reasonably determines that—

    a) an emergency situation exists with respect to conspiratorial activities threatening the national security interest or to conspiratorial activities characteristic of organized crime that requires a wire or oral communication to be intercepted before an order authorizing such interception can with due diligence be obtained, and

    b) there are grounds upon which an order could be entered under this chapter to authorize such interception,

may intercept such wire or oral communication if an application for an order approving the interception is made in accordance with this section within forty-eight hours after the interception has occurred, or begins to occur. . . ."

Sec. 2519 contains the requirements for reports concerning intercepted wire or oral communications.

Sec. 2520 provides that persons whose wire or oral communication has been intercepted, disclosed or used in violation of this chapter shall have a civil cause of action and be entitled to recover damages from the violator.

"A good faith reliance on a court order or on the provisions of section 2518 (7) of this chapter shall constitute a complete defense to any civil or criminal action brought under this chapter."

CASES FOR CHAPTER FIFTEEN

KATZ v. UNITED STATES
SUPREME COURT OF THE UNITED STATES
389 U.S. 347, 88 S. CT. 507, 19 L. ED. 2d 576 (1967)

Mr. Justice Stewart delivered the opinion of the Court.

The petitioner was convicted in the District Court for the Southern District of California under an eight-count indictment charging him with transmitting wagering information by telephone from Los Angeles to Miami and Boston, in violation of a federal statute. At trial the Government was permitted, over the petitioner's objection, to introduce evidence of the petitioner's end of telephone conversations, overheard by FBI agents who had attached an electronic listening and recording device to the outside of the public telephone booth from which he had placed his calls. In affirming his conviction, the Court of Appeals rejected the contention that the recordings had been obtained in violation of the Fourth Amendment, because "[t]here was no physical entrance into the area occupied by [the petitioner]." We granted certiorari in order to consider the constitutional questions thus presented.

The petitioner has phrased those questions as follows:

"A. Whether a public telephone booth is a constitutionally protected area so that evidence obtained by attaching an electronic listening recording device to the top of such a booth is obtained in
violation of the right to privacy of the user of the booth.
"B. Whether physical penetration of a constitutionally protected
area is necessary before a search and seizure can be said to be violative of the Fourth Amendment to the United States Constitution."

We decline to adopt this formulation of the issues. In the first place, the correct solution of Fourth Amendment problems is not necessarily promoted by incantation of the phrase "constitutionally protected area." Secondly, the Fourth Amendment cannot be translated into a general constitutional "right to privacy." That
Amendment protects individual privacy against certain kinds of governmental intrusion, but its protections go further, and often have nothing to do with privacy
at all. Other provisions of the Constitution protect personal privacy from other
forms of governmental invasion. But the protection of a person's *general* right to
privacy—his right to be let alone by other people—is, like the protection of his
property and of his very life, left largely to the law of the individual States.

Because of the misleading way the issues have been formulated, the parties
have attached great significance to the characterization of the telephone booth
from which the petitioner placed his calls. The petitioner has strenuously argued
that the booth was a "constitutionally protected area." The Government has maintained with equal vigor that it was not. But this effort to decide whether or not a
given "area," viewed in the abstract, is "constitutionally protected" deflects attention from the problem presented by this case. For the Fourth Amendment protects
people, not places. What a person knowingly exposes to the public, even in his
own home or office, is not a subject of Fourth Amendment protection. See *Lewis* v.
United States, 385 U. S. 206, 210; *United States* v. *Lee*, 274 U. S. 559, 563. But what
he seeks to preserve as private, even in an area accessible to the public, may be
constitutionally protected.

The Government stresses the fact that the telephone booth from which the
petitioner made his calls was constructed partly of glass, so that he was as visible
after he entered it as he would have been if he had remained outside. But what
he sought to exclude when he entered the booth was not the intruding eye—it
was the uninvited ear. He did not shed his right to do so simply because he made
his calls from a place where he might be seen. No less than an individual in a
business office, in a friend's apartment, or in a taxicab, a person in a telephone
booth may rely upon the protection of the Fourth Amendment. One who occupies
it, shuts the door behind him, and pays the toll that permits him to place a call,
is surely entitled to assume that the words he utters into the mouhpiece will not
be broadcast to the world. To read the Constitution more narrowly is to ignore
the vital role that the public telephone has come to play in private communication.

The Government contends, however, that the activities of its agents in this
case should not be tested by Fourth Amendment requirements, for the surveillance
technique they employed involved no physical penetration of the telephone booth
from which the petitioner placed his calls. It is true that the absence of such penetration was at one time thought to foreclose further Fourth Amendment inquiry,
for that Amendment was thought to limit only searches and seizures of tangible
property. But "[t]he premise that property interests control the right of the Government to search and seize has been discredited." *Warden* v. *Hayden*, 387 U. S. 294,
304. Thus, although a closely divided Court supposed in *Olmstead* that surveil-

lance without any trespass and without the seizure of any material object fell outside the ambit of the Constitution, we have since departed from the narrow view on which that decision rested. Indeed, we have expressly held that the Fourth Amendment governs not only the seizure of tangible items, but extends as well to the recording of oral statements, overhead without any "technical trespass under . . . local property law." Silverman v. United States, 365 US 505, 511. Once this much is acknowledged, and once it is recognized that the Fourth Amendment protects people—and not simply "areas"—against unreasonable searches and seizures, it becomes clear that the reach of that Amendment cannot turn upon the presence or absence of a physical intrusion into any given enclosure.

We conclude that the underpinnings of Olmstead and Goldman have been so eroded by our subsequent decisions that the "trespass" doctrine there enunciated can no longer be regarded as controlling. The Government's activities in electronically listening to and recording the petitioner's words violated the privacy upon which he justifiably relied while using the telephone booth and thus constituted a "search and seizure" within the meaning of the Fourth Amendment. The fact that the electronic device employed to achieve that end did not happen to penetrate the wall of the booth can have no constitutional significance.

The question remaining for decision, then, is whether the search and seizure conducted in this case complied with constitutional standards. In that regard, the Government's position is that its agents acted in an entirely defensible manner: They did not begin their electronic surveillance until investigation of the petitioner's activities had established a strong probability that he was using the telephone in question to transmit gambling information to persons in other States, in violation of federal law. Moreover, the surveillance was limited, both in scope and in duration, to the specific purpose of establishing the contents of the petitioner's unlawful telephonic communications. The agents confined their surveillance to the brief periods during which he used the telephone booth,[1] and they took great care to overhear only the conversations of the petitioner himself.[2]

Accepting this account of the Government's actions as accurate, it is clear that this surveillance was so narrowly circumscribed that a duly authorized magistrate, properly notified of the need for such investigation, specifically informed of the basis on which it was to proceed, and clearly apprised of the precise intrusion it would entail, could constitutionally have authorized, with appropriate safeguards, the very limited search and seizure that the Government asserts in fact took place. Only last Term we sustained the validity of such an authorization, holding that, under sufficiently "precise and discriminate circumstances," a federal court may empower government agents to employ a concealed electronic device "for the narrow and particularized purpose of ascertaining the truth of the . . . allegations" of a "detailed factual affidavit alleging the commission of a specific criminal offense." Osborn v. United States, 385 US 323, 329–330. Discussing that holding, the Court in Berger v. New York, 388 US 41, said that "the order authoriz-

---

[1] Based upon their previous visual observations of the petitioner, the agents correctly predicted that he would use the telephone booth for several minutes at approximately the same time each morning. The petitioner was subjected to electronic surveillance only during this predetermined period. Six recordings, averaging some three minutes each, were obtained and admitted in evidence. They preserved the petitioner's end of conversations concerning the placing of bets and the receipt of wagering information.

[2] On the single occasion when the statements of another person were inadvertently intercepted, the agents refrained from listening to them.

ing the use of the electronic device" in Osborn "afforded similar protections to those . . . of conventional warrants authorizing the seizure of tangible evidence." Through those protections, "no greater invasion of privacy was permitted than was necessary under the circumstances. Id., at 57.[3] Here, too, a similar judicial order could have accommodated "the legitimate needs of law enforcement"[4] by authorizing the carefully limited use of electronic surveillance.

The Government urges that, because its agents relied upon the decisions in Olmstead and Goldman, and because they did no more here than they might properly have done with prior judicial sanction, we should retroactively validate their conduct. That we cannot do. It is apparent that the agents in this case acted with restraint. Yet the inescapable fact is that this restraint was imposed by the agents themselves, not by a judicial officer. They were not required, before commencing the search, to present their estimate of probable cause for detached scrutiny by a neutral magistrate. They were not compelled, during the conduct of the search itself, to observe precise limits established in advance by a specific court order. Nor were they directed, after the search had been completed, to notify the authorizing magistrate in detail of all that had been seized. In the absence of such safeguards, this Court has never sustained a search upon the sole ground that officers reasonably expected to find evidence of a particular crime and voluntarily confined their activities to the least intrusive means consistent with that end. Searches conducted without warrants have been held un-

---

[3] Although the protections afforded the petitioner in Osborn were "similar . . . to those . . . of conventional warrants," they were not identical. A conventional warrant ordinarily serves to notify the suspect of an intended search. But if Osborn had been told in advance that federal officers intended to record his conversations, the point of making such recordings would obviously have been lost; the evidence in question could not have been obtained. In omitting any requirement of advance notice, the federal court that authorized electronic surveillance in Osborn simply recognized, as has this Court, that officers need not announce their purpose before conducting an otherwise authorized search if such an announcement would provoke the escape of the suspect or the destruction of critical evidence. See Ker v. California, 374 US 23, 37–41.

Although some have thought that this "exception to the notice requirement where exigent circumstances are present," id., at 39, should be deemed inapplicable where police enter a home before its occupants are aware that officers are present, id., at 55–58 (dissenting opinion of Mr. Justice Brennan), the reasons for such a limitation have no bearing here. However true it may be that "[i]nnocent citizens should not suffer the shock, fright or embarrassment attendant upon an unannounced police intrusion," id., at 57, and that "the requirement of awareness . . . serves to minimize the hazards of the officers' dangerous calling," id., at 57–58, these considerations are not relevant to the problems presented by judicially authorized electronic surveillance.

Nor do the Federal Rules of Criminal Procedure impose an inflexible requirement of prior notice. Rule 41(d) does require federal officers to serve upon the person searched a copy of the warrant and a receipt describing the material obtained, but it does not invariably require that this be done before the search takes place. Nordelli v. United States, 24 F2d 665, 666–667.

Thus the fact that the petitioner in Osborn was unaware that his words were being electronically transcribed did not prevent this Court from sustaining his conviction, and did not prevent the Court in Berger from reaching the conclusion that the use of the recording device sanctioned in Osborn was entirely lawful. 388 US 41, 57.

[4] Lopez v. United States, 373 US 427, 464 (dissenting opinion of Mr. Justice Brennan).

lawful "notwithstanding facts unquestionably showing probable cause," Agnello v. United States, 269 US 20, 33, for the Constitution requires "that the deliberate, impartial judgment of a judicial officer . . . be interposed between the citizen and the police. . . ." Wong Sun v. United States, 371 US 471, 481–482. "Over and again this Court has emphasized that the mandate of the [Fourth] Amendment requires adherence to judicial processes," United States v. Jeffers, 342 US 48, 51, and that searches conducted outside the judicial process, without prior approval by judge or magistrate, are per se unreasonable under the Fourth Amendment—subject only to a few specifically established and well-delineated exceptions.

It is difficult to imagine how any of those exceptions could ever apply to the sort of search and seizure involved in this case. Even electronic surveillance substantially contemporaneous with an individual's arrest could hardly be deemed an "incident" of that arrest.[5] Nor could the use of electronic surveillance without prior authorization be justified on grounds of "hot pursuit."[6] And, of course, the very nature of electronic surveillance precludes its use pursuant to the suspect's consent.[7]

The Government does not question these basic principles. Rather, it urges the creation of a new exception to cover this case.[8] It argues that surveillance of a telephone booth should be exempted from the usual requirement of advance authorization by a magistrate upon a showing of probable cause. We cannot agree. Omission of such authorization

> "bypasses the safeguards provided by an objective predetermination of probable cause, and substitutes instead the far less reliable procedure of an after-the-event justification for the . . . search, too likely to be subtly influenced by the familiar shortcomings of hindsight judgment." Beck v. Ohio, 379 US 89, 96.

And bypassing a neutral predetermination of the scope of a search leaves individuals secure from Fourth Amendment violations "only in the discretion of the police." Id., at 97.

These considerations do not vanish when the search in question is transferred from the setting of a home, an office, or a hotel room, to that of a telephone booth. Wherever a man may be, he is entitled to know that he will remain free from unreasonable searches and seizures. The government agents here ignored "the

---

[5] In Agnello v. United States, 269 US 20, 30, the Court stated: "The right without a search warrant contemporaneously to search persons lawfully arrested while committing crime and to search the place where the arrest is made in order to find and seize things connected with the crime as its fruits or as the means by which it was committed, as well as weapons and other things to effect an escape from custody, is not to be doubted."

[6] Although [t]he Fourth Amendment does not require police officers to delay in the course of an investigation if to do so would gravely endanger their lives or the lives of others," Warden v. Hayden, 387 US 294, 298–299, there seems little likelihood that electronic surveillance would be a realistic possibility in a situation so fraught with urgency.

[7] A search to which an individual consents meets Fourth Amendment requirements, Zap v. United States, 328 US 624, but of course "the usefulness of electronic surveillance depends on lack of notice to the suspect." Lopez v. United States, 373 US 427, 463 (dissenting opinion of Mr. Justice Brennan).

[8] Whether safeguards other than prior authorization by a magistrate would satisfy the Fourth Amendment in a situation involving the national security is a question not presented by this case.

procedure of antecedent justification . . . that is central to the Fourth Amendment,"[9] a procedure that we hold to be a constitutional precondition of the kind of electronic surveillance involved in this case. Because the surveillance here failed to meet that condition, and because it led to the petitioner's conviction, the judgment must be reversed.

It is so ordered.

LOPEZ v. UNITED STATES
SUPREME COURT OF THE UNITED STATES
373 U.S. 427, 83 S. CT. 1381, 10 L. ED. 2d 462 (1963)

The defendant was charged and convicted with the attempted bribery of an Internal Revenue Agent. While the defendant and the Internal Revenue Agent were alone in an office at the defendant's business place, the defendant gave the Agent $420. The Agent reported the meeting immediately to his superior and turned over the $420 to a Regional Inspector. The Agent was instructed to "pretend to play along with the scheme" and to keep an appointment with the defendant a few days later. The Agent was given a pocket wire recorder with which he recorded the conversation between himself and the defendant. The following issues were brought before the U.S. Supreme Court.

> *On the defense of entrapment the Court stated:*
> "The conduct with which the defense of entrapment is concerned is the manufacturing of crime by law enforcement officials and their agents. Such conduct, of course, is far different from the permissible stratagems involved in the detection and prevention of crime. Thus before the issue of entrapment can fairly be said to have been presented in a criminal prosecution there must have been at least some showing of the kind of conduct by government agents which may well have induced the accused to commit the crime charged. . . . In the case before us, we think that such a showing has not been made."

> *On whether the wire recording of the conversation was properly admitted into evidence,* the Court stated:
> "Indeed this case involves no 'eavesdropping' whatever in any proper sense of that term. The Government did not use an electronic device to listen in on conversations it could not otherwise have heard. Instead, the device was used only to obtain the most reliable evidence possible of a conversation in which the Government's own agent was a participant and which that agent was fully entitled to disclose. And the device was not planted by means of an unlawful physical invasion of petitioner's premises under circumstances which would violate the Fourth Amendment. It was carried in and out by an agent who was there with petitioner's assent and it neither saw nor heard more than the agent himself. . . . We think the risk that petitioner took in offering a bribe to Davis [the government agent] fairly included the risk that the offer would be accurately reproduced in court, whether by faultless memory or mechanical recording."

> *The conviction was affirmed.*

[9] See Osborn v. United States, 385 US 323, 330.

ON LEE v. UNITED STATES
SUPREME COURT OF THE UNITED STATES
343 U.S. 747, 72 S. CT. 967, 96 L. ED. 1270 (1952)

A Federal narcotics officer wired an "undercover agent" (one Chin Poy) for sound with a small microphone and a radio transmitter. Chin Poy was an acquaintance and former employee of the defendant, who ran a laundry. Conversations between Chin Poy and the defendant, On Lee, were not only overheard by the narcotic agent but the parties were also observed by the narcotic agent from some distance away. Incriminating statements were made in the front room of On Lee's laundry and also on the streets of New York. The defendant was charged and convicted with selling a pound of opium. Chin Poy did not testify at the trial but the narcotic agent testified as to what he heard and saw.

> *In affirming the conviction, the Court stated:*
> "The presence of a radio set is not sufficient to suggest more than the most attenuated analogy to wiretapping. Petitioner was talking confidentially and indiscreetly with one he trusted and he was overheard. This was due to aid from a transmitter and receiver, to be sure, but with the same effect on his privacy as if [narcotic] agent Lee had been eavesdropping outside an open window. The use of bifocals, field glasses or the telescope to magnify the object of a witness' vision is not a forbidden search or seizure, even if they focus without his knowledge or consent upon what one supposes to be private indiscretions.... No good reason of public policy occurs to us why the Government should be deprived of the benefit of On Lee's admissions because he made them to a confidante of shady character."

UNITED STATES v. WHITE
SUPREME COURT OF THE UNITED STATES
401 U.S. 746, 91 S. CT. 1122, 28 L. ED. 2d 453 (1971)

This case presents the same issue before the Court as the 1952 *On Lee* case. The Seventh Circuit Court of Appeals read *Katz v. United States* as overruling *On Lee v. United States* although all of the other Circuits in the United States held otherwise.

In this case a government informant, Harvey Jackson, carried a concealed radio transmitter on his person. Conversations were overheard by Federal narcotic agents. Conversations were overheard from Jackson's home, from a restaurant and from Jackson's car. On the four occasions when conversations were overheard in Jackson's home, an agent was concealed in a kitchen closet with Jackson's consent. Jackson could not be located to testify at the trial but narcotic agents testified as to what they heard.

> *The Court affirmed the conviction and the On Lee case, stating:*
> "... Concededly a police agent who conceals his police connections may write down for official use his conversations with a defendant and testify concerning them, without a warrant authorizing his encounters with the defendant and without otherwise violating the latter's Fourth Amendment rights. For constitutional purposes, no different result is required if the agent instead of immediately reporting

and transcribing the conversations with defendant, either (1) simultaneously records them with electronic equipment which he is carrying on his person, *Lopez v. United States;* (2) or carries radio equipment which simultaneously transmit the conversations either to recording equipment located elsewhere or to other agents monitoring the transmitting frequency. *On Lee v. United States.* If the conduct and revelations of an agent operating without electronic equipment do not invade the defendant's constitutionally justifiable expectations of privacy, neither does a simultaneous recording of the same conversations made by the agent or by others from transmissions received from the agent to whom the defendant is talking and whose trustworthiness the defendant necessarily risks. . . ."

QUESTIONS AND PROBLEMS

No court order or search warrant was obtained in the following problems. Choose the answer which best fits the situation described in each question.

Available Answers for Questions 1 to 13

1. This is a crime and would be the basis for a civil suit against the officer (or persons). The evidence obtained would be suppressed.
2. The evidence would be suppressed as being invalidly obtained.
3. This is a valid means of criminal investigation, and the evidence obtained could be used in court.

1. Law enforcement officers place a detectaphone against the wall of a motel room and record the conversation going on in the next room.
2. A woman who has been receiving obscene telephone calls requests an officer to listen in on one of the conversations.
3. Suspecting that he will be offered a bribe, a law enforcement officer carries a recording device on his person when he goes to the office of X. X offers the officer a bribe. May the recording of the conversation be used in a charge of bribery against X?
4. Three men wiretap telephone lines coming into a large apartment building. With the information they obtain, the men begin blackmail operations.
5. Officers use a parabolic mike to overhear conversations in an office 100 feet from the office which they are in (across the open court of the building).
6. An undercover officer carries a radio transmitter which transmits

the conversations around him to other officers outside the building he is in. At the right time, he transmits the signal to the waiting officers to make the raid which was planned.

7. It is suspected that threats will be made against a witness. Officers give the witness a tape recorder to record possible telephone threats.

8. A corporate executive bugs the office of the corporation auditor as he suspects embezzlement. The bugging provides evidence. May the evidence be used in a criminal trial?

9. Police bug a hotel room and obtain evidence which they wish to use in a criminal trial.

10. A jail cell in a prison is bugged, and conversation between prisoners is monitored and recorded.

11. Police wiretap the telephone of a defense attorney without a warrant or court order.

12. Police place a bug under a table in a restaurant with the consent of the restaurant owner. Suspects under investigation by the police eat regularly at the restaurant, and evidence is obtained from the bugging.

13. A private detective tells you that he has obtained a court order permitting him to wiretap a telephone line to obtain evidence for a divorce action. He also obtained criminal evidence which he offers to turn over to the police.

16

THE
RIGHT
AND THE
EXPECTATION
OF
PRIVACY

Each person in the United States has a right of privacy against certain types of governmental intrusions. This right to privacy is protected by the Fourth Amendment, which states:

> The right of the people to be secure in their persons, houses, papers, and effects, against unreasonable searches and seizures, shall not be violated. . . .

In the 1967 case of *Katz v. United States* (see Chap. 15), the United States Supreme Court defined and formulated the right of privacy test as follows:

> . . . In the first place the correct solution of Fourth Amendment problems is not necessarily promoted by incantation of the phrase "constitutionally protected area." Secondly, the Fourth Amendment cannot be translated into a general constitutional "right of privacy." That Amendment protects individual privacy against certain kinds of governmental intrusion, but its protections go further, and often have nothing to do with privacy at all. Other provisions of the Constitution protect personal privacy from other forms of governmental invasion. But the protection of a person's general right to privacy—his right to be let alone by other people—is, like the protection of his property and of his very life, left largely to the law of the individual States.
> . . . the Fourth Amendment protects people, not places. What a person knowingly exposes to the public, even in his own home or seeks to preserve as private, even in an area accessible to the public office, is not a subject of Fourth Amendment protection. But what he seeks to preserve as private, even in an area accessible to the public, may be constitutionally protected. . . .

RIGHT OF PRIVACY CASES

Curtilage

"What the term 'curtilage' means is that area near the dwelling itself which a person has a right to close off from public traffic...." *United States v. Blank*, 251 F. Supp. 166

PEOPLE v. BRADLEY, 81 CAL. RPTR. 457 (CAL. APP. 1969)

An experienced narcotics officer was told by an informant of unknown reliability that the defendant had marijuana in his house and was engaged in selling it. The informant also described the defendant's car. The next evening the same informant told the officer that the defendant was also growing marijuana in his backyard. The officer went to the home and when he did not see the defendant's car, the officer assumed that the defendant was not home and went into the backyard. The officer found the marijuana between two houses and about 20 feet from the defendant's door. The officer did not have a search warrant. (See Chap. 17 for the rest of the case and the entry into the defendant's home.)

THE COURT. "A number of cases in upholding searches in open fields or grounds around a house have stated their conclusions in terms of whether the place was a 'constitutionally protected area'. That phrase, however, does not afford a solution to every case involving a claim of an illegal search and seizure (see *Katz v. United States*) and we believe that an appropriate test is whether the person has exhibited a reasonable expectation of privacy, and if so, whether that expectation has been violated by unreasonable governmental intrusion.

"Measured by that test we are satisfied that the officer's discovery and seizure of the marijuana plants in the yard adjacent to defendant's residence did not violate the constitutional prohibitions against unreasonable searches and seizures. From the recited evidence it may be inferred that the marijuana plants were partially but not totally covered by foliage. It does not appear that the plants were covered by nontransparent material, and it may be inferred that at least part of the plants were in plain sight of anyone within a foot of the tree. Although they were in a rear yard that was fenced to an undisclosed extent, they were located a scant 20 feet from defendant's door to which presumably delivery men and others came, and the front house, as well as defendant's house, apparently had access to the yard. Under the circumstances it does not appear that defendant exhibited a subjective expectation of privacy as to the plants. Furthermore, any such expectation would have been unreasonable. (...see *Katz v. United States* concurring opinion by Harlan, J. containing statements to the effect that there is no reasonable expectation of privacy in an open field or with respect to 'conversations in the open.')"

WATTENBURG v. UNITED STATES, 388 F.2d 853 (9th CIR. 1968)

During a six-hour search, police uncovered a lumber pile and found the Christmas trees, which were seized. The stockpile was in the backyard of the motel where the defendant resided. There was no testimony that any of the objects seized were visible to a person standing nearby on the premises. The seized trees were covered by other trees. The court held that the defendant exhibited a subjective expectation of privacy. The court stated that the appropriate test "in determining if a search and seizure adjacent to a house is constitutionally forbidden is whether it constitutes an intrusion upon what the resident seeks to preserve as private even in an area which although adjacent to his home, is accessible to the public."

CARE v. UNITED STATES, 231 F.2d 22 (10th CIR. 1956), CERT. DENIED, 351 U.S. 932

THE COURT. "The applicable legal principles are well established and extended discussion of them would serve no useful purpose. As this court has stated 'the protection of the Fourth Amendment securing people in their persons, houses, papers and effects against unreasonable search and seizures does not apply to an open field'. (citing *Hester v. United States*, 265 U.S. 57) It does, however, apply to buildings within the curtilage which may include a garage, a barn, a smokehouse, a chicken house or similar property. Whether the place searched is within the curtilage is to be determined from the facts, including its proximity or annexation to the dwelling, its inclusion within the general enclosure surrounding the dwelling, and its use and enjoyment as an adjunct to the domestic economy of the family.

"The cave in the instant case was in a plowed field, across a road and more than a long city block from the home. It gave no evidence of ever having been used as a refuge from storms or for normal uses of a cave adjacent to a home such as the storage of foods or dairy products. The trial court chose to disbelieve the testimony of the defendant 'that it was used for a storm cave' or for the primary purpose of feeding hogs, stating: 'the evidence points conclusively to the fact it was used as a distillery ... separate and apart and distinct from his home as one could be.' As indicated above, we are not persuaded that the trial court erred in reaching its conclusion that the cave was not within the curtilage. The search has not been shown to have been within the prescription of the amendment relied upon. The evidence was therefore properly admitted. . . ."

PEOPLE v. EDWARDS, 458 P.2d 713 (CAL. 1969)

A search of a trash can near the back door of the defendant's home was held to be a violation of the defendant's right of privacy. The officers did not have a warrant to search and the marijuana was not visible without rummaging through the can. The Court rejected the "open fields" and "grounds around a house" tests and applied the test of whether the defendant had exhibited a reasonable expectation of privacy and whether this expectation of privacy was violated by an unreasonable governmental search.

CROKER v. STATE, 477 P.2d 122 (WYO. 1970)

City sanitation men turned the defendant's garbage over to the police after they collected it. The Court held that this did not constitute a search.

THE COURT. "Even assuming under the rationale of *Katz v. United States* that defendant did have a reasonable expectation of privacy to the contents of his garbage cans as long as the contents were on his premises it would be most unrealistic to hold that such reasonable expectation of privacy would reach beyond the confines of defendant's premises. It is our view that when defendant put his garbage in his garbage cans for purposes of removal he impliedly consented to entry upon his premises by the garbage collectors in the regular performances of their duties and to the removal of the garbage by them to the alley, which was open to the public (where the police took the contents of the cans). At that time the officers or anyone else, if the garbage collectors did not object, were free to examine the contents of the collector's barrel."

PEOPLE v. KRIVDA, 91 CAL. RPTR. 219 (CAL. APP. 1971)

In a divided opinion, the California Supreme Court held contrary to the Wyoming Supreme Court in the Croker case.

THE CALIFORNIA COURT. "We can readily ascribe many reasons why residents would not want their castaway clothing, letters, medicine bottles or telltale refuse and trash to be examined by neighbors or others, at least not until the trash had lost its identity and meaning by becoming part of a large conglomeration of trash elsewhere ... we hold that defendants had a reasonable expectation that their trash would not be rummaged through and picked over by police officers acting without a search warrant."

Authors' Note: The state of California appealed the Krivda decision to the United States Supreme Court, arguing that the defendant abandoned the refuse and trash and therefore lost any right of privacy in the property. The Supreme Court vacated and remanded the matter back to the Supreme Court of California in 93 S. Ct. 32 (Oct., 1972), stating, "... we are unable to say with any degree of certainty that the judgment of the California Supreme Court was not based on an adequate and independent nonfederal ground." At some future date this issue is likely to appear before the United States Supreme Court and will be decided upon the Fourth Amendment issue of the right and expectation of privacy.

Plain View or Open View

In *Harris v. United States*, 390 U.S. 234 (1968), the United States Supreme Court reaffirmed the principle that "objects falling in the plain view of an officer who has a right to be in the position to have that view are subject to seizure and may be introduced in evidence." The plain-view doctrine has been applied to anything which an officer becomes aware of by use of his five senses while in a lawful position.

KER v. CALIFORNIA, 374 U.S. 23 (U.S. S. CT. 1963) (SEE CASE IN CHAP. 8)

THE U.S. SUPREME COURT. "Probable cause for the arrest of petitioner Diane Ker, while not present at the time the officers entered the apartment to arrest her husband, was nevertheless present at the time of her arrest. Upon their entry and announcement of their identity, the officers were met not only by George Ker but also by Diane Ker, who was emerging from the kitchen. Officer Berman immediately walked to the doorway from which she emerged and, without entering, observed the brick-shaped package of marijuana in plain view...."

PEOPLE v. WRIGHT, 242 N.E. 2d 180 (ILL. 1968)

Chicago police officers obtained a search warrant for a second-floor apartment in Chicago where they were informed that a policy operation (numbers game) would be conducted at 10:00 or 10:30 P.M. The officers established a surveillance of the building at about 9:30 P.M. and saw persons known to be policy runners entering the first-floor apartment rather than the second-floor apartment. The building did not have a backyard and the officers were able to stand 1 to 3 feet from the rear window of the first-floor apartment and observe and hear what the people were doing in the apartment. The officers stood on the property of the Chicago Transit Authority. After ten minutes of watching and listening through the window, the officers had probable cause to believe that the policy operation was being conducted in the first-floor apartment. They went to the front door of the apartment and knocked. When the person who came to the door told them to "get lost," they forced their way into the apartment.

THE COURT. "We have here a law enforcement officer using his senses of vision and hearing to discover what is occurring inside a private residence. In three Federal cases (*Brock v. United States*, 5th Cir., 223 F. 2d 681; *California v. Hurst*, 9th Cir., 325 F 2d 891; *Texas v. Gonzales*, 5th Cir., 388 F 2d, 145) it was held that evidence procured by officers standing on the *defendants' premises* and peering into their windows constituted a search in violation of the defendants' fourth amendment 'right to be let alone'. This case differs from those on the physical facts because here the police officer watched and listened through the rear window of the first floor apartment while standing on public property, a C.T.A. right-of-way where he had a right to be, rather than trespassing on defendants' property; and the absence of a trespass under our reading of *Harris v. United States* is of major if not decisive importance in cases involving the plain-view doctrine. We need not make the resolution of this appeal turn on the absence of a trespass by Officer Waller, however, because the *Brock-Hurst-Gonzales* cases do not hold that officers can never acquire probable cause to arrest by looking in windows of private residences, 'but only that they must have probable cause to think that a crime is being or has been committed before they do so.' (388 F. 2d at 148) It is clear that when officer Waller peered through the rear window in question, he had ample cause to believe that a policy operation was being conducted on the premises. The officer knew that by issuing a search warrant for the second floor apartment of the two-story structure . . . a court had found there was sufficient cause to believe that a policy operation was being carried on in the building. Furthermore, he had been informed that those individuals involved in the gambling activity would not arrive at the apartment until 10:00 or 10:30 P.M. and when he observed persons known to him as policy runners whom he had arrested on many prior occasions enter the first floor apartment at about 10 o'clock that evening we hold that he had probable cause to believe that the policy operation was being conducted in that apartment on that particular night. Therefore the evidence which was seized incident to the arrest of the defendants was properly admitted."

PONCE v. CRAVEN, 409 F.2d 621 (9th CIR. 1969)

A motel manager called California police and informed them (1) that the defendant, who lived at the motel, made twenty to thirty telephone calls on the pay phone every day; (2) that the defendant rarely slept; (3) that he left the motel at all hours; (4) that he kept his blinds pulled at all times; (5) that he refused to allow the maid to enter the room; (6) that when the manager had been in the room, uninflated balloons were seen and children were not in the room; (7) that another guest had observed that "those people are loaded"; (8) that the tenants made frequent trips to Mexico; (9) that packages were passed out of the motel window to people who stopped by in a car. The manager then took the narcotics officers to a parking lot in the rear of the motel. While standing in the parking lot, the officers could look into the defendant's bathroom window and could overhear conversations taking place in the motel. An officer who could speak Spanish was called to the motel as the conversations were partly in English and partly in Spanish. From the conversations and noise, the officers concluded that the defendants were packaging narcotics. They also observed a man washing out a hypodermic needle. Considering all the information available to him, the officer concluded that he had at least probable cause to make an arrest for possession of narcotics paraphernalia. (See Chap. 17 for the method of entry used in this case.)

THE COURT. "If a person knowingly exposes his activities to public view and hearing, he is not entitled to have these activities protected against searches and seizure. *Katz v. United States.* Further if a person relies upon privacy in a given situation, that reliance must be reasonable and justified under the particular circumstances. *Katz v. United States.*

"Ponce's reliance on privacy in his motel room was not reasonable under the circumstances. If he did not wish to be observed, he could have drawn his blinds. The officers did not intrude upon any reasonable expectation of privacy in this case by observing with their eyes the activities visible through the window. Nor was there any unreasonable intrusion upon privacy when the officers overheard conversation from inside the motel room. As the court said in *United States v. Llanes*, 398 F. 2d 880, 884 (2nd Cir. 1968):

> 'We believe that conversations carried on in a tone of voice quite audible to a person standing outside the home are conversations knowingly exposed to the public'.

We agree; the conversation between Ponce and his woman companion was lawfully overheard by Officer Reed and admitted into evidence."

MARULLO v. UNITED STATES, 328 F.2d 361 (5th CIR. 1964)

THE COURT. "A private home is quite different from a place of business or from a motel cabin. A home owner or tenant has the exclusive enjoyment of his home, his garage, his barn or other buildings, and also the area around his home. But a transient occupant of a motel must share corridors, sidewalks, yards and trees with other occupants. Granted that a tenant has standing to protect the room he occupies, there is nevertheless an element of public or shared property in motel surroundings that is entirely lacking in the enjoyment of one's home."

PEOPLE v. WILLARD, 47 CAL. RPTR. 734 (1965)

An officer entered the side yard of a duplex through an open gate. The sidewalk went from the gate to a side porch. The officer stood on the first step of the porch and looked through a window into the interior of the house, where he observed certain matters. The California court held that under the circumstances, the officer's acts did not constitute an unconstitutional invasion of the defendant's privacy and that looking through a window does not become an unreasonable search merely because a police officer may be on the defendant's premises when he makes the observations. The court stated that, "the degree of privacy which defendant enjoyed in the place involved is an important factor in determining the reasonableness of the search...."

PEOPLE v. TERRY, 77 CAL. RPTR. 460 (1969)

The court held that the defendant's constitutional right of privacy was not violated when officers entered an apartment house garage, used in common by tenants of the apartment building and saw in plain sight marijuana on an open ashtray inside the defendant's car. The court stated that the Fourth Amendment prohibits unreasonable searches and seizures, not trespasses, and that, even if the officers' entry into the garage was a technical trespass, there was no violation of the Fourth Amendment.

STATE v. CLARKE, 242 SO. 2d 791 (FLA. APP. 1971)

A police officer standing on the fire escape of an apartment building looked through the window of an apartment and observed narcotics being prepared for injection. The court held that the officer was authorized to enter the apartment with other officers without knocking in order to seize the contraband before it was destroyed.

THE COURT. "Since the fire escape was open to use by others, the occupants of the apartment in question had no reasonable right to expect any privacy with relation to what they did inside the window within easy view of any person on that fire escape. They had no yard surrounding the premises which they could reasonably expect to protect their windows from visual intrusions by strangers. Those inside the apartment must be held to an expectation that those using the common facilities of the building would come across the window and look inside...."

PEOPLE v. SPROVIERI, 252 N.E.2d 531 (ILL. 1969)

Police were looking for the defendant to arrest him on a murder charge. When they found no one in his apartment, they entered his private garage at the rear of the premises to search for him. He was not in the garage, but the police found evidence in plain view in the garage which they seized.

THE COURT. "Normal precautionary measures require that the police eliminate all hiding places before moving on. An entry into the garage was proper under the circumstances in this case. The officers had reason to believe that Sprovieri and his companion might be hiding there or that Judith had suffered the same fate as Vana, whose body was found in an automobile. We therefore hold that once lawfully inside the garage, the police were not obligated to overlook those items which they reasonably thought were connected with the slaying of Vana and which lay in open view.... Judgment affirmed."

COOLIDGE v. NEW HAMPSHIRE, 403 U.S. 443 (U.S. S. CT. 1971)

Police suspected the defendant in the murder of a teen-age baby-sitter. Two witnesses placed him and his car at the site where the body was found on the night she disappeared. When the search warrant to seize the car failed, the state argued that the car was seized under the plain-view doctrine. The U.S. Supreme Court reversed, holding that the plain-view doctrine applied only when an officer came upon the evidence or contraband "inadvertently." In this case the officers not only had prior knowledge of the location of the evidence but also had the intention to seize the car before they went to the home of the defendant.

MR. JUSTICE STEWART. "... It is well established that under certain circumstances the police may seize evidence in plain view without a warrant. But it is important to keep in mind that, in the vast majority of cases, *any* evidence seized by the police will be in plain view, at least at the moment of seizure. The problem with the 'plain view' doctrine has been to identify the circumstances in which plain view has legal significance rather than being simply the normal concomitant of any search, legal or illegal.

"An example of the applicability of the 'plain view' doctrine is the situation in which the police have a warrant to search a given area for specified objects, and in the course of the search come across some other article of incriminating character. Where the initial intrusion which brings the police within plain view of such an article is supported not by a warrant, but by one of the recognized exceptions to the warrant requirement, the seizure is also legitimate. Thus the police may inadvertently come across evidence while in 'hot pursuit' of a fleeing suspect. *Warden* v. *Hayden, supra.* And an object which comes into view during a search incident to arrest that is appropriately limited in scope under existing law may be seized without a warrant. *Chimel* v. *California*, 395 U. S. 752, 762–763. Finally, the 'plain view' doctrine has been applied where a police officer is not searching for evidence against the accused, but nonetheless inadvertently comes across an incriminating object.

"What the 'plain view' cases have in common is that the police officer in each of them had a prior justification for an intrusion in the course of which he came inadvertently across a piece of evidence incriminating the accused. The doctrine serves to supplement the prior justification—whether it be a warrant for another object, hot pursuit, search incident to lawful arrest, or some other legitimate reason for being present unconnected with a search directed against the accused—and permits the warrantless seizure. Of course, the extension of the original justification is legitimate only where it is immediately apparent to the police that they have evidence before them; the 'plain view' doctrine may not be used to extend a general exploratory search from one object to another until something incriminating at last emerges.

"The rationale for the 'plain view' exception is evident if we keep in mind the two distinct constitutional protections served by the warrant requirement. First, the magistrate's scrutiny is intended to eliminate altogether searches not based on probable cause. The premise here is that *any* intrusion in the way of search or seizure is an evil, so that no intrusion at all is justified without a careful prior determination of necessity. . . .

"The second, distinct objective is that those searches deemed necessary should be as limited as possible. Here, the specific evil is the 'general warrant' abhorred by the colonists, and the problem is not that of intrusion *per se*, but of a general, exploratory rummaging in a person's belongings. The warrant accomplishes this second objective by requiring a 'particular description' of the things to be seized.

"The 'plain view' doctrine is not in conflict with the first objective because plain view does not occur until a search is in progress. In each case, this initial intrusion is justified by a warrant or by an exception such as 'hot pursuit' or search incident to a lawful arrest, or by an extraneous valid reason for the officer's presence. And given the initial intrusion, the seizure of an object in plain view is consistent with the second objective, since it does not convert the search into a general or exploratory one. As against the minor peril to Fourth Amendment protections, there is a major gain in effective law enforcement. Where, once an otherwise lawful search is in progress, the police inadvertently come upon a piece of evidence, it would often be a needless inconvenience, and sometimes dangerous—to the evidence or to the police themselves—to require them to ignore it until they have obtained a warrant particularly describing it.

"The limits on the doctrine are implicit in the statement of its rationale. The first of these is that plain view *alone* is never enough to justify the warrantless seizure of evidence. This is simply a corollary of the familiar principle discussed above, that no amount of probable cause can justify a warrantless search or seizure absent 'exigent circumstances.' Incontrovertible testimony of the senses that an incriminating object is on premises belonging to a criminal suspect may establish the fullest possible measure of probable cause. But even where the object is contraband, this Court has repeatedly stated and enforced the basic rule that the police may not enter and make a warrantless seizure.

"The second limitation is that the discovery of evidence in plain view must be inadvertent. The rationale of the exception to the warrant requirement, as just stated, is that a plain view seizure will not turn an initially valid (and therefore limited) search into a 'general' one, while the inconvenience of procuring a warrant to cover an inadvertent discovery is great. But where the discovery is anticipated, where the police know in advance the location of the evidence and intend to seize it, the situation is altogether different. The requirement of a warrant to seize imposes no inconvenience whatever, or at least none which is constitutionally cognizable in a legal system that regards warrantless searches as 'per se unreasonable' in the absence of 'exigent circumstances.'

"If the initial intrusion is bottomed upon a warrant which fails to mention a particular object, though the police know its location and intend to seize it, then there is a violation of the express constitutional requirement of 'warrants . . . particularly describing . . . [the] things to be seized.' The initial intrusion may, of course, be legitimated not by a warrant but by one of the exceptions to the warrant requirement, such as hot pursuit or search incident to lawful arrest. But to extend the scope of such an intrusion to the seizure of objects—not contraband nor stolen nor dangerous in themselves—which the police know in advance they will find in plain view and intend to seize, would fly in the face of the basic rule that no amount of probable cause can justify a warrantless seizure.

"In the light of what has been said, it is apparent that the 'plain view' exception cannot justify the police seizure of the Pontiac car in this case. The police had ample opportunity to obtain a valid warrant; they knew the automobile's exact description and location well in advance; they intended to seize it when they came upon Coolidge's property. And this is not a case involving contraband or stolen goods or objects dangerous in themselves.

"The seizure was therefore unconstitutional, and so was the subsequent search at the station house. Since evidence obtained in the course of the search was admitted at Coolidge's trial, the judgment must be reversed and the case remanded to the New Hampshire Supreme Court. *Mapp v. Ohio*, 367 U. S. 643."

[Concurring and dissenting opinions omitted.]

PEOPLE v. STONE, 265 N.E.2d 883 (ILL. 1970)

A Chicago narcotics officer, while standing on a common stairway, observed the defendant through a window. The defendant was packaging heroin in tinfoil packages. The Court held that "defendant was committing a criminal offense in plain view of Officer Parker, and the latter gained his view from the outside stairway of an apartment building, an area which, unlike the apartment itself, was not subject to the dominion and control of defendant."

UNITED STATES v. CASE, 435 F.2d 766 (7th CIR. 1970)

Government agents obtained a key to a building from the landlord. They stood outside the closed door of a printing shop and overheard defendants' conversations in the printing shop. It was held that the hallway was not a public place and that this was an invasion of the right of privacy guaranteed to the defendants, who sought to keep their discussion in the printing shop private.

PEOPLE v. SUPERIOR COURT FOR COUNTY OF LOS ANGELES, 82 CAL. RPTR. 507 (CAL. APP. 1969)

Police officers went into a pawnshop and examined a typewriter on a desk in the portion of the premises open to the public. The serial number showed the typewriter was stolen, and the court held that examining its serial number did not constitute a search.

THE COURT. "Prior to their entry, the police had probable cause to believe that at least one stolen electric machine had been sold by the real party in interest. Accordingly, it was reasonable for them to pursue their investigation as to office machines in plain view to determine if there might be other stolen goods on the premises. *People v. Roberts* (303 P. 2d 721) teaches us that the mere act of picking up and examining the exterior surface of an object in open and plain view for identifying marks or numbers does not constitute a search. 'The essence of a search is the viewing of that which was not only intended to be private or hidden, but that which was, so far as the one searched is able to do so, made concealed or closed from open viewing.'... The Fourth Amendment does not prohibit the seizure of evidence 'which is readily visible' and 'accessible' to the police.

"Under the facts of this case there was no search. The typewriter was not intentionally put out of the way or concealed in a private or hidden place. The cover was not on the typewriter when it was first viewed by the officers. Had the serial number been on a surface on top of the typewriter, the officer would have been able to examine it without touching it. The fortuitous circumstance that the serial number was placed in such a manner as to require that the typewriter be moved in order to be read cannot be construed to turn reasonable conduct into misconduct of constitutional dimensions."

PEOPLE v. GOLDBERG, 280 N.Y.S.2d 646 (S. CT. N.Y. 1967), CERT. DENIED, 390 U.S. 909

The arresting officer was standing in a public hallway and overheard telephone and other conversation indicating that a bookmaking operation was being conducted. When the door was open, he was able to see into the room. The officer entered and arrested those inside. The Court affirmed the conviction, stating that the "officer, acted on the evidence he perceived by means of his own senses, without any artificial aids. He relied on his own sight and hearing and not on any information supplied to him."

Abandonment

Abandonment is defined as the relinquishment, surrender, and giving up of property or the rights to the property. If it is found that a person has abandoned property, then he cannot object to the search or seizure of that property by a law enforcement officer.

Some states have enacted statutes (for example, Wisconsin's newly enacted statute 342.40) which forbid the owners of motor vehicles, trailers, semitrailers, or mobile homes from leaving such vehicles unattended on private or public property. If any vehicle is left unattended for more than forty-eight hours without permission, the statute provides that the vehicle is deemed abandoned and constitutes a public nuisance. The statute also provides for the impounding of such vehicle.

ABEL v. UNITED STATES, 362 U.S. 217 (U.S. S. CT. 1960)

The defendant is the famous Russian spy arrested in New York City in 1957. The arrest took place in the defendant's hotel room. He was told to dress himself, to assemble his things, and to choose what he wished to take with him. The defendant deliberately left items on a windowsill and threw other items into the room's wastepaper basket. After he was packed, the defendant paid his bill to the hotel. He was then handcuffed and taken with his baggage to a waiting automobile. After the defendant had left, an FBI agent received permission from the hotel management to search the room vacated by the defendant. The hotel's practice was to consider a room vacated whenever a guest removed his baggage and turned in his key. The agent spent three hours searching the room. In the wastebasket, he found a hollow pencil containing microfilm and a block of wood containing a "cipher pad." The defense challenges the admissibility of the evidence found in the room.

THE COURT. ". . . at the time of the search petitioner had vacated the room. The hotel then had the exclusive right to its possession, and the hotel management freely gave its consent that the search be made. Nor was it unlawful to seize the entire contents of the wastepaper basket, even though some of its contents had no connection with crime. So far as the record shows, petitioner had abandoned these articles. He had thrown them away. So far as he was concerned, they were bona vacantia. There can be nothing unlawful in the Government's appropriation of such abandoned property. The two items which were eventually introduced in evidence were assertedly means for the commission of espionage, and were themselves seizable as such. These two items having been lawfully seized by the Government in connection with an investigation of crime, we encounter no basis for discussing further their admissibility as evidence. Affirmed."

(*Authors' Note:* The Colonel Abel case illustrates the fact that all persons—even spies or persons illegally in the United States—have full rights to all the privileges and protections afforded by the United States Constitution. The Bill of Rights uses the terms "persons" and "people," so that officers who seek to question a person illegally in the United States as to his criminal activity would be required to first give him the Miranda warnings and receive a waiver of the person's constitutional rights.)

GONZALES v. STATE, 461 S.W.2d (TEX. 1970)

When the defendant was stopped for a traffic offense, he threw a bag away. One of the officers saw him and retrieved the bag, which was found to contain marijuana. It was held that the marijuana was found in plain view after it was abandoned by the defendant. The court held that the seizure was not incident to the arrest for the traffic offense.

PEOPLE v. HARRIS, 93 CAL. RPTR. 285 (CAL. APP. 1971)

Police officers were on routine patrol in an area noted for a high rate of both narcotics and other offenses. They saw the defendant walking very fast or running down an alley and across a street. They maneuvered the patrol car so the lights fell on the defendant and saw him throw away a handkerchief. While one of the officers stopped the defendant and frisked him, the other officer recovered the handkerchief. The handkerchief contained twenty-four balloons containing a substance later shown to be heroin.

THE COURT. "Clearly the officers were entitled to stop and question the defendant; the handkerchief and its contents, abandoned by him, were not the subject of any 'search'; since the action of the officers in turning their lights on defendant was lawful, it cannot be argued that they had illegally compelled or impelled him to disclose the fatal evidence. Whether or not the officers had a right to search defendant's person, either before or after discovering the balloons, is immaterial; no evidence (if any) obtained by that search was introduced at the trial."

HESTER v. UNITED STATES, 265 U.S. 57 (U.S. S. CT. 1924)

Officers suspected the defendants of bootlegging and concealed themselves 50 to 100 yards from the defendant's house. They saw Hester leave the house and hand a bottle to one Henderson. When the men saw the officers, they ran, Hester dropped a jug which broke, and Henderson threw away the bottle which he had. The officers recovered the jug and bottle and recognized their contents as moonshine.

THE COURT. "It is obvious that even if there had been a trespass, the [officers'] testimony was not obtained by an illegal search or seizure. The defendant's own acts, and those of his associates, disclosed the jug, the jar and the bottle and there was no seizure in the sense of the law when the officers examined the contents of each after it had been abandoned.... The only shadow of a ground for bringing up the case is drawn from the hypothesis that the examination of the vessels took place upon Hester's father's land. As to that, it is enough to say that, apart from the justification, the special protection accorded by the Fourth Amendment to the people in their 'persons, houses, papers and effects' is not extended to the open fields. The distinction between the latter and the house is as old as the common law."

The Use of Binoculars, Telescopes, Flashlights, Etc.

Such equipment may be used in surveillance or plain-view observations as long as there is no physical trespass onto the curtilage. Officers may listen to conversations and other sounds from premises and curtilages if there is no physical trespass onto the curtilage. If an electronic or mechanical device is used to listen, a warrant should first be obtained authorizing such use.

STATE v. WADE, 479 P.2d 811 (KAN. 1971)

Officers found the defendant in the rear of a service station at night. The door of the service station was damaged and the defendant's car was parked with the motor running. The officers shined a flashlight into the car and saw the hammer lying on the front seat. The court held that the officers had probable cause to believe contents of the automobile offended against the law and were authorized to seize the hammer as a burglary tool.

WALKER v. BETO, 437 F.2d 1018 (5th CIR. 1971)

Officers saw the defendant's vehicle turn around without lights at 3:45 A.M. The driver made a right-hand turn signal and then turned left. Passengers in the car could be seen and then would disappear from sight. The officers stopped the car, and the defendant immediately got out and met them before they reached the vehicle. The driver had a valid license. The officer walked to the car and shined a flashlight into the vehicle, which revealed criminal objects including burglary tools.

THE COURT. "The appellant's first contention is that the shining of a flashlight through the window of the car to aid the policeman's view of the contents within constituted an illegal search of the car. The answer to that assertion was given by the Second Circuit in *United States v. Barone* (1964) 330 F. 2d 543, simply "That which is in plain view is not the product of a search.' It is now settled law that criminal objects falling within the plain view of a police officer who has a right to be in a position to have the view are subject to seizure and may be introduced into evidence. (*Harris v. United States* 390 U.S. 234) We reject the proposition urged by appellant that nothing untoward had been observed by the officer when he inspected Walker's valid driver's license between the two cars and walked forward to take a better look at the car. The argument is that Officer Husketh should then have permitted Walker to depart in peace and violated Fourth Amendment rights by walking forward and looking into the car. We think the turning around of the car without lights, the misleading turn signal and the appearance and disappearance from view of the passengers were suspicious circumstances warranting further inspection of the vehicle by the officer. Precaution for his own safety as well as investigation of possible wrong doing required as much."

MARSHALL v. UNITED STATES, 422 F.2d 185 (5th CIR. 1970)

The Court held that "The plain view rule does not go into hibernation at sunset" and that using a flashlight did not transform a nighttime observation into a search.

UNITED STATES v. LEE, 274 U.S. 559 (U.S. S. CT. 1927)

A Coast Guard cutter shined a searchlight on a motorboat suspected of carrying illegal liquor while over 12 miles out to sea. The U.S. Supreme Court affirmed the conviction stating, "Such use of a searchlight is comparable to the use of a marine glass or a field glass. It is not prohibited by the Constitution."

ON LEE v. UNITED STATES, 343 U.S. 747 (1952) (SEE CHAP. 15)

The United States Supreme Court stated, "The use of bifocals, field glasses or the telescope to magnify the object of a witness' vision is not a forbidden search or seizure, even if they focus without his knowledge or consent upon what one supposes to be private indiscretions.... We find no violation of the Fourth Amendment here."

PEOPLE v. BOONE, 82 CAL. RPTR. 398 (CAL. APP. 1969)

Police were called because of loud music in an apartment at 2:25 A.M. One of the officers used his flashlight coming up the dark stairway and it was on when the defendant responded to the knock at the door. The police did not identify themselves as police officers, and when the defendenant opened the door "a foot and a half," they smelled the odor of marijuana smoke. The officer with the flashlight beamed it 5 feet or so inside the dimly lit apartment and observed marijuana in pans. The officers then pushed open the door and arrested the defendant and others in the apartment.

THE COURT. "... Officers are permitted to seek interviews of persons at their homes and there is nothing illegal about looking through the open door which is opened without any show of force or coercion. Looking through a partially open door is not an illegal search. Here the observation of the aluminum pan with green leafy material resembling marijuana was made by the officer from a place where he had a right to be and which was open to his eyes. What was in plain sight was also confirmed by the officer's sense of smell. The officer did not have to close his eyes to what was in plain sight. With this probable cause, the search lawfully could precede the arrests. It would run counter to common sense to hold that in this situation, the officer would have to reknock on the door and stop to tell defendant Boone why he was coming in and to step aside.

"Defendants argue that the use of the flashlight constituted an illegal intrusion by light beam. We do not agree. While we have found no California case dealing with the use of a flashlight in the factual context presented by this case, the decisions have uniformly held that use of a flashlight to look inside of a vehicle or a truck van from outside of the vehicle does not constitute an illegal search.... No cognizable legal factor why we should hold differently where the officer beamed his flashlight five feet or so inside an apartment, where the door was voluntarily opened by a defendant has been brought to our attention. Nor does such consideration come to mind. We, therefore, hold that the use of the flashlight in this instance did not constitute an illegal search...."

PEOPLE v. CERDA, 61 CAL. RPTR. 784 (CAL. APP. 1967)

While the defendant was looking in his wallet for his identification papers, the officer shined his flashlight on the wallet. This enabled the officer to observe a folded check which turned out to be forged. The court held that the use of the flashlight did not constitute a search.

PEOPLE v. LEES, 64 CAL. RPTR. 888 (CAL. APP. 1967)

The court held that the use of a flashlight through the cracks in a garage wall to ascertain from the adjoining garage that the defendant had stolen goods in his garage did not constitute an unlawful entry and a search.

Effect of Illegal Police Action

Illegal police action may cause the defendant to throw contraband or incriminating evidence away. Courts have held that the property thrown away was not abandoned or not in plain view.

HOBSON v. UNITED STATES, 226 F.2d 890 (8th CIR. 1955)

Officers knew that the defendant made an illegal sale of narcotics on March 22, 1955. No action was taken until April 20, 1955, when officers surrounded the home. The officers did not have a search warrant or arrest warrant. The officers requested entry into the house. There was a delay and the officers said they forced entry when the defendant threw a package out of a back window into his back yard. The defendant said he threw the package after the officers forced the entry. When the package was opened, it was found to contain heroin. The court suppressed the evidence stating, "The enclosed back yard in which the thrown package landed was part of the curtilage of the defendant's home and was subject to the same protection as the home itself ... we can not separate the throwing of the package from the unlawful search. The defendant's action in throwing the package was not voluntary but was forced by the actions of the officers...."

PEOPLE v. BALDWIN, 250 N.E.2d 62 (N.Y. 1969)

The defendant dropped a white envelope after he was illegally arrested. The envelope contained narcotics. The court held that the primary illegality tainted the abandonment and therefore abandonment would not justify the admission of the evidence.

COMMONWEALTH v. WATKINS, 272 A.2d 212 (PA. APP. 1970)

Defendant ran to a window and threw narcotics paraphernalia out when police illegally entered his apartment. The court held that "Where an entry or an arrest is illegal the 'plain view' doctrine is inapplicable. This is true even if the defendant himself reveals the illegal goods to police officers."

FLETCHER v. WAINWRIGHT, 399 F.2d 62 (5th CIR. 1968)

The defendant threw stolen jewelry out of the hotel room window when the police made an illegal entry into the room.

MOLINA v. STATE, 53 WIS.2d 662 (WIS. 1971)
CERT. DENIED BY U.S. S. CT. IN JUNE, 1972, 409 U.S. ....

THE COURT. "Can police officers pick up and use as evidence heroin powder that they have seen scattered on a public street from a speeding automobile by occupants fleeing police arrest? The commonsense answer would seem to be that they can. Not so, argue the defendants, for picking up the powder from the street constitutes a search and seizure incident to an arrest. As such, the validity of the search depends upon the legality of the arrest, and here, the argument continues, arrest was illegal because (1) the officers lacked probable cause for the arrest; and (2) if they had probable cause, they were required to procure an arrest warrant before placing the defendants in custody. Each link in that argumentative chain will be examined in its turn.

"... we conclude here that the officers' picking up the heroin strewn about the street (1) was not a search; (2) was not a seizure; and (3) was not dependent upon their right to arrest the defendants."

[*Authors' note:* The Wisconsin Supreme Court held that probable cause to arrest did exist in the Molina case. However, probable cause is not necessary to stop an automobile, and probable cause was not necessary to pick up heroin thrown out of the automobile.]

College Dormitory Room
PIASSOLA v. WATKINS, 442 F.2d 284 (5th CIR. 1971)

THE COURT. "... we must conclude that a student who occupies a college dormitory room enjoys the protection of the Fourth Amendment. True the University retains broad supervisory powers which permit it to adopt the regulation heretofore quoted, providing the regulation is reasonably construed and is limited in its application to further the University's function as an educational institution. The regulation cannot be construed or applied so as to give consent to a search for evidence for the primary purpose of a criminal prosecution. Otherwise the regulation itself would constitute an unconstitutional attempt to require a student to waive his protection from unreasonable searches and seizures as a condition to his occupancy of a college dormitory room.

"The right of privacy is 'no less important than any other right carefully and particularly reserved to the people.' *Mapp v. Ohio* The results of the search do not prove its reasonableness. This search was an unconstitutional invasion of the privacy both of the appellees and of the students in whose rooms no evidence of marijuana was found. The warrantless search of these students' dormitory rooms cannot be justified."

Public Jail, Police Building, or Police Car

LANZA v. NEW YORK, 370 U.S. 139 (U.S. S. CT. 1962)

THE COURT. "... to say that a public jail is the equivalent of a man's 'house' or that it is a place where he can claim constitutional immunity from search or seizure of his person, his papers, or his effects, is at best a novel argument. To be sure, the Court has been far from niggardly in construing the physical scope of Fourth Amendment protection. A business office is a protected area, and so may be a store. A hotel room in the eyes of the Fourth Amendment may become a person's 'house', and so, of course, may an apartment. An automobile may not be unreasonably searched. Neither may an occupied taxicab. Yet, without attempting either to define or to predict the ultimate scope of Fourth Amendment protection, it is obvious that a jail shares none of the attributes of privacy of a home, an automobile, an office, or a hotel room. In prison, official surveillance has traditionally been the order of the day...." (A conversation between the defendant and his brother was recorded without their knowledge in a public jail where the defendant was being held.)

PEOPLE v. CHANDLER, 68 CAL. RPTR. 645 (CAL. APP. 1968), CERT. DENIED, 393 U.S. 1043

The defendant contended that his constitutional right of privacy was violated when the police used an electronic device to record a conversation between him and his accomplice while they were alone in a police car in which they had been placed after their arrest.

THE COURT. "Defendant also claims a violation of his constitutional right of privacy in the recording of the conversation in question. It is now settled law that an inmate of a jail or prison may not successfully complain of such a recording even if its taking was not known to him at the time."

PEOPLE v. MORGAN, 16 CAL. RPTR. 838 (CAL. APP. 1962), CERT. DENIED, 370 U.S. 965

The court held that an electronic recording of conversations between a county jail prisoner and his sister was not an unlawful invasion of the prisoner's privacy and was not an illegal search and seizure.

THE COURT. "A man detained in jail cannot reasonably expect to enjoy the privacy afforded to a person in free society. His lack of privacy is a necessary adjunct to his imprisonment."

PEOPLE v. LOPEZ, 32 CAL. RPTR. 424 (CAL. APP. 1963)

THE COURT. "Except only insofar as concerns consultation with his attorney in a room designated for that purpose a prisoner has no right of privacy in a jail."

The following case concerns the Sixth Amendment right to privacy while seeking the assistance of counsel.

HOFFA v. UNITED STATES, 385 U.S. 293 (U.S. S. CT. 1966)
(SEE CASES IN CHAP. 19)

THE U.S. SUPREME COURT. "... an essential ingredient thereof [of the Sixth Amendment] is the right of a defendant and his counsel to prepare for trial without intrusion upon their confidential relationship by an agent of the Government, the defendant's trial adversary....

"The proposition that a surreptitious invasion by a government agent into the legal camp of the defense may violate the protection of the Sixth Amendment has found expression in two cases decided by the Court of Appeals for the District of Columbia Circuit, *Caldwell v. United States* 205 F. 2d 879 and *Coplon v. United States*, 191 F. 2d 749. Both of those cases dealt with government intrusion of the grossest kind upon the confidential relationship between the defendant and his counsel...."

Personal Property Held by Bailee

A bailment is an everyday business transaction in which temporary possession of personal property is transferred from the owner to another person for a specific purpose. Examples of bailments are: (1) a car taken to a garage for repairs or storage and (2) a package given to a common carrier for shipment from one city to another city. As the bailment contract is controlling, the bailee in many cases (such as common carriers) has the right of inspection. See also Chap. 3 in regard to searches by private persons. The Fourth Amendment applies only to government and to the agents of government.

PEOPLE v. HIVELY, 480 P.2d 558 (COLO. 1971)

A United Air Lines freight agent became suspicious of a package and feared that it might contain a bomb. The agent and his foreman, on their own initiative, opened the package and observed five plastic bags containing purple-colored tablets (LSD). They called the sheriff, who removed one bag and marked the others and the package. The package was forwarded to its destination, Denver, and law enforcement officers in Denver were notified. The defendant was arrested without warrant when he claimed the package and was convicted of (1) possession of dangerous drugs for sale and (2) possession of dangerous drugs. The Supreme Court of Colorado affirmed the convictions, stating that the airline freight agent's search was a lawful private inspection and that information obtained by officers after they had been notified by the airline employee was not "tainted" and could serve as foundation for probable cause to make the arrest and seizure at the destination in Denver.

CORNGOLD v. UNITED STATES, 367 F.2d 1 (9th CIR. 1966)

U. S. customs officers suspected the defendant of smuggling watches into the United States. The defendant shipped a package via TWA air freight and the customs officers requested a TWA freight agent to open the package under the airline's right of inspection. Together the customs officers and the TWA employee opened and inspected the package. They found the watches, and one of the customs officers wrote his initials inside the box containing the watches. The validity of the search is challenged.

THE COURT. "The owner of personal property may bring his right of privacy to an end by abandoning the property. He may expressly authorize another to acquiesce in a search of his personal property or he may give another such complete and unrestricted freedom over his property that he will be held to have accepted the risk that the person will consent to a search; he may, in other words, impliedly authorize another to consent to an invasion of his right of privacy.

"Appellant did not abandon his package; and mere surrender of custody to a carrier did not forfeit appellant's right of privacy. He did not expressly authorize TWA to consent to search of his package by customs agents. Therefore, unless appellant impliedly authorized TWA to acquiesce in such a search, TWA's consent could not bind appellant. The facts negate any intention to grant TWA such broad authority. Appellant's package, securely wrapped and tied, was delivered to the airline solely for transportation from Los Angeles to New York, and the inspection clause in TWA's tariff authorized examination only by the carrier itself.

"It is perhaps worth repeating that although this court may now be faced with the choice of justifying a warrantless search or letting a guilty man go free, that choice did not face the customs officers. They could have secured a warrant, or, if probable cause for search was lacking, continued their investigation until information establishing probable cause was obtained. . . . Reversed."

GOLD v. UNITED STATES, 378 F.2d 588 (1967)

Government agents informed United Air Lines employees that they had reason to believe that what was being shipped in a parcel was inaccurately described in the waybill and that the address of the shipper was nonexistent. The government agents would not reveal what they suspected to be the true contents of the package. They then left the airline office.

THE COURT. "The instant case differs from Corngold in several significant respects. After informing the manager of their suspicions regarding the shipment, the government agents left the premises. The manager, after attending to some other business, made the decision to investigate further. The shipment was taken from the freight area to the air freight room at the manager's direction. No one else was present while the manager and one other employee opened one of the packages. After finding the film and observing its nature, the manager determined that the matter 'should be someone else's business'. It was another 45 minutes to an hour after discovering the films before he got around to calling the government agents.

"We conclude that the initial search of the packages by the airline's employee was not a federal search, but was an independent investigation by the carrier for its own purposes. Unlike *Corngold*, here the agents did not request that the package be opened, and they were not present when it was opened. The agents had the same right as any citizen to point out what they suspected to be a mislabeled shipping document, and they exercised no control over what followed. What did follow was the discretionary action of the airline's manager and was not so connected with government participation or influence as to be fairly characterized, as was the search in *Corngold*, as a 'federal search cast in the form of a carrier inspection.'"

COMMONWEALTH v. PEREZ, 258 N.E.2d 1 (MASS. 1970)

In investigating a very bloody murder, police contacted cleaning establishments, requesting them to be on the lookout for bloody clothing. One of the cleaners contacted stated that a man who gave his name only as "Joe" with no address given had left blood-covered clothing at his firm, which was not far from the scene of the murder. This was six hours after the murder was committed. The police requested the clothing, and the owner of the store turned it over to the police. The clothing was traced to the defendant. The court held that there was no necessity for a warrant as the police conducted no search but at most seized items in plain view when they had probable cause to believe that the bloody clothing would aid in the identification of the murderer. The court stated that the defendant took the risk that the cleaner would inform the police when the bloody clothing was left to be cleaned with specific instructions to take out the bloodstains.

STATE v. CURLEY, 171 S.E.2d 699 (1970)

The court held that the general rule is that a bailor's constitutional rights are not violated in the case of a search of the bailed property consented to by the bailee.

Public Toilets

SMAYDA v. UNITED STATES, 352 F.2d 251 (9th CIR. 1965), CERT. DENIED, 86 S. CT. 555

Rangers at Yosemite National Park received complaints and information that rest room 600 in the park was being used for homosexual activities. Inspection showed that holes had been cut waist-high between the enclosed toilet stalls. The court stated, "We do not detail all of the evidence in this regard; it was ample to give the manager and the rangers reasonable cause to believe that the stalls in restroom 600 had been and would be used in violation of Penal Code section 288a."

The park rangers cut a hole in the roof of the rest room building for observation purposes. It was decided to begin surveillances on Saturday nights "after the family-type people had quit using the facility" because this was the most likely time the criminal acts would be committed. The rangers did not request or obtain a search warrant for this search.

The defendants were photographed and arrested on the second Saturday of the surveillance for the offense of oral copulation. Both defendants were convicted and appeal, alleging that their Fourth Amendment rights were violated.

THE COURT. "We agree that every person who enters an enclosed stall in a public toilet is entitled to believe that, while there, he will have at least the modicum of privacy that its design affords. We would not uphold a clandestine surveillance of such an area without cause. We are made as uncomfortable as the next man by the thought that our own legitimate activities in such a place may be spied upon by the police. We also think, however, that the nature of the places, the nature of the criminal activities that can and do occur in it, the ready availability therein of a receptacle for disposing of incriminating evidence, and the right of the public to expect that the police will put a stop to its use as a resort for crime all join to require a reasonable limitation upon the right of privacy involved. We hold that when, as here, the police have reasonable cause to believe that public toilet stalls are being used in the commission of crime, and when, as here, they confine their activities to the times when such crimes are most likely to occur, they are entitled to institute clandestine surveillance, even though they do not have probable cause to believe that the particular persons whom they may thus catch in flagrante delicto have committed or will commit the crime. The public interest in its privacy, we think, must to that extent be subordinated to the public interest in law enforcement. Affirmed."

[Concurring and dissenting opinion omitted]

PEOPLE v. YOUNG, 29 CAL. RPTR. 492 (CAL. APP. 1963)

There were no doors on the stalls and persons walking into the public toilet could have seen the offense.

THE COURT. "To hold that the public areas of such toilets are to be 'off limits' from clandestine surveillance by police would be to encourage the use of such places by perverts, panderers, pickpockets, addicts, and hoodlums. Such persons would seek asylum or refuge in such places with the assurance that they could conduct their illicit activities therein while fully protected from the secret surveillance of the vice squad. Should the areas of such toilets, where the members of the public are free to circulate, as distinguished from areas where one may seclude oneself from public view, such as in an enclosed commode or toilet stall, become areas removed from such secret surveillance by the police, the peril to immature and innocent youth would be increased immeasurably. By leaving a 'spotter' or 'lookout' at the door to warn other perverts or degenerates of the approach of police, such immoral persons could conduct their illicit activities in full view of impressionable youths. Parents would not rest secure that their youngsters could use such facilities without fear that they would witness scenes of shocking adult degeneracy such as witnessed by the police in the instant case."

BROWN v. STATE, 238 A.2d 147 (MD. APP. 1968)

An officer looked over the door of a toilet booth and saw narcotics paraphernalia on the commode. The defendant was a known drug addict. The door was about 5 feet 5 inches high. The court held that the officer's testimony was inadmissible.

THE COURT. "... We believe that a person who enters an enclosed stall in a public toilet, with the door closed behind him, is entitled, at least, to the modicum of privacy its design affords, certainly to the extent that he will not be joined by an uninvited guest or spied upon by probing eyes in a head physically intruding into the area."

STATE v. BRYANT, 177 N.W. 2d 800 (MINN. 1970)

The protection supervisor of a Montgomery Ward store in St. Paul became aware that unknown persons had cut a hole waist-high through the partition separating two toilet stalls in the men's public toilet in the store. The supervisor suspected that the toilet stalls were being illegally used by homosexuals and requested assistance from the St. Paul police. A police officer and the supervisor began surveillance by observing the toilet stalls through a ventilator in the ceiling. The defendant was arrested when he was observed performing an act of oral sodomy by means of the hole cut in the toilet partition. The only question before the Supreme Court of Minnesota is whether the testimony of the police officer and the store supervisor is admissible.

THE COURT after citing all the preceding public toilet cases: "We view as controlling the case of *Katz v. United States*. . . . It is understandable that a large department store would desire to eliminate a use of restrooms that would be revolting to most people who wished to use the facilities properly. There were, however, ways of eliminating such use of the facilities other than surreptitious surveillance. The store had known about the hole in the partition for some time before defendant was apprehended, but had not closed it. The store could have removed the doors if it saw fit, so that anyone using the facilities would have no expectation of privacy; or it could have posted signs warning anyone using the facilities that they were apt to be under surveillance. But once facilities are provided wherein those using them properly are assured of privacy, the store has no right to destroy that privacy without the consent, actual or implied, of one to whom it has been assured. In the very nature of things, in the process of protecting the innocent all search and seizure prohibitions inevitably afford protection to some guilty persons; but the rights of the innocent may not be sacrificed to apprehend the guilty.

"We think that those using the facilities provided by the store in a proper manner would have been quite shocked to know that they were under surveillance. We are convinced that the evidence obtained in this manner is inadmissible.... Reversed." [Three justices dissented in this case.]

BIELICKI v. SUPERIOR COURT, 371 P.2d 288 (CAL. APP. 1962)
BRITT v. SUPERIOR COURT, 374 P.2d 817 (CAL. APP. 1962)

The California courts also reversed convictions and held similar testimony inadmissible in factual situation similar to the Bryant case.

PEOPLE v. CRAFTS, 91 CAL. RPTR. 563 (CAL. APP. 1970)

The court held that the defendant did not have a reasonable expectation to privacy when he was found engaging in oral copulation in the public portion of public rest rooms.

KIRSCH v. STATE, 271 A.2d 770 (MD. APP. 1970)

A service station attendant called the police and gave them the key to the men's rest room. He had become suspicious of three men who had used the room for over thirty minutes. The police found that the three men had narcotics and narcotics paraphernalia in plain view and were apparently using the toilet as a "shooting gallery." The court held that "At best, the expectation of privacy in a free rest room facility, or any part of it which is intended to be accessible for public use cannot be other than temporary ... no reasonable person would be justified in expecting absolute privacy in, or exclusive use of, the whole of such a facility, particularly where the length of such occupancy and use far exceeded as here, normally permissible limits."

Motor Vehicles

In some respect, the motor vehicle is treated by the law in the same manner as the private premises. However, exceptions are made in the law concerning motor vehicles because of:

1. The mobility of the motor vehicles.
2. The extensive use of the motor vehicle as an instrumentality of crime.
3. The fact that over a half million motor vehicles are stolen every year in the United States.
4. The use by motor vehicles of streets and highways owned by the state. Such use is a privilege which may be and is licensed and regulated by the state.

COTTON v. UNITED STATES, 371 F.2d 385 (9th CIR. 1967)

THE COURT. "We have no doubt that here, even if the mere opening of the door [of the car] to look at the number was a search, it was a reasonable one. The agent had reliable information from the Las Vegas police that the car was stolen and it was entirely reasonable for him to check the car before sending out his inquiry. It was true that he could have obtained a warrant. And if he had found and used evidence that Cotton might have placed in the car, we would hold that he should have done so. But we are of the opinion that when a policeman or a federal agent having jurisdiction has reasonable cause to believe that a car has been stolen, or has any other legitimate reason to identify a car, he may open a door to check the serial number, or open the hood to check the motor number, and that he need not obtain a warrant before doing so in a case where the car is already otherwise lawfully available to him. We express no opinion as to whether he can break into a car without a warrant if the car be locked."

PEOPLE v. FRANK, 305 N.Y.S. 940 (S. CT. N.Y. 1970)

Police had probable cause to believe that the Cadillac in the defendant's possession was stolen. An officer raised the hood of the car to check the motor number. The defendant contends that the raising of the hood was a search covered by the Fourth Amendment and that it was not done with consent, or incident to a lawful arrest, or with warrant.

THE COURT. "The use of motor vehicles upon the highways or streets of the State is a privilege and not a right.... Thus if the privilege extended by the State to operate a motor vehicle may be denied, it follows that the legislature may circumscribe the exercise of that privilege by particular conditions.... Detective Rapp had ample probable cause, from the information he had received from the Bureau of Motor Vehicles, to believe that the Cadillac was a stolen one. He could have, in the circumstances, searched the automobile much more extensively than merely looking at the serial number on the motor to determine the true owner. What he did, he had the power to do even in the absence of a statute such as section 401...."

PEOPLE v. GOLDSTEIN, 304 N.Y.S.2d 106 (S. CT. QUEENS 1969)

A police officer observed the defendant seated behind the wheel of a car parked at the curb at 12:45 A.M. The officer observed the defendant for some time and suspected that the defendant might be there for a criminal purpose. The officer approached the defendant and questioned him as to what he was doing. The defendant stated that he had come from his girl friend's home and had stopped to rest because he was tired. Upon request, the defendant produced his driver's license and vehicle registration. The officer checked the registration with the license number of the car and then opened the front left door to examine the identification number mounted on the front left door jamb. When he opened the door, he observed in plain view a policeman's wooden billy club some 18 inches long lying on the floor next to the door jamb. The officer picked up the billy club, ordered the defendant out of the car, and arrested him for the possession of a dangerous instrument. The question of whether an officer is justified in opening a door of a motor vehicle to verify the serial number was considered by the court.

THE COURT. "...I hold that where the police have legitimate reason to believe that surreptitious circumstances may surround the operation of a vehicle, they may inquire into all areas of identification thereof to verify the accuracy of any document certifying the ownership of the operator, all without a warrant. Such conduct by them is not a search and it is not violative of the defendant's privilege under the Fourth Amendment. When such circumstances exist, and I deem them present in this case, the seizure of contraband in plain view is lawful."

QUESTIONS AND PROBLEMS

For each question choose the answer which best fits the situation.

Available Answers for Questions 1 to 14

1. There was *no* violation of the right of privacy as the plain-view or open-view doctrine would apply.
2. There was *no* violation of the suspect's right of privacy as the abandonment doctrine would apply.
3. This *violates* the Fourth Amendment right of privacy.
4. This *violates* the Sixth Amendment.

1. By using binoculars, police are able to observe the activities of the suspects in a hotel room.
2. While checking a driver's license, an officer sees the butt of a gun on the floor, protruding from under the driver's seat.
3. An exploratory search is made of hotel rooms by police officers going up and down the fire escape peeking into the windows to see if any criminal offenses can be observed.
4. By using a telescopic lens on a camera, police are able to photograph a marijuana party in a private home. They were given permission by the property owner next door to climb his tree for their observation post.
5. A police officer enters the men's toilet in a tavern frequented by homosexuals and observes a criminal act as he walks into the room.

6. Jail cells are bugged, and incriminating evidence is obtained.
7. An officer picks up and examines the exterior surface of an item on a display rack in a store to determine whether the object which is for sale has been stolen.
8. An off-duty officer who is not in uniform observes contraband in plain view in a home. The person who invited the officer into the home did not know he was an officer.
9. While standing on the defendant's property, officers saw and heard the criminal offense take place in the home. The officers were responding to a disturbance call from neighbors and were walking up the front walk.
10. Officers who suspected the defendant walked into his backyard from the alley and stood near a rear window. They were then able to observe and hear the criminal act in the single-family home.
11. Officers who were standing in a common hallway overheard incriminating conversations from inside an apartment. The officers were there with the consent of the landlord, and there were forty apartments in the building.
12. Conversations are overheard by using a parabolic mike. The officers do not have a warrant or court order permitting the placing of the mike against the door of the apartment.
13. Suspecting that a motor vehicle is one which has been stolen, officers examine the vehicle's identification number and the motor number. They do not have probable cause or a search warrant. The car is on the public street.
14. Officers bug the attorneys' conference room in a jail.
15. Note the illustration on p. 397. Indicate when and where a search warrant would be necessary if police wanted to search for and obtain evidence of a crime from:
    a. Curtilage which is enclosed by a fence.
    b. Curtilage which is not enclosed.
    c. Open fields which are owned by the suspect.
    d. Any of the buildings above.
16. Police seek to arrest X for armed robbery. Describe the procedure which may be used in searching the above (15 a, b, c, d) for X without a search warrant or arrest warrant. (See Chap. 17 for entry into private premises.)
17. An anonymous telephone caller states that there is a dead man in the barn above. The owner of the premises refuses to give consent for the search. Must a search warrant be obtained?

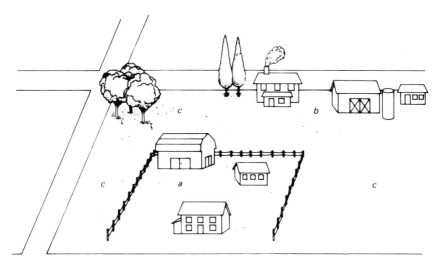

18. Police had probable cause to arrest the defendant for murder. When they arrived at the place where he lived, his landlady accompanied the officers to his room. The door was open (ajar) and the officers entered, seeking to find the defendant. He was not present, but the officers saw a bloody shirt on the bed and seized it as evidence of the crime. May the shirt be used in evidence in the trial of the defendant? (See *State v. Howard*, 162 S.E.2d 495 [N.C. 1968].)

19. A sheriff's department received an anonymous telephone call that X, who lived in a rural area, was bootlegging whiskey. Two officers were sent out to investigate. They parked their car in X's driveway and walked up to X's front door. While walking up to the porch and while on the porch, the officers were alert to anything they could see or smell which would confirm the report which had been received. No one answered their knock on the door and, apparently, no one was in the house. Thinking that X was somewhere on the premises, the officers went out to the barn in an effort to find X. The barn door was open, and they walked in calling for X. No one was in the barn, but they saw on the floor on one side of the barn a pile of freshly harvested marijuana.

    a. Did the officers violate X's right and expectation of privacy? Could the marijuana be used in evidence against X?

    b. Would the results be different if, in looking for X, the officers had not gone into the barn but had seen the marijuana from the open door of the barn?

17
ENTRY INTO PRIVATE PREMISES

The question of when an officer may lawfully enter private premises has presented itself in many of the cases of this text up to this point. This chapter will attempt to summarize and present the law of entry into private premises.

AUTHORITY TO ENTER

Entry into private premises may be made by law enforcement officers:

1. If consent to enter was given. (See Chap. 12.)
2. If the officers were responding to an exigency or emergency. (See Chap. 8.) In *McDonald v. United States*, 335 U.S. 451 (1948), it was held that "a shot and a cry for help" is justification for entry.
3. If the officers were in hot pursuit of a fleeing felon. (See Chap. 8 and *Warden v. Hayden* in that chapter.)
4. If the goods ultimately seized were in the process of being destroyed. (See Chap. 8 and *Schmerber v. California* and *Ker v. California* in that chapter.)
5. If the goods to be seized were about to be removed from the jurisdiction or were to be moved from a known place to an unknown place. (See the Dorman, Pino, and Hailes cases, where the "principle of urgent need" is discussed.)
6. If the officers have a valid search warrant to search the premises.

AUTHORITY TO ENTER PRIVATE PREMISES TO MAKE AN ARREST

In addition to the six authorities to enter which are listed above, there is the additional authority to enter to make an arrest. The requirements which follow are *also* applicable to *all* entries into private premises without consent.

Unless there are state statutes to the contrary, the general rule for entry has been held to be that the validity of the entry to execute an arrest must be tested by criteria identical with the standards required of forced entry to execute a search warrant. (See *Miller v. United States* in case section.)

BASIC CRITERIA FOR ENTRY

1. The authority to make a lawful arrest must exist (or one of the other six authorities must exist).
2. There must be a reasonable belief that the suspect is present and the officer must be reasonably sure that he has the right premises and the right man. In the event of a mistake or a challenge to the entry, the officer must be able to point to objective evidence justifying his belief that he had the right man, the right premises, and reasonable grounds to believe that the suspect was present. Such objective evidence could be:
   a. Actual observation of the suspect's entry by an officer or a witness (neighbor or person in the area).
   b. Tip from a reliable informant.
   c. In *Ker v. California* (see cases, Chap. 8) the car which the officers had followed with Ker in it was parked outside the apartment house with a warm engine.
3. The officer seeking to make the arrest should knock, identify himself, state his purpose, and await a refusal or silence before entering. There are two good reasons for imposing such requirements on unannounced police entries into private premises:
   a. Possibility of mistake: "... cases of mistaken identity are surely not novel in the investigation of crime. The possibility is very real that the police may be misinformed as to the name or address of a suspect, or as to other material information.... Innocent citizens should not suffer the shock, fright or embarrassment attendant upon an unannounced police intrusion" *Ker v. California* (see cases, Chap. 8).
   b. Protection of the officers: "... [It] is also a safeguard for the police themselves who might be mistaken for prowlers and be shot down by a fearful householder." *Miller v. United States* (see cases).
4. The entry may be made without announcing the identity and purpose of the police if the officer has reasonable grounds to believe that the suspect is present and also has reasonable grounds to believe that by announcing his presence:

a. Such notice is likely to endanger the life or the safety of the officer or another person.

b. Such notice is likely to result in the evidence subject to seizure being easily and quickly destroyed or disposed of (see *Ker v. California*, Chap. 8).

c. Such notice is likely to enable the party to be arrested to escape.

d. Such notice would be a useless gesture.

Note: The officer must be able to justify his action by pointing to objective evidence which gave him the authority to enter without announcement. The mere opportunity to hide evidence may not be sufficient justification for an unannounced entry where such evidence would be difficult to destroy.

> *Example:* Suppose that the evidence being sought was stolen truck tires. No court would accept the argument that the tires could quickly and easily be destroyed or hidden.

(See the 1970 federal knock or no-knock statute on p. 411 in this chapter.)

Types of Entry

For the purposes of this chapter, entry into private premises will be divided into the following categories with cases illustrating each category: (1) entry without force, (2) entry with force, and (3) entry by trick, ruse, or subterfuge.

ENTRY WITHOUT FORCE

PREVIOUS TEXT CASES WHERE ENTRY WITHOUT FORCE WAS AN ISSUE

Warden v. Hayden, Chap. 8: entry held valid
Ker. v. California, Chap. 8: entry held valid
Vale v. Louisiana, Chap. 9: entry held invalid
Wong Sun v. United States, Chap. 5: Blackie Toy entry held invalid
Fahy v. United States, Chap. 5: entry held invalid

MCDONALD v. UNITED STATES, 335 U.S. 451 (U.S. S. CT. 1948)

> The police suspected the defendant of gambling and had him under surveillance for two months. At a time when the numbers game was usually functioning, an officer who was outside of the defendant's boardinghouse thought he heard an adding machine. One of the officers entered the house through the landlady's window. The officer identified himself to the landlady and received her consent to admit the other officers. The officers went up to the second floor and by standing

on a chair could look into the defendant's room through the transom. Money, betting slips, and adding machines were in the room with the defendant and another man. The officers yelled to open the door, and when the defendant did, he and the other man were arrested. The Court reversed the conviction stating, "... We will not assume that where a defendant has been under surveillance for months, no search warrant could have been obtained.... When the officers heard the adding machine and, at the latest, when they saw what was transpiring in the room, they certainly had adequate grounds for seeking a search warrant."

STATE v. CHINN, 373 P.2d 392 (S. CT. OREG. 1962)

Portland police receive a report that a twelve-year-old girl was missing. The next day the mother told the police that the girl had returned and that she had been sexually abused by a man known only as "Ray." The girl told a police officer that she was taken to Ray's apartment (address given), was given beer, and had sexual relations with Ray in his bed. Ray then took her picture in his bed. On the basis of this information, the officer obtained an arrest warrant for Ray. No search warrant was obtained or sought. The officer then went to the apartment, but no one answered the door. The apartment was kept under surveillance for four hours until two men were seen entering. The officers knocked at the door and were admitted. The two men informed the officers that neither of them was Ray but that Ray would be along shortly. The officers looked through the apartment for Ray but did not find him. They saw the camera and the six-pack of empty beer bottles in plain view in Ray's bedroom but did not seize the items. After another wait, a man answering to the name of Ray entered the apartment. He was immediately placed under arrest, and the officers then seized the camera, the beer bottles, and a bed sheet. When the film in the camera was developed, a picture was obtained showing the twelve-year-old in the defendant's bed. The beer bottle had the girl's fingerprints on it, and the linen showed that sexual intercourse had occurred. The evidence was admitted as being obtained subsequent to a lawful arrest.

UNITED STATES v. MORRISON, 262 F.2d 449 (CT. APP. FOR D.C., 1958)

Washington, D.C., police officers were informed that a perverted sexual act was committed on a ten-year-old boy. When officers arrived at the boy's home, the boy and his older brother were taken in a police car to show the officers the premises where the alleged offense took place. The building was only partially completed, as the defendant was building his own home. The defendant, however, was living in the basement. The officers were told by another brother of the boy who was at the scene that he had been watching the house and that the defendant was in the building. The officers knocked at the front door several times but received no response. One of the officers walked around to the back of the house and entered the house through the basement. The officer then came upstairs through the structure and opened the front door for his brother officer. The officers searched the house for the defendant, but he was not in the building.

The boys then entered the house and the ten-year-old boy showed the officers the room in which he said the incident occurred. The boy pointed out a handkerchief which the boy said was used by defendant and which bore tangible evidence of the offense. The officers took the handkerchief. When the defendant arrived, he was arrested and the question on appeal is whether the handkerchief may be used in evidence against the defendant. The motion to suppress the evidence was granted.

PEOPLE v. BRADLEY, 81 CAL. RPTR. 457 (CAL. APP. 1969)

After an officer found marijuana growing in the defendant's yard, he attempted to obtain a search warrant but was unsuccessful because a judge was unavailable late at night. The officer and four other officers then went to the defendant's home at 3:15 A.M. The door of the residence was fully open. With the use of a flashlight, the officer could see a man on a bed. The officers entered the home and as they did, the man sat up in bed. The officers identified themselves and told the man that he was under arrest for the possession of marijuana. After informing the defendant of his "constitutional rights," the officer asked whether the defendant minded if a search was made of the house. The defendant told the officers to go ahead. The search disclosed more marijuana and narcotics paraphernalia. The court held that the entry was unlawful under California law (section 844). Therefore the arrest and search of the house were unlawful. The court stated, "Although section 844 codified the common law rule requiring peace officers to demand admittance and explain their purpose before they break open a door or window, the section is silent or inexplicit as to whether the officers must make such a demand and explanation before they enter a house through an open door. Even if at common law an unannounced intrusion through an open door was lawful, we are satisfied in view of the purposes of section 844 ... that the demand and explanation requirements of that section also apply where, as here, officers walk into a dwelling through an open door at nighttime where the occupant apparently is asleep. Under the circumstances here appearing there was a breaking within the meaning of the section. The consequences of such an unannounced intrusion could be resistance to the intruders and violent death or injury to them or others including innocent third parties. The burden of complying with the demand and explanation requirement of section 844 is slight...."

JOHNSON v. UNITED STATES, 333 U.S. 10 (U.S. S. CT. 1948)

This case is also discussed in Chap. 12, "Authority to Search with Consent." The officers in this case could smell the burning opium in the hall of the hotel. The Court held: "Entry to defendant's living quarters which was the beginning of the search, was demanded under color of office.... No reason is offered for not obtaining a search warrant except the inconvenience to the officers and some slight delay necessary to prepare papers and present the evidence to a magistrate. These are never very convincing reasons and, in these circumstances, are not enough to by-pass the constitutional requirement. No suspect was fleeing or likely to take flight. The search was of permanent premises, not of a movable vehicle. No evidence or contraband was threatened with removal or destruction, except perhaps the fumes which we suppose in time would disappear.... The Government, in effect, concedes that the arresting officer did not have probable cause to arrest petitioner until he had entered her room and found her to be the sole occupant. It points out specifically, referring to the time just before entry, 'For at that time just before entry, the agents did not know whether there was one or several persons in the room. It was reasonable to believe that the room might have been an opium smoking den.' And it says, '...that when the agents were admitted into the room and found only the petitioner present they had a reasonable basis for believing that she had been smoking opium and thus illicitly possessed the narcotics.' Thus the Government quite properly stakes the right to arrest, not on the informer's tip and the smell the officers recognized before entry, but on the knowledge that she was alone in the room, gained only after, and wholly by reason of, their entry of her home. It was therefore their observations inside of her quarters, after they had obtained admission under color of their police authority, on which they made the arrest."

[*Authors' Note:* The Johnson case is over twenty years old; it was a 5-4 decision in 1948. It is the opinion of the authors that with the new safeguards imposed by the U.S. Supreme Court in the 1960s, the probable-cause requirements have been lowered in recent years. The authors believe that if the Johnson case was heard before the Court today, it would be held that probable cause did exist *before* the entry of the officers into the hotel room.]

ENTRY WITH FORCE

PREVIOUS TEXT CASES WHERE ENTRY WITH FORCE WAS AN ISSUE

Mapp v. Ohio, Chap. 5: entry held invalid
Schmerber v. California, Chap. 8: entry into the body held valid
Dorman v. United States, Chap. 8: entry held valid

UNITED STATES v. BLANK, 251 F. SUPP. 166 (1966)

In a Cleveland gambling raid, Internal Revenue Service agents with a search warrant went to the apartment where the defendant lived. Instead of ringing for the apartment superintendent, they smashed a window and opened the lobby door. They then went to apartment 6 and began breaking the door down with an ax as they chanted, "Come on, Johnny Blank, we know that you are in there." The agents stumbled over the remains of the door and began the search. The court suppressed the evidence obtained stating, "...it is the opinion of this Court that agents who are executing a search warrant directed to a single apartment must act within reason in gaining entrance to the main premises. We further find that, if the outer doors are locked, the agents must afford some authorized person an opportunity to permit them to enter peacefully before force may be employed to effect entrance. We further find that each tenant in an apartment building has a constitutionally protected interest in the integrity of the entire apartment building.... We further find that the illegal character of their entry permeates the entire search with the taint of its illegality, so that all evidence which the agents obtained by reason of their presence on the premises must be suppressed."

HAILES v. UNITED STATES, 267 A.2d 363 (D.C. CT. APP. 1970)

About one o'clock in the morning, a Washington, D.C., officer received information from a reliable informant that one "Popeye" (known to the officer) had received a shipment of about a pound of heroin. The informant stated that "Popeye" and a man named "Gumdrop" were going to move the heroin elsewhere to cut it and cap it. The officer called an assistant U.S. attorney to obtain a search warrant for "Popeye's" apartment. The attorney told the officer that it would take three hours to obtain a warrant and suggested that under the circumstances the officers enter the apartment without a warrant. The officer then called his informant again and was told that heroin was still at the apartment but that the men had guns and were not afraid to use them. Six or eight officers met the informant, who pointed out "Popeye's" apartment. The officers knocked at the door and announced their purpose. When they received no response, they made a forced entry. No one was in the apartment. The officers searched and found the heroin, cocaine, and six pistols and ammunition. They seized these items. A few hours later, the defendant was arrested on the street. The court sustained the entry and search and seizure, stating, "We have no doubt that there was probable cause for the issuance of an arrest warrant based on the information Officer Hartford had. We are also convinced that there was sufficient information upon which a search warrant could have been issued for the appellant's apartment. Nonetheless, we think that the 'principle of urgent need' justified the warrantless entry. Certainly, reliable information in the early morning hours that a large supply of heroin is to be transported in a few hours from a certain to an uncertain location for processing demands immediate police action to apprehend the suspects. In this case, where no magistrate was available, there existed an urgent need for a warrantless entry to effect their arrest.... When the officers entered the apartment and discovered it empty, they could not know whether the heroin had yet been removed. It was imperative that they ascertain immediately whether it had been; otherwise, they would have been unable to determine whether further investigation was needed...."

[Note: The court in the Hailes case cited *Dorman v. United States*, which is in Chap. 8, as authority on the "principle of urgent need."]

TEXAS v. GONZALES, 388 F.2d 145 (1968)

Officers suspected the defendant and others of narcotics violations. They had a search warrant which proved to be invalid. The state argued that the raid followed by the search and seizure could be sustained without the warrant. The officers had the house under surveillance for a number of hours. During this time, the officers made three trips into the yard and onto the property to peek and peer into the windows of the house. When the officers concluded that the persons in the house were capping heroin, they rushed a door hollering "police." They broke the door down and after a short skirmish arrested the defendant and others. The court held that the conduct of the officers amounted to an unreasonable search and seizure because the trips into the yard to the window of the house were made at a time when they lacked probable cause to believe that narcotics were present in the home. The court stated, "The aversion to the exploratory search has deep roots and the fourth amendment condemnation of this practice refutes the State's circular argument that the fruits of the search can justify the arrest or that the search can be justified by the subsequent arrest."

ENTRY BY TRICK, RUSE, OR SUBTERFUGE

TEXT CASES WHERE ENTRY BY TRICK, RUSE, OR SUBTERFUGE IS AN ISSUE

Lewis v. United States, Chap. 19: entry held valid
Hoffa v. United States, Chap. 19: entry held valid
Osborn v. United States, Chap. 19: entry held valid

PONCE v. CRAVEN, 409 F.2d 621 (9th CIR. 1969)

After police officers had probable cause to believe that the defendant had narcotics paraphernalia in a motel room, they had the problem of entry. They had their police department telephone the motel and ask to talk to the woman in unit 12. As the rooms did not have telephones, the manager knocked on the door, telling the woman that she was wanted on the phone. When the woman opened the door, the police immediately entered the room and arrested her and the defendant. The California court and the federal courts held the police entry and arrest to be lawful. The appellate court stated, "The lawfulness of an arrest by state authorities for a state offense must be tested by resorting to applicable state law so long as it is not violative of the protection set forth in the Federal Constitution. . . . It is clear from the language of section 844 (California Code) that only if police resort to a breaking must they announce their purpose. The employment of a ruse which results in the occupant of a dwelling voluntarily opening the door and thereby allowing officers to enter without announcement of purpose, is not a breaking and, therefore, not violative of California arrest law. The California Court of Appeal held that the police entry in this case was not unlawful merely because a ruse was employed." The court cites *People v. Quilon*, 54 Cal. Rptr. 294 (1966), which states the rule: ". . . constitutionally proscribed trickery is that in which an officer obtains entry by subterfuge to a place where he has no right to be. Stratagem in itself is not illegal; it may be used, for example, to gain entry in order to effect a lawful arrest."

UNITED STATES v. ST. CLAIR, 240 F. SUPP. 338 (S.D. N.Y. 1965)

Two federal agents and a New York detective had the defendant under surveillance for narcotics violations. When they saw lights in his apartment, they rang the landlord's bell and, after identifying themselves, requested admission to the apartment building. The landlord refused, stating that all of his tenants were law-abiding. A discussion ensued, and there was a general commotion in the vestibule area. One of the officers circled the group and walked through the open vestibule door. He went down the hall to the defendant's door and knocked. When the defendant answered the door, the officer arrested him. The court held that the officer had properly announced his authority and purpose prior to entering the apartment. The court also held that there was no impropriety in the manner in which the agents gained entrance to the hallway.

GATEWOOD v. UNITED STATES, 209 F.2d 789 (U.S. APP. D.C. 1953)

Officers knocked on the defendant's door, announcing that they were from Western Union. The defendant opened the door partway and when he saw the officers, he attempted to close it. The officers forced the door open. The court held that fraud followed by force constituted a breaking. (*Authors' Note:* Before forcing the door, the officers should have identified themselves and stated their purpose. Then if there was a refusal or silence, a forceful entry could have been made.)

LEAHY v. UNITED STATES, 272 F.2d 487 (9th CIR. 1959), CERT. DENIED, 364 U.S. 945 (1961)

IRS agents had a warrant for the arrest of the defendant. They represented themselves as being agents from the county assessor's office. After they were admitted to the defendant's home, they arrested him. After the court cited *Miller v. United States* (see cases) and the preceding Gatewood case, it noted that "the element of force was present in each of the cited cases which distinguishes them from the instant case.... There is no constitutional mandate forbidding the use of deception in executing a valid arrest warrant." After quoting *Sherman v. United States*—"Criminal activity is such that stealth and strategy are necessary weapons in the arsenal of the police officer"—the court in this case stated, "Such weapons were necessary and wisely used here. The record discloses that the door to appellant's premises was a heavy one and would require much time and labor to break open. The officers feared that if they announced their identity before entry, evidence would be destroyed and other establishments which were simultaneously raided warned before entry could be made therein. Violence was also feared, and such fear was later supported by the finding of rifles, shotguns and eight pistols on the premises. In analogous cases and similar circumstances courts have refused to condemn the use of deception."

DICKEY v. UNITED STATES, 332 F.2d 773 (9th CIR. 1964), CERT. DENIED, 379 U.S. 948

Narcotics officers received information from an informant that the defendant was in a hotel room and was ready to sell narcotics to a man named Lacey. The officers did not have a search warrant or arrest warrant. They obtained a key to the room from the hotel manager. As an officer was inserting the key and before he turned the key, the defendant asked from inside the hotel room, "Who's there?" The officer with the key disguised his voice and said, "It's Lacey; open up." Dickey opened the door and when he saw the officers, he turned and tossed a package to his wife who was in the room. The officers entered the room and recovered the package, which contained heroin. Mr. and Mrs. Dickey were then arrested. The court sustained the entry, stating, "Had entry into Dickey's hotel room been gained by the use of the pass key, this would have been a 'breaking' of the door within the meaning of Sec. 3109. But entry was not gained by that means and the noise made when the key was inserted into the lock had no more significance than a knock at the door. Had the officers obtained, by ruse, a partial opening of Dickey's door, and if they had then forced open the door the rest of the way to gain entrance, this would have been a 'breaking' in the sense of section 3109 Gatewood v. U.S. But the employment of a ruse to obtain the full opening of the Dickeys' door unassociated with force was not a 'breaking'. Leahy v. U. S. And since the door was then wide open, the subsequent entry into Dickey's room for the purpose of arresting him did not involve a 'breaking' of the door. It is true that the officers seized the narcotics before effectuating the arrest. This was because exigent circumstances arose which made this course necessary in order to preserve the evidence. The officers already had probable cause to make the arrest and since it was made immediately after the seizure the latter was substantially contemporaneous with the valid arrest."

PEOPLE v. LAWRENCE, 308 P.2d 821 (CAL. 1957)

The officers gained entrance to the defendant's premises by having a friend of the defendant ring the bell and ask for admittance. The court held, "The fact that officers gained admittance to the entry hall by subterfuge in order to make the arrest is immaterial. The officers had reasonable cause to believe defendant had committed a felony and the fact that they resorted to trickery to get the door to defendant's apartment open in order to arrest him has no bearing upon the justification for the arrest."

PEOPLE v. SCOTT, 339 P.2d 162 (CAL. 1959)

In order to gain admittance to the home, the officers dressed in white smocks and carried a green leather couch. The defendant's wife opened the door, and the officers walked in and arrested the defendant. The court sustained the entry and the arrest.

GOULED v. UNITED STATES, 255 U.S. 298 (U.S. S. CT. 1921)

The defendant was suspected of defrauding the government through contracts for clothing and equipment. A U.S. Army private who was a business acquaintance of the defendant was instructed to contact him. The private was working with Army Intelligence. On the pretense of making a friendly call, the private was invited into the defendant's office. While the defendant was out of the room, the private took several papers. One of the papers was used in evidence against the defendant. The U.S. Supreme Court suppressed the use of this paper as evidence, stating, "The prohibition of the Fourth Amendment is against all unreasonable searches and seizures and if for a Government officer to obtain entrance to a man's house or office by force or by an illegal threat or show of force, amounting to coercion, and then to search for and seize his private papers would be an unreasonable and therefore a prohibited search and seizure, as it certainly would be, it is impossible to successfully contend that a like search and seizure would be a reasonable one if only admission were obtained by stealth instead of by force or coercion. . . ."

SUMMARY

Officers seeking entrance to private premises *must* have authority to make an entrance and must follow the statutory or common-law rules of their jurisdiction in making the entrance.

Example: X is wanted for recently committed robbery. Officers who do not have an arrest warrant or a search warrant go to his home. His mother answers the door and states that X is not in the house and refuses to give the officers permission to search the house. The officers may suspect that X is in the house but unless they have reasonable belief sustained by objective evidence, they do not have the authority to enter the house. They have the alternatives of keeping the house under surveillance and/or attempting to obtain a search warrant.

However, if an exigency arises or "the inherent necessities at the time" justify an entrance, then the officers may act. The following situation confronted Milwaukee officers in 1970.

Example: X was wanted for a recently committed burglary. Officers went to his home and were told that he was not there but might be at his girl friend's house. The officers went to his girl friend's house. She answered the door and told the officers that she was the only person in the house. She refused consent to search the house. As the officers were leaving, one of the officers looked through a window of the house and saw a young man matching X's description in the house. The officers then demanded admittance to the house and apprehended X. The girl friend was also taken in and charged with obstructing an officer.

Officers should inform and remind persons who state that wanted persons are not in the premises that they may be charged with a crime if they are not telling the truth. Depending upon the statutes of the jurisdiction, the crimes which may be charged are (1) harboring and aiding felons and (2) resisting or obstructing an officer.

BASIC CRITERIA FOR POLICE ENTRY INTO PRIVATE PREMISES

1. The authority to make a lawful arrest must exist, or one of the following justifications must exist:
   a. Consent to enter from a person authorized to give consent.
   b. Response to an exigency or emergency.
   c. Officers in hot pursuit of a fleeing felon.
   d. Contraband or evidence ultimately seized was in the process of being destroyed (*Schmerber v. California*).
   e. If the contraband to be seized is about to be removed from the jurisdiction. See Chap. 8 and the principle of urgent need in *Dorman v. United States* and *Pino v. United States*.
   f. If the officer has a valid search warrant to search the premises.

2. There must be a reasonable belief that the suspect is present and that the officer is reasonably sure that he has the right premises and the right man (officer must show by pointing to objective evidence).

3. The officer seeking to make the arrest should knock, identify himself, state his purpose, and await a refusal or silence before entering.
   Reasons for the knock requirement
   a. Possibility of mistake (see *Ker v. California*)
   b. Protection of the officer (*Miller v. United States*)

4. The entry may be made without announcing the identity and purpose of the police if the officer has reasonable grounds to believe that the suspect is present and also has reasonable grounds to believe that by announcing his presence:
   a. Such notice is likely to endanger the life or the safety of the officer or another person.
   b. Such notice is likely to result in the evidence subject to seizure being easily and quickly destroyed or disposed of (see *Ker v. California*).
   c. Such notice is likely to facilitate the escape of the person(s) to be arrested.

   (The 1970 federal knock or no-knock statute provides for a no-knock entry if such notice would be a useless gesture.)

District of Columbia Court Reform and Criminal Procedure Act of 1970 ("Knock or no-knock" section)

SUBCHAPTER VI—AUTHORITY TO BREAK AND ENTER UNDER CERTAIN CONDITIONS

§ 23–591. Authority to break and enter under certain conditions

(a) Any officer authorized by law to make arrests, or to execute search warrants, or any person aiding such an officer, may break and enter any premises, any outer or inner door or window of a dwelling house or other building, or any part thereof, any vehicle, or anything within such dwelling house, building, or vehicle, or otherwise enter to execute search or arrest warrants, to make an arrest where authorized by law without a warrant, or where necessary to liberate himself or a person aiding him in the execution of such warrant or in making such arrest.

(b) Breaking and entry shall not be made until after such officer or person makes an announcement of his identity and purpose and the officer reasonably believes that admittance to the dwelling house or other building or vehicle is being denied or unreasonably delayed.

(c) An announcement of identity and purpose shall not be required prior to such breaking and entry—

(1) if the warrant expressly authorizes breaking and entry without such a prior announcement, or

(2) if circumstances known to such officer or person at the time of breaking and entry, but, in the case of the execution of a warrant, unknown to the applicant when applying for such warrant, give him probable cause to believe that—

(A) such notice is likely to result in the evidence subject to seizure being easily and quickly destroyed or disposed of,

(B) such notice is likely to endanger the life or safety of the officer or another person,

(C) such notice is likely to enable the party to be arrested to escape, or

(D) such notice would be a useless gesture.

(d) Whoever, after notice is given under subsection (b) or after entry where such notice is unnecessary under subsection (c), destroys, conceals, disposes of, or attempts to destroy, conceal, or dispose of, or otherwise prevents or attempts to prevent the seizure of, evidence subject to seizure shall be fined not more than $5,000 or imprisoned for not more than 5 years, or both.

(e) As used in this section and in subchapters II and IV, the terms 'break and enter' and 'breaking and entering' include any use of physical force or violence or other unauthorized entry but do not include entry obtained by trick or stratagem.

CASES FOR CHAPTER SEVENTEEN

MILLER v. UNITED STATES
SUPREME COURT OF THE UNITED STATES
357 U.S. 301, 78 S. CT. 1190, 2 L. ED. 2d 1332 (1958)

Mr. Justice Brennan delivered the opinion of the Court.

Petitioner, William Miller, together with Bessie Byrd and her brother, Arthur R. Shepherd, was tried and convicted in the District Court for the District of Columbia for conspiracy to commit violations, and violations, of the federal narcotics laws. 26 U. S. C. (Supp. V) § 4704 (a), 21 U. S. C. § 174, 18 U. S. C. § 371. The Court of Appeals for the District of Columbia Circuit affirmed, one judge dissenting. We granted certiorari to determine whether evidence seized at the time of petitioner's arrest was properly admitted against the petitioner. The evidence was $100 of marked currency which was seized by the federal officers who arrested the petitioner and Bessie Byrd at their apartment.

On March 25, 1955, at 1:35 a. m., Clifford Reed was arrested, under an arrest warrant, on a Washington, D. C., street on suspicion of narcotics offenses. Reed revealed to Wilson, a federal narcotics agent, that he purchased heroin in 100-capsule quantities from the petitioner through Shepherd. Agent Wilson knew of the petitioner as one who had trafficked in narcotics and had been convicted for a narcotics offense in 1953. Reed said that he was to meet Shepherd later that morning to make a purchase. Agent Wilson enlisted his aid to apprehend Shepherd and the petitioner. About 3 a. m. another federal narcotics agent, Lewis, carrying $100 of marked currency, went with Reed in a taxicab to Shepherd's home. Reed introduced Lewis to Shepherd as a buyer. Shepherd accepted the $100 and agreed to secure 100 capsules of heroin from the petitioner and deliver them to Lewis at Reed's apartment. Shepherd proceeded alone in the taxicab to the petitioner's apartment.

The taxicab was followed by agent Wilson, officer Wurms of the Metropolitan Police Department, and other officers in police cars. Shepherd was seen to leave the taxicab in front of the apartment house where the petitioner and Bessie Byrd occupied a two-room-and-bath basement apartment. The taxicab waited. Shepherd entered the basement but agent Wilson, who looked into the basement hall, could not see where he went. Shepherd came out of the basement within a few minutes and re-entered the taxicab. The taxicab was proceeding toward Reed's apartment when the officers following in the police cars intercepted it. Shepherd was arrested and searched. He did not have the marked bills on his person but admitted to agent Wilson and officer Wurms that a package of 100 capsules of narcotics found under the taxicab's front seat was put there by him when the police cars stopped the taxicab. He said that he had taken the package from behind a fire extinguisher in the basement hall where he had been sent by a "fellow" with Reed who had promised him $10 for getting it.

The federal officers returned immediately to the apartment building. About 3:45 a. m. agent Wilson and officer Wurms went to the door of the petitioner's apartment. Officer Wurms knocked and, upon the inquiry from within—"Who's there?"—replied in a low voice, "Police." The petitioner opened the door on an attached door chain and asked what the officers were doing there. Before either responded, he attempted to close the door. Thereupon, according to officer Wurms, "we put our hands inside the door and pulled and ripped the chain off, and entered." The officers had no arrest or search warrant. They did not expressly demand admission or state their purpose for their presence, nor did they place the petitioner under arrest until after they entered the apartment.

Bessie Byrd was also arrested in the apartment and turned over the cash she had in her housecoat. The cash included $34 of the marked currency. After an extended search the remaining $66 of marked currency was found, some in a hatbox in a closet, and the rest within the covers of a bed in the bedroom.

The Government contends that there was probable cause for arresting the petitioner and that the marked currency was properly admitted in evidence because it was seized as an incident to a lawful arrest. *Harris* v. *United States*, 331 U. S. 145. The petitioner's argument breaks down into three contentions: (1) that the officers had no probable cause to arrest the petitioner without a warrant; (2) that the search was not justified as being an incident of a lawful arrest; (3) that the arrest, and therefore the search, was in any event unlawful because the officers broke the door of petitioner's home without first giving notice of their authority and purpose in demanding admission. If any one of these contentions prevails, it is agreed that the marked money was inadmissible in evidence. In the view we take, we need consider only petitioner's third contention.

The lawfulness of the arrest of petitioner depends upon the power of the arresting officers to "break" the doors of a home in order to arrest without warrant persons suspected of having committed narcotics offenses. Agent Wilson did not have statutory authority to arrest without a warrant although officer Wurms, as a member of the Metropolitan Police Department, did have such authority. This Court has said, in the similar circumstance of an arrest for violation of federal law by state peace officers, that the lawfulness of the arrest without warrant is to be determined by reference to state law. By like reasoning the validity of the arrest of petitioner is to be determined by reference to the law of the District of Columbia.

In making reference to that law we are mindful of our policy of not interfering with local rules of law fashioned by the courts of the District of Columbia. But the Government agrees with petitioner that the validity of the entry to execute the arrest without warrant must be tested by criteria identical with those embodied in 18 U. S. C. § 3109, which deals with entry to execute a search warrant. That section provides that an officer, executing a search warrant, may break open a door only if, "after notice of his authority and purpose," he is denied admittance. The Government states in its brief that, "where an arrest is made on probable cause rather than a warrant, these statutory requirements must be met before an officer can force entry into an apartment." These statutory requirements are substantially identical to those judicially developed by the Court of Appeals for the District of Columbia Circuit in *Accarino* v. *United States*, 85 U. S. App. D. C. 394, 403, 179 F. 2d 456, 465. Since the rule of *Accarino* bears such a close relationship to a statute which is not confined in operation to the District of Columbia, we believe that review is warranted here.

From earliest days, the common law drastically limited the authority of law officers to break the door of a house to effect an arrest. Such action invades the precious interest of privacy summed up in the ancient adage that a man's house is his castle. As early as the 13th Yearbook of Edward IV (1461–1483), at folio 9, there is a recorded holding that it was unlawful for the sheriff to break the doors of a man's house to arrest him in a civil suit in debt or trespass, for the arrest was then only for the private interest of a party. Remarks attributed to William Pitt, Earl of Chatham, on the occasion of debate in Parliament on the searches incident to the enforcement of an excise on cider, eloquently expressed the principle:

> "The poorest man may in his cottage bid defiance to all the forces of the Crown. It may be frail; its roof may shake; the wind may blow through it; the storm may enter; the rain may enter; but the King of England cannot enter—all his force dares not cross the threshold of the ruined tenement!"

But the common law recognized some authority in law officers to break the door of a dwelling to arrest for felony. The common-law authorities differ, however, as to the circumstances in which this was the case. Hawkins says: "where one lies under a probable Suspicion only, and is not indicted, it seems the better Opinion at this Day, That no one can justify the Breaking open Doors in Order to apprehend him." 2 Hawkins, Pleas of the Crown (1762), c. 14, § 7; see also Foster, Crown Law (1762), 320–321. Coke appears to have been of the same view, and to have thought that the breaking of a house was limited to cases in which a writ, now our warrant, had issued. Co. 4th Inst. 177. On the other hand, Hale says that "A man, that arrests upon suspicion of felony, may break open doors, if the party refuse upon demand to open them. . . ." 1 Hale, Pleas of the Crown (1736), 583.

Whatever the circumstances under which breaking a door to arrest for felony might be lawful, however, the breaking was unlawful where the officer failed first to state his authority and purpose for demanding admission. The requirement was pronounced in 1603 in *Semayne's Case*, 5 Co. Rep. 91a, 11 E. R. C. 629, 77 Eng. Repr. 194, at 195: "In all cases where the King is party, the sheriff (if the doors be not open) may break the party's house, either to arrest him, or to do other execution of the K[ing]'s process, if otherwise he cannot enter. *But before he breaks it, he ought to signify the cause of his coming, and to make request to open doors. . . ."* (Emphasis supplied.)

The requirement stated in *Semayne's Case* still obtains. It is reflected in 18 U. S. C § 3109, in the statutes of a large number of States, and in the American Law Institute's proposed Code of Criminal Procedures, § 28.[1] It applies, as the Government here concedes, whether the arrest is to be made by virtue of a warrant, or when officers are authorized to make an arrest for a felony without a warrant. There are some state decisions holding that justification for noncompliance exists in exigent circumstances, as, for example, when the officers may in good faith believe that they or someone within are in peril of bodily harm or that the person to be arrested is fleeing or attempting to destroy evidence.

But whether unqualified requirements of the rule admit of an exception justifying noncompliance in exigent circumstances is not a question we are called upon to decide in this case. The Government makes no claim here of the existence of circumstances excusing compliance. The Government concedes that compliance was required but argues that "compliance is evident from the events immediately preceding the officers' forced entry."

The rule seems to require notice in the form of an express announcement by the officers of their purpose for demanding admission. The burden of making an express announcement is certainly slight. A few more words by the officers would have satisfied the requirement in this case. It may be that, without an express

---

[1] Code of Crim. Proc., American Law Institute, Official Draft (1930), § 28:
"*Right of officer to break into building.* An officer, in order to make an arrest either by virtue of a warrant, or when authorized to make such arrest for a felony without a warrant, as provided in section 21, may break open a door or window of any building in which the person to be arrested is or is reasonably believed to be, if he is refused admittance after he has announced his authority and purpose."

announcement of purpose, the facts known to officers would justify them in being virtually certain that the petitioner already knows their purpose so that an announcement would be a useless gesture.[2] But even by that test the evidence upon which the Government relies was not sufficient to justify the officers' failure expressly to notify the petitioner that they demanded admission to his apartment for the purpose of arresting him.

The single fact known to the officers upon which the Government relies is the "split-second" occurrence in which the petitioner evinced "instantaneous resistance to their entry," an "almost instinctive attempt to bar their entry after they [the officers] had identified themselves as police...." It is argued that this occurrence "certainly points up that he knew their purpose immediately... [and], at once, realized that he had been detected and that the officers were there to arrest him"; that "[i]t would be wholly unrealistic to say that the officers had not made their purpose known because they did not more formally announce that they were there to arrest him."

But, first, the fact that petitioner attempted to close the door did not of itself prove that he knew their purpose to arrest him. It was an ambiguous act. It could have been merely the expected reaction of any citizen having this experience at that hour of the morning, particularly since it does not appear that the officers were in uniform, and the answer "Police" was spoken "in a low voice" and might not have been heard by the petitioner so far as the officers could tell.

Second, petitioner's reaction upon opening the door could only have created doubt in the officers' minds that he knew they were police intent on arresting him. On the motion to suppress, agent Wilson testified that "he wanted to know what we were doing there." This query, which went unanswered, is on its face inconsistent with knowledge. The majority of the Court of Appeals denied the import of the query by inferring that Miller knew Wilson and Wurms personally and recognized them as soon as he opened the door. That inference has no support in the record.[3] But even if this inference were supportable, Miller's recognition of Wilson and Wurms as police officers would not have justified them, in light of others facts known to them, in being virtually certain that Miller actually knew

[2] Professor Wilgus sums up his discussion of the breaking of doors thus: "Before doors are broken, there must be a necessity for so doing, and notice of the authority and purpose to make the arrest must be given and a demand and refusal of admission must be made, unless this is already understood, or the peril would be increased." 22 Mich. L. Rev. 798, 802. (Footnotes omitted.) The dissenting opinion herein, in footnote 1, mistakenly refers to this passage as if it were a holding "enunciated" by the Court of Appeals. In fact, this passage was merely quoted without approval. The holding was: "Upon one topic there appears to be no dispute in the authorities. Before an officer can break open a door to a home, he must make known the cause of his demand for entry. There is no claim in the case at bar that the officers advised the suspect of the cause of their demand before they broke down the door." Accarino v. United States, 85 U. S. App. D. C. 394, 403, 179 F. 2d 456, 465.

[3] Judge Holtzoff heard the motion to suppress over two months before the trial. Our examination of the record made at that time brings us into complete agreement with Judge Edgerton, who, dissenting in the Court of Appeals, said, "I find no evidence, and the court cites no evidence, that supports an inference that Miller even recognized the officers as the narcotics squad." Even if petitioner could have seen the officers sufficiently to make out their faces, there is no evidence that he knew them personally. The record at best supports an inference, not that either officer personally knew Miller, or that Miller had met, or even heard of, either officer, but only that the officers knew of him as a reputed narcotics violator. Judge Youngdahl presided at the trial and refused to hear a renewed motion to suppress be-

the reason for their presence. The officers knew that petitioner was unaware of Shepherd's arrest; they knew that he was unaware that the currency was marked; they knew that he was unaware that their presence was pursuant to a plan, initiated by Reed's disclosures, to catch the petitioner in a criminal act. Moreover, they did not actually know that petitioner had made a sale to Shepherd and received the marked money, for Shepherd had not talked and had not been seen to enter petitioner's apartment. The fact that the marked money was found in the apartment has no bearing upon the petitioner's knowledge of the officers' purpose since he did not know that the money was marked. This Court said in *United States v. Di Re*, 332 U.S. 581. "We have had frequent occasions to point out that a search is not to be made legal by what it turns up. In law it is good or bad when it starts and does not change character from its success." The most that can be said is that the petitioner's act in attempting to close the door might be the basis for the officers being virtually certain that the petitioner knew there were police at his door conducting an investigation. This, however, falls short of a virtual certainty that the petitioner knew of their purpose to arrest him. The requirement is not met except by notice of that purpose, for the Government admits that the officers had no authority to break the petitioner's door except to arrest him. We must, therefore, conclude that the petitioner did not receive the required notice of authority and purpose.

We are duly mindful of the reliance that society must place for achieving law and order upon the enforcing agencies of the criminal law. But insistence on observance by law officers of traditional fair procedural requirements is, from the long point of view, best calculated to contribute to that end. However much in a particular case insistence upon such rules may appear as a technicality that inures to the benefit of a guilty person, the history of the criminal law proves that tolerance of shortcut methods in law enforcement impairs its enduring effectiveness. The requirement of prior notice of authority and purpose before forcing entry into a home is deeply rooted in our heritage and should not be given grudging application. Congress, codifying a tradition embedded in Anglo-American law, has declared in § 3109 the reverence of the law for the individual's right of privacy in his house.[4] Every householder, the good and the bad, the guilty and the innocent, is entitled to the protection designed to secure the common interest against unlawful invasion of the house. The petitioner could not be lawfully arrested in his home by officers breaking in without first giving him notice of their authority and purpose. Because the petitioner did not receive that notice before the officers broke the door to invade his home, the arrest was unlawful, and the evidence seized should have been suppressed.

Reversed.

Mr. Justice Harlan concurs in the result.

Mr. Justice Clark, with whom Mr. Justice Burton concurs, dissenting.

---

cause he considered the matter settled by Judge Holtzoff's ruling. Agent Wilson's testimony at the trial was again at variance with his testimony before Judge Holtzoff as it had been on the question whether the officers had communicated their purpose to arrest. At the trial he testified that Miller had met him on one occasion before the night of the arrest. Apparently unwilling to rely on this testimony, in the face of its inconsistency, the majority of the Court of Appeals did not allude to it as the basis for its conclusion that Miller recognized the officers.

[4] Compliance is also a safeguard for the police themselves who might be mistaken for prowlers and be shot down by a fearful householder. See concurring opinion in *McDonald v. United States*, 335 U. S. 451, 460–461.

SABBATH v. UNITED STATES
SUPREME COURT OF THE UNITED STATES
391 U.S. 585, 88 S. CT. 1755, 20 L. ED. 2d 828 (1968)

Mr. Justice Marshall delivered the opinion of the Court.

The issue in this case is whether petitioner's arrest was invalid because federal officers opened the closed but unlocked door of petitioner's apartment and entered in order to arrest him without first announcing their identity and purpose. We hold that the method of entry vitiated the arrest and therefore that evidence seized in the subsequent search incident thereto should not have been admitted at petitioner's trial.

On February 19, 1966, one William Jones was detained at the border between California and Mexico by United States customs agents, who found in his possession an ounce of cocaine. After some questioning, Jones told the agents that he had been given the narcotics in Tijuana, Mexico, by a person named "Johnny," whom he had accompanied there from Los Angeles. He said he was to transport the narcotics to "Johnny" in the latter city.

Also found in Jones' possession was a card on which was written the name "Johnny" and a Los Angeles telephone number. On the following day at about 3 p. m., Jones made a call to the telephone number listed on the card; a customs agent dialed the number, and with Jones' permission, listened to the ensuing conversation. A male voice answered the call, and Jones addressed the man as "Johnny." Jones said he was in San Diego, and still had "his thing." The man asked Jones if he had "any trouble getting through the line." Jones replied that he had not. Jones inquired whether "Johnny" planned to remain at home, and upon receiving an affirmative answer, indicated that he was on his way to Los Angeles, and would go to the man's apartment.

At about 7:30 that evening, the customs agents went with Jones to an apartment building in Los Angeles. The agents returned to Jones the cocaine they had seized from him, and placed a small broadcasting device on him. The agents waited outside the building, listening on a receiving apparatus. Jones knocked on the apartment door; a woman answered. Jones asked if "Johnny" was in, and was told to wait a minute. Steps were heard and then a man asked Jones something about "getting through the line." Because of noise from a phonograph in the apartment, reception from the broadcasting device on Jones' person was poor, but agents did hear the word "package."

The customs agents waited outside for five to 10 minutes, and then proceeded to the apartment door. One knocked, waited a few seconds, and, receiving no response, opened the unlocked door, and entered the apartment with his gun drawn. Other agents followed, at least one of whom also had his gun drawn. They saw petitioner sitting on a couch, in the process of withdrawing his hand from under the adjacent cushion. After placing petitioner under arrest, an agent found the package of cocaine under the cushion, and subsequently other items (e. g., small pieces of tin foil) were found in the apartment; officers testified at trial they were adapted to packaging narcotics.

Petitioner and Jones were indicted for knowingly importing the cocaine into this country and concealing it, in violation of § 2 of the Narcotic Drugs Import and Export Act, as amended, 35 Stat. 614, 21 U. S. C. §§ 173 and 174. Petitioner was tried alone. The narcotics seized at petitioner's apartment were admitted into evidence, over objection. On appeal, following the conviction, the Court of Appeals for the Ninth Circuit ruled that the officers, in effecting entry to petitioner's apartment by opening the closed but unlocked door, did not "break open" the door within the meaning of 18 U. S. C. § 3109 and therefore were not required by that statute to make a prior announcement of "authority and purpose." 380 F. 2d 108. We granted certiorari to consider the somewhat uncomplicated but nonetheless significant issue of whether the agents' entry was consonant with federal law.[1] We hold that it was not, and therefore reverse.

The statute here involved, 18 U. S. C. § 3109,[2] deals with the entry of federal officers into a dwelling in terms only in regard to the execution of a search warrant. This Court has held, however, that the validity of such an entry of a federal officer to effect an arrest without a warrant "must be tested by criteria identical with those embodied in" that statute. We therefore agree with the parties and with the court below that we must look to § 3109 as controlling.

In *Miller v. United States, supra,* the common-law background to § 3109 was extensively examined.[3] The Court there concluded, *id.,* at 313:

> "The requirement of prior notice of authority and purpose before forcing entry into a home is deeply rooted in our heritage and should not be given grudging application. Congress, codifying a tradition embedded in Anglo-American law, had declared in § 3109 the reverence of the law for the individual's right of privacy in his house."

It was also noted, *id.,* at 313, n. 12, that another facet of the rule of announcement was, generally, to safeguard officers, who might be mistaken, upon an unannounced intrusion into a home, for someone with no right to be there.

Considering the purposes of § 3109, it would indeed be a "grudging application" to hold, as the Government urges, that the use of "force" is an indispensable element of the statute. To be sure, the statute uses the phrase "break open" and that connotes some use of force. But linguistic analysis seldom is adequate when a statute is designed to incorporate fundamental values and the ongoing development of the common law.[4] Thus, the California Supreme Court has recently inter-

---

[1] The Government contends in this Court that petitioner did not adequately raise at trial the issue of the agents' manner of entry, and therefore that it did not have sufficient opportunity to indicate the full circumstances surrounding the entry and petitioner's arrest. However, petitioner's trial counsel, in the course of objecting, clearly stated there were no facts "sufficient to justify this officer's breaking into" the apartment, and his objection was truncated by a ruling of the trial judge. In any event, the Government met the issue on the merits in the Court of Appeals, and apparently did not there contend the record was inadequate for its resolution; and the Court of Appeals decided the issue on the merits. In these circumstances, we are justified in likewise doing so.

[2] "The officer may break open any outer or inner door or window of a house, or any part of a house, or anything therein, to execute a search warrant, if, after notice of his authority and purpose, he is refused admittance or when necessary to liberate himself or a person aiding him in the execution of the warrant."

[3] See also *Ker v. California,* 374 U. S. 23, 47–59 (1963) (opinion of Brennan, J.).

[4] While distinctions are obvious, a useful analogy is nonetheless afforded by the common and case law development of the law of burglary: a forcible entry has generally been eliminated as an element of that crime under statutes using the word "break," or similar words. See R. Perkins, Criminal Law 149–150 (1957); J. Michael & H. Wechsler, Criminal Law and Its Administration 367–382 (1940); Note, A Rationale of the Law of Burglary, 51 Col. L. Rev. 1009, 1012–1015 (1951). Commentators on the law of arrest have viewed the development of that body of

preted the common-law rule of announcement codified in a state statute identical in relevant terms to § 3109 to apply to an entry by police through a closed but unlocked door. *People* v. *Rosales*, 68 Cal. 2d 299, 437 P. 2d 489 (1968). And it has been held that § 3109 applies to entries effected by the use of a passkey, which requires no more force than does the turning of a doorknob. An unannounced intrusion into a dwelling—what § 3109 basically proscribes—is no less an unannounced intrusion whether officers break down a door, force open a chain lock on a partially open door, open a locked door by use of a passkey, or, as here, open a closed but unlocked door.[5] The protection afforded by, and the values inherent in, § 3109 must be "governed by something more than the fortuitous circumstance of an unlocked door." *Keiningham* v. *United States*, 109 U. S. App. D. C. 272, 276, 287 F. 2d 126, 130 (1960).

The Government seeks to invoke an exception to the rule of announcement, contending that the agents' lack of compliance with the statute is excused because an announcement might have endangered the informant Jones or the officers themselves. However, whether or not "exigent circumstances," *Miller* v. *United States*, 357 U.S. 301, would excuse compliance with § 3109,[6] this record does not reveal any substantial basis for excusing the failure of the agents here to announce their authority and purpose. The agents had no basis for assuming petitioner was armed or might resist arrest, or that Jones was in any danger. Nor, as to the former, did the agents make any independent investigation of petitioner prior to setting the stage for his arrest with the narcotics in his possession.

The judgment of the Court of Appeals is reversed, and the case is remanded for further proceedings consistent with this opinion.

Reversed and remanded.

Mr. Justice Black dissents.

QUESTIONS AND PROBLEMS

In Questions 1 through 10, indicate the circumstances which would justify the type of entry stated in the question.

---

law as similar. See H. Voorhees, Law of Arrest §§ 159, 172–173 (1904); Wilgus, Arrest Without a Warrant, 22 Mich. L. Rev. 798, 806 (1924):

"What constitutes 'breaking' seems to be the same as in burglary: lifting a latch, turning a door knob, unhooking a chain or hasp, removing a prop to, or pushing open, a closed door of entrance to the house,—even a closed screen door ... is a breaking...." Footnotes omitted.)

See generally Blakey, The Rule of Announcement and Unlawful Entry, 112 U. Pa. L. Rev. 499 (1964).

[5] We do not deal here with entries obtained by ruse, which have been viewed as involving no "breaking." See e. g., *Smith* v. *United States*, 357 F. 2d 486 488 n. 1 (C. A. 5th Cir. 1966); *Leahy* v. *United States*, 272 F. 2d 487, 489 (C .A. 9th Cir. 1959). See also Wilgus, n. 5, *supra*, at 806.

[6] Exceptions to any possible constitutional rule relating to annnouncement and entry have been recognized, see *Ker* v. *California, supra*, at 47 (opinion of BRENNAN, J.), and there is little reason why those limited exceptions might not also apply to § 3109, since they existed at common law, of which the statute is a codification. See generally Blakey, n. 5, *supra*.

1. Obtaining a key to the suspect's apartment and quietly opening the door without first knocking and announcing the presence of a law enforcement officer and his purpose.
2. The officer finds that the door is unlocked and opens it and walks in without first knocking and announcing his presence.
3. Going into private premises where the door is standing wide open.
4. A pizza is being delivered to the apartment. The officers go through the apartment lobby door with the pizza boy. When the defendant opens his apartment door, the officers arrest him.
5. A person in the premises other than the defendant opens the door and admits the officers.
6. The door is opened by the defendant as a result of a ruse or trick unaccompanied by the use of force.
7. An officer hears a woman scream and call for help from within the premises. The officer opens the unlocked door and enters the premises.
8. Same as statement 7 except that the door is locked and the officer forces his way into the premises without knocking and announcing his presence and purpose.
9. An officer enters a tavern during business hours without first knocking at the door.
10. The officer obtains a partial opening of the door by ruse and trick but before he can arrest the defendant, the defendant closes the door. The officer then forces the door open without first identifying himself and stating his purpose.

11. In 1964, the known head of a gambling syndicate had a heart attack and Chicago police were called to his apartment to render assistance. While in the premises, they observed gambling paraphernalia and large amounts of money, some of which was wrapped in labels used by gambling organizations. They seized the gambling paraphernalia and over $750,000 in cash. (See the *Chicago Tribune*, February 20, 1964, and Sept. 16, 1965.)
    a. If the entry was valid, state the authority for the entry.
    b. If the seizure was valid, state the authority for the seizure.
12. In *State v. Chinn* (in this chapter) the Supreme Court of Oregon stated, "There is some dispute whether the officers were invited to examine the apartment. In any event, the officers entered and proceeded to look in the kitchen, bathroom, bedroom and living room."
    a. Assume that the officers were in the apartment but were told that they could *not* examine the other rooms of the apartment

to determine whether Ray was hidden in one of those rooms. Would they have the authority to make a search for Ray?

b. If the officers were given consent to examine the rest of the apartment and immediately seized the camera and beer bottles, would this be a valid seizure? If so, what would be the authority for the seizure?

13. Narcotics officers received information that X was selling heroin. Officers and a "special employee" went to the area where X lived. Before entering X's home, the special employee was searched for money and narcotics by the officers. He had no narcotics and only the marked money supplied by the officers when he entered the house. The special employee's intention in entering X's home was to make a purchase of heroin. When the special employee came out of X's house, he was again searched. He no longer had the marked money, but he did have three capsules which he had purchased as heroin. A preliminary field test made by the officers showed the presence of narcotics in the capsules.

The court stated that "The officers went to the rear door of the house, knocked on the door, and announced that they were police officers. When no one opened the door, they turned the knob and entered; they did not force their way in through the back door. The officers had no arrest or search warrant. No one had entered or left the premises. . . . They immediately placed appellant and certain other occupants of the house under arrest. Appellant at the time of the arrest, admitted to them the sale of narcotics. . . . The search of the appellant revealed the marked money. . . ." *Smith v. United States*, 254 F.2d 751 (D.C. Cir. 1958). Was the entry into the house a proper and valid entry?

14. What are the possible defense attacks upon:
   a. An entry by force into private premises?
   b. An entry without force into private premises?
   c. An entry by ruse or trick into private premises?

15. If the court rules that the entry was improper and unlawful, what would be the effect upon:
   a. An arrest made *after* the entry?
   b. Evidence seized *after* the entry?

18

ENTRAPMENT AND OTHER RELATED DEFENSES

Entrapment is a defense available to a defendant in which the defendant alleges that a law enforcement officer or his agent has used improper methods to induce him to commit the crime which he is charged with. In order to do this, the defendant must admit that he committed the act but would not have done so if the alleged improper methods had not been used. The fact that the defendant admits committing the crime indicates that the state has a strong case against him.

DETECTION PROCEDURES IN CRIMES OF VICE

Law enforcement agencies become aware of most crimes through complaints from victims and reports from witnesses. There are categories of crimes, however, where there are no victims as such and the crime is ordinarily committed under such clandestine circumstances that there seldom are witnesses who will report the incident to the police. These crimes are sometimes referred to as victimless crimes. In reality, the so-called willing victim is not a victim but is a party to the crime and as such is not likely to report the incident to the police because he will be incriminating himself. Most so-called victimless crimes are crimes of vice. They include narcotics offenses, gambling offenses, prostitution, homosexuality, and liquor violations.

Law enforcement agencies are legally bound to enforce the law within their jurisdiction. Because of the nature of vice crimes, the law enforcement agency must make an effort to determine whether these crimes are being committed. To detect crimes of vice, it is often necessary for law enforcement officials to set traps, make some inducements, or employ decoys to afford suspects an opportunity to commit a crime. An officer or his agent often acts in the capacity of a willing victim.

The defense of entrapment is most often used in crimes of vice because the detection and apprehension of the suspect is most often the result of the pretended willingness of an officer or his agent. To determine whether the defendant was entrapped by improper methods and procedures used by law enforcement officers, courts will use one or more of the following tests.

ORIGIN-OF-INTENT TEST OR INDUCEMENT TEST

The origin-of-intent test asks where the intent to commit the crime originated. Was the defendant predisposed to commit the crime and did the government offer him only the normal opportunity to commit the crime? Or did the officer or his agent originate the intent that a crime be committed?

Some encouragement, some pretended willingness, some persuasion, some solicitation, some inducement, some temptation can be used by law enforcement agencies, but it is improper for officers or their agents to use *excessive* inducement, encouragement, urging, or temptation which is likely to cause a person to commit an offense which he would not ordinarily be disposed to commit.

Example: A law enforcement agency hires five very pretty girls and instructs them to wear very provocative clothing. The girls are then sent out in the evenings to taverns and bars where they are told to flirt and act very suggestively with the men. When a man makes immoral suggestions, a nearby officer arrests the man making the proposition on a morals charge. This would clearly be excessive temptation and inducement and would be held to be entrapment.

Example: In cracking down on homosexuals, a large police department had officers dress effeminately and go into bars which were known to be frequented by homosexuals. The local branch of the American Civil Liberties Union became aware of this practice and challenged it as being excessive inducement and excessive temptation and therefore entrapment. As a result of the challenge, the police dropped the practice.

Law enforcement officers may create only the *usual* or *ordinary* opportunity to commit a crime. The task of law enforcement is *to detect* crime and *not to instigate* criminal activity.

Usual or *ordinary opportunity to commit a crime—*
     Mere offer to purchase a drink at the standard price in a bar after the closing hour

Excessive inducement and temptation to commit a crime—
> Pleading that a drink is desperately needed and offering to pay more than the regular price for the drink after the closing hour in a tavern

The court in *United States v. Sherman*, 200 F.2d 880 (2d Cir. 1952), defined the origin-of-intent test as follows:

> Therefore in such cases [where entrapment is raised as an issue] two questions of fact arise: 1) did the agent induce the accused to commit the offense charged in the indictment; 2) if so, was the accused ready and willing without persuasion and was he awaiting any propitious opportunity to commit the offense? On the first question the accused has the burden; on the second the prosecution has it. . . .

Probably most states require that the defendant show by a preponderance of the evidence that inducement occurred, while the burden on the state would be to show beyond a reasonable doubt that the accused had a prior disposition to commit the crime. To do this, most states using this test allow the prosecutor to show the past record of the defendant when entrapment is used as a defense. For example, a showing of three past convictions for gambling could indicate to a court or jury a prior disposition to commit such an offense again.

The defendant's immediate and ready compliance with the inducement of the agent would be an indication of a prior disposition. If the defendant did not immediately comply with the inducement and showed reluctance to commit the crime, the court or jury would have to determine whether the reluctance was due to fear of detection or whether it was a reluctance to commit a crime.

THE OBJECTIVE TEST

The majority of the United States Supreme Court adopted the origin-of-intent test in *Sorrells v. United States*, 287 U.S. 435 (1932), which was approved by the Supreme Court in the 1958 case of *Sherman v. United States*, 356 U.S. 369. Most states have probably adopted the origin-of-intent rule.

The objective test differs from the origin-of-intent test primarily in that the state cannot present the past record of the defendant on the issue of whether entrapment did exist or did not exist.

Minority concurring opinions in both the Sorrells and the Sherman cases favored adoption of the objective test. These concurring opinions thought the origin-of-intent test was improper.

SORRELLS (MINORITY CONCURRING OPINION)

"Whatever may be the demerits of the defendant or his previous infractions of law these will not justify the instigation and creation of a new crime, as a means to reach him and punish him for his past misdemeanors. He has committed the crime in question, but, by supposition, only because of instigation and inducement by a government officer. To say that such conduct by an official of government is condoned and rendered innocuous by the fact that the defendant had a bad reputation or had previously transgressed is wholly to disregard the reason for refusing the processes of the court to consummate an abhorrent transaction. . . ."

SHERMAN (MINORITY CONCURRING OPINION)

". . . a test that looks to the character and predisposition of the defendant rather than the conduct of the police loses sight of the underlying reason for the defense of entrapment. No matter what the defendant's past record and present inclinations to criminality, or the depths to which he has sunk in the estimation of society, certain police conduct to ensnare him into further crime is not to be tolerated by an advanced society. . . ."

Authors' Note: Read the rulings by the United States Supreme Court on the entrapment issues in the Lopez case in Chap. 15 and the Osborn case in Chap. 19.

ESSENTIAL-ELEMENT TEST

The essential-element test is used in *all* criminal cases. The state must prove all the essential elements of the crime beyond a reasonable doubt. Failure to prove an essential element of the crime charged beyond a reasonable doubt is fatal to the state's case.

FRAMEUP

The defendant who argues that he has been framed is asserting the defense that an essential element of the crime is not present—usually, the element of intent (in crimes in which intent is specifically required by statute).

Example: X is arrested and heroin is found in his pocket. X states that he did not know that the heroin was there and that someone must have placed it in his pocket.

Example: X is arrested and heroin is found in a box which he is carrying. X states that he was being paid to deliver the box and did not know the contents of the box.

In both of the examples given, X's defense is that the essential element of intent (intentional possession of heroin) is absent. The defense in a frameup goes further and alleges that X was framed by someone who wanted him arrested on a narcotics charge. If he alleges that the police framed him, then the defense is closely related to that of entrapment in that the police are alleged to have instigated the whole situation. A court or jury would have to make findings of fact to determine whether X was or was not framed.

TRAPS TO CATCH THIEVES

In order to catch thieves, traps are sometimes set with property used as bait with the consent of the owner of the property. However, an essential element of common-law larceny, which is written into state statutes, is that the taking of the property of another must be without the owner's consent and against his will.

Probably every state in the Union has had cases where an employee of a company is solicited with a plan to steal from his employer and then turn the property over to the outsider for money or other consideration. This type of planned criminal activity comes to the attention of law enforcement agencies when the employee pretends to go along with the scheme but instead tells his employer about it and the employer notifies the police.

A trap can be set with property used as bait, and the suspect is arrested when he has the property in his possession. The problem then is how to charge the arrested person. If the arrested person is charged with larceny or attempted larceny as was done in *People v. Rollino*, 233 N.Y.S.2d 580 (1962), the defense will argue that the state cannot prove the essential element that the taking was without the owner's consent and against his will. In the Rollino case, the New York court dismissed the case, stating that the state did not prove this essential element.

In *People v. Meyers*, 213 Cal. App. 2d 518 (1963), a similar situation occurred with a trap being set and the defendant arrested as he received the property. In the California case, however, the defendant was charged with attempting to receive stolen property and was convicted. The appellant court affirmed the conviction, holding that the state had proved all the essential elements of the crime which was charged.

A prosecutor could also successfully charge solicitation to commit a crime or, if there are more than two defendants, conspiracy to commit a crime. The state must prove all the essential elements of the crime it is charging.

PERMISSIBLE LIMITS FOR OFFICERS

In the enforcement of the law, officers are given a degree of freedom of action which is necessary to make them effective in their work. Undercover officers, with the permission of their department, might gamble and might actually participate in some criminal activity when necessary. But there are limits as to the extent of activity. If there is a question of what an officer can do, he should discuss the matter with his superiors and, if necessary, with the prosecuting officer of his jurisdiction. The following unusual case is one where officers exceeded the allowable limits.

REIGAN v. PEOPLE, 210 P.2d 991 (S. CT. COLO. 1949)

> Two game wardens were investigating the unlawful trapping of beaver. After talking with two boys (eighteen and nineteen years old) for an hour, the game wardens asked the boys why the boys didn't catch something that had some money in it. The game wardens represented themselves as fur buyers who wanted to buy "hot" beaver hides. They told the boys how to skin and stretch the hides out. They told the boys that they would be back to buy the hides when the boys had them. Instead of charging the boys, the prosecutor charged the game wardens. The Supreme Court of Colorado affirmed the convictions.

CASE FOR CHAPTER EIGHTEEN

UNITED STATES v. RUSSELL
SUPREME COURT OF THE UNITED STATES
.... U.S. ...., ...S.Ct. ...., 13 CrL 3055 (1973)

Mr. Justice Rehnquist delivered the opinion of the Court.

Respondent Richard Russell was charged in three counts of a five count indictment returned against him and codefendants John and Patrick Connolly. After a jury trial in the District Court, in which his sole defense was entrapment, respondent was convicted on all three counts of having unlawfully manufactured and processed methamphetamine ("speed") and of having unlawfully sold and delivered that drug in violation of 21 U. S. C. §§ 331 (q)(1), (2), 360a (a), (b) (Supp. V, 1964). He was sentenced to concurrent terms of two years in prison for each offense, the terms to be suspended on the condition that he spend six months in prison and be placed on probation for the following three years. On appeal the United States Court of Appeals for the Ninth Circuit, one judge dissenting, reversed the conviction solely for the reason that an undercover agent supplied an essential chemical for manufacturing the methamphetamine which formed the basis of respondent's conviction. The court concluded that as a matter of law "a defense to a criminal charge may be founded upon an intolerable degree of governmental participation in the criminal enterprise." *United States* v. *Russell*, 459 F. 2d 671, 673 (CA9 1972). We granted certiorari, 409 U. S. 911 (1972), and now reverse that judgment.

There is little dispute concerning the essential facts in this case. On December 7, 1969, Joe Shapiro, an undercover agent for the Federal Bureau of Narcotics and Dangerous Drugs, went to respondent's home on Whidbey Island in the State of Washington where he met with respondent and his two codefendants, John and Patrick Connolly. Shapiro's assignment was to locate a laboratory where it was believed that methamphetamine was being manufactured illicitly. He told the respondent and the Connollys that he represented an organization in the Pacific Northwest that was interested in controlling the manufacture and distribution of methamphetamine ["speed"]. He then made an offer to supply the defendants with the chemical phenyl-2-propanone, an essential ingredient in the manufacture of methamphetamine, in return for one-half of the drug produced. This offer was made on the condition that Agent Shapiro be shown a sample of the drug which they were making and the laboratory where it was being produced.

During the conversation Patrick Connolly revealed that he had been making the drug since May 1969 and since then had produced three pounds of it.[1] John Connolly gave the agent a bag containing a quantity of methamphetamine that he represented as being from "the last batch that we made." Shortly thereafter, Shapiro and Patrick Connolly left respondent's house to view the laboratory which was located in the Connolly house on Whidbey Island. At the house Shapiro observed an empty bottle bearing the chemical label phenyl-2-propanone.

By prearrangement Shapiro returned to the Connolly house on December 9, 1969, to supply 100 grams of propanone and observe the chemical reaction. When he arrived he observed Patrick Connolly and the respondent cutting up pieces of aluminum foil and placing them in a large flask. There was testimony that some of the foil pieces accidentally fell on the floor and were picked up by the respondent and Shapiro and put into the flask.[2] Thereafter Patrick Connolly added all of the necessary chemicals, including the propanone brought by Shapiro, to make two batches of methamphetamine. The manufacturing process having been completed the following morning, Shapiro was given one-half of the drug and respondent kept the remainder. Shapiro offered to buy, and the respondent agreed to sell, part of the remainder for $60.

About a month later Shapiro returned to the Connolly house and met with Patrick Connolly to ask if he was still interested in their "business arrangement." Connolly replied that he was interested but that he had recently obtained two additional bottles of phenyl-2-propanone and would not be finished with them for a couple of days. He provided some additional methamphetamine to Shapiro at that time. Three days later Shapiro returned to the Connolly house with a search warrant and, among other items, seized an empty 500-gram bottle of propanone and a 100-gram bottle, not the one he had provided, that was partially filled with the chemical.

---

[1] At trial Patrick Connolly admitted making this statment to Agent Shapiro but asserted that the statement was not true.

[2] Agent Shapiro did not otherwise participate in the manufacture of the drug or direct any of the work.

There was testimony at the trial of respondent and Patrick Connolly that phenyl-2-propanone was generally difficult to obtain. At the request of the Bureau of Narcotics and Dangerous Drugs, some chemical supply firms had voluntarily ceased selling the chemical.

At the close of the evidence, and after receiving the District Judge's standard entrapment instruction,[3] the jury found the respondent guilty on all counts charged. On appeal the respondent conceded that the jury could have found him predisposed to commit the offenses, 459 F. 2d, at 672, but argued that on the facts presented there was entrapment as a matter of law. The Court of Appeals agreed, although it did not find the District Court had misconstrued or misapplied the traditional standards governing the entrapment defense. Rather, the court in effect expanded the traditional notion of entrapment, which focuses on the predisposition of the defendant, to mandate dismissal of a criminal prosecution whenever the court determines that there has been "an intolerable degree of governmental participation in the criminal enterprise." In this case the court decided that the conduct of the agent in supplying a scarce ingredient essential for the manufacture of a controlled substance established that defense.

This new defense was held to rest on either of two alternative theories. One theory is based on two lower court decisions which have found entrapment, regardless of predisposition, whenever the government supplies contraband to the defendants. United States v. Bueno, 447 F. 2d 903 (CA5 1971); United States v. Chisum, 312 F. Supp. 1307 (CD Cal. 1970). The second theory, a nonentrapment rationale, is based on a recent Ninth Circuit decision that reversed a conviction because a government investigator was so enmeshed in the criminal activity that the prosecution of the defendants was held to be repugnant to the American criminal justice system. Greene v. United States, 454 F. 2d 783 (CA9 1971). The court below held that these two rationales constitute the same defense, and that only the label distinguishes them. In any event, it held that "[b]oth theories are premised on fundamental concepts of due process and evince the reluctance of the judiciary to countenance 'overzealous law enforcement.'" 459 F. 2d, at 674, quoting Sherman v. United States, 356 U. S. 369, 381 (1958) (Frankfurter, J., concurring).

This Court first recognized and applied the entrapment defense in Sorrells v. United States, 287 U. S. 435 (1932).[4] In Sorrells a federal prohibition agent visited the defendant while posing as a tourist and engaged him in conversation about their common war experiences. After gaining the defendant's confidence the agent asked for some liquor, was twice refused, but upon asking a third time the defendant finally capitulated, and was subsequently prosecuted for violating the National Prohibition Act.

Chief Justice Hughes, speaking for the Court, held that as a matter of statutory

---

[3] The District Judge stated the governing law on entrapment as follows: "Where a person has the willingness and the readiness to break the law, the mere fact that the government agent provides what appears to be a favorable opportunity is not entrapment." He then instructed the jury to acquit respondent if it had a "reasonable doubt whether the defendant had the previous intent or purpose to commit the offense . . . and did so only because he was induced or persuaded by some officer or agent of the government." No exception was taken by respondent to this instruction.

[4] The first case to recognize and sustain a claim of entrapment by government officers as a defense was apparently Woo Wai v. United States, 223 F. 412 (CA9 1915).

construction the defense of entrapment should have been available to the defendant. Under the theory propounded by the Chief Justice, the entrapment defense prohibits law enforcement officers from instigating criminal acts by persons "otherwise innocent in order to lure them to its commission and to punish them." 287 U. S., at 448. Thus, the thrust of the entrapment defense was held to focus on the intent or predisposition of the defendant to commit the crime. "[I]f the defendant seeks acquittal by reason of entrapment he cannot complain of an appropriate and searching inquiry into his own conduct and predisposition as bearing upon that issue." 287 U. S., at 451.

Justice Roberts concurred in the result but was of the view "that courts must be closed to the trial of a crime instigated by the government's own agents." 287 U. S., at 459. The difference in the view of the majority and the concurring opinions is that in the former the inquiry focuses on the predisposition of the defendant, whereas in the latter the inquiry focuses on whether the government "instigated the crime."

In 1958 the Court again considered the theory underlying the entrapment defense and expressly reaffirmed the view expressed by the *Sorrells* majority. *Sherman* v. *United States*, 356 U. S. 369 (1958). In *Sherman* the defendant was convicted of selling narcotics to a government informer. As in *Sorrells* it appears that the government agent gained the confidence of the defendant and, despite initial reluctance, the defendant finally acceded to the repeated importunings of the agent to commit the criminal act. On the basis of *Sorrells*, this Court reversed the affirmance of the defendant's conviction.

In affirming the theory underlying *Sorrells*, Chief Justice Warren for the Court, held that "[t]o determine whether entrapment has been established, a line must be drawn between the trap for the unwary innocent and the trap for the unwary criminal." 356 U. S., at 372. Justice Frankfurter stated in a concurring opinion that he believed Justice Roberts had the better view in *Sorrells* and would have framed the question to be asked in an entrapment defense in terms of "whether the police conduct revealed in the particular case falls below standards . . . for the proper use of governmental power." 356 U. S., at 382.

In the instant case respondent asks us to reconsider the theory of the entrapment defense as it is set forth in the majority opinions in *Sorrells* and *Sherman*. His principal contention is that the defense should rest on constitutional grounds. He argues that the level of Shapiro's involvement in the manufacture of the methamphetamine was so high that a criminal prosecution for the drug's manufacture violates the fundamental principles of due process. The respondent contends that the same factors that led this Court to apply the exclusionary rule to illegal searches and seizures, *Weeks* v. *United States*, 232 U. S. 383 (1914); *Mapp* v. *Ohio*, 367 U. S. 643 (1961), and confessions, *Miranda* v. *Arizona*, 384 U. S. 346 (1966), should be considered here. But he would have the Court go further in deterring undesirable official conduct by requiring that any prosecution be barred absolutely because of the police involvement in criminal activity. The analogy is imperfect in any event, for the principal reason behind the adoption of the exclusionary rule was the government's "failure to observe its own laws." *Mapp* v. *Ohio, supra*, 367 U. S., at 659. Unlike the situations giving rise to the holdings in *Mapp* and *Miranda*, the government's conduct here violated no independent constitutional right of the respondent. Nor did Shapiro violate any federal statute or rule or commit any crime in infiltrating the respondent's drug enterprise.

Respondent would overcome this basic weakness in his analogy to the exclusionary rule cases by having the Court adopt a rigid constitutional rule that would preclude any prosecution when it is shown that the criminal conduct would not have been possible had not an undercover agent "supplied an indispensable means to the commission of the crime that could not have been obtained otherwise, through legal or illegal channels." Even if we were to surmount the difficulties attending the notion that due process of law can be embodied in fixed rules, and those attending respondent's particular formulation, the rule he proposes would not appear to be of significant benefit to him. For on the record presented it appears that he cannot fit within the terms of the very rule he proposes.[5]

The record discloses that although the propanone was difficult to obtain it was by no means impossible. The defendants admitted making the drug both before and after those batches made with the propanone supplied by Shapiro. Shapiro testified that he saw an empty bottle labeled phenyl-2-propanone on his first visit to the laboratory on December 7, 1969. And when the laboratory was searched pursuant to a search warrant on January 10, 1970, two additional bottles labeled phenyl-2-propanone were seized. Thus, the facts in the record amply demonstrate that the propanone used in the illicit manufacture of methamphetamine not only could have been obtained without the intervention of Shapiro but was in fact obtained by these defendants.

While we may some day be presented with a situation in which the conduct of law enforcement agents is so outrageous that due process principles would absolutely bar the government from invoking judicial processes to obtain a conviction, cf. *Rochin* v. *California*, 342 U. S. 165 (1952), the instant case is distinctly not of that breed. Shapiro's contribution of propanone to the criminal enterprise already in process was scarcely objectionable. The chemical is by itself a harmless substance and its possession is legal. While the government may have been seeking to make it more difficult for drug rings, such as that of which respondent was a member, to obtain the chemical, the evidence described above shows that it nonetheless was obtainable. The law enforcement conduct here stops far short of violating that "fundamental fairness, shocking to the universal sense of justice," mandated by the Due Process Clause of the Fifth Amendment. *Kinsella* v. *United States ex rel. Singleton*, 361 U. S. 234, 246 (1960).

The illicit manufacture of drugs is not a sporadic, isolated criminal incident, but a continuing, though illegal, business enterprise. In order to obtain convictions for illegally manufacturing drugs, the gathering of evidence of past unlawful conduct frequently proves to be an all but impossible task. Thus in drug-related offenses law enforcement personnel have turned to one of the only practicable means of detection: the infiltration of drug rings and a limited participation in their unlawful present practices. Such infiltration is a recognized and permissible means of apprehension; if that be so, then the supply of some item of value that the drug ring requires must, as a general rule, also be permissible. For an agent will not be taken into the confidence of the illegal entrepreneurs unless he has something of value to offer them. Law enforcement tactics such as this can hardly be said to violate "fundamental fairness" or "shocking to the universal sense of justice," *Kinsella, supra.*

Respondent also urges, as an alternative to his constitutional argument, that we broaden the nonconstitutional defense of entrapment in order to sustain the judgment of the Court of Appeals. This Court's opinions in *Sorrells* v. *United States, supra,* and *Sherman* v. *United States, supra,* held that the principal element in the

---

[5] The language quoted above first appeared in the government's brief at 32, but was subsequently adopted by the respondent. Respondent's Brief, at 20–21.

defense of entrapment was the defendant's predisposition to commit the crime. Respondent conceded in the Court of Appeals, as well he might, "that he may have harbored a predisposition to commit the charged offenses," 459 F. 2d. at 672. Yet he argues that the jury's refusal to find entrapment under the charge submitted to it by the trial court should be overturned and the views of Justices Roberts and Frankfurter, concurring in *Sorrells* and *Sherman*, respectively, which make the essential element of the defense turn on the type and degree of governmental conduct, be adopted as the law.

We decline to overrule these cases. *Sorrells* is a precedent of long standing that has already been once reexamined in *Sherman* and implicitly there reaffirmed. Since the defense is not of a constitutional dimension, Congress may address itself to the question and adopt any substantive definition of the defense that it may find desirable.[6]

Critics of the rule laid down in *Sorrells* and *Sherman* have suggested that its basis in the implied intent of Congress is largely fictitious, and have pointed to what they conceive to be the anomalous difference between the treatment of a defendant who is solicited by a private individual and one who is entrapped by a government agent. Questions have been likewise raised as to whether "predisposition" can be factually established with the requisite degree of certainty. Arguments such as these, while not devoid of appeal, have been twice previously made to this Court, and twice rejected by it, first in *Sorrells* and then in *Sherman*.

We believe that at least equally cogent criticism has been made of the concurring views in these cases. Commenting in *Sherman* on Justice Roberts' position in *Sorrells* that "although the defendant could claim that the government had induced him to commit the crime, the government could not reply by showing the defendant's criminal conduct was due to his own readiness and not to the persuasion of government agents," *Sherman v. United States, supra,* 356 U. S., at 376–377, Chief Justice Warren quoted the observation of Judge Learned Hand in an earlier stage of that proceeding:

> " 'Indeed, it would seem probable that, if there were no reply [to the claim of inducement], it would be impossible ever to secure convictions of any offenses which consist of transactions that are carried on in secret.' *United States v. Sherman,* 200 F. 2d 880, 882." *Sherman v. United States, supra,* 356 U. S., at 377 n. 7.

Nor does it seem particularly desirable for the law to grant complete immunity from prosecution to one who himself planned to commit a crime, and then committed it, simply because government undercover agents subjected him to inducements which might have seduced a hypothetical individual who was not so predisposed. We are content to leave the matter where it was left by the Court in *Sherman:*

> "The function of law enforcement is the prevention of crime and the apprehension of criminals. Manifestly, that function does not include the manufacturing of crime. Criminal activity is such that stealth and strategy are necessary weapons in the arsenal of the police officer. However, 'A different question is presented when the criminal design originates with the officials of the government, and they implant in

---

[6] A bill currently before the Congress contemplates an express statutory formulation of the entrapment defense. S. 1, 93d Cong., 1st Sess., § 1–3B2 (1973).

the mind of an innocent person the disposition to commit the alleged offense and induce its commission in order that they may prosecute.' " 356 U. S., at 372, quoting *Sorrells* v. *United States, supra,* 287 U. S., at 442.

Several decisions of the United States district courts and courts of appeals have undoubtedly gone beyond this Court's opinions in *Sorrells* and *Sherman* in order to bar prosecutions because of what they thought to be for want of a better term "overzealous law enforcement." But the defense of entrapment enunciated in those opinions was not intended to give the federal judiciary a "chancellor's foot" veto over law enforcement practices of which it did not approve. The execution of the federal laws under our Constitution is confided primarily to the Executive Branch of the Government, subject to applicable constitutional and statutory limitations and to judicially fashioned rules to enforce those limitations. We think that the decision of the Court of Appeals in this case quite unnecessarily introduces an unmanageably subjective standard which is contrary to the holdings of this Court in *Sorrells* and *Sherman.*

Those cases establish that entrapment is a relatively limited defense. It is rooted not in any authority of the Judicial Branch to dismiss prosecutions for what it feels to have been "overzealous law enforcement," but instead in the notion that Congress could not have intended criminal punishment for a defendant who has committed all the elements of a prescribed offense, but who was induced to commit them by the government.

Sorrells and *Sherman* both recognize "that the fact that officers or employees of the government merely afford opportunities or facilities for the commission of the offense does not defeat the prosecution," 287 U. S., at 441; 356 U. S., at 372. Nor will the mere fact of deceit defeat a prosecution, see, e. g., *Lewis* v. *United States,* 385 U. S. 206, 208–209 (1966), for there are circumstances when the use of deceit is the only practicable law enforcement technique available. It is only when the government's deception actually implants the criminal design in the mind of the defendant that the defense of entrapment comes into play.

Respondent's concession in the Court of Appeals that the jury finding as to predisposition was supported by the evidence is, therefore, fatal to his claim of entrapment. He was an active participant in an illegal drug manufacturing enterprise which began before the government agent appeared on the scene, and continued after the government agent had left the scene. He was, in the words of *Sherman, supra,* not an "unwary innocent" but an "unwary criminal." The Court of Appeals was wrong, we believe, when it sought to broaden the principle laid down in *Sorrels* and *Sherman.* Its judgment is therefore

Reversed.

Mr. Justice Stewart, with whom Mr. Justice Brennan and Mr. Justice Marshall join, dissenting.

It is common ground that "[t]he conduct with which the defense of entrapment is concerned is the *manufacturing* of crime by law enforcement officials and their agents." *Lopez* v. *United States,* 373 U. S. 429, 434 (1963). For the Government cannot be permitted to instigate the commission of a criminal offense in order to prosecute someone for committing it. As Mr. Justice Brandeis put it, the Government "may not provoke or create a crime and then punish the criminal, its creature." *Casey* v. *United States,* 276 U. S. 413, 423 (1928) (dissenting opinion). It is to prevent this situation from occurring in the administration of federal criminal justice that the defense of entrapment exists. But the Court has been sharply divided as to the proper basis, scope, and focus of the entrapment defense, and as to whether, in the absence of a conclusive showing, the issue of entrapment is for the judge or the jury to determine.

I

In *Sorrells* v. *United States* and *Sherman* v. *United States* the Court took what might be called a "subjective" approach to the defense of entrapment. In that view, the defense is predicated on an unexpressed intent of Congress to exclude from its criminal statutes the prosecution and conviction of persons, "otherwise innocent," who have been lured to the commission of the prohibited act through the Government's instigation. *Sorrells* v. *United States.* The key phrase in this formulation is "otherwise innocent," for the entrapment defense is available under this approach only to those who would not have committed the crime but for the Government's inducements. Thus, the subjective approach focuses on the conduct and propensities of the particular defendant in each individual case: if he is "otherwise innocent," he may avail himself of the defense; but if he had the "predisposition" to commit the crime, or if the "criminal design" originated with him, then—regardless of the nature and extent of the Government's participation— there has been no entrapment. *Id.* And, in the absence of a conclusive showing one way or the other, the question of the defendant's "predisposition" to the crime is a question of fact for the jury. The Court today adheres to this approach.

. . . .

It cannot be doubted that if phenyl-2-propanone had been wholly unobtainable from other sources, the agent's undercover offer to supply it to the respondent in return for part of the illicit methamphetamine produced therewith—an offer initiated and carried out by the agent for the purpose of prosecuting the respondent for producing methamphetamine—would be precisely the type of governmental conduct that constitutes entrapment under any definition. For the agent's conduct in that situation would make possible the commission of an otherwise totally impossible crime, and, I should suppose, would thus be a textbook example of instigating the commission of a criminal offense in order to prosecute someone for committing it.

But assuming in this case that the phenyl-2-propanone was obtainable through independent sources, the fact remains that that used for the particular batch of methamphetamine involved in all three counts of the indictment with which the respondent was charged—i. e., that produced on December 10, 1969—was supplied by the Government. This essential ingredient was indisputably difficult to obtain, and yet that used in committing the offenses of which the respondent was convicted was offered to the respondent by the government agent, on the agent's own initiative, and was readily supplied to the respondent in needed amounts. If the chemical was so easily available elsewhere, then why did not the agent simply wait until the respondent had himself obtained the ingredients and produced the drug, and then buy it from him? The very fact that the agent felt it incumbent upon him to offer to supply phenyl-2-propanone in return for the drug casts considerable doubt on the theory that the chemical could easily have been procured without the agent's intervention, and that therefore the agent merely afforded an opportunity for the commission of a criminal offense.

In this case, the chemical ingredient was available only to licensed persons, and the Government itself had requested suppliers not to sell that ingredient even to people with a license. Yet the government agent readily offered and supplied that ingredient to an unlicensed person and asked him to make a certain illegal drug with it. The Government then prosecuted that person for making the drug produced *with the very ingredient* which its agent had so helpfully supplied. This strikes me as the very pattern of conduct that should be held to constitute entrapment as a matter of law.

It is the Government's duty to prevent crime, not to promote it. Here, the Government's agent asked that the illegal drug be produced for him, solved his quarry's practical problems with the assurance that he could provide the one essential ingredient that was difficult to obtain, furnished that element as he had promised, and bought the finished product from the respondent—all so that the respondent could be prosecuted for producing and selling the very drug for which the agent had asked and for which he had provided the necessary component. Under the objective approach that I would follow, this respondent was entrapped, regardless of his predisposition or "innocence."

[Dissenting opinion of Mr. Justice Douglas omitted.]

QUESTIONS AND PROBLEMS

Available Answers for Questions 1 to 13
Choose the answer which best fits the situation described in each question.

1. This would *not* be held to be entrapment.
2. This would be held to be entrapment (or a procedure which law enforcement agencies should not use).
3. The state *cannot* prove an essential element of the crime in this case.

1. A vice-squad officer in plain clothes goes into a bar *after* the closing hour and asks for a beer as he puts 50 cents on the bar.
2. A police officer in civilian clothes pretends that he is intoxicated (a drunk), and the accused tries to "roll" him.
3. Unmarked police cars are used for highway patrol.
4. A male police officer is dressed as a woman as a decoy for criminals who have been assaulting women.
5. Police officers are on duty in swimming suits at a beach where robberies have taken place.
6. $2,000 worth of cigarettes are used as bait, and as a result of the trap, the defendants are arrested and charged with theft. The cigarettes belong to a firm which consented to have them used as a bait for the trap.
7. Effeminately dressed male police officers go into bars known to be frequented by male homosexuals.
8. Urging a doctor to take the $1,000 which the undercover officer has in cash while he pleads with the doctor that he badly needs the narcotics fix.
9. A woman who has been receiving anonymous obscene telephone

calls agrees to meet the male caller. The meeting is a trap suggested by the police and the man is arrested.

10. An undercover police officer asks a woman who he knows has been previously convicted of prostitution to have sexual relations with him for money. She agrees and is arrested when she accepts the money.

11. The facts of the case show that the defendant was talked into committing the crime by his girl friend. The defendant pleads entrapment.

12. An undercover secret service agent gives 500 counterfeit bills to the defendant. A few hours later, another agent arrests the defendant for illegally receiving and possessing the contraband.

13. An informant who is being paid by a law enforcement agency uses excessive incitement, urging, and pleading to encourage the defendant to commit the crime which is being charged.

14. As the arrestee was leaving a YMCA building in downtown Washington, D.C., he noticed that a stranger was staring at him. The man made a hardly perceptible nod in the direction of the stairs and then went down toward the men's room. The arrestee turned around and followed him. The Court found that "A conversation ensued between them. It began with an exchange of innocuous remarks and then in rather vulgar phraseology, the stranger indicated to the [arrestee] that he was looking for a partner for a homosexual act. The [arrestee] made a reply that seemed to acquiesce in the stranger's suggestion and also touched the stranger's body through his clothing in an indecent manner. The stranger then identified himself as a police officer, exhibited his badge, and placed the [arrestee] under arrest." *Beard v. Stahr*, 200 F. Supp. 766 (1961). From the facts stated, was this entrapment?

15. The use of entrapment as a defense has increased in recent years. A controversy has risen as to the reason for the increase. Some argue that the primary reason is that law enforcement officers are bolder and more aggressive than they were in the past. Others state that the primary reason is that vice crimes such as narcotics and homosexual offenses have increased significantly. Discuss in view of enforcement practices and court requirements in your jurisdiction.

19
INFORMANTS AND THE USE OF HEARSAY INFORMATION AS AN ESSENTIAL ELEMENT OF PROBABLE CAUSE

The first part of this chapter (pages 439–445) was prepared by Mr. Richard C. Thompson of the Police Science Department of the Milwaukee Area Technical College. The authors sincerely thank Mr. Thompson and appreciate the fine insight which he gives to this difficult and much misunderstood subject.

A detective, in his efforts to locate a fugitive from justice, interviews relatives, friends, and acquaintances of the accused; he checks the old hangouts and may establish a stakeout in the hope of making the arrest. Often these methods succeed, after the expenditure of much time and the effort of numerous officers. But frequently success is elusive because no one will talk.

A burglary occurs. The crime scene yields evidence which could be connected with the burglars—if their identities were only known. The absence of a well-founded suspicion against any particular burglar or gang forces the diffusion of the work of the burglary squad over a broad area; their efforts are diluted insofar as they concern any one suspect. Their suspicion may never attach to those persons who committed the offense.

Commercial gamblers set up a book. Because they operate only by phone, their activities are unknown to the general public. No complaints are made to the police, who might remain ignorant of the operation if they relied solely on the complaint system.

In each of the three commonplace examples above, the experienced officer will recognize the need for confidential informants, i.e., cooperative persons who associate with criminals or, at their poorest, who are on the fringe of acquaintance with those who rather regularly violate the law.

Something may be read about confidential informants in textbooks, and they are occasionally referred to in articles in the daily papers. But there are few guides to the police officer in these writings, because—like the blind men describing the elephant—each writer is able only to set down his own impressions, and these impressions vary with individual experience. Some who write about informants do so in the half-light of vicarious experience.

On the other hand, informants have sometimes been written about as threats to personal privacy, academic freedom, or other of our liberties. Such treatment of the subject tends to be emotional rather than objective.

Others see the use of informants as a dirty business.

But the reality of the matter is that confidential informants are necessary to efficient crime detection. The problem lies in the development of reliable and willing informants, maintaining their anonymity over significant periods of time, and keeping relationships with informants on a plane which is morally and legally sound. It is the primary purpose here to suggest procedures for developing informants, and it should be clear throughout that the writer believes firmly that this can be done without compromise of moral or legal principles.

THE DEVELOPMENT OF CONFIDENTIAL INFORMANTS

The first premise to be recognized by the investigator who seeks to develop confidential informants is that purposeful effort is more apt to be successful than sheer chance. It is true, of course, that chance may open communication with a future informant, but it is purposeful effort which capitalizes on chance and converts it to opportunity. Officers meet and interview previously convicted felons as well as unconvicted offenders in the regular course of investigating crimes. They become acquainted with the proprietors of bars which are hangouts for criminals. They interview parolees who have served time and thus broadened their acquaintance with criminals while in prison. In pursuit of a fugitive from justice, officers may contact brothel keepers and gamblers. In this process they chance upon the individuals who obviously know a great deal which would be of use to the police. The officer who understands the value of informants will, while pursuing his investigation, evaluate the person he interviews in terms of his potential as an informant. He will, in accordance with good judgment, explore the scope of such a person's knowledge, or leave the door open for returning to do so later. He will develop the knack of finding a common ground for discussion with a person who has, in his opinion, the potential of becoming an informant. This potential is composed of two qualities: a knowledge of criminal activity and the ability to find things out, on the one hand, and the possibility of being induced to cooperate. Cooperation is seldom, if ever, immediate; in fact, it is usually obtained only through patient effort. Thus the role played by chance in the development of an informant is usually incidental.

On the other hand, persons who have the makings of good confidential informants may also be contacted by design. Such a person might be known to the officer only by reputation prior to a deliberate contact to explore his possibilities as an informant.

But whether by chance or design, the first step in developing a confidential informant involves communication with a person who has the potential previously spoken of. Obviously, such a person is seldom found among the pillars of society. On the contrary, he probably will have had some difficulty with the law.

The second step consists of renewing contact with a prospective informant for the purpose of developing a personal relationship with him. This relationship, about which there should be no false assumptions, will be like no other relationship in the life of the officer. It will never be extremely close, as circumstances will not permit; yet it will be personal. Approaching or attempting to develop this relationship, the officer should not be condescending, nor should he attempt to lower himself by crudeness or coarseness to what he assumes to be the level of the prospective informant. Nor should the officer play down his identity or purposes as a "cop." Experience says that not even the underworld respects the officer whose principles are suspect, whereas many a criminal has admitted his respect for a tough but fair and honest "cop." The officer should be himself, avoiding subterfuge. He should attempt to let the potential informant see him as he is. Conversation, intelligently directed, should promote an understanding of the potential informant as he is. Confidence can be promoted in no better way, and it is absolutely essential that an informant have confidence in the officer whom he may help and in whom he may confide. It may be a good tactic to listen to the troubles of the prospective informant and to show some sympathy, even to the extent of making suggestions or offering help. All potential informants, it seems, have troubles. Any help given should, of course, be within legal and moral limits. It may also be a good tactic to ask about people the prospect knows and to talk about innocuous things at the outset. The interview ought to terminate on a friendly note, with care taken to open the way for further contact.

Many may consider interviews with possible informants to be trying and pointless. The would-be informant may be scornful, because he knows the officer wants information he does not want to give. He may be hostile because he sees the officer as an adversary—a part of the system which has always given him trouble. He may be disrespectful. To take things like this to heart is self-defeating, and the officer should realize that heated argument will gain nothing. A verbal barb or two, in a joking way, might be in order, but anger or recrimination is without profit.

Should the procedure up to this point disclose the potential informant to be so low a character that the officer sees no prospect of trusting his work, common sense dictates that efforts at development should be broken off. Similarly, if it appears that a clash of personalities would prevent progress, there is no sense in continuing.

What has been said above lays the groundwork for the second premise in developing informants: that a confidential informant's cooperation depends on his confidence in the officer with whom he works. This confidence is built up over a period of time, just like Rome, which was not built in a day.

A number of suggestions, set out below, may assist the officer in building the confidence which is necessary to a working relationship between the informant and himself.

1. Be yourself, since nothing is so mistrusted as a false front.
2. Show interest in the prospective informant's life and problems.
3. Be a practical psychologist; guide conversation into areas about which the prospective informant is willing to talk; avoid discussing persons whom he wishes to protect, as there are plenty of others to talk about.
4. Discuss matters within the scope of the prospective informant's knowledge, as other things may not interest him and tend to destroy the continuity of the conversation.
5. Be willing to do the prospective informant a favor, but one which is not in conflict with the law.
6. If he is willing, give the informant easy tasks at first.
7. By word and attitude, show appreciation for assistance rendered; compliment him on his knowledge or ability, but don't use false flattery.
8. Use extreme care in contacting the prospective informant in order to avoid any suspicion on the part of others that he is talking with the police.

Some informants will accept pay for information delivered, particularly those who make a precarious living. However, an officer should not be misled into a belief that money is the best or only incentive for informants. Some will consider it a weakness to take money. Some would hardly be impressed by the amounts law enforcement agencies are able to pay.

If money is a motive, it should not be the only motive for assisting an officer. It is reasonable to suspect that the informant who acts only for pay may try to play a deceptive game for his own gain. There isn't room, in dealing with informants, for guessing games or false information. As security against deception, informants should be paid only for value received. Overpayments invite trouble. They put the officer on the defensive in justifying payments in terms of information delivered. Psychologically, this permits the informant to dominate the officer, rather than the other way around.

MAINTAINING RELATIONS WITH INFORMANTS

Once a satisfactory rapport has been built up between an officer and an informant, and the informant furnishes information on a somewhat regular basis, it might be supposed that no real serious problems remain. Nothing could be further from the truth. At best the relationship between officer and informant is delicate and sometimes complicated. Apprehension that his identity will somehow be disclosed, suspicion that the officer has somehow deceived him, or other reasons may contribute to strained relations. The informant may avoid the officer for a period. Renewing contact may be difficult without a breach of security.

The following are suggestions for maintaining relations with an informant:

1. Learn as much as possible about the informant so as to understand his personal life and problems; the interest shown should help maintain good relations, and the information will help the officer dominate his relationship with the informant and keep the latter from avoiding, deceiving, or taking advantage of the officer.
2. Learn, especially through conversation, something about the informant's values and traits of personality so that he may be treated like the individual he is, rather than as a stereotype; everyone has standards, and the officer must recognize those of the informant; it is probably not helpful to ridicule or "preach" to the informant about his private affairs, although in the long run the officer probably exerts a wholesome influence on the informant's conduct; on the other hand, the officer must insist on frankness and must not permit the informant to take the reins and try to run the investigation.
3. Never give the informant grounds to doubt one's sincerity, particularly in matters pertaining to his welfare; he should know that, if he is caught in a violation of the law, the officer will have to arrest

him; but he should also believe that the officer will not disclose his identity or call him as a witness.

4. During the interviews, the officer should be interesting to the informant. Bear in mind that he cooperates, not with the U.S. Constitution, but with an individual. Most officers have the capacity (investigation tends to make one an extrovert) to be interesting personalities; if they are not, perhaps they have chosen the wrong vocation.

5. In giving the informant assignments, the officer should work from the simple task to the difficult; success breeds further effort, whereas failure tends to discourage.

SOURCES OF INFORMANTS

Much has been said and written about obtaining informants from among those who are in trouble with the law and who volunteer to cooperate to avoid prosecution. Unquestionably informants are developed in this way; the charge may be minor and the prosecuting attorney willing to drop the case in consideration of information furnished about a more serious offense. Or perhaps this decision is made within the law enforcement agency, without going to the prosecutor. In any event, such an informant may be only a temporary one unless a working basis, along the lines referred to above, is established between himself and an officer. One reason for this is that this "informant" tends to measure his services in terms of the favor done him, and when he considers the debt paid, he wants no more of the arrangement. In fact, he may consciously work toward breaking off his connection with the police. This, obviously, makes for a rather temporary informant.

Other sources of informants are available. Almost every criminal an officer talks to can be evaluated as to his potential as an informant. Many will fail even the most superficial test—they belong in jail, not in circulation. But among them will be some who could be compatible and capable enough. It is suggested that persons over thirty-five may be more susceptible to development because by that time they have lost some of the ardor of youth and have learned to look at life a bit more seriously. By that time of life, the incidence of crime drops considerably, and the man over thirty-five is less apt to be lured by the excitement of the chase. Yet, the man over thirty-five may have a vast acquaintanceship among ex-cons and may be trusted alike by his older acquaintances and the younger crop of offenders.

As suggested in a previous paragraph, informants may also be found among relatively law-abiding citizens who come into regular contact with criminals through their occupations. Bartenders and tavern keepers often are privy to criminal information. Secondhand dealers may be offered stolen goods.

Those guilty of crimes against morality will often cooperate and may be able to furnish information in more serious cases. Prostitutes, for example. Gamblers often know about the gambling activities of others. The principle that the petty operator is not prosecuted anyway often is used to justify the development of minor lawbreakers in an effort to catch the big ones. This raises a number of questions which will not be treated here. Surely, it must be realized that there are potential risks here, as in other informant matters. The public and the press, when in a particularly puritanical mood, will not understand it. Contacts with informants of this type will be questioned. The individual officer ought not to climb out on a limb by being the only person who can vouch for the honesty of his position vis-à-vis an informant of dubious morality. Since rumors touching on bribery, sexual relations, and the like are apt to spring up, relations with all informants (particularly those involved in the vices) should be handled with the greatest discretion on the officer's part. A witness becomes a virtual necessity, which leads to the conclusion that, for safety's sake, all informants ought to be contacted by two officers together.

INFORMANT RECORDS

Since record keeping is primarily administrative in nature, little will be said about details. However, it is emphasized that records relating to informants should be confidential beyond the meaning of that word in the usual run of police business. What everyone knows is no longer a secret, and that which is open to every officer in the department will soon be known outside the department. Unless informant records are kept under lock and key, available only to high administrative personnel, it follows that the identity of informants cannot be protected. Whether by carelessness or design, their security will be violated.

Acceptance of this premise requires that informants be disguised in the writing of investigative reports. Assignment of code numbers or names will usually suffice. Several sound books on criminal investigation furnish details for the establishment and maintenance of confidential files relating to informants.

If the security of informants requires extreme care as to records, it also demands extreme care in conversation. It likewise demands that all contacts be made with forethought to avoid being seen by anyone who would recognize either the officers or the informants.

THE LAW IN REGARD TO THE CONFIDENTIAL INFORMANT

Most persons who have been privileged to observe the British police system on a firsthand basis are very impressed with the intelligence system which they have systematically developed over the years. Like an army in time of war, no democratic police organization can operate effectively without an informant system. This is particularly true in the battle which law enforcement agencies carry on to combat the narcotic and dangerous drug traffic which has grown alarmingly in recent years. The American courts have always recognized this reality and the rationale for an informant system can be found in the cases in this chapter.

THE GOVERNMENT'S PRIVILEGE NOT TO
DISCLOSE THE IDENTITY OF INFORMANTS

The U.S. Supreme Court pointed out in *Roviaro v. United States* (see cases) that it is the government's privilege to withhold the identity of the informant and it is not the informant's privilege to have his identity withheld as is sometimes thought. The Court in Roviaro stated the reason for the privilege;

> ...the purpose of the privilege is the furtherance and protection of the public interest in effective law enforcement. The privilege recognizes the obligation of citizens to communicate their knowledge of the commission of crimes to law enforcement officials and, by preserving their anonymity encourages them to perform that obligation.

The number of informants would drop drastically if identities were disclosed. In addition disclosure would, in most cases, put an end to any future use of the informant. And because the underworld of criminals hates and fears the informant, disclosure of identity would jeopardize the life of the informant and the safety of his family. (See *Shuster v. The City of New York* in Chap. 3 concerning the gangland slaying of an informant.)

TYPES OF INFORMANTS

The following is a general classification of the various types of informants who provide information to law enforcement agencies:

1. *Police informants:* Persons known to the police who for monetary or other considerations provide information on a regular or irregular basis. The establishment of a system of police informants pro-

vides law enforcement agencies with a source of information as to activities in the underworld of criminals.

2. *Nonpolice informants*, who would include:

    a. Ordinary citizens who provide information with no expectation of any compensation or consideration in return.

    b. Victims or witnesses to a crime.

    c. Fellow officers, officers from other departments, and information sent out through official channels.

3. *The anonymous informant* who provides information without revealing his identity. The police have no information as to who the person is and, ordinarily, do not know why he is providing the information.

TYPES OF INFORMATION PROVIDED

The types of information which is provided can be classified into the following groups:

1. *Information which leads to an investigation* but is not in itself the basis for an arrest or the issuance of a search warrant. Most information provided by informants would fall into this classification. A nationally known officer who lectured on informants would tell his audiences that informants don't ordinarily "make" cases. The officer puts together the evidence sufficient to charge and convict while informants merely point the officer and the investigation in the right direction. An example of this type of information is found in the following case.

STATE v. GRIDER, 479 P.2d 818 (KAN. 1971)

> Police received information from an informant that marijuana was hidden on a riverbank. Officers found the marijuana and kept the area under surveillance. When the defendant came to take the marijuana, he was arrested. The Supreme Court of Kansas held that it was immaterial how the officers happened to be on the riverbank and stated, "... the informant's information did not furnish the probable cause in this case for an arrest or a search. There was probable cause for an arrest independent of what the informant told the officer.... This case is quite different from situations where the informant's information provides all or a great part of the basis for the arrest, or a search."

2. *Information from informants which becomes an essential element in a finding of probable cause.* Examples of this type of information can be found in the U.S. Supreme Court cases of *Draper v. United States* and *McCray v. Illinois* (see case section).

THE USE OF HEARSAY INFORMATION
FROM AN UNDISCLOSED POLICE INFORMANT

Information from informants is hearsay information. When the information (or tip) is from a police informant, the officer is relying upon information provided by a person who could be very closely involved in criminal activity. If the information merely leads to further investigation, then the reliability of the informant and the source of the information are immaterial.

However, hearsay information from an undisclosed police informant may be used as an essential element for the establishment of probable cause to arrest or to issue a search warrant if two or more of the following tests are complied with.

1. *The prior-reliability test.* The United States Supreme Court has required that information from a police informant which is used as a necessary element of probable cause *must be supported* by some additional independent information tending to show that, in the past, the informant was proved credible and that his information has been reliable. This is usually done by the officer testifying as to accurate information which the informant has supplied in the past. The reason for this requirement is that the police informant in many instances has a past criminal record. He is sometimes a narcotics addict. His motivation in cooperating with the police is often a concession or money and is sometimes revenge.
2. *A showing of the reliability of the basis or source of the informant's information.* Generally when hearsay information is used as an essential element of probable cause, the officer has shown
   a. the underlying circumstances from which the officer concluded that the informant was reliable (the prior-reliability test)
   b. and the underlying circumstances or manner in which the informant obtained his information was reliable.

Consider the varying bases and sources of information in the following example:

Example: A large department store was burglarized and 100 valuable fur coats were taken. An informant who has previously provided reliable information to the police states that X burglarized the store and the reason for his statement is that:

a. He saw the coats in X's home (*reliable* for the establishment of probable cause).
b. He purchased one of the coats from X and produced the coat for the officer (*reliable* for the establishment of probable cause).

    c. He is a bartender and overheard unknown persons in his tavern state that X is trying to sell expensive fur coats (*not reliable* for probable cause but is a good lead for the officer).

    d. He states that X now has a good deal of money which he did not have before and suspects that X burglarized the store because it is the type of job that X would pull (*not reliable* for the establishment of probable cause but it is a possible lead for the officer).

3. *The test of corroboration* of the police informant's information. Where the information from a reliable informant is a necessary element in a finding of probable cause and the requirements set forth in test 2 above cannot be met, then additional information from independent sources which corroborate the tip and make it trustworthy may be considered. The corroborating information could be the result of further investigation or observations made by the officer or other officers. The Draper and McCray cases (see case section) are examples where observations by the arresting officers corroborated the information given by reliable informants. The U.S. Supreme Court in the McCray case stated:

> The arresting officers in this case testified, in open court, fully and in precise detail as to what the informer told them and as to why they had reason to believe his information was trustworthy. Each officer was under oath. Each was subjected to searching cross examination. The judge was obviously satisfied that each was telling the truth.

4. *The test used in United States v. Harris.* In June 1971, the U.S. Supreme Court *eased* the probable-cause requirements for the issuance of a search warrant based on the hearsay information from an undisclosed police informant (*United States v. Harris;* see cases, Chap. 13). In Harris, the officer could not testify as to prior reliability of the informant but only that he was a "prudent person." The U.S. Supreme Court held that there was sufficient corroboration of the informant's information because of two pieces of information in the affidavit of the officer:

    a. The officer's statement, together with other supporting information that the officer knew of the reputation of the suspect as a moonshiner.

    b. The informant's admission to the officer that he had committed a crime, and he admitted to having made several illegal moonshine purchases from the suspect. The Court stated, ". . . People do not lightly admit a crime and place critical evidence in the hands of the police in the form of their own admissions. . . ."

THE PROBABLE-CAUSE REQUIREMENT

The total amount of information available to the law enforcement officer *must* amount to such a quantum of evidence as would lead a reasonable officer to believe that the defendant has committed or is committing a crime. The requirements for using hearsay information from an undisclosed police informant to establish probable cause can be summarized as follows:

1. The basis for the informant's reliability and the underlying circumstances or manner in which the informant obtained his information are *both* shown to be reliable.
2. Even if the basis for the informant's information is not shown, hearsay information from a reliable informant may be sufficient as a necessary element of probable cause when the information from the informant is corroborated by independent observation.
3. Or there may be corroboration of the informant's information by evidence similar to that used in the 1971 case of *United States v. Harris.* It was held that probable cause was established primarily based on the hearsay information obtained from an unidentified "prudent person" who had recent "personal knowledge" of the suspect's illegal sale of bootlegged whiskey. The informant admitted to making several moonshine purchases from the suspect (an admission against penal interest).

THE USE OF HEARSAY INFORMATION
FROM A NONPOLICE INFORMANT

Hearsay information from a citizen or other person who is not a police informant may be used as a necessary element in the establishment of probable cause. The tests used to determine whether such information may be used as a necessary element to establish probable cause differ from the tests used in the case of the police informant.

The motivation for supplying the information differs greatly. The nonpolice informant is not receiving any compensation or concessions for his cooperation. Nor does he have a criminal record or close association with the underworld of criminals.

In most cases the officer has never seen the person before and therefore cannot testify as to past contacts with the person. Not only is the prior-reliability test not generally used, but courts have also held that a lesser degree of corroboration is required to verify information given by persons who are not police informants.

Citizen Informants

The reliability of information from a citizen informant is generally based upon (1) the nature of the information given to the officers, (2) the opportunity of the officer to appraise the information as to its reliability, and (3) corroboration of the information by police investigation and observation. The following cases illustrate the use of information from citizens. The question before the courts is whether the officer had probable cause based upon the information available to him.

PEOPLE v. HOFFMAN, 258 N.E.2d 326 (ILL. 1970)

During the 1968 Democratic convention in Chicago, an unidentified woman waved down a squad car in downtown Chicago. She informed the officers that a man who had just walked past her had the vulgarism "F....K" written in red letters on his forehead. She pointed the man out to the officers. The officers saw the man put on a hat and enter a restaurant. The officers followed the man into the restaurant and asked him what he had under his hat. The officers testified that the defendant removed his hat and they saw the word printed on his forehead. The defendant testified that the officers told him that he was under arrest and that he was to remove his hat. He testified that when he removed his hat, he was forcibly taken from the restaurant. The defendant testified that he offered no resistance, but the officers testified that he resisted the arrest. The defendant was tried and charged with disorderly conduct and resisting a police officer under Illinois statutes. The court acquitted him of the first charge and found him guilty of the second charge. The Supreme Court of Illinois held that "The officers here were justified in relying on the information received from the woman, and the usual requirement of prior reliability which must be met when police act upon 'tips' from professional informers does not apply to information supplied by ordinary citizens. Accordingly, we find that these officers had probable cause to arrest the defendant for disorderly conduct. The fact that the defendant was later discharged of this offense in no way detracts from the validity of the arrest."

STATE v. PASZEK, 50 WIS.2d 619 (WIS. 1971)

A drugstore clerk informed police that the defendant attempted to sell her marijuana. She described the defendant and stated that he would be back in the store at 1:00 P.M. The defendant entered the store at approximately 1:00 P.M. and matched the description given to the officers. After the clerk identified him, the officers arrested him. In the following search, the officers found marijuana on his person. The defendant appealed from his conviction, arguing that his arrest and search were invalid because probable cause did not exist. The court affirmed the conviction, stating, ". . . an ordinary citizen who reports a crime which has been committed in his presence, or that a crime is being or will be committed, stands on much different ground than a police informer. He is a witness to criminal activity who acts with an intent to aid the police in law enforcement because of his concern for society or for his own safety. He does not expect any gain or concession in exchange for his information."

TAYLOR v. STATE, 209 A.2d 595 (MD. CT. APP. 1965)

An unidentified eyewitness provided police with a description of the defendant. The Maryland Court of Appeals held that it was "reasonably trustworthy information" and admitted it in determining the probable cause for the felony arrest. The court stated that "it would be entirely impractical and unrealistic to require the officer to stop his investigation of the crime and inquire into the witness' trustworthiness."

FORD v. STATE, 460 S.W.2d 749 (ARK. 1970)

Eyewitnesses saw the defendant shoot a police officer and provided information to other officers. The court held that this information was sufficient to establish probable cause even though the arresting officer could not name his informants, had not used the informants in previous instances, and had no idea of their reliability.

Victims or Witnesses of a Crime

The source of information of a victim or witness to a crime is what he saw or observed. The test which is used is:

1. Whether the description of the suspect is specific enough to single out the likely suspect
2. Whether the person arrested by the officer reasonably matches the description given to him

The information that a crime was committed and the description of the suspect could be received by the officer directly from the victim or witness, or could be received by police radio or teletype.

BROWN v. UNITED STATES, 365 F.2d 976 (D.C. CIV. 1966)

At about 4:20 on the morning of September 21, 1964, a Howard Johnson Motor Lodge in Washington, D.C., was robbed. At about 4:30 that morning, two police officers in Washington stopped an old maroon Ford car because its tag light was out. One of the officers stayed in the squad car while the other officer left it to talk to the driver of the car which they had stopped. The officer in the squad car received the radio report of the robbery with a description of the suspect, stating that he was driving a maroon 1954 Ford. As the driver and car matched the report given to the officers, they placed the driver under arrest for robbery. A search was then made of the car which disclosed $178 found under the front seat on the passenger's side.

JUSTICE BURGER. "When one of the officers radioed back for more details of the person being sought for the robbery, he was told that the suspect was reported to be five feet, five inches, wearing a brown jacket and a cream-colored straw hat. Appellant was wearing blue and had only a felt hat in the car. He testified he was five feet eleven inches. The officer told the dispatcher that the man they had was wearing different clothes but fitted the general description; the dispatcher then repeated the 'lookout' for the benefit of other cruisers. These discrepancies, which can be the result of the victim's excitement or poor visibility or of the suspect's changing clothes, did not destroy the ascertainment made on the basis of the accurate portion of the identification, which was by itself enough to constitute probable cause, that Appellant was the one sought.

"The information received by the police was that the suspect was driving a 1954 maroon Ford; it turned out at trial that it was a 1952 car. One of the arresting officers testified that he thought Appellant was driving a 1952 or 1953 or 1954 Ford and that these model years were all pretty much identical to him. What they properly looked for —and found—was an 'old' maroon Ford car. Appellant and his car thus reasonably matched the description received.

"That the information came from an unknown victim of the crime did not preclude the policeman's having probable cause to arrest Appellant on the basis of it. Although the police could not here judge the reliability of the information on the basis of past experience with the informant, compare Draper v. United States, 358 U.S. 307 (1959), the victim's report has the virtue of being based on personal observation, a factor stressed in Aguilar v. United States, 378 U.S. 108 (1964), and is less likely to be colored by self-interest than is that of an informant. Admittedly a crime victim's observation may be faulty in some respects, as it may have been here; however, the mistakes are irrelevant if there is sufficient particularized information to constitute probable cause. Except in those few cases where cameras are part of a burglar alarm system, most reports are likely to be less than perfect. . . . Affirmed."

ROUNDTREE v. STATE, 272 A.2d 805 (MD. APP. 1971)

Two police officers received a radio broadcast of a holdup several blocks from where they were at the time. Within minutes the officers observed the defendant walking into a store. The officers arrested the defendant, frisked him, and found a revolver in his pants pocket. The only similarity between the described suspect on the radio broadcast and the defendant was that he was a black male, the height was similar, and both wore white tennis shoes. The defendant did not match the description given in age, weight, or clothing. Further investigation showed that the defendant was not involved in the holdup. The defendant was charged with carrying a concealed weapon and convicted.

THE COURT: "Assuming without deciding, that the broadcast description of the holdup suspect was sufficiently definite to furnish a basis for probable cause to single out an individual for arrest, we must conclude from our independent examination of the record before us that the facts adduced by the State do not measure up to that quantum of evidence which impels a finding that the police officers had probable cause, as above defined, to believe that appellant was the individual described in the lookout broadcast which the officers had received moments before the arrest. At best, the officers could have had no more than a suspicion that appellant was the individual described. To hold otherwise would be to arm the police with authority to apprehend, in this instance, any young negro of average height who happened to be wearing white tennis shoes.

"Lacking probable cause, the arrest was invalid. The search of the appellant's person incident to the unlawful arrest and the seizure of the concealed weapon found by the search was illegal and thus its admission into evidence was constitutionally impermissible and constituted reversible error. Judgment reversed."

[See *United States v. Kuntz* in Chap. 1, where bank holdup men had time to change their clothes and cars. One of them hid in the trunk while the other drove the Alfa Romeo. The court held that probable cause did exist from the police radio description of the suspects. The holdup loot of $99,000 was recovered by the arresting officer.]

Other Officers

Fellow officers and officers from other departments are reliable and credible sources of information.

EVANS v. STATE, 274 A.2d 653 (MD. APP. 1971)

THE COURT. "We have held that a report of a felony and a description of the perpetrators broadcast over a police radio may furnish probable cause for an arrest, it not being essential that the arresting officer himself have probable cause for the arrest, where information collectively within the knowledge of the police comprises probable cause and the arresting officer has been alerted over the police radio to make the arrest. The rationale in such case is that a police officer who is the source of the information is credible and reliable. But where another person and not a police officer is the source of the incriminating information, the officer who relays the information to an arresting officer is merely a conduit and the fact that he is a reliable person himself is not sufficient; it is the credibility and reliability of his informant that is involved and the State must establish it on the record."

The Anonymous Informant

Several cases up to this point had unidentified informants who at the scene of the crime or immediately after the crime provided information to officers. This was done on a face-to-face basis with the officer taking immediate action on the information provided to him. Because of the need for immediate action, the officer did not take the time to obtain the informant's name and address. Nor could the officer ascertain the reliability of the informant as he did not know the person and had never seen him before.

The term "anonymous informant" is used in this chapter to indicate a person who telephones or mails information to a law enforcement agency without disclosing his identity. The officer usually has no information on the reliability of the anonymous informant and usually does not know why the person is providing the information.

PEOPLE v. HOROWITZ, 233 N.E.2d 453 (N.Y. CT. APP. 1967)

An anonymous telephone call to the New York Police Department stated that the defendant (name given) had in his possession a brown paper bag containing stolen United States savings bonds and pornographic literature. The caller stated that the defendant worked in the mail room of the New York Times Building and described the defendant as being over 6 feet tall, weighing more than 200 pounds, and known as "Mr. Clean" because of the lack of hair on his head. This information was relayed from the officer receiving it to a detective who went to the New York Times Building. The detective found the defendant from the name and description given. He asked the defendant for the brown paper bag and a search of the bag produced United States savings bonds which were later identified as having been stolen. The defendant pleaded guilty to a charge of receiving stolen property after his motion to suppress illegally obtained evidence was denied.

THE COURT. "... the anonymous informer described the defendant correctly and had the right man as the sequel proved when he was found to have the stolen bonds in his possession. That is not the kind of evidence necessary to prove the reliability of the informer.... No ... evidence is in this record to support the reliability of this informer, which was demonstrated entirely by the fact that the man who was identified by the informer and arrested possessed of the stolen property. That is not enough (*Roviaro v. United States*).

"The controlling principle seems to be that it is not necessary for the officer making the arrest to know of the reliability of the informer or to be, himself, in possession of information sufficient to constitute probable cause provided that he acts upon the direction of or as a result of communication with a superior or brother officer or another police department provided that the police as a whole were in possession of information sufficient to constitute probable cause to make the arrest. This record does not show that any of the law enforcement officers had facts before them sufficient to indicate that this anonymous informer was reliable, or that the police had other information, not derived from the informer, which was sufficient, in itself to constitute probable cause...."

STATE v. LEO, 480 P.2d 456 (ORE. APP. 1971)

> An anonymous telephone caller told police that the defendant had marijuana in his home and was cutting it at the time in his kitchen. The police upon checking determined that the defendant was a student at Oregon State University and that a car registered in his name was parked in front of his home. A search warrant was issued on the basis of this information, and marijuana was found in the defendant's home. A motion to suppress was denied, and the issue of the legality of the search warrant is appealed.

> **THE COURT.** "Here we have an unseen and unknown informant with no prior history of reliability. The state concedes he was 'truly anonymous'. This informant did not tell the officer that he had himself seen the defendant or the contraband or that either the defendant or the person in possession of the house had told him about the narcotics being on the premises. The informant did not say from what source he had derived his information. He did not tell Officer Montgomery that he was then or ever had been at the house, nor that he had at any time seen the defendant or the person having control of the house in possession of the described or any other narcotics.... Merely, because the officer verified the presence at the house of a car registered to a Carl H. Leo and that one Carl H. Leo was registered as a student at Oregon State University does not in our opinion meet the Aguilar test of supplying to the magistrate sufficient 'underlying circumstances' upon which to base a conclusion 'that the informant ... was credible or his information reliable....' The officer's statement that 'I believe the caller was telling me the truth' is not a statement of an 'underlying circumstance' within the test of *Aguilar*. The motion to suppress should have been allowed. The judgment is reversed."

DISCLOSURE OF THE IDENTITY OF THE INFORMANT

Ordinarily, the government may and does invoke its privilege not to disclose the identity of the police informant or other informant (such as an undercover police officer). The public has a strong interest in not disclosing such identities in order to ensure a free flow of information necessary for effective law enforcement.

However, situations do arise when the state is faced with the alternatives of either dropping the charge (or charges) against the defendant or revealing the identity of the informant. The state is not obligated to use the informant as a witness. Some of the situations where the state would be obligated to disclose the identity of the informant would be:

1. If the disclosure is held to be essential or relevant and helpful to the defense of the accused. This would be a situation where the court finds that the informant may have evidence which may assist the accused in defending himself.

ROVIARO v. UNITED STATES (SEE CASES)

> "...The circumstances of this case demonstrate that John Doe's possible testimony was highly relevant and might have been helpful to the defense.... John Doe [the informant] was his one material witness...."

PEOPLE v. PEREZ, 44 CAL. RPTR. 326, 401 P.2d 934 (1965)

> The court held that where the defense seeks disclosure on cross-examination and it appears that the informant is a material witness on the issue of guilt, then the state must either disclose or suffer dismissal.

PEOPLE v. WILLIAMS, 230 N.E.2d 214, CERT. DENIED, 390 U.S. 983 (1967)

> When one of the Illinois officers called to the defendant, the defendant threw away a package of heroin. The informant was riding in the police car and pointed out the defendant to the officers. The court held that the informant's testimony would have been of little significance on the issue of the defendant's guilt or innocence. The critical question in the case was whether the defendant had thrown away the package containing heroin. There was no discrepancy in the officer's testimony.

STATE v. OLIVER, 231 A.2d 805 (1967)

> The New Jersey court held that the informant's identity need not be disclosed where the informant was no more than a witness to the criminal event.

2. If the informant participated in the criminal incident which is charged against the defendant, the defense may successfully demand disclosure of the informant's identity.
3. If entrapment is used as a defense and the informant is shown to have taken a part in bringing about the offense.

WRIGHT v. STATE, 420 S.W.2d 411 (1967)

> The Texas court held that if there was no proof that the informant was responsible for the defendant's possession of marijuana and that the informant played no material part in the offense, then the identity of the informant need not be disclosed.

TESTIMONY BY THE STATE BEFORE A JURY THAT INFORMATION FROM A POLICE INFORMANT WAS RELIED UPON

Ordinarily, the issue of the disclosure of the identity of a police informant and the issue of whether probable cause existed is determined in a motion to suppress (which is not heard before the jury). Disclosure before the jury is sometimes made on cross-examination that information from a police informant was relied upon either in the investigation of the case or in the establishment of probable cause. The following case demonstrates the risk which the state takes if the state shows on direct examination that an unidentified informant was relied upon in initiating the investigation and developing the case against the defendant.

GLOVER v. STATE, 251 N.E. 814 (IND. 1969)

> The Supreme Court of Indiana stated, "It is important to realize that this is not a case where, on cross examination, it is brought out that Officer Mize relied upon the informant in initiating the investigation and getting leads in the investigation. There may be a public policy in preventing the non-disclosure of informants used in such instances where at the trial, no evidence regarding the informant is presented to the jury. Hearsay testimony that law enforcement officers use and rely upon for investigation and the gathering of competent and material evidence, of course, is not evidence properly to be used in the trial of a criminal case. Here, however, we have the state opening up the matter and the activity of two informants played up in the case, and then the state seeks to close the door after it had shown that they were 'reliable' informants who put the finger of identity upon the appellant. The door cannot be closed once it is opened. If the identity of an informant is to be protected, then it is up to the prosecuting attorney not to bring into the case evidence relating to the informants."

THE USE OF FALSE NAMES OR ALIASES BY INFORMANTS

If an informant does appear in court as a witness or signs an affidavit supporting a search warrant, he must disclose his true identity. He cannot use an alias. If an informant has been using and is generally known by an alias or an assumed name, he cannot hide his identity by using his true name. See the Smith and Roviaro cases in the case section.

UNDERCOVER OFFICERS AND FALSE FRIENDS

Undercover officers and "false friends" can be classified as informants if the state invokes the privilege not to disclose their identity. However, in the Lewis, Hoffa, and Osborn cases, the undercover officer and the false friends appeared as witnesses. These important cases are in the case section, and the rules of law in each of the cases speak for themselves.

THE USE OF CONTINGENT FEES
FOR POLICE INFORMANTS

The method of payment of police informants has been an issue in cases which have come before courts. Informants are not paid by the hour, nor are they ordinarily salaried employees of the law enforcement agency. Therefore, the most practical method of payment is the "contingent fee." The police informant is being paid for a service or a commodity and payment is contingent upon the information which he provides.

The police informant can be on general assignment to keep his eyes and ears open for information of interest to the law enforcement agency. He (or she) may be requested to obtain any information possible in regard to a specific crime or type of crime (narcotics or gambling in a given area). Or the informant may be requested to make a purchase of contraband (such as narcotics) from the suspect.

In *Williamson v. United States*, 311 F.2d 441 (5th Cir. 1962), the court held that contingent-fee agreement to produce evidence against the defendants as to crimes not yet committed "might tend to a 'frame up' or cause an informer to induce or persuade innocent persons to commit crimes which they had no previous intent or purpose to commit. The opportunities for abuse are too obvious to require elaboration."

In *United States v. Grimes*, 438 F.2d 391 (6th Cir. 1971), the court rejected the Williamson rule and in reviewing the reported cases found that no other federal circuit had expressly followed Williamson. It also found that the Fifth Circuit itself had distinguished Williamson in many other cases. In affirming the conviction, the Sixth Circuit stated:

> Congress itself has authorized a form of contingent fee arrangement in certain cases. For example, an informer whose information leads to a conviction for violation of a revenue law may be awarded up to one-half of any fine levied as a result of that conviction. Internal Rev. Code of 1954, Sec. 7214(a)....
>
> It is well recognized that informers are an important and necessary aspect of our system of criminal justice. Although some critics view the difficult fight against crime as a game, we take a different view. "We are not persuaded that the impeccable manners and sportsmanship that would characterize dealings between members of the Westchester Saddle and Cycle Club must be exhibited by all federal agents when dealing with criminal suspects." *U.S. v. Costner*, 359 F. 2d at 973.

CASES FOR CHAPTER NINETEEN

ROVIARO v. UNITED STATES
SUPREME COURT OF THE UNITED STATES
353 U.S. 53, 77 S. CT. 623, 1 L. ED. 2d 639 (1957)

. . . .

In 1955, in the Northern District of Illinois, petitioner, Albert Roviaro, was indicted on two counts by a federal grand jury. The first count charged that on August 12, 1954, at Chicago, Illinois, he sold heroin to one "John Doe" in violation of 26 U. S. C. § 2554(a). The second charged that on the same date and in the same city he "did then and there fraudulently and knowingly receive, conceal, buy and facilitate the transportation and concealment after importation of . . . heroin, knowing the same to be imported into the United States contrary to law; in violation of Section 174. Title 21, United States Code."

. . . .

At the trial, the Government relied on the testimony of two federal narcotics agents, Durham and Fields, and two Chicago police officers, Bryson and Sims, each of whom knew petitioner by sight. On the night of August 12, 1954, these four officers met at 75th Street and Prairie Avenue in Chicago with an informer described only as John Doe. Doe and his Cadillac car were searched and no narcotics were found. Bryson secreted himself in the trunk of Doe's Cadillac, taking with him a device with which to raise the trunk lid from the inside. Doe then drove the Cadillac to 70th Place and St. Lawrence Avenue, followed by Durham in one government car and Field and Sims in another. After an hour's wait, at about 11 o'clock, petitioner arrived in a Pontiac, accompanied by an unidentfiied man. Petitioner immediately entered Doe's Cadillac, taking a front seat beside Doe. They then proceeded by a circuitous route to 74th Street near Champlain Avenue. Both government cars trailed the Cadillac but only the one driven by Durham managed to follow it to 74th Street. When the Cadillac came to a stop on 74th Street, Durham stepped out of his car onto the sidewalk and saw petitioner alight from the Cadillac about 100 feet away. Durham saw petitioner walk a few feet to a nearby tree, pick up a small package, return to the open right front door of the Cadillac, make a motion as if depositing the package in the car, and then wave to Doe and walk away. Durham went immediately to the Cadillac and recovered a package from the floor. He signaled to Bryson to come out of the trunk and then walked down the street in time to see petitioner re-enter the Pontiac, parked nearby, and ride away.

Meanwhile, Bryson, concealed in the trunk of the Cadillac, had heard a conversation between John Doe and petitioner after the latter had entered the car. He heard petitioner greet John Doe and direct him where to drive. At one point, petitioner admonished him to pull over to the curb, cut the motor, and turn out the lights so as to lose a "tail." He then told him to continue "further down." Petitioner asked about money Doe owed him. He advised Doe that he had brought him "three pieces this time." When Bryson heard Doe being ordered to stop the car, he raised the lid of the trunk slightly. After the car stopped, he saw petitioner walk to a tree, pick up a package, and return toward the car. He heard petitioner say, "Here it is," and "I'll call you in a couple of days." Shortly thereafter he heard Durham's signal to come out and emerged from the trunk to find Durham holding a small package found to contain three glassine envelopes containing a white powder.

A field test of the powder having indicated that it contained an opium derivative, the officers, at about 12:30 a. m., arrested petitioner at his home and took him, along with Doe, to Chicago police headquarters. There petitioner was confronted with Doe, who denied that he knew or had ever seen petitioner. Subsequent chemical analysis revealed that the powder contained heroin.

I.

Petitioner contends that the trial court erred in upholding the right of the Government to withhold the identity of John Doe. He argues that Doe was an active participant in the illegal activity charged and that, therefore, the Government could not withhold his identity, his whereabouts, and whether he was alive or dead at the time of trial. The Government does not defend the nondisclosure of Doe's identity with respect to Count 1, which charged a sale of heroin to John Doe, but it attempts to sustain the judgment on the basis of the conviction on Count 2, charging illegal transportation of narcotics. It argues that the conviction on Count 2 may properly be upheld since the identity of the informer, in the circumstances of this case, has no real bearing on that charge and is therefore privileged.

What is usually referred to as the informer's privilege is in reality the Government's privilege to withhold from disclosure the identity of persons who furnish information of violations of law to officers charged with enforcement of that law. The purpose of the privilege is the furtherance and protection of the public interest in effective law enforcement. The privilege recognizes the obligation of citizens to communicate their knowledge of the commission of crimes to law-enforcement officials and, by preserving their anonymity, encourages them to perform that obligation.

The scope of the privilege is limited by its underlying purpose. Thus, where the disclosure of the contents of a communication will not tend to reveal the identity of an informer, the contents are not privileged. Likewise, once the identity of the informer has been disclosed to those who would have cause to resent the communication, the privilege is no longer applicable.

A further limitation on the applicability of the privilege arises from the fundamental requirements of fairness. Where the disclosure of an informer's identity, or of the contents of his communication, is relevant and helpful to the defense of an accused, or is essential to a fair determination of a cause, the privilege must give way. In these situations the trial court may require disclosure and, if the Government withholds the information, dismiss the action. Most of the federal cases involving this limitation on the scope of the informer's privilege have arisen where the legality of a search without a warrant is in issue and the communications of an informer are claimed to establish probable cause. In these cases the Government has been required to disclose the identity of the informant unless there was sufficient evidence apart from his confidential communication.

Three recent cases in the Courts of Appeals have involved the identical problem raised here—the Government's right to withhold the identity of an informer who helped to set up the commission of the crime and who was present at its occurrence. In each case it was stated that the identity of such an informer must be disclosed whenever the informer's testimony may be relevant and helpful to the accused's defense.

We believe that no fixed rule with respect to disclosure is justifiable. The problem is one that calls for balancing the public interest in protecting the flow of information against the individual's right to prepare his defense. Whether a proper balance renders nondisclosure erroneous must depend on the particular circumstances of each case, taking into consideration the crime charged, the possible defenses, the possible significance of the informer's testimony, and other relevant factors.

II.

The materiality of John Doe's possible testimony must be determined by reference to the offense charged in Count 2 and the evidence relating to that count. The charge is in the language of the statute. It does not charge mere possession; it charges that petitioner did "fraudulently and knowingly receive, conceal, buy and facilitate the transportation and concealment after importation of . . . heroin, knowing the same to be imported into the United States contrary to law. . . ." While John Doe is not expressly mentioned, this charge, when viewed in connection with the evidence introduced at the trial, is so closely related to John Doe as to make his identity and testimony highly material.

It is true that the last sentence of subdivision (c) of § 2 authorizes a conviction when the Government has proved that the accused possessed narcotics, unless the accused explains or justifies such possession. But this statutory presumption does not reduce the offense to one of mere possession or shift the burden of proof; it merely places on the accused, at a certain point, the burden of going forward with his defense. The fact that petitioner here was faced with the burden of explaining or justifying his alleged possession of the heroin emphasizes his vital need for access to any material witness. Otherwise, the burden of going forward might become unduly heavy.

The circumstances of this case demonstrate that John Doe's possible testimony was highly relevant and might have been helpful to the defense. So far as petitioner knew, he and John Doe were alone and unobserved during the crucial occurrence for which he was indicted. Unless petitioner waived his constitutional right not to take the stand in his own defense, John Doe was his one material witness. Petitioner's opportunity to cross-examine Police Officer Bryson and Federal Narcotics Agent Durham was hardly a substitute for an opportunity to examine the man who had been nearest to him and took part in the transaction. Doe had helped to set up the criminal occurrence and had played a prominent part in it. His testimony might have disclosed an entrapment. He might have thrown doubt upon petitioner's identity or on the identity of the package. He was the only witness who might have testified to petitioner's possible lack of knowledge of the contents of the package that he "transported" from the tree to John Doe's car. The desirability of calling John Doe as a witness, or at least interviewing him in preparation for trial, was a matter for the accused rather than the Government to decide.

Finally, the Government's use against petitioner of his conversation with John Doe while riding in Doe's car particularly emphasizes the unfairness of the nondisclosure in this case. The only person, other than petitioner himself, who could controvert, explain or amplify Bryson's report of this important conversation was John Doe. Contradiction or amplification might have borne upon petitioner's knowledge of the contents of the package or might have tended to show an entrapment.

This is a case where the Government's informer was the sole participant, other than the accused, in the transaction charged. The informer was the only witness in a position to amplify or contradict the testimony of government witnesses. Moreover, a government witness testified that Doe denied knowing petitioner or ever having seen him before. We conclude that, under these circumstances, the trial court committed prejudicial error in permitting the Government to withhold the identity of its undercover employee in the face of repeated demands by the accused for his disclosure. . . .

The judgment of the Court of Appeals is reversed and the case is remanded to the District Court for proceedings not inconsistent with this opinion.

Reversed and remanded.

[Dissenting opinion omitted.]

OSBORN v. UNITED STATES
SUPREME COURT OF THE UNITED STATES
385 U.S. 323, 87 S. CT. 429, 17 L. ED. 2d 420 (1966)

Mr. Justice Stewart delivered the opinion of the Court.

. . . .

In late 1963, James R. Hoffa was awaiting trial upon a criminal charge in the federal court in Nashville, and the petitioner, as one of Hoffa's attorneys, was engaged in preparing for that trial. In connection with these preparations the petitioner hired a man named Robert Vick to make background investigations of the people listed on the panel from which members of the jury for the Hoffa trial were to be drawn. Vick was a member of the Nashville police department whom the petitioner had employed for similar investigative work in connection with another criminal trial of the same defendant a year earlier. What the petitioner did not know was that Vick, before applying for the job with the petitioner in 1963, had met several times with federal agents and had agreed to report to them any "illegal activities" he might observe.

The conviction which we now review was upon the charge that the petitioner "during the period from on or about November 6, 1963, up to and including November 15, 1963, . . . did unlawfully, knowingly, wilfully and corruptly endeavor to influence, obstruct and impede the due administration of justice . . ." in that he "did request, counsel and direct Robert D. Vick to contact Ralph A. Elliott, who was, and was known by the said Osborn to be, a member of the petit jury panel from which the petit jury to hear the [Hoffa] trial was scheduled to be drawn, and to offer and promise to pay the said Ralph A. Elliott $10,000 to induce the said Elliott to vote for an acquittal, if the said Elliott should be selected to sit on the petit jury in the said trial." The primary evidence against the petitioner on this charge consisted of Vick's testimony, a tape recording of a conversation between the petitioner and Vick, and admissions which the petitioner had made during the course of federal disbarment proceedings.

Vick testified that during a discussion with the petitioner at the latter's office on November 7, he mentioned that he knew some of the prospective jurors. At this, according to Vick, the petitioner "jumped up," and said, "You do? Why didn't you tell me?" The two then moved outside into the adjacent alley to continue the conversation. There, Vick testified, he told the petitioner that one of the prospective jurors, Ralph Elliott, was his cousin, and the petitioner told Vick to pay a visit to Elliott to see what arrangements could be made about the case. Vick also testified to meetings with the petitioner on November 8 and November 11, when he told the petitioner, falsely, that he had visited Elliott and found him "susceptible to money for hanging this jury," to which the petitioner responded by offering $5,000 to Elliott if he became a member of the jury and an additional $5,000 "when he hung the jury, but he would have to go all the way, and to assure Mr. Elliott that he would not be alone, that there would be some other jurors in there."

I.

No claim is made in this case that Vick's testimony about the petitioner's incriminating statements was inadmissible in evidence. What is challenged is the introduction in evidence of a tape recording of one of the conversations about which Vick testified, specifically the conversation which took place in the petitioner's office on November 11. The recording of this conversation was played for the jury, and a written transcript of it was introduced in evidence. We are asked to hold that the recording should have been excluded, either upon constitutional grounds, *Weeks v. United States*, 232 U. S. 383, or in the exercise of our supervisory power over the federal courts.

There is no question of the accuracy of the recording. The petitioner testified that it was a "substantially correct" reproduction of what took place in his office on November 11. There can be no doubt, either, of the recording's probative relevance. It provided strong corroboration of the truth of the charge against the petitioner.[1] The recording was made by means of a device concealed upon Vick's person during the November 11 meeting. We thus deal here not with surreptitious surveillance of a private conversation by an outsider but, as in *Lopez v. United States*, 373 U. S. 427, with the use by one party of a device to make an accurate record of a conversation about which the party later testified. Unless *Lopez v. United States* is to be disregarded, therefore, the petitioner cannot prevail.[2]

But we need not rest our decision here upon the broad foundation of the Court's opinion in *Lopez*, because it is evident that the circumstances under which the tape recording was obtained in this case fall within the narrower compass of the *Lopez* concurring and dissenting opinions. Accordingly, it is appropriate to set out with some precision what these circumstances were.

Immediately after his November 7 meeting with the petitioner, at which, according to Vick, the possibility of approaching the juror Elliott was first discussed, Vick reported the conversation to an agent of the United States Department of Justice. Vick was then requested to put his report in the form of a written statement under oath, which he did. The following day this sworn statement was shown by government attorneys to the two judges of the Federal District Court, Chief Judge Miller and Judge Gray. After considering this affidavit, the judges agreed to authorize agents of the Federal Bureau of Investigation to conceal a recorder on Vick's person in order to determine from recordings of further conversations between Vick and the petitioner whether the statements in Vick's affidavit were true. It was this judicial authorization which ultimately led to the recording here in question.[3]

The issue here, therefore, is not the permissibility of "indiscriminate use of such devices in law enforcement,"[4] but the permissibility of using such a device under the most precise and discriminate circumstances, circumstances which fully

---

[1] A transcript of the recording is reproduced as an Appendix to this opinion.

[2] It is argued that in *Lopez* the petitioner knew that the person to whom he offered a bribe was a federal officer. But, even assuming there might otherwise be some force to this distinction, it is enough to point out that in the present case the petitioner also knew he was talking to a law enforcement officer—a member of the Nashville police department.

[3] The recording device did not operate properly on the occasion of Vick's visit to the petitioner's office on November 8, and Vick made a written statement of what occurred during that meeting. The government lawyers reported these circumstances to District Judge Miller, who then authorized the use of the recorder on November 11, under the same conditions:

"I said on that second occasion the same as I did on the first occasion: that the tape recorder should be used under proper surveillance, supervision, to see that it was not faked in any way, and to take every precaution to determine that it was used in a fair manner, so that we could get at the bottom of it and determine what the truth was."

[4] "I also share the opinion of Mr. Justice Brennan that the fantastic advances in the field of electronic communication constitute a great danger to the privacy of the individual; that indiscriminate use of such devices in law enforcement raises grave constitutional questions under the Fourth and Fifth Amendments; and that these considerations impose a heavier responsibility on this Court in its supervision of the fairness of procedures in the federal court system. However, I do not believe that, as a result, all uses of such devices should be proscribed either as unconstitutional or as unfair law enforcement methods." *Lopez v. United States*, 373 U. S., at 441 (concurring opinion of the Chief Justice).

met the "requirement of particularity" which the dissenting opinion in *Lopez* found necessary.

The situation which faced the two judges of the District Court when they were presented with Vick's affidavit on November 8, and the motivations which prompted their authorization of the recorder are reflected in the words of Chief Judge Miller. As he put it, "The affidavit contained information which reflected seriously upon a member of the bar of this court, who had practiced in my court ever since I have been on the bench. I decided that some action had to be taken to determine whether this information was correct or whether it was false. It was the most serious problem that I have had to deal with since I have been on the bench. I could not sweep it under the rug."

So it was that, in response to a detailed factual affidavit alleging the commission of a specific criminal offense directly and immediately affecting the administration of justice in the federal court, the judges of that court jointly authorized the use of a recording device for the narrow and particularized purpose of ascertaining the truth of the affidavit's allegations. As the district judges recognized, it was imperative to determine whether the integrity of their court was being undermined, and highly undesirable that this determination should hinge on the inconclusive outcome of a testimonial contest between the only two people in the world who knew the truth—one an informer, the other a lawyer of previous good repute. There could hardly be a clearer example of " 'the procedure of antecedent justification before a magistrate that is central to the Fourth Amendment' " as "a precondition of lawful electronic surveillance." [5]

We hold on these facts that the use of the recording device was permissible, and consequently that the recording itself was properly admitted as evidence at the petitioner's trial.

II.

The petitioner's defense was one of entrapment, and he renews here the contention made in his motion for acquittal at the trial that entrapment was established as a matter of law. We cannot agree.

The validity of the entrapment defense depended upon what had transpired at the meetings between the petitioner and Vick which took place before the recorded conversation of November 11. According to the petitioner, Vick initiated the idea of making a corrupt approach to Elliott on October 28, and the petitioner at first resisted the suggestion and tried to discourage Vick from carrying it out. The petitioner conceded that he ultimately acquiesced in the scheme, out of "weakness" and because he was exhaustetd from overwork, but said that he never seriously intended actually to carry out the plan to bribe Elliott. But Vick's version of what had happened was, as stated above, quite different, and the truth of the matter was for the jury to determine. Surely it was not a "trap for the unwary innocent," *Sherman v. United States,* 356 U. S. 369, 372, for Vick to tell the petitioner, truthfully, that he knew some of the members of the jury panel and that one of them was his cousin. And according to Vick he had said no more when the petitioner "jumped up," went out into the alley with him, and initiated the effort

---

[5] "The requirements of the Fourth Amendment are not inflexible, or obtusely unyielding to the legitimate needs of law enforcement. It is at least clear that 'the procedure of antecedent justification before a magistrate that is central to the Fourth Amendment,' *Ohio ex rel. Eaton v. Price,* 364 U. S. 263, 272 (separate opinion); see *McDonald v. United States,* 335 U. S. 451, 455; *Abel v. United States,* 362 U. S. 217, 251–252 (dissenting opinion), could be made a precondition of lawful electronic surveillance...." *Lopez v. United States,* 373 U. S., at 464 (dissenting opinion of Mr. Justice Brennan).

to get Elliott "on our side." At the most, Vick's statement afforded the petitioner "opportunities or facilities" for the commission of a criminal offense, and that is a far cry from entrapment.

III.

Finally, the argument is made that even if the admissibility and truth of all the evidence against the petitioner be accepted, this conviction must be set aside because his conduct did not constitute a violation of 18 U. S. C. § 1503. The basis for this argument is that since Vick never in fact approached Elliott and never intended to do so, any endeavor on the petitioner's part was impossible of accomplishment.

We reject the argument. Whatever continuing validity the doctrine of "impossibility," with all its subtleties, may continue to have in the law of criminal attempt, that body of law is inapplicable here. The statute under which the petitioner was convicted makes an offense of any proscribed "endeavor." And almost 50 years ago this Court pointed out the significance of that word: "The word of the section is 'endeavor,' and by using it the section got rid of the technicalities which might be urged as besetting the word 'attempt,' and it describes any effort or essay to accomplish the evil purpose that the section was enacted to prevent. ...The section...is not directed at success in corrupting a juror but at the 'endeavor' to do so. Experimental approaches to the corruption of a juror are the 'endeavor' of the section."

If the evidence against the petitioner be accepted, there can be no question that he corruptly endeavored to impede the due administration of justice by instructing Robert Vick to offer a bribe to a prospective juror in a federal criminal case.

Affirmed.

Mr. Justice White took no part in the consideration or decision of this case.

HOFFA v. UNITED STATES
SUPREME COURT OF THE UNITED STATES
385 U.S. 293, 87 S. CT. 408, 17 L. ED. 2d 374 (1966)

This is a companion case to *Osborn v. United States*, as it grew out of the same circumstances. It is referred to as a "false friend" case, as Hoffa confided in another Teamster's Union official in his hotel suite, the hotel lobby, and elsewhere. The man was a paid government informer. Hoffa was charged and convicted of attempting to bribe members of a jury at his previous trial. The Court held that there were *no* violations of:

the Fourth Amendment—the informer's *entry* into his hotel suite without disclosing his true identity

the Fifth Amendment—Hoffa's conversations with the informer were entirely voluntary

the Sixth Amendment—no violations of Hoffa's right to counsel

On the question of the informer reporting on the activity and conversations of Hoffa's attorneys in preparing the defense, the court held as follows:

III.

UNITED STATES SUPREME COURT. The petitioner makes two separate claims under the Sixth Amendment, and we give them separate consideration.

A.

During the course of the Test Fleet trial the petitioner's lawyers used his suite as a place to confer with him and with each other, to interview witnesses, and to plan the following day's trial strategy. Therefore, argues the petitioner, Partin's presence in and around the suite violated the petitioner's Sixth Amendment right to counsel, because an essential ingredient thereof is the right of a defendant and his counsel to prepare for trial without intrusion upon their confidential relationship by an agent of the Government, the defendant's trial adversary. Since Partin's presence in the suite thus violated the Sixth Amendment, the argument continues, any evidence acquired by reason of his presence there was constitutionally tainted and therefore inadmissible against the petitioner in this case. We reject this argument.

In the first place, it is far from clear to what extent Partin was present at conversations or conferences of the petitioner's counsel. Several of the petitioner's Test Fleet lawyers testified at the hearing on the motion to suppress Partin's testimony in the present case. Most of them said that Partin had heard or had been in a position to hear at least some of the lawyers' discussions during the Test Fleet trial. On the other hand, Partin himself testified that the lawyers "would move you out" when they wanted to discuss the case, and denied that he made any effort to "get into or be present at any conversations between lawyers or anything of that sort," other than engaging in such banalities as "how things looked," or "how does it look?" He said he might have heard some of the lawyers' conversations, but he didn't know what they were talking about, "because I wasn't interested in what they had to say about the case." He testified that he did not report any of the lawyers' conversations to Sheridan, because the latter "wasn't interested in what the attorneys said." Partin's testimony was largely confirmed by Sheridan. Sheridan did testify, however, to one occasion when Partin told him about a group of prospective character witnesses being interviewed in the suite by one of the petitioner's lawyers, who "was going over" some written "questions and answers" with them. This information was evidently relayed by Sheridan to the chief government attorney at the Test Fleet trial.

The District Court in the present case apparently credited Partin's testimony, finding "there has been no interference by the government with any attorney-client relationship of any defendant in this case." The Court of Appeals accepted this finding. In view of Sheridan's testimony about Partin's report of the interviews with the prospective character witnesses, however, we proceed here on the hypothesis that Partin did observe and report to Sheridan at least some of the activities of defense counsel in the Test Fleet trial.

The proposition that a surreptitious invasion by a government agent into the legal camp of the defense may violate the protection of the Sixth Amendment has found expression in two cases decided by the Court of Appeals for the District of Columbia Circuit, *Caldwell* v. *United States*, 92 U. S. App. D. C. 355, 205 F. 2d 879, and *Coplon* v. *United States*, 89 U. S. App. D. C. 103, 191 F. 2d 749. Both of those cases dealt with government intrusion of the grossest kind upon the confidential relationship between the defendant and his counsel. In *Coplon*, the defendant alleged that government agents deliberately intercepted telephone consultations between the defendant and her lawyer before and during the trial. In *Caldwell*, the agent, "[i]n his dual capacity as defense assistant and Government agent . . . gained free access to the planning of the defense. . . . Neither his dealings with the defense nor his reports to the prosecution were limited to the proposed unlawful acts of the defense: they covered many matters connected with the impending trial."

It is possible to imagine a case in which the prosecution might so pervasively insinuate itself into the councils of the defense as to make a new trial on the same charges impermissible under the Sixth Amendment. But even if it were further arguable that a situation could be hypothesized in which the Government's previous activities in undermining a defendant's Sixth Amendment rights at one trial would make evidence obtained thereby inadmissible in a different trial on other charges, the case now before us does not remotely approach such a situation.

This is so because of the clinching basic fact in the present case that none of the petitioner's incriminating statements which Partin heard were made in the presence of counsel, in the hearing of counsel, or in connection in any way with the legitimate defense of the Test Fleet prosecution. The petitioner's statements related to the commission of a quite separate offense—attempted bribery of jurors—and the statements were made to Partin out of the presence of any lawyers.

Even assuming, therefore, as we have, that there might have been a Sixth Amendment violation which might have made invalid a conviction, if there had been one, in the Test Fleet case, the evidence supplied by Partin in the present case was in no sense the "fruit" of any such violation. In *Wong Sun v. United States*, 371 U. S. 471, a case involving exclusion of evidence under the Fourth Amendment, the Court stated that "the more apt question in such a case is 'whether, granting establishment of the primary illegality, the evidence to which instant objection is made has been come at by exploitation of that illegality or instead by means sufficiently distinguishable to be purged of the primary taint.' Maguire, Evidence of Guilt, 221 (1959)." 371 U. S., at 488.

Even upon the premise that this same strict standard of excludability should apply under the Sixth Amendment—a question we need not decide—it is clear that Partin's evidence in this case was not the consequence of any "exploitation" of a Sixth Amendment violation. The petitioner's incriminating statements to which Partin testified in this case were totally unrelated in both time and subject matter to any assumed intrusion by Partin into the conferences of the petitioner's counsel in the Test Fleet trial. These incriminating statements, all of them made out of the presence or hearing of any of the petitioner's counsel, embodied the very antithesis of any legitimate defense in the Test Fleet trial.

B.

The petitioner's second argument under the Sixth Amendment needs no extended discussion. That argument goes as follows: Not later than October 25, 1962, the Government had sufficient ground for taking the petitioner into custody and charging him with endeavors to tamper with the Test Fleet jury. Had the Government done so, it could not have continued to question the petitioner without observance of his Sixth Amendment right to counsel. Therefore, the argument concludes, evidence of statements made by the petitioner subsequent to October 25 was inadmissible, because the Government acquired that evidence only by flouting the petitioner's Sixth Amendment right to counsel.

Nothing in *Massiah*, in *Escobedo*, or in any other case that has come to our attention, even remotely suggests this novel and paradoxical constitutional doctrine, and we decline to adopt it now. There is no constitutional right to be arrested. The police are not required to guess at their peril the precise moment at which they have probable cause to arrest a suspect, risking a violation of the Fourth Amendment if they act too soon, and a violation of the Sixth Amendment if they wait too long. Law enforcement officers are under no constitutional duty to call a halt to a criminal investigation the moment they have the minimum evidence to establish probable cause, a quantum of evidence which may fall far short of the amount necessary to support a criminal conviction.

LEWIS v. UNITED STATES
SUPREME COURT OF THE UNITED STATES
385 U.S. 206, 87 S. CT. 424, 17 L. ED. 2d 312 (1966)

Mr. Chief Justice Warren delivered the opinion of the Court.

The question for resolution here is whether the Fourth Amendment was violated when a federal narcotics agent, by misrepresenting his identity and stating his willingness to purchase narcotics, was invited into petitioner's home where an unlawful narcotics transaction was consummated and the narcotics were thereafter introduced at petitioner's criminal trial over his objection. We hold that under the facts of this case it was not. Those facts are not disputed and may be briefly stated as follows:

On December 3, 1964, Edward Cass, an undercover federal narcotics agent, telephoned petitioner's home to inquire about the possibility of purchasing marihuana. Cass, who previously had not met or dealt with petitioner, falsely identified himself as one "Jimmy the Pollack [sic]" and stated that a mutual friend had told him petitioner might be able to supply marihuana. In response, petitioner said, "Yes. I believe, Jimmy, I can take care of you," and then directed Cass to his home where, it was indicated, a sale of marihuana would occur. Cass drove to petitioner's home, knocked on the door, identified himself as "Jim," and was admitted. After discussing the possibility of regular future dealings at a discounted price, petitioner led Cass to a package located on the front porch of his home. Cass gave petitioner $50, took the package, and left the premises. The package contained five bags of marihuana. On December 17, 1964, a similar transaction took place, beginning with a phone conversation in which Cass identified himself as "Jimmy the Pollack" and ending with an invited visit by Cass to petitioner's home where a second sale of marihuana occurred. Once again, Cass paid petitioner $50, but this time he received in return a package containing six bags of marihuana.

Petitioner was arrested on April 27, 1965, and charged by a two-count indictment with violations of the narcotics laws relating to transfers of marihuana. 26 U. S. C. § 4742(a). A pretrial motion to suppress as evidence the marihuana and the conversations between petitioner and the agent was denied, and they were introduced at the trial. The District Court, sitting without a jury, convicted petitioner on both counts and imposed concurrent five-year penitentiary sentences. The Court of Appeals for the First Circuit affirmed and we granted certiorari.

Petitioner does not argue that he was entrapped, as he could not on the facts of this case; nor does he contend that a search of his home was made or that anything other than the purchased narcotics was taken away. His only contentions are that, in the absence of a warrant, any official intrusion upon the privacy of a home constitutes a Fourth Amendment violation and that the fact the suspect invited the intrusion cannot be held a waiver when the invitation was induced by fraud and deception.

Both petitioner and the Government recognize the necessity for some undercover police activity and both concede that the particular circumstances of each case govern the admissibility of evidence obtained by stratagem or deception. Indeed, it has long been acknowledged by the decisions of this Court that, in the detection of many types of crime, the Government is entitled to use decoys and to conceal the identity of its agents. The various protections of the Bill of Rights, of course, provide checks upon such official deception for the protection of the individual. . . .

Petitioner argues that the Government ovsrstepped the constitutional bounds in this case and places principal reliance on *Gouled* v. *United States*, 255 U. S. 298 (1921). But a short statement of that case will demonstrate how misplaced his reliance is. There, a business acquaintance of the petitioner, acting under orders of federal officers, obtained entry into the petitioner's office by falsely representing that he intended only to pay a social visit. In the petitioner's absence, however, the intruder secretly ransacked the office and seized certain private papers of an incriminating nature. This Court had no difficulty concluding that the Fourth Amendment had been violated by the secret and general ransacking, notwithstanding that the initial intrusion was occasioned by a fraudulently obtained invitation rather than by force or stealth.

In the instant case, on the other hand, the petitioner invited the undercover agent to his home for the specific purpose of executing a felonious sale of narcotics. Petitioner's only concern was whether the agent was a willing purchaser who could pay the agreed price. Indeed, in order to convince the agent that his patronage at petitioner's home was desired, petitioner told him that, if he became a regular customer there, he would in the future receive an extra bag of marihuana at no additional cost; and in fact petitioner did hand over an extra bag at a second sale which was consummated at the same place and in precisely the same manner. During neither of his visits to petitioner's home did the agent see, hear, or take anything that was not contemplated, and in fact intended, by petitioner as a necessary part of his illegal business. Were we to hold the deceptions of the agent in this case constitutionally prohibited, we would come near to a rule that the use of undercover agents in any manner is virtually unconstitutional *per se*. Such a rule would, for example, severely hamper the Government in ferreting out those organized criminal activities that are characterized by covert dealings with victims who either cannot or do not protest.[1] A prime example is provided by the narcotics traffic.

The fact that the undercover agent entered petitioner's home does not compel a different conclusion. Without question, the home is accorded the full range of Fourth Amendment protections. But when, as here, the home is converted into a commercial center to which outsiders are invited for purposes of transacting unlawful business, that business is entitled to no greater sanctity than if it were carried on in a store, a garage, a car, or on the street. A government agent, in the same manner as a private person, may accept an invitation to do business and may enter upon the premises for the very purposes contemplated by the

---

[1] "Particularly, in the enforcement of vice, liquor or narcotics laws, it is all but impossible to obtain evidence for prosecution save by the use of decoys. There are rarely complaining witnesses. The participants in the crime enjoy themselves. Misrepresentation by a police officer or agent concerning the identity of the purchaser of illegal narcotics is a practical necessity. . . . Therefore, the law must attempt to distinguish between those deceits and persuasions which are permissible and those which are not." Model Penal Code § 2.10, comment, p. 16 (Tent. Draft. No. 9, 1959). See also Donnelly, Judicial Control of Informants, Spies, Stool Pigeons and Agent Provocateurs, 60 Yale L. J. 1091, 1094 (1951); Note, 73 Harv. L. Rev. 1333, 1338–1339 (1960).

occupant. Of course, this does not mean that, whenever entry is obtained by invitation and the locus is characterized as a place of business, an agent is authorized to conduct a general search for incriminating materials; a citation to the *Gouled* case, *supra*, is sufficient to dispose of that contention.

Finally, petitioner also relies on *Rios* v. *United States*, 364 U. S. 253 (1960); *Jones* v. *United States*, 362 U. S. 257 (1960); *McDonald* v. *United States*, 335 U. S. 451 (1948); and *Johnson* v. *United States*, 333 U. S. 10 (1948). But those cases all dealt with the exclusion of evidence that had been forcibly seized against the suspects' desires and without the authorization conferred by search warrants. A reading of them will readily demonstrate that they are inapposite to the facts of this case; and, in this area, each case must be judged on its own particular facts. Nor is *Silverman* v. *United States*, 365 U. S. 505 (1961), in point; for there, the conduct proscribed was that of eavesdroppers, unknown and unwanted intruders who furtively listened to conversations occurring in the privacy of a house. The instant case involves no such problem; it has been well summarized by the Government at the conclusion of its brief as follows:

> "In short, this case involves the exercise of no governmental power to intrude upon protected premises; the visitor was invited and willingly admitted by the suspect. It concerns no design on the part of a government agent to observe or hear what was happening in the privacy of a home; the suspect chose the location where the transaction took place. It presents no question of the invasion of the privacy of a dwelling; the only statements repeated were those that were willingly made to the agent and the only things taken were the packets of marihuana voluntarily transferred to him. The pretense resulted in no breach of privacy; it merely encouraged the suspect to say things which he was willing and anxious to say to anyone who would be interested in purchasing marihuana."

Further elaboration is not necessary. The judgment is

Affirmed.

DRAPER v. UNITED STATES
SUPREME COURT OF THE UNITED STATES
358 U.S. 307, 79 S. CT. 329, 3 L. ED. 2d 327 (1959)

Mr. Justice Whittaker delivered the opinion of the Court.

Petitioner was convicted of knowingly concealing and transporting narcotic drugs in Denver, Colorado, in violation of 35 Stat 614, as amended, 21 USC § 174. His conviction was based in part on the use in evidence against him of two "envelopes containing [865 grains of] heroin" and a hypodermic syringe that had been taken from his person, following his arrest, by the arresting officer. Before the trial, he moved to suppress that evidence as having been secured through an unlawful search and seizure. After hearing, the District Court found that the arresting officer had probable cause to arrest petitioner without a warrant and that the subsequent search and seizure were therefore incident to a lawful arrest, and overruled the motion to suppress. At the subsequent trial, that evidence was offered and, over petitioner's renewed objection, was received in evidence, and the trial resulted, as we have said, in petitioner's conviction. The Court of Appeals affirmed the conviction, and certiorari was sought on the sole ground that the search and seizure violated the Fourth Amendment and therefore the use of the heroin in evidence vitiated the conviction. We granted the writ to determine that question.

The evidence offered at the hearing on the motion to suppress was not substantially disputed. It established that one Marsh, a federal narcotic agent with 29 years' experience, was stationed at Denver; that one Hereford had been engaged as a "special employee" of the Bureau of Narcotics at Denver for about six months, and from time to time gave information to Marsh regarding violations of the narcotic laws, for which Hereford was paid small sums of money, and that Marsh had always found the information given by Hereford to be accurate and reliable. On September 3, 1956, Hereford told Marsh that James Draper (petitioner) recently had taken up abode at a stated address in Denver and "was peddling narcotics to several addicts" in that city. Four days later, on September 7, Hereford told Marsh "that Draper had gone to Chicago the day before [September 6] by train [and] that he was going to bring back three ounces of heroin [and] that he would return to Denver either on the morning of the 8th of September or the morning of the 9th of September also by train." Hereford also gave Marsh a detailed physical description of Draper and of the clothing he was wearing, and said that he would be carrying "a tan zipper bag," and that he habitually "walked real fast."

On the morning of September 8, Marsh and a Denver police officer went to the Denver Union Station and kept watch over all incoming trains from Chicago, but they did not see anyone fitting the description that Hereford had given. Repeating the process on the morning of September 9, they saw a person, having the exact physical attributes and wearing the precise clothing described by Hereford, alight from an incoming Chicago train and start walking "fast" toward the exit. He was carrying a tan zipper bag in his right hand and the left was thrust in his raincoat pocket. Marsh, accompanied by the police officer, overtook, stopped and arrested him. They then searched him and found the two "envelopes containing heroin" clutched in his left hand in his raincoat pocket, and found the syringe in the tan zipper bag. Marsh then took him (petitioner) into custody. Hereford died four days after the arrest and therefore did not testify at the hearing on the motion.

. . . .

The crucial question for us then is whether knowledge of the related facts and circumstances gave Marsh "probable cause" within the meaning of the Fourth Amendment, and "reasonable grounds" within the meaning of § 104(a), supra, to believe that petitioner had committed or was committing a violation of the narcotic laws. If it did, the arrest without a warrant, was lawful and the subsequent search of petitioner's person and the seizure of the found heroin were validly made incident to a lawful arrest, and therefore the motion to suppress was properly overruled and the heroin was competently received in evidence at the trial.

Petitioner does not dispute this analysis of the question for decision. Rather, he contends (1) that the information given by Hereford to Marsh was "hearsay" and, because hearsay is not legally competent evidence in a criminal trial, could not legally have been considered, but should have been put out of mind, by Marsh in assessing whether he had "probable cause" and "reasonable grounds" to arrest petitioner without a warrant, and (2) that, even if hearsay could lawfully have been considered, Marsh's information should be held insufficient to show "probable cause" and "reasonable grounds" to believe that petitioner had violated or was violating the narcotic laws and to justify his arrest without a warrant.

Considering the first contention, we find petitioner entirely in error. Brinegar v United States, 338 US 160, has settled the question the other way. There, in a similar situation, the convict contented "that the factors relating to inadmissibility of the evidence [for] *purposes of proving guilt at the trial,* deprive[d] the evidence as a whole of sufficiency to show probable cause for the search...." (Emphasis added.) But this Court, rejecting that contention, said:

> "[T]he so-called distinction places a wholly unwarranted emphasis upon the criterion of admissibility in evidence, to prove the accused's guilt, of the facts relied upon to show probable cause. That emphasis, we think, goes much too far in confusing and disregarding the difference between what is required to prove guilt in a criminal case and what is required to show probable cause for arrest or search. It approaches requiring (if it does not in practical effect require) proof sufficient to establish guilt in order to substantiate the existence of probable cause. There is a large difference between the two things to be proved [guilt and probable cause], as well as between the tribunals which determine them, and therefore a like difference in the quanta and modes of proof required to establish them."

Nor can we agree with petitioner's second contention that Marsh's information was insufficient to show probable cause and reasonable grounds to believe that petitioner had violated or was violating the narcotic laws and to justify his arrest without a warrant. The information given to narcotic agent Marsh by "special employee Hereford may have been hearsay to Marsh, but coming from one employed for that purpose and whose information had always been found accurate and reliable, it is clear that Marsh would have been derelict in his duties had he not pursued it. And when, in pursuing that information, he saw a man, having the exact physical attributes and wearing the precise clothing and carrying the tan zipper bag that Hereford had described, alight from one of the very trains from the very place stated by Hereford and start to walk at a "fast" pace toward the station exit, Marsh had personally verified every facet of the information given him by Hereford except whether petitioner had accomplished his mission and had the three ounces of heroin on his person or in his bag. And surely, with every other bit of Hereford's information being thus personally verified, Marsh had "reasonable grounds" to believe that the remaining unverified bit of Hereford's information—that Draper would have the heroin with him—was likewise true.

"In dealing with probable cause,... as the very name implies, we deal with probabilities. These are not technical; they are the factual and practical considerations of everyday life on which reasonable and prudent men, not legal technicians, act." Brinegar v United States, supra (338 US at 175). Probable cause exists where "the facts and circumstances within [the arresting officers'] knowledge and of which they had reasonably trustworthy information [are] sufficient in themselves to warrant a man of reasonable caution in the belief that" an offense has been or is being committed. Carroll v United States, 267 US 132.

We believe that, under the facts and circumstances here, Marsh had probable cause and reasonable grounds to believe that petitioner was committing a violation of the laws of the United States relating to narcotic drugs at the time he arrested him. The arrest was therefore lawful, and the subsequent search and seizure, having been made incident to that lawful arrest, were likewise valid. It follows that petitioner's motion to suppress was properly denied and that the seized heroin was competent evidence lawfully received at the trial.

Affirmed.

[Dissenting opinion omitted.]

McCRAY v. ILLINOIS
SUPREME COURT OF THE UNITED STATES
386 U.S. 300, 87 S. CT. 1056, 18 L. ED. 2d 62 (1967)

Mr. Justice Stewart delivered the opinion of the Court.

The petitioner was arrested in Chicago, Illinois, on the morning of January 16, 1964, for possession of narcotics. The Chicago police officers who made the arrest found a package containing heroin on his person and he was indicted for its unlawful possession. Prior to trial he filed a motion to suppress the heroin as evidence against him, claiming that the police had acquired it in an unlawful search and seizure in violation of the Fourth and Fourteenth Amendments. After a hearing, the court denied the motion, and the petitioner was subsequently convicted upon the evidence of the heroin the arresting officers had found in his possession. The judgment of conviction was affirmed by the Supreme Court of Illinois, and we granted certiorari to consider the petitioner's claim that the hearing on his motion to suppress was constitutionally defective.

The petitioner's arrest occurred near the intersection of 49th Street and Calumet Avenue at about seven in the morning. At the hearing on the motion to suppress, he testified that up until a half hour before he was arrested he had been at "a friend's house" about a block away, that after leaving the friend's house he had "walked with a lady from 48th to 48th and South Park," and that, as he approached 49th Street and Calumet Avenue, "[t]he Officers stopped me going through the alley." "The officers," he said, "did not show me a search warrant for my person or an arrest warrant for my arrest." He said the officers then searched him and found the narcotics in question. The petitioner did not identify the "friend" nor the "lady," and neither of them appeared as a witness.

The arresting officers then testified. Officer Jackson stated that he and two fellow officers had had a conversation with an informant on the morning of January 16 in their unmarked police car. The officer said that the informant had told them that the petitioner, with whom Jackson was acquainted, "was selling narcotics and had narcotics on his person and that he could be found in the vicinity of 47th and Calumet at this particular time." Jackson said that he and his fellow officers drove to that vicinity in the police car and that when they spotted the petitioner, the informant pointed him out and then departed on foot. Jackson stated that the officers observed the petitioner walking with a woman, then separating from her and meeting briefly with a man, then proceeding alone, and finally, after seeing the police car, "hurriedly walk[ing] between two buildings." "At this point," Jackson testified, "my partner and myself got out of the car and informed him we had information he had narcotics on his person, placed him in the police vehicle at this point." Jackson stated that the officers then searched the petitioner and found the heroin in a cigarette package.

Jackson testified that he had been acquainted with the informant for approximately a year, that during this period the informant had supplied him with information about narcotics activities "fifteen, sixteen times at least," that the information had proved to be accurate and had resulted in numerous arrests and convictions. On cross-examination, Jackson was even more specific as to the informant's previous reliability, giving the names of people who had been convicted of narcotics violations as the result of information the informant had supplied. When Jackson was asked for the informant's name and address, counsel for the State objected, and the objection was sustained by the court.[1]

Officer Arnold gave substantially the same account of the circumstances of the petitioner's arrest and search, stating that the informant had told the officers that the petitioner "was selling narcotics and had narcotics on his person now in the vicinity of 47th and Calumet." The informant, Arnold testified, "said he had observed [the petitioner] selling narcotics to various people, meaning various addicts, in the area of 47th and Calumet." Arnold testified that he had known the informant "roughly two years," that the informant had given him information concerning narcotics "20 or 25 times," and that the information had resulted in convictions. Arnold too was asked on cross-examination for the informant's name and address, and objections to these questions were sustained by the court.... It is the petitioner's claim ... that even though the officers' sworn testimony fully supported a finding of probable cause for the arrest and search, the state court nonetheless violated the Constitution when it sustained objections to the petitioner's questions as to the identity of the informant. We cannot agree.

In permitting the officers to withhold the informant's identity, the court was following well-settled Illinois law. When the issue is not guilt or innocence, but, as here, the question of probable cause for an arrest or search, the Illinois Supreme Court has held that police officers need not invariably be required to disclose an informant's identity if the trial judge is convinced, by evidence submitted in open court and subject to cross-examination, that the officers did rely in good faith upon credible information supplied by a reliable informant. This Illinois evidentiary rule is consistent with the law of many other States. In California, the State Legislature in 1965 enacted a statute adopting just such a rule for cases like the one before us:

> "[I]n any preliminary hearing, criminal trial, or other criminal proceeding, for violation of any provision of Division 10 (commencing with Section 11000) of the Health and Safety Code, evidence of information communicated to a peace officer by a confidential informant, who is not a material witness to the guilt or innocence of the accused of the

---

[1] "Q. What is the name of this informant that gave you this information?

"Mr. Engerman: Objection, your Honor.

"The Court: State for the record the reasons for your objection.

"Mr. Engerman: Judge, based upon the testimony of the officer so far that they had used this informant for approximately a year, he has worked with this individual, in the interest of the public, I see no reason why the officer should be forced to disclose the name of the informant, to cause harm or jeopardy to an individual who has cooperated with the police. The City of Chicago have a tremendous problem with narcotics. If the police are not able to withhold the name of the informant they will not be able to get informants. They are not willing to risk their lives if their names become known.

"In the interest of the City and the law enforcement of this community, I feel the officer should not be forced to reveal the name of the informant. And I also cite People vs. Durr.

"The Court: I will sustain that.

"Mr. Adam: Q. Where does this informant live?

"Mr. Engerman: Objection, your Honor, same basis.

"The Court: Sustained."

offense charged, shall be admissible on the issue of reasonable cause to make an arrest or search without requiring that the name or identity of the informant be disclosed if the judge or magistrate is satisfied, based upon evidence produced in open court, out of the presence of the jury, that such information was received from a reliable informant and in his discretion does not require such disclosure." California Code of Evidence, § 1042(c).

The reasoning of the Supreme Court of New Jersey in judicially adopting the same basic evidentiary rule was instructively expressed by Chief Justic Weintraub in State v. Burnett, 42 N.J. 377, 201 A.2d 39:

"If a defendant may insist upon disclosure of the informant in order to test the truth of the officer's statement that there is an informant or as to what the informant related or as to the informant's reliability, we can be sure that every defendant will demand disclosure. He has nothing to lose and the prize may be the suppression of damaging evidence if the State cannot afford to reveal its source, as is so often the case. And since there is no way to test the good faith of a defendant who presses the demand, we must assume the routine demand would have to be routinely granted. The result would be that the State could use the informant's information only as a lead and could search only if it could gather adequate evidence of probable cause apart from the informant's data. Perhaps that approach would sharpen investigatorial techniques, but we doubt that there would be enough talent and time to cope with crime upon that basis. Rather we accept the premise that the informer is a vital part of society's defensive arsenal. The basic rule protecting his identity rests upon that belief. . . .

"We must remember also that we are not dealing with the trial of the criminal charge itself. There the need for a truthful verdict outweighs society's need for the informer privilege. Here, however, the accused seeks to avoid the truth. The very purpose of a motion to suppress is to escape the inculpatory thrust of evidence in hand, not because its probative force is diluted in the least by the mode of seizure, but rather as a sanction to compel enforcement officers to respect the constitutional security of all of us under the Fourth Amendment. State v. Smith, 37 N.J. 481, 486, 181 A.2d 761 (1962). If the motion to suppress is denied, defendant will still be judged upon the untarnished truth. . . .

"The Fourth Amendment is served if a judicial mind passes upon the existence of probable cause. Where the issue is submitted upon an application for a warrant, the magistrate is trusted to evaluate the credibility of the affiant in an ex parte proceeding. As we have said, the magistrate is concerned, not with whether the informant lied, but with whether the affiant is truthful in his recitation of what he was told. If the magistrate doubts the credibility of the affiant, he may require that the informant be identified or even produced. It seems to us that the same approach is equally sufficient where the search was without a warrant, that is to say, that it should rest entirely with the judge who hears the motion to suppress to decide whether he needs such disclosure as to the informant in order to decide whether the officer is a believable witness."

What Illinois and her sister States have done is no more than recognize a well-established testimonial privilege, long familiar to the law of evidence. Professor Wigmore, not known as an enthusiastic advocate of testimonial privileges generally, has described that privilege in these words:

> "A genuine privilege, on...fundamental principle...must be recognized for the *identity of persons supplying the government with information concerning the commission of crimes*. Communications of this kind ought to receive encouragement. They are discouraged if the informer's identity is disclosed. Whether an informer is motivated by good citizenship, promise of leniency or prospect of pecuniary reward, he will usually condition his cooperation on an assurance of anonymity—to protect himself and his family from harm, to preclude adverse social reactions and to avoid the risk of defamation or malicious prosecution actions against him. The government also has an interest in nondisclosure of the identity of its informers. Law enforcement officers often depend upon professional informers to furnish them with a flow of information about criminal activities. Revelation of the dual role played by such persons ends their usefulness to the government and discourages others from entering into a like relationship.
>
> "That the government has this privilege is well established, and its soundness cannot be questioned." (Footnotes omitted.) 8 Wigmore, Evidence § 2374 (McNaughton rev. 1961).

In the federal courts the rules of evidence in criminal trials are governed "by the principles of the common law as they may be interpreted by the courts of the United States in the light of reason and experience." This Court, therefore, has the ultimate task of defining the scope to be accorded to the various common law evidentiary privileges in the trial of federal criminal cases. This is a task which is quite different, of course, from the responsibility of constitutional adjudication. In the exercise of this supervisory jurisdiction the Court had occasion 10 years ago, in Roviaro v. United States, to give thorough consideration to one aspect of the informer's privilege, the privilege itself having long been recognized in the federal judicial system.

The *Roviaro* case involved the informer's privilege, not at a preliminary hearing to determine probable cause for an arrest or search, but at the trial itself where the issue was the fundamental one of innocence or guilt. The petitioner there had been brought to trial upon a two-count federal indictment charging sale and transportation of narcotics. According to the prosecution's evidence, the informer had been an active participant in the crime. He "had taken a material part in bringing about the possession of certain drugs by the accused, had been present with the accused at the occurrence of the alleged crime, and might be a material witness as to whether the accused knowingly transported the drugs as charged." The trial court nonetheless denied a defense motion to compel the prosecution to disclose the informer's identity.

This Court held that where, in an actual trial of a federal criminal case, "the disclosure of an informer's identity ... is relevant and helpful to the defense of an accused, or is essential to a fair determination of a cause, the privilege must give way. In these situations the trial court may require disclosure and, if the Government withholds the information, dismiss the action....

"We believe that no fixed rule with respect to disclosure is justifiable. The problem is one that calls for balancing the public interest in protecting the flow of information against the individual's right to prepare his defense. Whether a proper balance renders nondisclosure erroneous must depend on the particular circumstances of each case, taking into consideration the crime charged, the possible defenses, the possible significance of the informer's testimony, and other relevant factors."

The Court's opinion then carefully reviewed the particular circumstances of Roviaro's trial, pointing out that the informer's "possible testimony was highly relevant ...," that he "might have disclosed an entrapment ...," "might have thrown doubt upon petitioner's identity or on the identity of the package ...," "might have testified to petitioner's possible lack of knowledge of the contents of the package that he 'transported' ...," and that the "informer was the sole participant, other than the accused, in the transaction charged." The Court concluded "that, under these circumstances, the trial court committed prejudicial error in permitting the Government to withhold the identity of its undercover employee in the face of repeated demands by the accused for his disclosure."

What *Roviaro* thus makes clear is that this Court was unwilling to impose any absolute rule requiring disclosure of an informer's identity even in formulating evidentiary rules for federal criminal trials. Much less has the Court ever approached the formulation of a federal evidentiary rule of compulsory disclosure where the issue is the preliminary one of probable cause, and guilt or innocence is not at stake. Indeed, we have repeatedly made clear that federal officers need *not* disclose an informer's identity in applying for an arrest or search warrant. As was said in United States v. Ventresca, 380 U.S. 102, 108, 85 S.Ct. 741, 745, we have "recognized that 'an affidavit may be based on hearsay information and need not reflect the direct personal observations of the affiant,' so long as the magistrate is 'informed of some of the underlying circumstances' supporting the affiant's conclusions and his belief that any informant involved *whose identity need not be disclosed* ... was "credible" or his information "reliable." ' Aguilar v. State of Texas, supra, 378 U.S., at 114, 84 S.Ct., at 1514." (Emphasis added.) And just this Term we have taken occasion to point out that a rule virtually prohibiting the use of informers would "severely hamper the Government" in enforcement of the narcotics laws.

In sum, the Court in the exercise of its power to formulate evidentiary rules for federal criminal cases has consistently declined to hold that an informer's identity need always be disclosed in a federal criminal trial, let alone in a preliminary hearing to determine probable cause for an arrest or search. Yet we are now asked to hold that the Constitution somehow compels Illinois to abolish the informer's privilege from its law of evidence, and to require disclosure of the informer's identity in every such preliminary hearing where it appears that the officers made the arrest or search in reliance upon facts supplied by an informer they had reason to trust. The argument is based upon the Due Process Clause of the Fourteenth Amendment, and upon the Sixth Amendment right of confrontation, applicable to the States through the Fourteenth Amendment. We find no support for the petitioner's position in either of those constitutional provisions.

The arresting officers in this case testified, in open court, fully and in precise detail as to what the informer told them and as to why they had reason to believe his information was trustworthy. Each officer was under oath. Each was subjected to searching cross-examination. The judge was obviously satisfied that each was telling the truth, and for that reason he exercised the discretion conferred upon him by the established law of Illinois to respect the informer's privilege.

Nothing in the Due Process Clause of the Fourteenth Amendment requires a state court judge in every such hearing to assume the arresting officers are committing perjury. "To take such a step would be quite beyond the pale of this Court's proper function in our federal system. It would be a wholly unjustifiable encroachment by this Court upon the constitutional power of States to promulgate their own rules of evidence . . . in their own state courts. . . ."

The petitioner does not explain precisely how he thinks his Sixth Amendment right to confrontation and cross-examination was violated by Illinois' recognition of the informer's privilege in this case. If the claim is that the State violated the Sixth Amendment by not producing the informer to testify against the petitioner, then we need no more than repeat the Court's answer to that claim a few weeks ago in Cooper v. State of California:

> "Petitioner also presents the contention here that he was unconstitutionally deprived of the right to confront a witness against him, because the State did not produce the informant to testify against him. This contention we consider absolutely devoid of merit."

On the other hand, the claim may be that the petitioner was deprived of his Sixth Amendment right to cross-examine the arresting officers themselves, because their refusal to reveal the informer's identity was upheld. But it would follow from this argument that no witness on cross-examination could ever constitutionally assert a testimonial privilege, including the privilege against compulsory self-incrimination guaranteed by the Constitution itself. We have never given the Sixth Amendment such a construction, and we decline to do so now.

Affirmed.

[Dissenting opinion omitted.]

SMITH v. ILLINOIS
SUPREME COURT OF THE UNITED STATES
390 U.S. 129, 88 S. CT. 748, 19 L. ED. 2d 956 (1968)

OPINION OF THE COURT BY MR. JUSTICE STEWART. At the trial the principal witness against the petitioner was a man who identified himself on direct examination as "James Jordan." This witness testified that he had purchased a bag of heroin from the petitioner in a restaurant with marked money provided by two Chicago police officers. The officers corroborated part of this testimony, but only this witness and the petitioner testified to the crucial events inside the restaurant, and the petitioner's version of those events was entirely different. The only real question at the trial, therefore, was the relative credibility of the petitioner and this prosecution witness.

On cross-examination this witness was asked whether "James Jordan" was his real name. He admitted, over the prosecutor's objection, that it was not. He was then asked what his correct name was, and the court sustained the prosecutor's objection to the question.

As the Court said in *Pointer*, "It cannot seriously be doubted at this late date that the right of cross-examination is included in the right of an accused in a criminal case to confront the witnesses against him." Even more recently we have repeated that "a denial of cross-examination without waiver . . . would be constitutional error of the first magnitude and no amount of showing of want of prejudice would cure it."

In the present case there was not, to be sure, a complete denial of all right of cross-examination. But the petitioner was denied the right to ask the principal prosecution witness either his name or where he lived, although the witness admitted that the name he had first given was false. Yet when the credibility of a witness is in issue, the very starting point in "exposing falsehood and bringing out the truth" through cross-examination must necessarily be to ask the witness who he is and where he lives. The witness' name and address open countless avenues of in-court examination and out-of-court investigation. To forbid this most rudimentary inquiry at the threshold is effectively to emasculate the right of cross-examination itself.

In *Alford v. United States*, 282 U. S. 687, this Court almost 40 years ago unanimously reversed a federal conviction because the trial judge had sustained objections to questions by the defense seeking to elicit the "place of residence" of a prosecution witness over the insistence of defense counsel that "the jury was entitled to know 'who the witness is, where he lives and what his business is.'" What the Court said in reversing that conviction is fully applicable here:

> "It is the essence of a fair trial that reasonable latitude be given the cross-examiner, even though he is unable to state to the court what facts a reasonable cross-examination might develop. Prejudice ensues from a denial of the opportunity to place the witness in his proper setting and put the weight of his testimony and his credibility to a test, without which the jury cannot fairly appraise them. . . . To say that prejudice can be established only by showing that the cross-examination, if pursued, would necessarily have brought out facts tending to discredit the testimony in chief, is to deny a substantial right and withdraw one of the safeguards essential to a fair trial. . . .
>
> ". . . The question 'Where do you live?' was not only an appropriate preliminary to the cross-examination of the witness, but on its face, without any such declaration of purpose as was made by counsel here, was an essential step in identifying the witness with his environment, to which cross-examination may always be directed. . . .
>
> . . . .
>
> "The extent of cross-examination with respect to an appropriate subject of inquiry is within the sound discretion of the trial court. It may exercise a reasonable judgment in determining when the subject is exhausted. . . . But no obligation is imposed on the court, such as that suggested below, to protect a witness from being discredited on cross-examination, short of an attempted invasion of his constitutional protection from self incrimination, properly invoked. There is a duty to protect him from questions which go beyond the bounds of proper cross-examination merely to harass, annoy or humiliate him. . . . But no such case is presented here. . . ." 282 U.S., at 692–694.

In *Pointer* v. *Texas, supra,* the Court made clear that "the right of an accused to be confronted with the witnesses against him must be determined by the same standards whether the right is denied in a federal or state proceeding...." In this state case we follow the standard of *Alford* and hold that the petitioner was deprived of a right guaranteed to him under the Sixth and Fourteenth Amendments of the Constitution.

Reversed.

WARDEN v. WILLIAMS
SUPREME COURT OF THE UNITED STATES
407 U.S. 143, 92 S. CT. 1921, 32 L. ED. 2d 612 (JUNE 1972)

MR. JUSTICE REHNQUIST. ... Police Sgt. John Connolly was alone early in the morning on car patrol duty in a high crime area of Bridgeport, Connecticut. At approximately 2:15 a.m. a person known to Sgt. Connolly approached his cruiser and informed him that an individual seated in a nearby vehicle was carrying narcotics and had a gun at his waist.

After calling for assistance on his car radio, Sgt. Connolly approached the vehicle to investigate the informant's report. Connolly tapped on the car window and asked the occupant, Robert Williams, to open the door. When Williams rolled down the window instead, the sergeant reached into the car and removed a fully loaded revolver from Williams' waistband. The gun had not been visible to Connolly from outside the car, but it was in precisely the place indicated by the informant. Williams was then arrested by Connolly for unlawful possession of the pistol. A search incident to that arrest was conducted after other officers arrived. They found substantial quantities of heroin on Williams' person and in the car, and they found a machete and a second revolver hidden in the automobile.

Respondent contends that the initial seizure of his pistol, upon which rested the later search and seizure of other weapons and narcotics, was not justified by the informant's tip to Sgt. Connolly. He claims that absent a more reliable informant, or some corroboration of the tip, the policeman's actions were unreasonable under the standards set forth in *Terry* v. *Ohio.*

. . . .

The Court recognized in *Terry* that the policeman making a reasonable investigatory stop should not be denied the opportunity to protect himself from attack by a hostile suspect. "When an officer is justified in believing that the individual whose suspicious behavior he is investigating at close range is armed and presently dangerous to the officer or to others," he may conduct a limited protective search for concealed weapons. *Id.,* at 24. The purpose of this limited search is not to discover evidence of crime, but to allow the officer to pursue his investigation without fear of violence, and thus the frisk for weapons might be equally necessary and reasonable whether or not carrying a concealed weapon violated any applicable state law. So long as the officer is entitled to make a forcible stop and has reason to believe that the suspect is armed and dangerous, he may conduct a weapons search limited in scope to this protective purpose. *Id.,* at 30.

Applying these principles to the present case we believe that Sgt. Connolly acted justifiably in responding to his informant's tip. The informant was known to him personally and had provided him with information in the past. This is a stronger case than obtains in the case of an anonymous telephone tip. The informant here came forward personally to give information that was immediately verifiable at the scene. Indeed, under Connecticut law, the informant herself might have been subject to immediate arrest for making a false complaint had Sgt. Connolly's investigation proven the tip incorrect. Thus, while the Court's decisions indicate that this informant's unverified tip may have been insufficient for a narcotics arrest or search warrant, see, e. g., *Spinelli v. United States*, 393 U. S. 410 (1969); *Aguilar v. Texas*, 378 U. S. 108 (1964), the information carried enough indicia of reliability to justify the officer's forcible stop of Williams.

In reaching this conclusion, we reject respondent's argument that reasonable cause for a stop and frisk can only be based on the officer's personal observation, rather than on information supplied by another person. Informants' tips, like all other clues and evidence coming to a policeman on the scene, may vary greatly in their value and reliability. One simple rule will not cover every situation. Some tips, completely lacking in indicia of reliability, would either warrant no police response or require further investigation before a forcible stop of a suspect would be authorized. But in some situations—for example, when the victim of a street crime seeks immediate police aid and gives a description of his assailant, or when a credible informant warns of a specific impending crime—the subtleties of the hearsay rule should not thwart an appropriate police response.

While properly investigating the activity of a person who was reported to be carrying narcotics and a concealed weapon and who was sitting alone in a car in a high crime area at 2:15 in the morning, Sgt. Connolly had ample reason to fear for his safety. When Williams rolled down his window, rather than complying with the policeman's request to step out of the car so that his movements could more easily be seen, the revolver allegedly at Williams' waist became an even greater threat. Under these circumstances the policeman's action in reaching to the spot where the gun was thought to be hidden constituted a limited intrusion designed to insure his safety, and we conclude that it was reasonable. The loaded gun seized as a result of this intrusion was therefore admissible at Williams' trial. *Terry v. Ohio, supra,* at 30.

Once Sgt. Connolly had found the gun precisely where the informant had predicted, probable cause existed to arrest Williams for unlawful possession of the weapon. Probable cause to arrest depends "upon whether, at the moment the arrest was made . . . the facts and circumstances within [the arresting officers'] knowledge and of which they had reasonably trustworthy information were sufficient to warrant a prudent man in believing that the [suspect] had committed or was committing an offense." *Beck v. Ohio,* 379 U. S. 89, 91 (1964). In the present case the policeman found Williams in possession of a gun in precisely the place predicted by the informant. This tended to corroborate the reliability of the informant's further report of narcotics, and together with the surrounding circumstances certainly suggested no lawful explanation for possession of the gun. Probable cause does not require the same type of specific evidence of each element of the offense as would be needed to support a conviction. See *Draper v. United States,* 358 U. S. 307, 311–312 (1959). Rather, the court will evaluate generally the circumstances at the time of the arrest to decide if the officer had probable cause for his action:

> "In dealing with probable cause, however, as the very name implies, we deal with probabilities. These are not technical; they are the factual and practical considerations of everyday life on which reasonable and prudent men, not legal technicians, act." *Brinegar v. United States,* 338 U. S. 160, 175 (1949).

See also *id.*, at 177. Under the circumstances surrounding Williams' possession of the gun seized by Sgt. Connolly, the arrest on the weapons charge was supported by probable cause, and the search of his person and of the car incident to that arrest was lawful. See *Brinegar v. United States, supra; Carroll v. United States,* 267 U. S. 132 (1925). The fruits of the search were therefore properly admitted at Williams' trial, and the Court of Appeals erred in reaching a contrary conclusion.

[Defendant's conviction was affirmed.]
[Dissenting opinions omitted.]

QUESTIONS AND PROBLEMS

Available Answers for Questions 1 to 9

For each question, choose the answer which best fits the situation.

1. This *alone* is sufficient to establish probable cause for the issuance of a search warrant or to make an arrest.

2. This is *not* sufficient to establish probable cause. (If you choose answer 2, state the alternative courses of action available to the investigating officer based upon the information available to him.)

1. A man with a past criminal record comes into the district attorney's office and states that he wants to sign a criminal complaint that X has heroin in his home. He states that he has seen the heroin and will appear as a witness in the criminal action.

2. An anonymous telephone caller states that X now has heroin in his home. The caller will not give his name or the basis for his information.

3. An undercover officer telephones and states that X has heroin in his home at the present time. The officer states that he saw the heroin while he was in the home.

4. The same facts as in problem 3 except that the officer states that he received the information from a narcotics addict who has not previously cooperated with the police.

5. A heroin addict is arrested and states that X is his supplier and that X now has heroin in his apartment. The addict has never provided information to the police before and does not want his identity as an informant disclosed.

6. A factory worker, M, informs a police officer friend that a worker in the factory is selling LSD. Under instructions from his superior, the officer provides money to M and requests M to purchase LSD. M makes the purchase and turns the LSD over to the officer. M requests that his identity not be disclosed.

7. An anonymous telephone caller states that a man (description given) who is now walking down Fifth Street is carrying a concealed weapon (a gun).

8. A squad car receives a radio message that two men (twenty-three to twenty-five years old) in a green 1965 Ford have just robbed a liquor store which is a mile away from the squad car. The officers see a green 1965 Ford with three men of that age driving in a direction away from the liquor store. See *Bailey v. United States*, 389 F.2d 305 (1967).

9. A clerk in a store tells police that a man tried to sell her narcotics. She describes the man and tells the officers that he said that he would be back at 3 P.M. At about that time, a man matching the description given walks into the store. The clerk indicates to the officers that the man is the man she complained of. Does probable cause to arrest exist?

SEARCH AND SEIZURE OF OBSCENITY

The question as to what is obscene and what is not obscene has been the issue of many cases in recent years. Not only do courts vary from state to state on this determination, but also enforcement practices vary from city to city and county to county within states. The Supreme Court of Virginia stated in 1972 that "In light of the diversity of opinion that exists in our nation, it would be impossible to establish a workable national standard." (*Alexander v. Commonwealth*, 186 S.E. 43)

IS OBSCENITY CONSTITUTIONALLY PROTECTED?

The issue of whether obscenity is protected by the First Amendment, however, is clear. Obscenity is *not* constitutionally protected. States and communities may enact and enforce policies for adults (with stricter standards for children) within the guidelines of the Roth-Memoirs rule established in *Roth v. United States*, 354 U.S. 476 (1957), and *Memoirs v. Massachusetts*, 383 U.S. 413 (1966). In setting the criteria for determining whether material is obscene or not, the Court held that a state may not constitutionally inhibit the distribution of material unless (1) the dominant theme of the material taken as a whole appeals to a prurient interest in sex, (2) the material is patently offensive because it affronts contemporary community standards relating to the description or representation of sexual matters, and (3) the material is utterly without redeeming social value. Material may be held to be obscene if these three elements "coalesce" (that is, come together into a body). Therefore if tests 1 and 2 are met but the material has some social value, it would not be held to be obscene.

OBSCENITY AS CONTRABAND

Free speech, free press, and the freedom to read nonobscene material are highly cherished rights in our democracy. Because of the danger that these basic freedoms may be infringed upon in attempts to search and seize obscene material, the U.S. Supreme Court has established procedural safeguards which must be complied with. (See *A Quantity of Copies of Books v. Kansas,* 378 U.S. 205 (1964), *Freedman v. Maryland,* 380 U.S. (1965), and *Lee Art Theatre v. Virginia,* 392 U.S. 636 [1968]). Examples of these procedures which give obscenity a special contraband status are:

Example: A merchant has on display in his store a certain publication which the police believe to be obscene. The police, believing that a crime is being committed in their presence, seize the publication and all the copies of that publication in the store. A judge later determines that the publication is not obscene.

    The merchant's First Amendment rights have been violated by the police. The police, in effect, have imposed a restraint on the sale of the seized publication prior to a judicial finding of obscenity. (Even had the judge determined that the publication was obscene, the result would be the same.)

Example: Police observe a certain publication offered for sale in a store. The officers examine the publication and conclude that it is obscene. They do not take the publication, but instead report their observations of the contents of the publication to a judge. Relying upon the officers' description of the contents of the book, the judge issues a search warrant for the publication described and all copies of the same publication on the premises. The books are seized.

    The merchant's First Amendment rights have been violated. Even though there was a judicial determination, it was based on the officers' observations and conclusions. The judge himself must examine the publication in its entirety and make his own determination as to whether or not there is redeeming social value in the publication which would save it from being obscene. In addition, the merchant must be given an opportunity for an adversary hearing on the question of obscenity. (See the following example.)

Example: Officers purchase a copy of a publication from a merchant, which they feel is obscene. They take the publication to a judge who personally examines its contents and concludes that the publication is obscene. The judge issues an arrest warrant for the merchant, charging him with the sale of obscene matter and also issues a search warrant directing the officers to seize all other copies of the same publication on the merchant's premises. Other copies of the publication are seized pursuant to the search warrant.

    The arrest warrant is valid because the publication was validly obtained by purchase from the merchant and not seized. Since there was no seizure, the question of restraint of speech or press is not involved. The arrest is valid.

The search warrant seizure of other copies of the same publication is a violation of the merchant's First Amendment rights. Even though the judge determines that the publication is obscene, that determination is often a difficult one to make because of the various factors which must be taken into consideration (part of the definition of obscenity is based on contemporary community standards). The merchant must be given the opportunity to present testimony or evidence as to whether or not the publication is obscene or whether or not to the average person in the community, applying contemporary community standards, the dominant theme of the material taken as a whole appeals to prurient interest and is without socially redeeming value. Since the merchant was not given the opportunity to be heard before the search warrant was issued, the seizure on the authority of the search warrant amounted to a prior restraint of speech and press.

Example: Officers purchase a magazine from a merchant, which they believe to be obscene. They take the magazine to the prosecuting attorney who agrees that it is obscene. The prosecuting attorney causes to be served on the merchant a summons ordering the merchant to appear before a named judge with all the copies of the publication believed to be obscene; an order to show cause why the magazine should not be held to be obscene; a restraining order requiring the merchant not to sell, destroy, or otherwise dispose of the publications in question until a determination of obscenity has been made.

After a hearing before a judge in which both sides are given the opportunity to present their point of view on the question of obscenity of the magazine, the judge finds that there is probable cause to believe that the publication is obscene. The judge issues a search warrant. The copies of the magazines in the possession of the merchant are seized and held as evidence for trial.

The proceedings are valid. The merchant's right of free speech and press was not restrained prior to a judicial determination at an adversary proceeding.

OTHER ASPECTS OF OBSCENITY

In *Stanley v. Georgia*, 394 U.S. 557 (1969), the defendant was convicted for the possession of pornographic films which were found in his home. The U.S. Supreme Court reversed the conviction, stating that "a state has no business telling a man, sitting alone in his own house, what books or what films he may watch. Our whole constitutional heritage rebels at the thought of giving government the power to control men's minds."

The Supreme Court has refused in subsequent cases to expand the doctrine established in *Stanley v. Georgia* and stated in the 1970 case of *United States v. Reidel*, 402 U.S. 351, that "... *Roth* has squarely placed obscenity and its distribution outside the reach of the First Amendment and they remain there today. *Stanley* did not overrule *Roth* and we decline to do so now."

In the Reidel case, the defendant was convicted of knowingly using the mails for the delivery of obscene matter. In affirming the conviction, the Supreme Court commented on the defense argument that adults should have complete freedom to read anything and everything which they wish to purchase and read as long as the material is not made available to children or thrust upon unwilling adults. The Court stated that such a rule "may prove to be the desirable and eventual legislative course. But if it is, the task of restructuring the obscenity laws lies with those who pass, repeal and amend statutes and ordinances. *Roth* and like cases pose no obstacle to such development."

Authors' Note: In December 1972, the United States Supreme Court ruled in *California v. LaRue*, 409 U.S. ...., 34 L. Ed. 2d 342, 93 S.Ct. 390, 12 CrL 3027, that a state could prohibit the sale of liquor by the drink in establishments presenting nude entertainment or filmed explicit sexual entertainment even if some of the entertainment was not obscene. The Court stated that "While the States, vested as they are with general police power, require no specific grant of authority in the Federal Constitution to legislate with respect to matters traditionally within the scope of the police power, the broad sweep of the Twenty-first Amendment has been recognized as conferring something more than the normal state authority over public health, welfare and morals."

Justice Stewart, in a separate concurring opinion, stated that "A State has broad power under the Twenty-first Amendment to specify the times, places and circumstances where liquor may be dispensed within its borders."

21

CIVIL AND CRIMINAL LIABILITY OF LAW ENFORCEMENT OFFICERS

In electing a career in law enforcement, the officer has chosen a proud and honored profession. His profession performs some of the most vital services in a democratic society. He enforces the law. He is sometimes the thin blue line between order and anarchy. Cicero wrote long ago in *Pro Cluentio* 53 that "We are in bondage to the law in order that we may be free." Calvin Coolidge made the following observations while he was the President of the United States:

> The duties which a police officer owes to the State are of a most exacting nature. No one is compelled to choose the profession of a police officer, but having chosen it everyone is obliged to perform its duties and live up to the high standards of its requirements. To join in that high enterprise means the surrender of much individual freedom. The police officer has chosen a profession that he must hold to at all peril. He is the outpost of civilization. He cannot depart from it until he is relieved. A great and honorable duty, to be greatly and honorably fulfilled.
>
> But there is toward the officer a corresponding duty of the State. It owes him generous compensation for the perils he endures for the protection of society. It owes him the knowledge of security that is to be his from want in his declining years. It owes him that measure which is due to the great importance of the duties he discharges.
>
> Wherever the law goes, there civilization goes and stays. When the law fails, barbarism flourishes. Whoever scouts the law, whoever brings it into disrespect, whoever connives at its evasion, is an enemy of civilization. Change it if you will . . . but observe it always. That is government.

Because of the nature of his work, the law enforcement officer has unusual powers vested in him. And because of the effect that officers' actions can have on others, the law provides many types of reviews of the acts and performances of law enforcement officers.

WHO REVIEWS THE ACTS OF THE
LAW ENFORCEMENT OFFICER?

1. The officer's superior and his department are usually the first to review what the officer has done and are usually the first to reprimand him if his actions do not conform to those required by the department and the law.
2. Any person in the community may go into the office of the local prosecuting attorney and complain in regard to alleged misconduct or criminal conduct of law enforcement officers. In this manner, the prosecuting attorney may review an officer's acts and can, if necessary, issue a criminal complaint.
3. Any deaths caused by unexplained or suspicious circumstances or by gunshot wounds, etc., are automatically reviewed in accordance with state statute by the prosecuting attorney. A coroner's inquest could be ordered to investigate the circumstances of the death by the district attorney.
4. A complaint may be filed with the police and fire commission against a police officer. Disciplinary action could be taken by the commission under the powers vested in it.
5. A civil suit could be filed against an officer in the state courts under the laws of that state (a) alleging negligence and requesting compensatory damages and/or (b) alleging willful misconduct on the part of the officer and requesting punitive damages in addition to the compensatory damages.
6. Title 42 of the *U.S. Code*, section 1983, creates a right whereby a person may sue a law enforcement officer personally in a U.S. district court for depriving the plaintiff of "... any rights, privileges or immunities secured by the U.S. Constitution and laws...." The history of this Civil War statute is presented in the U.S. Supreme Court case of *Monroe v. Pape*. The Court held in this case that a plaintiff did not have to exhaust the remedy available to him in his state before coming into a federal court.
7. Other review actions are:
   Grand jury or "John Doe" inquiries conducted in federal or state courts.
   Federal grand jury or FBI investigations to determine whether civil rights or other statutes have been violated.
8. Some jurisdictions have civilian police review boards which can hear complaints against law enforcement officers or agencies.

CRIMINAL LIABILITY

All persons, *including law enforcement officers*, are subject to the law. The offenses listed below are criminal offenses which might be more applicable to law enforcement officers than to persons in other walks of life.

Excessive or unauthorized use of force (assault and battery)

False imprisonment

Unauthorized wiretapping (felony) or bugging (see state statute)

Extortion or accepting a bribe

Misconduct in public office or official misconduct (using the power of his office to obtain a dishonest advantage for himself or falsifying an entry in a record or report, etc.)

Perjury and subornation of perjury (perjury is to knowingly testify falsely under oath while subornation of perjury is to induce another to testify falsely)

Aiding, assisting, or permitting escape of any prisoner

Communicating with or harassing witnesses or jurors

Intimidation of witnesses or prisoners

Coercing a confession

Denial or violation of the rights of persons held in custody (denial of the opportunity to call an attorney, etc.)

Criminal statutes vary from state to state, and the specific statute of your jurisdiction should be checked as to these and other offenses.

CIVIL SUITS

In civil suits, the plaintiff must carry the burden of showing that:

1. The law enforcement officer either was negligent or intentionally committed the act (or acts) which are alleged.
2. Rights or the person of the plaintiff were violated.
3. Money damages should be awarded:
    a. To compensate the plaintiff for the injuries or wrongs received. To justify this, the plaintiff must show the extent of the injury or wrong. (Was it five days in jail or a five-minute detention? Was it a broken arm or a small scratch?)
    b. To punish the defendant for his alleged intentional acts, punitive damages should be awarded. To justify punitive damages, the plaintiff must show bad faith, malice, or willful misconduct on the part of the defendant officer.

Beginning in the August 1968 issue of the *FBI Law Enforcement Bulletin* is a three-part article on police liability. It states:

> A survey of these cases reveals what most officers could have guessed. Practically all routine law enforcement chores have the potential of becoming the subject of complaint by an irate citizen who demands satisfaction by way of a civil suit under this statute (Sec. 1983 of the Ku Klux Act of 1871).

The *FBI Bulletin* offers the following advice to law enforcement officers:

> Keep in mind the constitutional protections that are available to all and enforce the law vigorously without bias or favor. Arrest only when you have probable cause. Search whenever necessary, but do so under the authority of a valid warrant, incidental to lawful arrest, by appropriate consent, or, in the case of mobile vehicles, search on probable cause alone.
>
> As much as possible, allow the courts first to decide, by applying for a warrant, whether there is probable cause to justify an arrest, a search, or the seizure and destruction of property *before* any such action occurs....
>
> When executing an arrest, rely on probable cause or a valid warrant instead of the mere promise of a citizen to file a complaint "later." Do not accede to the demand of any person, whether he be an official or a private citizen, that such action be taken without probable cause. The resulting civil suit will name the officer and not those whose interests he was protecting.

The article concludes that there are two practical alternatives available to protect officers in civil suits. They are indemnification by the government and insurance. Of the two, the *FBI Bulletin* states, "... insurance designed to protect individual officers may be the most useful means of softening the impact of 1983 liability."

As many medical doctors in the United States have discovered, civil suits can be very costly even if the defendant doctor or officer is the eventual winner. If an officer loses a civil suit, he generally does not have the financial resources necessary to compensate a plaintiff who was awarded a judgment (see *Sauls v. Hutto and Ruppert* in the case section of Chap. 4). It is therefore important that officers be aware of their civil liability and are adequately protected either by indemnification or by insurance.

THE USE OF DEPARTMENT REPORTS
IN CIVIL OR CRIMINAL COURTS

As a condition of employment, officers must submit reports when ordered by superior officers. To prevent such reports from being used in civil or criminal actions against them, police associations suggest the following preface to such required reports:

> On _____ (date) _____ (time) _____ at _____ (place) _____, I was ordered to submit this report (and/or statement) by _____ (name and rank of superior officer) _____. I submit this report (and/or statement) at his order as a condition of employment. In view of possible job forfeiture, I have no alternative but to abide by this order.

It is my belief and understanding that the department requires this report (and/or statement) solely and exclusively for internal purposes and will not release it to any other agency. It is my further belief that this report (and/or statement) will not and cannot be used against me in any subsequent proceedings other than disciplinary proceedings within the confines of the department itself.

For any and all other purposes, I hereby reserve my constitutional right to remain silent under the Fifth and Fourteenth Amendments to the United States Constitution.

QUESTIONS AND PROBLEMS

Available Answers for Questions 1 to 12
Choose the answer which applies to each situation.

1. You may be held civilly liable as a law enforcement officer under state law or sec. 1983 of Title 42 of the *U.S. Code.*

2. You would *not* be held liable under state or federal law.

1. You are enforcing a valid statute in such a way as to deprive an individual of constitutional rights.
2. You act in good faith and on reasonable ground assume that the law which you are enforcing is constitutional.
3. You are enforcing a statute, which you know or reasonably should know to be unconstitutional, in such a way as to deprive constitutional rights.
4. You fail or refuse to act and you had no legal duty to act in regard to the complainant.
5. You deprive an individual of his constitutional rights although you did not have the specific intent to deprive him of a known constitutional right.
6. You violate the state constitution and deprive a person of a constitutional right of that state.
7. A husband is taken into custody on a Saturday night upon the verbal complaint of his wife. The wife promises to sign a complaint on Monday. However, on Monday she denies the story she told you on Saturday and refuses to sign a written complaint. The husband is released from jail on Monday.
8. The mayor of your city orders you to arrest X and to close his tavern with a promise that he will give you the reason for this action and a written order as soon as he has time. X is held for eighteen hours and then released when the mayor fails to provide probable cause for the arrest.

9. A prisoner in jail pleads for medical attention and a doctor. You believe that he is faking his illness and do not call a doctor. The prisoner dies that night.
10. You place a bug in the home of a suspected gambler without a warrant to do so.
11. You wiretap the telephone of a lawyer without the authority of a court to do so.
12. You order a citizen to block a highway by placing a truck across the highway and then fail to light the roadblock properly. A motorist crashes into the unlighted roadblock.

ANSWERS TO THE ABOVE QUESTIONS

1-1   2-2   3-1   4-2   5-1   6-1   7-1   8-1   9-1   10-1   11-1   12-1

APPENDIX A PERTINENT SECTIONS OF THE U.S. CONSTITUTION

PREAMBLE

WE THE PEOPLE of the United States, in Order to form a more perfect Union, establish Justice, insure domestic Tranquility, provide for the common defence, promote the general Welfare, and secure the Blessings of Liberty to ourselves and our Posterity, do ordain and establish this CONSTITUTION for the United States of America.

Article I

Section 1. All legislative Powers herein granted shall be vested in a Congress of the United States, which shall consist of a Senate and House of Representatives. . . .

. . . .

Article II

Section 1 The executive Power shall be vested in a President of the United States of America. . . .

. . . .

Article III

Section 1 The judicial Power of the United States, shall be vested in one supreme Court, and in such inferior Courts as the Congress may from time to time ordain and establish. . . .

. . . .

Article IV

. . . .

Section 4   The United States shall guarantee to every State in this Union a Republican Form of Government, and shall protect each of them against Invasion; and on Application of the Legislature, or of the Executive (when the Legislature cannot be convened) against domestic Violence.

. . . .

Article VI

. . . .

This Constitution, and the Laws of the United States which shall be made in Pursuance thereof; and all Treaties made, or which shall be made, under the Authority of the United States, shall be the supreme Law of the Land; and the Judges in every State shall be bound thereby, any Thing in the Constitution or Laws of any State to the Contrary notwithstanding. . . .

. . . .

AMENDMENTS

Amendment I

Congress shall make no law respecting an establishment of religion, or prohibiting the free exercise thereof; or abridging the freedom of speech, or of the press; or the right of the people peaceably to assemble and to petition the Government for a redress of grievances.

Amendment II

A well regulated Militia, being necessary to the security of a free State, the right of the people to keep and bear Arms, shall not be infringed.

Amendment III

No Soldier shall, in time of peace be quartered in any house, without the consent of the Owner, nor in time of war, but in a manner to be prescribed by law.

Amendment IV

The right of the people to be secure in their persons, houses, papers, and effects, against unreasonable searches and seizures, shall not be violated, and no Warrants shall issue, but upon probable cause, supported by Oath, or affirmation, and particularly describing the place to be searched, and the persons or things to be seized.

Amendment V

No person shall be held to answer for a capital, or otherwise infamous crime, unless on a presentment or indictment of a Grand Jury, except in cases arising in the land or naval forces, or in the Militia, when in actual service in time of War or public danger; nor shall any person be subject for the same offence to be twice put in jeopardy of life or limb; nor shall be compelled in any criminal case to be a witness against himself, nor be deprived of life, liberty, or property, without due process of law; nor shall private property be taken for public use, without just compensation.

Amendment VI

In all criminal prosecutions, the accused shall enjoy the right to a speedy and public trial, by an impartial jury of the State and district wherein the crime shall have been committed, which district shall have been previously ascertained by law, and to be informed of the nature and cause of the accusation; to be confronted with the witnesses against him; to have compulsory process for obtaining witnesses in his favor, and to have the Assistance of Counsel for his defence.

Amendment VII

In suits at common law, where the value in controversy shall exceed twenty dollars, the right of trial by jury shall be preserved, and no fact tried by jury, shall be otherwise reexamined in any Court of the United States, than according to the rules of the common law.

Amendment VIII

Excessive bail shall not be required, nor excessive fines imposed, nor cruel and unusual punishments inflicted.

Amendment IX

The enumeration in the Constitution, of certain rights, shall not be construed to deny or disparage others retained by the people.

Amendment X

The powers not delegated to the United States by the Constitution, nor prohibited by it to the States, are reserved to the States respectively, or to the people.

. . . .

Amendment XIV

Section 1. All persons born or naturalized in the United States, and subject to the jurisdiction thereof, are citizens of the United States and of the State wherein they reside. No State shall make or enforce any law which shall abridge the privileges or immunities of citizens of the United States; nor shall any State deprive any person of life, liberty, or property, without due process of law; nor deny to any person within its jurisdiction the equal protection of the laws.

. . . .

APPENDIX B
THE LAW
ENFORCEMENT
CODE OF
ETHICS

"As a Law Enforcement Officer, my fundamental duty is to serve mankind; to safeguard lives and property; to protect the innocent against deception, the weak against oppression or intimidation, and the peaceful against violence or disorder; and to respect the Constitutional Rights of all men to Liberty, Equality, and Justice.

"I will keep my private life unsullied as an example to all; maintain courageous calm in the face of danger, scorn, or ridicule; develop self-restraint; and be constantly mindful of the welfare of others. Honest in thought and deed in both my personal and official life, I will be exemplary in obeying the laws of the land and the regulations of my Department. Whatever I see or hear of a confidential nature or that is confided to me in my official capacity will be kept ever secret unless revelation is necessary in the performance of my duty.

"I will never act officiously or permit personal feelings, prejudices, animosities, or friendships to influence my decisions with no compromise for crime and with relentless prosecution of criminals. I will enforce the law courteously and appropriately without fear or favor, malice or ill will, never employing unnecessary force or violence and never accepting gratuities.

"I recognize the badge of my office as a symbol of public faith, and I accept it as a public trust to be held so long as I am true to the ethics of the police service. I will constantly strive to achieve these objectives and ideals, dedicating myself before God to my chosen profession—Law Enforcement."

[Adopted by the National Conference of Police Associations and by many law enforcement organizations.]

INDEX

INDEX OF CASES

* An asterisk indicates a Supreme Court case. Pages numbers in italics indicate that all or most of the decision is given on those pages.